Lecture Notes in Computer S

Commenced Publication in 1973
Founding and Former Series Editors:
Gerhard Goos, Juris Hartmanis, and Jan van Leeuwen

T0250822

Lecture Notes in Computer Science

Commenced Publication in 1973
Founding and Former Series Editors:
Gerhard Goos, Juris Hartmanis, and Jan van Leeuwen

Editorial Board

David Hutchison
Lancaster University, UK

Takeo Kanade
Carnegie Mellon University, Pittsburgh, PA, USA

Josef Kittler
University of Surrey, Guildford, UK

Jon M. Kleinberg
Cornell University, Ithaca, NY, USA

Friedemann Mattern
ETH Zurich, Switzerland

John C. Mitchell
Stanford University, CA, USA

Moni Naor
Weizmann Institute of Science, Rehovot, Israel

Oscar Nierstrasz
University of Bern, Switzerland

C. Pandu Rangan
Indian Institute of Technology, Madras, India

Bernhard Steffen
University of Dortmund, Germany

Madhu Sudan
Massachusetts Institute of Technology, MA, USA

Demetri Terzopoulos
University of California, Los Angeles, CA, USA

Doug Tygar
University of California, Berkeley, CA, USA

Moshe Y. Vardi
Rice University, Houston, TX, USA

Gerhard Weikum
Max-Planck Institute of Computer Science, Saarbruecken, Germany

Massimo Marchiori   Jeff Z. Pan
Christian de Sainte Marie (Eds.)

Web Reasoning and Rule Systems

First International Conference, RR 2007
Innsbruck , Austria, June 7-8, 2007
Proceedings

 Springer

Volume Editors

Massimo Marchiori
UNIPD and UTILABS
Via Trieste, 63, 35121 Padova, Italy
E-mail: massimo@math.unipd.it

Jeff Z. Pan
University of Aberdeen, Department of Computing Science
Aberdeen AB24 3UE, UK
E-mail: jpan@csd.abdn.ac.uk

Christian de Sainte Marie
ILOG S.A., Bureaux R&D
1681 Route des Dolines, Les Taissounières HB2, 06560 Valbonne, France
E-mail: csma@ilog.fr

Library of Congress Control Number: 2007927817

CR Subject Classification (1998): H.4, H.3, I.2, C.2, H.5, D.2, F.3

LNCS Sublibrary: SL 3 – Information Systems and Application, incl. Internet/Web
and HCI

ISSN   0302-9743
ISBN-10   3-540-72981-X Springer Berlin Heidelberg New York
ISBN-13   978-3-540-72981-5 Springer Berlin Heidelberg New York

Typesetting: Camera-ready by author, data conversion by Scientific Publishing Services, Chennai, India
Printed on acid-free paper   SPIN: 12074211   06/3180   5 4 3 2 1 0

Preface

This volume contains the proceedings of the 1st International Conference on Web Reasoning and Rule Systems (RR2007). This conference was special in that it is the first in a series whose ambitious goal is to be the major forum for discussion and dissemination of new results on all topics concerning Web reasoning and rule systems.

The importance of Web reasoning and rule systems has been constantly growing in the recent years, becoming more and more crucial for the future of the Web and of information handling. However, discussions on these aspects were, so far, distributed among a number of different events, lacking a common focus event. The new RR series fills this gap, and provides such a unified forum, giving reasoning and rules the first-class role they deserve, and offering the place for the best research on these topics to be presented, discussed, and advanced.

In its unifying role, RR2007 brought together three previously separate events: the International Workshop on Principles and Practice of Semantic Web Reasoning (PPSWR), the International Conference on Rules and Rule Markup Languages for the Semantic Web (RuleML), and the International Workshop on Reasoning on the Web (RoW). Every merge needs effort, but we have to remark how, in this case, there was an enthusiastic support that made it possible, rather exceptionally, for this conference to take place as early as this year, whereas the initial planning was for 2008: this witnesses the big need for such a common forum, bringing together initially different communities as soon as possible, overcoming all the timing difficulties for a higher goal.

Starting early had its risks: the short time reflected on a very short announcement and deadline, aggravated by the fact this was a first edition (and as such, it has yet to build up a success history). Despite all of these difficulties, we were very pleased to receive more than 60 submissions, which showed that the expectations were justified, and made us confident that the subsequent events in this series will be even more successful, making RR the unifying forum in the area. The Program Committee also did an exceptional job, managing to complete the paper selection in record time, eventually selecting 14 full papers, 15 short papers, and 7 selected posters. This great selection truly represents the state of the art in Web reasoning and rule systems.

Finally, we would like to thank all the people who made this possible. The people from PPSWR (including the REWERSE Executive Committee), from the RuleML organization, from RoW, from the newly founded RR Steering Committee, who put their enthusiasm in to making this event live as soon as possible. The people from the Program Committee and the reviewers, who faced the challenge of completing the paper selection even within a time-critical situation. The authors who submitted their works at the conference, believing in a first edition like this, and in the idea it brings forth. Last but not least, we would like to thank Andrei Voronkov, the author of the Easychair system, who made possible the handling of this conference even within such constrained timing, and Nick Cercone, the Editor-in-Chief of the *International Journal of Knowledge and Information Systems* (KAIS), who accepted to have the best papers of RR2007 submitted to a top journal even with RR in its first edition.

April 2007

Massimo Marchiori
Jeff Z. Pan
Christian de Sainte Marie

Organization

Program Chairs

Massimo Marchiori   UNIPD and UTILABS (Italy)
Jeff Z. Pan   University of Aberdeen (UK)
Christian de Sainte Marie   ILOG (France)

General Chair

Riccardo Rosati   Università di Roma La Sapienza (Italy)

Steering Committee

Harold Boley   University of New Brunswick (Canada)
Francois Bry   University of Munich (Germany)
Thomas Eiter   Technische Universität Wien (Austria)
Pascal Hitzler   University of Karlsruhe (Germany)
Michael Kifer   State University of New York (USA)
Massimo Marchiori   UNIPD and UTILABS (Italy)
Jeff Z. Pan   University of Aberdeen (UK)
Riccardo Rosati   Università di Roma La Sapienza (Italy)
Christian de Sainte Marie   ILOG (France)
Michael Schroeder   TU Dresden (Germany)
Bruce Spencer   University of New Brunswick (Canada)
Holger Wache   Vrije Universiteit Amsterdam (The Netherlands)

Program Committee

Maristella Agosti   University of Padova (Italy)
Dean Allemang   TopQuadrant (USA)
Jürgen Angele   ontoprise GmbH, Karlsruhe (Germany)
Helen Ashman   University of Nottingham (UK)
Grigoris Antoniou   University of Crete (Greece)
Jos de Bruijn   DERI (Austria)
Ernesto Damiani   University of Milan (Italy)
Stan Devitt   Agfa (Germany)
Kurt Godden   General Motors R&D Center (USA)
Christine Golbreich   University of Versailles-Saint Quentin (France)
Ramanathan Guha   Google (USA)
Paul Haley   Haley Systems (USA)
Frank van Harmelen   Free University of Amsterdam (The Netherlands)

Ian Horrocks	University of Manchester (UK)
Vipul Kashyap	Clinical Informatics R&D, Partners Healthcare System (USA)
Georg Lausen	Freiburg University (Germany)
Jiming Liu	Hong Kong Baptist University (KR)
Thomas Meyer	NICTA (Australia)
Toyoaki Nishida	Kyoto University (Japan)
Axel Polleres	DERI Galway, National University of Ireland, Galway (Ireland)
Dave Reynolds	HP (UK)
Amit Sheth	Kno.e.sis Center, Wright State University (USA)
Derek Sleeman	University of Aberdeen (UK)
Silvie Spreeuwenberg	LibRT (The Netherlands)
Giorgos Stamou	National Technical University of Athens (Greece)
Susie Stephens	Oracle (USA)
Heiner Stuckenschmidt	University of Mannheim (Germany)
Katia Sycara	Carnegie Mellon (USA)
Loïc Trégan	eBay (USA)
Paul Vincent	Tibco (USA)
David Warren	Stony Brook University (USA)
Guizhen Yang	SRI (USA)
Ning Zhong	Maebashi Institute (Japan)

Additional Reviewers

Antonis Bikakis, David Corsar, David Fowler, Alfredo Gabaldon, Aurona Gerber, Birte Glimm, Guido Governatori, Hassan Hait-Kaci, Thomas Hornung, Matthew Perry, Livia Predoiu, Edward Thomas, Dmitry Tsarkov.

Supporting Organizations

REWERSE
(http://www.rewerse.net/)

RuleML
(http://www.ruleml.org/)

Table of Contents

I Full Papers

II   Short Papers

III   Selected Posters

Well-Founded Semantics for Hybrid Rules

Włodzimierz Drabent[1,2] and Jan Małuszyński[2]

[1] Institute of Computer Science, Polish Academy of Sciences,
ul. Ordona 21, Pl – 01-237 Warszawa, Poland
[2] Deptartment of Computer and Information Science,
Linköping University, S – 581 83 Linköping, Sweden
wdr@ida.liu.se, janma@ida.liu.se

Abstract. The problem of integration of rules and ontologies is addressed in a general framework based on the well-founded semantics of normal logic programs and inspired by the ideas of Constraint Logic Programming (CLP). *Hybrid rules* are defined as normal clauses extended with *constraints* in the bodies. The constraints are formulae in a language of a first order theory defined by a set T of axioms. Instances of the framework are obtained by specifying a language of constraints and providing T. A hybrid program is a pair (P, T) where P is a finite set of hybrid rules. Thus integration of (non-disjunctive) Datalog with ontologies formalized in a Description Logic is covered as a special case.

The paper defines a declarative semantics of hybrid programs and a formal operational semantics. The latter can be seen as an extension of SLS-resolution and provides a basis for hybrid implementations combining Prolog with constraint solvers. In the restricted case of positive rules, hybrid programs are formulae of FOL. In that case the declarative semantics reduces to the standard notion of logical consequence. The operational semantics is sound and it is complete for a restricted class of hybrid programs.

1 Introduction

This paper is motivated by the ongoing discussion on the integration of rules and ontologies (see e.g. [8,14,15,16,13] and references therein), where rules are usually based on Datalog. Our primary interest is in the hybrid approach, where existing ontology reasoners and rule reasoners are re-used for reasoning in the extended rule languages. We present a framework for hybrid integration of axiomatic first-order theories with normal logic programs with well-founded semantics. Integration of Datalog rules with ontologies specified in a Description Logic is considered as a special instance of the framework. Going beyond Datalog makes it possible to use data structures like lists for programming in the extended rule language. The choice of the well-founded semantics as the basis for our approach is motivated by the fact that under this semantics a logic program has a unique well-founded model and well-established query answering algorithms. We introduce a notion of hybrid program; such a program is a tuple (P, T) where T is a set of axioms in a first order language $\mathcal{L}$ and P is a

M. Marchiori, J.Z. Pan, and C. de Sainte Marie (Eds.): RR 2007, LNCS 4524, pp. 1–15, 2007.

set of *hybrid rules*. A hybrid rule is a normal clause whose body may include a formula in $\mathcal{L}$, called *the constraint* of the rule. We define the declarative semantics of hybrid rules as a natural extension of the well-founded semantics of logic programs. The operational semantics presented in this paper combines a variant of SLS-resolution with checking satisfiability of the constraints wrt $\mathcal{T}$, which is assumed to be done by a reasoner of $\mathcal{T}$. Thus, it provides a basis for development of prototypes integrating LP reasoners supporting/approximating the well-founded semantics (such as XSB Prolog [19]) with constraint solvers. The operational semantics is sound wrt the declarative one. It is complete for a restricted class of *safe* hybrid programs and goals. Generally query answering in hybrid programs is undecidable, since they include normal logic programs as a special case. Decidable subclasses of hybrid programs can be defined using the safeness conditions. In the special case of hybrid rules where the negation does not appear the rules can be seen as the usual formulae of the FOL, thus as additional axioms extending $\mathcal{T}$. In that case the declarative semantics of the hybrid rules defined in this paper is compatible with the semantics of FOL.

The paper is organized as follows. Section 2 gives an (informal) introduction to well-founded semantics of normal logic programs, and presents the notion of constraint used in this paper. A simple example of a Datalog program is presented to illustrate well-founded semantics and its extension to Datalog rules with ontological constraints. Section 3 gives a formal presentation of the syntax and semantics, both declarative and operational, of the generic language of hybrid rules, parameterized by the constraint domain. Soundness and completeness results relating the declarative semantics and the operational semantics are stated. Section 4 includes discussion of related work, and conclusions.

2   Preliminaries

2.1   Normal Logic Programs and the Well-Founded Semantics

The language of hybrid rules will be defined as an extension of *normal logic programs*. We assume that the programs are built over a first-order alphabet including a set P_R of predicates, a set V of variables and a set F of function symbols including a non-empty finite set of *constants*. Our main interest is in the case where the only function symbols are constants. However the presented approach is sound without this restriction, so it is interesting to present a general case.

Atomic formulae (or *atoms*) and *terms* are built in a usual way. A *literal* is an atomic formula (*positive literal*) or a negated atomic formula (*negative literal*). A literal (a term) not including variables is called *ground*.

A normal logic program P is a finite set of rules (called *normal clauses*) of the form

$$H \leftarrow B_1, ..., B_n \qquad \text{where } n \geq 0$$

where h is an atomic formula, and $B_1, ..., B_n$ are *literals*. The rules with empty bodies $n = 0$ are called *facts*. A normal clause is called *definite clause* iff all literals of its body are positive. A definite program is a finite set of definite clauses.

In the case where the alphabet of function symbols consists only of constants, normal logic programs are called *Datalog programs*.

The *Herbrand base* $\mathcal{H}_P$ is the set of all ground atoms built with the predicates, constants, and function symbols of P. For a subset $S \subseteq \mathcal{H}_P$, by $\neg S$ we denote the set of negations of the elements of S, $\neg S = \{ \neg a \mid a \in S \}$. A ground instance of a rule r is a rule r' obtained by replacing each variable of r by a ground term over the alphabet. The set of all ground instances of the rules of a program P will be denoted $ground(P)$. Notice that in the case of Datalog $ground(P)$ is a finite set of ground rules. A *3-valued Herbrand interpretation* (shortly – interpretation) $\mathcal{I}$ of P is a subset of $\mathcal{H}_P \cup \neg\mathcal{H}_P$ such that for no ground atom A both A and $\neg A$ are in $\mathcal{I}$. Intuitively, the set $\mathcal{I}$ assigns the truth value $\mathbf{t}$ (true) to all its members. Thus A is false (has the truth value $\mathbf{f}$) in $\mathcal{I}$ iff $\neg A \in \mathcal{I}$, and $\neg A$ is false in $\mathcal{I}$ iff $A \in \mathcal{I}$. If $A \notin \mathcal{I}$ and $\neg A \notin \mathcal{I}$ then the truth value of A (and that of $\neg A$) is $\mathbf{u}$ (undefined). An interpretation $\mathcal{I}$ is a model of a ground instance $H \leftarrow B_1, \ldots, B_n$ of a rule iff H is true in $\mathcal{I}$, or H is undefined in $\mathcal{I}$ and some B_i is not true in $\mathcal{I}$, or H is false in $\mathcal{I}$ and some B_i is false in $\mathcal{I}$. An interpretation is a model of a rule $H \leftarrow B_1, \ldots, B_n$ iff it is a model of all its ground instances.

As usual, a 2-valued Herbrand interpretation is a subset of $\mathcal{H}_P$. It assigns the value $\mathbf{t}$ to all its elements and the value $\mathbf{f}$ to all remaining elements of the Herbrand universe. It is well known that any definite program P has the least[1] 2-valued Herbrand model. We will denote it $\mathcal{M}_P$. A normal program may not have the least Herbrand model. The well-founded semantics of logic programs [18] assigns to every program P a unique (three valued) Herbrand model, called the *well-founded* model of P. Intuitively, the facts of a program should be true, and the ground atoms which are not instances of the head of any rule should be false. This information can be used to reason which other atoms must be true and which must be false in any Herbrand model. Such a reasoning gives in the limit the well-founded model, where the truth values of some atoms may still be undefined. Well-founded semantics has several equivalent formulations. We briefly sketch here a definition following that of [11]. It will be extended in Section 3 to the case of hybrid programs.

For every predicate symbol p we will treat $\neg p$ as a new distinct predicate symbol. A normal program can thus be treated as a definite program over Herbrand base $\mathcal{H} \cup \neg\mathcal{H}$. A 3-valued interpretation over $\mathcal{H}$ can be treated as a 2-valued interpretation over $\mathcal{H} \cup \neg\mathcal{H}$.

Let I be such an interpretation. We define two ground, possibly infinite, definite programs $P/_t I$ and $P/_{tu} I$. For a given program P, $P/_t I$ is the ground instantiation of P together with ground facts that show which negative literals are true in I.

$$P/_t I = ground(P) \cup \{ \neg A \mid \neg A \in I \}$$

$P/_{tu} I$ is similar but all the negative literals that are true or undefined in I are made true here:

$$P/_{tu} I = ground(P) \cup \{ \neg A \mid A \notin I, A \in \mathcal{H} \}$$

---

[1] In the sense of set inclusion.

Now we define an operator $\Psi_P(I)$ which produces a new Herbrand interpretation of P:

$$\Psi_P(I) = (\mathcal{M}_{P/_t I} \cap \mathcal{H}) \cup \neg(\mathcal{H} \setminus \mathcal{M}_{P/_{tu} I})$$

This operator is monotonic. Its least fixed point is called the *well-founded model* $WF(P)$ of program P. For some countable ordinal α we have $WF(P) = \Psi_P^\alpha(\emptyset)$. The notation $I \models_3 F$ will be used to denote that a formula F is true in a 3-valued interpretation I. The following example shows a simple Datalog program and its well-founded model.

Example 1. A two person game consists in moving a token between vertices of a (finite) directed graph. Each move consists in traversing one edge from the actual position. Each of the players in order makes one move. The graph is described by a Datalog database of facts $m(X, Y)$ corresponding to the edges of the graph. A position X is said to be a *winning position* X if there exists a move from X to a position Y which is a losing (non-winning) position:

$$w(X) \leftarrow m(X, Y), \neg w(Y)$$

Consider the graph

$$
\begin{array}{c}
d \rightarrow e \\
\uparrow \quad \downarrow \\
b \leftrightarrow a \rightarrow c \rightarrow f
\end{array}
$$

and assume that it is encoded by the facts $m(b, a), m(a, b), \ldots, m(e, f)$ of the program. The winning positions are e, c. The losing positions are d, f. Position a is not a losing position since the player has an option of moving to b from which the partner can only return to a. This intuition is properly reflected by the well-founded model of the program, it contains the following literals with the predicate symbol w: $w(c), w(e), \neg w(d), \neg w(f)$.

2.2 External Theories

This section discusses logical theories to be integrated with logic programs.

Constraints. Our objective is to define a general framework for extending normal logic programs, which, among others, can also be used for integration of Datalog rules with ontologies. Syntactically, the clauses of a logic program are extended by adding formulae (called *constraints*) of a certain logical theory. We use this term due to similarities with constraint logic programming [12]. We will consider an external 2-valued theory, also called *constraint theory*. The function symbols and the variables of the language of the constraint theory are the same as those of the language of rules, but the predicate alphabets of both languages (denoted P_C and P_R) are disjoint. The predicates are called, respectively, *constraint predicates* and *rule predicates*. We assume that the constraint theory is given by a set of axioms $\mathcal{T}$. Formally, the theory is the set of logical consequences of $\mathcal{T}$. We will however often use $\mathcal{T}$ as the name of the theory.

Constraints are distinguished formulae in the language of the constraint theory. The set of constraints is closed under conjunction, disjunction, negation and existential quantification. We assume that P_C contains the equality symbol $=$ and $\mathcal{T}$ includes axioms of syntactic equality, known as CET (Clark's equality theory) [3]. CET implies that any different ground terms have different values in any model of $\mathcal{T}$. The latter property, reduced to constants, is called unique name assumption. Informally, each function symbol is treated as a constructor.

The requirement on equality in $\mathcal{T}$ may seem too restrictive. However such requirement appears in most of CLP implementations and is not found inconvenient in practice. When one needs functions not satisfying CET (eg. 2+4 and 4 denoting the same number) one introduces another equality predicate $='$ (eg. numerical equality of CLP(FD)). Formally, $='$ is an equivalence relation. It is a congruence of the relevant constraint predicates (eg. of numerical predicates of CLP(FD)). Informally, these predicates do not distinguish equivalent values. The intuition is that we deal both with the Herbrand interpretation and with a non Herbrand one. We may treat arguments of certain constraint predicates as interpreted by the latter interpretation, and the arguments of the other predicates as interpreted by the Herbrand interpretation. In particular, the Herbrand interpretation applies to rule predicates.

Ontologies and Ontological Constraints. An important special case of external theories consists of ontologies formalized in Description Logics (DL's) (see e.g. [2]). The syntax of a DL is built over distinct alphabets of *class names*(also known as *concepts*), *property names* (also known as *roles*) and individual names. Depending on the kind of DL, different constructors are provided to build class expressions (or briefly *classes*) and property expressions (or briefly *properties*). Intuitively, classes are used to represent sets of individuals of a domain and properties are used to represent binary relations over individuals. Individual names are used to represent individuals of a domain and can be seen as logical constants. Following the assumption about $\mathcal{T}$ we consider DL's where different names represent different individuals of the domain (*unique name assumption*).

By an *ontology* we mean a finite set of DL axioms of the form: $A := C$ (*concept definition*), $C \sqsubseteq D$ (*concept inclusion*), $R := S$ (*role definition*), $R \sqsubseteq S$ (*role inclusion*), $C(a)$ (*concept assertion*) and $R(a, b)$ (*role assertion*), where A is an atomic concept, C, D arbitrary concepts, R, S roles and a, b individuals. An ontology is thus a DL knowledge base in which one can distinguish two different kinds of axioms: a *T-Box* (terminology) consisting of concept (resp. role) definitions and inclusions; and an *A-Box* (assertions) describing concept (resp. role) assertions relating to individuals.

Class expressions, property expressions and axioms can be seen as an alternative representation of FOL formulae. Thus, the semantics of DL's is defined by referring to the usual notions of interpretation and model.

Due to the restricted syntax, DL's are decidable. There exist well developed automatic reasoning techniques. Some DL's also support reasoning with concrete data types, such as strings or integers. In that case one distinguishes between individual-valued properties and data-valued properties.

Given an ontology $\mathcal{T}$ in a DL one can use a respective reasoner for checking if a formula C is a logical consequence of $\mathcal{T}$. If $\mathcal{T} \not\models C$ and $\mathcal{T} \not\models \neg C$ then C is true in some models of the ontology and false in some other models. However, generally the syntax of DL's puts restriction on the use of negation: classes are closed under complement (negation) but the properties are not. So the language of ontological constraints is to be defined with care if the constraints are to be closed under negation, as required in Section 2.2.

Example 2. Consider a classification of geographical locations. For example the classification may concern the country (Finland (Fi), Norway (No), etc.), the continent (Europe (E), etc.), and possibly other categories. We specify a classification by axioms in a DL logic. The ontology provides, among others, the following information

- subclass relations (T-box axioms): e.g. $(Fi \sqsubseteq E)$;
- classification of some given locations represented by constants (A-box axioms). For instance, assuming that the positions of Example 1 represent locations we may have: b is a location in Finland $(Fi(b))$, c is a location in Europe $(E(c))$.

2.3 Datalog with Constraints: An Example

We now illustrate the idea of adding constraints to rule bodies on a simple example. The intention is to give an informal introduction to the formal definitions of Section 3.

Example 3. We now describe a variant of the game Example 1 where the rules are subject of additional restrictions. Assume that the positions of the graph represent geographical locations described by the ontology of Example 2. The restrictions will be expressed as ontological constraints added in rule bodies. For instance the facts $m(e, f)$ and $m(c, f)$ of Example 1 can be modified, respectively, to $m(e, f) \leftarrow E(f)$ and to $m(c, f) \leftarrow \neg Fi(f)$. Intuitively, this would mean that the move from e to f is allowed only if f is in Europe and the move from c to f – only if f is not in Finland. These restrictions may influence the outcome of the game: f will still be a losing position but if the axioms of the ontology do not allow to conclude that f is in Europe, we cannot conclude that e is a winning position. However, we can conclude that if f is not in Europe then it cannot be in Finland. Thus, at least one of the conditions $E(f), \neg Fi(f)$ holds. Therefore c is a winning position: If $E(f)$ then, as in Example 1, e is a winning position, d is a losing one, hence c is a winning position. On the other hand, if $\neg Fi(f)$ the move from c to f is allowed in which case c is a winning position. This intuitive explanation gives an informal introduction to the formal semantics discussed in Section 3.

3   Hybrid Integration of Rules and External Theories

This section defines the syntax and the semantics (both declarative and operational) of hybrid programs, integrating normal rules with axiomatically defined first-order theories. The general principles discussed here apply in a special case to integration of Datalog with ontologies specified in Description Logics.

3.1   The Syntax

We consider a first-order alphabet including, as usual, disjoint alphabets of predicate symbols P, function symbols F (including a non-empty set of constants) and variables V. We assume that P consists of two disjoint sets P_R (*rule predicates*) and P_C (*constraint predicates*). The atoms and the literals constructed with these predicates will respectively be called *rule atoms (rule literals)* and *constraint atoms (constraint literals)*. We will combine rules over alphabets P_R, F, V with constraints over alphabets P_C, F, V.

Definition 1. *A* hybrid rule *(over P_R, P_C, F, V) is an expression of the form:*

$$H \leftarrow C, L_1, \ldots, L_n$$

where, $n \geq 0$ each L_i is a rule literal and C is a constraint (over P_C, F, V); C is called the constraint *of the rule.*

A hybrid program *is a pair $(\mathcal{P}, \mathcal{T})$ where $\mathcal{P}$ is a set of hybrid rules and $\mathcal{T}$ is a set of axioms over P_C, F, V.* □

We adopt the convention that a constraint **true**, which is a logical constant interpreted as **t**, is omitted. Notation $\overline{L}$ will be used to denote a sequence of rule literals (similarly $\overline{t}$ a sequence of terms, etc.); $\overline{t} = \overline{u}$ will denote a conjunction of equalities $t_1 = u_1, \ldots, t_k = u_k$. Hybrid rules are illustrated in Example 3.

3.2   The Declarative Semantics

The declarative semantics of hybrid programs is defined as a generalization of the well-founded semantics of normal programs; it refers to the models of the external theory $\mathcal{T}$ of a hybrid program. Given a hybrid program $(\mathcal{P}, \mathcal{T})$ we cannot define a unique well-founded model of $\mathcal{P}$ since we have to take into consideration the logical values of the constraints in the rules. However, a unique well-founded model can be defined for any given model of $\mathcal{T}$. Roughly speaking, the constraints in the rules are replaced by their values in the model; then the well-founded model of the obtained logic program is taken. The well-founded models are over the Herbrand universe, but the models of $\mathcal{T}$ are arbitrary.

By a ground instance of a hybrid rule $H \leftarrow C, L_1, \ldots, L_n$ we mean any rule $H\theta \leftarrow C\theta, L_1\theta, \ldots, L_n\theta$ where θ is a substitution replacing the variables of $H, L_1, \ldots, L_n$ by ground terms. Here $C\theta$ means applying θ to the free variables of C. (So $C\theta$ is not ground if it contains a bound variable or a free variable not occurring in $H, L_1, \ldots, L_n$.) By $ground(\mathcal{P})$ we denote the set of all ground instances of the hybrid rules in $\mathcal{P}$.

Definition 2. *Let $(\mathcal{P}, \mathcal{T})$ be a hybrid program and let M_0 be a model of $\mathcal{T}$. Let $\mathcal{P}/M_0$ be the normal program obtained from $ground(\mathcal{P})$ by*

- *removing each rule constraint C which is satisfiable in M_0 (i.e. $M_0 \models \exists C$),*
- *removing each rule whose constraint C is unsatisfiable in M_0.*

The well-founded model of $\mathcal{P}/M_0$ is called the well-founded model of $\mathcal{P}$ based on M_0. A formula F holds in the well-founded semantics of a hybrid program (P,T) (denoted $(P,T) \models_{\mathrm{wf}} F$ iff $M \models_3 F$ for each well-founded model M of (P,T). □

Example 4. For the hybrid program $(\mathcal{P},\mathcal{T})$ of Example 3 we have to consider models of the ontology $\mathcal{T}$. For every model M_0 of $\mathcal{T}$ such that $M_0 \models E(f)$ the program $\mathcal{P}/M_0$ includes the fact $m(e,f)$. The well-founded model of $\mathcal{P}/M_0$ includes thus the literals $\neg w(f), w(e), \neg w(d), w(c)$ (independently of whether $M_0 \models Fi(f)$).

On the other hand, for every model M_1 of the ontology such that $M_1 \models \neg Fi(f)$ the program $\mathcal{P}/M_1$ includes the fact $m(c,f)$. The well-founded model of P/M_0 includes thus the literals $\neg w(f), w(c)$ (independently of whether $M_0 \models E(f)$).

Notice, that each of the models of the ontology falls in one of the above discussed cases. Thus, $w(c)$ and $\neg w(f)$ hold in the well-founded semantics of the hybrid program, while $w(e), \neg w(e), w(d)$ and $\neg w(d)$ do not hold in it (provided that $M \models E(f)$ does not hold in every model M of $\mathcal{T}$).

As the well-founded semantics of normal programs is undecidable, so is the well-founded semantics of hybrid programs.

3.3   The Operational Semantics

The operational semantics is based on the constructive negation approach presented in [5,6].

We will consider goals of the form $C, L_1, \ldots, L_n$, $(n \geq 0)$ where each L_i is a rule literal and C is a constraint. By the restriction $F|_V$ of a formula F to a set of variables V we mean the formula $\exists x_1, \ldots, x_n F$ where $x_1, \ldots, x_n$ are those free variables of F that are not in V. By $F|_{F'}$ we mean $F|_V$, where V are the free variables of F'.

Consider a goal $G = C, \overline{L}, p(\overline{t}), \overline{L'}$ and a rule $R = p(\overline{u}) \leftarrow C', \overline{K}$, such that no variable occurs both in G and R. We say that the goal

$$G' \;=\; \overline{t} = \overline{u}, C, C', \overline{L}, \overline{K}, \overline{L'}$$

is **derived** from G by R, with the selected atom $p(\overline{t})$, if $\overline{t} = \overline{u}, C, C'$ is satisfiable.

We inductively define two kinds of derivation trees: t-trees and tu-trees. Informally, their role is to find out when a given goal is **t**, or respectively when it is **t** or **u**. An answer C of a t-tree with the root G means that if C holds then G is **t** (in the well-founded models of the program). On the other hand, if G is **t** or **u** under some variable valuation ν then in a tu-tree for G there exists a leaf C which is true under ν.

For correctness of the definition we use the standard notion of a rank. In the general case ranks are countable ordinals, but for a language where the function symbols are constants natural numbers are sufficient. The children of nodes with an atom selected are defined as in the standard SLD-resolution. The only difference is that instead of explicit unification we employ equality constraints. The children of nodes with a negative literal selected are constructed employing the results of tu- (t-) trees of lower rank. A t-tree refers to tu-trees and vice versa. This is basically just a simplification of the corresponding definitions of [5,6].

Definition 3 (Operational semantics). *A t-tree (tu-tree) of rank $k \geq 0$ for a goal G w.r.t. a program $(\mathcal{P}, \mathcal{T})$ satisfies the following conditions. The nodes of the tree are (labelled by) goals. In each node a rule literal is selected, if such a literal exists. A node containing no rule literal is called* successful, *a branch of the tree with a successful leaf is also called* successful.

1. *A constraint $(C_1 \vee \cdots \vee C_n)|_G$ $(n \geq 0)^2$ is an* **answer** *of the t-tree if $C_1, \ldots, C_n$ are (some of the) successful leaves of the t-tree. (It is not required that all the successful leaves are taken.)*

2. *By a* **cross-section** *(or frontier) of a tu-tree we mean a set F of tree nodes such that each successful branch of the tree has a node in F. Let F be a cross-section of the tu-tree and $CF = \{C_1, \ldots\}$ the constraints of the nodes in F.*

   If $CF = \{C_1, \ldots, C_n\}$ is finite then the constraint $\neg(C_1|_G), \ldots, \neg(C_n|_G)$ (the negation of $\bigvee(C_i|_G)$) is called a **negative answer** *of the tu-tree.*

   If CF is infinite then a constraint C which implies $\neg(C_i|_G)$ for each $C_i \in CF$ is called a **negative answer** *of the tu-tree. Moreover it is required that each free variable of C is a free variable of G.*

3. *If (in the t-tree or tu-tree) the selected literal A in a node G' is an atom then, for each rule R of P, a goal derived from G' with A selected by a variant R' of R is a child of G', provided such a goal exists. Moreover it is required that no variable in R' occurs in the tree on the path from the root to G'.*

4. *Consider a node $G' = C, \overline{L}, \neg A, \overline{L'}$ of the t-tree (tu-tree), in which the selected literal $\neg A$ is negative. The node is a leaf or has one child, under the following conditions.*

   (a) *If the tree is a t-tree then*
      i. *G' is a leaf, or*
      ii. *G' has a child $C', C, \overline{L}, \overline{L'}$, where C' is a negative answer of a tu-tree for C, A of rank $< k$, and C', C is satisfiable.*

   (b) *If the tree is a tu-tree then*
      i. *G' has a child $C, \overline{L}, \overline{L'}$, or*
      ii. *G' has a child $C', C, \overline{L}, \overline{L'}$, where $C' = \neg C''$ is the negation of an answer C'' of a t-tree for C, A of rank $< k$, and C', C is satisfiable, or*
      iii. *G' is a leaf and there exists an answer C'' of a t-tree for C, A of rank $< k$ such that $\neg C'', C$ is unsatisfiable.*

---

[2] If $n = 0$ then by $C_1 \vee \cdots \vee C_n$ we mean **false**, and by $C_1 \wedge \cdots \wedge C_n$ we mean **true**.

An informal explanation for case 2 is that the constraints of the cross-section include all the cases in which G is $\mathbf{t}$ or $\mathbf{u}$, thus their negation implies that G is $\mathbf{f}$. Notice that if C is the negative answer considered in case 2 then C, C_i is unsatisfiable for any $C_i \in CF$. Hence C, C' is unsatisfiable for any constraint C' which is a leaf of the tu-tree (as C' is of the form C_i, C'', where $C_i \in CF$).

An informal explanation for case 4 is that in a t-tree C' implies that A is $\mathbf{f}$, equivalently $\neg A$ is $\mathbf{t}$. In a tu-tree $\neg C''$ includes all the cases in which C, A is not $\mathbf{t}$, and C, A being not $\mathbf{t}$ is equivalent to $\neg(C, A)$ being $\mathbf{t}$ or $\mathbf{u}$.

Notice that in case 4 the node $G' = C, \overline{L}, \neg A, \overline{L'}$ may unconditionally be a leaf of a t-tree (of any rank). This corresponds to the fact that $C' = \neg C$ is a negative answer for any tu-tree for C, A. (Take the cross-section $\{\, C, A\,\}$). Hence the constraint $\neg C, C$ in the supposed child of G' is unsatisfiable. Conversely, G' in a tu-tree may have $C, \overline{L}, \overline{L'}$ as the child. This corresponds to the fact that $C'' = \mathbf{false}$ is an answer of any t-tree. Hence C is equivalent to $\neg C'', C$ (which is the constraint obtained in 4(b)ii).

Example 5. Consider a query $w(c)$ for the hybrid program of Example 3. It can be answered by the operational semantics by construction of the following trees. (Sometimes we replace a constraint by an equivalent one.)

1. A t-tree for $w(c)$:

$$w(c)$$
$$|$$
$$X = c, m(X, Y), \neg w(Y)$$

$$X = c, Y = f, \neg Fi(f), \neg w(Y) \qquad\qquad X = c, Y = d, \neg w(Y)$$
$$| \qquad\qquad\qquad\qquad\qquad |$$
$$X = c, Y = f, \neg Fi(f) \qquad X = c, Y = d, \neg(X = c, Y = d, E(f))$$

The tree refers to negative answers derived in the cases 2, 4 below. The answer obtained from the two leaves of the tree is $\neg Fi(f) \vee E(f)$. As this is a logical consequence of the ontology, $w(c)$ holds in each well-founded model of the program.

2. A tu-tree for $Y = d, w(Y)$, employing an answer from the t-tree from case 3:

$$Y = d, w(Y)$$
$$|$$
$$Y = d, X' = Y, m(X', Y'), \neg w(Y')$$
$$|$$
$$Y = d, X' = Y, Y' = e, \neg w(Y')$$
$$|$$
$$Y = d, X' = Y, Y' = e, \neg(Y = d, X' = Y, Y' = e, E(f))$$

The negative answer (obtained from the cross-section containing the leaf) is $\neg \exists X', Y'\, \big(Y = d, X' = Y, Y' = e, \neg(Y = d, X' = Y, Y' = e, E(f))\big)$ which is equivalent to $\neg(Y = d, \neg E(f))$. Similarly, if a constraint $C, Y = d$ is satisfiable then $\neg(C, Y = d, \neg E(f))$ is a negative answer of a tu-tree for $C, Y = d, w(Y)$.

3. A t-tree for $Y' = e, w(Y')$ employing a negative answer from case 4:

$$Y' = e, w(Y')$$
$$|$$
$$Y' = e, X'' = Y', m(X'', Y''), \neg w(Y'')$$
$$|$$
$$Y' = e, X'' = Y', Y'' = f, E(Y''), \neg w(Y'')$$
$$|$$
$$Y' = e, X'' = Y', Y'' = f, E(Y'')$$

The corresponding answer is (equivalent to) $Y' = e, E(f)$. Similarly, any satisfiable constraint $C, Y' = e, E(f)$ is an answer for $C, Y' = e, w(Y')$.

4. A tu-tree for $Y = f, w(Y)$:

$$Y = f, w(Y)$$
$$|$$
$$Y = f, Y = X', m(X', Y'), \neg w(Y')$$

From the empty cross-section a negative answer **true** is obtained. Similarly, **true** is a negative answer for $C, Y = f, w(Y)$, where C is an arbitrary constraint.

3.4 Soundness and Completeness

Now we show that the operational semantics from the previous section is sound, and under certain conditions, complete. Due to lack of space we omit the actual proofs.

By a *grounding substitution* for the variables of a formula F (or just "for F") we mean a substitution replacing the free variables of F by ground terms. Notice that this differs from substitutions used to define $ground(\mathcal{P})$.

Theorem 1 (Soundness). *Consider a program $(\mathcal{P}, \mathcal{T})$ and a model M_0 of T*

1. If C is an answer of a t-tree of rank k for G then for any grounding substitution θ (for the variables of G) $M_0 \models C\theta$ implies $\Psi^k_{P/M_0}(\emptyset) \models_3 G\theta$.

2. If C is a negative answer of a tu-tree of rank k for G then for any grounding substitution θ (for the variables of G) $M_0 \models C\theta$ implies $\Psi^k_{P/M_0}(\emptyset) \models_3 \neg G\theta$.

Intuitively the soundness result shows that for any model M_0 of the external theory the answers (the negative answers) obtained by construction of a t-tree (of a tu-tree) are correct in the well-founded model of the program which is based on M_0.

Generally t-trees and tu-trees may have infinite branches and infinite cross-sections, resulting in infinite sets of constraints. In that case there is no effective way of finding a negative answer of the tu-tree. Thus the operational semantics is not complete.

Our operational semantics turns out to be complete for the case where the program and goals are *safe* in the sense defined below and the alphabet does not contain function symbols of arity > 0, in other words the Herbrand universe is finite.

A rule $R = H \leftarrow C_1, \ldots, C_l, \overline{L}$, where $C_1, \ldots, C_l$ is the constraint of R, is *safe* if

- each variable of H,
- each variable of a negative literal of $\overline{L}$, and
- each free variable of $C_1, \ldots, C_l$

is bound in $C_1, \ldots, C_l$ to a constant or to a variable appearing in a positive literal in $\overline{L}$. A variable x_0 is *bound* in $C_1, \ldots, C_l$ to a variable x_n (respectively to a constant c) if the set $\{C_1, \ldots, C_l\}$ contains equalities $x_0 = x_1, \ldots, x_{n-1} = x_n$ (resp. $x_0 = x_1, \ldots, x_{n-1} = x_n, x_n = c$), where $n \geq 0$. (We do not distinguish here equivalent equalities, like $x = y$ and $y = x$.) Notice that x_0 is bound to itself independently of the constraint.

A hybrid program is safe if all its rules are safe. A goal $G = C_1, \ldots, C_l, \overline{L}$ is *safe* if the rule $p \leftarrow G$ is safe (where p is a 0-argument predicate symbol). It can be proved that if the root of a t-tree (tu-tree) for a safe program is safe then any node of the tree is safe.

Intuitively, safeness guarantees that in a node of a tree that does not include positive literals all free variables of its constraints and all variables of the negative literals are bound to constants of the program. For safe programs we have the following completeness result.

Theorem 2 (Completeness). Assume that the Herbrand universe is finite. Consider a safe program $(\mathcal{P}, \mathcal{T})$ and a model M_0 of $\mathcal{T}$. Let $\mathcal{R}$ be a selection rule, G be a safe goal, and C_0 be the constraint of G. Let $k \geq 0$ and θ be a grounding substitution for the variables of G such that $C_0\theta$ is satisfiable.

1. If $\Psi^k_{P/M_0}(\emptyset) \models_3 G\theta$ then there exists a t-tree for G via R with an answer C such that $M_0 \models C\theta$.

2. If $\Psi^k_{P/M_0}(\emptyset) \models_3 \neg G\theta$ then there exists a tu-tree for G via R with a negative answer C such that $M_0 \models C\theta$.

4   Conclusions and Related Work

We presented a generic scheme for integration of normal logic programs with axiomatically defined external theories. For every instance of the scheme the declarative semantics is defined by combining the well-founded semantics of normal programs with the logical semantics of the axioms of the external theory. In the special case of a positive logic programs the hybrid rules become formulae of FOL and the declarative semantics reduces to their logical semantics. We defined an operational semantics which opens for re-use of existing rule reasoners and constraint solvers for implementation of sound reasoners for hybrid programs. The operational semantics is based on the constructive negation of [5,6] (an extension of SLS-resolution, for references see e.g. the survey [1]) combined with the ideas of Constraint Logic Programming [12]. We proved the soundness of the operational semantics in general and its completeness for safe hybrid rules based on Datalog and safe goals. A way of implementing the proposed approach, combining XSB Prolog with any DIG compatible reasoner is presented in [7].

Our work addresses integration of rules and ontologies as a special case of the problem of integration normal logic programs with external theories. The related work on integration of rules and ontologies is instead focused on integration of various variants of Datalog with Description Logics. Below we discuss only those approaches to integration of rules and ontologies which in our opinion are more closely related to our work. This is not intended as a survey of all work done on this topic.

Our work is strongly motivated by the early $\mathcal{AL}$-log approach [4] where positive Datalog was extended by allowing the concepts of $\mathcal{ALC}$ DL as constraints in safe Datalog rules, thus restricting the Herbrand model of the underlying Datalog program. The operational semantics of $\mathcal{AL}$-log relies on an extension of SLD-resolution where the disjunction of constraints from different derivations is to be submitted for validity check to the DL-reasoner. We adopted the $\mathcal{AL}$-log idea of extending rules with constraints in the body and applied it to more expressive rules including non-monotonic negation and to more expressive constraints than those used in $\mathcal{AL}$-log.

In our approach the heads of the hybrid rules are atoms built with rule predicates. Thus the semantics of the rule predicates depends on the external theory which is assumed to be given a priori and to not depend on the rules. The rationale for that is that the rules describe a specific application while the theory (for example an ontology) provides a knowledge common for an application domain. In contrast to that, several recent papers [14,15,16,17] allow the use of ontology predicates in the heads of rules, defining thus an integrated language where rule predicates and ontology predicates may be mutually dependent, and ontology predicates can be (re-)defined by rules.

The paper [14] defines *DL rules*, a decidable combination of disjunctive Datalog not allowing a non-monotonic negation, with OWL-DL. In contrast to that our primary concern is non-monotonic reasoning.

The r-hybrid knowledge bases [15] and the more recent DL+log [16,17] are based on disjunctive Datalog with non-monotonic negation under the stable model semantics. The objective is to define a generic integration scheme of this variant of Datalog with an arbitrary Description Logic. The DL-rules defined under this scheme may include DL predicates not only in their bodies but also in the heads. A hybrid DL+log knowledge base consists of a DL knowledge base $\mathcal{K}$ and a set of hybrid rules $\mathcal{P}$. A notion of *model* of such a knowledge base is defined by referring to the models of $\mathcal{K}$ and to the stable models of disjunctive Datalog. This is similar to our definition of declarative semantics in that that models of $\mathcal{K}$ are used to transform the set of grounded hybrid rules into a set of ground Datalog rules, not including DL-atoms. However, as the heads of the hybrid rules may include DL-atoms, the transformation is more elaborate than our $\mathcal{P}/M_0$ transformation. Also the semantics of DL+log is based on stable models of the transformed ground rules, while our semantics is based on the well-founded semantics of $\mathcal{P}/M_0$. Last but not least, we adopt the unique name assumption, while in DL+log the notion of stable model is modified so that unique names need not be assumed. In this modification the interpretation of constants must be considered in the definition of stable model. No implementation of DL+log has been presented in [16,17]. The discussed general reasoning algorithm relies on guessing a partition of a set of Boolean conjunctive queries obtained by (partial) grounding of DL-atoms that occur in the program.

An important objective of our work has been to facilitate re-use of existing rule reasoners and constraint solvers for reasoning with hybrid rules. A similar objective has been achieved in the project "Answer Set Programming for the Semantic Web"[8]. The language of Description Logic Programs (DLP's), defined in this project, allows for integration of ontologies defined in OWL DL with Datalog rules with negation by extending the latter with so called *dl-queries* to a given ontology. The queries may locally modify the ontology. Two kinds of declarative semantics are considered for the integrated language. The semantics of choice [9] extends the stable model semantics of Datalog with negation, but an extension of the well-founded semantics is also considered [10]. In both variants of the declarative semantics the *truth value* of a rule wrt to an interpretation depends on dl-queries in the rule being *logical consequences* of the respective ontologies. This makes the semantics incompatible with the standard semantics of the first order logic. For example consider two dl-queries Q_1, Q_2 such that in each model of the ontology at least one of them is true, but none of them is a logical consequence of the ontology. Add the rules $p \leftarrow Q_1$ and $p \leftarrow Q_2$, which can be seen as axioms in FOL. Then p is a logical consequence of the ontology and rules, but will not follow from the declarative semantics of DLP. In contrast to that our approach is compatible with FOL. For achieving this our operational semantics requires storing of constraints which makes possible reasoning by cases. In contrast to DLP our integration scheme does not provide a possibility of modifying the external theory by rule constraints.

Acknowledgement. This research has been co-funded by the European Commission and by the Swiss Federal Office for Education and Science within the 6th Framework Programme project REWERSE number 506779 (cf. http://rewerse.net).

References

1. Apt, K.R., Bol, R.N.: Logic programming and negation: A survey. J. Log. Program. 19/20, 9–71 (1994)
2. Baader, F., Calvanese, D., McGuiness, D., Nardi, D., Patel-Schneider, P. (eds.): The Description Logic Handbook. Cambridge University Press, Cambridge (2003)
3. Clark, K.: Negation as failure. In: Logic and Data Bases, pp. 293–322 (1978)
4. Donini, F., Lenzerini, M., Nardi, D., Schaerf, A.: AL-Log: Integrating datalog and description logics. Intelligent Information Systems 10(3), 227–252 (1998)
5. Drabent, W.: SLS-resolution without floundering. In: Pereira, L.M., Nerode, A. (eds.) Proc. 2nd International Workshop on Logic Programming and Non-Monotonic Reasoning, pp. 82–98. MIT Press, Cambridge, MA (1993)
6. Drabent, W.: What is failure? An approach to constructive negation. Acta Informatica 32(1), 27–59 (1995)

7. Drabent, W., Henriksson, J., Maluszynski, J.: Hybrid reasoning with rules and constraints under well-founded semantics. In: Marchiori, M., Pan, J.Z., de Sainte Marie, C. (eds.) RR 2007. LNCS, vol. 4524, pp. 348–357. Springer, Heidelberg (2007)
8. Eiter, T., Ianni, G., Schindlauer, R., Tompits, H.: Effective integration of declarative rules with external evaluations for semantic-web reasoning. In: Sure, Y., Domingue, J. (eds.) ESWC 2006. LNCS, vol. 4011, pp. 273–287. Springer, Heidelberg (2006)
9. Eiter, T., Lukasiewicz, T., Schindlauer, R., Tompits, H.: Combining answer set programming with description logics for the semantic web. In: Proc. of the International Conference of Knowledge Representation and Reasoning (KR'04) (2004)
10. Eiter, T., Lukasiewicz, T., Schindlauer, R., Tompits, H.: Well-founded semantics for description logic programs in the semantic web. In: Antoniou, G., Boley, H. (eds.) RuleML 2004. LNCS, vol. 3323, pp. 81–97. Springer, Heidelberg (2004)
11. Ferrand, G., Deransart, P.: Proof method of partial correctness and weak completeness for normal logic programs. J. Log. Program 17(2/3&4), 265–278 (1993)
12. Marriott, K., Stuckey, P.J., Wallace, M.: Constraint logic programming. In: Handbook of Constraint Programming, Elsevier, Amsterdam (2006)
13. Motik, B., Rosati, R.: A faithful integration of description logics with logic programming. In: IJCAI, pp. 477–482 (2007)
14. Motik, B., Sattler, U., Studer, R.: Query answering for OWL-DL with rules. J. Web. Sem. 3(1), 41–60 (2005)
15. Rosati, R.: On the decidability and complexity of integrating ontologies and rules. Journal of Web Semantics 3, 61–73 (2005)
16. Rosati, R.: DL+log: Tight integration of description logics and disjunctive datalog. In: Doherty, P., Mylopoulos, J., Welty, C.A. (eds.) KR, pp. 68–78. AAAI Press, California (2006)
17. Rosati, R.: Integrating ontologies and rules. Semantic and computational issues. In: Barahona, P., Bry, F., Franconi, E., Henze, N., Sattler, U. (eds.) Reasoning Web. LNCS, vol. 4126, pp. 128–151. Springer, Heidelberg (2006)
18. van Gelder, A., Ross, K.A., Schlipf, J.S.: Unfounded sets and well-founded semantics for general logic programs. In: Principles of Database Systems, pp. 221–230. ACM, New York (1988)
19. XSB. XSB Prolog. Available at http://xsb.sourceforge.net

Rule-Based Composite Event Queries: The Language XChange^{EQ} and Its Semantics

François Bry and Michael Eckert

University of Munich, Institute for Informatics
Oettingenstr. 67, 80538 München, Germany
{bry,eckert}@pms.ifi.lmu.de
http://www.pms.ifi.lmu.de

Abstract. Reactive Web systems, Web services, and Web-based publish/subscribe systems communicate events as XML messages, and in many cases require composite event detection: it is not sufficient to react to single event messages, but events have to be considered in relation to other events that are received over time.

Emphasizing language design and formal semantics, we describe the rule-based query language XChange^{EQ} for detecting composite events. XChange^{EQ} is designed to completely cover and integrate the four complementary querying dimensions: event data, event composition, temporal relationships, and event accumulation. Semantics are provided as model and fixpoint theories; while this is an established approach for rule languages, it has not been applied for event queries before.

1 Introduction

Emerging Web technologies such as reactive Web systems [9,4,7,23], Web-based publish/subscribe systems [25,15], and Web services communicate by exchanging messages. These messages usually come in an XML format such as SOAP [20] or Common Base Event (CBE) [14] and signify some application-level event, e.g., an update on a Web document, publication of new information, a request for some service, or a response to a request.

For many applications it is not sufficient to query and react to only single, atomic events, i.e., events signified by a single message. Instead, events have to be considered with their relationship to other events in a stream of events. Such events (or situations) that do not consist of one single atomic event but have to be inferred from some pattern of several events are called *composite events*.

Examples for such composite events are omnipresent. An application for student administration might require notification when "a student has both handed in her thesis and given the defense talk." A library application might send a monition when "a book has been borrowed and not returned or extended within one month." A stock market application might require notification if "the average of the reported stock prices over the last hour raises by 5%."

This article describes work on the rule-based high-level event query language XChange^{EQ} for the Web, focusing on language design and formal semantics.

M. Marchiori, J.Z. Pan, and C. de Sainte Marie (Eds.): RR 2007, LNCS 4524, pp. 16–30, 2007.
© Springer-Verlag Berlin Heidelberg 2007

XChange^{EQ} has been introduced in [3]; we extend on this work by providing formal semantics in the form of model and fixpoint theories for stratified programs. XChange^{EQ} is developed as a part (sub-language) of the reactive, rule-based Web language XChange [9].[1] It is however designed so that it can also be deployed as a stand-alone event mediation component in an event-driven architecture [16] or in the General Semantic Web ECA Framework described in [23].

The contributions of this article are as follows. (1) We discuss language design issues of event query languages for the Web (Section 2). We identify four complementary dimensions that need to be considered for querying events. While they might have been implicit in some works on composite event queries, we are not aware of any works stating them explicitly before.

(2) We shorty introduce XChange^{EQ} (Section 3). XChange^{EQ} is significantly more high-level and expressive than previous (composite) event query languages. To the best of our knowledge, XChange^{EQ} is the first language to deal with complex structured data in event messages, support rules as an abstraction and reasoning mechanism for events, and build on a separation of concerns that gives it ease-of-use and a certain degree of expressive completeness.

(3) We provide formal semantics for XChange^{EQ} in the form of model and fixpoint theories (Section 4). While this approach is well-explored in the world of rule-based and logic programming, its application to an event query language is novel and should be quite beneficial for research on composite event queries: semantics of earlier event query languages often have been somewhat ad hoc, generally with an algebraic and less declarative flavor, and did not accommodate rules. In our discussion, we highlight where we deviate from traditional model theories to accommodate the temporal notions required by event queries.

2 Design Considerations

Our work on XChange^{EQ} is motivated by previous work on XChange [9], a language employing Event-Condition-Action rules to program distributed, reactive Web applications. Similar to composite event detection facilities found in active databases [19,18,13,12,1], XChange provides composition operators such as event conjunction, sequence, repetition, or negation. Our experiences with programming in XChange [10,7] has taught us that there is a considerable gap between the requirements posed by applications and the expressivity of composition operators. Further, event querying based on composition operators is prone to misinterpretations as discussions in the literature show [29,17,1]. This experience has lead us to reconsider and analyze the requirements for event query languages, which we present here, and to the development of XChange^{EQ}.

A sufficiently expressive event query language should cover (at least) the following four complementary dimensions. How well an event query language covers each of these dimensions gives a practical measure for its expressiveness.

---

[1] Accordingly, the superscript EQ stands for **E**vent **Q**ueries. XChange^{EQ} replaces the original composite event query constructs [8] of XChange. It has a different design and is an improvement both in expressivity and ease-of-use.

Data extraction: Events contain data that is relevant for applications to decide whether and how to react to them. For events that are received as XML messages, the structure of the data can be quite complex (semi-structured). The data of events must be extracted and provided (typically as bindings for variables) to test conditions (e.g., arithmetic expressions) inside the query, construct new events, or trigger reactions (e.g., database updates).

Event composition: To support composite events, i.e., events that consist out of several events, event queries must support composition constructs such as the conjunction and disjunction of events (more precisely, of event queries). Composition must be sensitive to event data, which is often used to correlate and filter events (e.g., consider only stock transactions from the *same* customer for composition). Since reactions to events are usually sensitive to timing and order, an important question for composite events is *when* they are detected. In a well-designed language, it should be possible to recognize when reactions to a given event query are triggered without difficulty.

Temporal (and causal) relationships: Time plays an important role in event-driven applications. Event queries must be able to express temporal conditions such as "events A and B happen within 1 hour, and A happens before B." For some applications, it is also interesting to look at causal relationships, e.g., to express queries such as "events A and B happen, and A has caused B." In this article we concentrate only on temporal relationships since causal relationships can be queried in essentially the same manner.[2]

Event accumulation: Event queries must be able to accumulate events to support non-monotonic features such as negation of events (understood as their absence) or aggregation of data from multiple events over time. The reason for this is that the event stream is (in contrast to extensional data in a database) unbounded (or "infinite"); one therefore has to define a scope (e.g., a time interval) over which events are accumulated when aggregating data or querying the absence of events. Application examples where event accumulation is required are manifold. A business activity monitoring application might watch out for situations where "a customer's order has *not* been fulfilled within 2 days" (negation). A stock market application might require notification if "the *average* of the reported stock prices over the last hour raises by 5%" (aggregation).

3   The Language XChange^{EQ}

XChange^{EQ} is designed on the following foundations.

(1) Its syntax enforces a separation of the four querying dimensions described above, yielding a clear language design, making queries easy to read and understand, and giving programmers the benefit of a separation of concerns.

---

[2] While temporality and causality can be treated similarly in queries, causality raises interesting questions about how causal relationships can be *defined* and *maintained*. Investigation of these issues is planned for the future.

Even more importantly, this separation allows to argue that the language reaches a certain degree of expressive completeness. Our experience, stemming from attempts to express queries with existing event query languages, shows us that without such a separation not all dimensions are fully covered.

(2) It embeds the Web and Semantic Web query language Xcerpt [28] to specify classes of relevant events, extract data (in the form of variable bindings) from them, and construct new events.

(3) It supports rules as an abstraction and reasoning mechanism for events, with the same motivation and benefits of views in traditional database systems.

These foundations lead to improvements on previous work on composite event query languages in the following ways: XChange^{EQ} is a high-level language with a clear design that is easy to use and provides the appropriate abstractions for querying events. It emphasizes the necessity to query data in events, which has been neglected or over-simplified earlier. Being targeted for semi-structured XML messages as required for CBE, SOAP, and Web Services, it is particularly suitable for use in business applications domains. We make an attempt towards expressive completeness by fully covering all four query dimensions explained earlier using a separation of concerns in XChange^{EQ}. Arguably, in previous languages that do not use such a separation, some (usually simple) queries might be expressed more compactly. This compactness then however leads easily to misinterpretations (as discussed in [29,17,1]) and comes in previous work at the price of a serious lack in expressiveness (incomplete coverage of the four dimensions), where less simple queries cannot be expressed.

Using the example of a stock market application, we now introduce the syntax of our event query language XChange^{EQ}.

3.1   Querying Atomic Events

Application-level events are nowadays often represented as XML, especially in the formats Common Base Event [14] and SOAP [20]. Skipping details of such formats for the sake of brevity, we will be using four atomic events in our stock market example: stock *buys*, stock *sells*, and *orders* to buy or sell stocks. Involved applications may also generate further events without affecting our examples.

The left side of Figure 1 depicts a *buy order* event in XML. For conciseness and human readability, we use a "term syntax" for data, queries, and construction of data instead of the normal tag-based XML syntax. The right side of Figure 1 depicts the XML event as a (data) term. The term syntax is slightly more general than XML, indicating whether the order of children is relevant (square brackets []), or not (curly braces {}).

Querying such single event messages is a two-fold task: one has to (1) specify a class of relevant events (e.g., all *buy* events) and (2) extract data from the events (e.g., the price). XChange^{EQ} embeds the XML query language Xcerpt [28] for both. Figure 2 shows an exemplary *buy* event (left) and an event query that recognizes such *buy* events with a price total of $10 000 or more (right).

Xcerpt queries describe a pattern that is matched against the data. Query terms can be partial (indicated by double brackets or braces), meaning that a

```
<order>                                        order [
  <orderId >4711</orderId >                       orderId  {  4711  },
  <customer>John</customer>                        customer  {  "John"  },
  <buy>    <stock>IBM</stock>                      buy  [    stock  {  "IBM"  },
          <limit >3.14</limit >                             limit  {  3.14  },
          <volume >4000</volume>                            volume  {  4000  }      ]
</buy> </order>                                ]
```

Fig. 1. XML and term representation of an event

```
buy  [   orderId  {  4711  },              buy  {{   tradeId  {  var  I  },
         tradeId  {  4242  },                        customer  {  var  C  },
         customer  {  "John"  },                     stock  {  var  S  },
         stock  {  "IBM"  },                         price  {  var  P  },
         price  {  2.71  },                          volume  {  var  V  }
         volume  {  4000  }   ]             }}  where  {  var  P  *  var  V  >=  10000  }
```

Fig. 2. Atomic event query

matching data term can contain subterms not specified in the query, or total (indicated by single brackets or braces). Queries can contain variables (keyword **var**), which will be bound to the matching data, and a **where**-clause can be attached to specify non-structural (e.g., arithmetic) conditions. In this article, we will stick to simple queries as above. Note however that Xcerpt supports more advanced constructs for (subterm) negation, incompleteness in breadth and depth, and queries to graph-shaped data such as RDF. An introduction to Xcerpt is given in [28].

The result of evaluating an Xcerpt query on an event message is the set Σ of all possible substitutions for the free variables in the query (non-matching is signified by $\Sigma = \emptyset$). Our example query does not match the *order* event from Figure 1, but matches the *buy* event on the left of Fighre 2 with $\Sigma = \{\sigma_1\}$, $\sigma_1 = \{I \mapsto 4242, C \mapsto \text{John}, S \mapsto \text{IBM}, P \mapsto 2.71, V \mapsto 4000\}$.

In addition to event messages, XChange^{EQ} event queries can query for timer events. Absolute timer events are time points or intervals (possibly periodic) defined without reference to the occurrence time of some other event. They are specified in a similar way as queries to event messages and we refer to [3] for details. Relative timer events, i.e., time points or intervals defined in relation to some other event, will be looked at in Section 3.3 on event composition.

3.2   Reactive and Deductive Rules for Events

XChange^{EQ} uses two kinds of rules: deductive rules and reactive rules. Deductive rules allow to define new, "virtual" events from the events that are received. They have no side effects and are analogous to the definition of views for database data. Figure 3 (left) shows a deductive rule deriving a new *bigbuy* events from *buy* events satisfying the earlier event query of Figure 2. Deductive rules follow the syntax **DETECT** *event construction* **ON** *event query* **END**. The event construction in the rule head is simply a data term augmented with variables which are replaced during construction by their values obtained from evaluating the event

```
DETECT bigbuy {
        tradeId { var I },              RAISE
        customer { var C },               to(recipient=
        stock { var S }  }                  "http://auditor.com",
ON buy {{                                   transport=
    tradeId { var I },                      "http://.../HTTP/")
    customer { var C },                   {
    stock { var S },                        var B
    price { var P },                      }
    volume { var V }                    ON var B -> bigbuy {{ }}
    }} where { var P * var V >= 10000 }  END
END
```

Fig. 3. Deductive rule (left) and reactive rule (right)

query in the rule body. (Several variables bindings will lead to the construction of several events if no grouping or aggregation constructs are used.) The event construction is also called a construct term; more involved construction will be seen in Section 3.5 when we look at aggregation of data. Recursion of rules is restricted to stratifiable programs, see Section 4.2 for a deeper discussion.

Reactive rules are used for specifying a reaction to the occurrence of an event. The usual (re)action is constructing a new event message (as with deductive rules) and use it to call some Web Service. Note that this new event leaves the system and that it is up to the receiver to decide on the occurrence time (typically such events are considered to happen only at the time *point* when the corresponding message is received). For tasks involving accessing and updating persistent data, our event queries can be used in the Event-Condition-Action rules of the reactive language XChange.

An example for a reactive rule is in Figure 3 (right); it forwards every *big-buy* event (as derived by the deductive rule on the left) to a Web Service http://auditor.com using SOAP's HTTP transport binding. The syntax for reactive rules is similar to deductive rules, only they start with the keyword RAISE; in the rule head to() is used to indicate recipient and transport.

The distinction between deductive and reactive rules is important. While it is possible to "abuse" reactive rules to simulate or implement deductive rules (by sending oneself the result), this is undesirable: it is difficult with events that have a duration, misleading for programmers, less efficient for evaluation, and could allow arbitrary recursion (leading, e.g., to non-terminating programs or non-stratified use of negation).

3.3 Composition of Events

So far, we have only been looking at queries to single events. Since temporal conditions are dealt with separately, only two operators, or and and, are necessary to compose event queries into *composite event queries*. (Negation falls under event accumulation, see Section 3.5.) Both composition operators are multi-ary, allowing to compose any (positive) number of event queries (without need for nesting), and written in prefix notation. Disjunctions are a convenience in practical programming but not strictly necessary: a rule with a (binary) disjunction can be written as two rules. We therefore concentrate on conjunctions here.

```
DETECT  buyorderfulfilled  {  orderId  { var O },
                               tradeId  { var I },
                               stock    { var S } }
ON and  {
      order   {  orderId  { var O },
                 buy {{    stock  { var S }  }} },
      buy     {{  orderId  { var O },
                  tradeId  { var I }  }}  }
END
```

Fig. 4. Conjunction of event queries

```
and  {  event o:  order {{ orderId  { var O } }},
        event t:  extend[o, 1 min]  }
```

Fig. 5. Composition with relative timer event

When two event queries are composed with **and**, an answer to the composite event query is generated for every pair of answers to the constituent queries. If the constituent queries share free variables, only pairs with "compatible" variable bindings are considered. (This generalizes to composition of three and more event queries in the obvious manner.) Figure 4 illustrates the use of the **and** operator. The *buy order fulfilled* event is detected for every corresponding pair of *buy order* and *buy* event. The events have to agree on variable O (the orderId). The occurrence time of the detected *order fulfilled* event is the time interval enclosing the respective constituent events.

Composition of events gives rise to defining relative timer events, i.e., time points or intervals defined in relation to the occurrence time of some other event. Figure 5 shows a composite event query asking for an *order* event and a timer covering the whole time interval from the *order* event until one minute after. This timer event will be used later in Section 3.5 when querying for the absence of a corresponding *buy* event in this time interval.

An event identifier (o) is given to the left of the event query after the keyword **event**. It is then used in the definition of the relative timer extend[o, 1 min] which specifies a time interval one minute longer than the occurrence interval of o. (The time point at which o occurs is understood for this purpose as a degenerated time interval of zero length.) The event identifier t is not necessary here, but can be specified anyway. Event identifiers will also be used in temporal conditions and event accumulation (Sections 3.4 and 3.5).

Further constructors for relative timers are: shorten[e,d] (subtracting d from the end of e), extend-begin[e,d], shorten-begin[e,d] (adding or subtracting d at the begin of e), shift-forward[e,d], shift-backward[e,d] (moving e forward or backward by d).

3.4 Temporal Conditions

Temporal conditions on events and causal relationships between events play an important role in querying events. We concentrate in this paper on temporal conditions, though the approach generalizes to causal relationships. Just like

```
DETECT  earlyResellWithLoss  {   customer { var C },
                                 stock { var S }  }
ON and {
      event b: buy  {{   customer { var C },
                         stock { var S },
                         price { var P1 }  }},
      event s: sell {{   customer { var C },
                         stock { var S },
                         price { var P2 }  }}
      } where { b before s, timeDiff(b,s)<1hour, var P1>var P2 }
END
```

Fig. 6. Event query with temporal conditions

conditions on event data, temporal conditions are specified in the **where**-clause of an event query and make use of the event identifiers introduced above.

The event query in Figure 6 involves temporal conditions. It detects situations where a customer first buys stocks and then sells them again within a short time (less than 1 hour) at a lower price. The query illustrates that typical applications require both qualitative conditions (**b before s**) and quantitative (or metric) conditions (**timeDiff(b,s) < 1 hour**). In addition, the query also includes a data condition for the price (**var P1 > var P2**).

In principle, various external calendar and time reasoning systems could be used to specify and evaluate temporal conditions. However, many optimizations for the evaluation of event queries require knowledge about temporal conditions. See [6] for an initial discussion of temporal optimizations.

XChange^{EQ} deals with non-periodic time intervals (time points are treated as degenerated intervals of zero length), periodic time intervals (i.e., sequences of non-periodic intervals), and durations (lengths of time). An overview of the built-in constructs for temporal conditions can be found in [3].

Note that there is an important difference between timer events used in queries and references to time as part of **where**-conditions. Timer events have to happen for the event query to yield an answer (i.e., they are waited for), while time references in conditions can lie in the future and only restrict the possible answers to an event query.

3.5 Event Accumulation

Event querying displays its differences to traditional querying most perspicuously in non-monotonic query features such as negation or aggregation. For traditional database queries, the data to be considered for negation or aggregation is readily available in the database and this database is *finite*.[3] In contrast, events are received over time in an event stream which is unbounded, i.e., potentially infinite. Applying negation or aggregation on such a (temporally) infinite event stream would imply that one has to wait "forever" for an answer because events received at a later time might always change the current answer. We therefore need a way to restrict the event stream to a finite temporal extent (i.e., a finite

---

[3] Recursive rules or views may allow to define infinite databases intensionally. However, the extensional data (the "base facts") is still finite.

```
DETECT buyOrderOverdue {
          orderId { var I }  }
ON and {
     event o: order {{
        orderId { var I }
        buy {{ }}  }},
     event t: extend[o, 1 min],
     while t: not buy {
        orderId { var I }  }
  }
END
```

```
RAISE to (...) {
     reportOfDailyAverages {
     all entry {
        stock { var S },
        avgPrice { avg(all var P) }
     } group-by var S  }  }
ON and {
     event t: tradingDay{{ }},
     while t: collect sell {
        stock { var S },
        price { var P }  }
  }
END
```

Fig. 7. Event accumulation for negation (left) and aggregation (right)

time interval) and apply negation and aggregation only to the events collected in this accumulation window.[4]

It should be possible to determine the accumulation window dynamically depending on the event stream received so far. Typical cases of such accumulation windows are: "from event a until event b," "one minute until event b," "from event a for one minute," and (since events can occur over time intervals, not just time points) "while event c." Here we only look at the last case because it subsumes the first three (they can be defined as composite events).

Negation is supported by applying the **not** operator to an event query. The window is specified with the keyword **while** and the event identifier of the event defining the window. The meaning is as one might expect: the negated event query **while** t: **not** q is successful if no event satisfying q occurs during the time interval given by t. An example can be seen in Figure 7 (left): it detects buy orders that are overdue, i.e., where no matching buy transaction has taken place within one minute after placing the order. The accumulation window is specified by the event query t, which is a timer relative to the *order* event. Observe that the negated query can contain variables that are also used outside the negation; the example reveals the strong need to support this.

Following the design of the embedded query language Xcerpt, aggregation constructs are used in the *head* of a rule, since they are related to the construction of new data. The task of the *body* is only *collecting* the necessary data or events. Collecting events in the body of a rule is similar to negation and indicated by the keyword **collect**. The rule in Figure 7 (right) has an event query collecting *sell* events over a full *trading day*. The actual aggregation takes place in the head of the rule, where all sales prices (P) for the same stock (S) are averaged and a report containing one entry for each stock is generated. The report is sent at the end of each trading day; this is reflected in the syntax by the fact that **tradingDay{{ }}** must be written as an event, i.e., must actually occur.

Aggregation follows the syntax and semantics of Xcerpt (see [27] for a full account), again showing that it is beneficial to base an event query language on a data query language. The keyword **all** indicates a structural aggregation,

---

[4] Keep in mind that accumulation here refers to the way we specify queries, not the way evaluation is actually performed. Keeping all events in the accumulation windows in memory is generally neither desirable nor necessary for query evaluation.

generating an **entry** element for each distinct value of the variable S (indicated with **group-by**). Inside the **entry**-element an aggregation function **avg** is used to compute the average price for each individual stock.

Aggregation has rarely been considered in work on composite events, though it is clearly needed in many applications, including our stock market example. A notable exception is [24], which however applies only to relational data (not semi-structured or XML) and does not have the benefits of a separation of the query dimensions as XChange^{EQ}.

4 Formal Semantics

Having introduced XChange^{EQ} informally above, we now supply formal, declarative semantics for stratified programs in the form of model and fixpoint theories. While this is a well-established approach for rule-based languages [22,2], including traditional database query languages supporting views or deductive rules, it has not been applied to event query languages before. Related work on semantics for event queries usually has an "algebraic flavor" (as the languages themselves do), where the semantics for operators are given as functions between sequences (or histories or traces) of events, e.g., [30,21]. Further, these approaches often neglect *data* in events (especially semi-structured data) and it is not clear how they could be extended to support deductive *rules* (or views) over events.

In addition to accommodating both rules and data, the model theoretic approach presented here can be argued to be more declarative than previous algebraic approaches, expressing *how* an event is to be to detected rather than *what* event is to be detected, making programs easier to understand and optimize.

The following specifics of querying events as opposed to pure (database) data have to be arranged for in our semantics and make it novel compared their counterpart in the logic programming literature [22,2]: (1) in addition to normal variables, event identifiers are accommodated, (2) answers to composite event queries have an occurrence time, (3) temporal relations have a fixed interpretation. Finally, the model theory must be (4) sensible for potentially *infinite* streams of events (this also entails that negation and aggregation of events must be "scoped" over a time window as we have seen earlier in Section 3.5).

4.1 Model Theory

Our model theory is Tarskian-style [11], i.e., it uses a valuation function for free variables and defines an entailment relation between an interpretation and sentences (rules and queries) from the language *recursively over the structure* of the sentences.[5] Tarskian model theories have the advantage of being highly declarative, theoretically well-understood, and relatively easy to understand.

An **event** happens over a given time interval and has a representation as message (as data term). Formally it is a tuple of a (closed and convex) time interval t and a data term e, written e^t. The set of all events is denoted *Events*.

---

[5] This recursive definition over the structure allows to consider sub-formulas of a formula in isolation, which is beneficial for both understanding and evaluation.

Time is assumed to be a linearly[6] ordered set of time points $(\mathbb{T}, <)$. The time intervals over which events happen are closed and convex, i.e., have the form $t = [b, e] = \{p \mid b \leq p \leq e\}$ (where $b \in \mathbb{T}$ and $e \in \mathbb{T}$). For convenience we define: $begin([b, e]) = b$, $end([b, e]) = e$, $[b_1, e_1] \sqcup [b_2, e_2] = [min\{b_1, b_2\}, max\{e_1, e_2\}]$, and $[b_1, e_1] \sqsubseteq [b_2, e_2]$ iff $b_2 \leq b_1$ and $e_1 \leq e_2$.

Matching of **Atomic Event Queries** against single incoming events is based on a non-standard unification that is especially designed for the variations and incompleteness in semi-structured data. Atomic Event Queries are single query terms q that match only for the data term part e of events e^t; this does not involve time or multiple events. Note that the query terms usually contain free variables. The matching of query terms and data terms is based on **Simulation**, which is a relation between ground terms, denoted $\preceq$. Intuitively, $q \preceq d$ means that the nodes and structure of q can be found in d. Simulation naturally extends to a non-ground query term q' by asking whether there is a (grounding) substitution σ for the free variables in q' such that the ground query term $q = \sigma(q')$ obtained by applying the substitution σ to q' simulates with the given data term d. Further details can be found in [27]; they are not important for understanding the presented model theory and thus not discussed here.

Substitution sets Σ rather than single substitutions σ are used in our model theory to accommodate grouping and aggregation in the construction in rule heads. Application $\Sigma(c)$ of Σ to a construct term c results in a set of data terms. For convenience we also define the application to query terms q with $\Sigma(q) = \{\sigma(q) \mid \sigma \in \Sigma\}$.

An **interpretation** for a given XChange^{EQ} query, rule, or program is a 3-tuple $M = (I, \Sigma, \tau)$, where (1) $I \subseteq Events$ is the set of events e^t that "happen," i.e., are either in the stream of incoming events or derived by some deductive rule. (2) $\Sigma \neq \emptyset$ is a grounding substitution set containing substitutions for the "normal" variables (i.e., data variables, but not event identifiers). (3) τ is a substitution for the event identifiers, i.e., a mapping from event variables to $Events$. The substitution τ for event identifiers (cf. Section 3.3) is the first unusual features of our model theory. Since τ signifies the events that contributed to the answer of some query, we also call it an "event trace."

The **satisfaction** $M \models F^t$ of an XChange^{EQ} expression F over an occurrence time t in an interpretation M is defined recursively in Figure 8. The time stamping of expressions is the second unusual feature of our model theory.

Given an XChange^{EQ} program P and a stream of incoming events E, we call an interpretation $M = (I, \Sigma, \tau)$ a **model** of P under E if (1) M satisfies all rules $(c \leftarrow Q) \in P$ for all time intervals t and (2) contains the stream of incoming events, i.e., $E \subseteq I$. Note that here the event stream simply corresponds to the notion of base facts or extensional data found of traditional model theories.

The satisfaction relation uses a fixed interpretation W for all conditions that can occur in the `where`-clause of a query. This includes the temporal relations

---

[6] Linear time is chosen because we are interested in event that actually happened, not in potential futures (where a branching time would be more apt).

$I, \Sigma, \tau \models (\text{event } i : q)^t$ iff exists $e^{t'} \in I$ with $\tau(i) = e^{t'}$, $t' = t$,
and for all $e' \in \Sigma(q)$ we have $e' \preceq e$

$I, \Sigma, \tau \models (\text{event } i : \text{extends}[j, d])^t$ iff exists $e^{t'}$ with $\tau(j) = e^{t'}$, $\tau(i) = e^t$, $t = t' + d$
...   (Definitions for other temporal events are similar and skipped.)

$M \models (q_1 \wedge q_2)^t$ iff $M \models q_1^{t_1}$ and $M \models q_2^{t_2}$ and $t = t_1 \sqcup t_2$

$M \models (q_1 \vee q_2)^t$ iff $M \models q_1^t$ or $M \models q_2^t$

$I, \Sigma, \tau \models (Q \text{ where } C)^t$ iff $I, \Sigma, \tau \models Q^t$ and $W_{\Sigma,\tau}(C) = true$

$I, \Sigma, \tau \models (\text{while } j : \text{ not } q)^t$ iff exists $e^{t'}$ with $\tau(j) = e^{t'}$, $t' = t$,
and for all $t'' \sqsubseteq t$ we have $I, \Sigma, \tau \not\models q^{t''}$

$I, \Sigma, \tau \models (\text{while } j : \text{ collect } q)^t$ iff exists $e^{t'}$ with $\tau(j) = e^{t'}$, $t' = t$, and exist $n \geq 0$,
$\Sigma_1, \ldots \Sigma_n$, $t_1 \sqsubseteq t, \ldots t_n \sqsubseteq t$ with $\Sigma = \bigcup_{i=1..n} \Sigma_i$,
and for all $i = 1..n$ we have $I, \Sigma_i, \tau \models q^{t_i}$

$I, \Sigma, \tau \models (c \leftarrow Q)^t$ iff (1) $\Sigma'(c)^t \subseteq I$ for Σ' maximal (w.r.t. $FreeVars(Q)$) and τ'
such that $I, \Sigma', \tau' \models Q^t$, or (2) $I, \Sigma', \tau' \not\models Q^t$ for all Σ', τ'

$W_{\Sigma,\tau}(i \text{ before } j) = \textbf{true}$ iff $end(\tau(i)) < begin(\tau(j))$
$W_{\Sigma,\tau}(i \text{ during } j) = \textbf{true}$ iff $begin(\tau(j)) < begin(\tau(i))$ and $end(\tau(i)) < end(\tau(j))$
$W_{\Sigma,\tau}(i \text{ overlaps } j) = \textbf{true}$ iff $begin(\tau(j)) < begin(\tau(i)) < end(\tau(j)) < end(\tau(i))$

Fig. 8. Model Theory for XChange^{EQ}

like `before` and is the third unusual feature of our model theory. W is a function that maps a substitution set Σ, an event trace τ, and an atomic condition C to true or false; we usually write Σ and τ in the index. $W_{\Sigma,\tau}$ extends straightforwardly to boolean formulas of conditions. The definition of W is left outside the "core model theory" to make it more modular and allow to easily integrate different temporal reasoners. In Figure 8, we have given only the definitions for `before`, `during`, and `overlaps` for space reasons.

Our fourth requirement on the model theory was that it is sensible on (potentially) infinite streams of events. The basic idea for this is that to evaluate a program P over a time interval t, we only have to consider events happening during t. We will state this formally after giving the fixpoint theory.

4.2 Fixpoint Theory

A model theory, such as the one presented above, has the issue of allowing many models for a given program. A common and convenient way to obtain a unique model is to define it as the solution of a fixpoint equation (which is based on the model theory). A fixpoint theory also describes an abstract, simple, forward-chaining evaluation method, which can easily be extended to work incrementally as is required for event queries [4].

Our fixpoint theory requires XChange^{EQ} programs to be stratifiable [2]. **Stratification** restricts the use of recursion in rules by ordering the rules of a program P into so-called strata (sets P_i of rules with $P = P_1 \uplus \cdots \uplus P_n$) such that a rule in a given stratum can only depend on (i.e., access results from) rules in lower strata (or the same stratum, in some cases). The restriction to stratifiable programs could be partially lifted at the cost of a more involved semantics (and evaluation). This is however outside the scope of this paper.

Three types of stratification are required: (1) Negation stratification, i.e., events that are negated in the query of a rule may only be constructed by rules in lower strata, events that occur positively may only be constructed by rules in lower strata or the same stratum. (2) Grouping stratification, i.e., rules using grouping constructs like `all` in the construction may only query for events constructed in lower strata. (3) Temporal stratification, i.e., if a rule queries a relative temporal event like `extends[i, 1min]` then the anchoring event (here: i) may only be constructed in lower strata. While negation and grouping stratification are fairly standard, temporal stratification is a requirement specific to complex event query programs like those expressible in XChange^{EQ}. We are not aware of former consideration of the notion of temporal stratification. For a formal definition of our stratification, we refer to [5].

The **fixpoint operator** T_P for an XChange^{EQ}-Program P is defined as:

$$T_P(I) = I \cup \{e^t \mid \text{there exist a rule } c \leftarrow Q \in P, \text{ a maximal substitution set } \Sigma,$$
$$\text{and a substitution } \tau \text{ such that } I, \Sigma, \tau \models Q^t \text{ and } e \in \Sigma(c)\}$$

The repeated application of T_P until a fixpoint is reached is denoted T_P^ω.

The **fixpoint interpretation**[7] $M_{P,E}$ of a program P with stratification $P = P_1 \uplus \cdots \uplus P_n$ under and event stream E is defined by computing fixpoints stratum by stratum: $M_0 = E = T_\emptyset^\omega(E)$, $M_1 = T_{\overline{P_1}}^\omega(M_0) \ldots$, $M_{P,E} = M_n = T_{\overline{P_n}}^\omega(M_{n-1})$. Here, $\overline{P_i} = \bigcup_{j \leq j} P_j$ denotes the set of all rules in strata P_i and lower.

Theorem 1 justifies our definition as usual for fixpoint semantics: For a stratifiable program P and an event stream E, $M_{P,E}$ is a minimal model of P under E. Further, $M_{P,E}$ is independent of the stratification of P.

More interestingly, we can show that the model theory and fixpoint semantics are sensible on infinite event streams. The next theorem justifies a streaming evaluation, where answers to composite event queries are generated "online" and we never have to wait for the stream to end (which it will not if infinite). This is the last feature of our semantics that is peculiar for event queries.

Theorem 2: Let $E \mid t$ denote the restriction of an event stream E to a time interval t, i.e., $E \mid t = \{e^{t'} \in E \mid t' \sqsubseteq t\}$. Similarly, let $M \mid t$ denote the restriction of an interpretation M to t. Then the result of applying the fixpoint procedure to $E \mid t$ is the same as applying it to E for the time interval t, i.e., $M_{P,E|t} \mid t = M_{P,E} \mid t$. In other words to evaluate a program over a time interval t, we do not have to consider any events happening outside of t.

Proofs for both theorems are presented in an extended version of this paper [5]. The proof for theorem 1 is an adoption of a proof in [22].

5   Conclusions and Future Work

This article has introduced the high-level event query language XChange^{EQ}, emphasizing language design and formal semantics. XChange^{EQ} deviates from previous event query languages in a separation of the query dimensions data extraction, event composition, temporal relationships, and event accumulation.

---

[7] Since we consider whole programs P now, only the set I of events that happen is relevant for the fixpoint interpretation of P; Σ and τ are thus skipped from now on.

This separation allows a complete coverage of each of the dimensions, yielding a language that can be argued to have reached a degree of expressive completeness.

The ability to query events represented in XML and other Web formats, makes XChange^{EQ} suited for use in service-oriented and event-driven architectures based on Web Services. Important for practical use, rules are supported as an abstraction and reasoning mechanism for events. Rule-based reasoning about events is also expected to become relevant in efforts to bring rules, including reactive rules, to the (Semantic) Web [26,4].

Efficient evaluation methods that utilize temporal conditions [6] and query optimization for large numbers of event queries are the current focus of our research. Implementation of our language in the scope of XChange is ongoing work.

Acknowledgments

This research has been funded by the European Commission and by the Swiss Federal Office for Education and Science within the 6th Framework Programme project REWERSE number 506779 (http://rewerse.net).

References

1. Adaikkalavan, R., Chakravarthy, S.: SnoopIB: Interval-based event specification and detection for active databases. Data and Knowledge Eng. In press (2005)
2. Apt, K.R., Blair, H.A., Walker, A.: Towards a theory of declarative knowledge. In: Foundations of Deductive Databases and Logic Programming, Morgan Kaufmann, Washington (1988)
3. Bry, F., Eckert, M.: A high-level query language for events. In: Proc. Int. Workshop on Event-driven Architecture, Processing and Systems (2006)
4. Bry, F., Eckert, M.: Twelve theses on reactive rules for the Web. In: Proc. Int. Workshop Reactivity on the Web (2006)
5. Bry, F., Eckert, M.: Rule-based composite event queries: The language XChange^{EQ} and its semantics [extended version]. Technical report, Inst. f. Informatics, U. of Munich, 2007. Available at www.pms.ifi.lmu.de/publikationen/
6. Bry, F., Eckert, M.: Temporal order optimizations of incremental joins for composite event detection. Technical report, Inst. f. Informatics, U. of Munich, 2007. Available at www.pms.ifi.lmu.de/publikationen/
7. Bry, F., Eckert, M., Grallert, H., Pătrânjan, P.-L.: Evolution of distributed Web data: An application of the reactive language XChange. In: Proc. Int. Conf. on Data Engineering (Demonstrations) (2006)
8. Bry, F., Eckert, M., Pătrânjan, P. L.: Querying composite events for reactivity on the Web. In: Proc. Int. Workshop on XML Research and Applications (2006)
9. Bry, F., Eckert, M., Pătrânjan, P.-L.: Reactivity on the Web: Paradigms and applications of the language XChange. J. of Web Engineering, vol. 5(1) (2006)
10. Bry, F., Eckert, M., Pătrânjan, P.-L., Romanenko, I.: Realizing business processes with ECA rules: Benefits, challenges, limits. In: Alferes, J.J., Bailey, J., May, W., Schwertel, U. (eds.) PPSWR 2006. LNCS, vol. 4187, Springer, Heidelberg (2006)
11. Bry, F., Marchiori, M.: Ten theses on logic languages for the Semantic Web. In: Fages, F., Soliman, S. (eds.) PPSWR 2005. LNCS, vol. 3703, Springer, Heidelberg (2005)

12. Buchmann, A.P., Zimmermann, J., Blakeley, J.A., Wells, D.L.: Building an integrated active OODBMS: Requirements, architecture, and design decisions. In: Proc. Int. Conf. on Data Engineering (1995)
13. Chakravarthy, S., Krishnaprasad, V., Anwar, E., Kim, S.-K.: Composite events for active databases: Semantics, contexts and detection. In: Proc. Int. Conf. on Very Large Data Bases (1994)
14. Common Base Event. `www.ibm.com/developerworks/webservices/library/ws-cbe`
15. Diao, Y., Rizvi, S., Franklin, M.J.: Towards an internet-scale XML dissemination service. In: Proc. Int. Conf. on Very Large Data Bases (2004)
16. Etzion, O.: Towards an event-driven architecture: An infrastructure for event processing (position paper). In: Proc. Int. Conf. on Rules and Rule Markup Languages for the Semantic Web (2005)
17. Galton, A., Augusto, J.C.: Two approaches to event definition. In: Proc. Int. Conf. on Database and Expert Systems Applications (2002)
18. Gatziu, S., Dittrich, K.R.: Events in an active object-oriented database system. In: Proc. Int. Workshop on Rules in Database Systems (1993)
19. Gehani, N.H., Jagadish, H.V., Shmueli, O.: Composite event specification in active databases: Model and implementation. In: Proc. Int. Conf. on Very Large Data Bases (1992)
20. Gudgin, M., et al.: SOAP 1.2. W3C recommendation (2003)
21. Hinze, A., Voisard, A.: A parameterized algebra for event notification services. In: Proc. Int. Symp. on Temporal Representation and Reasoning (2002)
22. Lloyd, J.W.: Foundations of Logic Programming. Springer, Heidelberg (1993)
23. May, W., Alferes, J.J., Amador, R.: Active rules in the Semantic Web: Dealing with language heterogeneity. In: Proc. Int. Conf. on Rules and Rule Markup Languages for the Semantic Web (2005)
24. Motakis, I., Zaniolo, C.: Temporal aggregation in active database rules. In: Proc. Int. Conf. on Management of Data (SIGMOD) (1997)
25. Pereira, J., Fabret, F., Jacobsen, H.-A., Llirbat, F., Shasha, D.: WebFilter: A high-throughput XML-based publish and subscribe system. In: Proc. Int. Conf. on Very Large Databases (2001)
26. Rule Interchange Format WG Charter. `www.w3.org/2005/rules/wg/charter`
27. Schaffert, S.: Xcerpt: A Rule-Based Query and Transformation Language for the Web. PhD thesis, Inst. f. Informatics, U. of Munich (2004)
28. Schaffert, S., Bry, F.: Querying the Web reconsidered: A practical introduction to Xcerpt. In: Proc. Extreme Markup Languages (2004)
29. Zhu, D., Sethi, A.S.: SEL, a new event pattern specification language for event correlation. In: Proc. Int. Conf. on Computer Communications and Networks (2001)
30. Zimmer, D., Unland, R.: On the semantics of complex events in active database management systems. In: Proc. Int. Conf. on Data Engineering (1999)

On the Semantics of Service Compositions

Harald Meyer

Hasso-Plattner-Institute for IT-Systems-Engineering
Prof.-Dr.-Helmert-Strasse 2-3, 14482 Potsdam, Germany
harald.meyer@hpi.uni-potsdam.de

Abstract. Supporting service discovery by semantic service specifications is currently an important research area. While the approaches for the annotation of individual services are well researched, determining the semantics of compositions of services remains an open research issue.

In this paper, we present an approach to generate the semantics of service compositions from the semantics of the contained services. To do this we assume a formal Workflow net model of the service composition. With an example use case we show how this works in practice.

1 Introduction

Discovery, composition, and management of services are the most important tasks in a service-oriented architecture (SOA) [1,2]. To perform them successfully in a large service landscape, semantic specifications of service functionality are important [3,4,5]. While several approaches for the description of individual service functionality exist, how to determine the functionality of service compositions remains largely unclear. It is the aggregation of the functionality of the individual services inside the composition. But determining this in the presence of complex control flow constructs is challenging. In this paper, we provide a formal model for the calculation of service composition functionality based on Petri nets that allows us to calculate the functionality for processes containing and- or xor- splits and joins.

There a several approaches for the description of individual service functionality through semantic service specification. The two most prominent approaches are OWL-S [6] and WSMO [7]. In OWL-S a service has a service profile that contains the functionality description consisting of input, output, precondition, and effect. These four elements describe the functionality of the service. The input describes the input parameters of the service; the output describes what the service returns. With precondition and effect logical expressions can be formulated to describe the states in which the service is invokable and that are reached by invoking the service. WSMO has a very similar model: A service has capability consisting of precondition, assumption, postcondition, and effect. While precondition and postcondition correspond to input and output in OWL-S, assumption and effect correspond to precondition and effect in OWL-S. So while they differ in syntax, terminology, and in the logical foundations used to express service functionality, they both agree on extending service descriptions

M. Marchiori, J.Z. Pan, and C. de Sainte Marie (Eds.): RR 2007, LNCS 4524, pp. 31–42, 2007.

by logical expressions to describe the situation in which a service is invokable and the effects on the situation by invoking the service [8]. Having semantic service specifications, facilitates the discovery of services. As the functionality of services is known, matchmaking can be used to find services matching given preconditions and effects. Composition and management both heavily rely on discovery so semantic service specifications support them as well.

We argue that knowing what a service composition does is equally important as knowing what individual services do. A service composition is not the task of creating the process but the resulting process that can be enacted. Knowing the functionality of a service composition is important if discovery is not only performed on individual services but also on service compositions. While no individual service fulfills the request, an existing composition might fulfill it. Finding it, saves us from re-modeling it. Also service compositions can be exposed as services again. This service requires a semantic service specification. By giving means to calculate the functionality of the new service from the functionality of the services it is composed of, the publication of the new service is simplified.

One might be interested in what a service composition does to verify that it works as expected. After modeling a service composition, one can calculate the functionality and check, manually or automated, whether it provides the desired functionality. This verification task can also be part of a semi-automated service composition approach. In [9] and [10] we introduced three mixed initiative features for semi-automated composition: filter inappropriate services, suggest partial plans, and check validity. While the two first features can be implemented using existing service matchmaking and automated service composition approaches, the last one can be realized by the work presented in this paper. A last use case for the verification of service composition is the verification of automated service composition results. While proofs for the correctness of automated service composition approaches exist, bugs in the implementation or incorrect service specifications can lead to erroneous service compositions. Checking whether the created service composition serves the intended purpose, can detect some of problems.

In the next section, we will give a short overview of Petri nets and workflow nets. Then in Section 3 we will present our formal model on how to express the semantics of services inside a Petri net. This model will serve as the foundations for the algorithms presented in Section 4 for the calculation of service composition preconditions and effects. Afterwards, in Section 5, we will show how this algorithm works with a service composition example and demonstrate our tool that implements these algorithms. The paper closes with an overview of related work in Section 6 and the conclusion in Section 7.

2   Preliminaries: Petri Nets and Workflow Nets

This section describes the notions of Petri nets and workflow nets. A Petri net is a directed bipartite graph. It contains two sets of vertices: places and transitions.

The directed edges connect either a place with a transition or a transition with a place.

Definition 1. *A Petri net is a triple* $n = (P, T, f)$ *with:*

- *P: set of places*
- *T: set of transitions*
- $f \subseteq (P \times T) \cup (T \times P)$

The sets of places and transitions are disjoint : $P \cap T = \emptyset$

The input and output places of a transition t are denoted with $\cdot t$ and $t \cdot$. Each place can host multiple token. The assignment of tokens to the places of a Petri net is called the marking:

Definition 2. *A marking is function* $m : P \to N$ *that assigns to each place the number of tokens in this place.*

The marking represents the state of the Petri net. State changes of the Petri net result in different markings. State changes can occur when an *enabled* transition *fires*:

Definition 3. *A transition* t *is enabled if all its input places* $\cdot t$ *contain at least one token.*

If a transition t *fires one token is removed from each input place and one token is added to each output place.*

Petri nets are a very generic concept to describe processes. Workflow nets restrict the notation of Petri nets to a subset sufficient for modeling the control flow of workflows:

Definition 4. *A Petri net* $n = (P, T, f)$ *is a workflow net iff:*

- *The net has one input place* i *(no incoming transitions)*
- *The net has one output place* o *(not outgoing transitions)*
- *Every vertex* $v \in P \cap T$ *is on a path from the input place to the output pace.*

A workflow net is sound if it terminates with one token in place o and no tokens in any other place and it does not contain any dead tasks. In the following we will limit ourselves to sound workflow nets to model service compositions.

3   Formal Model

To support the calculation of service composition functionality, workflow nets need to be extended to incorporate service semantics. Before this can be done, we first need to define a few basic concepts. A service is a discrete business functionality. It is described by a service specification:

Definition 5. *A service specification* $s = (\mathcal{I}, \mathcal{O}, pre, eff)$ *is a tuple with*

- $\mathcal{I}$: *List of input parameters consisting of variables* $\in V$
- $\mathcal{O}$: *List of output parameters consisting of variables* $\in V$
- *pre: The precondition of the service is a logical expression and must be satisfied in order to invoke the service.*
- *eff: The effect of the service is a logical expression. It describes the changes to the current state resulting from the invocation of the service.*

A **service invocation** $i = (s, z)$ *is a pair consisting of a service specification* s *and a variable assignment* $z : V \rightarrow \mathcal{T}_{ground}$ *that assigns every variable a ground term. Variables* $v \in V$ *are all the elements from* $\mathcal{I}$ *and* $\mathcal{O}$ *plus the variables in pre and eff.*

INV is the set of all possible service invocations for a given set of service specifications.

Service invocations represent the atomic elements of service compositions. They are ordered in such a way to reach the goal of the service composition. In a workflow net they are the transitions. Hence, to represent them in a workflow net, the definition for workflow nets needs to be extended:

Definition 6. *A semantic workflow net is a 4-tuple* $sn = (P, T, f, l_s)$ *is a Petri net* $n = (P, T, f)$ *with a function* $l_s : T \rightarrow INV$ *that maps each transition to a service invocation.*

Finally, we need to refine the concept of states. In a workflow net the state is the marking assigning tokens to the place of the net. But given logically specified service semantics, a logical state exists as well. The logical state is a logical expression assigned to each marking of a workflow net. How these states are calculated will be presented in the next section.

4   Calculation of Service Composition Precondition and Effect

How to calculate the precondition and effect of given a semantic workflow net is described in this section. First the effect calculation will be introduced. Afterwards it is shown how this algorithm can be modified and extended to calculate preconditions. To do this, we need to define what happens when a service is invoked:

Definition 7. *A service invocation* $i = (s, z)$ *with* $s = (\mathcal{I}, \mathcal{O}, pre, eff)$ *is **invokable** in state* a *if* $a \models pre$. ***Invoking service*** s *variable assignment* z *in state* a *leads to a state transition. This can be defined by the state transition function*

$\gamma(a, i) = a \bigcup eff \setminus (\{x | \neg x \in eff\} \bigcup \{\neg x | if x \in eff\})$. γ *is a partial function only defined if* $a \models pre$.

If an invokable service is invoked, all its effects are added to the state. Then all the facts of the state which are negated in the effects and all negated facts of the state which are not negated in the effects are removed from the new state.

4.1   Calculation of Effects

The calculation of the effects of a service composition works by recursively defining the current state for markings of the workflow net. Before we can show how this is done, we need to introduce the *reachability graph*:

Definition 8. *Given a semantic workflow net* $n = (P, T, f, l_s)$ *and an initial marking* m_1 *the reachability graph is a directed, labeled graph* $mg = (V, E, l_V, l_E)$. *The vertices* V *represent the possible markings. The labeling function* $l_V : V \rightarrow M$ *assigns to each vertex the according marking. The edges* E *represent the transitions of the Petri net. The labeling function* $l_E : E \rightarrow T$ *assigns a transition to every edge.*

Given this notion of a reachability graph the logical state for a given marking can be defined based on the logical states of its preceding markings:

Definition 9. *The logical state* s *for a marking* m *is given as* $s = \bigvee \gamma(s_{m'}, i')$ *with* $i' = l_s(l_E(e))$ *and* $e = (m', m) \in E$ *where* $s_{m'}$ *is the logical state of* m'. *The initial marking has the empty logical state* s_0.

The effect of a service composition is the logical state assigned to its final marking.

This means that the state for a marking is given by the states of its preceding markings and the effects of the transitions leading from them to the current marking. If a marking has more than one incoming marking, several actual states are possible. To express this in one state, all possible states are combined disjunctively. With this possibility to calculate the logical state for a marking, the effect of a workflow net is the state assigned to its final marking. To show how this works we will now look at three prominent examples: sequence, and-split and -join, xor-split and join. For each, its effect will be calculated.

First, Figure 1 shows a workflow net containing a sequence and all possible markings. The initial marking is $m_1 T$ with $s_{m_1} = \{\}$; m_3 is the final marking and we want to calculate s_3. To calculate it we need to solve $\gamma(s_{m_2}, t_2)$ which can be reduced to $\gamma(\gamma(s_{m_1}, t_1), t_2) = \gamma(\gamma(\{\}, t_1), t_2) = a \wedge b$.

Similarly compositions with and-splits and -joins work (Fig. 2). This process has the following markings:

- $m_1 = p_1$ (initial marking)
- $m_2 = p_2 + p_3$
- $m_3 = p_3 + p_4$
- $m_4 = p_2 + p_5$
- $m_5 = p_4 + p_5$
- $m_6 = p_6$ (final marking)

This results in the reachability graph displayed in Figure 3. To calculate the service composition effect, the logical state assigned to the final marking M_6 needs to be calculated. This state is given by $s_{m_6} = \gamma(s_{m_5}, t_4) = \gamma(\gamma(s_{m_3}, t_3) \vee \gamma(s_{m_4}, t_2), t_4) = \gamma(\gamma(\gamma(s_{m_2}, t_2), t_3) \vee \gamma(\gamma(s_{m_2}, t_3), t_2), t_4) =$

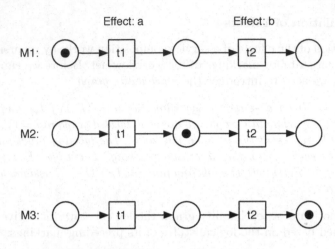

Fig. 1. Workflow net with a sequence

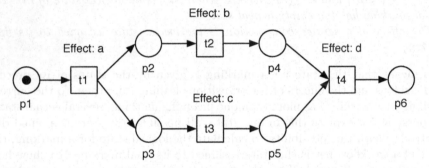

Fig. 2. Workflow Net with And-split and-join

$\gamma(\gamma(\gamma(\gamma(s_{m_1}, t_1), t_2), t_3) \vee \gamma(\gamma(\gamma(s_{m_1}, t_1), t_3), t_2), t_4) = ((a \wedge b \wedge c) \vee (a \wedge c \wedge b)) \wedge d = a \wedge b \wedge c \wedge d$. As you can see, even though the algorithm introduced a disjunction, it can be reduced to the expected outcome.

Finally, let us look at a composition with xor-splits and -joins. This composition is depicted in Figure 4. It has the following markings:

- $m_1 = p_1$ (initial marking)
- $m_2 = p_2$
- $m_3 = p_3$
- $m_4 = p_4$ (final marking)

The initial marking has two succeeding markings: m_2 and m_3. And both markings have exactly one succeeding marking m_4, the final marking. Calculating the state s_{m_4} works as follows: $s_{m_4} = \gamma(s_{m_2}, t_3) \vee \gamma(s_{m_3}, t_4) = \gamma(\gamma(s_{m_1}, t_1), t_3) \vee \gamma(\gamma(s_{m_1}, t_2), t_4) = (a \wedge c) \vee (b \wedge d)$. So this results in an effect for the composition one might expected. Either t_1 and t_3 or t_2 and t_4 are invoked. Actually, the service effect also allows for a third possibility: all four transitions are invoked.

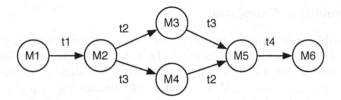

Fig. 3. Reachability Graph for And-split and -join

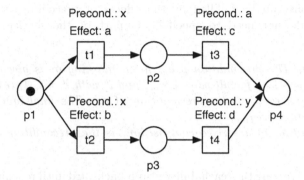

Fig. 4. Workflow Net with Xor-split and-join

This does not map exactly to the semantics of the Workflow net, which forbids this possibility. While using exclusive or would solve this problem, it opens up another one. The previous Workflow net contained an and-split and an and-join. In it the transitions t_2 and t_3 can fire in arbitrary order leading to distinct markings. In logics, the order of propositions is irrelevant, rendering $(a \wedge b \wedge c)$ and $(a \wedge c \wedge b)$ equivalent. Using inclusive or, this means that they can be merged. But with an exclusive or this results in a contradiction. Therefore, we choose the inclusive or leading to composition effects that are less restrictive than implied by the Workflow net. One possible solution to overcome this problem, is to replace the inclusive or by an exclusive or only after the whole calculation is finished and possible contradictions are resolved. This is allowed if only those axioms of the boolean algebra $(A, \wedge, \vee)$ are used that are also defined in the corresponding boolean ring $(A, \oplus, \wedge)$ plus idempotence.

In all examples listed above, the service effects were quite simple consisting of a singular fact. But service effects can be more complicated. They can contain conjunctions and disjunctions. In the next section, we will look at such a more complicated example. They may also contain first-order literals containing variables. Of course, these variables must be grounded in the service invocations assigned to the transitions.

The main restriction the algorithm currently has is that it does not allow for cycles in the workflow net. Because if it encounters a workflow net with cycles, the algorithm is not guaranteed to terminate. But for acyclic workflow nets termination is guaranteed.

4.2   Precondition Calculation

If it is possible to calculate the effects of a service composition, calculating
the precondition should work similarly. In principle, this works like the effect calculation in reverse. Instead of calculating the state achieved when invoking the service composition, we want to determine the requirements on a
state necessary to invoke the service. This works by starting from the initial
marking and adding up all the preconditions until reaching the final marking. But there is one important distinction. Preconditions of services inside
the compositions can be fulfilled by the effects of preceding services. These
preconditions do not need to specified as part of the service composition
precondition.

Definition 10. *The precondition pre_m for a marking m is given by $pre_m =$
$\bigvee pre_{m'} \cup (pre_{i'} - s_m)$ for all pairs $pre_{m'}$ and i' with $i' = l_s(l_E(e))$ where $e =$
$(m, m') \in E$ and $pre_{m'}$ is the precondition of m'. The final marking has the
empty precondition pre_{final}.*

*The precondition of a service composition, is the precondition pre_{m_1} of its
initial marking.*

So instead of traversing the reachability graph backward until reaching the initial
marking, the graph is traversed forward until the final marking is reached. Before
adding the precondition of a service to the precondition of a marking, all the
facts already known in the current logical state are removed. This ensures that
preconditions satisfied by other services are not added to the precondition of
the service composition. The current logical state can be calculated given the
method for service composition effects described earlier.

As this algorithm is quite similar to the effect calculation algorithm, only
one example will be demonstrated: the process with and-splits and -joins from
Figure 4. In contrast to the other figures, it also lists the preconditions for the
services. To calculate the precondition of composition, we need to calculate the
precondition for m_1. It is given by $m_1 = (pre_{m_2} \cup (pre_{t_1} - s_{m_1})) \vee (pre_{m_3} \cup$
$(pre_{t_2} - s_{m_1})) = ((pre_{m_4} \cup (pre_{t_3} - s_{m_2})) \cup (pre_{t_1} - s_{m_1})) \vee ((pre_{m_4} \cup (pre_{t_4} -$
$s_{m_3})) \cup (pre_{t_1} - s_{m_1})) = (\{\} \cup (p_{t_3} - s_{m_2})) \cup (pre_{t_1} - s_{m_1})) \vee (\{\} \cup (pre_{t_4} - s_{m_3})) \cup$
$(pre_{t_2} - s_{m_1})) = (\{\} \cup (\{a\} - s_{m_2})) \cup (\{x\} - s_{m_1})) \vee (\{\} \cup (\{y\} - s_{m_3})) \cup (\{x\} -$
$s_{m_1})) = (\{\} \cup (\{a\} - \{a\})) \cup (\{x\} - \{\})) \vee (\{\} \cup (\{y\} - \{b\})) \cup (\{x\} - \{\})) =$
$(\{\} \cup \{\} \cup \{x\}) \vee (\{\} \cup \{y\} \cup \{x\}) = (x) \vee (x \wedge y)$. Intuitively, we connect the
two possible paths disjunctively and remove the precondition of t_3 because it is
already fulfilled by the effect of t_1.

To sum up, in this section we have seen how service composition preconditions and effects can be calculated. Both algorithms, are based on traversing
the reachability graph containing all possible state transitions. The algorithm
to calculate service composition preconditions requires the calculation of logical
states for each marking except for the final marking. Having calculated the precondition, the effect calculation is reduced to determining the logical state for
this final marking without traversing the reachability graph.

5   Example and Tooling

In this section a more complicated example is introduced and it is shown how it can be analyzed with our tool. The tool is a command line tool implemented in Java that reads Petri nets specified in the LoLA format [11]. We extended this format to incorporate preconditions and effects of transitions. An extract from our example looks like this:

```
PLACE s1, s2, s3, s4, s5, s6, s7,s8;

MARKING s1: 1;

TRANSITION order
CONSUME s1: 1;
PRODUCE s2: 1, s3: 1;
PRECONDITION ;
EFFECT ordered;

...

TRANSITION close
CONSUME s6: 1, s7: 1;
PRODUCE s8: 1;
PRECONDITION rsent and shipped;
EFFECT order_closed;
```

Such a file defines places, transitions and the initial marking for a Petri net. Each TRANSITION contains two additional sub-elements, PRECONDITION and EFFECT, describing the semantics of this transition. The example used in this section is an order process (Fig. 5). After ordering, shipment and sending the receipt are done in parallel. Depending on the requested shipper, one out of two allowed shippers is selected. Preceding the two shipment services are empty transitions. They do not perform any functionality but just decide which route should be taken. This example contains an and-split, an and-join, an xor-split, and an xor-join. To not overload the diagram, it does not contain the semantics for the transitions. They are instead depicted in Table 5.

Table 1. Preconditions and Effects of the Services

Transition	Precondition	Effect
order		*ordered*
send_receipt	*ordered*	*rsent*
shipping1	*ordered ∧ shipper1*	*shipped*
shipping2	*ordered ∧ shipper2*	*shipped*
close	*rsent ∧ shipped*	*order_closed*

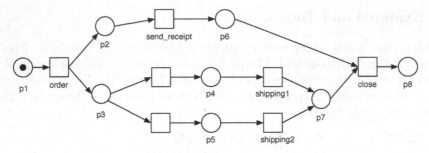

Fig. 5. Petri net of Order Service Composition

Using the tool, it is possible to calculate the semantics of the composition. As the effect it calculates $order_closed \wedge ordered \wedge rsent \wedge shipped$. The interesting fact about this effect is that it does not contain a xor even though the composition contained an xor-split. But as both possible paths have the same semantics (the order is shipped) this is explainable. The calculated precondition is $(ordered \wedge rsent \wedge shipped \wedge shipper1) \oplus (ordered \wedge rsent \wedge shipped \wedge shipper2)$. Obviously, the preconditions fulfilled by preceding services are not removed from the composition's precondition. This is a weakness of the current implementation. It uses a simplistic, propositional reasoner developed specifically for this tool. One of the next steps, is to replace it by a full fledged reasoner like Pellet.

6   Related Work

The algorithms presented allow the calculation of service composition preconditions and effects. This allows for the automated generation of service specification and the verification of service compositions.

In spite of these possible applications, only a few similar approaches exist. Koschmider and Ried [12] present a work that sounds quite similar to the one we present in this paper: *Semantic Annotation of Petri nets*. They show how Petri nets can be expressed in OWL to allow reasoning about their properties. So they are using Semantic Web technologies to prove properties about the syntactic structure of the process. Our approach instead extends the syntactic structure by semantic service annotations and uses known syntactic properties of the control flow to derive the semantics of the whole composition. In [13] they apply their formalism to allow for the auto completion of business processes.

Much more similar is the work by Narayanan and McIlraith [14]. They present an execution semantics for DAML-S (now OWL-S) based on Petri nets. The main difference to our approach is that they express atomic DAML-S processes (or services) as Petri nets. Each service consists of several places and transitions mapping the preconditions and effects to Petri net constructs. In our approach each service corresponds to exactly one transition in the Petri net. Another difference is that we define formally how the Petri net is build up from the atomic services whereas Narayanan and McIlraith only state this informally.

Many approaches for the automated composition of services exist [15,16,17,18,19]. They can be seen as related work as their algorithms create a service composition with a requested functionality. But they all fail to make this explicit. This gap is filled by this paper.

In the Tools4BPEL project the relationship between Petri nets and service compositions in general is investigated. This includes the mapping of BPEL processes to Petri nets [20]. This work can be used to create the Workflow nets necessary for the presented algorithm.

7 Conclusion

In this paper we presented an approach to calculate the preconditions and effects of service compositions based on semantics of individual services and a Petri net representation of the service composition. Using this approach it is now possible to automatically calculate the preconditions and effects for service compositions. This allows us to verify the correctness of compositions and their publication as services. We also introduced a tool that implements the described algorithms.

In the future we want to extend the precondition and effect calculation to cyclic Workflow nets. To reach this goal, both algorithms need to be adjusted to detect previously visited markings in the reachability graph. This functionality can then be used to ensure termination of the algorithm. Additionally, it needs to be discussed what a cycle or loop means semantically. If the only modification to the algorithms is to prevent visiting the same marking multiple times, the semantics of a composition with loops is equivalent to the semantics of an identical composition without the backward transition. This is not very useful.

Reasoning about loops only makes sense if service preconditions and effects are described using first-order logic. Otherwise, multiple runs through the same loop do not change anything. Therefore, a new reasoner is necessary as the very simple reasoner currently used is not sufficient for this. So a next step is to integrate a full-fledged reasoner.

References

1. Burbeck, S.: The tao of e-business services. IBM developerWorks (2000)
2. Papazoglou, M.P., Georgakopoulos, D.: Service-oriented computing: Introduction. Communications of the ACM 46, 24–28 (2003)
3. McIlraith, S.A., Son, T.C., Zeng, H.: Semantic web services. IEEE Intelligent Systems 16, 46–53 (2001)
4. Paolucci, M., Kawamura, T., Payne, T.R., Sycara, K.P.: Semantic matching of web services capabilities. In: Proceedings of the First International Semantic Web Conference on The Semantic Web, London, UK, pp. 333–347. Springer, Heidelberg (2002)
5. Li, L., Horrocks, I.: A software framework for matchmaking based on semantic web technology. In: Proceedings of the 12th International Conference on World Wide Web (WWW03), New York, NY, USA, pp. 331–339. ACM Press, New York (2003)
6. http://www.daml.org/services/owl-s/1.0/: OWL-S 1.0 Release (2003)

7. http://wsmo.org: Web Service Modeling Ontology (2005)
8. Keller, U., Lausen, H., Stollberg, M.: On the semantics of functional descriptions of web services. In: Sure, Y., Domingue, J. (eds.) ESWC 2006. LNCS, vol. 4011, Springer, Heidelberg (2006)
9. Schaffner, J., Meyer, H.: Mixed initiative use cases for semi-automated service composition: A survey. In: Proceedings of the International Workshop on Service Oriented Software Engineering (2006)
10. Schaffner, J., Meyer, H., Tosun, C.: A semi-automated orchestration tool for service-based business processes. In: Proceedings of the 2nd International Workshop on Engineering Service-Oriented Applications: Design and Composition (2006)
11. Schmidt, K.: LoLA: A Low Level Analyser. In: Nielsen, M., Simpson, D. (eds.) ICATPN 2000. LNCS, vol. 1825, pp. 465–474. Springer, Heidelberg (2000)
12. Koschmider, A., Ried, D.: Semantische annotation von petri-netzen. In: Proceedings des 12. Workshops Algorithmen und Werkzeuge fr Petrinetze (AWPN'05), pp. 66 – 71 (2006)
13. Betz, S., Klink, S., Koschmider, A., Oberweis, A.: Automatic user support for business process modeling. In: Proceedings of the Workshop on Semantics for Business Process Management, pp. 1–12 (2006)
14. Narayanan, S., McIlraith, S.: Simulation, verification and automated composition of web services. In: Proceedings of the 11th International Conference on World Wide Web, New York, NY, USA, pp. 77–88. ACM Press, New York (2002)
15. Zeng, L., Benatallah, B., Lei, H., Ngu, A., Flaxer, D., Chang, H.: Flexible Composition of Enterprise Web Services. Electronic Markets – Web. Services 13, 141–152 (2003)
16. Pistore, M., Barbon, F., Bertoli, P., Shaparau, D., Traverso, P.: Planning and monitoring web service composition. In: Workshop on Planning and Scheduling for Web and Grid Services held in conjunction with The 14th International Conference on Automated Planning and Scheduling, pp. 70 – 71 (2004)
17. Sirin, E., Parsia, B., Wu, D., Hendler, J., Nau, D.: HTN planning for web service composition using shop2. Journal of Web Semantics 1, 377–396 (2004)
18. Berardi, D., Calvanese, D., Giacomo, G.D., Mecella, M.: Composition of services with nondeterministic observable behaviour. In: Benatallah, B., Casati, F., Traverso, P. (eds.) ICSOC 2005. LNCS, vol. 3826, pp. 520–526. Springer, Heidelberg (2005)
19. Meyer, H., Weske, M.: Automated service composition using heuristic search. In: Dustdar, S., Fiadeiro, J.L., Sheth, A. (eds.) BPM 2006. LNCS, vol. 4102, pp. 81–96. Springer, Heidelberg (2006)
20. Hinz, S., Schmidt, K., Stahl, C.: Transforming BPEL to Petri Nets. In: van der Aalst, W.M.P., Benatallah, B., Casati, F., Curbera, F. (eds.) BPM 2005. LNCS, vol. 3649, pp. 220–235. Springer, Heidelberg (2005)

Expressive Reasoning with Horn Rules and Fuzzy Description Logics

Theofilos Mailis, Giorgos Stoilos, and Giorgos Stamou

Department of Electrical and Computer Engineering,
National Technical University of Athens, Zographou 15780, Greece

Abstract. This essay describes fuzzy CARIN, a knowledge representation language combining fuzzy description logics with Horn rules. Fuzzy CARIN integrates the management of fuzzy logic into the non-recursive CARIN system. It provides a sound and complete algorithm for representing and reasoning about fuzzy $\mathcal{ALCNR}$ extended with non-recursive Horn rules. Such an extension is most useful in realistic applications dealing with uncertainty and imprecision, such as multimedia processing and medical applications. Additionally, it provides the ability of answering to union of conjunctive queries, which is a novelty not previously addressed by fuzzy DL systems.

1 Introduction

Over the last two decades fragments of first order logic, called Description Logics (DLs) [1], have been brought into focus by the Artificial Intelligence community. DLs well formed semantics and great expressivity has enforced their utilization in numerous domains, such as multimedia [2,3,4] and medical [5] applications, as knowledge representation and reasoning languages. More importantly DLs provide the formal foundation for the standard web ontology language OWL [6] which is a milestone for the Semantic Web [7].

DLs main asset, their class-based knowledge representation formalism, also sets a limit to their expressive power as they are incapable of providing complex descriptions about role predicates. Expressive DLs such as $\mathcal{SHOIQ}$ are incapable of expressing even a simple composition between roles.[1] For this reason, as visualized in the Semantic Web stack diagram,[2] there is a need for integrating DLs with rules. A natural choice for such integration would be classes of rule languages originating from logic programming and non-monotonic reasoning [10].

In [10], the "cream" of systems combining rules and DLs is presented. Systems such as DLP [11], SWRL [12], $\mathcal{AL}$-log [13], F-logic [14] and CARIN [15] present different approximations for intergrading DLs with rules. These are divided into the hybrid systems, where there is a distinction between the predicates in the rule and the DL part, and the homogeneous where there is no such distinction. CARIN is such an hybrid system that combines the DL $\mathcal{ALCNR}$ with

---

[1] Recent systems such as EL^{++} [8], $SROIQ$ [9] are such extensions.
[2] http://www.w3.org/2003/Talks/05-gartner-tbl/slide29-0.html

M. Marchiori, J.Z. Pan, and C. de Sainte Marie (Eds.): RR 2007, LNCS 4524, pp. 43–57, 2007.
© Springer-Verlag Berlin Heidelberg 2007

Horn rules and through its existential entailment algorithm *offers a sound and complete inference procedure for non-recursive knowledge bases, can answer to arbitrary conjunctive queries and provides an algorithm for rule subsumption over $\mathcal{ALCNR}$* [15].

Though CARIN offers great expressivity in order to represent a fragment of our universe, it is incapable of encoding knowledge with some degree of uncertainty and imprecision. Uncertainty emerges from our lack of knowledge about a certain fact e.g. we assume that the black dot in the background of a picture is a lion, while imprecision refers to the intrinsic inability to strictly classify a fact or a state of an object e.g. a half-empty glass of water can neither be characterized as full, nor as empty.

Fuzzy logic is a mean to represent knowledge containing uncertainty and imprecision. Several systems, such as fuzzy $\mathcal{ALC}$ [16], fuzzy $f_{KD} - \mathcal{SI}$ [4], f_{KD}-$\mathcal{SHIN}$ [17], have been proposed for combining fuzzy logic with description logics. Based on these systems we propose fuzzy CARIN, which is an extension of non-recursive CARIN, in order to represent uncertainty and imprecision. Related work combining DLs with Rules has been presented in [18,19], providing fuzzy extensions of DL programs [20].

The need for fuzzy extensions of systems combining DLs with rules is most obvious in multimedia applications:

Example 1. Suppose that we have a, rather "optimistic", algorithm for object recognition. This algorithm is divided into an image processing and a DL extended with rules part. Assume it contains the following rules and implications:

$$leaf(x) \wedge nextTo(x,y) \wedge trunk(y) \Rightarrow tree(x,y)$$
$$\exists hascolor.green \sqcup \exists hascolor.yellow \sqsubseteq leafs \ldots$$

The algorithm implies that a tree is an object consisting of leafs and a trunk and that leafs is an object of either green or yellow color. Obviously an object described by another shade of green would never have been characterized as being leafs by a crisp system. That's where fuzzy logic fits in, allowing assertions of the form $(object : green) \geq 0.7$ that imply an object being green to a certain degree. As it will be demonstrated this degree plays an important role throughout the whole reasoning procedure.

The rest of the paper is organized as follows: section 2 provides some preliminary report on the CARIN system and fuzzy logic, section 2 provides the syntax and semantics of our system, section 4 describes the inference problems addressed by our system, section 5 presents a consistency checking algorithm for fuzzy $\mathcal{ALCNR}$ and finally section 6 presents an algorithm for answering to conjunctive queries and union of conjunctive queries.

2   Preliminaries

2.1   CARIN

The CARIN language combines the DL $\mathcal{ALCNR}$ with Horn rules. CARIN' s structural elements are concept names, role names, individuals and ordinary predicates. Individuals reflect the objects of our universe while concepts and roles correspond to unary and binary predicates. Ordinary predicates refer to predicates of any arity that are found only in the ABox and in the Horn rule component. CARIN enables us to create concept descriptions using the following constructors:

$$C, D \rightarrow A \mid \top \mid \bot \mid C \sqcap D \mid C \sqcup D \mid \neg C \mid \forall R.C \mid \exists R.C \mid \geq nR \mid \leq nR$$

where A is a concept name (primitive concept), R is a role name and C, D denote concept descriptions.

A CARIN knowledge base K consists of an ABox, TBox and a Horn rule component. The ABox consists of a set of concept, role and ordinary predicate assertions of the form: $C(a)$, $R(a, b)$ and $q(a_1, \ldots, a_k)$ where q is an ordinary predicate and $a, b, a_1, \ldots, a_k$ are individuals in K. The TBox is a set of concept inclusions or definitions of the form $C \sqsubseteq D$, $C := D$ and role definitions $P_1 \sqcap \ldots \sqcap P_k \equiv R$, where $P_1, \ldots P_k$ are role names. Finally the Horn rules component consists of a set of Horn rules of the form $p_1(\overline{X}_1) \wedge \ldots \wedge p_k(\overline{X}_k) \Rightarrow q(\overline{Y})$ where $p_1, \ldots, p_k$ are either concept descriptions, role definitions or ordinary predicates of the appropriate arity.

The semantics of CARIN are given via interpretations. An interpretation consists of a domain and an interpretation function $(\Delta^{\mathcal{I}}, \cdot^{\mathcal{I}})$, where the domain is a non-empty set of objects and the interpretation function maps: each individual name a to an object $a^{\mathcal{I}} \in \Delta^{\mathcal{I}}$, each concept name C to a subset of $\Delta^{\mathcal{I}}$, $C^{\mathcal{I}} \subseteq \Delta^{\mathcal{I}}$, each role name R to a binary relation $R^{\mathcal{I}} \subseteq \Delta^{\mathcal{I}} \times \Delta^{\mathcal{I}}$ and each ordinary predicate q to a n-ary relation $q^{\mathcal{I}} \subseteq \Delta^{\mathcal{I}} \times \ldots \times \Delta^{\mathcal{I}}$. An interpretation $\mathcal{I}$ satisfies $C(a)$, $R(a, b)$ and $q(a_1, \ldots, a_k)$ if $a^{\mathcal{I}} \in C^{\mathcal{I}}$, $\langle a^{\mathcal{I}}, b^{\mathcal{I}} \rangle \in R^{\mathcal{I}}$ and $\langle a_1^{\mathcal{I}}, \ldots, a_k^{\mathcal{I}} \rangle \in q^{\mathcal{I}}$. TBox axioms $C \sqsubseteq D$, $C := D$ and $R := P_1 \sqcap \ldots \sqcap P_k$ imply that $C^{\mathcal{I}} \subseteq D^{\mathcal{I}}$, $C^{\mathcal{I}} := D^{\mathcal{I}}$ and $R^{\mathcal{I}} \equiv P_1^{\mathcal{I}} \sqcap \ldots \sqcap P_k^{\mathcal{I}}$. Finally Horn rules of the form $p_1(\overline{X}_1) \wedge \ldots \wedge p_k(\overline{X}_k) \Rightarrow q(\overline{Y})$ imply that for any mapping $\psi : VarsIndivs(\overline{X}_1 \cup \ldots \cup \overline{X}_k) \rightarrow \Delta^{\mathcal{I}}$, if $\psi(\overline{X}_i) \in p_i^{\mathcal{I}}$, then $\psi(\overline{Y}) \in q^{\mathcal{I}}$.

2.2   Fuzzy Sets

Fuzzy set theory and fuzzy logic enables to represent uncertain and imprecise knowledge [21]. In classical set theory an element x which belongs to the universe Ω, $x \in \Omega$, may or may not belong to a subset A of Ω. This can be represented by a mapping $\chi_A : \Omega \rightarrow \{0, 1\}$, if $\chi_A(x) = 1$ then $x \in A$ else if $\chi_A(x) = 0$ then $x \notin A$. In fuzzy set theory, a fuzzy subset A of Ω has a mapping $\mu_A : \Omega \rightarrow [0, 1]$ which means that instead of saying that $x \in A$ we can claim that x belongs to A to a certain degree. Additionally a binary fuzzy relation over two crisp sets Ω_1, Ω_2 is a mapping $R : \Omega_1 \times \Omega_2 \rightarrow [0, 1]$ and a n-ary relation q over n crisp sets $\Omega_1, \ldots \Omega_n$ is a mapping $q : \Omega_1 \times \ldots \times \Omega_n \rightarrow [0, 1]$.

The classical set theoretical operations of complement, union intersection and implication are also extended in fuzzy set theory by using triangular norm operations [21]. Because of the difficulty of extending DLs with arbitrary fuzzy set operations our system uses some standard norm operations [16]. These norms are: the Lukasiewicz negation $c(a) = 1 - a$, the Gödel $t - norm$ for conjunction,

$t(a, b) = \min(a, b)$, the Gödel t-conorm for disjunction $u(a, b) = \max(a, b)$ and the Kleene-Dienes fuzzy implication, $J(a, b) = \max(1 - a, b)$.

3   The Language of Fuzzy Carin

As stated, *non recursive fuzzy CARIN* is a language, which combines the description logic fuzzy $\mathcal{ALCNR}$ with non recursive Horn Rules. A fuzzy CARIN knowledge base K is composed of three components $K = \langle \mathcal{T}, \mathcal{H}, \mathcal{A} \rangle$, a DL terminology component $\mathcal{T}$ also called a TBox, a Horn rules component $\mathcal{H}$ and a ground facts component $\mathcal{A}$ also called an ABox. In the syntax and semantics that we propose, we consider that fuzziness exists only in the ground facts component.

3.1   Syntax

Fuzzy CARIN's structural elements are a set of individuals **I**, an alphabet of concept names **C**, role names **R** and ordinary predicate names **Q**. Elements of **I** represent the objects in our universe, while **C** and **R** correspond to unary and binary fuzzy relationships between individuals in **I**. Elements of **Q** correspond to relationships, between individuals, of any arity.

Terminological component in fuzzy CARIN: The fuzzy CARIN terminological component $\mathcal{T}$ has the same syntax as the crisp. Complex concepts are built from concept and role names using the constructors of $\mathcal{ALCNR}$ as described in Equation 1 where A is a concept name, C and D are concept descriptions and R is a role definition.

$$C, D \longrightarrow A \mid \top \mid \bot \mid C \sqcap D \mid C \sqcup D \mid \neg C \mid \forall R.C \mid \exists R.C \mid (\geq m\ R) \mid (\leq m\ R) \quad (1)$$

The TBox contains *concept definitions* $A := D$, concept inclusions $C \sqsubseteq D$ and role definitions of the form $R := P_1 \sqcap \ldots \sqcap P_k$, where P_is are role names.[3]

Horn rules in fuzzy CARIN: The Horn rule component $\mathcal{H}$ of a fuzzy CARIN knowledge base K contains a set of Horn rules that are logical sentences of the form:

$$p_1(\overline{X}_1) \wedge \ldots \wedge p_k(\overline{X}_k) \Rightarrow q(\overline{Y}) \quad (2)$$

where $\overline{X}_1, \cdots, \overline{X}_k$ and $\overline{Y}$ are tuples of variables and individuals and $p_1, \cdots p_k$ may be concept names, roles or ordinary predicates while q is *always* an ordinary predicate. The antecedents of a Horn rule are called its body and the consequents are called its head.

Fuzzy as well as the classic CARIN are, as stated before, hybrid systems, which means that there is a clear distinction between their DL and Horn rule part. For this reason ordinary predicates are defined as predicates of any arity that locate only in $\mathcal{H}$ and $\mathcal{A}$ and cannot be part of a concept description, even if they are unary or binary predicates. Additionally in order to have a sound and complete algorithm, variables located in $\overline{Y}$ must also be located in one of the $\overline{X}_i$'s and only non-recursive Horn rules are adopted. A set of rules is said

---

[3] In some bibliography role definitions may be a part of an RBox $\mathcal{R}$ instead of a TBox.

to be recursive if there is a cycle in the dependency relation among ordinary predicates, i.e an ordinary predicate q depends on a predicate p when p appears in the body of a rule whose head is q and dependency is a transitive relation.

Ground fact component: The ground fact component $\mathcal{A}$ of a fuzzy CARIN knowledge base contains a set of fuzzy assertions as shown in table 1:

Table 1. Fuzzy CARIN assertions

$(a : C) \bowtie n$	where $a \in \mathbf{I}$, $\bowtie \in \{\geqslant, >, \leqslant, <\}$, $n \in [0,1]$ and C is a concept description
$(\langle a,b \rangle : R) \rhd n$	where $a, b \in \mathbf{I}$, $\rhd \in \{\geqslant, >\}$, $n \in [0,1]$ and R is a role name
$(\overline{a} : p) \rhd n$	where $\overline{a}$ is a tuple of individuals, $\rhd \in \{\geqslant, >\}$, $n \in [0,1]$ and p is an ordinary predicate of any arity.

Intuitively a fuzzy assertion of the form $(weather : cloudy) \geqslant 0.5$ means that the weather is cloudy with a degree at least equal to 0.5. We call assertions defined by $\geqslant, >$ *positive assertions*, denoted with $\rhd$, while those defined by $\leqslant, <$ *negative assertions*, denoted with $\lhd$. $\bowtie$ stands for any type of inequality. In fuzzy CARIN, we consider only positive role assertion, since negative assertions would imply the existence of role negation and union of roles in $\mathcal{ALCNR}$, which would lead to undecidability. Similarly for ordinary predicates we use only positive assertions since negation cannot be expressed in simple Horn Rules.

3.2 Semantics

The semantics of the terminological component are given via fuzzy interpretations which use membership functions that range over the interval $[0,1]$. A fuzzy interpretation is a pair $\mathcal{I} = \langle \Delta^{\mathcal{I}}, \cdot^{\mathcal{I}} \rangle$, where the domain $\Delta^{\mathcal{I}}$ is a non empty set of objects and $\cdot^{\mathcal{I}}$ is a *fuzzy interpretation function*, which maps:

1. An individual name $a \in \mathbf{I}$ to an element $a^{\mathcal{I}} \in \Delta^{\mathcal{I}}$,
2. A concept name $A \in \mathbf{C}$ to a membership function $A^{\mathcal{I}} : \Delta^{\mathcal{I}} \rightarrow [0,1]$,
3. A role name $R \in \mathbf{R}$ to a membership function $R^{\mathcal{I}} : \Delta^{\mathcal{I}} \times \Delta^{\mathcal{I}} \rightarrow [0,1]$,
4. An ordinary predicate $q \in \mathbf{Q}$ of l-arity to a membership function $q^{\mathcal{I}} : \underbrace{\Delta^{\mathcal{I}} \times \ldots \times \Delta^{\mathcal{I}}}_{l} \rightarrow [0,1]$,
5. Finally, we make the unique names assumption, i.e. for each tuple of elements $a, b \in \mathbf{I}$, $a^{\mathcal{I}} \neq b^{\mathcal{I}}$ holds.

The semantics of concept descriptions are given by the equations in table 2 where $a, b \in \Delta^{\mathcal{I}}$ and C, D are concept descriptions, R is a role description and A is a concept name. *Terminological component satisfiability:* An interpretation $\mathcal{I}$ satisfies the terminological component $\mathcal{T}$, iff

- $\forall a \in \Delta^{\mathcal{I}}$, $C^{\mathcal{I}}(a) \leqslant D^{\mathcal{I}}(a)$ for each concept inclusion axiom $C \sqsubseteq D$ in $\mathcal{T}$,
- $\forall a \in \Delta^{\mathcal{I}}$, $C^{\mathcal{I}}(a) = D^{\mathcal{I}}(a)$ for each concept definition axiom $C := D$ in $\mathcal{T}$,

Table 2. Semantics

Syntax	Semantics
A	$A^{\mathcal{I}}(a) = n$ where $n \in [0,1]$
$\top$	$\top^{\mathcal{I}}(a) = 1$
$\bot$	$\bot^{\mathcal{I}}(a) = 0$
$\neg C$	$(\neg C)^{\mathcal{I}}(a) = 1 - C^{\mathcal{I}}(a)$
$C \sqcap D$	$(C \sqcap D)^{\mathcal{I}}(a) = \min(C^{\mathcal{I}}(a), D^{\mathcal{I}}(a))$
$C \sqcup D$	$(C \sqcup D)^{\mathcal{I}}(a) = \max(C^{\mathcal{I}}(a), D^{\mathcal{I}}(a))$
$\forall R.C$	$(\forall R.C)^{\mathcal{I}}(a) = \inf_{b \in \Delta^{\mathcal{I}}}\{\max(1 - R^{\mathcal{I}}(a,b), C^{\mathcal{I}}(b))\}$
$\exists R.C$	$(\exists R.C)^{\mathcal{I}}(a) = \sup_{b \in \Delta^{\mathcal{I}}}\{\min(R^{\mathcal{I}}(a,b), C^{\mathcal{I}}(b))\}$
$(\geq m\ R)$	$(\geq mR)^{\mathcal{I}}(a) = \sup_{b_1,\cdots,b_m \in \Delta^{\mathcal{I}}} \min_{i=1}^{m}\{R^{\mathcal{I}}(a,b_i)\}$
$(\leq m\ R)$	$(\leq mR)^{\mathcal{I}}(a) = \inf_{b_1,\cdots,b_{m+1} \in \Delta^{\mathcal{I}}} \max_{i=1}^{m+1}\{1 - R^{\mathcal{I}}(a,b_i)\}$

- $\forall a,b \in \Delta^{\mathcal{I}}$, $\min(P_1^{\mathcal{I}}(a,b), \ldots, P_k^{\mathcal{I}}(a,b)) = R^{\mathcal{I}}(a,b)$ for each role definition axiom $P_1 \sqcap \ldots \sqcap P_k := R$ in $\mathcal{T}$.

Horn rule satisfiability: An interpretation $\mathcal{I}$ satisfies a Horn rule $p_1(\overline{X}_1) \wedge \ldots \wedge p_k(\overline{X}_k) \Rightarrow q(\overline{Y})$ iff for every mapping ψ from the variables and individuals of $\overline{X}_1, \ldots, \overline{X}_k, \overline{Y}$ to the objects of $\Delta^{\mathcal{I}}$, where each individual a is mapped to $a^{\mathcal{I}}$, $\min\big(p_1^{\mathcal{I}}(\psi(\overline{X}_1)), \ldots, p_k^{\mathcal{I}}(\psi(\overline{X}_k))\big) \leq q(\psi(\overline{Y}))$ holds. The Horn rule component is satisfied iff all rules in it are satisfied.

Ground fact component satisfiability: A fuzzy interpretation satisfies the *ground fact component* $\mathcal{A}$ iff it satisfies all fuzzy assertions in $\mathcal{A}$ as described in table 3. In this case we say $\mathcal{I}$ is *a model* of $\mathcal{A}$ and it is denoted as $\mathcal{I} \models \mathcal{A}$. If $\mathcal{A}$ has a model we then say that it is *consistent*.

Table 3. Fuzzy assertion satisfiability

$\mathcal{I}$ satisfies	iff
$(a : C) \bowtie n$	$C^{\mathcal{I}}(a^{\mathcal{I}}) \bowtie n$
$(\langle a,b \rangle : R \rhd n)$	$R^{\mathcal{I}}(a^{\mathcal{I}}, b^{\mathcal{I}}) \rhd n$
$(\langle a_1, \ldots, a_k \rangle : q \rhd n)$	$q^{\mathcal{I}}(a_1^{\mathcal{I}}, \ldots, a_k^{\mathcal{I}}) \rhd n$

In fuzzy CARIN we consider that each concept assertion is in its positive inequality formal, negation normal, normalized form i.e. only concept assertions of the form $(a : C) \geq n$ are allowed, where C is in its negation normal form. The same applies for role and ordinary predicate assertions.

Negative assertions can be converted to their Positive Inequality Normal Form (PINF) by applying the fuzzy complement in both sides of the inequality as described in [22]. For example $(a : C) \leq n$ and $(a : C) < n$ are being transformed into $(a : \neg C) \geq 1 - n$ and $(a : \neg C) > 1 - n$.

We also assume that all concepts are in their Negation Normal Form. A concept can be transformed into its NNF by pushing negation inwards making use of the following concept equivalences [16,17]:

$$\neg(C \sqcup D) \equiv (\neg C \sqcap \neg D) \qquad \neg(C \sqcap D) \equiv (\neg C \sqcup \neg D)$$
$$\neg \exists R.C \equiv \forall R.(\neg C) \qquad \neg \forall R.C \equiv \exists R.(\neg C)$$
$$\neg \geq p_1 R \equiv \leq (p_1 - 1)R \qquad \neg \leq p_2 R \equiv \geq (p_2 + 1)R$$
$$\neg \neg C = C$$

where $p_1 \in \mathbb{N}^*$ and $p_2 \in \mathbb{N}$ in the above equations.

Normalized assertions, are assertions where $>$ is eliminated with $\geq$. This can be achieved by introducing a positive, infinitely small value ϵ which, from an analysis point of view, would be equal to 0^+. Following [23] each concept assertion $a : C > n$ is normalized to $a : C \geq n + \epsilon$. The same kind of normalization holds for role and ordinary predicate assertions. It has been proven in [23] that each model $\mathcal{I}$ of K is also a model of K's normalized form and vice versa.

Finally following [17] a conjugated pair of fuzzy assertions is a pair of assertions whose semantics are contradicted. If ϕ represents a crisp concept assertion and $\neg\phi$ its negation (e.g. if $\phi \equiv a : C$ then $\neg\phi \equiv a : \neg C$) the instances of conjugated pairs are seen in table 4. An ABox $\mathcal{A}$ with a conjugated pair of fuzzy assertions has no model $\mathcal{I}$.

Table 4. Conjugated pairs of fuzzy assertions

	$\neg\phi > m$	$\neg\phi \geq m$
$\phi \geq n$	$n + m \geq 1$	$n + m > 1$
$\phi > n$	$n + m \geq 1$	$n + m \geq 1$

Knowledge base satisfiability: An ABox $\mathcal{A}$ is consistent w.r.t. a TBox $\mathcal{T}$ and a Horn rules component $\mathcal{H}$ if it has a model, $\mathcal{I} \models \mathcal{A}$, that satisfies every concept, role inclusion and definition in $\mathcal{T}$ as well as each Horn rule in $\mathcal{H}$. A knowledge base $K = \langle \mathcal{A}, \mathcal{T}, \mathcal{H} \rangle$ is satisfiable when there exists such a model $\mathcal{I}$ which is called a model of a knowledge base K and denoted as $\mathcal{I} \models K$.

4   Reasoning

The most common inference problems addressed by previous fuzzy DL systems are the satisfiability, n-satisfiability, subsumption and the entailment problem [16]. It has been proven in [16,17] that each one of the previous problems can be reduced to the problem of a knowledge base satisfiability.

Another kind of inference problem interwoven with relational databases is the conjunctive query answering problem. Following [24] we present the definition of the conjunctive query problem for fuzzy DLs.

Definition 1 (Conjunctive Query). *A conjunctive query (CQ) over a knowledge base K is a set of atoms of the form*

$$CQ = \{p_1(\overline{Y}_1) \rhd n_1 \wedge \ldots \wedge p_k(\overline{Y}_k) \rhd n_k\}$$

where $p_1, \ldots, p_k$ are either concept names in $\mathbf{C}$, role names in $\mathbf{R}$ or ordinary predicates in $\mathbf{Q}$ and $\overline{Y}_1, \ldots, \overline{Y}_k$ are tuples of variables and individuals in $\mathbf{I}$ matching each p_i's arity.

Similarly to assertions, conjunctive queries are also transformed to their normalized form by substituting each $p_i(\overline{Y}_i) > n_i$ in CQ with $p_i(\overline{Y}_i) \geq n_i + \epsilon$.

Definition 2 (Union of Conjunctive Queries). *A union of conjunctive queries (UCQ) over a knowledge base K is a set of conjunctive queries:*

$$UCQ = \{Q_1, \dots, Q_l\}$$

where Q_i is a CQ for each $1 \leq i \leq l$.

To say that Q is either a CQ or an UCQ, we simply say that Q is a *query*. We denote by *varsIndivs(Q)* the set of variables and individuals in a query Q, by *vars(Q)* the set of variables in Q and by *Indivs(Q)* the set of individuals in Q.

Queries are interpreted in the standard way. For a CQ, we say that $\mathcal{I}$ models CQ, $\mathcal{I} \models CQ$, iff there exists a mapping $\sigma : varsIndivs(CQ) \rightarrow \Delta^{\mathcal{I}}$ such that $\sigma(a) = a^{\mathcal{I}}$ for each $a \in Indivs(CQ)$ and $p_i^{\mathcal{I}}(\sigma(\overline{Y}_i)) \geq n$ for each $p(\overline{Y}_i) \geq n$ in CQ. For a union of conjunctive queries $UCQ = \{Q_1, \dots, Q_l\}$, $\mathcal{I} \models UCQ$ iff $\mathcal{I} \models Q_i$ for some $Q_i \in UCQ$. For a knowledge base K and a query Q, we say that K entails Q, denoted $K \models Q$, iff $\mathcal{I} \models Q$ for each model $\mathcal{I}$ of K.

Definition 3 (Query Entailment). *Let K be a knowledge base and Q a query. The query entailment problem is to decide whether $K \models Q$.*

It is important to notice that the query entailment, contrary to the entailment problem, cannot be reduced to consistency checking, since the negation of a query cannot be expressed as part of a knowledge base. For this reason consistency checking does not suffice for answering to conjunctive queries.

5   Consistency Checking for Fuzzy CARIN

To say that $K \models Q$ it has to hold that $\mathcal{I} \models Q$ for each model $\mathcal{I}$ of K. Instead of checking an infinite number of interpretations $\mathcal{I}$ satisfying K, our algorithm checks a finite number of completion forests. A completion forest $\mathcal{F}$ is an abstraction of an interpretation $\mathcal{I}$ and in most tableaux algorithms a complete and clash free $\mathcal{F}$ is the proof of the existence of a model of K. In 5.1 we provide an algorithm for consistency checking in $\mathcal{ALCNR}$ and based on this algorithm the conjunctive query answering problem is solved as described in 6.

5.1 $\mathcal{ALCNR}$ Completion Forests

The completion forest introduced is based on the completion forest presented in [15]. As in [15] the application of the expansion rules for the completion forest could lead to an arbitrary number of nodes due to the existence of cyclic concept inclusions. In order to ensure the termination of the expansion rules a blocking condition should be adopted. Contrary to the simple blocking condition embraced by $\mathcal{ALCNR}$ [25] our algorithm adopts the q-blocking condition, introduced in [15], in order to cope with union of conjunctive queries. In the next paragraphs the notions of completion forest, q-blocking and the expansion rules are explained in detail.

Definition 4 (Completion Tree). *A completion tree for fuzzy $\mathcal{ALCNR}$ is a tree, all nodes of which are variables, except from the root node which might be an individual. Each node x is labelled with a set $\mathcal{L}(x) = \{\langle C, \geq, n \rangle\}$, where $C \in sub(K)$ and $n \in [0,1]$. Each edge is labelled with a set $\mathcal{L}(x,y) = \{\langle R, \geq, n \rangle\}$, where $R \in \mathbf{R}$ are roles occurring in K.*

(Completion Forest). A completion forest $\mathcal{F}$ is a collection of trees whose roots, which correspond to individuals, are arbitrarily connected by arcs. As before, edges between root nodes are labelled with the set $\mathcal{L}(x,y) = \{\langle R, \geq, n \rangle\}$, where $R \in \mathbf{R}$.

In the previous definition $sub(K)$ denotes the set of concepts occurring in K along with their sub-concepts.

Example 2. In Figure 1 we see a completion forest for fuzzy $\mathcal{ALCNR}$ where r_1, r_2 correspond to root nodes while $o_1, \ldots, o_8$ are variable nodes created by node generating rules. Each node must be labelled with a set of concepts with degrees and each edge must be labelled with a set of roles with degrees. In this example only nodes r_1, o_1 and edges $\langle r_1, o_1 \rangle, \langle r_1, r_2 \rangle$ are labelled due to space limitations.

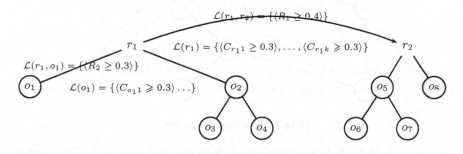

Fig. 1. A fuzzy $\mathcal{ALCNR}$ completion forest

Definition 5 (nodes, vars, R-successor, successor, descendant). *For a completion forest $\mathcal{F}$: (i) $nodes(\mathcal{F})$ denotes the set of nodes in $\mathcal{F}$, (ii) $vars(\mathcal{F})$ denotes the set of variable nodes in $\mathcal{F}$, (iii) v is an $R_{\geq n}$-successor of w when nodes v and w are connected by an edge $\langle v, w \rangle$ with $\{\langle P_1, \geq, n_1 \rangle, \ldots, \langle P_k, \geq, n_k \rangle\} \subseteq \mathcal{L}(\langle x, y \rangle)$, $R := P_1 \sqcap \ldots \sqcap P_k$ and $\min(n_1, \ldots, n_k) \geq n$, (iv) v is a successor of w, when v is an $R_{\geq n}$-successor of w with $n > 0$, (v) descendent is the transitive closure of successor.*

Example 3. In figure 1, o_1 is a $R_{2 \geq 0.3}$ successor of r_1.

Definition 6 (q-tree equivalence). *The q-tree of a variable v is the tree that includes the node v and its successors, whose distance from v is at most q direct-successors arcs. We denote the set of nodes in the q-tree of v by $V_q(v)$. Two nodes $v, w \in \mathcal{F}$ are said to be q-tree equivalent in $\mathcal{F}$ if there exists an isomorphism $\psi : V_q(v) \to V_q(w)$ such that (i) $\psi(v) = w$, (ii) for every $s \in V_q(v)$, $\langle C, \geq, n \rangle \in$*

$\mathcal{L}(s)$ iff $\langle C, \geq, n \rangle \in \mathcal{L}(\psi(s))$ *(iii) for every* $s, t \in V_q(v)$, $\langle R, \geq, n \rangle \in \mathcal{L}(\langle s, t \rangle)$ *iff* $\langle R, \geq, n \rangle \in \mathcal{L}(\langle \psi(s), \psi(t) \rangle)$. *Intuitively, two variables are q-tree equivalent if the trees of depth q of which they are roots are isomorphic.*

Definition 7 (q-Witness). *A node v is the q-witness of a node w when (i) v is an ancestor of w, (ii) v and w are q-tree equivalent, (iii) $w \notin V_n(v)$.*

Definition 8 (q-blocking). *A node x is q-blocked when it is the leaf of a q-tree in $\mathcal{F}$ whose root w has a q-witness v and $w \in vars(\mathcal{F})$ or when $\mathcal{L}(x) = \emptyset$.*

Example 4. In Figure 2 o_1 is a 1-witness of o_4, since the 1-tree of o_1 is equivalent of the 1-tree of o_4 because $\mathcal{L}(o_1) = \mathcal{L}(o_4)$, $\mathcal{L}(o_2) = \mathcal{L}(o_5)$, $\mathcal{L}(o_3) = \mathcal{L}(o_6)$ and $\mathcal{L}(o_1, o_2) = \mathcal{L}(o_4, o_5)$, $\mathcal{L}(o_1, o_3) = \mathcal{L}(o_4, o_6)$. For this reason o_5 is blocked by o_2 and o_3 is blocked by o_6.

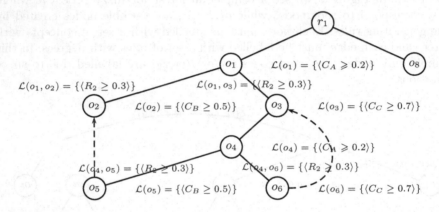

Fig. 2. Blocking Example

Definition 9 (Clash free completion forest). *For a node x, $\mathcal{L}(x)$ contains a clash if it contains: (i) A conjugated pair of triples. Conjugated pairs of triples are identical to conjugated pairs of fuzzy assertions described in table 4, (ii) one of the triples $\langle \bot, \geq, n \rangle$, with $n > 0$, or $\langle C, \geq, n \rangle$ with $n > 1$, or (iii) some triple $\langle \leq pR, \geq, n \rangle$, x has $p + 1$ $R_{\geq n'}$-successors $y_0, \ldots, y_p$, with $n' = 1 - n + \epsilon$ and $y_i \neq y_j$ for all $0 \leq i < j \leq p$. A completion forest $\mathcal{F}$ is clash free if none of its nodes contains a clash.*

For an $\mathcal{ALCNR}$ ABox $\mathcal{A}$, the algorithm initializes a completion forest $\mathcal{F}_K$ to contain (i) a root node x_0^i, for each individual $a_i \in \mathbf{I}$ in $\mathcal{A}$, labelled with $\mathcal{L}(x_0^i)$ such that $\{\langle C_i, \geq, n \rangle\} \subseteq \mathcal{L}(x_0^i)$ for each assertion of the form $(a_i : C_i) \geq n \in \mathcal{A}$, (ii) an edge $\langle x_0^i, x_0^j \rangle$, for each assertion $(\langle a_i, a_j \rangle : R_i) \geq n \in \mathcal{A}$, labelled with $\mathcal{L}(\langle x_0^i, x_0^j \rangle)$ such that $\{\langle R_i, \geq n \rangle\} \subseteq \mathcal{L}(\langle x_0^i, x_0^j \rangle)$, (iii) the relation $\neq$ as $x_0^i \neq x_0^j$ for each two different individuals $a_i, a_j \in \mathbf{I}$ and the relation $\doteq$ to be empty. $\mathcal{F}$ is expanded by repeatedly applying the completion rules from table 5.

In table 5 rules $\sqcap_{\geq}, \sqcup_{\geq}, \exists_{\geq}, \forall_{\geq}$ are first introduced in [16] and then modified for completion forests in [4], rules $\geq_{\geq}$ and $\leq_{\geq}$ are presented in [17], while rule

Table 5. Tableaux expansion rules for fuzzy $\mathcal{ALCNR}$

Rule	Description
$\sqcap_\geq$	if 1. $\langle C_1 \sqcap C_2, \geq, n\rangle \in \mathcal{L}(x)$, x is not blocked,
	2. $\{\langle C_1, \geq, n\rangle, \langle C_2, \geq, n\rangle\} \not\subseteq \mathcal{L}(x)$
	then $\mathcal{L}(x) \to \mathcal{L}(x) \cup \{\langle C_1, \geq, n\rangle, \langle C_2, \geq, n\rangle\}$
$\sqcup_\geq$	if 1. $\langle C_1 \sqcup C_2, \geq, n\rangle \in \mathcal{L}(x)$, x is not blocked,
	2. $\{\langle C_1, \geq, n\rangle, \langle C_2, \geq, n\rangle\} \cap \mathcal{L}(x) = \emptyset$
	then $\mathcal{L}(x) \to \mathcal{L}(x) \cup \{C\}$ for some $C \in \{\langle C_1, \geq, n\rangle, \langle C_2, \geq, n\rangle\}$
$\exists_\geq$	if 1. $\langle \exists R.C, \geq, n\rangle \in \mathcal{L}(x)$, x is not blocked,
	2. x has no $R_{\geq n}$-successor y with $\langle C, \geq, n\rangle \in \mathcal{L}(y)$
	then create a new node y with $\mathcal{L}(\langle x,y\rangle) = \{\langle R, \geq, n\rangle\}$, $\mathcal{L}(y) = \{\langle C, \geq, n\rangle\}$
$\forall_\geq$	if 1. $\langle \forall R.C, \geq, n\rangle \in \mathcal{L}(x)$, x is not blocked,
	2. x has an $R_{\geq n'}$-successor y with $n' = 1 - n + \epsilon$
	then $\mathcal{L}(y) \to \mathcal{L}(y) \cup \{\langle C, \geq, n\rangle\}$
$\geq_\geq$	if 1. $\langle \geq mR, \geq, n\rangle \in \mathcal{L}(x)$, x is not blocked,
	2. there are no m $R_{\geq n}$-successors $y_1, \dots, y_p$ of x
	3. with $y_i \neq y_j$ for $1 \leq i < j \leq m$
	then create m new nodes $y_1, \dots, y_m$, with $\mathcal{L}(\langle x, y_i\rangle) = \{\langle R, \geq, n\rangle\}$ and
	$y_i \neq y_j$ for $1 \leq i < j \leq m$
$\leq_\geq$	if 1. $\langle \leq mR, \geq, n\rangle \in \mathcal{L}(x)$, x is not blocked,
	2. there are more then m $R_{\geq n'}$-successors of x with $n' = 1 - n + \epsilon$ and
	there are two of them y, z, with no $y \neq z$,
	3. y is not a root node
	then (a) $\mathcal{L}(z) \to \mathcal{L}(z) \cup \mathcal{L}(y)$
	(b) $\mathcal{L}(\langle x, z\rangle) \to \mathcal{L}(\langle x, z\rangle) \cup \mathcal{L}(\langle x, y\rangle)$
	(c) $\mathcal{L}(\langle x, y\rangle) \to \emptyset$, $\mathcal{L}(y) \to \emptyset$
	(d) Set $u \neq z$ for all u with $u \neq y$
$\sqsubseteq$	if 1. $C \sqsubseteq D \in \mathcal{T}$ and
	2. $\{\langle \neg C, \geq, 1 - n + \epsilon\rangle, \langle D, \geq, n\rangle\} \cap \mathcal{L}(x) = \emptyset$ for $n \in N^{\mathcal{A}}$ [a]
	then $\mathcal{L}(x) \to \mathcal{L}(x) \cup \{E\}$ for some $E \in \{\langle \neg C, \geq, 1 - n + \epsilon\rangle, \langle D, \triangleright, n\rangle\}$

[a] $N^{\mathcal{A}}$ denotes the set of degrees in ABox assertions as well as the set of degrees in conjunctive queries.

$\sqsubseteq$ is first introduced in [23]. The $\leq_{r\geq}$ presented in [17] cannot be applied, since $a^{\mathcal{I}} \neq b^{\mathcal{I}}$ holds for every pair of individuals $a, b \in \mathbf{I}$.

Definition 10 (q-complete completion forest). *We denote by* $\mathbb{F}_K$ *the set of completion forests* $\mathcal{F}$ *obtained by applying the expansion rules in table 5 to* $\mathcal{F}_K$. *A completion forest* $\mathcal{F}$ *is q-complete when none of the rules in table 5 can be applied to it. We denote by* $\mathrm{ccf}(\mathbb{F}_K^q)$ *the set of completion forests in* $\mathbb{F}_K$ *that are q-complete and clash free.*

It can be proven that each $\mathcal{F} \in \mathrm{ccf}(\mathbb{F}_K^q)$ can be mapped to a model $\mathcal{I}$ of K and vice versa (detailed proofs can be found in [17]). In section 6 we show how the set $\mathrm{ccf}(\mathbb{F}_K^q)$ can be exploited in order to answer to unions of conjunctive queries.

6   Union of Conjunctive Queries

In this section we will introduce an algorithm for answering to union of conjunctive queries over an $\mathcal{ALCNR}$ knowledge base K, where we exam the finite set of clash free completion forests $ccf(\mathcal{F}_{\mathbb{K}}^{|Q|})$. Our algorithm is first presented for union of conjunctive queries free of ordinary predicates (6.1) and then extended for query answering with ordinary predicates (6.2).

6.1   Answering to Conjunctive Queries Without Ordinary Predicates

In order to have a complete algorithm for answering to conjunctive queries we must add to our $TBox$ the rule $C \sqsubseteq C$ for each concept name C appearing in a conjunctive query. This ensures that in each completion forest either $(x : C) \geq n$ or $(x : C) < n$ [4] holds and consequently it can be checked if a node can be mapped to a variable of our conjunctive query.

Additionally we have to show why q-blocking is adopted instead of simple blocking. A conjunctive query CQ as presented in definition 1 can be mapped to a graph G_{CQ} whose nodes correspond to variables and individuals, each node is labelled with a set $\mathcal{L}(x) = \{\langle C, \geq, n \rangle\}$ and each edge is labelled with a set $\mathcal{L}(x, y) = \{\langle R, \geq, n \rangle\}$ where C and R are concepts and roles in CQ. Suppose that d_{xy} is the length of the lengthiest acyclic path between nodes x and y, we define $|CQ|$ to be the maximum d_{xy} between the set of pairs of connected nodes in CQ. Naturally we deduce that a conjunctive query CQ cannot be mapped to a subtree of a completion forest $\mathcal{F}$ that has more than $|CQ|$ arcs height. The $|CQ|$-blocking condition ensures that a possible mapping from CQ to $\mathcal{F}$ wont be blocked. In case of a union of conjunctive queries UCQ we will consider that $|UCQ|$ coincidents with the value of the maximum $|CQ|$.

Example 5. The conjunctive query:

$$CQ = \left\{ \begin{array}{l} friend(John, x) \geq 0.3, \, tall(x) \geq 0.7, \\ likes(x, Mary) \geq 0.2, \, friend(John, y) \geq 0.6, \\ hates(y, Mary) \geq 0.8, \, loves(z, w) \geq 0.4 \end{array} \right\} \text{ [5]}$$

is represented by the graph in figure 3. For this conjunctive query $|CQ| = 2$.

Definition 11. *Suppose we have a query* $Q = C_1(x_1) \geq n_1 \wedge \ldots \wedge C_k(x_k) \geq n_k \wedge R_1(y_1, z_1) \geq n_{k+1} \wedge \ldots \wedge R_l(y_l, z_l) \geq n_{k+l}$. *For a completion forest* $\mathcal{F}$ *we say that* $Q \hookrightarrow \mathcal{F}$ *iff there exists a mapping* $\sigma : varsIndivs(Q) \rightarrow \text{nodes}(\mathcal{F})$ *such that* $\{\langle C_i, \geq, n_i \rangle\} \in \mathcal{L}(\sigma(x_i))$ *and* $\sigma(y_j)$ *is an* $R_{\geq n_j}$-*successor of* $\sigma(z_j)$ *for each* $1 \leq i \leq k$ *and* $k+1 \leq j \leq l$. *For a union of conjunctive queries* $UCQ = \{Q_1, \ldots, Q_l\}$ *we say that* $UCQ \hookrightarrow \mathcal{F}$ *iff* $Q_i \hookrightarrow \mathcal{F}$ *for some* $Q_i \in UCQ$.

It can be proven that if a mapping $Q \hookrightarrow \mathcal{F}$ exists for each $\mathcal{F} \in ccf(\mathcal{F}_{\mathbb{K}}^{|Q|})$, then $K \models Q$.

---

[4] $(a : \neg C) > 1 - n + \epsilon$ is its PINF, normalized form.

[5] Here we claim that someone may like, hate, love or be a friend of someone else at certain degree.

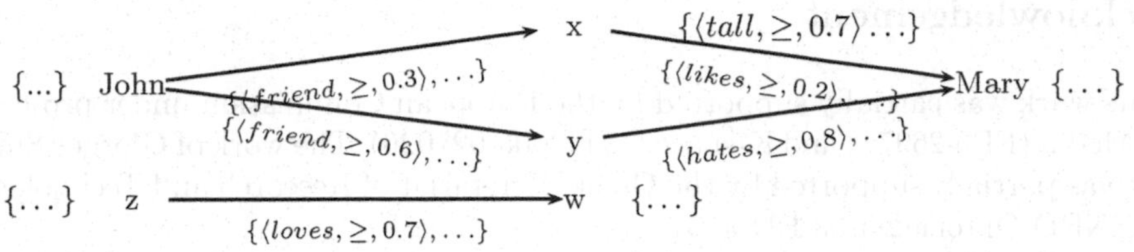

Fig. 3. Conjunctive query mapped to a graph

6.2   Answering to Conjunctive Queries with Ordinary Predicates

Initially, we will consider conjunctive queries containing no assertions about ordinary predicates, in such a case it holds:

Proposition 1. *Suppose that we have a conjunctive query of the form* $Q = \{p_1 \geq n_1 \wedge \ldots \wedge p_k \geq n_k \wedge \ldots \wedge p_m \geq n_m\}$ *and a set of Horn Rules related to* p_k:

$$
\mathcal{H}_{p_k} = \left\{ \begin{array}{c} p_k \leftarrow p_{11} \wedge \ldots \wedge p_{1l_1}, \\ \vdots \\ p_k \leftarrow p_{m1} \wedge \ldots \wedge p_{ml_m} \end{array} \right\}
$$

Q can be replaced with a union of conjunctive queries $UCQ = \{Q_1, \ldots, Q_m\}$ *where in each* Q_j, $p_k \geq n_k$ *is replaced with* $p_{k1} \geq m_k \wedge \ldots \wedge p_{kl_k} \geq m_k$.

Fuzzy assertions about ordinary predicates can be introduced by the use of pseudo-roles and pseudo-concepts. For example an assertion about an ordinary predicate $q(a_1, \ldots, a_m) \geq n$ can be substituted by a set of role assertions $\mathcal{A}_q = \{R_{q1}(a_1, a_2) \geq n, \ldots, R_{q(m-1)}(a_{m-1}, a_m) \geq n\}$ and a Horn rule $q \leftarrow R_{q1} \wedge \ldots \wedge R_{q(m-1)}$. In such a case conjunctive queries and union of conjunctive queries can be recurrently stretched to union of conjunctive queries containing only concepts and roles (pseudo or not) since only acyclic Horn Rules are allowed in $\mathcal{H}$. So the problem is reduced to the problem described in section 6.1.

7   Conclusions

Till now we have presented the integration of fuzzy logic, description logics and Horn rules, into fuzzy CARIN. The acquired system matches the benefits of its ancestors, providing a very expressive language for handling uncertainty and imprecision, with the counterweight of its high complexity, resulting from the high complexity of its structural elements. Future directions concern the study of fuzzy CARIN's complexity and its extension with more expressive DLs (a guide towards that direction is provided in [24]). It should also be extended to answer to other kind of inference problems, originating from the fuzzy DL domain, such as *glb* queries [16].

Acknowledgement

This work was partially supported by the European Commission under projects X-Media (FP6-26978) and K-space (IST-2005-027026). The work of Giorgos Stoilos was partially supported by the Greek Secretariat of Research and Technology (PENED Ontomedia 03 ED 475).

References

1. Baader, F., Calvanese, D., McGuinness, D.L., Nardi, D., Patel-Schneider, P.F. (eds.): The Description Logic Handbook: Theory, Implementation, and Applications. Cambridge University Press, Cambridge (2003)
2. Meghini, C., Sebastiani, F., Straccia, U.: A model of multimedia information retrieval. J. ACM 48, 909–970 (2001)
3. Goble, C.A., Haul, C., Bechhofer, S.: Describing and classifying multimedia using the description logic grail. In: Storage and Retrieval for Image and Video Databases (SPIE). pp. 132–143 (1996)
4. Stoilos, G., Stamou, G., Tzouvaras, V., Pan, J., Horrocks, I.: A fuzzy description logic for multimedia knowledge representation. In: Proc. of the International Workshop on Multimedia and the Semantic Web (2005)
5. Golbreich, C., Bierlaire, O., Dameron, O., Gibaud, B.: Use case: Ontology with rules for identifying brain anatomical structures. In: Rule Languages for Interoperability, W3C (2005)
6. Herman, J.H.I.: Web ontology language (OWL). technical report (2004) http://www.w3.org/2004/OWL/
7. Herman, I.: Semantic web. technical report http://www.w3.org/2001/sw/ (2007)
8. Baader, F., Brandt, S., Lutz, C.: Pushing the el envelope. In: Kaelbling, L.P., Saffiotti, A.,(eds.): IJCAI, Professional Book Center, pp. 364–369 (2005)
9. Horrocks, I., Kutz, O., Sattler, U.: The even more irresistible SROIQ. In: Doherty, P., Mylopoulos, J., Welty, C.A. (eds.) KR, pp. 57–67. AAAI Press, California (2006)
10. Antoniou, G., Damasio, C.V., Grosof, B., Horrocks, I., Kifer, M., Maluszynski, J., Patel-Schneider, P.F.: Combining rules and ontologies. A survey (2006)
11. Grosof, B.N., Horrocks, I., Volz, R., Decker, S.: Description logic programs: combining logic programs with description logic. In: WWW, pp. 48–57 (2003)
12. Horrocks, I., Patel-Schneider, P.F.: A proposal for an OWL rules language. In: Feldman, S.I., Uretsky, M., Najork, M., Wills, C.E. (eds.) WWW, pp. 723–731. ACM, New York (2004)
13. Donini, F.M., Lenzerini, M., Nardi, D., Schaerf, A.: Al-log: Integrating datalog and description logics. J. Intell. Inf. Syst. 10, 227–252 (1998)
14. Kifer, M., Lausen, G., Wu, J.: Logical foundations of object-oriented and frame-based languages. J. ACM 42, 741–843 (1995)
15. Levy, A.Y., Rousset, M.C.: Combining horn rules and description logics in carin. Artif. Intell. 104, 165–209 (1998)
16. Straccia, U.: Reasoning within fuzzy description logics. J. Artif. Intell. Res. (JAIR) 14, 137–166 (2001)
17. Stoilos, G., Stamou, G.B., Tzouvaras, V., Pan, J.Z., Horrocks, I.: The fuzzy description logic f-SHIN. In: da Costa, P.C.G., Laskey, K.B., Laskey, K.J., Pool, M. (eds.) ISWC-URSW, pp. 67–76 (2005)

18. Lukasiewicz, T.: Fuzzy description logic programs under the answer set semantics for the semantic web. In: Eiter, T., Franconi, E., Hodgson, R., Stephens, S. (eds.) RuleML, pp. 89–96. IEEE Computer Society, Washington (2006)

19. Straccia, U.: Fuzzy description logic programs. In: Proceedings of the 11th International Conference on Information Processing and Management of Uncertainty in Knowledge-Based Systems, (IPMU-06), pp. 1818–1825 (2006)

20. Eiter, T., Lukasiewicz, T., Schindlauer, R., Tompits, H.: Well-founded semantics for description logic programs in the semantic web. In: Antoniou, G., Boley, H. (eds.) RuleML 2004. LNCS, vol. 3323, pp. 81–97. Springer, Heidelberg (2004)

21. Klir, G.J., Yuan, B.: Fuzzy Sets and Fuzzy Logic: Theory and Applications. vol. 567 of [26]

22. Straccia, U.: Description logics with fuzzy concrete domains. In: Bachus, F., Jaakkola, T. (eds.) 21st Conference on Uncertainty in Artificial Intelligence (UAI-05), (Edinburgh, Scotland) pp. 559–567

23. Stoilos, G., Straccia, U., Stamou, G.B., Pan, J.Z.: General concept inclusions influzzy description logics. In: Brewka, G., Coradeschi, S., Perini, A., Traverso, P. (eds.) ECAI, pp. 457–461. IOS Press, Amsterdam (2006)

24. Ortiz, M., Calvanese, D., Eiter, T.: Characterizing data complexity for conjunctive query answering in expressive description logics. In: AAAI, AAAI Press, California (2006)

25. Baader, F., Hollunder, B.: A terminological knowledge representation system with complete inference algorithms. [26], pp. 67–86

26. Boley, H., Richter, M.M.: Processing Declarative Knowledge, International Workshop PDK'91. In: Boley, H., Richter, M.M. (eds.) PDK 1991, LNCS, vol. 567, pp. 1–3. Springer, Heidelberg (1991)

Quantified Equilibrium Logic and Hybrid Rules*

Jos de Bruijn[3], David Pearce[1], Axel Polleres[1,4], and Agustín Valverde[2]

[1] Universidad Rey Juan Carlos, Madrid, Spain
[2] Universidad de Málaga, Málaga, Spain
[3] DERI Innsbruck, Innsbruck, Austria
[4] DERI Galway, National University of Ireland, Galway
jos.debruijn@deri.org, davidandrew.pearce@urjc.es,
axel@polleres.net, a_valverde@ctima.uma.es

Abstract. In the ongoing discussion about combining rules and Ontologies on the Semantic Web a recurring issue is how to combine first-order classical logic with nonmonotonic rule languages. Whereas several modular approaches to define a combined semantics for such hybrid knowledge bases focus mainly on decidability issues, we tackle the matter from a more general point of view. In this paper we show how Quantified Equilibrium Logic (QEL) can function as a unified framework which embraces classical logic as well as disjunctive logic programs under the (open) answer set semantics. In the proposed variant of QEL we relax the unique names assumption, which was present in earlier versions of QEL. Moreover, we show that this framework elegantly captures the existing modular approaches for hybrid knowledge bases in a unified way.

1 Introduction

In the current discussions on the Semantic Web architecture a recurring issue is how to combine a first-order classical theory formalising an ontology with a nonmonotonic rule base. In this context, nonmonotonic rule languages have received considerable attention and achieved maturity over the last few years due to the success of Answer Set Programming (ASP), a nonmonotonic, purely declarative logic programming and knowledge representation paradigm with many useful features such as aggregates, weak constraints and priorities, supported by efficient implementations (for an overview see [1]). As a logical foundation for the answer set semantics and a tool for logical analysis in ASP, the system of Equilibrium Logic was presented in [14] and further developed in subsequent works (see [15] for an overview and references). We will show how Equilibrium Logic can be used as a logical foundation for the combination of ASP and Ontologies.

In the quest to provide a formal underpinning for a nonmonotonic rules layer for the Semantic Web which can coexist in a semantically well-defined manner with the Ontology layer, various proposals for combining classical first-order logic with different variants of ASP have been presented in the literature.[1] We distinguish three kinds

---

* This research has been partially supported by the Spanish MEC under the projects TIC-2003-9001, TIN2006-15455-CO3 and the Acción Integrada "Formal Techniques for Reasoning about Ontologies in E-Science", and by the European Commission under the projects Knowledge Web (IST-2004-507482) and DIP (FP6-507483).

[1] Most of these approaches focus on the Description Logics fragments of first-order logic underlying the Web Ontology Language OWL.

M. Marchiori, J.Z. Pan, and C. de Sainte Marie (Eds.): RR 2007, LNCS 4524, pp. 58–72, 2007.
© Springer-Verlag Berlin Heidelberg 2007

of approaches: At the one end of the spectrum there are approaches which provide an entailment-based query interface to the Ontology in the bodies of ASP rules, resulting in a loose integration (e.g. [5,4]). At the other end there are approaches which use a unifying nonmonotonic formalism to embed both the Ontology and the rule base (e.g. [2,13]), resulting in a tight coupling. Hybrid approaches (e.g. [18,19,20,9]) fall between these extremes. Common to hybrid approaches is the definition of a modular semantics based on classical first-order models, on the one hand, and stable models, on the other hand. Additionally, they require several syntactical restrictions on the use of classical predicates within rules. With further restrictions of the classical part to decidable Description Logics (DLs), these semantics support straightforward implementation using existing DL reasoners and ASP engines, in a modular fashion. In this paper, we focus on such hybrid approaches.

Example 1. Consider a hybrid knowledge base consisting of a classical theory $\mathcal{T}$:
$$\forall x.PERSON(x) \rightarrow (AGENT(x) \wedge (\exists y.HAS\text{-}MOTHER(x,y)))$$
$$\forall x.(\exists y.HAS\text{-}MOTHER(x,y)) \rightarrow ANIMAL(x)$$
which says that every $PERSON$ is an $AGENT$ and has some (unknown) mother, and everyone who has a mother is an $ANIMAL$, and a nonmonotonic logic program $\mathcal{P}$:
$$PERSON(x) \leftarrow AGENT(x), \neg machine(x)$$
$$AGENT(DaveB)$$
which says that $AGENT$s are by default $PERSON$s, unless *known* to be *machine*s, and $DaveB$ is an $AGENT$.

Using a hybrid knowledge base which includes both $\mathcal{T}$ and $\mathcal{P}$, we intuitively would conclude $PERSON(DaveB)$ since he is not known to be a *machine*, further that $DaveB$ has some (unknown) mother, and thus $ANIMAL(DaveB)$.

We see two important shortcomings in current hybrid approaches:

(1) Current approaches to hybrid knowledge bases differ not only in terms of syntactic restrictions, motivated by decidability considerations, but also in the way they deal with more fundamental issues which arise when classical logic meets ASP, such as the domain closure and unique names assumptions.[2] In particular, current proposals implicitly deal with these issues by either restricting the allowed models of the classical theory, or by using variants of the traditional answer set semantics which cater for open domains and non-unique names. So far, little effort has been spent in a comparing the approaches from a more general perspective.

(2) The semantics of current hybrid knowledge bases is defined in a modular fashion. This has the important advantage that algorithms for reasoning with this combination can be based on existing algorithms for DL and ASP satisfiability. A single underlying logic for hybrid knowledge bases which, for example, allows to capture notions of equivalence between combined knowledge bases in a standard way, is lacking though.

Our main contribution with this paper is twofold. First, we survey and compare different (extensions of the) answer set semantics, as well as the existing approaches to hybrid knowledge bases. Second, we propose to use Quantified Equilibrium Logic (QEL)

---

[2] See [3] for a more in-depth discussion of these issues.

as a unified logical foundation for hybrid knowledge bases: As it turns out, the equilibrium models of the combined knowledge base coincide exactly with the modular nonmonotonic models for all approaches we are aware of [18,19,20,9].

The remainder of this paper is structured as follows: Section 2 recalls some basics of classical first-order logic. Section 3 reformulates different variants of the answer set semantics introduced in the literature using a common notation and points out correspondences and discrepancies between these variants. Next, definitions of hybrid knowledge bases from the literature are compared and generalised in Section 4. QEL and its relation to the different variants of ASP are clarified in Section 5. Section 6 describes an embedding of hybrid knowledge bases into QEL and establishes the correspondence between equilibrium models and nonmonotonic models of hybrid KBs. Implications of our results and further work are discussed in the concluding Sections 6.1, 6.2, and 7.

2 First-Order Logic (FOL)

A *function-free first-order language* $\mathcal{L} = \langle C, P \rangle$ with equality consists of disjoint sets of constant and predicate symbols C and P. Moreover, we assume a fixed countably infinite set of variables, the symbols '$\rightarrow$', '$\vee$', '$\wedge$', '$\neg$', '$\exists$', '$\forall$', and auxiliary parentheses '$($','$)$'. Each predicate symbol $p \in P$ has an assigned arity $ar(p)$. Atoms and formulas are constructed as usual. Closed formulas, or *sentences*, are those where each variable is bound by some quantifier. A *theory* $\mathcal{T}$ is a set of sentences. Variable-free atoms, formulas, or theories are also called *ground*. If D is a non-empty set, we denote by $At_D(C, P)$ the set of ground atoms constructible from $\mathcal{L}' = \langle C \cup D, P \rangle$.

Given a first-order language $\mathcal{L}$, an $\mathcal{L}$-structure consists of a pair $\mathcal{I} = \langle U, I \rangle$, where the *universe* $U = (D, \sigma)$ (sometimes called pre-interpretation) consists of a non-empty domain D and a function $\sigma: C \cup D \rightarrow D$ which assigns a domain value to each constant such that $\sigma(d) = d$ for every $d \in D$. For tuples we write $\sigma(\boldsymbol{t}) = (\sigma(d_1), \ldots, \sigma(d_n))$. We call $d \in D$ an *unnamed* individual if there is no $c \in C$ such that $\sigma(c) = d$. The function I assigns a relation $p^I \subseteq D^n$ to each n-ary predicate symbol $p \in P$ and is called the $\mathcal{L}$-*interpretation over D* . The designated binary predicate symbol eq, occasionally written '$=$' in infix notation, is assumed to be associated with the fixed interpretation function $eq^I = \{(d, d) \mid d \in D\}$. If $\mathcal{I}$ is an $\mathcal{L}'$-structure we denote by $\mathcal{I}|_\mathcal{L}$ the restriction of $\mathcal{I}$ to a sublanguage $\mathcal{L} \subseteq \mathcal{L}'$.

An $\mathcal{L}$-structure $\mathcal{I} = \langle U, I \rangle$ *satisfies* an atom $p(d_1, \ldots, d_n)$ of $At_D(C, P)$, written $\mathcal{I} \models p(d_1, \ldots, d_n)$, iff $(\sigma(d_1), \ldots, \sigma(d_n)) \in p^I$. This is extended as usual to sentences and theories. $\mathcal{I}$ is a *model* of an atom (sentence, theory, respectively) φ, written $\mathcal{I} \models \varphi$, if it satisfies φ. A theory $\mathcal{T}$ *entails* a sentence φ, written $\mathcal{T} \models \varphi$, if every model of $\mathcal{T}$ is also a model of φ. A theory is *consistent* if it has a model.

In the context of logic programs, the following assumptions often play a role: We say that the *parameter names assumption (PNA)* applies in case σ is surjective, i.e., there are no unnamed individuals in D; the *unique names assumption (UNA)* applies in case σ is injective; in case both the PNA and UNA apply, the *standard names assumption (SNA)* applies, i.e. σ is a bijection. In the following, we will speak about PNA-, UNA-, or SNA-structures, (or PNA-, UNA-, or SNA-models, respectively), depending on σ.

An $\mathcal{L}$-interpretation I over D can be seen as a subset of $At_D(C, P)$. So, we can define a subset relation for $\mathcal{L}$-structures $\mathcal{I}_1 = \langle (D, \sigma_1), I_1 \rangle$ and $\mathcal{I}_2 = \langle (D, \sigma_2), I_2 \rangle$ over the same domain by setting $\mathcal{I}_1 \subseteq \mathcal{I}_2$ if $I_1 \subseteq I_2$.[3] Whenever we speak about subset minimality of models/structures in the following, we thus mean minimality among all models/structures over the same domain.

3 Answer Set Semantics

In this paper we assume non-ground disjunctive logic programs with negation allowed in rule heads and bodies, interpreted under the answer set semantics [12].[4] A program $\mathcal{P}$ consists of a set of rules of the form

$$a_1 \vee a_2 \vee \ldots \vee a_k \vee \neg a_{k+1} \vee \ldots \vee \neg a_l \leftarrow b_1, \ldots, b_m, \neg b_{m+1}, \ldots, \neg b_n \quad (1)$$

where a_i ($i \in \{1, \ldots, l\}$) and b_j ($j \in \{1, \ldots, n\}$) are atoms, called head (body, respectively) atoms of the rule, in a function-free first-order language $\mathcal{L} = \langle C, P \rangle$ without equality. By $C_\mathcal{P} \subseteq C$ we denote the set of constants which appear in $\mathcal{P}$. A rule with $k = l$ and $m = n$ is called *positive*. Rules where each variable appears in $b_1, \ldots, b_m$ are called *safe*. A program is *positive* (*safe*) if all its rules are positive (safe).

For the purposes of this paper, we give a slightly generalised definition of the common notion of the *grounding* of a program: The *grounding* $gr_U(\mathcal{P})$ of $\mathcal{P}$ wrt. a universe $U = (D, \sigma)$ denotes the set of all rules obtained as follows: For $r \in \mathcal{P}$, replace (i) each constant c appearing in r with $\sigma(c)$ and (ii) each variable with some element in D. Observe that thus $gr_U(\mathcal{P})$ is a ground program over the atoms in $At_D(C, P)$.

For a ground program $\mathcal{P}$ and first-order structure $\mathcal{I}$ the *reduct* $\mathcal{P}^\mathcal{I}$ consists of rules

$$a_1 \vee a_2 \vee \ldots \vee a_k \leftarrow b_1, \ldots, b_m$$

obtained from all rules of the form (1) in $\mathcal{P}$ for which hold that $\mathcal{I} \models a_i$ for all $k < i \leq l$ and $\mathcal{I} \not\models b_j$ for all $m < j \leq n$.

Answer set semantics is usually defined in terms of *Herbrand structures* over $\mathcal{L} = \langle C, P \rangle$. Herbrand structures have a fixed universe, the *Herbrand universe* $\mathcal{H} = (C, id)$, where id is the identity function. For a Herbrand structure $\mathcal{I} = \langle \mathcal{H}, I \rangle$, I can be viewed as a subset of the *Herbrand base*, $\mathcal{B}$, which consists of the ground atoms of $\mathcal{L}$. Note that by definition of $\mathcal{H}$, Herbrand structures are SNA-structures. A Herbrand structure $\mathcal{I}$ is an *answer set* [12] of $\mathcal{P}$ if $\mathcal{I}$ is subset minimal among the structures satisfying $gr_\mathcal{H}(\mathcal{P})^\mathcal{I}$. Two variations of this semantics, the open [8] and generalised open answer set [9] semantics, consider open domains, thereby relaxing the PNA. An *extended Herbrand structure* is a first-order structure based on a universe $U = (D, id)$, where $D \supseteq C$.

Definition 1. *A first-order $\mathcal{L}$-structure $\mathcal{I} = \langle U, I \rangle$ is called a* generalised open answer set *of $\mathcal{P}$ if $\mathcal{I}$ is subset minimal among the structures satisfying all rules in $gr_U(\mathcal{P})^\mathcal{I}$. If, additionally, $\mathcal{I}$ is an extended Herbrand structure, then $\mathcal{I}$ is an* open answer set *of $\mathcal{P}$.*

---

[3] Note that this is not the substructure or submodel relation in classical model theory, which holds between a structure and its restriction to a subdomain.

[4] By $\neg$ we mean negation as failure and not classical, or strong negation, which is also sometimes considered in ASP.

In the open answer set semantics the UNA applies. Note that every answer set of a program is also an open answer set [8], but the converse does not hold in general:

Example 2. Consider $\mathcal{P} = \{p(a); \ ok \leftarrow \neg p(x); \ \leftarrow \neg ok\}$ over $\mathcal{L} = \langle \{a\}, \{p, ok\} \rangle$. We leave it as an exercise to the reader to show that $\mathcal{P}$ is inconsistent under the answer set semantics, but $\mathcal{M} = \langle (\{a, c_1\}, id), \{p(a), ok\} \rangle$ is an open answer set of $\mathcal{P}$.

An alternative approach to relax the UNA has been presented by Rosati in [19]: Instead of grounding with respect to U, programs are grounded with respect to the Herbrand universe $\mathcal{H} = (C, id)$, and minimality of the models of $gr_{\mathcal{H}}(\mathcal{P})^{\mathcal{I}}$ wrt. U is redefined: $\mathcal{I}|_{\mathcal{H}} = \{p(\sigma(c_1), \ldots, \sigma(c_n)) \mid p(c_1, \ldots, c_n) \in \mathcal{B}, \mathcal{I} \models p(c_1, \ldots, c_n)\}$, i.e., $\mathcal{I}|_{\mathcal{H}}$ is the restriction of $\mathcal{I}$ to ground atoms of $\mathcal{B}$. Given $\mathcal{L}$-structures $\mathcal{I}_1 = (U_1, I_1)$ and $\mathcal{I}_2 = (U_2, I_2)$, the relation $\mathcal{I}_1 \subseteq_{\mathcal{H}} \mathcal{I}_2$ holds if $\mathcal{I}_1|_{\mathcal{H}} \subseteq \mathcal{I}_2|_{\mathcal{H}}$.

Definition 2. *An $\mathcal{L}$-structure $\mathcal{I}$ is called a* generalised answer set *of $\mathcal{P}$ if $\mathcal{I}$ is $\subseteq_{\mathcal{H}}$-minimal among the structures satisfying all rules in $gr_{\mathcal{H}}(\mathcal{P})^{\mathcal{I}}$.*

The following Lemma establishes that, for safe programs, all atoms of $At_D(C, P)$ satisfied in an open answer set of a safe program are ground atoms over $C_{\mathcal{P}}$:

Lemma 1. *Let $\mathcal{P}$ be a safe program over $\mathcal{L} = \langle C, P \rangle$ with $\mathcal{M} = \langle U, I \rangle$ a (generalised) open answer set over universe $U = (D, \sigma)$. Then, for any atom from $At_D(C, P)$ such that $\mathcal{M} \models p(d_1, \ldots, d_n)$, there exist $c_i \in C_{\mathcal{P}}$ such that $\sigma(c_i) = d_i$ for each $1 \leq i \leq n$.*

From this Lemma, the following correspondence follows directly.

Proposition 1. *$\mathcal{M}$ is an (generalised) answer set of a safe program $\mathcal{P}$ if and only if $\mathcal{M}$ is an (generalised) open answer set of $\mathcal{P}$.*

If the SNA applies, consistency with respect to all semantics introduced so far boils down to consistency under the original definition of answer sets:

Proposition 2. *A program $\mathcal{P}$ has an answer set if and only if $\mathcal{P}$ has a generalised open answer under the SNA.*

Answer sets under SNA may differ from the original answer sets since also non-Herbrand structures are allowed. Further, we observe that there are programs which have generalised (open) answer sets but do not have (open) answer sets, even for safe programs:

Example 3. Consider $\mathcal{P} = \{p(a); \ \leftarrow \neg p(b)\}$ over $\mathcal{L} = \langle \{a, b\}, \{p\} \rangle$. $\mathcal{P}$ is ground, thus obviously safe. However, although $\mathcal{P}$ has a generalised (open) answer set – the reader may verify this by, for instance, considering the one-element universe $U = (\{d\}, \sigma)$, where $\sigma(a) = \sigma(b) = d$ – it is inconsistent under the open answer set semantics.

4   Hybrid Knowledge Bases

We now turn to the concept of hybrid knowledge bases, which combine classical theories with the various notions of answer sets. We define a notion of hybrid knowledge bases which generalizes definitions in the literature [18,19,20,9]. We then compare and discuss the differences between the various definitions. It turns out that the differences are mainly concerned with the notion of answer sets, and syntactical restrictions, but do not change the general semantics. This will allow us to base our embedding into Quantified Equilibrium Logic on a unified definition.

A *hybrid knowledge base* $\mathcal{K} = (\mathcal{T}, \mathcal{P})$ over the function-free language $\mathcal{L} = \langle C, P_{\mathcal{T}} \cup P_{\mathcal{P}} \rangle$ consists of a classical first-order theory $\mathcal{T}$ (also called the *structural* part of $\mathcal{K}$) over the language $\mathcal{L}_{\mathcal{T}} = \langle C, P_{\mathcal{T}} \rangle$ and a program $\mathcal{P}$ (also called *rules* part of $\mathcal{K}$) over the language $\mathcal{L}$, where $P_{\mathcal{T}} \cap P_{\mathcal{P}} = \emptyset$, i.e. $\mathcal{T}$ and $\mathcal{P}$ share a single set of constants, and the predicate symbols allowed to be used in $\mathcal{P}$ are a superset of the predicate symbols in $\mathcal{L}_{\mathcal{T}}$. Intuitively, the predicates in $\mathcal{L}_{\mathcal{T}}$ are interpreted classically, whereas the predicates in $\mathcal{L}_{\mathcal{P}}$ are interpreted nonmonotonically under the (generalised open) answer set semantics. With $\mathcal{L}_{\mathcal{P}} = \langle C, P_{\mathcal{P}} \rangle$ we denote the restricted language of $\mathcal{P}$.

We define the *projection* of a ground program $\mathcal{P}$ with respect to an $\mathcal{L}$-structure $\mathcal{I} = \langle U, I \rangle$, denoted $\Pi(\mathcal{P}, \mathcal{I})$, as follows: for each rule $r \in \mathcal{P}$, r^{Π} is defined as:

1. $r^{\Pi} = \emptyset$ if there is a literal over $At_D(C, P_T)$ in the head of r of form $p(t)$ such that $p(\sigma(t)) \in I$ or of form $\neg p(t)$ with $p(\sigma(t)) \notin I$;
2. $r^{\Pi} = \emptyset$ if there is a literal over $At_D(C, P_T)$ in the body of r of form $p(t)$ such that $p(\sigma(t)) \notin I$ or of form $\neg p(t)$ such that $p(\sigma(t)) \in I$;
3. otherwise r^{Π} is the singleton set resulting from r by deleting all occurrences of literals from $\mathcal{L}_{\mathcal{T}}$,

and $\Pi(\mathcal{P}, \mathcal{I}) = \bigcup \{r^{\Pi} : r \in \mathcal{P}\}$. Intuitively, the projection "evaluates" all classical literals in $\mathcal{P}$ with respect to $\mathcal{I}$.

Definition 3. *Let $\mathcal{K} = (\mathcal{T}, \mathcal{P})$ be a hybrid knowledge base over the language $\mathcal{L} = \langle C, P_{\mathcal{T}} \cup P_{\mathcal{P}} \rangle$. An NM-model $\mathcal{M} = \langle U, I \rangle$ (with $U = (D, \sigma)$) of $\mathcal{K}$ is a first-order $\mathcal{L}$-structure such that $\mathcal{M}|_{\mathcal{L}_{\mathcal{T}}}$ is a model of $\mathcal{T}$ and $\mathcal{M}|_{\mathcal{L}_{\mathcal{P}}}$ is a generalised open answer set of $\Pi(gr_U(\mathcal{P}), \mathcal{M})$.*

Analogous to first-order models, we speak about PNA-, UNA-, and SNA-NM-models.

Example 4. Consider the hybrid knowledge base $\mathcal{K} = (\mathcal{T}, \mathcal{P})$, with $\mathcal{T}$ and $\mathcal{P}$ as in Example 1, with the capitalised predicates being predicates in $P_{\mathcal{T}}$. Now consider the interpretation $\mathcal{I} = \langle U, I \rangle$ (with $U = (D, \sigma)$) with $D = \{DaveB, k\}$, σ the identity function, and $I = \{AGENT(DaveB), HAS\text{-}MOTHER(DaveB, k), ANIMAL(DaveB), machine(DaveB)\}$. Clearly, $\mathcal{I}|_{\mathcal{L}_{\mathcal{T}}}$ is a model of $\mathcal{T}$. The projection $\Pi(gr_U(\mathcal{P}), \mathcal{I})$ is

$$\leftarrow \neg machine(DaveB),$$

which does not have a stable model, and thus $\mathcal{I}$ is not an NM-model of $\mathcal{K}$. In fact, the logic program $\mathcal{P}$ ensures that an interpretation cannot be an NM-model of $\mathcal{K}$ if there is an $AGENT$ which is neither a $PERSON$ nor known (by conclusions from $\mathcal{P}$) to be a $machine$. It is easy to verify that, for any NM-model of $\mathcal{K}$, the atoms $AGENT(DaveB)$, $PERSON(DaveB)$, and $ANIMAL(DaveB)$ must be true, and are thus entailed by $\mathcal{K}$. The latter cannot be derived from $\mathcal{T}$ or $\mathcal{P}$ individually.

We now proceed to compare our definition of NM-models with the various definitions in the literature. The first kind of hybrid knowledge base we consider was introduced by Rosati in [18] (and extended in [20] under the name $\mathcal{DL+log}$), and was labeled *r-hybrid* knowledge base. Syntactically, *r-hybrid* KBs do not allow negated atoms in rule heads, i.e. for rules of the form (1) $l = k$, and do not allow atoms from $\mathcal{L_T}$ to occur negatively in the rule body.[5] Moreover, in [18], Rosati deploys a restriction which is stronger than standard safety: each variable must appear in at least one positive body atom with a predicate from $\mathcal{L_P}$. We call this condition $\mathcal{L_P}$-*safe* in the remainder. In [20] this condition is relaxed to *weak* $\mathcal{L_P}$-*safety*: there is no special safety restriction for variables which occur only in body atoms from P_T.

Definition 4. *Let* $\mathcal{K} = \langle T, \mathcal{P} \rangle$ *be an r-hybrid knowledge base, over the language* $\mathcal{L} = \langle C, P_T \cup P_{\mathcal{P}} \rangle$, *where* C *is countably infinite, and* $\mathcal{P}$ *is a (weak)* $\mathcal{L_P}$-*safe program. An* r-NM-*model* $\mathcal{M} = \langle U, I \rangle$ *of* $\mathcal{K}$ *is a first-order* $\mathcal{L}$-SNA-*structure such that* $\mathcal{M}|_{\mathcal{L_T}}$ *is a model of* T *and* $\mathcal{M}|_{\mathcal{L_P}}$ *is an answer set of* $\Pi(gr_U(\mathcal{P}), \mathcal{M})$.

In view of the (weak) $\mathcal{L_P}$-safety condition, we observe that r-NM-model existence coincides with SNA-NM-model existence on r-hybrid knowledge bases, by Lemma 1 and Proposition 2. In [19], Rosati relaxes the UNA for what we will call here r^+-*hybrid* knowledge bases.

Definition 5. *Let* $\mathcal{K} = \langle T, \mathcal{P} \rangle$ *be an* r^+-*hybrid knowledge base consisting of a theory* T *and an* $\mathcal{L_P}$-*safe program* $\mathcal{P}$. *An* r^+-NM-*model,* $\mathcal{M} = \langle U, I \rangle$ *of* $\mathcal{K}$ *is a first-order* $\mathcal{L}$-*structure such that* $\mathcal{M}|_{\mathcal{L_T}}$ *is a model of* T *and* $\mathcal{M}|_{\mathcal{L_P}}$ *is a generalised answer set of* $\Pi(gr_U(\mathcal{P}), \mathcal{M})$.

$\mathcal{L_P}$-safety guarantees safety of $\Pi(gr_U(\mathcal{P}), \mathcal{M})$. Thus, by Proposition 1, we can conclude that r^+-NM-models coincide with NM-models on r-hybrid knowledge bases.

G-hybrid knowledge bases [9] allow a different form of rules in the program. In order to regain decidability, rules are not required to be safe, but they are required to be *guarded* (hence the 'g' in g-hybrid): All variables in a rule are required to occur in a single positive body atom, the *guard*, with the exception of unsafe choice rules of the form

$$p(c_1, \ldots, c_n) \vee \neg p(c_1, \ldots, c_n) \leftarrow$$

are allowed. Moreover, disjunction in rule heads is limited to at most one positive atom, i.e. for rules of the form (1) we have that $k \leq 1$, but an arbitrary number of negated head atoms is allowed. The definition of NM-models in [9] coincides precisely with our Definition 3.

5   Quantified Equilibrium Logic (QEL)

Equilibrium logic for propositional theories and logic programs was presented in [14] as a foundation for answer set semantics, and extended to the first-order case in [16], as well as, in slightly more general, modified form, in [17]. For a survey of the main properties of equilibrium logic, see [15]. Usually in quantified equilibrium logic we

---

[5] Note that by projection, negation of predicates from P_T is treated classically, whereas negation of predicates from $P_{\mathcal{P}}$ is treated nonmonotonically. The negative occurrence of classical predicates in the body is equivalent to the positive occurrence of the predicate in the head.

consider a full first-order language allowing function symbols and we include a second, strong negation operator as occurs in several ASP dialects. For the present purpose of drawing comparisons with approaches to hybrid knowledge bases, it will suffice to consider the function-free language with a single negation symbol, '¬'. In particular, we shall work with a quantified version of the logic HT of *here-and-there*. In other respects we follow the treatment of [17].

5.1   General Structures for Quantified Here-and-There Logic

As before, we consider a function-free first order languages $\mathcal{L} = \langle C, P \rangle$ built over a set of *constant* symbols, C, and a set of *predicate* symbols, P. The sets of $\mathcal{L}$-formulas, $\mathcal{L}$-sentences and atomic $\mathcal{L}$-sentences are defined in the usual way.

Again, we only work with *sentences*, and, as in Section 2, by an $\mathcal{L}$-interpretation I over a set D we mean a subset I of $At_D(C, P)$. A here-and-there $\mathcal{L}$-structure with static domains, or $\mathbf{QHT}^s(\mathcal{L})$*-structure*, is a tuple $\mathcal{M} = \langle (D, \sigma), I_h, I_t \rangle$ where

- D is a non-empty set, called the *domain* of $\mathcal{M}$.
- σ is a mapping: $C \cup D \to D$ called the *assignment* such that $\sigma(d) = d$ for all $d \in D$. If $D = C$ and $\sigma = id$, $\mathcal{M}$ is a *Herbrand structure*.
- I_h, I_t are $\mathcal{L}$-interpretations over D such that $I_h \subseteq I_t$.

We can think of $\mathcal{M}$ as a structure similar to a first-order classical model, but having two parts, or components, h and t that correspond to two different points or "worlds", 'here' and 'there', in the sense of Kripke semantics for intuitionistic logic [22], where the worlds are ordered by $h \leq t$. At each world $w \in \{h, t\}$ one verifies a set of atoms I_w in the expanded language for the domain D. We call the model static, since, in contrast to say intuitionistic logic, the same domain serves each of the worlds.[6] Since $h \leq t$, whatever is verified at h remains true at t. The satisfaction relation for $\mathcal{M}$ is defined so as to reflect the two different components, so we write $\mathcal{M}, w \models \varphi$ to denote that φ is true in $\mathcal{M}$ with respect to the w component. Evidently we should require that an atomic sentence is true at w just in case it belongs to the w-interpretation. Formally, if $p(t_1, \ldots, t_n) \in At_D$ then

$$\mathcal{M}, w \models p(t_1, \ldots, t_n) \quad \text{iff} \quad p(\sigma(t_1), \ldots, \sigma(t_n)) \in I_w. \tag{2}$$

Then $\models$ is extended recursively as follows:[7]

- $\mathcal{M}, w \models \varphi \wedge \psi$ iff $\mathcal{M}, w \models \varphi$ and $\mathcal{M}, w \models \psi$.
- $\mathcal{M}, w \models \varphi \vee \psi$ iff $\mathcal{M}, w \models \varphi$ or $\mathcal{M}, w \models \psi$.
- $\mathcal{M}, t \models \varphi \to \psi$ iff $\mathcal{M}, t \not\models \varphi$ or $\mathcal{M}, t \models \psi$.
- $\mathcal{M}, h \models \varphi \to \psi$ iff $\mathcal{M}, t \models \varphi \to \psi$ and $\mathcal{M}, h \not\models \varphi$ or $\mathcal{M}, h \models \psi$.
- $\mathcal{M}, w \models \neg\varphi$ iff $\mathcal{M}, t \not\models \varphi$.
- $\mathcal{M}, t \models \forall x \varphi(x)$ iff $\mathcal{M}, t \models \varphi(d)$ for all $d \in D$.
- $\mathcal{M}, h \models \forall x \varphi(x)$ iff $\mathcal{M}, t \models \forall x \varphi(x)$ and $\mathcal{M}, h \models \varphi(d)$ for all $d \in D$.
- $\mathcal{M}, w \models \exists x \varphi(x)$ iff $\mathcal{M}, w \models \varphi(d)$ for some $d \in D$.

---

[6] Alternatively it is quite common to speak of a logic with *constant* domains.

[7] The reader may easily check that the following correspond exactly to the usual Kripke semantics for intuitionistic logic given our assumptions about the two worlds h and t and the single domain D, see e.g. [22].

Truth of a sentence in a model is defined as follows: $\mathcal{M} \models \varphi$ iff $\mathcal{M}, w \models \varphi$ for each $w \in \{h, t\}$. A sentence φ is valid if it is true in all models, denoted by $\models \varphi$. A sentence φ is a consequence of a set of sentences Γ, denoted $\Gamma \models \varphi$, if every model of Γ is a model of φ. In a model $\mathcal{M}$ we often use the symbols H and T, possibly with subscripts, to denote the interpretations I_h and I_t respectively; so, an $\mathcal{L}$-structure may be written in the form $\langle U, H, T \rangle$, where $U = (D, \sigma)$.

The resulting logic is called *Quantified Here-and-There Logic with static domains*, denoted by $\mathbf{QHT}^s$, and can be axiomatised as follows.

Let $\mathbf{INT}^=$ denote first-order intuitionistic logic [22] with the usual axioms for equality:

$$x = x,$$
$$x = y \rightarrow (F(x) \rightarrow F(y))$$

for every formula $F(x)$ such that y is substitutable for x in $F(x)$. To this we add the axiom of Hosoi

$$\alpha \vee (\neg \beta \vee (\alpha \rightarrow \beta))$$

which determines 2-element here-and-there models in the propositional case, and the axiom:

SQHT $\exists x (F(x) \rightarrow \forall x F(x))$.

The notation SQHT stands for "static quantified here-and-there". Lastly we add the "decidable equality" axiom

DE $x = y \vee x \neq y$.

For a completeness proof for $\mathbf{QHT}^s$, see [11].

As usual in first order logic, satisfiability and validity are independent from the language. If $\mathcal{M} = \langle (D, \sigma), H, T \rangle$ is an $\mathbf{QHT}^s(\mathcal{L}')$-structure and $\mathcal{L} \subset \mathcal{L}'$, we denote by $\mathcal{M}|_{\mathcal{L}}$ the restriction of $\mathcal{M}$ to the sublanguage $\mathcal{L}$: $\mathcal{M}|_{\mathcal{L}} = \langle (D, \sigma|_{\mathcal{L}}), H|_{\mathcal{L}}, T|_{\mathcal{L}} \rangle$.

Proposition 3. *Suppose that $\mathcal{L}' \supset \mathcal{L}$, Γ is a theory in $\mathcal{L}$ and $\mathcal{M}$ is an $\mathcal{L}'$-structure such $\mathcal{M} \models \Gamma$. Then $\mathcal{M}|_{\mathcal{L}}$ is a model of Γ in $\mathbf{QHT}^s_=(\mathcal{L})$.*

Proposition 4. *Suppose that $\mathcal{L}' \supset \mathcal{L}$ and $\varphi \in \mathcal{L}$. Then φ is valid (resp. satisfiable) in $\mathbf{QHT}^s_=(\mathcal{L})$ if and only if is valid (resp. satisfiable) in $\mathbf{QHT}^s_=(\mathcal{L}')$.*

Analogous to the case of classical models we can define special kinds of $\mathbf{QHT}^s$ (resp. $\mathbf{QHT}^s_=$) models. Let $\mathcal{M} = \langle (D, \sigma), H, T \rangle$ be an $\mathcal{L}$-structure that is a model of a universal theory T. Then, we call $\mathcal{M}$ a PNA-, UNA-, or SNA-model if the restriction of σ to constants in $\mathcal{C}$ is surjective, injective or bijective, respectively.

5.2   Equilibrium Models and Their Relation to Answer Sets

As in the propositional case, quantified equilibrium logic is based on a suitable notion of minimal model.

Definition 6. *Among $\mathbf{QHT}^s_=(\mathcal{L})$-structures we define the order $\trianglelefteq$ as: $\langle (D, \sigma), H, T \rangle \trianglelefteq \langle (D', \sigma'), H', T' \rangle$ if $D = D'$, $\sigma = \sigma'$, $T = T'$ and $H \subseteq H'$. If the subset relation is strict, we write '$\triangleleft$'.*

Definition 7. *Let Γ be a set of sentences and $\mathcal{M} = \langle (D,\sigma), H, T \rangle$ a model of Γ.*
1. *$\mathcal{M}$ is said to be* total *if $H = T$.*
2. *$\mathcal{M}$ is said to be an* equilibrium *model of Γ (or short, we say: "$\mathcal{M}$ is in equilibrium") if it is minimal under $\unlhd$ among models of Γ, and it is total.*

Notice that a total $\mathbf{QHT}^s_=$ model of a theory Γ is equivalent to a classical first order model of Γ.

Proposition 5. *Let Γ be a theory in $\mathcal{L}$ and $\mathcal{M}$ an equilibrium model of Γ in $\mathbf{QHT}^s_=(\mathcal{L}')$ with $\mathcal{L}' \supset \mathcal{L}$. Then $\mathcal{M}|_{\mathcal{L}}$ is an equilibrium model of Γ in $\mathbf{QHT}^s_=(\mathcal{L})$.*

The above version of QEL is described in more detail in [17]. If we assume all models are UNA-models, we obtain the version of QEL found in [16]. There, the relation of QEL to (ordinary) answer sets for logic programs with variables was established (in [16, Corollary 7.7]). For the present version of QEL the correspondence can be described as follows.

Proposition 6 ([17]). *Let Γ be a universal theory in $\mathcal{L} = \langle C, P \rangle$. Let $\langle U, T, T \rangle$ be a total $\mathbf{QHT}^s_=$ model of Γ. Then $\langle U, T, T \rangle$ is an equilibrium model of Γ iff $\langle T, T \rangle$ is a propositional equilibrium model of $gr_U(\Gamma)$.*

By convention, when $\mathcal{P}$ is a logic program with variables we consider the models and equilibrium models of its universal closure expressed as a set of logical formulas. So, from Proposition 6 we obtain:

Corollary 1. *Let $\mathcal{P}$ be a logic program. A total $\mathbf{QHT}^s_=$ model $\langle U, T, T \rangle$ of $\mathcal{P}$ is an equilibrium model of $\mathcal{P}$ iff it is a generalised open answer set of $\mathcal{P}$.*

6 Relation Between Hybrid KBs and QEL

In this section we show how equilibrium models for hybrid knowledge bases relate to the NM models defined earlier and we show that QEL captures the various approaches to the semantics of hybrid KBs in the literature [18,19,20,9].

Given a hybrid KB $\mathcal{K} = (\mathcal{T}, \mathcal{P})$ we call $\mathcal{T} \cup \mathcal{P} \cup st(\mathcal{T})$ the *stable closure* of $\mathcal{K}$, where $st(\mathcal{T}) = \{\forall x(p(x) \vee \neg p(x)) : p \in \mathcal{L}_{\mathcal{T}}\}$.[8] From now on, unless otherwise clear from context, the symbol '$\models$' denotes the truth relation for $\mathbf{QHT}^s_=$. Given a ground program $\mathcal{P}$ and an $\mathcal{L}$-structure $\mathcal{M} = \langle U, H, T \rangle$, the *projection* $\Pi(\mathcal{P}, \mathcal{M})$ is understood to be defined relative to the component T of $\mathcal{M}$.

Lemma 2. *Let $\mathcal{M} = \langle U, H, T \rangle$ be a $\mathbf{QIIT}^s_=$-model of $\mathcal{T} \cup st(\mathcal{T})$. Then $\mathcal{M} \models \mathcal{P}$ iff $\mathcal{M}|_{\mathcal{L}_{\mathcal{P}}} \models \Pi(gr_U(\mathcal{P}), \mathcal{M})$.*

Proof. By the hypothesis $\mathcal{M} \models \{\forall x(p(x) \vee \neg p(x)) : p \in \mathcal{L}_{\mathcal{T}}\}$. It follows that $H|_{\mathcal{L}_{\mathcal{T}}} = T|_{\mathcal{L}_{\mathcal{T}}}$. Consider any $r \in \mathcal{P}$, such that $r^\Pi \neq \emptyset$. Then there are four cases to consider. (i) r has the form $\alpha \to \beta \vee p(t)$, $p(t) \in \mathcal{L}_{\mathcal{T}}$ and $p(\sigma(t)) \notin T$, so $\mathcal{M} \models \neg p(t)$. W.l.o.g. assume that $\alpha, \beta \in \mathcal{L}_{\mathcal{P}}$, so $r^\Pi = \alpha \to \beta$ and

---

[8] Evidently $\mathcal{T}$ becomes *stable* in $\mathcal{K}$ in the sense that $\forall \varphi \in \mathcal{T}$, $st(\mathcal{T}) \models \neg\neg\varphi \to \varphi$. The terminology is drawn from intuitionistic logic and mathematics.

$$\mathcal{M} \models r \Leftrightarrow \mathcal{M} \models r^{\Pi} \Leftrightarrow \mathcal{M}|_{\mathcal{L}_{\mathcal{P}}} \models r^{\Pi} \tag{3}$$

by the semantics for $\mathbf{QHT}^s_=$ and Theorem 3. (ii) r has the form $\alpha \rightarrow \beta \vee \neg p(t)$, where $p(\sigma(t)) \in T$; so $p(\sigma(t)) \in H$ and $\mathcal{M} \models p(t)$. Again it is easy to see that (3) holds. Case (iii): r has the form $\alpha \wedge p(t) \rightarrow \beta$ and $p(\sigma(t)) \in H, T$, so $\mathcal{M} \models p(t)$. Case (iv): r has the form $\alpha \wedge \neg p(t) \rightarrow \beta$ and $\mathcal{M} \models \neg p(t)$. Clearly for these two cases (3) holds as well. It follows that if $\mathcal{M} \models \mathcal{P}$ then $\mathcal{M}|_{\mathcal{L}_{\mathcal{P}}} \models \Pi(gr_U(\mathcal{P}), \mathcal{M})$.

To check the converse condition we need now only examine the cases where $r^{\Pi} = \emptyset$. Suppose this arises because $p(\sigma(t)) \in H, T$, so $\mathcal{M} \models p(t)$. Now, if $p(t)$ is in the head of r, clearly $\mathcal{M} \models r$. Similarly if $\neg p(t)$ is in the body of r, by the semantics $\mathcal{M} \models r$. The cases where $p(\sigma(t)) \notin T$ are analogous and left to the reader. Consequently if $\mathcal{M}|_{\mathcal{L}_{\mathcal{P}}} \models \Pi(gr_U(\mathcal{P}), \mathcal{M})$, then $\mathcal{M} \models \mathcal{P}$.   □

We now state the relation between equilibrium models and NM-models.

Theorem 1. *Let $\mathcal{K} = (\mathcal{T}, \mathcal{P})$ be a hybrid knowledge base. Let $\mathcal{M} = \langle U, T, T \rangle$ be a total here-and-there model of the stable closure of $\mathcal{K}$. Then $\mathcal{M}$ is in equilibrium if and only if $\langle U, T \rangle$ is an NM-model of $\mathcal{K}$.*

Proof. Assume the hypothesis and suppose that $\mathcal{M}$ is in equilibrium. Since T contains only predicates from $\mathcal{L}_T$ and $\mathcal{M} \models \mathcal{T} \cup st(\mathcal{T})$, evidently

$$\mathcal{M}|_{\mathcal{L}_T} \models \mathcal{T} \cup st(\mathcal{T}) \tag{4}$$

and so in particular $(U, \mathcal{M}|_{\mathcal{L}_T})$ is a model of $\mathcal{T}$. By Lemma 2,

$$\mathcal{M} \models \mathcal{P} \Leftrightarrow \mathcal{M}|_{\mathcal{L}_{\mathcal{P}}} \models \Pi(gr_U(\mathcal{P}), \mathcal{M}). \tag{5}$$

We claim (i) that $\mathcal{M}|_{\mathcal{L}_{\mathcal{P}}}$ is an equilibrium model of $\Pi(gr_U(\mathcal{P}), \mathcal{M})$. If not, there is a model $\mathcal{M}' = \langle H', T' \rangle$ with $H' \subset T' = T|_{\mathcal{L}_{\mathcal{P}}}$ and $\mathcal{M}' \models \Pi(gr_U(\mathcal{P}), \mathcal{M})$. Lift $(U, \mathcal{M}')$ to a (first order) $\mathcal{L}$-structure $\mathcal{N}$ by interpreting each $p \in \mathcal{L}_T$ according to $\mathcal{M}$. So $\mathcal{N}|_{\mathcal{L}_T} = \mathcal{M}|_{\mathcal{L}_T}$ and by (4) clearly $\mathcal{N} \models \mathcal{T} \cup st(\mathcal{T})$. Moreover, by Lemma 2 $\mathcal{N} \models \mathcal{P}$ and by assumption $\mathcal{N} \lhd \mathcal{M}$, contradicting the assumption that $\mathcal{M}$ is an equilibrium model of $\mathcal{T} \cup st(\mathcal{T}) \cup \mathcal{P}$. This establishes (i). Lastly, we note that since $\langle T|_{\mathcal{L}_{\mathcal{P}}}, T|_{\mathcal{L}_{\mathcal{P}}} \rangle$ is an equilibrium model of $\Pi(gr_U(\mathcal{P}), \mathcal{M})$, $\mathcal{M}|_{\mathcal{L}_{\mathcal{P}}}$ is a generalised open answer set of $\Pi(gr_U(\mathcal{P}), \mathcal{M})$ by Corollary 1, so that $\mathcal{M} = \langle U, T, T \rangle$ is an NM-model of $\mathcal{K}$.

For the converse direction, assume the hypothesis but suppose that $\mathcal{M}$ is not in equilibrium. Then there is a model $\mathcal{M}' = \langle U, H, T \rangle$ of $\mathcal{T} \cup st(\mathcal{T}) \cup \mathcal{P}$, with $H \subset T$. Since $\mathcal{M}' \models \mathcal{P}$ we can apply Lemma 2 to conclude that $\mathcal{M}'|_{\mathcal{L}_{\mathcal{P}}} \models \Pi(gr_U(\mathcal{P}), \mathcal{M}')$. But clearly

$$\Pi(gr_U(\mathcal{P}), \mathcal{M}') = \Pi(gr_U(\mathcal{P}), \mathcal{M}).$$

However, since evidently $\mathcal{M}'|_{\mathcal{L}_T} = \mathcal{M}|_{\mathcal{L}_T}$, thus $\mathcal{M}'|_{\mathcal{L}_{\mathcal{P}}} \lhd \mathcal{M}|_{\mathcal{L}_{\mathcal{P}}}$, so this shows that $\mathcal{M}|_{\mathcal{L}_{\mathcal{P}}}$ is not an equilibrium model of $\Pi(gr_U(\mathcal{P}), \mathcal{M})$ and therefore $T|_{\mathcal{L}_{\mathcal{P}}}$ is not an answer set of $\Pi(gr_U(\mathcal{P}), \mathcal{M})$ and $\mathcal{M}$ is not an NM- model of $\mathcal{K}$.   □

This establishes the main theorem relating to the various special types of hybrid KBs discussed earlier.

Theorem 2 (Main Theorem). *(i) Let $\mathcal{K} = (\mathcal{T}, \mathcal{P})$ be a g-hybrid (resp. an r^+-hybrid) knowledge base. Let $\mathcal{M} = \langle U, T, T \rangle$ be a total here-and-there model of the stable closure of $\mathcal{K}$. Then $\mathcal{M}$ is in equilibrium if and only if $\langle U, T \rangle$ is an NM-model (resp. r^+-NM-model) of $\mathcal{K}$.*

(ii) Let $\mathcal{K} = (\mathcal{T}, \mathcal{P})$ *be an r-hybrid knowledge base. Let* $\mathcal{M} = \langle U, T, T \rangle$ *be an Herbrand model of the stable closure of* $\mathcal{K}$. *Then* $\mathcal{M}$ *is in equilibrium in the sense of [16] if and only if* $\langle U, T \rangle$ *is an r-NM-model of* $\mathcal{K}$.

Example 5. Consider again the hybrid knowledge base $\mathcal{K} = (\mathcal{T}, \mathcal{P})$, with $\mathcal{T}$ and $\mathcal{P}$ as in Example 1. The stable closure of $\mathcal{K}$, $st(\mathcal{K}) = \mathcal{T} \cup st(\mathcal{T}) \cup \mathcal{P}$ is

$\forall x. PERSON(x) \rightarrow (AGENT(x) \wedge (\exists y. HAS\text{-}MOTHER(x, y)))$
$\forall x. (\exists y. HAS\text{-}MOTHER(x, y)) \rightarrow ANIMAL(x)$
$\forall x. PERSON(x) \vee \neg PERSON(x)$
$\forall x. AGENT(x) \vee \neg AGENT(x)$
$\forall x. ANIMAL(x) \vee \neg ANIMAL(x)$
$\forall x, y. HAS\text{-}MOTHER(x, y) \vee \neg HAS\text{-}MOTHER(x, y)$
$\forall x. AGENT(x) \wedge \neg machine(x) \rightarrow PERSON(x)$
$AGENT(DaveB)$

Consider the total HT-model $\mathcal{M}_{HT} = \langle U, I, I \rangle$ of $st(\mathcal{K})$, with U, I as in Example 4. $\mathcal{M}_{HT}$ is *not* an equilibrium model of $st(\mathcal{K})$, since $\mathcal{M}_{HT}$ is not minimal among all models: $\langle U, I', I \rangle$, with $I' = I \backslash \{machine(DaveB)\}$, is a model of $st(\mathcal{K})$. Furthermore, it is easy to verify that $\langle U, I', I' \rangle$ is not a model of $st(\mathcal{K})$.

Now, consider the total HT-model $\mathcal{M}'_{HT} = \langle U, M, M \rangle$, with U as before, and

$M = \{AGENT(DaveB), PERSON(DaveB),$
    $ANIMAL(DaveB), HAS\text{-}NAME(DaveB, k)\}.$

$\mathcal{M}'_{HT}$ is an equilibrium model of $st(\mathcal{K})$. Indeed, consider any $M' \subset M$. It is easy to verify that $\langle U, M', M \rangle$ is not a model of $st(\mathcal{K})$.

6.1 Discussion

We have seen that quantified equilibrium logic captures three of the main approaches to integrating classical, first-order or DL knowledge bases with nonmonotonic rules under the answer set semantics, in a modular, hybrid approach. However, QEL has a quite distinct flavor from those of r-hybrid, r^+-hybrid and g-hybrid KBs. Each of these hybrid approaches has a semantics composed of two different components: a classical model on the one hand and an answer set on the other. The style of QEL is different. There is one semantics and one kind of model that covers both types of knowledge. The only distinction we make is that for that part of the knowledge base considered to be classical and monotonic we add a stability condition to obtain the intended interpretation.

There are other features of the approach using QEL that are worth highlighting. First, it is based on a simple minimal model semantics in a known non-classical logic. No reducts are involved and, consequently, the equilibrium construction applies directly to arbitrary first-order theories. The rule part $\mathcal{P}$ of a knowledge base might therefore comprise, say, a nested logic program, where the heads and bodies of rules may be arbitrary boolean formulas, or perhaps rules permitting nestings of the implication connective. While answer sets have recently been defined for such general formulas, more work would be needed to provide integration in a hybrid KB setting.[9] Evidently QEL in the

---

[9] For a recent extension of answer sets to first-order formulas, see [6].

general case is undecidable, so for extensions of the rule language syntax for practical applications one may wish to study restrictions analogous to safety or guardedness. Second, the logic $\mathbf{QHT}^s_=$ can be applied to characterise properties such as the strong equivalence of programs and theories [11,17]. While strong equivalence and related concepts have been much studied recently in ASP, their characterisation in the case of hybrid KBs remains uncharted territory. The fact that QEL provides a single semantics for hybrid KBs means that a simple concept of strong equivalence is applicable to such KBs and characterisable using the underlying logic, $\mathbf{QHT}^s_=$. We now describe briefly how $\mathbf{QHT}^s_=$ can be applied in this context.

6.2   An Application to the Strong Equivalence of Knowledge Bases

Generally speaking it is important to know when different reconstructions of a given body of knowledge or state of affairs are equivalent and lead to essentially the same solutions. In the case of knowledge reconstructed in classical logic, ordinary logical equivalence can serve as a suitable concept when applied to theories formulated in the same vocabulary. In the case where nonmonotonic rules are present, however, one would like to know that equivalence between KBs is also robust, since two sets of rules may have the same answer sets yet behave very differently once they are embedded in some larger context. A robust or modular notion of equivalence for logic programs should therefore require that programs behave similarly when extended by any further programs. This leads to the following concept of *strong* equivalence: programs Π_1 and Π_2 are strongly equivalent if and only if for any set of rules Σ, $\Pi_1 \cup \Sigma$ and $\Pi_2 \cup \Sigma$ have the same answer sets. This concept of strong equivalence for logic programs in ASP was introduced and studied in [10] and has given rise to a substantial body of further work looking at different characterisations, new variations and applications of the idea, as well as the development of systems to test for strong equivalence.

In the case of hybrid knowledge bases $\mathcal{K} = (\mathcal{T}, \mathcal{P})$, various kinds of equivalence can be specified, according to whether one or other or both of the components $\mathcal{T}$ and $\mathcal{P}$ are allowed to vary. Let us illustrate for simplicity the case where $\mathcal{T}$ is fixed and $\mathcal{P}$ may vary; the extension to other cases is straightforward.

Definition 8. *Let $\mathcal{K}_1 = (\mathcal{T}, \mathcal{P}_1)$ and $\mathcal{K}_2 = (\mathcal{T}, \mathcal{P}_2)$ be two hybrid KBs based on the same classical theory $\mathcal{T}$. $\mathcal{K}_1$ and $\mathcal{K}_2$ are said to be* strongly equivalent *if for any set of rules $\mathcal{P}$, $(\mathcal{T}, \mathcal{P}_1 \cup \mathcal{P})$ and $(\mathcal{T}, \mathcal{P}_2 \cup \mathcal{P})$ have the same NM-models.*

The following characterisation of strong equivalence is an immediate consequence of Theorem 1 and the main theorem of [11].

Proposition 7. *Hybrid KBs $\mathcal{K}_1 = (\mathcal{T}, \mathcal{P}_1)$ and $\mathcal{K}_2 = (\mathcal{T}, \mathcal{P}_2)$ are strongly equivalent if and only if $\mathcal{P}_1$ and $\mathcal{P}_2$ are logically equivalent in $\mathbf{QHT}^s_=$.*

In other words, although we consider the effect of adding arbitrary nonmonotonic rules to a knowledge base, ordinary logical equivalence in $\mathbf{QHT}^s_=$ is a necessary and sufficient condition for strong equivalence.

It is interesting to note here that meaning-preserving relations among ontologies have recently become a topic of interest in the DL community where logical concepts such as that of conservative extension are currently being studied and applied [7]. A unified, logical approach to hybrid KBs such as that developed here should lend itself well to the application of such concepts.

7   Related Work and Conclusions

We have provided a general notion of hybrid knowledge base, combining first-order theories with nonmonotonic rules, with the aim of comparing and contrasting some of the different variants of hybrid KBs found in the literature [18,19,20,9]. We presented a version of quantified equilibrium logic, QEL, without the unique names assumption, as a unified logical foundation for hybrid knowledge bases. We showed how for a hybrid knowledge base $\mathcal{K}$ there is a natural correspondence between the nonmonotonic models of $\mathcal{K}$ and the equilibrium models of what we call the *stable closure* of $\mathcal{K}$. This yields a way to capture in QEL the semantics of the g-hybrid KBs of Heymans et al. [9] and the r-hybrid KBs of Rosati [19], where the latter is defined without the UNA but for safe programs. Similarly, the version of QEL with UNA captures the semantics of r-hybrid KBs as defined in [18,20]. It is important to note that the aim of this paper was not that of providing new kinds of safety conditions or decidability results; these issues are ably dealt with in the literature reviewed here. Rather our objective has been to show how classical and nonmonotonic theories might be unified under a single semantical model. In part, as [9] show with their reduction of DL knowledge bases to open answer set programs, this can also be achieved (at some cost of translation) in other approaches. What distinguishes QEL is the fact that it is based on a standard, nonclassical logic, $\mathbf{QHT}^s_=$, which can therefore provide a unified logical foundation for such extensions of (open) ASP. To illustrate the usefulness of our framework we showed how the logic $\mathbf{QHT}^s_=$ also captures a natural concept of strong equivalence between hybrid knowledge bases.

There are several other approaches to combining languages for Ontologies with non-monotonic rules which can be divided into two main streams [3]: approaches which define integration of rules and ontologies (a) by entailment, ie. querying classical knowledge bases through special predicates the rules body, and (b) on the basis of single models, ie. defining a common notion of combined model.

The most prominent of the former kind of approaches are dl-programs [5] and their generalization, HEX-programs [4]. Although these approaches both are based on Answer Set programming like our approach, the orthogonal view of integration by entailment can probably not be captured by a simple embedding in QEL. Another such approach which allows querying classical KBs from a nonmonotonic rules language is based on Defeasible Logic [21].

As for the second stream, variants of Autoepistemic Logic [2], and the logic of minimal knowledge and negation as failure (MKNF) [13] have been recently proposed in the literature. Similar to our approach, both these approaches embed a combined knowledge base in a unifying logic. Remarkably however, both [2] and [13] use modal logics which syntactically and semantically extend first-order logics. Thus, in these approaches, embedding of the classical part of the theory is trivial, whereas the nonmonotonic rules part needs to be rewritten in terms of modal formulae. Our approach is orthogonal, as we base on a non-classical logic where the nonmonotonic rules are trivially embedded, but the stable closure guarantees classical behavior of certain predicates.

In future work we hope to consider further aspects of applying QEL to the domain of hybrid knowledge systems. Extending the language with functions symbols and with strong negation is a routine task, since QEL includes these items already. We also plan to consider in the future how QEL can be used to define a catalogue of logical relations between hybrid KBs.

References

1. Baral, C.: Knowledge Representation, Reasoning and Declarative Problem Solving. CUP, Cambridge (2002)
2. de Bruijn, J., Eiter, T., Polleres, A., Tompits, H.: Embedding Non-Ground Logic Programs into Autoepistemic Logic for Knowledge-Base Combination. IJCAI (2007)
3. de Bruijn, J., Eiter, T., Polleres, A., Tompits, H.: On Representational Issues about Combinations of Classical Theories with Nonmonotonic Rules. In: Lang, J., Lin, F., Wang, J. (eds.) KSEM 2006. LNCS (LNAI), vol. 4092, Springer, Heidelberg (2006)
4. Eiter, T., Ianni, G., Schindlauer, R., Tompits, H.: A Uniform Integration of Higher-Order Reasoning and External Evaluations in Answer-Set Programming. IJCAI (2005)
5. Eiter, T., Lukasiewicz, T., Schindlauer, R., Tompits, H.: Combining Answer Set Programming with Description Logics for the Semantic Web. KR (2004)
6. Ferraris, P., Lee, J., Lifschitz, V.: A new perspective on stable models. IJCAI (2007)
7. Ghilardi, S., Lutz, C., Wolter, F.: Did I damage my ontology: A Case for Conservative Extensions of Description Logics. KR (2006)
8. Heymans, S., van Nieuwenborgh, D., Vermeir, D.: Open answer set programming with guarded programs. ACM Transactions on Computational Logic. Accepted for Publication
9. Heymans, S., Predoiu, L., Feier, C., de Bruijn, J., van Nieuwenborgh, D.: G-hybrid Knowledge Bases. ALPSWS (2006)
10. Lifschitz, V., Pearce, D., Valverde, A.: Strongly equivalent logic programs. ACM Transactions on Computational Logic 2, 526–541 (2001)
11. Lifschitz, V., Pearce, D., Valverde, A.: A Characterization of Strong Equivalence for Logic Programs with Variables. In: Proceedings LPNMR 2007, Springer, Heidelberg (to appear 2007)
12. Lifschitz, V., Woo, T.: Answer Sets in General Nonmonotonic Reasoning (preliminary report). KR (1992)
13. Motik, B., Rosati, R.: A faithful integration of description logics with logic programming. IJCAI (2007)
14. Pearce, D.: A new Logical Characterization of Stable Models and Answer Sets. NMELP96(1997)
15. Pearce, D.: Equilibrium logic. Annals of Mathematics and Artificial Intelligence. In press, available at http://dx.doi.org/10.1007/s10472-006-9028-z (2006)
16. Pearce, D., Valverde, A.: A First-Order Nonmonotonic Extension of Constructive Logic. Studia Logica, 80 (2005)
17. Pearce, D., Valverde, A.: Quantified Equilibrium Logic. Tech. report, Univ. Rey Juan Carlos, http://www.satd.uma.es/matap/investig/tr/ma06_02.pdf. (2006)
18. Rosati, R.: On the Decidability and Complexity of Integrating Ontologies and Rules. Journal of Web Semantics, 3(1) (2005)
19. Rosati, R.: Semantic and Computational Advantages of the Safe Integration of Ontologies and Rules. In: Fages, F., Soliman, S. (eds.) PPSWR 2005. LNCS, vol. 3703, Springer, Heidelberg (2005)
20. Rosati, R.: DL+log: Tight Integration of Description Logics and Disjunctive Datalog. KR (2006)
21. Wang, K., Billington, D., Blee, J., Antoniou, G.: Combining Description Logic and Defeasible Logic for the Semantic Web. In: Antoniou, G., Boley, H. (eds.) RuleML 2004. LNCS, vol. 3323, Springer, Heidelberg (2004)
22. van Dalen, D.: Logic and Structure. Springer, Heidelberg (1983)

Web Services Discovery and Constraints Composition*

Debmalya Biswas

IRISA-INRIA, Campus Universitaire de Beaulieu,
35042 Rennes, France
dbiswas@irisa.fr

Abstract. The most promising feature of the Web services platform is its ability to form new (composite) services by combining the capabilities of already existing (component) services. The existing services may themselves be composite leading to a hierarchical composition. In this work, we focus on the discovery aspect. We generalize the characteristics of a service, which need to be considered for successful execution of the service, as constraints. We present a predicate logic model to specify the corresponding constraints. Further, composite services are also published in a registry and available for discovery (hierarchical composition). Towards this end, we show how the constraints of a composite service can be derived from the constraints of its component services in a consistent manner. Finally, we present an incremental matchmaking algorithm which allows bounded inconsistency.

Keywords: Web Services, Composition, Discovery, Constraints, Matchmaking.

1 Introduction

Web services, also known in a broader context as Service Oriented Architecture (SOA) based applications, are based on the assumption that the functionality provided by an enterprise (provider) are exposed as services. The World Wide Web Consortium (W3C) defines Web Services as "a software application identified by a URI, whose interfaces and bindings are capable of being defined, described, and discovered as XML artifacts. A Web service supports direct interactions with other software agents using XML-based messages exchanged via Internet-based protocols". The most promising aspect of the Web services platform is the composability aspect, that is, its ability to form new services (hereafter, referred to as composite services) by combining the capabilities of already existing services (hereafter, referred to as component services). The existing services may themselves be composite leading to a hierarchical composition. The services which do not depend on any other services for their execution are referred to as primitive services.

There are mainly two approaches to composing a service: dynamic and static. In the dynamic approach [1], given a complex user request, the system comes up with a plan to fulfill the request depending on the capabilities of available Web services at run-time. In the static approach [2], given a set of Web services, composite services are defined manually at design-time combining their capabilities. In this paper, we

---

* This work is supported by the ANR DOCFLOW and CREATE ACTIVEDOC projects.

M. Marchiori, J.Z. Pan, and C. de Sainte Marie (Eds.): RR 2007, LNCS 4524, pp. 73–87, 2007.

consider a mix [3] of the two approaches where the composite services are defined statically, but the matchmaking with providers is performed dynamically depending on the user request. The above approach is typical of a group of organizations collaborating to provide recurring general services, usually, requested by users. Thus, we assume that the organizations (providers) agree on some of the compositional aspects, such as, ontology used to describe their services, underlying state transition model, logging format, etc.

As mentioned earlier, the main focus of this paper is on the discovery aspect for Web services composition. The current industry standard, Universal Description, Discovery and Integration (UDDI) [4], only supports classification (keyword) based-search and does not capture the semantics of Web services functionality. To overcome this, work has already been initiated towards a semantic description specification for Web services, especially, the Web Ontology Language for Services (OWL-S) [5] specification. The OWL-S specification allows a service to be specified in terms of its IOPE: Inputs, Outputs (required input and expected output values of the service parameters, respectively), Pre-conditions (the state of the world as it should be before execution), and Effects (the state of the world as it would be after execution). We generalize the above as *constraints,* that is, *characteristics of a service which need to be considered for successful execution of the service.* For example, let us consider a house painting contractor C whose services can be reserved online (via credit card). Given this, the fact that the user requires a valid credit card is a pre-condition; and the fact that the user's house will be painted along with the painting charges deducted from his/her account, are the effects. In addition, we also need to consider any limitations of C during the actual execution phase, e.g., the fact that C works only on weekdays (and not on weekends). The above restriction might be a problem if the user would like to get the work done during weekends. In general, pre-conditions refer to the conditions required to initiate an execution and effects reflect the expected conditions after the execution terminates. Constraints attempt to capture the conditions necessary for the entire execution lifecycle (initiate-terminate).

A significant contribution of this paper is the aspect of constraint composition and its impact on service discovery. This aspect has been mostly overlooked till now as, according to most specifications, the description of a composite service resembles that of a primitive service externally (or at an abstract level). However, determining the description of a complex composite service, by itself, is non-trivial. Given their inherent non-determinism (allowed by the "choice" operators within a composition schema), it is impossible to statically determine the subset of component services which would be invoked at run-time. The above implies the difficulty in selecting the component services, whose constraints should be considered, while defining the constraints of the composite service. Basically, the constraints of a composite service should be consistent with the constraints of its component services. In this paper, we take the bottom-up approach and discuss how the constraints of a composite service can be consistently derived from the constraints of its component services. Towards this end, we consider four approaches: optimistic, pessimistic, probabilistic and relative. Finally, we discuss how matchmaking can be performed based on the constraints model. Current matchmaking algorithms focus on "exact" matches (or the most optimum match). They do not consider the scenario where a match does not exist. We try to overcome the above by allowing inconsistencies during the matchmaking process (does not have to be an exact match) up to a "bounded" limit.

Before proceeding, we would like to mention that the work in this paper is part of ongoing work to provide a lightweight discovery mechanism for ActiveXML (AXML) [6] systems. AXML systems provide an elegant way to combine the power of XML, Web services and Peer to Peer (P2P) paradigms by allowing (active) Web service calls to be embedded in XML documents. An AXML system consists of the following main components:

- AXML documents: XML documents with embedded Web service calls. The embedded services may be AXML services (defined below) or generic Web services.
- AXML Services: Web services defined as queries/updates over AXML documents. An AXML service is also exposed as a regular Web service (with a WSDL description file).
- AXML peers: Nodes where the AXML documents and services are hosted.

Currently, the provider for an embedded service call is hard coded in the AXML document. The objective is to let AXML systems also benefit from the additional flexibility offered by dynamic selection (among the available AXML peers). As obvious, this can be achieved by replacing the hard coding with a query to select the provider at run-time. Given this, we needed a mechanism for discovery in an environment, which is more homogeneous as compared to dynamic Web services compositions (and allows us to assume the presence of a shared ontology, state transition model, etc.). As the proposed concepts are valid for Web services compositions in general, we present them in a Web services context (in the sequel); and only mention their usage with respect to AXML to show their practical relevance.

The rest of the paper is organized as follows: Section 2 deals with the constraints aspect in detail, starting with a predicate logic specification of constraints (sub-section 2.1) followed by the constraints composition model (sub-section 2.2). The incremental matchmaking algorithm is presented in section 3. Sections 4 and 5 discuss related works and conclude the paper, respectively.

2 Constraints

As mentioned earlier, constraints refer to the characteristics of a service which need to be considered for a successful execution of the service. Before proceeding, we would like to discuss some heuristics to decide if a characteristic should (or should not) be considered as a constraint. If we consider constraints as limitations, then the fact that an Airline ABC cannot provide booking for a particular date is also a limitation (and hence, a constraint). However, we do not expect such characteristics to be expressed as constraints as they keep changing frequently. Similarly, we do not expect characteristics which depend on internal business rules (sensitive or confidential information) to be exposed as constraints. Thus, what should (or should not) be expressed as constraints is very much context-specific, and we simply consider constraints as a level of filtering during the discovery process.

2.1 Constraint Specification

Constraints are specified as first order predicates associated with the service definitions. For example, the fact that an airline ABC provides vegetarian meals and has facilities for handicapped people on only some of its flights (to selected destinations) can be represented as follows:

flight(Airlines,X,Y):-
      veg_meals(Airlines,Destination_List), member(X,Destination_List),
      hnd_facilities(Airlines,Destination_List), member(Y,Destination_List).
veg_meals('ABC',['Paris','Rennes']).
hnd_facilities('ABC',['Paris','Grenoble']).

In the above snippet, 'member(X,Y)' is a system defined predicate which holds if X is an element of the set Y. Now, let us consider "related" constraints or scenarios where there exists a relationship among the constraints. By default, the above example assumes an AND relation among the constraints (both veg_meals and hnd_facilities predicates have to be satisfied). The operators studied in literature for the composition of logic programs are: AND, OR, ONE-OR-MORE, ZERO-OR-MORE and any nesting of the above. We only consider the operators AND, OR and any level of nesting of both to keep the framework simple (ONE-OR-MORE and ZERO-OR-MORE can be expressed in terms of OR). An example of an OR relation among the constraints is as follows: Airline ABC allows airport lounge access at intermediate stopovers only if the passenger holds a business class ticket or is a member of their frequent flier programme. The above scenario can be represented as follows:

lounge_access(Airlines,X):-
      ticket_type('ABC',X,'Business').
lounge_access(Airlines,Y):-
      frequent_flier(Airlines,FF_List), member(Y,FF_List).

We briefly consider the following qualifiers which may be specified in conjunction with the constraints:

- Validity period: Period until when the constraints are valid. The validity period qualifier can be used to optimize matchmaking. Basically, there is no need to repeat the entire matchmaking process for each and every request. Once a service provider is found suitable, it remains so till the validity period of at least one of its "relevant" constraints expires.
- Commitment: The commitment of a provider towards providing a specific service (levels of commitment [7]). For example, a provider may be willing to accept the responsibility of providing its advertised services under any circumstance; or that it is capable of providing the services, but not willing to accept responsibility if something goes wrong.
- Non-functional: Qualifiers related to non-functional aspects, such as, transactions, security, monitoring (performance), etc. From a transactional point of view, we need to know the protocols supported for concurrency control (e.g., 2PL), atomic commit (e.g., 2PC), and the following attributes required for recovery: idempotent (the effect of executing a service once is the same as executing it more than once), compensatable (its effects can be semantically canceled), pivot (non-compensatable).

From a security perspective, it is important to know the protocols supported for message exchange (e.g., X.509), and if any part of the interaction or service description needs to be kept confidential. The relevant qualifiers, from a monitoring point of view, would be the time interval between successive snapshots of the system state, snapshot format, etc. It is obviously possible to have qualifiers which overlap between the aspects, e.g., it may be required to specify if part of the monitored data (snapshot) cannot be exposed due to security issues.

2.2 Constraints Composition

2.2.1 Broker
The composite provider aggregates services offered by different providers and provides a unique interface to them (without any modification to the functionality of the services, as such). In other words, the composite provider acts as a broker for the aggregated set of services [8]. The accumulated services may have different functionalities or the same functionality with different constraints (as shown by the following example scenario). Scenario: Provider XYZ composing the flight services offered by Airlines ABC and DEF.

Airlines ABC:
flight(Airlines,X):-
    hnd_facilities(Airlines,Destination_List), member(X,Destination_List).
hnd_facilities('ABC',['Marseilles','Grenoble']).

Airlines DEF:
flight(Airlines,X):-
    hnd_facilities(Airlines,Destination_List), member(X,Destination_List).
hnd_facilities('DEF',['Rennes','Paris']).

Composite provider XYZ:
flight(Airlines,X):-
    hnd_facilities(Airlines,Destination_List), member(X,Destination_List),
    Airlines:= 'XYZ'.
hnd_facilities('ABC',['Marseilles','Grenoble']).
flight(Airlines,X):-
    hnd_facilities(Airlines,Destination_List), member(X,Destination_List),
    Airlines:= 'XYZ'.
hnd_facilities('DEF',['Rennes','Paris']).

The addition of the clauses *Airlines:= 'XYZ'* in the above code snippet ensures that the binding returned to the outside world is provider XYZ while the provider XYZ internally delegates the actual processing to the providers ABC/DEF. Another point highlighted by the above example is that composition may lead to *relaxation* of constraints, e.g., the composite provider XYZ can offer flights with facilities for handicapped people to more destinations (Marseilles, Grenoble, Rennes and Paris) than offered by either of the component providers ABC (Marseilles, Grenoble)/DEF (Rennes, Paris).

2.2.2 Mediator

Two or more services offered by (the same or) different providers are composed to form a new composite service with some additional logic (if required) [8]. We assume that the composition schema is specified using some conversation language, e.g., Business Process Execution Language for Web Services (BPEL) [2], OWL-S Service Model [5], etc. We show how the constraints of component services, composed in sequence or parallel, can be composed. Given an Airline ABC with facilities for handicapped people on its flights to selected destinations,

flight(Airlines,X):-
      hnd_facilities(Airlines,Destination_List), member(X,Destination_List).
hnd_facilities('ABC',['Marseilles','Grenoble']).

and a transport company DEF which has facilities for handicapped people on its local bus networks in selected cities,

bus(Transport_C,X):-
      hnd_facilities(Transport_C,Cities_List), member(X, Cities_List).
hnd_facilities('DEF',['Marseilles','Rennes']).

the constraints of the composite service provider Travel Agent XYZ can be defined as follows:

flight_bus(Agent,X):-
      sequence(_flight(Agent1,X),_bus(Agent2,X)),
      Agent:= XYZ.
_flight(Airlines,X):-
      hnd_facilities(Airlines,Destination_List), member(X,Destination_List).
hnd_facilities('ABC',['Marseilles','Grenoble']).
_bus(Transport_C,X):-
      hnd_facilities(Transport_C,Cities_List), member(X, Cities_List).
hnd_facilities('DEF',['Marseilles','Rennes']).

The point to note in the above code snippet is the *flight_bus* predicate representing the newly formed composite service. Also, the original predicates of the primitive services are prefixed with _ to indicate that those services are no longer available (exposed) for direct invocation. The above scenario highlights the *restrictive* nature of constraint composition. For example, the newly composed service flight_bus can provide both flight and bus booking with facilities for handicapped people to fewer destinations (Marseilles) as compared to the destinations covered by the component services separately: flight (Marseilles, Grenoble) and bus (Marseilles, Rennes). Finally, we discuss the usage of the *sequence* predicate (in the above code snippet). For a group of constraints, the sequence relationship implies that all the constraints in the group need to hold (analogous to AND), however, they do not need to hold simultaneously, and it is sufficient if they hold in the specified sequence. For example, let us assume that the premium (constraint) of an insurance policy is €10,000, payable over a period of 10 years. The above constraint is, in reality, equivalent to a sequence of €1000 payments each year (the user does not have to pay €10,000 upfront). The sequential relationship among the constraints can be derived from the ordering of their respective services in the composition schema. Note that we do not consider the "parallel" relationship explicitly as it is equivalent to AND.

2.2.3 Mediator with Non-determinism

Till now, we have only considered deterministic operators in the composition schema, that is, sequential and parallel composition. With *non-deterministic operators*, the situation is slightly more complicated. Some of the component services, composed via non-deterministic operators, may never be invoked during an execution instance. As such, we need some logic to determine if the constraints of a component service should (or should not) be considered while defining the constraints of the composite service. For example, let us consider the e-shopping scenario illustrated in Fig. 1. There are two non-deterministic operators (choices) in the composition schema: Check Credit and Delivery Mode. The choice "Delivery Mode" indicates that the user can either pick-up the order directly from the store or have it shipped to his/her address. Given this, shipping is a non-deterministic choice and may not be invoked during the actual execution. As such, the question arises "if the constraints of the shipping service, that is, the fact that it can only ship to certain countries, be projected as constraints of the composite e-shopping service (or not)". Note that even component services composed using deterministic operators (Payment and Shipping) are not guaranteed to be invoked if they are preceded by a choice. We consider some approaches to overcome the above issue:

- *Optimistic:* Consider the constraints of only those services, which are guaranteed to be invoked in any execution, while defining the constraints of the composite service. The set of such services (hereafter, referred to as the strong set) can be determined by computing all the possible execution paths and selecting services which occur in all the paths. For example, with reference to the e-shopping scenario in Fig. 1, the strong set = {Browse, Order}. We call this approach optimistic as it assumes that the services in the strong set are sufficient to represent the constraints of the composite service. The concept of a strong set is analogous to the notion of strong unstable predicates [9] or predicates which will "definitely" hold [10] in literature. Strong unstable predicates are true if and only if the predicate is true for all total orders. For example, strong unstable predicates can be used to check if there was a point in the execution of a commit protocol when all the processes were ready to commit. Intuitively, strong unstable predicates allow us to verify that a desirable state will always occur.
- *Pessimistic:* In this approach, we take the pessimistic view and consider the constraints of all those services which are in at least one of the possible execution paths (while defining the constraints of the composite service). We refer to such a set of component services as the weak set. Note that the weak set would consist of all the component services if there are no "unreachable" services in the composition schema. Again, with reference to the e-shopping scenario in Fig. 1, the weak set = {Browse, Order, Cancel Order & Notify Customer, Arrange for Pick-up, Payment, Shipping}. We refer to this approach as pessimistic as it considers the constraints of those services also which may not even be invoked during the actual execution. The corresponding notion in literature is weak unstable predicates [11] or predicates which will "possibly" occur [10]. A weak unstable predicate is true if

and only if there exists a total order in which the predicate is true. For example, weak unstable predicates can be used to verify if a distributed mutual exclusion algorithm allows more than one process to be in the critical region simultaneously. Intuitively, weak unstable predicates can be used to check if an undesirable state will ever occur.

– *Probabilistic:* Another option would be to consider the most frequently invoked component services (or the component services in the most frequently used execution path) as the representative set of the composite service. Such a set can be determined statically from the execution logs or dynamically with the help of some mathematical model (such as, Markov Decision Processes [12]) to assign probabilities to the component services based on previous executions. Again, with reference to the e-shopping scenario in Fig. 1, a probable set of most frequently used component services would be {Browse, Order, Arrange for Pick-up}. While this option appears the most attractive at first sight, developing and solving a Markovian model is non-trivial for a complex composition schema (especially, if it involves a lot of choices).

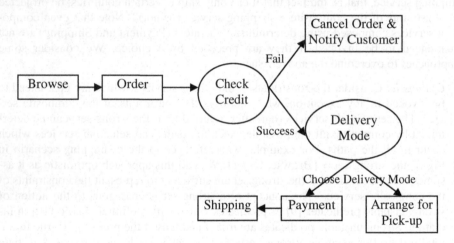

Fig. 1. An e-shopping scenario

The trade-off between the various options (discussed till now) can be summarized as follows: (a) Optimistic: A successful initial match does not guarantee a successful execution (as the constraints of all the component services are not considered initially, it might not be feasible to find a provider for one of the component services at a later stage). Thus, the cost to consider for this case is in terms of failed contractual agreements or simply the loss of user faith. (b) Pessimistic: "Pseudo" constraints may lead to the corresponding composite service becoming ineligible for (an otherwise successful match with) a user request. (c) Probabilistic: For this approach, the cost is in terms of the complexity in finding the adequate probabilities and distribution functions to define the probabilistic model. While the above approaches can be considered as extremes; next, we consider an intermediate, but more practical, approach to determine the representative set of component services (of a composite service).

Relative: In this approach, we consider an incremental construction of the set of component services whose constraints need to be considered (while defining the constraints of the composite service). Basically, we start with the strong set and keep on adding the "related" services as execution progresses. We define related services as follows:

Related services: Let X and Y be component services of a composition schema CS. Given this, X and Y are related if and only if the occurrence of X in an execution path P of CS implies the occurrence of Y in P.

Intuitively, if a component service X of CS is executed then all the component services till the next choice in CS will definitely be executed. For example, with reference to the e-shopping scenario in Fig. 1, services Payment and Shipping are related. As mentioned earlier, the execution of both Payment and Shipping are not guaranteed. However, if Payment is executed, then Shipping is also guaranteed to be executed. The above definition of related services can also be extended to non-invocation of a component service X as follows:

Related services (extended): Let X and Y be component services of a composition schema CS. Given this, X and Y are related if and only if the (non-) occurrence of X in an execution path P of CS implies the (non-) occurrence of Y in P.

Intuitively, if a component service X of CS is not executed then all the component services till the next merge in CS will also not be executed – Fig. 2. The extension is useful if we consider matching for more than one composite service simultaneously (not considered here). Given this, prior knowledge that a component service will not be invoked during a particular execution instance allows better scheduling of the providers among instances.

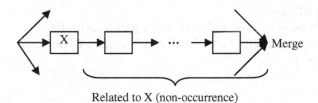

Related to X (non-occurrence)

Fig. 2. Related services (based on non-occurrence)

Till now, we have only considered component services related by functional dependencies (as specified by the composition schema). Other relationships between component services can also be (statically) determined based on the application or domain semantics. For example, with reference to an e-shopping scenario, the choice of € as the currency unit implies the (future) need for a shipping provider capable of delivering within countries of the European Union (EU).

AXML application scenario. We discuss an implementation of the "related" approach in the context of query evaluation by AXML systems. Given a query q on an AXML document d, the system returns the subset of nodes of d which satisfy the query criterion. There are two possible modes for query evaluation: lazy and eager. Of the two, lazy evaluation is the preferred mode and implies that only those services are invoked whose results are required for evaluating the query. Now, a query q on a document d may require invoking some of the embedded services in d. The invocation results are

```
<?xml version="1.0" encoding="UTF-8"?>
<ATPList date="18042005">
   <player rank=1>
      <name>
         <firstname>Roger</firstname>
         <lastname>Federer</lastname>
      </name>
      <citizenship>Swiss</citizenship>
      <axml:sc mode="replace" serviceNameSpace="getPoints"
      serviceURL="..." methodName="getPoints">
         <axml:params>
            <axml:param name="name">
            <axml:value>Roger Federer</axml:value>
         </axml:params>
         <points>475</points>
      </axml:sc>
      <axml:sc mode="merge" serviceNameSpace="getGrandSlamsWonbyYear"
      serviceURL="..." methodName="getGrandSlamsWonbyYear">
         <axml:params>
            <axml:param name="name">
            <axml:value>Roger Federer</axml:value>
            <axml:param name="year">
            <axml:value>$year (external value)</axml:value>
         </axml:params>
         <grandslamswon year="2003">W</grandslamswon>
         <grandslamswon year="2004">A, W, U</grandslamswon>
      </axml:sc>
   </player>...
</ATPList>
```

Fig. 3. Sample AXML document ATPList.xml

inserted as children of the embedded service node (modifying d). For example, let us consider the AXML document ATPList.xml in Fig. 3. The document ATPList.xml contains two embedded services "getPoints" and "getGrandSlamsWonbyYear". Now, let us consider the following query:

Query A:
```
<action type = "query">
   <location>Select p/citizenship, p/grandslamswon from p in ATPList//player
where p/name/lastname = Federer;</location>
</action>
```

Lazy evaluation of the above query would result in the invocation of the embedded service "getGrandSlamsWonbyYear" *(and not "getPoints")*. However, if the query were defined as follows:

Query B:
<action type = "query">
    <location>Select p/citizenship, p/points from p in ATPList//player where p/name/lastname = Federer;</location>
    </action>

Lazy evaluation of query B would result in the invocation of the embedded service call "getPoints" *(and not "getGrandSlamsWonbyYear")*.

Thus, given a q and d, (at a high level) the following three step process is used for query evaluation:

1. Determine the set of relevant embedded services in d to evaluate q.
2. Invoke them and insert their results in d (leading to a modified d).
3. Apply steps 1 and 2 iteratively on the modified d, till step 1 cannot find any relevant calls to evaluate q.

Step 3 is necessary because of the following reasons: (a) The result of a service invocation maybe another service. (b) The invocation results may affect the document d in such a way that formerly non-relevant embedded services become relevant after a certain stage. For more details on the above AXML query evaluation aspects, the interested reader is referred to [13].

To summarize, it is not feasible to statically determine the set of services, which would be invoked during an execution instance (depends on the query and corresponding invocation results). However, for each iteration, we can at least consider the constraints of the relevant ("related") embedded services determined by step 1 together for discovery.

3 Matchmaking

3.1 Basic Matchmaking

Here, we consider incremental matchmaking, that is, the provider for a service is selected as and when it needs to be executed. For a (composite) service X, let P(X) denote the constraints associated with X. Given this, the required matching for X can be accomplished by posing P(X) as a goal against the providers' constraints. A logic program execution engine specifies not only if a goal can be satisfied but also all the possible bindings for the unbounded variables in the goal. The bindings correspond to the providers capable of executing X. In case of multiple possible bindings (multiple providers capable of executing the same service), the providers are ranked using some user defined preference criteria or the user may be consulted directly to select the most optimum amongst them.

3.2 Approximate Matchmaking

Now, let us consider the scenario where the matchmaking is unsuccessful, that is, there does not exist a set of providers capable of executing a set of component services. Given this, it makes sense to allow some inconsistency while selecting a provider. Note that inconsistency is often allowed by real-life systems, e.g., flight reservation system allow flights to be overbooked, but only up to a limited number of seats. Thus, the key here is "bounded" inconsistency. Basically, for a given set of component services SC = {A_{SC1}, A_{SC2}, ..., A_{SCn}}, the selected provider for one of the component services A_{SCx} does not have to be a perfect match as long as their accumulated inconsistency is within a specified limit. Again (in the presence of non-determinism), the given set SC of component services implies that all the services in SC will be executed if at least one of the services in SC is executed (related services). Note that the inconsistency induced by a component service A_{SCx} may also have a counter effect on (reduce) the inconsistency induced by another component service A_{SCy}. We use the composition schema CS in Fig. 4 as a running example to illustrate our intuition behind the steps. X enclosed by a rectangle denotes a component service X of CS. Services can be invoked in sequence (D, E) or in parallel (B, C). As before, ovals represent choices.

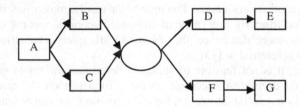

Fig. 4. Sample composition schema CS

For each set of component services SC = {A_{SC1}, A_{SC2}, ..., A_{SCn}} considered for matchmaking, perform the following:

1. Determine the common qualifiers: A qualifier q_{SC} is common for SC if a pair of constraints of services A_{SCx} and A_{SCy}, respectively, are based on q_{SC}. For example, if component services D and E need to be completed within 3 and 4 days, respectively; then D and E have constraints based on the common qualifier time. Studies [14] have shown that most constraints in real-life scenarios are based on the qualifiers: price, quantity or time.
2. For each q_{SC}, define a temporary variable C_{qSC} (to keep track of the inconsistency with respect to q_{SC}). *Initially, $C_{qSC} = 0$.*
3. For each A_{SCx} and a common qualifier q_{SC}: Let v_{qSCx} denote the constraint value of A_{SCx} with respect to q_{SC}. For example, $v_{tD} = 3$ denotes the completion time constraint value of D. *Delete the constraint of A_{SCx}, based on q_{SC}, from the goal.*
4. Perform matchmaking on the reduced goal (as discussed earlier in the previous sub-section).
5. If the matchmaking (above) is successful: [Note that if matchmaking is unsuccessful for the reduced goal then it would definitely have been unsuccessful for the original goal.] Let $p(A_{SCx})$ denote the provider selected to execute A_{SCx}. *For each deleted constraint of A_{SCx} based on q_{SC} (step 3), get the best possible value v_{best_qSCx} of $p(A_{SCx})$ with respect to q_{SC} and compute $C_{qSC} = C_{qSC} + (v_{qSCx} - v_{best\_qSCx})$. For*

example, let us assume that p(D) and p(E) can complete their work in 5 and 1 days, respectively. Given this, $C_t = 0 + (v_{tD} - v_{best\_tD}) + (v_{tE} - v_{best\_tE}) = (3 - 5) + (4 - 1) = 1$.
6. The selections as a result of the matchmaking in step 4 are valid if and only if, for all q_{SC}, $C_{qSC} \geq 0$. For example, p(D) and p(E) are valid matches for the component services D and E, respectively, as $C_t \geq 0$.

Note that this matching would not have been possible without the above extension as p(D) violates (takes 5 days) the completion time constraint (3 days) of D.

AXML application scenario. We consider a replicated architecture where copies of an AXML document d exist on more than one peer. With respect to each document d, there exists a primary copy of d (and the rest are referred to as secondary copies). Any updates on d occur on the primary copy of d, and are propagated to the secondary copies in a lazy fashion. Let us assume that the system guarantees a maximum propagation delay (of any update to all secondary copies of the affected document) of 1 hour. Given this, a query of the form "List of hotels in Rennes" can be evaluated on any of the secondary copies (that is, inconsistency is allowed). However, a query of the form "What is the current traffic condition on street X?" needs to be evaluated on the primary copy (that is, no inconsistency) or the system needs to be tuned to lower the maximum propagation delay guarantee (that is, inconsistency up to a bounded limit).

4 Related Works

The concept of "constraints" has been there for quite some time now, especially, in the field of Software Engineering as functional and non-functional features associated with components [15]. While studies [16] have identified their need with respect to Web services computing, there hasn't been much work towards trying to integrate them in a model for Web services composition. [17] and [18] describe preliminary works towards integrating the notion of constraints with WSDL/SOAP and OWL-S, respectively. However, their focus is towards trying to represent the operational specifications (e.g., if a service supports the Two Phase Commit protocol, authentication using X.509, etc.) of a Web service using features/constraints in contrast to our approach of trying to capture the functional requirements for a successful execution.

[19] allows each activity to be associated with a constraint c, which is composed of a number of variables ranging over different domains and over which one can express linear constraints. In [20], Vidyasankar et. al. consider "bridging" the incompatibility between providers selected (independently) for the component services of a composite service. In general, the issue of Web services discovery has been studied widely in literature based on different specification formalisms: Hierarchical Task Planning (HTN) [1], Situation Calculus [21], π-Calculus [22], etc. However, none of the above approaches consider composability of the component services' constraints (which is essential to reason about the constraints of the composite service). The notion of bounded inconsistency and its application to matchmaking is also a novel feature of our work.

5 Conclusion and Future Work

In this work, we focused on the discovery aspect of Web services compositions. To enable hierarchical composition, it is required to capture and publish the constraints of the composite services (along with, and in the same manner, as primitive services). We introduced a constraints based model for Web services description. We showed how the constraints of a composite service can be derived and described in a consistent manner with respect to the constraints of its component services. We discussed four approaches: optimistic, pessimistic, probabilistic and relative, to overcome the composition issues introduced by the inherent non-determinism. Finally, we discussed matchmaking for the constraints based description model. We showed how the notion of bounded inconsistency can be exploited to make the matchmaking more efficient.

An obvious extension of the matchmaking algorithm would to consider simultaneous matching for more than one composite service. Doing so, leads to some interesting issues like efficient scheduling of the available providers (touched upon briefly in section 2.2.3). We are already working towards translating the proposed concepts (in this paper) to compose service descriptions specified in OWL-S. In future, we would also like to consider the top-down aspect of constraint composition, that is, to define the constraints of a composite service independently and verifying their consistency against the constraints of its corresponding component services.

Acknowledgments. I would like to thank Krishnamurthy Vidyasankar, Blaise Genest, Holger Lausen and the anonymous referees for their helpful suggestions which helped to improve the paper considerably.

References

1. Wu, D., Parsia, B., Sirin, E., Hendler, J., Nau, D.: HTN planning for Web service composition using SHOP2. Web Semantics 1(4), 377–396 (2004)
2. Business Process Execution Language for Web Services (BPELFWS) Specification v1.1. http://www-128.ibm.com/developerworks/library/ws-bpel/
3. Casati, F., Ilnicki, S., Jin, L., Krishnamoorthy, V., Shan, M.-C.: Adaptive and Dynamic Service Composition in eFlow. HP Technical Report, HPL-2000-39 (March 2000)
4. Universal Description, Discovery and Integration (UDDI) Specification. http://www.uddi.org
5. Web Ontology Language for Services (OWL-S) Specification http://www.daml.org/services/owl-s/
6. Abiteboul, S., Bonifati, A., Cobena, G., Manolescu, I., Milo, T.: Dynamic XML Documents with Distribution and Replication. In: proceedings of 2003 ACM SIGMOD International Conference on Management of Data, pp. 527–538
7. Singh, M.P., Yolum, P.: Commitment Machines. In: Revised Papers from the 8th International Workshop on Intelligent Agents VIII, pp. 235–247 (2001)
8. Hull, R., Benedikt, M., Christophides, V., Su, J.: Eservices: A look behind the curtain. In: proceedings of the 22nd ACM Symposium on Principles of Database Systems (PODS), pp. 1–14 (2003)

9. Garg, V.K., Waldecker, B.: Detection of Strong Unstable Predicates in Distributed Programs. IEEE Transactions on Parallel and Distributed Systems, pp. 1323-1333 (Decemder 1996)
10. Cooper, R., Marzullo, K.: Consistent detection of global predicates. ACM SIGPLAN Notices 26(12) pp. 163–173
11. Garg, V.K., Waldecker, B.: Detection of Weak Unstable Predicates in Distributed Programs. IEEE Transactions on Parallel and Distributed Systems, pp. 299–307 (1994)
12. Doshi, P., Goodwin, R., Akkiraju, R., Verma, K.: Dynamic Workflow Composition: Using Markov Decision Processes. Intl. Journal of Web Services Research 2(1), 1–17 (2005)
13. Benjelloun, O.: Active XML: A data centric perspective on Web services. INRIA PhD dissertation, http://www.activexml.net/reports/omar-thesis.ps (2004)
14. Grosof, B., Labrou, Y., Chan, H.: A Declarative Approach to Business Rules in Contracts: Courteous Logic Programs in XML. In: proceedings of the 1st ACM International Conference on Electronic Commerce (EC), pp. 68–77 (1999)
15. Chung, L., Nixon, B., Yu, E.: Using Non-Functional Requirements to Systematically Select Among Alternatives in Architectural Design. In: proc. of the 1st International Workshop on Architectures for Software Systems, pp. 31–43 (1995)
16. O'Sullivan, J., Edmond, D., Hofstede, A.: What's in a Service? Towards Accurate Description of Non-Functional Service Properties. In: the Journal of Distributed and Parallel Databases, Vol. 12(2/3) (2002)
17. W3C Position Paper. Constraints and capabilities of Web services agents. In: proc. of the W3C Constraints and Capabilities Workshop, http://www.w3.org/2004/07/12-hh-ccw (2004)
18. OWL-S Coalition. OWL-S Technology for Representing Constraints and Capabilities of Web Services. In: proc. of the W3C Constraints and Capabilities Workshop, http://www.w3.org/2004/08/ws-cc/dmowls-20040904 (2004)
19. Aiello, M., Papzoglou, M., Yang, J., Carman, M., Pistore, M., Serafini, L., Traverso, P.: A Request Language for Web-Services based on Planning and Constraint Satisfaction. In: proc. of the 3rd VLDB Workshop on Technologies for E-Services (TES), pp. 76–85 (2002)
20. Vidyasankar, K., Ananthanarayana, V.S.: Binding and Execution of Web Service Compositions. In: proceedings of 6th International Conference on Web Information Systems Engineering (WISE), pp. 258–272 (2005)
21. Narayanan, S., Mcllraith, S.A.: Simulation, Verification and Automated Composition of Web Services. In: proceedings of the 11th ACM International Conference on the World Wide Web (WWW), pp. 77–88 (2002)
22. Rao, J., Kungas, P., Matskin, M.: Logic Based Web Services Composition: From Service Description to Process Model. In: proceedings of the 2nd IEEE International Conference on Web Services (ICWS), pp. 446–453 (2004)

Ontological Reasoning to Configure Emotional Voice Synthesis

Virginia Francisco, Pablo Gervás, and Federico Peinado

Departamento de Inteligencia Artificial e Ingeniería del Software
Universidad Complutense de Madrid, Spain
virginia@fdi.ucm.es, pgervas@sip.ucm.es, email@federicopeinado.com

Abstract. The adequate representation of emotions in affective computing is an important problem and the starting point of studies related to emotions. There are different approaches for representing emotions, selecting one of this existing methods depends on the purpose of the application. Another problem related to emotions is the amount of different emotional concepts which makes it very difficult to find the most specific emotion to be expressed in each situation. This paper presents a system that reasons with an ontology of emotions implemented with semantic web technologies. Each emotional concept is defined in terms of a range of values along the three-dimensional space of emotional dimensions. The capabilities for automated classification and establishing taxonomical relations between concepts are used to provide a bridge between an unrestricted input and a restricted set of concepts for which particular rules are provided. The rules applied at the end of the process provide configuration parameters for a system for emotional voice synthesis.

1 Introduction

An important challenge in addressing issues of affective computing is having an adequate representation of emotions. Existing approaches vary between identifying a set of basic categories - with a name tag assigned to each one of them - to designing a multi-dimensional space in terms of primitive elements - or emotional dimensions - such that any particular emotion can be defined in terms of a tuple of values along the different dimensions. For different purposes, one approach is better suited than the other. For instance, when attempting to synthesize voice utterances that reflect emotion to some extent, it is easier to identify the parameters for voice production associated with conveying a particular emotion. For assigning emotional values to given utterances, on the other hand, human evaluators find it much easier to provide numbers along given dimensions. If one were to operate computationally with a representation of emotions expressed in more than one format, one is faced with the task of being able to convert from one to another. This task is reasonably easy when converting from emotional categories to emotional dimensions: it would suffice to assign a particular tuple of values for the emotional dimensions of each emotional category. When trying

M. Marchiori, J.Z. Pan, and C. de Sainte Marie (Eds.): RR 2007, LNCS 4524, pp. 88–102, 2007.

to convert from emotional values expressed in terms of emotional dimensions to a representation in terms of emotional categories this is not so simple. The problem lies in the fact that, given the subjectivity associated with emotional perception, the particular values assigned to a given impression by one person usually deviate slightly from what a different person would have assigned. This suggests that the process of converting from emotional dimensions to emotional categories should be carried out in a manner that allows a certain tolerance, so that a region of space in the universe of emotional dimensions is assigned to each emotional category, rather than just a single point in the universe.

A separate problem arises from the fact that there is a large number of emotional categories, and the differences and similarities between them are not clear cut. In some cases, it is reasonable to assume that certain emotional categories may be subsumed by others. For example, the emotion *anger* subsumes the emotions *sulking, displeasure* and *annoyance* which may be seen as different types of *anger*. This suggests that a taxonomy of emotional categories as a hierarchy might be useful in finding correspondence between more specific emotional categories and more general emotional categories.

In this context, the development of an ontology of emotional categories based on description logics, where each element is defined in terms of a range of values along the space of emotional dimensions, provides a simple and elegant solution. The ability to carry out automatic classification of concepts simplifies the addition of new concepts - possibly expressed only in terms of their values along the axes of emotional dimensions - without having to worry explicitly about where in the ontology they should be placed. Thanks to a taxonomical reasoning system an implicit hierarchy for the concepts represented in the ontology can be inferred automatically.

This paper describes the development of such a system, together with its application as an interface between a text input marked up in terms of emotional dimensions and a set of rules for configuring an emotionally-enabled voice synthesizer. By reasoning over the ontology, insertion of new instances of emotional concepts into the ontology results in their automatic classification under the corresponding branch of the hierarchy. The system can then trace the ascendants in the ontology of the corresponding value, until a more general concept is found that satisfies the condition that specific rules are available for generating an appropriate voice synthesis configuration for expressing the intended emotional impression. Section 2 provides a basic introduction to the representation of emotions. Section 3 summarises the Semantic Web technologies employed in this approach. Section 4 describes how input texts are tagged with information describing their emotional content in terms of emotional dimensions. Section 5 gives an overview of the ontology of emotions we have developed. Section 6 describes the operation of the emotional synthesizer. Section 7 provides an example of the complete process for a particular input. Finally, section 8 discusses the technological issues that have arisen, and section 9 summarises our conclusions and future work.

2   State of the Art: Representation of Emotions

This section provides a brief review of the different methods used in the study of emotions in order to classify them. Interested readers can find more detail in the work of Randolph Cornelius [1] and Marc Schröder [2].

Emotions are not an easy reaction, there are a lot of factors that contribute to them. For Izard [3] a good definition of Emotion must take into account: conscious feeling of emotion, process which takes place in the nervous system and in the brain and expressive models of emotion. Emotions take place when something unexpected happens and the so-called "emotional effects" begin to take control.

Many of the terms used to describe emotions and their effects are difficult to tell apart from one another, as they are usually not well defined. This is due to the fact that the abstract concepts and the feelings associate with such concepts are very difficult to express with words. For this reason, there are a lot of methods for describing the characteristics of emotions.

There are different methods in order to represent emotions: *emotional categories* - based on the use of emotion-denoting words -, *descriptions based on psychology* [4] and *evaluation* [1], *circumflex models* - emotional concepts are represented by means of a circular structure [5], so that two emotional categories close in the circle are conceptually similar - and *emotional dimensions* which represent the essential aspects of emotional concepts.

In the following subsections we describe in detail the two methods which are employed in our work: *emotional categories* and *emotional dimensions*.

Emotional Categories. The most common method for describing emotions is the use of emotional words or affective labels. Different languages provide assorted labels of varying degrees of expressiveness for the description of emotional states. There are significant differences between languages in terms of the granularity with which these labels describe particular areas of emotional experience. Even within a given language, some areas of emotional experience have a higher density of labels than others. This diversity presents an additional difficulty. A lot of methods have been proposed in order to reduce the number of labels used to identify emotions. Some of them are listed below:

- Basic emotions: There is a general agreement that there are some emotions that are more basic than others. The number of basic emotions generally is small (in early studies 10, in more recent ones between 10 and 20), so it is possible to characterize each emotional category in terms of its intrinsic properties [1].
- Super ordinate emotional categories: Some emotional categories have been proposed as more fundamental than others on the grounds that they include the others. Scherer [6] and Ortony suggest that an emotion A is more fundamental than other emotion B if the set of evaluation components of the emotion A are a subset of the evaluation components of the emotion B.
- Essential everyday emotion terms: A pragmatic approach is to ask for the emotion terms that play an important role in everyday life. The approach is

exemplified by the work of Cowie [7], who proposed a Basic English Emotion Vocabulary. Starting from lists of emotional terms from the literature, subjects were asked to select a subset which appropriately represents the emotions relevant in everyday life. A subset of 16 emotion terms emerged.

Emotional Dimensions. Emotional dimensions represent the essential aspects of emotional concepts. There are two basic dimensions: *evaluation* and *activation*, occasionally these two dimensions are completed with a third dimension: *power*. *Evaluation* represents how positive or negative is an emotion. For example in a scale for the evaluation dimensions at one extreme we have emotions such as happy, satisfied, hopeful ... the other end of the scale is for emotions such as unhappy, unsatisfied, despaired ... *Activation* represents an active / passive scale for emotions, at one extreme of the activation are emotions such as excited, aroused ... At the other end of this scale are emotions such as calm, relaxed .... The last dimension, *power*, represent the control which exerts the emotion, at one end of the scale we have emotions characterized as completely controlled, such as care for, submissive ... At the opposite end of this scale we have emotions such as dominant, autonomous ... For all dimensions, if the emotion is completely neutral with respect to the emotional dimensions it should be assigned to the middle point of the scale.

This method is very useful because it provides a way of measuring the similarity between emotional states. Another important property of that method is that shifting the representational weight away from the actual labels employed allows for a relative arbitrariness when naming the different dimensions.

3   State of Art: Semantic Web Technologies

The Semantic Web is being developed with the intention of providing a global framework for describing data, its properties and relationships in a standard fashion. Many developers and researchers on knowledge systems are taking the approach of using Semantic Web technologies in order to obtain more interoperability and reusability with existing software and to take advantage of the strong trend of development that these technologies are living nowadays.

In this section we review the tools used in our project explaining what were the technological choices and the different criteria behind them.

Ontology Web Language. Semantic Web relies heavily on ontologies. Concretely, ontologies based on Description Logics paradigm include definitions of concepts –OWL classes–, roles –OWL properties– and individuals. The most common language to formalize Semantic Web ontologies is OWL (Ontology Web Language [8]), a proposal of the W3C. The goal of this standard is to formalize the semantics that was created *ad hoc* in old frame systems and semantic networks. OWL has three increasingly-expressive sublanguages: OWL Lite, OWL DL, and OWL Full.

OWL Full is powerful for representing complex statements but not useful for reasoning with them due to their computational properties.

OWL DL is the subset of OWL designed for applications that need the maximum expressiveness without losing computational completeness and decidability. It is based on Description Logics, a particular fragment of first order logic, in which concepts, roles, individuals and axioms that relate them (using universal and existential restrictions, negation, etc.) are defined. These entailments may be based on a single document or multiple distributed documents that we combine using the import OWL mechanisms. The OWL DL reasoning capabilities relies on the good computational properties of DLs. OWL DL has support for polihierarchical automatic classification.

Frameworks and APIs. The first thing a novice Semantic Web application developer is searching for is an all-in-one framework or a versatile application programming interface. Java is probably the most important general-purpose language for developing Semantic Web applications, and it is also the language in which the original voice synthesizer was made, so the choice was obvious. But there are at least two very promising Java frameworks available. One of them is Sesame [9], an open source RDF framework with support for RDF Schema inferencing and querying. The other one is Jena [10], another open source framework with a programmatic environment for RDF, RDFS, OWL, SPARQL and its own rule-based inference engine.

Sesame has a local and remote access API, several query languages (recently added SPARQL) and it is more oriented to offer flexible and fast connections with storage systems.

Jena has also RDF and OWL APIs, tools to deal with RDF/XML, N3 and N-Triples formats, an SPARQL query engine and also some persistent storage functionality.

For our purposes performance issues can be ignored and only inference support for Description Logics is taken into account. The architecture of Sesame is probably easier to extend than the architecture of Jena, but from the point of view of a client building a wrapper for Jena has been the easiest way of working.

DLModel [11] is a very straightforward open source API for accessing a Description Logic model instantiated in an external ontology and knowledge base. Although it has an abstract DL interface (called DLModel), it can act as a wrapper on top of Jena (called JenaModel), offering simple methods to access concepts, roles and invididuals of the knowledge base of our Java application .

Ontology Editor. Another important tool is the Integrated Development Environments (IDE) used to edit the ontology and the knowledge base. During our review of the state-of-art we found two interesting editors able to perform this task: SWOOP and Protégé.

SWOOP [12] is a hypermedia-based OWL ontology browser and editor written in Java. Is is open souce and it tries to simplify the ontology development using an interface similtar to a web browser. It includes some advanced features as ontology partitioning, debugging and different kinds of visualization, so it makes ontologies more scalable, maintainable and easy to use.

Protégé [13], specially the Protégé-OWL version, focuses on editing OWL ontologies. It is a powerful Java open source tool with a user-friendly interface that let you edit and visualize ontologies in a very easy way. It can be seen as a framework for developing Semantic Web applications itself. The number of plugins (including some plugins for knowledge adquisition), the stability of the last version, the extensibility of its architecture (plug-and-play environment) software allows rapid prototyping and application development, just what we were looking for. But this choice was not an easy decision.

Reasoner. Two different reasoners were considered for this project: Pellet [14] and Racer Pro [15].

Pellet is an open source DL reasoner completely implemented in Java. It deals not only with taxonomical reasoning but also with datatype reasoning, which is very important for our project. Pellet is the default reasoner integrated with SWOOP.

Compared to Racer Pro, a well-know commercial system for OWL/RDF which claims to be the most efficient and robust DL reasoner available, Pellet may have drawbacks, but ignoring again the problem of performance, Pellet is certainly one of the most feature-rich OWL reasoners. It is also supported by a strong development team and community, which is important if you are looking for different approaches and uses of the same tool. There are educational licenses for Racer Pro, but we have chosen Pellet as a tool for our prototype.

4   Tales Marked Up with Emotions

As a starting point of our approach we have some texts marked up with emotions. In these texts every emotional unit is marked up with the three emotional dimensions (activation, evaluation and power). We are currently using as emotional units the sentences of the text. This implies that every sentence has a value for each of the three dimensions. The emotions associated to each of the sentences try to rate how the listener will feel while listening each sentence as it is read out aloud by the synthesizer.

Texts are marked up with emotions by means of EmoTag [16] a tool for automated mark up of texts with emotional labels. The approach considers the representation of emotions as emotional dimensions. A corpus of example texts previously annotated by human evaluators was mined for an initial assignment of emotional features to words. This results in a List of Emotional Words (LEW) which becomes a useful resource for later automated mark up. EmoTag employs for the assignment of emotional features a combination of the LEW resource, the ANEW word list [17][1], and WordNet [18] for knowledge-based expansion of words not occurring in either.

A sample part of a marked tale by EmoTag is given in Table 1.

---

[1] The ANEW word list is a set of normative emotional ratings for a large number of words in the English language. Words are rated in terms of evaluation, activation and power.

Table 1. Fragment of a Marked Up Tale

```
...
<emotion act=9 eval=7 pow=5>"How well you are looking today: how glossy your feathers; how
bright your eye."</emotion>
<emotion act=9 eval=7 pow=5>"I feel sure your voice must surpass that of other birds, just
as your figure does;</emotion>
<emotion act=9 eval=7 pow=5>let me hear but one song from you that I may greet you as the
Queen of Birds."</emotion>
<emotion act=3 eval=9 pow=1>The Crow lifted up her head and began to caw her best, but the
moment she opened her mouth the piece of cheese fell to the ground, only to be snapped up
by Master Fox.</emotion>
...
```

5   Emotional Ontology

We have developed an ontology for all the emotional categories. They are structured in a taxonomy that covers from the basic emotions to the most specific emotional categories. Each of the emotional categories are related with the three emotional dimensions by means of data ranges.

5.1   Structure

Our ontology has two root concepts:

- Emotion: This is the root for all the emotional concepts which are used to refer to emotions. Each of the emotional concepts are subclasses of the root concept Emotion. Some examples of these subclasses are: *Anger, Annoyance, Displeasure, Sad, Happy, Surprise, Fright, Horror ...*
- Word: This is the root for the emotion-denoting words, the specific words which each language provides for denoting emotions. Our ontology is currently available for two different languages: English and Spanish. In order to classify the words into their corresponding language the root concept Word has two subclasses: *EnglishWord* and *SpanishWord*.

As instances of the *EnglishWord* and *SpanishWord* subclasses there are emotion-denoting words, which are all the words used for denoting *Anger, Annoyance, Displeasure, Terror ...* Each of these instances has two parents: a concept from the Emotion hierarchy (which indicates the type of abstract emotion denoted by the word) and a concept from the Word hierarchy (which indicates the language of the word).

It is important to note here that, because the ontology is intended to operate over input in the form of language utterances, the ontology must include the means for representing words. Therefore it includes the specific concept of Word. All actual words handled by the system must be instances of this concept or one of its subclasses. Specific subhierarchies are added to group together all words in a given language.

Figure 1 shows a fragment of the ontology. In this fragment it can be seen how the words are related both to one emotional concept and to one word concept, for example the word *unhappiness* is an instance of the emotional concept *Sadness*

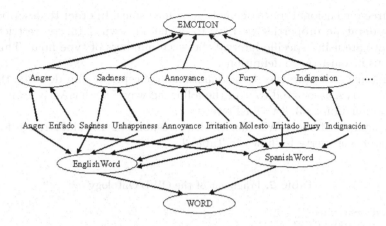

Fig. 1. Fragment of the emotional ontology

at the same time it is an instance of the word concept *EnglishWord*, which means that *unhappiness* is an English word for denoting the emotion sadness.

Another valid way of representing these relations might be to create a new property called "language" to connect each word with an instance of the language it belongs. We have chosen the in-built "type" relation because individuals with many different types are considered natural in OWL DL, and it is easier to retrieve every word of a specific type than "every word that has a relation with a specific individual".

In handling words, the system may need to identify synonyms for a particular words, that is, other words which may be used to refer to the same concept. Given the semantics we have chosen for our ontology, two instances of the Word-concept can be considered to be synonyms if they are also instances of the same single Emotion-concept from the parallel Emotion subhierarchy. For example, in the figure above, we can find that the words *annoyance* and *irritation* are synonyms because they are both instances of the Emotion-concept *Annoyance*.

5.2 Datatype Properties

Once we have a hierarchy of emotions, relations between the emotion-denoting words and their language and the concept they represent, we want to link the emotional concepts with the three emotional dimensions. Numeric data can be represented in OWL using datatype properties. To achieve this we have declared three datatype properties: *hasEvaluation*, *hasActivation* and *hasPower*. Each of the emotional concepts is defined by specifying appropriate data ranges for these properties as described in the following section.

5.3 Data Range

We have defined each of the emotional concepts through the emotional dimensions defined as datatype properties. Each emotional concept takes up a region in the three-dimensional space of emotional dimensions. In order to describe this with the datatype properties we have to define our own datatype restrictions, because we are using specific intervals between numbers of type float. This can be done using data range definitions.

For example, we have the *Anger* emotional concept, we can describe the region of the space associated to it in the following way: 7<=hasActivation<=10, 0<=hasEvaluation<=3, 3<=hasPower<=5.

The fragment of the OWL file which correspond to the data range for the *hasActivation* property is shown in Table 2.

Table 2. Fragment of the OWL Ontology

```
<owl:Restriction>
 <owl:allValuesFrom>
  <owl:DataRange>
   <owl:onDataRange rdf:resource=''http://www.w3.org/2001/XMLSchema#float''/>
   <owl:minInclusive rdf:datatype=''http://www.w3.org/2001/XMLSchema#float''>
   7.0</owl:minInclusive>
  </owl:DataRange
 </owl:allValuesFrom>
 <owl:onProperty>
  <owl:FunctionalProperty rdf:about=''#hasActivation''/>
 </owl:onProperty>
</owl:Restriction>
<owl:Restriction>
 <owl:onProperty>
  <owl:FunctionalProperty  rdf:about=''#hasActivation''/>
 </owl:onProperty>
 <owl:allValuesFrom>
  <owl:DataRange>
   <owl:onDataRange rdf:resource=''http://www.w3.org/2001/XMLSchema#float''/>
   <owl:maxInclusive rdf:datatype=''http://www.w3.org/2001/XMLSchema#float''>
   10.0</owl:maxInclusive>
  </owl:DataRange>
 </owl:allValuesFrom>
</owl:Restriction>
```

In this way, by means of the data ranges on the datatype properties, the link between the abstract emotional concepts and the three-dimensional space of emotional dimensiones is established.

5.4 Automatic Classification of Emotions Using Datatype Properties

A requirement to be taken into account when representing emotions using numerical data is to have some reasoning device capable of processing such data in an appropriate way. Pellet is able to classify concepts with restrictions formed by combinations of user-defined datatypes.

Once we have defined the emotional concepts by means of the emotional dimensions, Pellet automatically classifies the concepts into a hierarchy of emotional concepts. This means that Pellet obtains a hierarchy of emotions in which the most basic concepts are at the top of the hierarchy and the concepts which are more specific appear as descendants of the more general ones.

Datatype properties transform the classification of the emotional concepts into a relatively simple task. It is not necessary for the designer of the ontology to know which concepts are more specific than others because it is the reasoner that carries out the task automatically. For example, we have the following emotional concepts: *Anger, Annoyance, Fury* and *Indignation*. Anger is one of the basic emotions and Annoyance, Indignation and Fury are different forms of anger that differ from one another in their intensity of arousal. We define the four concepts as subclasses of the root concept Emotion, and we define the following ranges for the three datatype properties:

- Anger: $7<=$hasActivation$<=10;0<=$hasActivation$<=3;3<=$hasPower$<=5$
- Annoyance: $7<=$hasActivation$<8;0<=$hasActivation$<=3;3<=$hasPower$<=5$
- Indignation: $8<=$hasActivation$<9;0<=$hasActivation$<=3;3<=$hasPower$<=5$
- Fury: $9<=$hasActivation$<=10;0<=$hasActivation$<=3;3<=$hasPower$<=5$

Just by loading the ontology in DLModel, the reasoner automatically classifies the concepts *Annoyance, Indignation* and *Fury* as subclasses of the emotional concept *Angry* which is automatically identified as more general.

6 Emotional Synthesizer

EmoSpeech [19] is a system capable of modulating the voice quality of a synthesizer while reading out aloud children's tales, so that the voice conveys at least part of the emotions expressed by the corresponding text. This is achieved by controlling those parameters in the synthesizer that have been identified as having more relevance in the expression of emotions in human voice. EmoSpeech operates with five basic emotions:*anger, happiness, sadness, fear* and *surprise*. The aspects of the voice that act as personality identifiers are: volume, rate, pitch baseline and pitch range. EmoTag uses a group of rules which relates the five basic emotions to the specific changes on voice parameters involved in the communication of emotion in human voice utterances. The values of these parameters for every emotion were obtained by refining an original proposal by Schröder [2], based on the analysis of emotional material generated by actors. The optimal values were obtained through the systematic variation of the parameters during the synthesis. Table 3 summarizes the rules of the synthesizer for the basic emotions.

Table 3. Configuration Parameters for Emotional Voice Synthesis

	Volume	Rate	Pitch Baseline	Pitch Range
Anger	+10%	+21%	+0%	+173%
Surprise	+10%	+0%	+25%	+82%
Happiness	+10%	+29%	+35%	+27%
Sadness	-10%	-8%	-10%	-36%
Fear	+10%	+12,5%	+75%	+118%

7   Example of the Entire Process

The complete process from text input to voice output is described in this section. We have a text as the input of our system. EmoTag marks up this text with the emotional dimensions (*activation*, *evaluation* and *power*). Each sentence of the marked up text is related to a point in the three-dimensional space of emotions. This point is the input to our ontology of emotions, which by means of the datatype properties and the dataRange restrictions, automatically classifies this point under a given emotional concept. Once we have identified the specific emotional concept

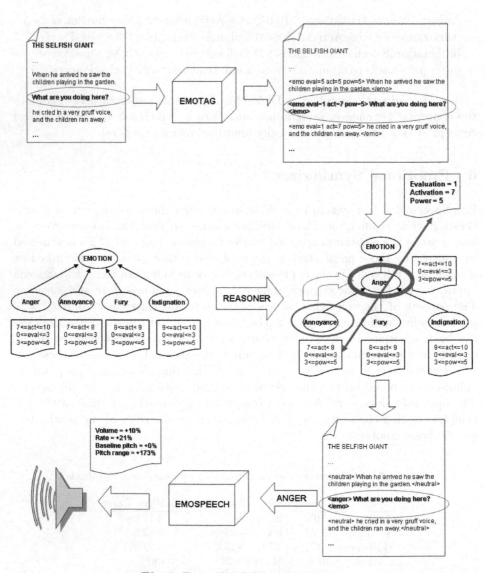

Fig. 2. Example of the entire process

to which the input point is related, by means of DLModel we recursively obtain its ancestors until we locate the one which correponds to one of the five basic emotions (*anger, happiness, sadness, fear* and *surprise*). Using the particular configuration of parameters for that particular basic emotion, the synthesizer reads out aloud the text with the emotion assigned by EmoTag to the sentences.

In Figure 2 we can see how this process works for a concrete example.

In the example, we have a sentence of input text which EmoTag marks up with the following values: activation = 7, evaluation = 1 and power = 5. This point is classified by means of the ontology under the *annoyance* emotional concept. We ask DLModel for the parents of *annoyance* and the *anger* emotional concept is returned. EmoSpeech then receives the sentence of the input text and the emotion *anger* as the one associated to the sentence, so it selects the rules corresponding to this basic emotions. Once EmoSpeech has the suitable rules for the emotional meaning of the sentence, the synthesizer reads out aloud the sentence in an angry way.

8 Discussion

Because the ontology is being used only as interface between the emotional mark up application and the voice synthesizer, its effect on the quality of speech output is limited.[2] For inputs originally tagged with emotional categories, the addition of the ontology has little impact. Nevertheless, emotional categories as a method of representing emotions provide only very limited granularity, restricted to the five basic emotions. On the other hand, emotional dimensions provide a much more flexible means of representing emotions, with greater expressive power. The main obstacle in switching from one representation to another lies in the fact that there is no easy way of converting from emotional dimensions to voice synthesizer configurations. At best, the three dimensional space of emotional dimensions could be partitioned into restricted volumes of space, and a particular configuration of the synthesizer assigned to each volume. The option of using a description logic ontology - and the associated abilities to carry out instance recognition and automatic classification - as an interface to achieve this conversion as proposed in this paper, presents two distinct advantages:

- It provides a method for the automatic association of any point in the three dimensional space to whatever is the closest available configuration of the speech synthesizer, based on information that is defined at the conceptual level - even if it relies on an underlying level of geometrical representation.
- Any subsequent refinement of the set of configurations available for the synthesizer - for instance, if the existing configurations are refined into a larger set of options by fine tuning them to better represent more specific emotions -, it would be enough to associate the new configurations to the corresponding concepts, and to refine the search algorithm to stop at the first ancestor that has some configuration data associated to it.

---

[2] The quality and emotional precision of the resulting voice has been discussed elsewhere. Details can be found in [19].

Regarding the technologies that have been applied in this proposal, some of these are not generally accepted as standard. Datatypes (and "reasoning" with numbers and strings) are not part of the essence of Description Logics. OWL DL considers datatypes properties disjoint with every object property. It seems that in the next version of OWL (1.1) support for datatypes is going to be improved, because they are useful for many applications. But the current version of OWL just supports some standard XML Schema datatypes and not a standard solution for representing user-defined datatypes. DIG 1.1, being a standard designed for the communication with DL reasoners, does not accept restrictions over datatype properties. This obstacle makes it impossible for us to send an ontology that includes such restrictions directly from Protégé to Pellet for its automatic classification. DIG 2.0, with support for the new OWL 1.1 will offer those features, but for now other shortcuts must be used in order to reason with restrictions on datatype properties . Protégé 3.2.1 now has a proprietary solution to represent user-defined datatypes, which allows the creation of restrictions with interesting datatype properties and even visualization of the limits of a numeric interval and things like that in the GUI. However, DIG does not allow that kind of information to travel to a DL reasoner. Pellet 1.4, by itself, can deal with user-defined datatype restrictions, and now the last version supports the inline syntax proposed by OWL 1.1 [3] So because we are using Protégé as the editor for our ontology and knowledge base, we have to edit the files manually to add those restrictions before loading everything in DLModel using the "Pellet-Java" default configuration. We hope that some of these shortcomings might be solved in later versions of the technologies.

9   Conclusions

An emotional ontology based on description logics has been implemented using semantic web technologies. Each emotional concept is defined in terms of a range of values along the three-dimensional space of emotional dimensions, that allows the system to make inferences concerning the location of new concepts with respect to the taxonomy. This constitutes a valid solution to the problem of finding a relationship between an arbitrary point in a space of emotional dimensions and the set of basic emotional categories usually identified with specific names. The importance of being able to identify such relationships is strengthened by the fact that configuration of synthesizer parameters for artificially producing emotional voice tends to be established in terms of basic emotional categories.

The ontology described in this paper has demonstrated its usefulness as part of a complex process of converting unmarked input text to emotional voice, resolving the problems that originated at the interface between the emotional tagging in terms of emotional dimensions and the synthesis of emotional voice in terms of basic emotional categories. In this process, both the capability for automatic classification provided by the reasoner, and the hierarchical structure provided by the ontology played important roles.

---

[3] http://owl1_1.cs.manchester.ac.uk/owl_specification.html#4.3

Although reasoning support for datatype properties in OWL DL is still not standard, technologies are available that let us experiment with these features and allow us to develop affective computing applications like the emotional voice synthesizer described in the paper. OWL, Jena, DLModel, Protégé and Pellet are the choices we made before developing this new iteration of the software.

Still more improvements are needed in editors as Protégé to be compatible with reasoners as Pellet. Testing SWOOP is going to be one of our next steps in order to facilitate the adquisition of knowledge for the emotional knowledge base.

Acknowledgements

This research is funded by the Spanish Ministry of Education and Science (TIN2006-14433-C02-01 project) and a joint research group grant (UCM-CAM-910494) from the Universidad Complutense de Madrid and the Dirección General de Universidades e Investigación of the Comunidad Autónoma de Madrid.

References

1. Cowie, R., Cornelius, R.: Describing the emotional states that are expressed in speech. In: Speech Communication Special Issue on Speech and Emotion (2003)
2. Schroder, M.: Dimensional emotion representation as a basis for speech synthesis with non-extreme emotions. In: Proc. Workshop on Affective Dialogue Systems, Kloster Irsee, Germany (2004)
3. Izard, C.: The face of emotion. Appleton-Century-Crofts, New York (1971)
4. Alter, K., Rank, E., Kotz, S., Toepel, U., Besson, M., Schirmer, A., Friederici, A.: Accentuation and emotions - two different systems? In: Proceedings of the ISCA Workshop on Speech and Emotion, pp.138–142 Northern Ireland (2000)
5. Russell, J.: A circumflex model of affect. Journal of Personality and Social Psychology 39, 1161–1178 (1980)
6. Scherer, K.R.: On the nature and function of emotion: A component process approach. Approaches to emotion, pp. 293–317 (1984)
7. Cowie, R., Douglas-Cowie, E., Romano, A.: Changing emotional tone in dialogue and its prosodic correlates. In: Proc ESCA International Workshop on Dialogue and prosody, Veldhoven, The Netherlands (1999)
8. Bechhofer, S., van Harmelen, F., Hendler, J., Horrocks, I., McGuinness, D.L., Patel-Schneider, P.F., Stein, A.: OWL web ontology language reference. http://www.w3.org/TR/2004/REC-owl-ref-20040210/
9. Aduna, NLnet-Foundation: Sesame.http://www.openrdf.org
10. Hewlett-Packard: Jena: A semantic web framework for java. http://jena.sourceforge.net/
11. Peinado, F.: Dlmodel, a tool for dealing with description logics. http://federicopeinado.com/projects/dlmodel/
12. Mindswap: Swoop: A hypermedia-based featherweight OWL ontology editor. http://www.mindswap.org/2004/SWOOP/
13. Crubézy, M., Dameron, O., Fergerson, R.W., Knublauch, H., Musen, M.A., Noy, N.F., Rubin, D., Tu, S.W., Vendetti, J.: Protégé project. http://protege.stanford.edu/

14. Mindswap: Pellet OWL reasoner.http://pellet.owldl.com/
15. Racer-Systems: Racerpro. http://www.racer-systems.com/
16. Francisco, V., Gervás, P.: Exploring the compositionality of emotions in text: Word emotions, sentence emotions and automated tagging. In: Proceedings of the AAAI-06 Workshop on Computational Aesthetics: AI Approaches to Beauty and Happiness, Boston (2006)
17. Bradley, M., Lang, P.: Affective norms for English words (ANEW): Stimuli, instruction manual and affective ratings. technical report c-1. Technical report, The Center for Research in Psychophysiology, University of Florida (1999)
18. Miller, G.: Wordnet: a lexical database for english. Communications of the ACM 38, 39–41 (1995)
19. Francisco, V., Hervás, R., Gervás, P.: Análisis y síntesis de expresión emocional en cuentos leídos en voz alta. In: Sociedad Española para el Procesamiento del Lenguaje Natural, Procesamiento de Lenguaje Natural, Granada, Spain (2005)

A Semantic Framework for Language Layering in WSML*

Jos de Bruijn and Stijn Heymans

DERI, University of Innsbruck, Technikerstraße 21a, 6020, Innsbruck, Austria
{jos.debruijn,stijn.heymans}@deri.org

Abstract. WSML presents a framework encompassing different language variants, rooted in Description Logics and (F-)Logic Programming. So far, the precise relationships between these variants have not been investigated. We take the nonmonotonic *first-order autoepistemic logic*, which generalizes both Description Logics and Logic Programming, and extend it with frames and concrete domains, to capture all features of WSML; we call this novel formalism FF-AEL. We consider two forms of language layering for WSML, namely *loose* and *strict* layering, where the latter enforces additional restrictions on the use of certain language constructs in the rule-based language variants, in order to give additional guarantees about the layering. Finally, we demonstrate that each WSML variant semantically corresponds to its target formalism, i.e. WSML-DL corresponds to $\mathcal{SHIQ}(\mathbf{D})$, WSML-Rule to the Stable Model Semantics for Logic Programs (the Well-Founded Semantics can be seen as an approximation), and WSML-Core to $\mathcal{DHL}(\mathbf{D})$ (without nominals), a Horn subset of $\mathcal{SHIQ}(\mathbf{D})$.

1 Introduction

The Web Service Modeling Language WSML[1] [6] is a language for modeling ontologies and Web services. In this paper we are only concerned with WSML ontologies. Thus, when referring to WSML in the remainder, we mean WSML ontologies. References to the ongoing work on the semantics of the functional and behavioral description of Web services can be found in [5].

WSML encompasses a framework of variants based on Description Logics [1] and (F-)Logic Programming [8,9,13]. Each WSML variant has a *target formalism*: *WSML-Core* is based on an intersection of the Description Logic $\mathcal{SHIQ}(\mathbf{D})$ and Horn Logic (without equality), called $\mathcal{DHL}(\mathbf{D})$ [10]. *WSML-DL* captures the Description Logic $\mathcal{SHIQ}(\mathbf{D})$. *WSML-Flight* is based on the Datalog subset of F-Logic, extended with (locally) stratified negation, for which the Well Founded and Stable Model Semantics correspond [8,9]. *WSML-Rule* is based on F-Logic Programming, extended with negation under the Well-Founded Semantics [8]. *WSML-Full* extends both WSML-DL and WSML-Rule towards first-order logic with nonmonotonic extensions.

WSML has two alternative *layerings*: Core $\Rightarrow$ DL $\Rightarrow$ Full and Core $\Rightarrow$ Flight $\Rightarrow$ Rule $\Rightarrow$ Full. For both layerings, WSML-Core and WSML-Full mark the least and

---

* This work was partially supported by the European Commission under the projects Knowledge Web (IST-2004-507482), DIP (FP6-507483), and SUPER (FP6-026850).

[1] http://www.wsmo.org/wsml/wsml-syntax

M. Marchiori, J.Z. Pan, and C. de Sainte Marie (Eds.): RR 2007, LNCS 4524, pp. 103–117, 2007.
© Springer-Verlag Berlin Heidelberg 2007

most expressive variants, respectively. The original WSML specification [6] did not demonstrate any semantic properties of this layering, nor did it include a specification of the semantics for WSML-Full; this was considered an open research topic.

In this paper, we specify an abstract syntax for WSML logical expressions, and define the WSML variants as subsets of this syntax. In order to give a semantics to WSML-Full and to investigate the language layering features of WSML, we specify a novel semantic framework for all WSML variants, based on first-order autoepistemic logic (FO-AEL) [14,3], extended with frames [13] and concrete domains [2]. Our approach to concrete domains is a generalization of the approaches typically followed in Description Logics [2] and Datalog [19]. We call this extended language FF-AEL. We define the semantics of each individual WSML variant through an embedding in FF-AEL. This embedding translates a given WSML description to FF-AEL, and, depending on the language variants, includes a number of sentences which axiomatize the semantics of certain WSML constructs. As an example, we show the difference in the treatment of the subclass (*subConceptOf*) construct in WSML-DL and WSML-Rule.

A subclass statement is of the form $A :: B$, where A, B are terms. In F-Logic, this statement has an *intentional* (only if) semantics: whenever $A :: B$ is true, then every instance of A must be an instance of B. In Description Logics, however, subclass statements (of the form $A \sqsubseteq B$) have an *extensional* (if and only if) semantics: $A \sqsubseteq B$ is true *if and only if* every instance of A is an instance of B. In order to guarantee the correspondence between WSML-DL and Description Logics, this extensional semantics needs to be axiomatized. However, such extensional semantics cannot be axiomatized in a typical rules language such as WSML-Rule, because it would require universal quantification in the body of a rule, which is beyond the expressiveness of a rules language. For example, the following entailment is valid in WSML-DL and WSML-Full ($x : A$ stands for "x is an instance of A"):

$$\forall x (x : A \supset x : B) \models A :: B,$$

whereas it is not valid in WSML-Rule.

This distinction between intentional and extensional treatment of language constructs leads us to the definition of two approaches to language layering in WSML. When considering *loose* layering, a variant L_2 is layered on a variant L_1 if, considering an arbitrary theory of L_1, every L_1-formula which is a consequence under L_1 semantics, is also a consequence under L_2 semantics. When considering *strict* layering, additionally every L_1-formula which is a consequence under L_2 semantics must be a consequence under L_1 semantics. Considering these notions of language layering in the context of OWL, we observe that OWL Lite and OWL DL are strictly layered, and that OWL DL and OWL Full are not strictly, but loosely layered (cf. [12]).

It turns out that when considering strict language layering in WSML, certain restrictions on the use of ontology modeling constructs (e.g. subclass statements ::) must be enforced for the rule-based WSML variants.

In the remainder of the paper we first review the Description Logic $\mathcal{SHIQ}(\mathbf{D})$ in Section 2. We proceed with our definitions of F-Logic with concrete domains, F-Logic Programming, and FF-AEL, in Sections 3, 4, and 5. We then proceed to describe the abstract syntax for WSML variants, and define strict and loose language layering, in

Section 6. We demonstrate the correspondence between the variants and the intended target formalisms in Section 7. Finally, we conclude the paper in Section 8.

2 The Description Logic $\mathcal{SHIQ}(\mathrm{D})$

The signature $\Sigma = \langle \mathcal{C}, \mathcal{D}, \mathcal{R}_a, \mathcal{R}_c, \mathcal{F}_a, \mathcal{F}_c \rangle$ of a $\mathcal{SHIQ}(\mathbf{D})$ [1] language consists of pairwise disjoint sets of concept ($\mathcal{C}$), datatype ($\mathcal{D}$), abstract role ($\mathcal{R}_a$), concrete role ($\mathcal{R}_c$), individual ($\mathcal{F}_a$), and data value ($\mathcal{F}_c$) identifiers. $\mathcal{SHIQ}(\mathbf{D})$ descriptions are defined as follows, with A a concept identifier, D a datatype identifier, C, C' descriptions, R, R' role identifiers, S, S' abstract role identifiers, U, U' concrete role identifiers, a, b individual identifiers, o a data value identifier, and n a non-negative integer.

$$C, C' \longrightarrow \bot \mid A \mid C \sqcap C' \mid \neg C \mid \geqslant nS.C \mid \geqslant nU.D \mid \leqslant nS.C \mid \leqslant nU.D$$

A $\mathcal{SHIQ}(\mathbf{D})$ ontology is a set of axioms of the following forms.

$$C \sqsubseteq C' \mid S \sqsubseteq S' \mid U \sqsubseteq U' \mid S \equiv S'^- \mid (S)^+ \mid C(a) \mid S(a,b) \mid U(a,o) \mid a = b \mid a \neq b$$

Additionally, we have that in *number restrictions* $\geqslant nS.C$ and $\leqslant nS.C$, S has to be *simple*, i.e., S and its sub-roles may not be transitive (with $(S)^+$ denoting transitivity).

For reasons of space, we do not present the $\mathcal{SHIQ}(\mathbf{D})$ semantics here, but refer to [1]. Given a $\mathcal{SHIQ}(\mathbf{D})$ axiom ϕ (resp., ontology Φ), we denote the FOL-equivalent of π (resp., Φ) with $\pi(\phi)$ (resp., $\pi(\Phi)$); by [1] we know that such equivalents exist.

$\mathcal{DHL}(\mathbf{D})$ ([10]) is a Horn subset of $\mathcal{SHIQ}(\mathbf{D})$, which means that every $\mathcal{DHL}(\mathbf{D})$ ontology is equivalent to a Horn theory. For the complete definition of $\mathcal{DHL}(\mathbf{D})$, see [5].

3 Frame Logic with Concrete Domains

In this section we review F-Logic, following [4], and define a novel extension with concrete domains, which is similar to, but more general than, the concrete domains extensions usually considered in Description Logics [2] and Datalog [19].

A language $\mathcal{L}$ has a signature of the form $\Sigma_{\mathcal{L}} = \langle \mathcal{F}, \mathcal{P}, \mathcal{F}^D, \mathcal{P}^D \rangle$, with $\mathcal{F}$ and $\mathcal{P}$ sets of function- and predicate-symbols, and $\mathcal{F}^D$ and $\mathcal{P}^D$ sets of concrete function and predicate symbols, each with an associated arity n, which is a nonnegative integer; $\mathcal{F}$ and $\mathcal{F}^D$ (resp., $\mathcal{P}$ and $\mathcal{P}^D$) are pairwise disjoint. Notice that the symbols in $\mathcal{F}$ and $\mathcal{P}$ do not have associated arities.

Let $\mathcal{V}$ be a set of variable symbols, disjoint from all sets of symbols in $\Sigma_{\mathcal{L}}$. Abstract terms are constructed using symbols from $\mathcal{F}$ and $\mathcal{V}$ as usual. Concrete terms are constructed using symbols from $\mathcal{F}^D$ and $\mathcal{V}$. Terms are either abstract or concrete terms. Abstract atomic formulas (atoms) are $\top, \bot$ or are constructed from terms and symbols in $\mathcal{P}$ in the usual way. Concrete atoms are constructed from concrete terms and symbols in $\mathcal{P}^D$. Atoms are either abstract or concrete atoms. Molecules are *isa* molecules of the form $t_1 : t_2$, *subclass* molecules of the form $t_1 :: t_2$, or *attribute value* molecules of the form $t_1[t_2 \twoheadrightarrow t_3]$, with t_1, t_2, t_3 terms.

Formulas are constructed in the usual way from atoms and molecules using the symbols $\neg, \wedge, \vee, \supset, \equiv, \forall, \exists,), ($, with the difference that abstract quantifiers are indexed with $_a$ ($\exists_a, \forall_a$) and concrete quantifiers are indexed with $_c$ ($\exists_c, \forall_c$). Finally, variables quantified using an abstract quantifier ($\exists_a, \forall_a$) may not occur in a concrete term or atom.

An interpretation is a tuple $\mathbf{I} = \langle U, U^D, \prec_U, \in_U, \mathbf{I}_F, \mathbf{I}_P, \mathbf{I}_{\twoheadrightarrow} \rangle$. U and U^D are disjoint non-empty countable sets, called the *abstract* and *concrete* domains, $\prec_U$ is an irreflexive partial order over $U \cup U^D$, and $\in_U$ is a binary relation over $U \cup U^D$. We write $a \preceq_U b$ when $a \prec_U b$ or $a = b$, for $a, b \in U \cup U^D$. For each interpretation holds that if $a \in_U b$ and $b \preceq_U c$ then $a \in_U c$. Thus, if $b \preceq_U c$, then $\{k \mid k \in_U b, k \in U \cup U^D\} \subseteq \{k \mid k \in_U c, k \in U \cup U^D\}$. We call the set $\{k \mid k \in_U b, k \in U \cup U^D\}$ the *class extension* of b. Thus, if $b \preceq_U c$, then the class extension of b is a subset of the class extension of c. However, the converse of this statement is not universally true.

An abstract function symbol $f \in \mathcal{F}$ is interpreted as a function over the domain U: $\mathbf{I}_F(f) : U^i \to U$, for every $i \geq 0$. An n-ary concrete function symbol $f \in \mathcal{F}^D$ is interpreted as a function over the domain U^D: $\mathbf{I}_F(f) : (U^D)^n \to U^D$. An abstract predicate symbol $p \in P$ is interpreted as a relation over the domain $U \cup U^D$: $\mathbf{I}_P(p) \subseteq (U \cup U^D)^i$, for every $i \geq 0$. An n-ary concrete predicate symbol $p \in P^D$ is interpreted as a relation over the domain U^D: $\mathbf{I}_P(p) \subseteq (U^D)^n$. $\mathbf{I}_{\twoheadrightarrow}$ associates a binary relation over $U \cup U^D$ with each $u \in U \cup U^D$: $\mathbf{I}_{\twoheadrightarrow}(u) \subseteq (U \cup U^D) \times (U \cup U^D)$.

A *concrete domain scheme* $\mathfrak{S}$ is a tuple $\mathfrak{S} = \langle U^{\mathfrak{S}}, \mathcal{F}^{\mathfrak{S}}, \mathcal{P}^{\mathfrak{S}}, \cdot^{\mathfrak{S}} \rangle$, where $U^{\mathfrak{S}}$ is a non-empty countable set of concrete values, $\mathcal{F}^{\mathfrak{S}}$ and $\mathcal{P}^{\mathfrak{S}}$ are disjoint sets of concrete function and predicate symbols, each with an associated nonnegative arity n, and $\cdot^{\mathfrak{S}}$ is an interpretation function which assigns a function $f^{\mathfrak{S}} : (U^{\mathfrak{S}})^n \to U^{\mathfrak{S}}$ to every $f \in \mathcal{F}^{\mathfrak{S}}$ and a relation $p^{\mathfrak{S}} \subseteq (U^{\mathfrak{S}})^n$ to every $p \in \mathcal{P}^{\mathfrak{S}}$. A language $\mathcal{L}$ with signature $\Sigma_{\mathcal{L}} = \langle \mathcal{F}, \mathcal{P}, \mathcal{F}^D, \mathcal{P}^D \rangle$ *conforms to* a concrete domains scheme $\mathfrak{S} = \langle U^{\mathfrak{S}}, \mathcal{F}^{\mathfrak{S}}, \mathcal{P}^{\mathfrak{S}}, \cdot^{\mathfrak{S}} \rangle$ if $\mathcal{F}^D = \mathcal{F}^{\mathfrak{S}}$ and $\mathcal{P}^D = \mathcal{P}^{\mathfrak{S}}$. An interpretation $\mathbf{I} = \langle U, U^D, \prec_U, \in_U, \mathbf{I}_F, \mathbf{I}_P, \mathbf{I}_{\twoheadrightarrow} \rangle$ of $\mathcal{L}$ *conforms to* $\mathfrak{S}$ if $U^D = U^{\mathfrak{S}}$, and $\mathbf{I}_F(f) = f^{\mathfrak{S}}, \mathbf{I}_P(p) = p^{\mathfrak{S}}$ for every $f \in \mathcal{F}^{\mathfrak{S}}, p \in \mathcal{P}^{\mathfrak{S}}$, respectively. In the remainder we assume that every language conforms to the concrete domain scheme under consideration. We illustrate the concept through the definition of a concrete domain scheme for integers and strings.

Example 1. We define the concrete domain scheme $\mathfrak{S} = \langle U^{\mathfrak{S}}, \mathcal{F}^{\mathfrak{S}}, \mathcal{P}^{\mathfrak{S}}, \cdot^{\mathfrak{S}} \rangle$ as follows: $U^{\mathfrak{S}}$ is the union of the sets of integer numbers and finite-length sequences of Unicode characters. $\mathcal{F}^{\mathfrak{S}}$ is the union of the set of finite-length sequences of decimal digits, optionally with a leading minus ($-$), and the set of finite-length sequences of Unicode characters, delimited with " (for simplicity, we assume that the character " does not occur in such strings), all with arity 0. $\mathcal{P}^{\mathfrak{S}}$ consists of unary predicate symbols *integer* and *string*, and the binary predicate symbol *numeric-equals*. The interpretation function $\cdot^{\mathfrak{S}}$ interprets (signed) sequences of decimal digits and "-delimited sequences of characters as integers and strings, respectively, in the natural way; $\cdot^{\mathfrak{S}}$ interprets *integer* and *string* as the set of integers and strings; finally, $\cdot^{\mathfrak{S}}$ interprets *numeric-equals* as identity over the set of integers.

Our approach to integrating concrete domains is a generalization of the usual approaches to integrating concrete domains in Description Logics [2], as well as extensions such as [17], and Datalog [19] (where they are called *built-ins*). In DLs, all predicate symbols are sorted (using the sorts *abstract* and *concrete*; binary predicates with the sort *abstract* × *concrete* are usually called *features*) and certain restrictions apply on the concrete domain schemes in order to guarantee decidability of reasoning and the existence of effective algorithms. In Datalog concrete predicates are only allowed to occur in rule bodies, and variables must occur in abstract atoms in the body of the rule; this guarantees the existence of effective terminating reasoning methods.

A variable assignment B assigns each variable $x \in \mathcal{V}$ to an individual $x^B \in U \cup U^D$. A variable assignment B' is an abstract (resp., concrete) x-variant of B if $x^{B'} \in U \cup U^D$ (resp., $x^{B'} \in U^D$) and $y^{B'} = y^B$ for $y \neq x$. The interpretation of a term t in some $\mathbf{I}$ with respect to some variable assignment B, written $t^{\mathbf{I},B}$, is defined as: $t^{\mathbf{I},B} = t^B$ if $t \in \mathcal{V}$, and $t^{\mathbf{I},B} = \mathbf{I}_F(f)(t_1^{\mathbf{I},B}, \ldots, t_n^{\mathbf{I},B})$ if t is of the form $f(t_1, \ldots, t_n)$. A variable substitution β, usually written in postfix notation, is a partial mapping from variable symbols to ground terms. A variable substitution β is *associated with* (cf. [3]) a variable assignment B if for every variable symbol x such that $x^B = k$ and there exists a ground term t such that $t^{\mathbf{I},B} = k$, then $x\beta = t'$ for some ground term t' such that $t'^{\mathbf{I},B} = k$; otherwise $x\beta$ is not defined.

Satisfaction of atomic formulas and molecules ϕ in $\mathbf{I}$, given the variable assignment B, denoted $(\mathbf{I}, B) \models_f \phi$, is defined as: $(\mathbf{I}, B) \models_f \top$, $(\mathbf{I}, B) \not\models_f \bot$, $(\mathbf{I}, B) \models_f p(t_1, \ldots, t_n)$ iff $(t_1^{\mathbf{I},B}, \ldots, t_n^{\mathbf{I},B}) \in \mathbf{I}_P(p)$, $(\mathbf{I}, B) \models_f t_1 : t_2$ iff $t_1^{\mathbf{I},B} \in_U t_2^{\mathbf{I},B}$, $(\mathbf{I}, B) \models_f t_1 :: t_2$ iff $t_1^{\mathbf{I},B} \preceq_U t_2^{\mathbf{I},B}$, $(\mathbf{I}, B) \models_f t_1[t_2 \twoheadrightarrow t_3]$ iff $\langle t_1^{\mathbf{I},B}, t_3^{\mathbf{I},B} \rangle \in \mathbf{I}_{\twoheadrightarrow}(t_2^{\mathbf{I},B})$, and $(\mathbf{I}, B) \models_f t_1 = t_2$ iff $t_1^{\mathbf{I},B} = t_2^{\mathbf{I},B}$.

This extends to arbitrary formulas as follows: $(\mathbf{I}, B) \models_f \phi_1 \wedge \phi_2$ (resp. $(\mathbf{I}, B) \models_f \phi_1 \vee \phi_2$, $(\mathbf{I}, B) \models_f \neg\phi_1$) iff $(\mathbf{I}, B) \models_f \phi_1$ and $(\mathbf{I}, B) \models_f \phi_2$ (resp. $(\mathbf{I}, B) \models_f \phi_1$ or $(\mathbf{I}, B) \models_f \phi_2$, $(\mathbf{I}, B) \not\models \phi_1$); $(\mathbf{I}, B) \models_f \forall_a x(\phi_1)$ (resp. $(\mathbf{I}, B) \models_f \exists_a x(\phi_1)$) iff for every (resp. for some) B'_a which is an abstract x-variant of B, $(\mathbf{I}, B'_a) \models_f \phi_1$; $(\mathbf{I}, B) \models_f \forall_c x(\phi_1)$ (resp. $(\mathbf{I}, B) \models_f \exists_c x (\phi_1)$) iff for every (resp. for some) B'_c which is a concrete x-variant of B, $(\mathbf{I}, B'_c) \models_f \phi_1$. If a variable x is quantified using a concrete quantifier $(\forall_c, \exists_c)$, x is a *concrete variable*; otherwise, x is an *abstract variable*.

Given a concrete domain scheme $\mathfrak{S}$, an interpretation $\mathbf{I}$ is a *model* of a formula ϕ if $\mathbf{I}$ conforms to $\mathfrak{S}$ and for every variable assignment B, $(\mathbf{I}, B) \models_f \phi$. A formula ϕ is *satisfiable* if it has a model; ϕ is *valid* if every interpretation which conforms to $\mathfrak{S}$ is a model of ϕ. These notions extend to theories $\Phi \subseteq \mathcal{L}$ in the natural way. A theory $\Phi \subseteq \mathcal{L}$ *entails* a formula $\phi \in \mathcal{L}$ if every model of Φ is also a model of ϕ.

Contextual FOL is F-Logic without molecules. *Classical FOL* is contextual first-order logic in which each function symbol and predicate symbol has one associated arity n, which is a nonnegative integer. We denote satisfaction and entailment in classical FOL with the symbol $\models$.

The following correspondence between $\mathcal{SHIQ}(\mathbf{D})$ and F-Logic ontologies is a straightforward extension of a result in [4]. Given an FOL formula (resp. theory) ϕ (resp., Φ), then $\delta(\phi)$ (resp., $\delta(\Phi)$) is the F-Logic formula (resp., theory) obtained from ϕ (resp., Φ) by replacing all atoms of the forms $A(t)$ and $R(t_1, t_2)$, where t, t_1, t_2 are terms, with molecules of the forms $t : A$ and $t_1[R \twoheadrightarrow t_2]$, respectively.

Proposition 1. *Given a concrete domain scheme* $\mathfrak{S}$, *let* Φ, ϕ *be a* $\mathcal{SHIQ}(\mathbf{D})$ *theory and formula, respectively. Then,* $\Phi \models \phi$ *iff* $\delta(\pi(\Phi)) \models_f \delta(\pi(\phi))$.

4   F-Logic Programs

Given a concrete domain scheme $\mathfrak{S}$ and a language $\mathcal{L}$ with at least one 0-ary function symbol, a rule is of the form

$$h \;\leftarrow\; b_1, \;\ldots, \; b_m, \; not \; c_1, \;\ldots, \; not \; c_n, \tag{1}$$

where $h, b_1, \ldots, b_m, c_1, \ldots, c_n$ are (equality-free) atoms or molecules, and h is not a concrete atom. h is the *head atom* of r, $B^+(r) = \{b_1, \ldots, b_m\}$ is the *positive body* of r, and $B^-(r) = \{c_1, \ldots, c_n\}$ is the *negative body* of r. If $B^-(r) = \emptyset$, then r is *positive*. If every variable in r occurs in an abstract atom in $B^+(r)$, then r is *safe*. If a variable occurs in a concrete atom, it is a concrete variable; otherwise, it is an abstract variable. The following rules axiomatize the semantics of subclass molecules: (∗) $x :: z \;\leftarrow\; x :: y, y :: z$, (∗∗) $x : z \;\leftarrow\; x : y, y :: z$, and (∗ ∗ ∗) $x :: x$, where (∗) axiomatizes transitivity of the subclass relation; (∗∗) axiomatizes inheritance of class membership; and (∗ ∗ ∗) axiomatizes the fact that every class is a subclass of itself[2]. A *normal F-Logic program* P is a set of rules of the form (1) which includes the rules (∗, ∗∗, ∗ ∗ ∗). If every rule $r \in P$ is positive (resp., safe), then P is positive (resp., safe).

The *Herbrand base* of $\mathcal{L}$ is the set of ground atomic formulas and molecules of $\mathcal{L}$. Subsets of the Herbrand base are called *Herbrand interpretations*.

The *grounding* of a logic program P, denoted $gr(P)$, is the union of all possible ground instantiations of P, obtained by replacing each abstract (resp., concrete) variable in a rule r with a ground (resp., ground concrete) term of $\mathcal{L}$, for each rule $r \in P$.

Let P be a positive program. A Herbrand interpretation M of P is a *model* of P if M conforms to $\mathfrak{S}$, $\top \in M, \bot \notin M$, and, for every rule $r \in gr(P)$, $B^+(r) \subseteq M$ implies $H(r) \cap M \neq \emptyset$. A Herbrand model M is *minimal* iff for every model M' such that $M' \subseteq M, M' = M$.

Following [9], the *reduct* of a logic program P with respect to an interpretation M, denoted P^M, is obtained from $gr(P)$ by deleting (i) each rule r with $B^-(r) \cap M \neq \emptyset$, and (ii) *not c* from the body of every remaining rule r with $c \in B^-(r)$. If M is a minimal Herbrand model of P^M, then M is a *stable model* of P.

If P is a positive logic program, then the corresponding Horn F-Logic theory Φ is obtained by replacing the arrow $\leftarrow$ and comma (,) in every rule with the symbols $\supset$ and $\wedge$ in the usual way, and prefixing the formula with a concrete (resp., abstract) universal quantifier ($\forall_c$ or $\forall_a$, resp.) for every concrete (resp., abstract) variable x. The following proposition follows straightforwardly from the definition, and the classical results by Herbrand.

Proposition 2. *Given a concrete domain scheme* $\mathfrak{S}$, *let* P *be a positive logic program and* Φ *be the corresponding Horn F-Logic theory, then*

– P *has a stable model iff* Φ *is satisfiable, and*
– *if* P *has a stable model* M, *it is unique, and for every ground atom or molecule* α, $\alpha \in M$ *iff* $\Phi \models_f \alpha$.

---

[2] Note that the rule (4) is not safe. However, (∗ ∗ ∗) is not necessary in case subclass statements (::) do not occur in rule bodies and are not considered when determining consequences.

5   First-Order Autoepistemic Logic with Frames and Concrete Domains

First-Order Autoepistemic Logic (FO-AEL) [14,3] is an extension of first-order logic with a modal belief operator L, which is interpreted nonmonotonically. We specify an extension of FO-AEL, based on F-Logic with concrete domains, called FF-AEL.

An FF-AEL language $\mathcal{L}_L$ is defined relative to a language $\mathcal{L}$:

- any atomic formula or molecule in $\mathcal{L}$ is a formula in $\mathcal{L}_L$,
- if ϕ is a *formula* in $\mathcal{L}_L$, then $L\phi$, called a *modal atom*, is a formula in $\mathcal{L}_L$, and
- *complex formulas* are constructed as in F-Logic with concrete domains.

A formula without modal atoms is an *objective* formula.

An *autoepistemic interpretation* is a pair $\langle I, \Gamma \rangle$, where $I = \langle U, U^D, \prec_U, \in_U, I_F, I_P, I_{\rightarrow} \rangle$ is an interpretation, and $\Gamma \subseteq \mathcal{L}_L$ is a set of sentences, called the *belief set*. Satisfaction of objective atomic formulas in $\langle I, \Gamma \rangle$ corresponds to satisfaction in I.

Satisfaction of a formula $L\phi$ ($\phi \in \mathcal{L}_L$) in an interpretation $\langle I, \Gamma \rangle$ with respect to a variable assignment B under the *any-name semantics*[3], denoted $(I, B) \models_\Gamma L\phi$, is defined as follows:

$(I, B) \models_\Gamma L\phi$ iff, for some variable substitution(s) β, associated with B, $\phi\beta$ has no free variables and $\phi\beta \in \Gamma$.

This extends to arbitrary formulas in the usual way (see also Section 3).

$\langle I, \Gamma \rangle$ is a *model* of ϕ, denoted $I \models_\Gamma \phi$, if $(I, B) \models_\Gamma \phi$ for every variable assignment B. This extends to sets of formulas in the usual way. A set of formulas $A \subseteq \mathcal{L}_L$ *entails* a sentence ϕ with respect to a belief set Γ, denoted $A \models_\Gamma \phi$, if for every interpretation I such that $I \models_\Gamma A$, $I \models_\Gamma \phi$.

A central notion in FF-AEL is the *stable expansion*, which is the set of beliefs of an ideally introspective agent, given some base set. A belief set $T \subseteq \mathcal{L}_L$ is a *stable expansion* of a base set $A \subseteq \mathcal{L}_L$ iff $T = \{\phi \mid A \models_T \phi\}$.

A formula ϕ is an *autoepistemic consequence* of A if ϕ is included in every stable expansion of A. In the remainder, when referring to consequences of a theory A we mean *objective autoepistemic consequences*, unless specified otherwise. The following proposition is a straightforward generalization of a result in [14].

Proposition 3. *Given a concrete domain scheme $\mathfrak{S}$, let $\Phi \subseteq \mathcal{L}$ be a satisfiable F-Logic theory. Then, Φ has one consistent stable expansion T, and $T \cap \mathcal{L} = \{\phi \mid \Phi \models_f \phi\}$.*

Embedding Logic Programs. Following [3], we define an embedding as a function which takes a normal F-Logic program P as its argument and returns a set of FF-AEL sentences. Since the unique-names assumption does not hold in FF-AEL, it is necessary to axiomatize default uniqueness of names. With UNA_Σ we denote the set of axioms

$$\neg L(t_1 = t_2) \supset t_1 \neq t_2, \quad \text{for all pairs of distinct ground terms } t_1, t_2.$$

---

[3] [14] presents also the all-names semantics, but we follow [14,3] in their choice for the any-name semantics.

Let r be a normal rule of the form (1). Then,

$$\tau_{HP}(r) = (\forall) \bigwedge_{1 \leq i \leq m} b_i \wedge \bigwedge_{1 \leq j \leq n} \neg \mathsf{L} c_j \supset h,$$

such that each concrete variable is quantified using $\forall_c$, and all other variables are quantified using $\forall_a$. For a normal F-Logic program P, we define:

$$\tau_{HP}(P) = \{\tau_{HP}(r) \mid r \in P\} \cup UNA_{\Sigma_P}.$$

Recall the three rules (*), (**) and (***), which are part of every F-Logic program. These rules translate to FF-AEL as follows: (*) $\forall_a x, y, z\ (x :: y \wedge y :: z \supset x :: z)$, (**) $\forall_a x, y, z\ (x : y \wedge y :: z \supset x : z)$ and (***) $\forall_a x\ (x :: x)$. It can be easily verified, using the definition of interpretations and satisfaction in F-Logic, that the embeddings of these formulas are all valid in F-Logic and thus in FF-AEL (i.e. they are included in every stable expansion). Faithfulness of the embedding is established in the following proposition, which generalizes a result in [3].

Proposition 4. *Given a concrete domain scheme $\mathfrak{S}$, a Herbrand interpretation M of a normal F-Logic program P is a stable model of P iff there is a consistent stable expansion T of $\tau_{HP}(P)$ such that M coincides with the set of objective ground atoms and molecules in T.*

6   WSML Logical Expressions

In this section we present an abstract syntax for WSML logical expressions, and define their semantics through an embedding in FF-AEL. We use this abstract syntax to discuss two forms of language layering between the WSML variants. Note that this abstract syntax for WSML formulas differs from the more verbose (logical expression) surface syntax in the original specification. There is, however, a straightforward mapping from the syntax we use here to the surface syntax; see [5, Section 4.3].

Given a concrete domain scheme $\mathfrak{S}$ [4], the signature of a WSML language $\mathcal{L}$ is of the form $\Sigma = \langle \mathcal{F}, \mathcal{P}, \mathcal{F}^{\mathfrak{S}}, \mathcal{P}^{\mathfrak{S}} \rangle$, as in F-Logic with concrete domains (cf. Section 3).

Terms and atoms are defined as in Section 3. Molecules are defined analogously to F-Logic: if t_1, t_2, t_3 are terms, then $t_1 : t_2$, $t_1 :: t_2$ and $t_1[t_2 \times t_3]$, with $\times \in \{ \mathsf{ot}, \mathsf{it}, \mathsf{hv} \}$, are molecules. The symbol ot stands for the WSML construct *ofType*; a statement $t_1[t_2 \,\mathsf{ot}\, t_3]$ requires all values for the attribute t_2 to be *known* to be a member of the type t_3; it stands for the WSML construct *impliesType*; a statement $t_1[t_2 \,\mathsf{it}\, t_3]$ implies that all values for the attribute t_2 are a member of the class t_3; hv stands for the WSML construct *hasValue*; a molecule $t_1[t_2 \,\mathsf{hv}\, t_3]$ says that the individual t_1 has an attribute t_2 with value t_3.

WSML formulas are inductively defined as follows, with $\phi, \psi \in \mathcal{L}$:

– atoms and molecules are formulas;
– $\sim \phi$, with $\sim \in \{\neg, not\ \}$, is a formula;

---

[4] It is assumed in WSML that such a concrete domain scheme incorporates at least the XML Schema datatypes *string*, *integer*, and *decimal* [6, Appendix C].

$- \phi \star \psi$, with $\star \in \{\wedge, \vee, \supset, \equiv\}$, is a formula; and

$- Q\, x(\phi)$, with $Q \in \{\forall_a, \exists_a, \forall_c, \exists_c\}$ and $x \in \mathcal{V}$, is a formula.

Additionally, no variable quantified using an abstract quantifier ($\forall_a, \exists_a$) may be used in a concrete atom. We assume that the predicate symbols $\_it, \_ot$ are not used in any WSML formula. As usual, WSML sentences are WSML formulas with no free variables.

The semantics of WSML formulas is defined through a translation to FF-AEL: let Φ be a set of WSML formulas, then $tr(\Phi)$ is the FF-AEL theory obtained as follows: for each $\phi \in \Phi$, $tr(\phi)$ is obtained from ϕ by replacing each occurrence of *not* with $\neg \mathsf{L}$, replacing hv with $\longrightarrow$, and replacing molecules of the forms $t_1[t_2\,\mathsf{ot}\,t_3]$ and $t_1[t_2\,\mathsf{it}\,t_3]$, with t_1, t_2 and t_3 terms, with atoms of the forms $\_ot(t_1, t_2, t_3)$ and $\_it(t_1, t_2, t_3)$, respectively. Finally, the following formulas are used to axiomatize the *intentional* (only if) semantics of the ot and it molecules:

$$\forall_a\, x, y, z, v, w\ (\_ot(x, y, z) \wedge v:x \wedge v[y\!\longrightarrow\!w] \wedge \neg\mathsf{L}w:z \supset \bot); \tag{2}$$

$$\forall_a\, x, y, z, v, w\ (\_it(x, y, z) \wedge v:x \wedge v[y\!\longrightarrow\!w] \supset w:z), \tag{3}$$

and the following formulas are used to axiomatize the *extensional* (if and only if) semantics of the it and :: molecules, necessary for DL-like languages:

$$\forall_a\, x, y, z\ (\forall_a v, w(v:x \wedge v[y\!\longrightarrow\!w] \supset w:z)) \supset \_it(x, y, z), \text{ and} \tag{4}$$

$$\forall_a\ x, y\ (\forall_a v(v:x \supset v:y)) \supset x::y. \tag{5}$$

WSML-Full and -FOL Any WSML sentence is a WSML-Full sentence. A *WSML-Full theory* is a set of WSML-Full sentences. The semantics of a WSML-Full theory Φ is given through the embedding $tr_{Full}(\Phi) = tr(\Phi) \cup \{(2), (3), (4), (5)\}$.

A WSML-FOL sentence is a WSML-Full sentence which neither contains ot-molecules, nor occurrences of the default negation operator *not*. A *WSML-FOL theory* is a set of WSML-FOL sentences. The semantics of a WSML-FOL theory Φ is given through the embedding $tr_{FOL}(\Phi) = tr(\Phi) \cup \{(3), (4), (5)\}$.

WSML-Rule. WSML-Rule formulas are of the form

$$(\forall)b_1 \wedge \ldots \wedge b_l \wedge not\ c_1 \wedge \ldots \wedge not\ c_m \supset h \tag{6}$$

where $b_1, \ldots, b_l, c_1, \ldots, c_m$ are atoms or hv, ot, or *isa* (:) molecules, with l, m nonnegative integers, and h an abstract equality-free atom or molecule; if $h = \bot$, then we call the rule an *integrity constraint*. Additionally, each quantifier is either abstract ($\forall_a$) or concrete ($\forall_c$). A *WSML-Rule theory* is a set of WSML-Rule sentences. The semantics of a WSML-Rule theory Φ is given through the embedding $tr_{Rule}(\Phi) = tr(\Phi) \cup \{(2), (3)\}$.

Concrete atoms in WSML-Rule correspond to the common built-in atoms in Logic Programming.

Notice that there is a natural correspondence between WSML-Rule formulas of the form (6) and rules in a logic program of the form (1). Thus, WSML-Rule formulas are essentially rules with a head and a body. Notice that, whereas the embedding $tr_{Full}(\Phi)$ includes the sentences (4) and (5), the embedding $tr_{Rule}(\Phi)$ does not, because there is no natural correspondence to rules due to the universal quantification in the antecedent of the formulas (4) and (5). The it- and ::-molecules may not be used in the body of a rule in order to maintain a strict correspondence between the WSML-Rule semantics and the WSML-Full semantics, as illustrated in the following example.

Example 2. Consider the theory Φ consisting of the formulas

$$\forall_a x(x:A \supset x:B) \text{ and}$$
$$A::B \supset q.$$

The theory $tr_{Rule}(\Phi)$ neither has $A::B$ nor q among its consequences. In contrast, it is easy to verify that, by (5), $tr_{Full}(\Phi)$ has both $A::B$ and q among its consequences.

WSML-Flight. A *WSML-Flight theory* is a WSML-Rule theory for which holds that, for every formula of the form (6), every variable occurs in a positive abstract body atom b_i, no function symbol in (6) is used with an arity higher than 0, and the theory is *locally stratified*[5].[6] The semantics of a WSML-Flight theory Φ is given through the embedding $tr_{Flight}(\Phi) = tr_{Rule}(\Phi)$.

WSML-DL. Given an FOL formula ϕ, $\delta'(\phi)$ is obtained from ϕ by replacing atoms of the forms $A(t_1)$, $R(t_1, t_2)$, with t_1, t_2 terms, with molecules of the forms $t_1 : A, t_1$ $[R \text{ hv } t_2]$.

Given a $\mathcal{SHIQ}(\mathbf{D})$ signature $\Sigma = \langle \mathcal{C}, \mathcal{D}, \mathcal{R}_a, \mathcal{R}_c, \mathcal{F}_a, \mathcal{F}_c \rangle$, the corresponding WSML signature is $\langle \mathcal{C} \cup \mathcal{D} \cup \mathcal{R}_a \cup \mathcal{R}_c \cup \mathcal{F}_a, \emptyset, \mathcal{F}'_c, \mathcal{D}' \rangle$, where $\mathcal{F}'_c$ is the set of 0-ary functions symbols obtained from $\mathcal{F}_c$ and $\mathcal{D}'$ is the set of 1-ary predicate symbols obtained from $\mathcal{D}$. A WSML-DL formula is a WSML formula of the form

- $\delta'(\phi)$, where ϕ is the FOL equivalent of a $\mathcal{SHIQ}(\mathbf{D})$ axiom of the signature Σ,
- $a::b$, with $a, b \in \mathcal{C}$,
- $a[s \text{ it } b]$, with $s \in \mathcal{R}_a$ and $a, b \in \mathcal{C}$, or
- $a[u \text{ it } d]$, with $u \in \mathcal{R}_c$, $a \in \mathcal{C}$ and $d \in \mathcal{D}$.

Given a $\mathcal{SHIQ}(\mathbf{D})$ signature Σ, a *WSML-DL theory* is a set of WSML-DL sentences. The semantics of a WSML-DL theory Φ is given through the embedding $tr_{DL}(\Phi) = tr_{FOL}(\Phi)$.

WSML-Core. A WSML-DL formula which is also a Flight formula is a WSML-Core formula. *WSML-Core theory* is a set of WSML-Core sentences. The semantics of a WSML-Core theory Φ is given through the embedding $tr_{Core}(\Phi) = tr_{Flight}(\Phi) = tr_{Rule}(\Phi)$.

Let $\mathfrak{S}$ be a concrete domain scheme and $x \in \{Core, Flight, Rule, DL, FOL, Full\}$ a WSML variant. We say that a WSML-x theory Φ is *consistent* if $tr_x(\Phi)$ has a consistent stable expansion an WSML-x formula ϕ, and is a WSML-x consequence of Φ if $\phi \in T$ for every stable expansion T of $tr_x(\Phi)$.

---

[5] Each atom or molecule in $gr(\Phi)$ is assigned a stratum, which is an integer. We say that $gr(\Phi)$ is stratified if there is an assignment of atoms and molecules to strata such that: if an atom or molecule p occurs positively in a rule with an atom or molecule q as its head, then p has the same or a lower stratum, and if p occurs negatively in a rule with q as its head, then p has a lower stratum than q. If $gr(\Phi)$ is stratified, then Φ is locally stratified.

[6] These conditions correspond to the usual safety condition which must hold for Datalog programs, and the usual local stratification for logic programs.

WSML Language Layering. We now turn to the relationships between the language variants. Certain relationships are straightforward, because of equivalence of the embeddings in FF-AEL (e.g. given a WSML-Core theory Φ, $tr_{Core}(\Phi) = tr_{Flight}(\Phi) = tr_{Rule}(\Phi)$); however, there are also certain differences between embeddings (e.g. given a WSML-Core theory Φ, $tr_{Core}(\Phi) \neq tr_{DL}(\Phi) \neq tr_{Full}(\Phi)$). We consider two forms of language layering: *strict* and *loose* language layering.

Admissible consequences under strict/loose language layering are subsets of all formulas of a given WSML variant. Intuitively, admissible consequences are the formulas allowed to be considered when checking consequences of a given a theory.

The admissible consequences under strict language layering for WSML are as follows: every it- and ::-free WSML-(Core/Flight/Rule) sentence is an admissible consequence of WSML-(Core/Flight/Rule), and every WSML-(DL/FOL/Full) sentence is an admissible consequence of WSML-(DL/FOL/Full) under strict language layering. Under loose layering, additionally every WSML-(Core/Flight/Rule) sentence is an admissible consequence of WSML-(Core/Flight/Rule). We denote the set of admissible consequences under strict (resp., loose) language layering of a given WSML variant L with $L|_{as}$ (resp., $L|_{al}$).

Definition 1. *Let L_1, L_2 be two WSML variants with associated embeddings (semantics) tr_1, tr_2. Then,*

- *L_2 is strictly layered on top of L_1, denoted $L_1 \Rightarrow_s L_2$, if for every theory $\Phi \subseteq L_1$ and every formula $\phi \in L_1|_{as}$, ϕ is a consequence of $tr_1(\Phi)$ if and only if ϕ is a consequence of $tr_2(\Phi)$, and*
- *L_2 is loosely layered on top of L_1, denoted $L_1 \Rightarrow_l L_2$, if for every theory $\Phi \subseteq L_1$ and every formula $\phi \in L_1|_{al}$, ϕ is a consequence of $tr_2(\Phi)$ whenever ϕ is a consequence of $tr_1(\Phi)$.*

It turns out that when considering loose language layering, we can consider *generalized* WSML-(Core/Flight/Rule) formulas, which are WSML-(Core/Flight/Rule) formulas which additionally allow it- and ::-molecules in the body, i.e. for formulas of the form (6) holds that b_i, c_i may be atoms or *arbitrary* molecules. This notion naturally extends to WSML-(Core/Flight/Rule) theories. We thus obtain the *generalized* WSML-(Core/Flight/Rule) language variants.

Theorem 1 (WSML Language Layering)

- *WSML-Core $\Rightarrow_s$ WSML-Flight $\Rightarrow_s$ WSML-Rule $\Rightarrow_s$ WSML-Full.*
- *WSML-Core $\Rightarrow_s$ WSML-DL $\Rightarrow_s$ WSML-FOL $\Rightarrow_s$ WSML-Full*
- *Gen. WSML-Core $\Rightarrow_l$ gen. WSML-Flight $\Rightarrow_l$ gen. WSML-Rule $\Rightarrow_l$ WSML-Full.*
- *Gen. WSML-Core $\Rightarrow_l$ WSML-DL $\Rightarrow_l$ WSML-FOL $\Rightarrow_l$ WSML-Full.*

An important distinction between the strict and the loose language layering, is that in the strict language layering setting certain schema-level formulas (i.e. those involving it- and ::- molecules) are not among the admissible consequences. Therefore, it is not possible in WSML-Flight and WSML-Rule to reason about subclass and certain typing relationships, when adhering to strict layering. We illustrate the differences between the two forms of layering with an example.

Example 3. Consider the WSML-Core theory $\Phi = \{Person[hasChild \text{ it } Person],$ $Astronaut :: Person, \forall_a \ x(x : Person \supset x : Animal)\}$ which says that, for every instance of the class $Person$, each value of the attribute $hasChild$ is an instance of $Person$, $Astronaut$ is a subclass of $Person$, and every instance of $Person$ is also an instance of $Animal$. Now consider the formulas $\phi_1 = Astronaut[hasChild$ it $Person]$ and $\phi_2 = Person :: Animal$; ϕ_1 and ϕ_2 are both consequences of $tr_{DL}(\Phi)$, but neither is a consequence of $tr_{Core}(\Phi)$ (or indeed $tr_{Flight}(\Phi)$ or $tr_{Rule}(\Phi)$). One can verify that, in fact, the set of consequences of $tr_{Core}(\Phi)$ is a subset of the set of consequences of $tr_{DL}(\Phi)$. Observe also that ϕ_1 and ϕ_2 are not admissible WSML-Core consequences under strict language layering. In fact, the sets of consequences of $tr_{Core}(\Phi)$ and $tr_{DL}(\Phi)$ coincide with respect to admissible WSML-Core consequences under strict language layering, as was demonstrated with Theorem 1.

Comparing strict and loose language layering, we observe that if strict language layering is considered, the definitions of WSML-Flight and WSML-Rule formulas are more restrictive, and there are certain (some may argue, unintuitive) restrictions on the kinds of consequences which are admissible. In fact, under strict language layering, the Core, Flight, and Rule variants are significantly less expressive than the corresponding generalized variants under loose layering, because inferences of it- and :: statements may not be considered. Therefore, the use of loose language layering seems more attractive. Indeed, the use of loose language layering is common in Semantic Web standards; for example, RDFS is loosely layered on top of RDF, OWL Full is loosely layered on top of RDFS, and OWL Full is loosely layered on top of OWL DL. However, one could imagine scenarios in which strict language layering is more attractive. For example, when directly using a WSML-DL reasoner for reasoning with WSML-Core theories, one needs to be sure that the semantics correspond; otherwise, certain inferences might be incorrect with respect to the WSML-Core semantics.

7   Correspondence with Target Formalisms

In this section we show the correspondences between the WSML language variants and the logical language formalisms which have originally motivated the definition of these variants, with respect to the reasoning tasks relevant in the formalism. The *target formalisms* for WSML-Core, WSML-DL, WSML-Flight, WSML-Rule and WSML-FOL are $\mathcal{DHL}(\mathbf{D})$, $\mathcal{SHIQ}(\mathbf{D})$, the Well-Founded Semantics for stratified and general logic programs, and (F-Logic-extended) classical first-order logic, respectively.

WSML-Full and WSML-FOL. The usual reasoning tasks for autoepistemic logic are existence of stable expansions, inclusion of a formula in some stable expansion, and inclusion of a formula in all stable expansions (autoepistemic consequence) (cf. [16]). We expect these reasoning tasks to be relevant for WSML-Full as well.

From the definition we can see that WSML-FOL does not make use of the non-monotonic modal operator L and thus basically corresponds to F-Logic with concrete domains. The following theorem follows straightforwardly from Proposition 3.

Theorem 2 (WSML-FOL correspondence). *Given a concrete domain scheme* $\mathfrak{S}$, *a WSML language* $\mathcal{L}$, *a WSML-FOL theory* $\Phi \in \mathcal{L}$ *and a formula* $\phi \in \mathcal{L}$, *then* $tr_{FOL}(\Phi)$ $\models_f tr(\phi)$ *iff* $tr(\phi)$ *is a consequence of* $tr_{FOL}(\Phi)$.

WSML-DL and -Core The usual reasoning tasks for the Description Logic $\mathcal{SHIQ}(\mathbf{D})$ are concept satisfiability, knowledge base satisfiability and logical entailment (usually restricted to formulas of a specific shape, such as ground atoms and subsumption axioms). Since these problems can all be reduced to each other [1], we only need to consider the entailment problem.

Theorem 3 (WSML-DL correspondence). *Given a concrete domain scheme $\mathfrak{S}$, if Φ is a WSML-DL theory and ϕ is a WSML-DL axiom, then there are a corresponding $\mathcal{SHIQ}(\mathbf{D})$ theory Φ' and $\mathcal{SHIQ}(\mathbf{D})$ axiom ϕ' (and vice versa) such that $\Phi' \models \phi'$ iff $tr(\phi)$ is a consequence of $tr_{DL}(\Phi)$.*

Proof (Sketch). By definition of WSML-DL we have that for each $\mathcal{SHIQ}(\mathbf{D})$ theory Ψ there is an equivalent WSML-DL theory Φ.

Let Φ be a WSML-DL theory and ϕ be a WSML-DL axiom, and let ϕ' be the (FOL equivalent of a) $\mathcal{SHIQ}(\mathbf{D})$ axiom obtained from ϕ by replacing each molecule of the form $t : f$ with an atom of the form $f(t)$, each molecule of the form $t_1[r \text{ hv } t_2]$ with an atom of the form $r(t_1, t_2)$, each formula of the form $t_1 :: t_2$ with a formula of the form $\forall x(t_1(x) \supset t_2(x))$, each formula of the form $t_1[t_2 \text{ it } t_3]$ with a formula of the form $\forall x, y(t_1(x) \wedge t_2(x, y) \supset t_3(y))$, and let Φ' be obtained from Φ in the same way, discarding the formulas (3,4,5). It is easy to verify that Φ' and ϕ' are FOL equivalents of a $\mathcal{SHIQ}(\mathbf{D})$ theory and axiom. Using Proposition 1 it is can be verified that $tr_{DL}(\Phi) \models_f tr(\phi)$ iff $\Phi' \models \phi'$ (under standard FOL semantics). The theorem then follows immediately from Theorem 2.   □

The following Theorem follows straightforwardly from the proof of Theorem 3 and the definition of WSML-Core.

Theorem 4 (WSML-Core correspondence). *Given a concrete domain scheme $\mathfrak{S}$, if Φ is a WSML-Core theory and ϕ is a $::-$ and it-free WSML-Core axiom, then there are a corresponding $\mathcal{DHL}(\mathbf{D})$ theory Φ' and $\mathcal{DHL}(\mathbf{D})$ axiom ϕ' (and vice versa) such that $\Phi' \models \phi'$ iff $tr(\phi)$ is a consequence of $tr_{Core}(\Phi)$.*

WSML-Rule and -Flight. The usual reasoning task for the Well-Founded Semantics is ground entailment, i.e. inclusion in the well-founded model. Additionally, as WSML-Flight and WSML-Rule have integrity constraints, consistency checking is also an important reasoning task.

Reasoning in the Well-Founded Semantics can be seen as an approximation to reasoning in the Stable Model Semantics. In fact, given a logic program P, if a ground atom α is true in the well-founded model of P, then α is included in every stable model of P, and thus is entailed under cautious inferencing. In the remainder we consider the Stable Model Semantics because of its close relation to autoepistemic logic.

In the following theorem we establish a correspondence between the stable expansions of a WSML-Rule theory and the stable models of the corresponding logic program. Correspondence with respect to all relevant reasoning tasks follows immediately. For example, cautious reasoning corresponds to autoepistemic consequence, and consistency checking corresponds to existence of a consistent stable expansion. The theorem follows straightforwardly from Proposition 4.

Theorem 5 (WSML-Rule and WSML-Flight correspondence). *Given a concrete domain scheme* $\mathfrak{S}$, *if* Φ *is a WSML-Rule theory, then there is a corresponding normal F-Logic Program* P *(and vice versa) such that a Herbrand interpretation* M *of* P *is a stable model of* P *iff there is a consistent stable expansion* T *of* $tr_{Rule}(\Phi)$ *such that* M *coincides with the set of objective ground atoms and molecules in* T.

If, additionally, Φ *is a WSML-Flight theory, then* P *has at most one stable model, and* Φ *is consistent iff* P *has exactly one model.*

8 Conclusions

In this paper we have presented a novel semantic framework for WSML based on FF-AEL, which is first-order autoepistemic logic [14,3] extended with Frames [13] and concrete domains [2]. Using this framework we have defined a semantics for WSML-Full, and have proposed two paradigms for language layering in WSML. *Strict* language layering requires additional restrictions on the syntax of the WSML variants, but gives more guarantees on the preservation of consequences than *loose* language layering. The WSML group is considering adopting loose language layering for future versions of the language; the main motivation is that it is considered unintuitive to disallow certain inferences (i.e. those involving it- and ::-molecules).

The approach for defining concrete domains in FF-AEL is very general, and might be applied in the area of Logic Programming, to extend current approaches to built-ins such as the one in Datalog [19], and might be used to extend the support for concrete domains in WSML-DL towards customized data types [17].

Two alternative embeddings for logic programs in FO-AEL have been considered in [3], besides the one we used in this paper (τ_{HP}). The distinguishing feature between the embedding we have considered in this paper, and these two alternative embeddings, is that, using the embedding τ_{HP}, positive rules are translated to Horn formulas, which means that there is a very tight integration between the axioms originating from a DL knowledge base and the rules originating from the logic program, corresponding to our intuition behind WSML-Full as a unifying integrating language.

An alternative formalism which has been used for combining rules and ontologies in a unifying semantics is MKNF [15]. This approach is very similar to ours (however, frames are not considered in MKNF), although the precise relationship between FF-AEL and MKNF remains to be investigated. The embedding of logic programs used in [15] is quite different from the embedding τ_{HP} which we considered in this paper, but it is very close in spirit to the embedding τ_{EH}, which is one of the alternative embeddings considered in [3]. Investigating the relationship between FF-AEL and MKNF, as well as other formalisms which combine Description Logics and Logic Programming (e.g. [7,18,11]) is future work. Since positive rules are interpreted as Horn formulas, we conjecture that our semantics corresponds to that of SWRL [11], provided only positive programs are considered, and certain restrictions apply to the allowed concrete domain schemes.

Acknowledgements

We would like to thank the members of the WSML working group, especially Axel Polleres, for valuable discussions about WSML language layering, and we would like to thank two anonymous reviewers for valuable comments on an earlier version of this paper.

References

1. Baader, F., Calvanese, D., McGuinness, D.L., Nardi, D., Patel-Schneider, P.F.: The Description Logic Handbook. Cambridge Univ. Press, Cambridge (2003)
2. Baader, F., Hanschke, P.: A scheme for integrating concrete domains into concept languages. In: IJCAI (1991)
3. de Bruijn, J., Eiter, T., Polleres, A., Tompits, H.: Embedding non-ground logic programs into autoepistemic logic for knowledge-base combination. In: IJCAI (2007)
4. de Bruijn, J., Heymans, S.: Translating ontologies from predicate-based to frame-based languages. In: RuleML (2006)
5. de Bruijn, J., Heymans, S.: WSML ontology semantics. WSML Final Draft d28.3 (2007)
6. de Bruijn, J. et al.: The web service modeling language WSML. WSML Final Draft D16.1v0.21 (2005)
7. Eiter, T., Lukasiewicz, T., Schindlauer, R., Tompits, H.: Combining answer set programming with description logics for the semantic web. In: KR2004 (2004)
8. van Gelder, A., Ross, K., Schlipf, J.S.: The well-founded semantics for general logic programs. JACM 38(3), 620–650 (1991)
9. Gelfond, M., Lifschitz, V.: Classical negation in logic programs and disjunctive databases. New Generation Computing 9(3/4), 365–386 (1991)
10. Grosof, B.N., Horrocks, I., Volz, R., Decker, S.: Description logic programs: Combining logic programs with description logic. In: WWW (2003)
11. Horrocks, I., Patel-Schneider, P.F., Bechhofer, S.: Tsarkov. OWL rules: A proposal and prototype implementation. J. Web Sem. 3(1), 23–40 (2005)
12. Horrocks, I., Patel-Schneider, P.F., van Harmelen, F.: From SHIQ and RDF to OWL: The making of a web ontology language. J. Web Sem. 1(1), 7–26 (2003)
13. Kifer, M., Lausen, G., Wu, J.: Logical foundations of object-oriented and frame-based languages. JACM 42(4), 741–843 (1995)
14. Konolige, K.: Quantification in autoepistemic logic. Fundamenta Informaticae 15(3–4), 275–300 (1991)
15. Motik, B., Rosati, R.: A faithful integration of description logics with logic programming. In: IJCAI (2007)
16. Niemelä, I.: On the decidability and complexity of autoepistemic reasoning. Fundamenta Informaticae 17(1,2), 117–155 (1992)
17. Pan, J.Z., Horrocks, I.: OWL-Eu: Adding customised datatypes into OWL. J. Web Sem. 4(1), 29–39 (2006)
18. Rosati, R.: DL+log : Tight integration of description logics and disjunctive datalog. In: KR2006 (2006)
19. Ullman, J.D.: Principles of Database and Knowledge-Base Systems, Vol. I. Computer Science Press (1988)

Merging Model Driven Architecture and Semantic Web for Business Rules Generation

Mouhamed Diouf, Sofian Maabout, and Kaninda Musumbu

Université de Bordeaux I, LaBRI (UMR 5800 du CNRS), Domaine Universitaire 351, cours de la Libration 33405 Talence Cedex, France
{diouf,maabout,musumbu}@labri.fr

Abstract. Business rules are statements that express (certain parts of) a business policy, defining terms and defining or constraining the operation of an entreprise, in a declarative manner. The business rule approach is more and more used due to the fact that in such systems, business experts can maintain the complex behavior of their application in a "zero development" environment. There exist more and more business rule management systems (BRMS) and rule engines, adding new needs in the business rules community. Currently the main requirement in this domain is having a standard language for representing business rules, facilitating their integration and share. Works for solving this lack are in progress at e.g OMG and W3C.

The aim of this paper is to propose a way to automatically generate a part of the business rules by combining concepts coming from Model Driven Architecture and Semantic Web using the Ontology Definition Metamodel.

Keywords: Artificial Intelligence, Business rules, knowledge based systems, Model Driven Architecture, knowledge representation, reasoning, ontology, Semantic Web.

1 Introduction

Business rules are statements that express (certain parts of) a business policy, defining terms and defining or constraining the operations of an entreprise, in a declarative manner [1,2,3,4]. The business rule approach is more and more used due to the fact that in such systems, business experts can maintain the complex behavior of their applications in a "zero development" environment. There exist more and more business rule management systems (BRMS) and rule engines, adding new needs in the business rules community. Currently the main need in this domain is having a standard language for representing business rules, facilitating their integration and share. Works for solving this lack is in progress at OMG and W3C [5,6,7,8,9] as well as other initiatives [10,11].

In another side, an enough heavy step during business rules bases systems implementation is the step of elicitation of rules from the business. Entreprises, generally, have (legacy) models in a UML or Entity Relationship like model. A

M. Marchiori, J.Z. Pan, and C. de Sainte Marie (Eds.): RR 2007, LNCS 4524, pp. 118–132, 2007.

question which results from this is, when using models, is it possible to automatically generate a part of business rules? For doing so by machines, they need to understand formally (semantics) terms and concepts they are manipulating.

We are working on a system of E-Government web application's generator from specifications. The system offers to business experts a way for specifying a part of the web application's behavior using business rules in a natural language editor. When we joined this project the first need was to solve the problem of none flexibility of the business rule's approach due to the lack of a standard recognized formalism. So, our firsts contribution was to create a rule's formalism independently of any rules engine (JRules [12], Drools [13], Jess [14], etc.). The principle was to save rules in our formalism (named ERML) and to generate the rulesets in the target rule engine at generation's step. Doing this offers to our application the possibility of changing rule engine target in a flexible way.

In Model Driven Architecture (MDA) [15] every concept is expressed by a model, but it does not say anything about semantics [16]. In another side, researches in Semantic Web, especially the use of ontologies, give many possibilities for adding semantics to semi-structured data, making automatic reasoning possible.

In this paper, we focus in "how can business rules be automatically generated from conceptual models semantically enriched? And what is the interest in doing so?"

This paper will first discuss Model Driven Architecture and semantics. We will present potential solutions for enriching MDA models with semantics. We will also discuss the possibilities and the benefits provided by mixing models and web reasoning. At last we will present an implementation of our previous works on business rules formalism and also our approach presented in this paper.

2   Model Driven Architecture

The Model-Driven Architecture starts with the well-known and long established idea of separating the specification of the operation of systems from the details of the way that these ones use the capabilities of their platform [15]. Figure 3 gives a general view of the MDA approach. We can see that a construction of a new Information System begins with the development of one or more requirement models called Computation Independent Model (CIM). Then we may develop models independent from any platform called Platform Independent Model (PIM). In theory, the latter models must be partially generated from the former. Platform independent models must be permanent, i.e. they do not contain any information about execution platform (is it a J2EE or .NET etc. application).

For constructing the concrete application, we must have Platform Specific Models (PSM). These models are obtained by transforming PIM and adding technical informations relative to platforms. PSM are not permanent models. All these models are for facilitating code generation. The MDA approach is widely used and advanced generators do exist.

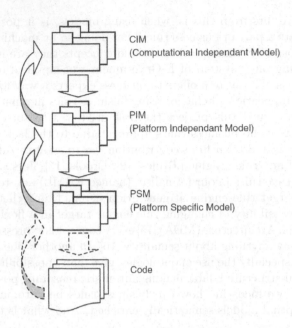

Fig. 1. Global view of the Model Driven Architecture approach

2.1 MDA Models and Semantics

MDA principals are very interesting and allow economizing time during application life cycle by code and model generation. However, MDA specification does not tell anything about semantics on models. MDA is only interested by content and not context. So adding semantics will offer a more interesting way for automatic generation.

Why should MDA take care about semantics: Making transformations between CIM and PIM, between PIM and PSM, and between PSM and code are done by specifying transformation rules. Nowadays these rules are handwritten and machines cannot generate them because there is no notion of semantics between the entities that are concerned by transformations.

Business rules are about meanings and act on models. Generating all business rules is impossible but it would be possible to generate a large part of them. For example for the model in Figure 2, we should want to generate business rules like:

1. Every *Human* must have a father and a mother.
2. IF a *Human* is the mother of a *Human* then this *Human* is a *Woman*.
3. IF a *Human* is the father of a *Human* then this *Human* is a *Man*.

For doing this automatically, it is clear that adding semantics in models is needed.

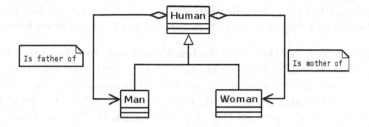

Fig. 2. A little human model

Potential solutions for adding semantics to models: In MDA, an instance of MOF (Meta Object Facilities) [17] is used for representing models but our works are only concerned by UML models. For adding semantics to UML models we can use:

1. *UML profile:* UML can be used for modeling many domains. The problem with this is that UML models are so generic that it is impossible to know either it is an object application, a metamodel, a model, a database structure or anything else just by looking at it [16]. For adding precision, the OMG has standardized the concept of UML profile [18]. A UML profile is a set of technics and mechanisms allowing to adapt UML to a particular and specific domain. UML profile can be used in any UML models and does not modify the structure of the metamodel. UML profiles are stereotypes or labels which can be pasted on models. After having pasted labels on models, we can make inference using then. As we can see, doing this can solve our problem of semantics lack on models in a low level, but this is not exploitable by machines because there is no notion of logic and taxonomy and semantics is not formally defined.

2. *Object Constraint Language:* In UML it was not possible to define the body of an operation (or a method) so the OCL [19] was standardized by OMG for this purpose. OCL allows expressing many kinds of constraints on UML models. For example, we can express constraints like: "before renting a car to a person one must be sure that this person is ok". OCL seems to be a good solution for our problem but it is not the case. Indeed, the first problem with OCL is that it does not offer automatic inference for machines and the second is that it does not support side effect operations. However OCL 2.0 does permit reference to operations that change the state of the system in a constraint expression, but the semantics of such a reference is that the operation will have been invoked when the truth of the constraint is tested. This semantics, which is permitted only in post-conditions, does not satisfy the requirements of the action clause of production rules, which cannot be used as postconditions of operations.

3. *Action Semantics:* Remember that the main constraint with OCL was that it only supports no side effects operations. To solve this constraint, the OMG standardized Action Semantics [20]. Now we have a formalism which is able to express any kind of operations and constraints but it is not enough. Indeed, this

formalism is too complicated to be used [16], was not created while thinking to machine comprehension and self-use, and do not have a textual formalism.

As we can see, none of the UML "technics" proposed so far is suitable for our purpose, which we recall, consists in exploiting semantics by machines.

In another side a new domain of computer science is growing more and more: Semantic Web. The aim of the Semantic Web is to make the web comprehensible by both humans and machines [21]. A part of Semantic Web is about ontology and reasoning. Modeling concepts defined by ontologies can be used to model the concepts in a domain, the relationships between them, and the properties that can be used to describe instances of those concepts [22]. In addition, the Web Ontology Language (OWL)[24] supports the inclusion of certain types of constraint in ontologies, allowing new information to be deduced when combining instance data with these description logics [22]. At this point our dilemma was how can we use MDA models and Semantic Web? Ontology Definition Metamodel (ODM) was the response to our need.

2.2   The Ontology Definition Metamodel

The MDA and its four-layer architecture provides a solid basis for defining the metamodels of any modeling language, and thus a language for modeling ontologies based on the MOF [23]. ODM is a proposal for an OMG's RFP (Request For Proposal) [24] resulting from an extensive previous research in the fields of the MDA and ontologies [25,26,27,28,29,30,31]. The main goal of ODM is to bridge the gap between traditional software tools for modeling (like UML) and artificial intelligence technics (Description Logics) for making ontologies. The principle of ODM is to merge two big domains of research which are Model Driven Architecture and Semantic Web. ODM is still in standardization process at the OMG [32] when this paper was being written. Basically the ODM allows

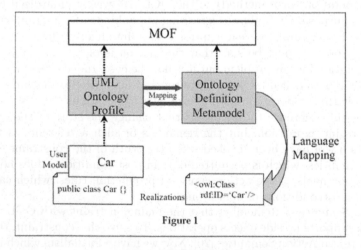

Fig. 3. ODM principle

making ontologies using UML (by using an UML profile with existing tools like Rational Rose or Poseidon) and transforming it to OWL/RDF, Topic Map or Common Logic (Figure 3).

In next sections, we will see how ontology reasoning can be used to solve the lack of semantics in models.

3   Ontology Reasoning

Ontology is an area of great importance for the semantic web. An ontology establishes the things that a system can talk about and makes reasoning on [21]. Describing concepts and relationships between them formally, offers to machines the ability of making some varieties of logic, formally or not. Ontology supplies the concepts and terms; logic provides ways to make statements that define and use them, and to reason about collections of statements that use the concepts and terms. In the semantic web, logic plays many different roles:

1. Firing rules: having a set of facts, take a decision.
2. Making inference on facts: for example if we know that Adam's wife is Eve, we can infer that Eve is a woman.
3. Explaining why a particular decision has been reached.
4. Detecting contradictory statements and claims.

OWL exploits results of more than 15 years of Description Logics (DL) research [33,8]. Indeed, for OWL a semantics was defined such that very large fragments of the language can be directly expressed using so called Description Logics [34]. Description Logics is a family of logic based Knowledge Representation formalisms descendants of semantic networks and [35]. It describes domains in terms of concepts (classes), roles (properties, relationships) and individuals. In description logics terminology, a tuple of a T-box and an A-box is referred to as a knowledge base. An individual is a specific named object. With some restrictions, one can state that the logical basis of OWL can be characterized with the description logics $SHIQ(D_n)^-$ [36]. This means, with some restrictions, OWL documents can be automatically translated to $SHIQ(D_n)^-$ T-boxes. The RDF-Part of OWL documents can be translated to $SHIQ(D_n)^-$ A-boxes [37].

The logic $SHIQ(D_n)^-$ is interesting for practical applications because highly optimized inference systems are available (e.g., Racer). In such systems, the following reasoning can be made with T-box :

1. Concept consistency. Is the set of objects described by a concept empty?
2. Concept subsumption: Is there a subset relationship between the set of objects described by two concepts?
3. Find all incoherences between the concepts mentioned in a T-box. Inconsistent concepts might be the result of modeling errors.
4. Determine the parents and children of a concept: The parents of a concept are the most specific concept names mentioned in a T-box which subsume the concept. The children of a concept are the most general concept names mentioned in a T-box that the concept subsumes.

With A-box we can answer the following questions :

1. Check the consistency of an A-box: Are the restrictions given in an A-box w.r.t. a T-box too strong, i.e. do they contradict each other? Other queries are only possible w.r.t. consistent A-boxes.
2. Instance testing: Is an individual instance of a concept? The individual is then called an instance of the query concept.
3. Instance retrieval: Find all individuals from an A-box such that the objects they stand for can be proven to be members of a set of objects described by a certain query concept.
4. Computation of the direct types of an individual: Find the most specific concept names from a T-box of which a given individual is an instance.
5. Computation of the roles which make reference to an individual.

Given the background of Description Logic, these inference services can be used to solve actual problems with OWL knowledge bases.

4   Adding Semantics to Models for Automatic Business Rules Generation

MDA technologies and Semantic web are complementary; the former is concerned about automating the physical management and interchange of metadata, while the latter is focused on the semantics embodied in the content of the metadata as well as on automated reasoning over that content [38]. The Semantic Web is the new-generation Web that tries to represent information such that it can be used by machines not just for display purposes, but also for automation, integration, and reuse across applications [39]. Model Driven Development (MDD) is being developed in parallel with the Semantic Web [40]. Emerging applications in finance, healthcare, security, communications, business intelligence, and many other vertical markets are content and context sensitive (semantics), and require entreprise scalability and performance [38]. Merging Semantic Web and MDA technologies can fill this lack. Merging these two domains will be beneficial to both:

1. MDA is only interested by content and not by context (semantics), semantic web will resolve this important problem.
2. For semantic web: an interesting thing is that so mature UML tools could be used for making ontologies rather than using so theoretical languages from Artificial Intelligence domain. In companies software engineers usually are doing models with UML, so it will be a good thing for allowing them using their preferred UML tools for making Ontology. Doing so will facilitate the use of ontologies.

Merging MDA and Semantic Web technologies allows more automatic processing like generation of constraints and business rules from models. To illustrate this let us consider the model in Figure 2 to which we add the OWL ontology in Figure 4. We must note that we take this example very simple for easy explanation and rapid comprehension but more complicated rules are generated. In this example

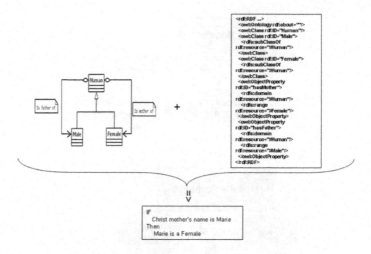

Fig. 4. A little ontology for a little model

of ontology, we declare that a human must have a mother that must be a human too. Therefore, with qualified "reasoners" and mechanism we can generate that: IF a *Human* is the mother of a *Human* then that *Human* is a *Woman*.

Therefore, we can infer that *"IF Christ mother's name is Marie THEN Marie is a Woman"*.

4.1   Our Approach for Business Rules Automatic Generation

Our principle is to use the advanced researches in Semantic Web, to combine it with Model Driven Architecture in order to make automatic business rules generation.

For generating business rules automatically, we will use principally the semantics in OWL format. In OWL reasoning, we can make automatic reasoning both with structures (TBox) and assertions on individuals and properties (ABox) [41]. In our case for example, if we have:

$$Predicate : Domain1 \longmapsto Domain2$$

This declaration means that we have a property *Predicate* going from the domain *Domain1* to the range *Domain2*.

So we want to generate that:

> *IF*
> *Object1 Predicate Object2*
> *THEN*
> *Object1 is of type Domain1*
> *AND*
> *Object2 is of type Domain2*

Reasonings are done using both domain and range restrictions, individuals and also properties's characteristics (functional, transitivity, symmetric, inverse, etc.)

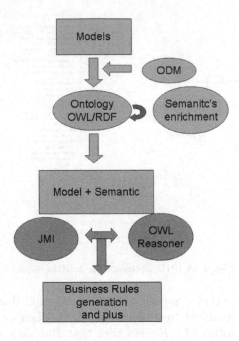

Fig. 5. Our approach

The Figure 5 describes our approach: using ODM, our model is generated in OWL/RDF model and this last one is enriched with semantics. With this semantically rich model two solutions are possible for generating rules: serialize the rich model in XMI [42] and use e.g JMI [2] for parsing it manually. Another solution is making inference directly with the OWL model using an OWL reasoner. We have adopted the last solution because there exist good OWL Reasoners and this solution uses less intermediary steps.

Recall that on gaol is not to generate all kinds of business rules. Indeed, this is infeasible. However, the part of them that able to generate will save time for business experts. Figure 6 summarizes our approach throughout MDA layers. As we can see the first step will be a generation according to the Computation Independent Model (CIM) in an OMG SBVR [5] like syntax (in strict natural language), the next step will be to generate executive rules according to the Platform Independent Model using our rule language [43] and models based on XMI like standard.At the PIM level either our business rules language ERML, the RIF W3C standard, the PRR OMG proposal or RuleML [6,7,11] may be used. At this step we use our "translators" for generating rules at the PSM level for a specific rule engine. If in the future, a standard business rules language is adopted, we'll either make a "translator" from our language towards the new standard or either store directly rules in the new formalism.

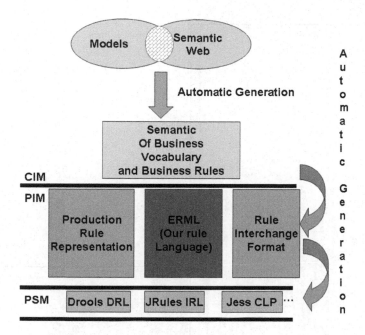

Fig. 6. Our approach throughout the MDA layers

4.2   Implementation

Our approach is being implemented in a system of E-Government web application's generator from specifications. Figure 7 describes its architecture. A studio is used for allowing business experts to specify the future web application. During specification, business experts can use an integrated rule editor in natural

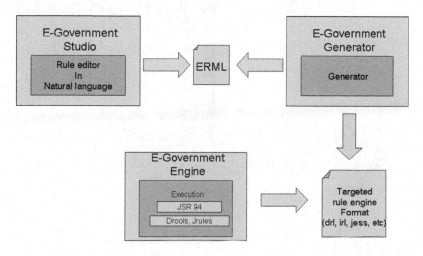

Fig. 7. Architecture of our E-Government web application

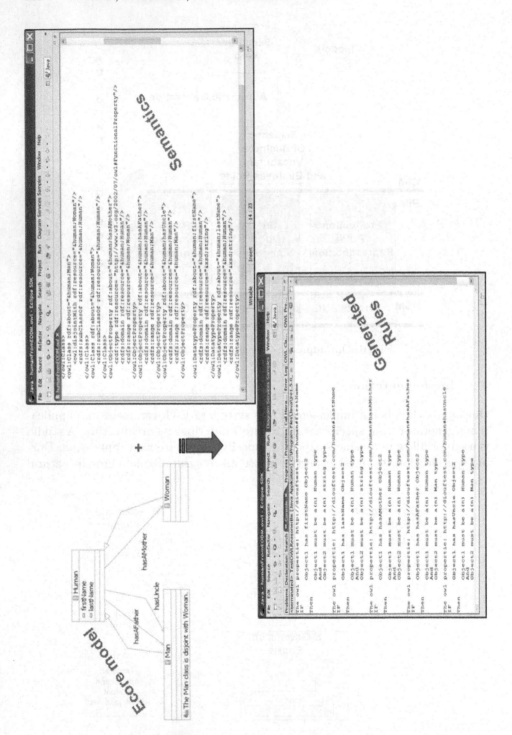

Fig. 8. Prototyping our approach

language for writing business rules. First, we have worked on creating a rule language independently of any rule engine after having studied the previous attempts of rule's standardization. From the beginning we have chosen to implement our own rule language together with translators from this language to some other ones. Few attempts for standardizing rule languages were proposed in the past without success. CommonRules [10] and RuleML [11] were the most promising.

It's important to note that our goal was not to add a new rule language to the standardization process but, as we work in an industrial project, it was simpler to develop our own rule language than using one which may be accepted or not in this standardization process which is only in its beginning phase [43]. ERML is also used in another project for automating ergonomic rules guideline inspection for web sites [44]. The process of standardizing business rules formalism is in serious progress with OMG and W3C workgroups [5,6,7,8,9].

After this step of getting business rule formalism the next step was to implement our approach on business rules automatic generation. Figure 8 shows a first prototype of our approach in an eclipse environment. Our model is an ECore model [45], our semantics is in OWL [46]. For us, the Ontology Definition Metamodel (ODM) arrives just in time, while we were thinking about how to use directly our semantics in OWL with MOF models (here ECore). We use an eclipse implementation of ODM (EODM) [47]. The process is the following: use EODM for transforming our ECore model to OWL model. This OWL model is a simple ontology (taxonomy) model. After this, using the UML profile of ODM, we enrich the OWL model with Abox and Tbox assertions, this is done using any UML tool (in our case MagicDraw) supporting profiles. The next step was to use an OWL reasoner like Racer or EODM reasoner for making inferences according to the domains, ranges and properties for generating business rules. At this state of the implementation, business rules are generated in a Semantics of Business Vocabulary and Business Rules (SBVR) [5] like format.

5   Conclusion

A business rules application is intentionally built to accommodate continuous changes in business rules. The ability to change them effectively, is fundamental for improving business adaptability. The platform on which the application runs should support such continuous changes. Offering to knowledgeable business people (experts) the possibilities to formulate, validate, and manage rules in a "zero-development" environment brings more value-added to this notion of "computer sciences in humanity's service". Allowing an automatic generation part of this business rules will be of valuable help. In this paper, we have seen that, by combining the two domains, Model Driven Architecture and Semantic Web, a solution is possible.

Right now we can only make generation according to the Computation Independent Model (CIM) in a OMG SBVR like syntax (in natural language). Due to the fact that the standardization of SBVR is recent, no implementation does exist. The best to our knowledge, the only free implementation we know is SBeaVER [48] which is not at an advanced level and, at this moment, can only express Business vocabulary and not Business Rules. The next step will be to generate executive rules according to the Platform Independent Model using our rule language [43] and models based on XMI like format. The last step will be to have an editor allowing to edit both models and semantics.

Making simple generic business rules generation possible from models facilitates the use of the business rules approach which allows easier systems maintenance. It's clear that generating all kinds of business rules is an utopia and we must delimit the degree of generation we want to obtain.

Adding semantics to conceptual models open exciting and interesting domains of applications like information merge.

Acknowledgment. We would like to thank the Genigraph company (Genitech Group) and especially the e-Citiz R&D team to support our research effort both financially and also by providing an industrial playground for our work.

References

1. von Halle, B.: Business Rules Applied. John Wiley & Sons, New York, USA (2002)
2. Java Community Process(JCP). Java Metadata Interface (JMI). Sun Java Specification Request (JSR 40) (2002)
3. Ross, R.G.: Principles of the Business Rule Approach. Addison-Wesley, Boston, USA (2003)
4. Taveter, K., Wagner, G.: Agent-Oriented Enterprise Modeling Based on Business Rules. In: Kunii, H.S., Jajodia, S., Sølvberg, A. (eds.) ER 2001. LNCS, vol. 2224, Springer, Heidelberg (2001)
5. The Object Management Group OMG. Semantics of Business Vocabulary and Business Rules (SBVR). OMG Specification (March 2006)
6. The Object Management Group OMG. Rule Interchange Format (RIF). W3C Workgroup (2005)
7. The Object Management Group OMG. Production Rule Representation (PRR) RFP. OMG Request For Proposal (br/2003-09-03) (2003)
8. Horrocks, I., Patel-Schneider, P.F., Boley, H., Tabet, S., Grosof, B., Dean, M.: SWRL: A Semantic Web Rule Language Combining OWL and RuleML. W3C Member Submission (May 2004)
9. W3C. Rule interchange format Workgroup, http://www.w3.org/2005/rules/ (2005)
10. IBM T.J. Watson Research Center. CommonRules project. Intelligent Agents project (1994-97) (1997)
11. RuleML. The RuleML initiative
12. Ilog Jrules. Ilog Jrules, http://www.ilog.com
13. Drools. Drools rule engine, http://www.drools.org
14. Friedman-Hill, E.: JESS in Action. Manning Publications Co, Greenwich, UK (2003)
15. The Object Management Group OMG. Model Driven Archtecture Guide Version 1.0.1. OMG Specification (June 2003)
16. Blanc, X.: MDA en action. Eyrolles, France (2005)

17. The Object Management Group OMG. Meta Objec tFacility (MOF) Specification Version 1.4. OMG Specification (formal/02-04-03) (April 2002)
18. The Object Management Group. Unified Modeling Language: Superstructure. OMG Specification (February 2004)
19. The Object Management Group OMG. UML 2.0 OCL Specification. OMG Specification (October 2003)
20. The Action Semantics Consortium. Action semantics for the uml. OMG Specification (ad/2001-03-01) (March 2001)
21. Passin, T.B.: Explorer's guide to the Semantic Web. Manning Publications Co, Greenwich, UK (2004)
22. Cranefield, S., Pan, J.: Bridging the Gap Between the Model-Driven Architecture and Ontology Engineering. In: Odell, J.J., Giorgini, P., Müller, J.P. (eds.) AOSE 2004. LNCS, vol. 3382, Springer, Heidelberg (2005)
23. Gaěvič, D., Djurié, D., Devedžić, V.: Model Driven Architecture and Ontology Development. Springer-Verlag, Berlin, DE (2006)
24. The Object Management Group OMG. Request For Proposal for Ontology Definition Metamodel. OMG Request For Proposal (March 2003)
25. Baclawski, K., Kokar, M.K., Kogut, P.A., Hart, L., Smith, J., Holmes III, W.S., Letkowski, I.,J., Aronson, M.L.: Extending UML to Support Ontology Engineering for the Semantic Web. In: Gogolla, M., Kobryn, C. (eds.) UML 2001 - The Unified Modeling Language. Modeling Languages, Concepts, and Tools. LNCS, vol. 2185, p. 342. Springer, Heidelberg (2001)
26. Baclawski, K., Kokar, M.M., Smith, J.E., Wallace, E., Letkowski, J., Koethe, M.R., Kogut, P.: UOL: Unified Ontology Language. Assorted paper discussed at the DC Ontology SIG Meeting (November 2002)
27. Brockmans, S., Volz, R., Eberhart, A., Löffler, P.: Visual Modeling of OWL DL Ontologies Using UML. In: International Semantic Web Conference, pp. 198–213 (2004)
28. Cranefield, S.: Networked Knowledge representation and exchange using UML and RDF. Journal of digital information, vol.1(8) (2001)
29. Djuric, D., Gasevic, D., Devedzic, V.: Ontology Modeling and MDA. Journal of Object Technology 4(1), 109–128 (2005)
30. Falkovych, K., Sabou, M., Stuckenschmidt, H.: UML for the Semantic Web: Transformation-Based Approaches. In: Knowledge Transformation for the Semantic Web, pp. 92–106 (2003)
31. Kendall, E.F., Dutra, M.E., McGuinness, D.L.: Towards A Commercial Ontology Development Environment. In: Proceedings of the 1st International Semantic Web Consference (Posters and Demos) (2002)
32. The Object Management Group OMG, IBM, and Sandpiper Software. Ontology Definition Metamodel. OMG Specification (June 2006)
33. Baader, F., Horrocks, I., Sattler, U.: Description logics as ontology languages for the semantic web (2003)
34. Baader, F., Calvanese, D., McGuinness, D.L., Nardi, D., Patel-Schneider, P.F. (eds.): The Description Logic Handbook: Theory, Implementation, and Applications. Cambridge University Press, Cambridge (2003)
35. Brachman, R.J., Schmolze, J.G.: An Overview of the KL-ONE Knowledge Representation System. Cognitive Science 9(2), 171–216 (1985)
36. Baader, F., Horrocks, I., Sattler, U.: Description Logics as Ontology Languages for the Semantic Web. In: Mechanizing Mathematical Reasoning, pp. 228–248 (2005)
37. Haarslev, V., Moller, R.: Racer: An owl reasoning agent for the semantic web (2003)

38. Knublauch, H.: Ontology-Driven Software Development in the Context of the Semantic Web: An Example Scenario with Protege/OWL. In: 1st International Workshop on the Model-Driven Semantic Web (MDSW2004) (2004)
39. Boley, H., Tabet, S., Wagner, G.: Design Rationale for RuleML: A Markup Language for Semantic Web Rules. In: SWWS, pp. 381–401 (2001)
40. Mellor, S.J., Clark, A.N., Futagami, T.: Guest Editors' Introduction: Model-Driven Development. IEEE Software 20(5), 14–18 (2003)
41. Volz, R.: Web Ontology Reasoning with Logic Databases. PhD thesis, Universität Karlsruhe (TH), Universität Karlsruhe (TH), Institut AIFB, D-76128 Karlsruhe (2004)
42. The Object Management Group OMG. MOF 2.0/XMI Mapping Specification, v2.1. OMG Specification (formal/05-09-01) (2005)
43. Diouf, M., Musumbu, K., Maabout, S.: Standard Business Rules Language: why and how? The 2006 International Conference on Artificial Intelligence (June 2006)
44. Diouf, M., Xiong, J., Farenc, C., Winckler, M.: AUTOMATING GUIDELINES INSPECTION From Web site Specification to Deployment. CADUI (2006)
45. Wu, C.G.: Modeling Rule-Based Systems with EMF. Eclipse Corner Article (2004)
46. W3C OWL's workgroup Smith, M. K., Welty, C., McGuinness, D. L.: OWL Web Ontology Language Reference. W3C Standard (February 2004)
47. Eclipse project. Eclipse Ontology Definition Metamodel project. Eclipse project (2006)
48. De Tommasi, M., Corallo, A.: SBEAVER: A Tool for Modeling Business Vocabularies and Business Rules. In: KES (3), pp. 1083–1091 (2006)

A Framework for Combining Rules and Geo-ontologies

Philip D. Smart[1], Alia I. Abdelmoty[1], Baher A. El-Geresy[2],
and Christopher B. Jones[1]

[1] Cardiff School of Computer Science,
Cardiff University, Wales, UK
[2] School of Computing,
University of Glamorgan, Wales, UK

Abstract. Geo-ontologies have a key role to play in the development of
the geospatial-semantic web, with regard to facilitating the search for geographical information and resources. They normally hold large amounts
of geographic information and undergo a continuous process of revision
and update. Hence, means of ensuring their integrity are crucial and
needed to allow them to serve their purpose. This paper proposes the
use of qualitative spatial reasoning as a tool to support the development
of a geo-ontology management system. A new framework for the representation of and reasoning over geo-ontologies is presented using the
web ontology language (OWL) and its associated reasoning tools. Spatial
reasoning and integrity rules are represented using a spatial rule engine
extension to the reasoning tools associated with OWL. The components
of the framework are described and the implementation of the spatial
reasoning engine is presented. This work is a step towards the realisation
of a complete geo-ontology management system for the semantic web.

1 Introduction

Retrieval of geographically-referenced information on the Internet is now a common activity. A large number of documents stored and retrieved on the web
include references to geographic information, typically by means of place names.
Also, the web is increasingly being seen as a medium for the storage and exchange of geographic data sets in the form of maps. The geospatial-semantic
web (GeoWeb) is being developed to address the need for access to current and
accurate geo-information [6]. The potential applications of the GeoWeb are numerous, ranging from specialised application domains for storing and analysing
geo-information to more common applications by casual users for querying and
visualising geo-data, e.g. finding locations of services, descriptions of routes, etc.

At the heart of the GeoWeb are geographic ontologies or geo-ontologies. These
are models of terminology and structure of geographic space as well as records
of entities in this space. An example of such an ontology has been proposed
recently in the SPIRIT project [14] and was shown to play a central role in the
development of a geographical search engine. Building geo-ontologies involves a

M. Marchiori, J.Z. Pan, and C. de Sainte Marie (Eds.): RR 2007, LNCS 4524, pp. 133–147, 2007.

continuous process of update to the originally modeled data to reflect change over time as well as to allow for ontology expansion by integrating new data sets, possibly from different sources. One of the main challenges in this process is finding means of ensuring the integrity of the geo-ontology and maintaining its consistency upon further evolution. Developing methods for the management of the spatial integrity of geo-ontologies will contribute towards the development of reliable geographical search engines and to the success of the GeoWeb in general.

In this paper we propose a new framework for the management of geo-ontologies for the purpose of geo-information retrieval. In particular, we build upon and utilise research results in the area of qualitative spatial reasoning (QSR). Composition tables for different types of qualitative spatial relations are used to derive general rules that govern the structure of the geographic entities and their interaction in space. A spatial integrity rule language has been developed, as an extension to OWL , for the expression of these rules. OWL and the popular semantic web reasoning engine Jena, are used for the representation and reasoning over the geo-ontology. This paper describes the new framework proposed and the implementation of the spatial reasoning engine. The presentation is limited only to the main distinguishing characteristics and extensions realised. The design of the language, its syntax and semantics are outside the scope of this paper.

Section 2 introduces the need of rules for supporting the representation and management of geo-ontologies and summarises the requirements of a spatial rule language for geo-ontologies. An overview of the new proposed framework proposed is given in section 3. Section 4 describes in some detail the implementation of the spatial rule engine, followed by section 5 which shows some examples to demonstrate the developed system. Conclusions and a view of ongoing research work is presented in section 6.

2   Rules for Geo-ontologies

Work is ongoing on the development of geo-ontologies to capture the conceptualisations of geographic domains and to facilitate the reuse and sharing of the geo-referenced information on the web. Several examples of geo-ontology developments have recently been proposed [9,5].

The following are some of the particular distinguishing characteristics of geo-ontologies of interest to this work.

1. Geo-ontologies are normally associated with large instance bases (or A-boxes). A geo-object can have one or multiple spatial representations to define its location in space. For example, a city may be associated with a polygon object made up of hundreds of points representing its boundary, a simplified bounding box approximating its shape, as well as a point representing its centre. Large instance bases and multiple spatial representation lead to large ontology files and associated overheads.

2. Much of the semantics in geo-ontologies are implicit and evident only at the instance level. For example, different types of spatial relationships exist between every object and all other objects in space; an object may be inside,

north-of, near to, larger than another object, etc. Some of those relationships may be captured on the concept level but most others are implicit, evident only by visual interpretation and geometric computation. Explicit representation of such relationships is not practically possible and means for their automatic extraction are needed.

3. Maintaining the logical as well as spatial integrity of geo-ontologies is crucial for maintaining their soundness and viability. Spatial integrity is different, and perhaps more complex, than logical integrity. Logical consistency does not automatically enforce spatial consistency. For example, a part-of semantic relationship between two geo-objects does not imply directly the correct relationships between the objects' spatial representations. The boundary of the child object might intersect with the parent or the area of the child might be larger than the parent, etc. If a third object exists that is located completely outside the parent object, then it is an error to insert a fact that this object intersects the child.

An understanding of the rules that govern space and spatial relationships is needed for the specification of spatial integrity rules to maintain the consistency of geo-ontologies. The problem is also evident when integrated utilisation of multiple geo-ontologies is considered, where processes such as comparison and merging assume the consistency of the candidate ontologies.

In [1], we reviewed the potential and limitations of OWL for representing geo-ontologies, the challenges indicated above can't be addressed directly using OWL. Recently, rule languages have been proposed that complement and enhance the expressiveness of standard ontology languages. Rule expression over geo-ontologies is needed for the representation of the following types of rules:

- Spatial reasoning rules for the deduction of implicit geo-semantics.
- Spatial integrity rules for representing different type of spatial integrity constraints to maintain the consistency of geo-ontologies.

In the rest of this section, spatial reasoning techniques are reviewed that allow for the identification and expression of both of the above rule types.

2.1 Qualitative Spatial Reasoning Tools

In this section, we demonstrate examples of the use and adaptation of some types of spatial reasoning techniques and the derivation of spatial rules, that are used as a basis for the spatial reasoning engine in the framework described later in the paper. A possible classification of the types of spatial rules is as follows.

- Rules representing constraints over object properties in space, in particular, spatial properties of dimension, shape and size. Examples of these types of rules include the fact that a polygon must have at least three different points and that a polygon must be closed, etc. These types of constraints are normally used in spatial databases and GIS.
- Rules for reasoning over spatial relationships between objects in space. For example, the fact that an object A is located inside another object B and

that B is inside object C, implies that object A is also inside C. It also implies that C is larger than A and B. This is an example of qualitative spatial reasoning (QSR). Here, we utilise the results of the large body of research in this field, where automated methods have been proposed for the derivation of spatial composition tables for different types of spatial objects and relationships. Table 1 shows part of a composition table for topological relations between two simple regions.

Table 1. Composition table for the set of base topological relations between simple regions

	$d(y,z)$	$m(y,z)$	$i(y,z)$	$ct(y,z)$	$o(y,z)$
$d(x,y)$	all	$d \vee m \vee$ $i \vee o$	$d \vee m \vee$ $i \vee o$	d	$d \vee m \vee$ $i \vee o$
$m(x,y)$	$d \vee m \vee$ $ct \vee o$	$d \vee m \vee$ $i \vee ct \vee o$	$i \vee o$ o	d	$d \vee m \vee$ $i \vee o$
$i(x,y)$	d	d	i	all	$d \vee m \vee$ $i \vee o$

Entries in the composition tables can be encoded into rules that can be used as deduction rules for the automatic derivation of implicit spatial relationships, as well as constraints for enforcing the integrity of the spatial data sets. These constraints are the building blocks of the proposed spatial reasoning engine as described later in the paper.

When reasoning over networks of spatial objects as with a typical geo-ontology, QSR becomes a more general constraint satisfaction problem. A path consistency algorithm was proposed earlier to address this problem [18,15]. The main function of this algorithm is denoted *REVISE* which deduces the consistency of region triples {A,B,C} by performing the following operation.[1]

$$A_r C = A_r C \cap (A_r B \otimes B_r C)$$

The equation validates whether the known or explicitly specified relationship(s) between A and C, contradicts the relationship(s) that may be derived between the same two objects, using the composition of their relationships with other objects in the scene (B in this case). The function was first used in the temporal domain by Allen [2] in his work on interval calculi. The implementation of the algorithm relies on the existence of pre-specified spatial composition tables. If the composition returns an empty set, the scene is inconsistent, otherwise other regions are selected and the process of spatial composition and intersection is repeated for the rest of the objects in the scene.

---

[1] where $\otimes$ represents the composition of spatial relationships.

2.2 Requirements for a Spatial Rule Language for Geo-ontologies

From the above section a list of requirements can be drawn for the design of a spatial rule language. Standard characteristics of a general rule language, designed to work with ontology languages, e.g. SWRL [13] or RuleML [22], are assumed. The following list are desirable additional characteristics for rule languages in the spatial domain. The specification of the language design and the language semantics is out of the scope of the current paper.

- Assumes a standard spatial data model (conforming with OGC or ISO spatial models). Predicates in the language will represent different types of geo-features, their associated geometric representations as well as different types of spatial operators and relationships.
- Can represent absolute spatial constraints on geographic features.
- Can represent relative spatial constraints between geographic features, including, topological, directional and proximity.
- Allows for external calls to geometric processing functions for the evaluation of pre-specified types of spatial relationships. As explained in the above section, only some spatial relationships can be stored a priori in the fact base. The application of spatial reasoning rules will occasionally require the evaluation of some of the implicit relationships using computational geometry algorithms supported by spatial database systems or GIS.
- Allows for the expression of rule exceptions. This characteristic is particularly useful for the expression of application specific rules, where in some cases exceptions to general spacial rules are required. See section 4.4 for an example.

The language should also have a formal logical underpinning, clear semantics and be serializable into a RuleML representation in order to interface with existing semantic web technologies.

3   Geo-ontology Management System Framework

The main objectives for the geo-ontology management system proposed here are to support the representation and storage of geo-ontologies and to allow for the expression and realisation of spatial integrity maintenance and deduction rules over the geo-ontologies.

Hence, the new framework proposed consists of three main component subsystems that together demonstrates an architecture for a system that allows for the spatial integrity maintenance management of geo-ontologies. These systems are: 1. the geo-ontology system and associated geo-location storage system, 2. the spatial rules management and the spatial inference engine, and 3. the error management system. The framework is shown in Figure 1. The system has been implemented using OWL , the Jena toolkit and Oracle Spatial.

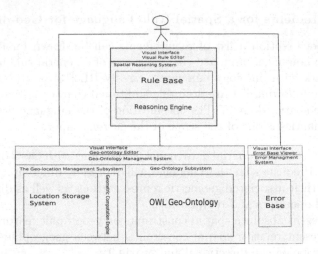

Fig. 1. A new framework for representing and maintaining geo-ontologies

3.1   The Geo-ontology Management System

Given the limitations of current web ontology languages for representing geographic features and their geometry, a dual model of representation will be used. The geographic concepts and features in the geo-ontology will be represented using OWL, while the spatial representations of the geo-features will be modeled using an external geometric processing or spatial database system. Such a dichotomy of representation does not affect the validity of the overall framework and is proposed as a practical solution to overcome the limitations of the current semantic web tools. The same spatial integrity maintenance framework will operate on geo-ontologies completely represented in OWL.

Geo-Ontology Subsystem. The geo-ontology's spatial data model conforms to the OGC abstract feature specification . The model also assumes a predefined set of qualitative spatial relationship properties including topological, directional as well as relative proximity and size relationships.

The Geo-location Management Subsystem. The types of geometric computation operations, such as distance or area, required to operate over locational information are not supported using OWL's schema or functions. Hence, the representation and management of the absolute locational information are delegated to an external geometric processor or a spatial database system, referred to as the Location Storage System (LSS) in Figure 1. Such systems have efficient spatial indexing techniques and optimised geometric processing capabilities.

A unique reference between features in the ontology and their corresponding locational information represented in the LSS is maintained. As URIs provide, what we will assume to be, a unique name to the features of the ontology, they will be mapped directly into the LSS as primary keys. Note that a single interface is used in the framework to both the OWL geo-ontology and the LSS that together form the complete geo-ontology used by the rest of the framework components.

3.2 The Error Management System

Errors mined from the geo-ontology by integrity rules are stored in a separate error ontology. Building an error ontology is interesting as it provides opportunities for reasoning over errors and would, for example, give insight to the types of integrity problems, their frequency and guide the error management process.

3.3 The Spatial Reasoning System

The spatial reasoning system (SRS) is at the heart of the framework. The system provides the functionality to represent spatial rules in their native format. the SRS is implemented in Java and sits alongside the Jena toolkit. Jena is an open source Java-based semantic web toolkit. Jena provides an API to access, manipulate and reason with RDF and OWL ontologies. Jena's rule reasoning engine uses a Rete-based forward production rule engine [24] , along with an XSB [23] based backward chaining logic programming engine.

Jena's reasoning subsystem is limited when it comes to the authoring of rule sets. The SRS implements a complete rule authoring system to construct, store, modify and visualise a spatial rule set. As the spatial rule set is syntactically and semantically different from a Jena rule set, SRS translates spatial rule sets into a format compliant with Jena for the purpose of execution. It also defines extensions to the rule engine in Jena to realise the full expressive extent of spatial reasoning rules. A more detailed overview of this system is presented below.

4   The Spatial Reasoning Engine

As mentioned, our proposed spatial rule language and reasoning engine have been implemented using the Jena toolkit. In what follows we describe the specific extensions to the toolkit needed to address the requirements of the rule language identified earlier. A more exhaustive treatment of the extensions described and their logical underpinnings are the subject of another report.

4.1 Interleaved Execution Extension

Typically, all rule body antecedents are matched from existing stored facts (that being facts derived by rules or explicitly represented). By interleaving forward and backward reasoning modes, facts can be derived, or proven, on the fly by a set of one or more backward rules. This is useful is minimising storage overheads. Consider for example the following rule:

$$[Region(?x) \wedge Region(?y) \wedge Region(?c) \wedge Inside(?x?c) \wedge Inside(?c?y) \rightarrow Inside(?x?y)]$$

The conclusion of `Inside(?x ?c)` would only be inferred if both the atoms `Inside(?x ?c)` and `Inside(?c ?y)` can be satisfied. These atoms are either satisfied by facts directly stored in the ontology (explicit), or inferred using

QSR rules (implicit),[2] or as a last resort satisfied by a rule that calls an external geo-computation engine.

For example, the following is a subset of QSR rules used to derive the inside relationship between two regions. The fifth rule is a call to external geo-computation (*exInside* predicate).

$Inside(?x\ ?y) \leftarrow Region(?x) \wedge Region(?y) \wedge Region(?c) \wedge Inside(?x\ ?c) \wedge Equal(?c\ ?y)$

$Inside(?x\ ?y) \leftarrow Region(?x) \wedge Region(?y) \wedge Region(?c) \wedge Inside(?x\ ?c) \wedge Inside(?c\ ?y)$

$Inside(?x\ ?y) \leftarrow Region(?x) \wedge Region(?y) \wedge Region(?c) \wedge Inside(?x\ ?c) \wedge CoveredBy(?c\ ?y)$

$Inside(?x\ ?y) \leftarrow Region(?x) \wedge Region(?y) \wedge Region(?c) \wedge CoveredBy(?x\ ?c) \wedge Inside(?c\ ?y)$

$Inside(?x\ ?y) \leftarrow Region(?x) \wedge Region(?y) \wedge Region(?c) \wedge exInside(?c\ ?y)$

Besides using builtins to evaluate spatial relationships, the engine supports a standardised set of predefined spatial builtins, such as for example, simple arithmetic and comparison operators that are evaluated using the external geometric processor. The restriction that variables must be bound applies to any external call, i.e. all variable must be bound and the call surmounts to a test of truth (returning either True or False). Interleaved logic programs have been implemented to varying degrees in Algernon, the M.4 system, MIKE, ECLIPSE and Harlequin.

Interleaved Implementation. Jena, more specifically Rete, does not inherently provide a means to call a backward rule during the course of antecedent pattern matching. To support this feature a backward call is added as a builtin (such a predicate is henceforth denoted a reserved spatial relation predicate). That is, the reserved spatial relationship predicates are not represented as triple patterns, but are added to the engine as builtins. The builtins are coded in Java and are registered with Jena's forward engine.

Once the builtin is called, the backward rule engine is initialised over the current set of intentional and extensional triples. For efficiency of retrieval using the external geometric processor, calls to backward rules must only contain ground variables. Thus backward rules only evaluate one relationship between two features at a time, and as such will either return true or false. For example, consider the following forward rule.

$$Region(?x) \wedge Region(?y) \wedge Region(?c) \wedge Inside(?x\ ?c) \rightarrow \cdots$$

`Inside(?A ?B)` represents a query to the backward QSR rule set. The nature of builtins in Jena, and the two class predicates, ensures that the variables ?A and ?B will be bound before the backward query is executed. Hence, `Inside(?A ?B)` will return either true or false, based on whether that relationship exists in the ontology, can be inferred, or whether it can be determined from the geometry.

Jena's Backward Engine: The reserved spatial relation predicates are executed in Jena's integrated XSB backward engine. XSB is based on a modified version of SLD resolution, namely SLG resolution. The following features of XSB are of particular interest to this work.

---

[2] Spatial reasoning rules are defined using composition tables as described earlier.

1. SLG tabling allows the transitive closure of a property to be computed without entering an infinite loop - as would be the case with SLD resolution. This is very useful for example when computing the containment hierarchy of geofeatures.
2. SLG's left to right top to bottom procedural reading (first in first out, also a feature of SLD resolution). The efficiency of the system is heavily affected by this. Rules with shallow inference chains can be evaluated before rules with deeper inference chains, lastly followed by rules with external calls to spatial relationship computation.

The order with which rules in the backward rule set are executed is explicitly defined by the rule execution metadata tag. In Jena, the order of rule evaluation is determined by the order in which the rules are encoded in the rule string sent to the backward reasoning engine. Therefore during conversion from the rule system to Jena, the rule string is constructed in the order that is represented by the backward meta tags.

4.2   Integrity Rules

The bodies of integrity and deduction rules are identical in both specification and functionality. An integrity rule differs from a deduction rule in the use of its head atom. That is, an integrity rule does not assert new information into the ontology,[3] instead it asserts errors into an error ontology (thus permitting the storage of errors). Positive and negative errors can be concluded, as explained below.

Default Integrity Rules. As indicated in the requirements earlier, it is desirable for the rule language to represent default integrity rules and their exceptions. This is a form of default reasoning [21,17,20]. That is, a default rule is assumed true until its contrary can be proved. For example:

$$body \rightarrow error(X)$$
$$body2 \rightarrow \neg error(X)$$

where X is a variable. The error of the first rule is assumed until there is enough evidence to support body2, and the error (where both errors have the same variable substitution for X) is refuted.

A large body of research in the area of prioritised default reasoning has studied this problem. Courteous logic [10] is a popular type of prioritised default reasoning which is expressive enough to capture our integrity requirements. Courteous logic provides us with a natural and intuitive way to provide rule priority to capture the requirement of rule defaults and rule exceptions.

---

[3] As is common in logic programming literature, a rule without head is referred to as an integrity rule.

Example: The following is an example of a spatial integrity constraint with both a default rule and an exception to that rule.

$$Road(?x) \land River(?y) \land Crosses(?x?y) \rightarrow$$
$$error(roadRiverCrossError\ ?xCrosses\ ?y\ doNotCross\ riverRCross) \qquad (1)$$
$$Road(A40) \land River(Taff) \land Crosses(A40\ Taff) \rightarrow$$
$$notError(roadRiverCrossError\ A40\ Crosses\ Taff$$
$$roadsRiversDoCross\ riverRCrossException) \qquad (2)$$

Rule (1) is the default rule and (2) its exception. Intuitively, The ground instantiation of the first rule which substitutes variables ?x and ?y for A40 and Taff respectively is overridden by the second rule.

An often used first step to the implementation of Courteous Logic in current reasoning engines is through the use of a courteous compiler. A courteous compiler compiles away the expressive Courteous logic extensions, leaving a semantically equivalent ordinary logic program [11], which can then be implemented in common logic program reasoning engines such as PROLOG. Here, we adapt such an implementation by placing some expressive restrictions on the courteous logic component, thus removing the need for a courteous compiler. Instead, we employ a simple algorithm denoted, the Prioritized Conflict Handling Engine ($PCHEng$), to perform a post processing cleanup. The following are the expressive restrictions to the full Generalised Courteous Logic as described in [12].

1. As with a basic courteous logic program we permit only the classical mutex.
2. Classical negation is restricted to integrity rule head atoms only, i.e. to infer *error* and its negation ¬*error*. Negation as failure is completely removed.

We have, however, in part extended the Courteous Logic specification. That is, we have supplemented the rule label with additional types of rule meta data or tags, which can be used to infer priorities amongst integrity rules.

With the above restrictions, a rule is definite. That is, it does not contain negation as failure and the limited form of classical negation can be dealt with by the $PCHEng$ post processing transform. Our simplified version of Courteous Logic will be henceforth denoted CLP^-. The advantages of using the CLP^- approach are two fold. Firstly, we need not deal with the rather complex semantics of a logic program that contains negation as failure (stable models [8] etc). Secondly, it allows the dynamic generation of rule priorities based on reasoning over rule meta tags and inferring *Overrides* predicates.

There are a number of implementations of default or defeasible reasoning, namely DR-Prolog [3], DR-Device [4], DELORES -a Defeasible Logic Reasoning System [16]. Both DR-Prolog and DR-Device handle non-monotonic rules over RDFS ontologies. DR-Prolog is implemented by transforming information into PROLOG, and DR-Device works by transforming information into JESS. All lack procedural attachment. Defeasible reasoning with procedural attachments is supported by the SweetRules project [19]. SweetRules supports Situated Courteous Logic, that is, Courteous Logic with cleanly formalised procedural attachments.

***CLP⁻* Implementation.** The implementation of CLP^- can be divided into two stages:

Stage 1: Jena's implementation of Rete [7] for forward inferencing does not support strong negation (¬, more akin to classical negation) - indeed Rete in general lacks support for classical negation. Therefore the first step involves the removal of all appearances of classical negation. This is an easy step and is a common way of adding a limited form of classical negation in ordinary or definite logic programs [11]. The step involves: for each error predicate *error*, each appearance of ¬*error* is replaced by an appearance of a new predicate notError; and a new explicit mutex between *error* and *notError* is introduced - or assumed (as we only deal with the classical mutex).

Stage 2: At the end of the inferencing stage, when Rete's match-resolve-act cycle has halted, a potentially inconsistent error base may result. That is, for all predicates in the error base, some may be negatively and positively represented. The error base is then fed into the Prioritised Conflict Handling Engine (*PCHEng*) along with the *Overrides* sub program, see figure 2. Stage 2 is performed by the following algorithm.

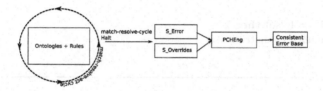

Fig. 2. *PCHEng* Information Flow

Algorithm: In overview, the *PCH* engine removes two conflicting error predicates by checking for a relevant *Overrides* predicate with which to resolve the conflict. As is the norm with a CLP, if an *Overrides* can't be found, then both positive and negative versions of the error are removed - treated skeptically.

4.3 Metadata

Rule metadata serves two purposes in our system. The first is as a form of reflection to derive *overrides* facts used by the CLP^- component. Secondly, to facilitate the visualisation and authoring of large spatial rule sets. Syntactically rule meta data is represented during the rules preamble. For example:

```
[<meta-data> : BODY -> HEAD]
```

The syntactical representation of rules separates the appearance of the rules meta data from the rules logic. However, in order to reason over rule meta data during the reasoning process, the tags must be translated to syntactically reserved, variable free predicates.

Algorithm 1. PCHEng

Let S = array of all error individuals in the error ontology
Let P = array of 2-tuple records representing conflicting errors (error, error) - conflict set
Let Ov = array of all overrides predicates
for (i =0; i < sizeof(S);i++) **do**
    for (int j=0; j < sizeof(S);j++) **do**
        if (i ≠ j) **then**
            if (s[i] complementof s[j]) **then**
                add s[i] and s[j] to P
            end if
        end if
    end for
end for
for (int i=0; i < sizeof(P); i++) **do**
    Let found = FALSE
    for (int j =0; j < sizeOf(Ov); j++) **do**
        if (Ov[j] represents priority over P[i]) **then**
            Remove defeated error triple
            Set found = true
        end if
    end for
    if (found == false) **then**
        remove both error triples
    end if
end for

Our rule language supports the following spatial meta tags.

```
forward_meta_data = "<" rule_Name "> "<" rule_Level "> "<" rule_Type ">
                "<" rule_Class "> "<" spatial_Rule_Group ">
backward_meta_data = forward_meta_data "<" backward_Rule_Group ">
                "<" backward_Rule_Order ">
```

Overrides predicate inference example: Meta level reasoning can be used to infer a general prioritisation between level 0 and level 1 rules, for example:

$$[ruleLevel(?A\ 0)\ AND\ ruleLevel(?B\ 1) \rightarrow overrides(?A\ ?B)]$$

As a result, all rules that have a rule level of 0 will override rules having a level of 1 - providing they have conflicting error predicates.

4.4   Example of Default Reasoning

In this example consider the domain specific knowledge that roads and rivers do not cross in the general case. There are, however, exceptions to this rule. A road may pass through a river where the river is shallow enough (a forge). Without modeling forges directly, integrity rules can be used to capture this situation using a form of default reasoning.

Consider for example, that roads A40, A50 and the rivers Taff and Tywn are instantiated into a geo-ontology, and that the spatial relationships {A40 crosses Taff} and {A50 crosses Tywn } are also added. The following rule is then added to the rule base as a default.

[< *label* > *riverRoadCross* < */label* >< *ruleLevel* > 0 < */ruleLevel* >< *ruleGroup* > *Topo* − *Semantic* < */ruleGroup* >< *ruleType* > 0 < */ruleType* >< *ruleClass* > 1 < */ruleClass* >: Road(?x) AND River(?y) AND Cross(?x ?y) → error(roadRiverCrossError ?x Crosses ?y roads_rivers_do_not_cross riverRoadCross)]

With only the default rule in the rule base, both the A40 and A50 are added to the error base as shown in figure 3. I.e. roads should not cross rivers.

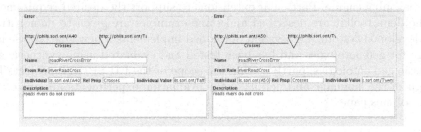

Fig. 3. Error Base Without Exception Rule(s)

A further rule is asserted into the knowledge base that contradicts the default rule by specifying the negation of the error that occurs when the individuals assigned to the variables ?x and ?y are A40 and Taff respectively.

[< *label* > *riverRoadCrossException* < */label* >< *ruleLevel* > 1 < */ruleLevel* >< *ruleGroup* > *Topo* − *Semantic* < */ruleGroup* >< *ruleType* > 0 < */ruleType* >< *ruleClass* > 0 < */ruleClass* >: Road(A40) AND River(Taff) AND Cross(A40 Taff) → notError(roadRiverCrossError http://phils.sorl.ont/A40 Crosses http://phils.sorl.ont/Taff roads_rivers_do_cross riverRoadCrossException)]

A rule is used to represent the fact that all level 1 rules override all level 0 rules. As a result, because the exception being at a lower level than the default, the error for that instance is eliminated.

[< *label* > *overrides* < */label* >:ruleLevel(?x 0) AND ruleLevel(?y 1) → overrides(?x ?y)]

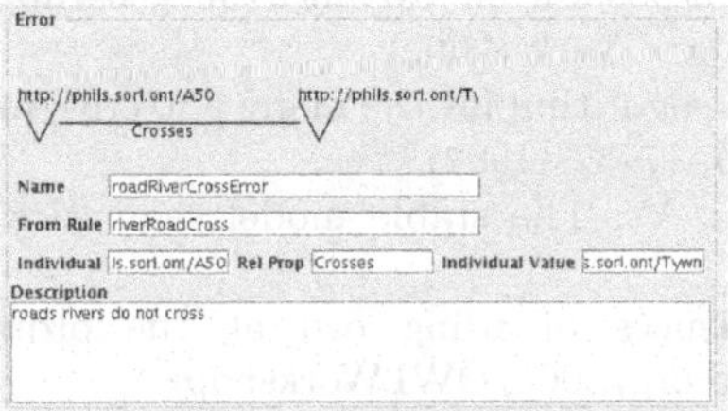

Fig. 4. Error Base After Exception Rule(s) Added

With both the rule exception and the overrides rule now added to the rule system, only the error between the A50 and Twyn is detected as shown in figure 4.

5 Conclusions

A new framework for the representation and management of geo-ontologies is proposed. Rules for geo-ontologies were shown to serve two primary purposes, namely, deduction of implicit spatial semantics and expressions of spatial integrity constraints. Requirements for a spatial rule language for geo-ontologies are identified and are used as a base for the design and development of a spatial reasoning engine. Particular extensions to support the desired requirements to the Jena toolkit are described and some examples are given to demonstrate the developed system. The system developed implements a new spatial rule language for geo-ontologies and has been tested and evaluated using synthetic and realistic geo-ontologies, partly within the scope of the EU SPIRIT project. The design of the language and details of the evaluation experiments are out of the scope of this paper.

References

1. Abdelmoty, A.I., Smart, P.D., Jones, C.B., Fu, G., Finch, D.A.: Critical evaluation of ontology languages for geographic information retrieval on the Internet. Journal of Visual Languages and Computing. pp. 331–358 (August 2005)
2. Allen, J.F.: Maintaining knowledge about temporal intervals. Tech. rep. University of Rochester, Department of Computer Science (1981)
3. Antoniou, G., Bikakis, A.: DR-prolog: A system for defeasible reasoning with rules and ontologies on the semantic web. IEEE Trans. Knowl. Data Eng. 19(2), 233–245 (2007)
4. Bassiliades, N., Antoniou, G., Vlahavas, I.P.: DR-DEVICE: A defeasible logic system for the semantic web. In: Ohlbach, H.J., Schaffert, S. (eds.) PPSWR 2004. LNCS, vol. 3208, Springer, Heidelberg (2004)
5. Bernard, L., Einspanier, U., Haubrock, S.: Ontology-based discovery and retrieval of geographic information in spatial data infrastructures. In: Geotechnologien Science Report No. 4 (2004). http://www.delphi-imm.de/meanings/index_eng.html
6. Egenhofer, M.J.: Toward the semantic geospatial web. In: Proceedings of the tenth ACM international symposium on Advances in geographic information systems, pp. 1–4. ACM Press, New York (2002)
7. Forgy, C.: Rete: A fast algorithm for the many patterns/many objects match problem. Artif. Intell 19(1), 17–37 (1982)
8. Gelfond, M., Lifschitz, V.: The stable model semantics for logic programming, pp.1070–1080
9. Goodwin, J.: Experiences of using owl at the ordnance survey. pp. 1–11 http://www.mindswap.org/2005/OWLWorkshop/
10. Grosof, B.N.: Prioritized conflict handling for logic programs. pp. 197–211
11. Grosof, B.N.: Compiling prioritized default rules into ordinary logic programs (June 23, 1999)

12. Grosof, B.N.: DIPLOMAT: Compiling prioritized default rules into ordinary logic programs, for E-commerce applications. In: AAAI/IAAI. pp. 912–913 (1999)
13. Horrocks, I., Patel-Schneider, P.F., Tabet, H.B.S., Grosof, B., Dean, M.: Swrl: A semantic web rule language combining owl and ruleml. Internet Report, http://www.w3.org/Submission/2004/SUBM-SWRL-20040521/ (May 2004)
14. Jones, C., Abdelmoty, A., Fu, G.: Maintaining ontologies for geographical information retrieval on the web (2003)
15. Mackworth, A.: Consistency in networks of constraints. Artificial Intelligence vol. 8 (1977)
16. Maher, M., Miller, T.: Delores a defeasible logic reasoning system. Internet, http://www.nothingisreal.com/dfki/delores/ (2007)
17. McCarthy, J.: Circumscription, a form of non-monotonic reasoning. Artificial Intelligence 13, 27–39 (1990)
18. Montanari, U.: Networks of constraints: Fundamental properties and application to picture processing. In: Information Science vol. 7 (1974)
19. Neogy, C. C., (UMBC), S. G., Grosof, B., Dean, M., Tabet, S.: Sweetrules. Internet, http://sweetrules.projects.semwebcentral.org/ (2006)
20. Nute, D.: General Defeasible Logic. Tech. Rep. forthcoming, University of Georgia (1989)
21. Reiter, R.: A logic for default reasoning. AI 13, 81–132 (1980)
22. RuleML. Ruleml web site. Internet, http://www.ruleml.org/ (2006)
23. Sagonas, K., Swift, T., Warren, D.S.: Xsb: An overview of its use and implementation. Tech. rep. (November 02, 1993)
24. Schneier, B.: The rete matching algorithm. AI Expert 7(12), 24–29 (1992)

Domain Ontology Learning and Consistency Checking Based on TSC Approach and Racer

Xi Bai[1,2], Jigui Sun[1,2], Zehai Li[1,2], and Xianrui Lu[3]

[1] College of Computer Science and Technology, Jilin University,
Changchun 130012, China
[2] Key Laboratory of Symbolic Computation and Knowledge Engineering of Ministry
of Education, Jilin University, Changchun 130012, China
[3] College of Mathematics, Jilin University, Changchun 130012, China
xibai@email.jlu.edu.cn, {jgsun,zhli,lvxr}@jlu.edu.cn

Abstract. Building domain ontology is time consuming and tedious since it is usually done by domain experts and knowledge engineers manually. This paper proposes a two-stage clustering approach for semi-automatically building ontologies from the Chinese-document corpus based on SOM neural network and agglomerative hierarchical clustering and automatically checking the ontology consistency. Chinese lexical analysis and XML Path Language(XPath) are used in the process of extracting resources from Web documents. In our experiment, this two-stage clustering approach is used for building an automobile ontology. Experimental results and the comparison with the more conventional ontology-generation method are presented and discussed, indicating the high performance of our approach. A Racer-based consistency-checking method of reasoning is presented in this paper. An ontology evolution method and performance evaluation are also given.

Keywords: Ontology learning, consistency checking, ontology reasoning, hierarchical clustering.

1 Introduction

How to build ontologies becomes one of the hottest problems for researchers in information community nowadays. Ontologies are usually built by knowledge engineers and domain experts manually. This is unsuitable for building large ontologies and sometimes inconsistencies are generated inevitably. With the emergence of the Semantic Web, designing automatic or semi-automatic approaches for constructing and maintaining domain ontologies becomes more and more important. However, there is no "correct" way or methodology for developing ontologies [1].

Some work has contributed to the ontology learning from tabular structures with the help of relational database [2]. However, besides structured content, there is a great deal of free content which contains ontologies. Moreover, to the best of our knowledge, much less work has further researched ontology learning from Chinese Web documents. As the author's known, no solutions exist, which

M. Marchiori, J.Z. Pan, and C. de Sainte Marie (Eds.): RR 2007, LNCS 4524, pp. 148–162, 2007.

learn ontologies from both structured content and free content. Learning ontologies from Chinese Web documents has not been further researched and it still face many difficulties nowadays.

In this paper, we propose a novel Two-Stage Clustering(TSC) approach for building ontologies based on Self-Organizing Maps (SOM) and agglomerative hierarchical clustering from Chinese Web Documents. The remainder of this paper is organized as follows. Section 2 describes the general framework for building domain ontologies by using our two-stage clustering approach. Meanwhile, basic concepts of SOM neural network and Hierarchical clustering are given respectively. Section 3 describes the mechanism of the two-stage clustering approach and gives a method of checking the ontology consistency. This section also gives the performance evaluation for our approach. Section 4 describes our method for ontology evolution. Section 5 gives an example of validating our approach in the automobile domain by building an automobile ontology. The performance comparing between TSC approach and the conventional ontology-generation method is also given in our experiment. Section 6 briefly describes the related work. Section 7 describes the conclusions and our future research directions.

2   Building Domain Ontologies Based on TSC

In this section, we present a general two-stage clustering framework based on SOM neural network and agglomerative hierarchical clustering to build domain ontologies. Figure 1 describes this TSC framework. Firstly, Web documents in some domain from which we want to extract ontologies are retrieved. Secondly, they are send to SOM neural network [3] and classified into several sorts. Then, for each sort, objects and properties in paragraphs are identified by lexical analysis and those in the structured content are extracted by using Extensible Markup

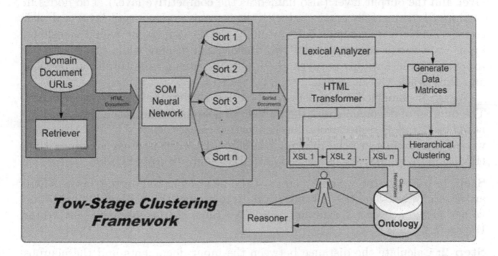

Fig. 1. TSC framework

Language Transformation(XSLT) [4]. Date matrices are built based on the associated properties of individuals and the Euclidean distances between each two individuals are also calculated. By using the above two-stage clustering, ontologies are described by trees which can reflect the relationships of classes and their subclasses(the subclass can represent concepts that are more specific than the superclass). Finally, ontologies are checked by a reasoner and modified manually if there are some inconsistencies.

2.1 Model Domain Documents

In order to build domain ontologies, we collect documents about this domain from Web first of all. Thereafter, these documents should be transformed into the formation suitable for SOM neural network. Boolean Model, Naive Bayes Model [6] and Vector Space Model(VSM) [7] are all widely used models for doing this transformation at present. Boolean Model is simple in structure but strict in its expression. VSM takes the appearance frequencies of words in documents as the elements of feature vectors. We use VSM to model the Web documents. In VSM, every document is denoted by a feature vector $(tf_{W_1}, tf_{W_2}, \cdots, tf_{W_N})$. Here, N denotes the number of words which appear in a document(stop words have been removed after word segment). tf_{W_i} denotes the frequency of the ith word. After modeling, we get a set of feature vectors which indicates the documents to be trained.

2.2 Train SOM Neural Network – The First-Stage Clustering

SOM neural network is more suitable for implementing the process of learning instances compared with other Artificial Neural Networks (ANN). It is proposed by Kononen in University of Helsinki in 1981. SOM is a kind of competitive neural network without supervision [3]. It is formed by two layers: the input layer and the output layer (also named as the competitive layer). The nodes in the input layer are fully connected with the neurons in the output layer and each connection has a weight vector. By training, SOM can map the high dimensional input data vector onto a usually two dimensional display while preserving the topological relationships between the input data items as faithfully as possible and thus utilize the clustering.

We use the modeled documents in subsection 2.1 to train SOM neural network. The number of documents and the number of neurons in the output layer are denoted by K and M respectively. The connection value is denoted by W_i. Moreover, we get the winning area by drawing a square area with the Best Matching Unit (BMU) in the center. We can use following five steps to train SOM:

Step 1: Initialize the weight vectors of the neurons in the output layer. There are several ways to do this initialization. Here, we use the method of generating values between 0 and 1 randomly and give them to the initial weight vector $W_i(i = 1, 2, ..., M)$.

Step 2: Calculate the distance between the input documents and the neurons in the output layer. We use *Euclidean distance* here and its formula is as follows:

$$d_{ki}(t) = \sqrt{\sum_{j=1}^{N}(C_{kj} - W_{ij}(t))^2} \qquad (i = 1, 2, ..., M; k = 1, 2, ..., K) \qquad (1)$$

$d_{ki}(t)$ denotes the Euclidean distance between the feature vector of the kth input document and the connection value of the ith neutron at the time t; C_{kj} denotes the value at the jth bit in the kth document's feature vector; $W_{ij}(t)$ denotes the value at the ith bit in the ith neuron's weight vector at time t.

Step 3: Find the BMU and adjust the weight vectors of neurons in the neighbors of BMU. We select the neuron with the shortest distance as the BMU (also named as winner). We can randomly select a BMU from the neurons when their distances are shortest and have the same value.

$$d_{ki}^{*}(t) = min(d_{ki}^{(t)}) \qquad (i = 1, 2, ..., M; k = 1, 2, ..., K) \qquad (2)$$

The $d_{ki}^{*}(t)$ denotes Euclidean distance between the BMU and the input document. The neighbors of BMU can be determined by using several methods. Here we determine it by drawing a square area with the BMU in the center. Then we adjust the weight vectors of neurons in neighboring area(each border will include 7 neurons) according to the following equation.

$$W_{ij}(t + 1) = W_i(t) + \eta(t)(C_{kj} - W_{ij}(t))$$
$$(i = 1, 2, ..., M; j = 1, 2, ..., N; k = 1, 2, ..., K) \qquad (3)$$

$\eta(t)$ denotes the learning rate at time t, which decreases as t increases, and $0 < \eta(t) < 1$.

Step 4: Update the learning rate $\eta(t)$ and re-scale the boundary of the winning area.

$$\eta(t) = \eta(0)(1 - \frac{t}{T}) \qquad (4)$$

$\eta(0)$ denotes the learning rate at the beginning. T denotes the number of times for learning. Suppose that the coordinates of the winner are (x_{win}, y_{win}). $R(t-1)$ denotes the radius of the winning area at the time $t - 1$:

$$R(t) = R(t - 1)\rho \qquad (0 < \rho < 1) \qquad (5)$$

Then the winning area is the square with the $(x_{win} - R(t), y_{win} - R(t))$ on the top left corner, and $(x_{win} + R(t), y_{win} + R(t))$ on the bottom right corner at the time t.

Step 5: Decide whether the training terminates or not. When all the training documents have been input and the algorithm satisfies $max(|W_{ij}(t + 1) - W_{ij}(t)|) < \varepsilon$, or it has finished the pre-appointed training times, the algorithm ends. Otherwise it goes to *step 2*.

By virtue of visualization method (U-matrix method or distance mapping method) we can get the clustering result. The method for visualization has been studied in our previous work [5] and will not described here for brevity. Then for each sort we calculate the summations of the frequencies of every word which appears in documents belonging to this sort. We arrange these words according to their frequencies in descending order and get a new feature vector of the sort.

As we know, some documents contain structured content (like tables). However, we cluster documents just according to the paragraphs outside the structured content here and leave the structured content to the second clustering stage.

2.3 Arrange Classes in Taxonomic Hierarchy – The Second-Stage Clustering

An ontology is a specification of a conceptualization, used to help programs and humans share knowledge [21]. According to this definition, we can use the tree structure to express an ontology. In this tree, the nodes denote concepts. Every concept has its properties. The edges denote IS-A relations, which are the relations between classes and subclasses. Each concept has a set of its individual. So every individual can be denoted by $\{\langle property1, value\rangle, \langle property2, value\rangle, ..., \langle property n, value\rangle\}$. Clustering is a kind of data mining technique and its objective is to classify a set of objects without supervision. That means there is no preappointed class before the classification. Since hierarchical clustering [8] is an early developed and widely used clustering method, in this paper, we use agglomerative hierarchical clustering and extract information from paragraphs and structured content in different ways in this subsection.

Extract Information From Paragraphs. Usually, the dimension of the feature vectors generated in subsection 2.2 is so large that it contains several words which do not actually reflect the document's sort. Therefore, for the paragraphs case, we employ a pruning strategy which can safely eliminate the words whose appearing frequencies are less than the average frequency of all words. Then we select the documents whose feature vectors contain not less than 80% of words in this sort's bag of words. These documents in themselves constitute the feature-document corpus which can actually represent the sort. Now we do lexical analysis by using ICTCLAS [9]. ICTCLAS is developed by Institute of Computing Technology at the Chinese Academy of Sciences and its frame is based on Hierarchical Hidden Markov Model(HHMM) [10].

In [1], Noy and McGuinness given ontology-building rules described as follows.

Rule 1. *There is no one correct way to model a domain and there are always viable alternatives. The best solution almost always depends on the application that you have in mind and the extensions that you anticipate.*

Rule 2. *Ontology development is necessarily an iterative process.*

Rule 3. *Concepts in the ontology should be close to objects (physical or logical) and relationships which are most likely to nouns (objects) or verbs (relationships) in sentences that describe your domain.*

Based on above rules, after lexical analysis, we can identify nouns and verbs and find the corresponding objects and properties. Then we identify the individuals and associate them with their properties by using the reference-resolution technique. Here, each individual has an ID number. Since the values of properties may be numerals or characters, we generate values according to two cases respectively. For the numerals case, we take them as the values of properties. As we all know, property has two kinds: Object property and Datatype property. The values of them are generated in different ways. For the characters case, if a property has a literal value and in some matrix there is one individual which matches this literal, we take the ID number of this individual as the value of the property instead of the literal. Otherwise, the programme generates a new individual and we take its ID number as the property's value. Note that different individuals have different ID numbers. Finally, we save individuals to XML files.

Extract Information From Structured Content. Besides paragraphs, there may be some structured content in documents. For this case, we use XPaths to extract resources. Since much of the HTML content on the Web is ill-formed, first of all, we pass the HTML documents through a transformer that can repair the broken syntax and generate well-formed HTML documents (also a kind of XML documents). Then, we write some XSLT files to do the extraction. Every XSLT file extracts some kind of information from certain structure. For instance, table XSLT file can extract all the records and attributes from table structure and produce a XML file to describe them. Finally, we can simply translate the XML files containing individuals into data matrices by using another XSLT file.

Cluster Individuals. Now we create classes for ontologies by using agglomerative hierarchical clustering method based on the aforementioned extracted individuals and their properties. Suppose that there are m individuals and each individual has n properties. We can get a $m \times n$ data matrix $M = \begin{pmatrix} x_{11} & x_{12} & \cdots & x_{1n} \\ x_{21} & x_{22} & \cdots & x_{2n} \\ \vdots & \vdots & & \vdots \\ x_{m1} & x_{m2} & \cdots & x_{mn} \end{pmatrix}$.

In this matrix, we can recognize each individual as a point in the space with n dimensions. So this matrix denotes m points in the space.

We use some distance to describe the degree of the individuals' similarities when we do the clustering analysis. There are several methods for defining this distance such as *Absolute distance, Euclidean distance, Minkowski distance* and *Chebyshev distance*. Whichever type the distance belongs to, it should satisfy following four conditions: **a.** $d_{ij} \geqslant 0$; **b.** $d_{ij} = 0$ $(i = j)$; **c.** $d_{ij} = d_{ji}$; **d.** $d_{ij} \leqslant d_{ik} + d_{ki}$. Here, $i = 1, 2, \cdots, m; j = 1, 2, \cdots, m; k = 1, 2, \cdots, m$. Since $d_{ij} \leqslant \max\{d_{ik}, d_{kj}\} \leqslant d_{ik} + d_{kj}$, sometimes condition **d** is reinforced as condition **e:** $d_{ij} \leqslant \max\{d_{ik}, d_{kj}\}$. The distance which satisfies all of **a, b, c** and **e** conditions is named as *Extreme distance*.

This paper uses *Euclidean distance* to describe the similarity of every two individuals. So the clustering algorithm is described as follows:

Step 1: Calculate the distances between every two individuals, marked as $d_{ij}(i = 1, 2, ..., m$ and $j = 1, 2, ..., m)$;

Step 2: Create n classes and make sure that every class contains only a single individual;

Step 3: Incorporate the two classes into one according to some strategy;

Step 4: Calculate the distances between this new class and other classes respectively. If the number of the classes is equal to one, the algorithm goes to *Step 5*; Otherwise, it goes to *Step 3*;

Step 5: Draw the hierarchical diagram of classes;

Step 6: Determine the number of classes.

In *Step 3*, "some strategy" means *single linkage, complete linkage, average linkage, centroid method* or *Ward's method*. Here, we use *Ward's method* proposed by Ward [11]. It was derived from the analysis of the Error Sum-of-Squares(ESS): If the classification is reasonable, the ESSs of the individuals in the same sort should be small and the ESSs of different sorts should be large. Suppose that m individuals are classified into l sorts $G_1, G_2, ..., G_l$ at present. The ESS of individuals in sort G_p is defined as follows:

$$ESS_p = \sum_{\alpha=1}^{N_p} (x_{p\alpha} - \overline{x}_p)'(x_{p\alpha} - \overline{x}_p) \tag{6}$$

Algorithm 1. Two-Stage Clustering

Input: A document corpus d used for training.
Output: The class hierarchies of all the sorts.

```
TSC1(Document[] d){
    TermVector[] tv = new TermVector[d.length()];
    for(i = 0;i < tv.length();i++)
        tv[i] = Spliter.split(d[i]);
    SOM som = new SOM();
    som.train(Normalizer.normalize(tv));
    som.distanceMapping();
}//split() method does word segment and word frequency statistics;
//normalize() method does feature vector generation.

extractResource(Sort[] s){
    for(int i = 0;i < s.length();i++){
        Extractor.prune(s[i].getDocument());
        Extractor.extractInfo(s[i]);
        Extractor.saveToXML();
    }
}//prune() method does pruning strategy; extractInfo() method does resource ex-
traction.
//Note that paragraphs and structured content have different extractInfo() methods.

TSC2(XMLFile[] f){
    HierarchicalClusterer[] hc = new HierarchicalClusterer[f.length()];
    EuclideanDistanceMatrix edm = new EuclideanDistanceMatrix();
    for(int i = 0;i < f.length();i++){
        edm.setMatrix(f[i].getXMLFile());
        hc[i].linkageByWardMethod(edm);
        hc[i].getClassHierarchy();
    }//getClassHierarchy() method does the class hierarchy generation.
}
```

Here, $x_{p\alpha}$ denotes the αth individual in G_p; N_p denotes the number of individuals in G_p; $\overline{x}_p$ denotes the centroid of G_t. Moreover, the ESS of l sorts is:

$$ESS = \sum_{p=1}^{l} ESS_p = \sum_{p=1}^{l} \sum_{\alpha=1}^{N_p} (x_{p\alpha} - \overline{x}_p)'(x_{p\alpha} - \overline{x}_p) \tag{7}$$

When l is fixed, we should choose the incorporation which can minimize ESS. Suppose that sort G_a and sort G_b are chosen and they are incorporated into a new sort G_r. We can calculate the distances between this new sort and other sorts $G_t(t \neq a, t \neq b)$ by the following equation:

$$d_{rt}^2 = \frac{N_t + N_a}{N_r + N_t} d_{ta}^2 + \frac{N_t + N_b}{N_r + N_t} d_{tb}^2 - \frac{N_t}{N_r + N_t} d_{ab}^2 \tag{8}$$

We describe three most important methods in the algorithm for the two-stage clustering approach in Algorithm 1. Here, $TSC1()$ and $TSC2()$ correspond to the 1st clustering procedure and the 2nd clustering procedure respectively. $extractResource()$ corresponds to the information extraction procedure.

3 Performance Evaluation and Consistency Analysis

3.1 Performance Evaluation of TSC Approach

In our ontology-building process, we use the clustering technique twice. Since one domain may contain several sorts and one sort may contain several classes and subclasses, we use SOM to cluster the domain documents first of all. Actually, the ontology is larger with the increasing of the domain. So we should avoid building complex ontologies which are unnecessary for our use [1]. By using bags of words, we select a corpus which can represent its sort well. The bags of words also exclude the documents which represent their sorts weakly. Therefore, the researched range can be restrained. The later Chinese lexicon analysis can provide us with the individuals and relationships which are very important for creating the classes in the ontology base. Thereafter, in the second clustering stage, we use agglomerative hierarchical clustering to get the class hierarchy for each sort.

Here we use the cophenetic correlation to evaluate the performance of agglomerative hierarchical clustering. It is the linear correlation coefficient between the original distances used to construct the hierarchy and the cophenetic distances obtained from the hierarchy. The larger the correlation coefficient is, the more satisfying the hierarchical clustering is. Suppose that the original distance matrix is Y and the value of $linkage(Y)$ for generating the hierarchy is Z, the cophenetic correlation is defined as follows:

$$c = \frac{\sum_{i<j}(Y_{ij} - y)(Z_{ij} - z)}{\sqrt{\sum_{i<j}(Y_{ij} - y)^2 \sum_{i<j}(Z_{ij} - z)^2}} \tag{9}$$

Here, Y_{ij} is the distance between individual i and individual j; Z_{ij} is the cophenetic distance between individual i and individual j; y is the average of elements in matrix Y and z is the average of elements in matrix Z.

We evaluate the performance of our TSC ontology learning approach by using *Recall*, *Precision*, and *E-measure*.

$$Recall_{ind} = \frac{DOC_{cor\_extracted}}{DOC_{total}} \quad , \quad Precision_{ind} = \frac{DOC_{cor\_extracted}}{DOC_{all\_extracted}} \quad (10)$$

Here, $Recall_{ind}$ denotes the ratio of the documents from which correct individuals are extracted($DOC_{cor\_extracted}$) to total documents(DOC_{total}) in the corpus. $Precision_{ind}$ denotes the ratio of the documents from which correct individuals are extracted to all the documents from which individuals are extracted ($DOC_{all\_extracted}$).

$$E_{measure}(Recall_{ind}, Precision_{ind}) = 1 - \frac{2}{\frac{1}{Recall_{ind}} + \frac{1}{Precision_{ind}}} \quad (11)$$

$E_{measure}$ a number with a value range from 0 to 1 and the smaller $E_{measure}$ is, the more accurate the individual extraction is. The ontologies extracted by TSC approach and those manually extracted by experts from the same domain corpus is also compared. Assume the ontology build by domain experts is sound and complete. The *Recall* and *Precision* of classes and properties are as follows.

$$Recall_{Class} = \frac{|Set_{ontC_{TSC}} \bigcap Set_{ontC_{MAN}}|}{|Set_{ontC_{MAN}}|} \quad (12)$$

$$Precision_{Class} = \frac{|Set_{ontC_{TSC}} \bigcap Set_{ontC_{MAN}}|}{|Set_{ontC_{TSC}}|} \quad (13)$$

$$Recall_{Property} = \frac{|Set_{ontP_{TSC}} \bigcap Set_{ontP_{MAN}}|}{|Set_{ontP_{MAN}}|} \quad (14)$$

$$Precision_{Property} = \frac{|Set_{ontP_{TSC}} \bigcap Set_{ontP_{MAN}}|}{|Set_{ontP_{TSC}}|} \quad (15)$$

Here, $Set_{ontC_{TSC}}$ and $Set_{ontP_{TSC}}$ are the set of classes and the set of Properties extracted by TSC approach respectively. $Set_{ontC_{MAN}}$ and $Set_{ontP_{MAN}}$ are the set of classes and the set of properties extracted by domain experts respectively.

3.2 Class Consistency Analysis

After learning, we can get the class hierarchies of the domain ontology. However, these classes may be inconsistent and can not be used correctly. For instance, suppose Class A and Class B are disjoint, and Class C is a subclass of both Class A and Class B. Then Class C is an inconsistent class and can not have any individuals since something can not be the individual of disjoint classes. Therefore, we should check the consistence before using the newly generated ontology.

Here, we use Jena's DIG interface [12] to invoke Racer [13] and perform the consistency check. The ontology can be sent to Racer which then automatically computes the class hierarchies and checks the logical consistency of the ontology. If some inconsistent classes are found, we modify their superclasses or themselves. Finally, we edit the consistent ontology in ontology editors.

4   Ontology Evolution

With the update of the Web documents, the corresponding ontologies should evolve as well. In this paper, we propose a semi-automatic method to perform ontology evolution. We take the current domain ontology as an *ontology seed*. When new documents in this domain are retrieved, we calculate the similarities between documents and sorts which have been saved in SOM neural network. If the similarities are no less than a preappointed threshold value, then the corresponding documents are classified into these sorts. Then, we annotate them based on the *ontology seed* and add the generated individuals into the ontology. If the similarities are less than the threshold value, there may be some individuals which the *ontology seed* can not describe. In this case, we take these unsorted documents as the input and use our TSC approach again to update the ontology schema. Then, we add the generated classes, properties and individuals into the ontology.

However, the newly added content may provoke inconsistencies. So we should use Racer to check the updated ontologies and fix possible inconsistencies. There are two ways of doing this checking. One way is that after all the changes executed, the reasoner is invoked to do a single checking. The other is that the change and checking are performed by turns. We use the later method since checking the entire ontology is costly. Moreover, when the inconsistency are found, the roll back of the ontology into the initial consistent state is inevitable. This also occupy lots of the system resource. By using the later method, if the inconsistency is found by the reasoner, we can easily know which change induces this inconsistency and fix it in time before the next change.

5   Experiment

Our two-stage clustering approach is carried out on a PC with an Intel Pentium $1.8GHz$ CPU and $512M$ of RAM. We use a sample set containing 212 documents about automobiles and build the automobile ontology. We use feature vectors with 105 dimensions to represent documents. These documents are firstly used for training SOM neural network described in section 2. Its parameters setting is as follows: the dimension of input nodes is 105; the number of neurons in the output layer is 20×20; the winning area is a square (12 neurons in each side) with the BMU in the center; the number of the training step is 1000 and the initial learning-rate is 0.97.

After training, we find these documents belonging to six sorts. By analyzing their labels, we define the six sorts are *Model, Participants in Automobile Market, Performance, News, Technology* and *Automobile Culture*. Then for each sort, we calculate the total frequency of each word and get the feature vector by cutting the long vector whose values are arranged by descending order to a new feature vector with 20 dimensions. We re-collect the feature documents which contain not less than 80% of the words appearing in the new feature vector of the sort and build an ontology based on them.

By lexical analysis, we can identify the nouns and verbs in the feature documents. Now, we use agglomerative hierarchical clustering to build the class hierarchies for our automobile ontology. In order to compare our TSC approach to the conventional ontology-generation method, we select 35 common individuals contained in every sort. In *Model* sort, each individual has 12 properties denoted as *Price, Length, Width, Height, Air Capacity, Gears, Top Speed, Acceleration, Fuel Consumption, Category, Max. Output* and *Production Place*(value 1 denotes "homemade" and value 2 denotes "imports"). Based on these properties, we get the class hierarchy which is shown in Figure 2 after clustering.

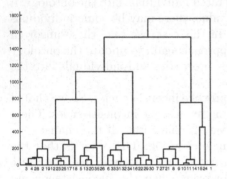

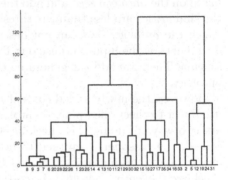

Fig. 2. Hierarchical clustering in *Model* sort

Fig. 3. Hierarchical clustering in *Performance* sort

Moreover, by running our program, we know that the value of cophenetic correlation of this clustering is 0.600. For another instance, in *Performance* sort, each individual has 6 properties denoted as *Safety Index, Power Index, Cross-Country Index, Economy Index, Comfort Index* and *Brand Index*, which are evaluated using float numbers respectively. The corresponding class hierarchy is shown in Figure 3 and the value of cophenetic correlation is 0.804.

We compare the performance of our TSC approach to that of conventional ontology-generation method which relies on hierarchical clustering. For comparison, we select documents containing aforementioned 35 individuals here. After clustering, We can get the value of cophenetic correlation is 0.571. From Table 1, we can find that the values of cophenetic correlations associated with our TSC approach are all higher than the value of cophenetic correlation associated with the conventional hierarchical clustering. However, from the class hierarchy, we can not identify the classes easily since the clustering is rough. Traditional ontology-generation method clusters all the individuals in the domain without pre-classification. Contrarily, by using two-stage clustering, TSC can pre-classify

Table 1. TSC approach versus conventional hierarchical clustering

Method		Cophenetic Correlation
TSC	Sort 1	0.755
	Sort 2	0.804
	Sort 3	0.796
	Sort 4	0.680
	Sort 5	0.665
	Sort 6	0.600
Conventional HC		0.571

Table 2. Performance evaluation for TSC approach

resource	Recall/%	Precision/%	$E_{measure}$
Individual	62.32	80.27	0.298
Class	65.82	84.16	0.261
Property	63.59	90.37	0.253

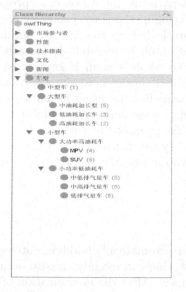

Fig. 4. Class hierarchy for *Model* sort

Fig. 5. Class hierarchy for *Performance* sort

the documents which contain individuals into several sorts and generate the class hierarchies of domain ontologies more reasonably and accurately.

From Figure 3, we can find that *Automobile 3*, *Automobile 4*, *Automobile 28*, *Automobile 2* and *Automobile 19* are classified into one class named *LowAirCapacityAuto*. Thereafter, this class, *HighAirCapacityAuto* class and *ModerateAirCapacityAuto* class are incorporated into a new class *LowOutputLowFuelConsumptionAuto*. Therefore, we can get the ontology corresponding to *Model* sort from the bottom to the top according to the class hierarchy in Figure 2. Likewise, the class hierarchies of other sorts can be generated in the same way. The results of TSC approach's performance evaluation stage are shown in Table 2. Then, we send the automobile ontology to Racer to checking its consistency. Some inconsistencies are found during the reasoning. Finally, we edit our automobile ontology in protégé [14]. The class hierarchies of Model and Performance in protégé are shown in Figure 4 and Figure 5.

6 Related Work

Ontology can be built from various sources, such as documents(structured, un-structured, or semi-structured), relational databases and existing preliminaries. Most methods for learning ontology from documents employ statistics and a document corpus. The corpus is usually obtained from World Wide Web and WordNet is usually used to construct topic signature. Patterns are also involved to mining relations between words. Cimiano et al. cluster nouns based on similar-ities and construct a hierarchy by using Hearst-patterns [15]. Agirre et al. propose a framework to define hierarchical term clustering methods to specific syntactic constructions [16]. Since knowledge is not static but evolves timely, ontology extending become an very important part of ontology research. In Zurawski's approach [17], when the ontology evolves, the whole system is kept coherent using lightweight methods for maintaining global consistency. Moreover, many researchers build ontologies with limited human effort by using formal concept analysis [18], natural language processing [19] and the clustering technique [20]. Some automatic tools for learning ontologies are proposed recently, such as On-toLT, TextToOnto or OntoLearn. However, they can not deal with the Chinese corpus and lack the interaction with users who are usually most familiar with the domain.

7 Conclusion

This paper proposes a TSC approach for semi-automatically building ontologies from Chinese Web documents. The first clustering can roughly classify domain documents into several sorts without supervision. After the identification of in-dividuals and their properties, ontologies can be built according to the class hierarchies automatically generated by the second clustering. The experimen-tal result indicates that TSC can overcome the interfere brought by the docu-ments which are unhelpful for building domain ontologies. Moreover, TSC does not need much artificial interventions comparing to the conventional ontology-building methods. Our long-term goal is to add rules for finding and handling incorrect and conflicting information automatically in the information extraction process.

Acknowledgements

This work is supported by the National Science Foundation of China (60496321, 60473003), Ministry of Education Program for New Century Excellent Tal-ents in University(NECT) and Doctor Point Founds of Educational Department (20050183065).

References

1. Noy, N.F., McGuinness, D.L.: Ontology development a guide to creating your first ontology, Technical Report KSL-01-05, Stanford Knowledge Systems Laboratory vol.101 (2001)
2. Astrova, I.: Reverse engineering of relational databases to ontologies. In: Bussler, C.J., Davies, J., Fensel, D., Studer, R. (eds.) ESWS 2004. LNCS, vol. 3053, pp. 327–341. Springer, Heidelberg (2004)
3. Zhiqing, M., Hongcan, Z., Yihua, Z., Gengui, Z.: A clustering algorithm for Chinese text based on SOM neural network and density. In: Wang, J., Liao, X.-F., Yi, Z. (eds.) ISNN 2005. LNCS, vol. 3497, pp. 251–256. Springer, Heidelberg (2005)
4. Bex, G.J., Maneth, S., Neven, F.: A formal model for an expressive fragment of XSLT. Information Systems 28(1), 21–39 (2002)
5. Bai, X., Sun, J.G., Luo, H.: WDM: A new efficient visualization method of classifying Web documents based on SOM. In: Proceedings of CIS'06, pp. 809–814. IEEE Computer Society Press, Washington (2006)
6. Schneider, K.M.: On word frequency information and negative evidence in Naive Bayes text classification. In: Vicedo, J.L., Martínez-Barco, P., Muñoz, R., Saiz Noeda, M. (eds.) EsTAL 2004. LNCS (LNAI), vol. 3230, pp. 474–485. Springer, Heidelberg (2004)
7. Goncalves, A., Jianhan, Z., Dawei, S., Uren, V., Pacheco, R.: LRD: Latent relation discovery for vector space expansion and information retrieval. In: Yu, J.X., Kitsuregawa, M., Leong, H.V. (eds.) WAIM 2006. LNCS, vol. 4016, pp. 122–133. Springer, Heidelberg (2006)
8. Dasgupta, S.: Performance guarantees for hierarchical clustering. In: Kivinen, J., Sloan, R.H. (eds.) COLT 2002. LNCS (LNAI), vol. 2375, pp. 351–363. Springer, Heidelberg (2002)
9. Zhang, H.P., Yu, H.K., Xiong, D.Y., Liu, Q.: HHMM-based chinese lexical analyzer ICTCLAS. In: Proceedings of the 2nd SIGHAN Workshop, Sapporo, Japan, pp. 184-187 (July 2003)
10. Panuccio, A., Bicego, M., Murino, V.: A hidden Markov model-based approach to sequential data clustering. In: Caelli, T.M., Amin, A., Duin, R.P.W., Kamel, M.S., de Ridder, D. (eds.) SPR 2002 and SSPR 2002. LNCS, vol. 2396, pp. 734–742. Springer, Heidelberg (2002)
11. Ward, J.H.: Hierarchical grouping to optimize an objective function. Journoal of the American Statistical Association 58, 236–244 (1963)
12. Jena APIs, http://jena.sourceforge.net/downloads.html
13. RacerPro, http://www.sts.tu-harburg.de/~ r.f.moeller/racer/
14. Noy, N., Fergerson, R., Musen, M.: The knowledge model of Protégé-2000: Combining interoperability and flexibility. In: Dieng, R., Corby, O. (eds.) EKAW 2000. LNCS (LNAI), vol. 1937, pp. 17–32. Springer, Heidelberg (2000)
15. Cimiano, P., Staab, S.: Learning by googling. SIGKDD Explorations 6(2), 24–34 (2004)
16. Agirre, E., Ansa, O., Hovy, E., Martinez, D.: Enriching very large ontologies using the WWW. In: Proceedings of the ECAI'00 Workshop on Ontology Learning, Berlin, Germany (2000)
17. Zurawski, M.: Distributed multi-contextual ontology evolution–a step towards semantic autonomy. In: Staab, S., Svátek, V. (eds.) EKAW 2006. LNCS (LNAI), vol. 4248, pp. 198–213. Springer, Heidelberg (2006)

18. Cimiano, P., Stumme, G., Hotho, A., Tane, J.: Conceptual knowledge processing with formal concept analysis and ontologies. In: Eklund, P.W. (ed.) ICFCA 2004. LNCS (LNAI), vol. 2961, pp. 189–207. Springer, Heidelberg (2004)
19. Bandini, S., Calegari, S., Radaelli, P.: Towards fuzzy ontology handling vagueness of natural languages. In: Wang, G.-Y., Peters, J.F., Skowron, A., Yao, Y. (eds.) RSKT 2006. LNCS (LNAI), vol. 4062, pp. 693–700. Springer, Heidelberg (2006)
20. Pirrone, R., Cossentino, M., Pilato, G., Rizzo, R., Russo, G.: Discovering learning paths on a domain ontology using natural language interaction. In: Ali, M., Esposito, F. (eds.) IEA/AIE 2005. LNCS (LNAI), vol. 3533, pp. 310–314. Springer, Heidelberg (2005)
21. Gruber, T.R.: A translation approach to portable ontology specifications. Knowledge Acquisition 5(2), 199–220 (1993)

$\mathcal{ALC}_{\mathbb{P}}^{u}$: An Integration of Description Logic and General Rules

Jing Mei[1], Zuoquan Lin[1], and Harold Boley[2]

[1] Department of Information Science
Peking University, Beijing 100871, China
{mayyam,lz}@is.pku.edu.cn
[2] Institute for Information Technology - e-Business
National Research Council of Canada
Fredericton, NB, E3B 9W4, Canada
Harold.Boley@nrc.gc.ca

Abstract. A unifying logic is built on top of ontologies and rules for the revised Semantic Web Architecture. This paper proposes $\mathcal{ALC}_{\mathbb{P}}^{u}$, which integrates a description logic (DL) that makes a *unique* names assumption with general rules that have the form of Datalog $\mathbb{P}$rograms permitting default negation in the body. An $\mathcal{ALC}_{\mathbb{P}}^{u}$ knowledge base (KB) consists of a TBox $\mathcal{T}$ of subsumptions, an ABox $\mathcal{A}$ of assertions, and a novel PBox $\mathbb{P}$ of general rules that share predicates with DL concepts and DL roles. To model open answer set semantics, extended Herbrand structures are used for interpreting DL concepts and DL roles, while open answer sets hold for general rules. To retain decidability, a well-known weak safeness condition is employed. We develop DL tableaux-based algorithms for decision procedures of the KB satisfiability and the query entailment problems.

1 Introduction

Based on input from the Semantic Web Rules community, the Semantic Web Architecture has been recently reconsidered by Tim Berners-Lee [3]: ontologies and rules are now sitting side by side between RDF(S) and a unifying logic layer. The Web Ontology Language (OWL), whose formalization relies directly on Description Logic (DL) [2], dates back to a W3C Recommendation released on 10 February 2004 [23]. Subsequently, W3C announced the formation of the Rule Interchange Format (RIF [24]) Working Group on 7 November 2005, aiming to specify a format for rules in the Semantic Web chartered to allow "knowledge expressed in OWL and in rules to be easily used together". Not surprisingly, how to best combine OWL/DL and rules has become a topic of heated discussions in the Semantic Web community.

At the top-level, those integration approaches are either homogeneous or hybrid [1]. Early work in the *hybrid* direction comprises AL-log [7] and CARIN [16], both of which extend Datalog rules with DL constraints. Recent work prefers a

M. Marchiori, J.Z. Pan, and C. de Sainte Marie (Eds.): RR 2007, LNCS 4524, pp. 163–177, 2007.
© Springer-Verlag Berlin Heidelberg 2007

more general and tight integration, such as $\mathcal{DL} + log$ [22] (originating from r-hybrid KBs [21]) and HEX-programs [8] (originating from dl-programs [9]). Their generality appeals to negation and disjunction in rules, namely Datalog$^{\neg,\vee}$, while their tightness calls for certain *safeness* conditions that limit the interaction between the DL component and rules.

In hybrid approaches, ontology and rule predicates are always kept distinct. Homogeneous frameworks instead permit predicate sharing in a syntactically and semantically coherent manner. DLP (Description Logic Programs [11]) has been proposed as the intersection of DL and Datalog rules, while SWRL (Semantic Web Rule Language [25]) is their union. Unfortunately, DLP seems too restrictive, and SWRL seems too expressive (hence is undecidable).

Reduction is another way to build a homogeneous platform. The paper [15] works on reducing DL KBs to disjunctive Datalog programs, getting ready for an extension with DL-safe rules [19] and even MKNF rules [18]. There, DL-safeness is imposed as the condition for grounding rule variables with named individuals.

Summarizing, from a practical perspective, hybrid approaches are component-based, using plug-ins of both DL reasoners and rule engines, in addition to well-defined interfaces. Most homogeneous approaches make use of translators from the DL component into rules (even first-order formulae), followed by running rule engines (even first-order provers) with support for those reduced languages. We totally agree that reusing existing reasoning tools (e.g., DL reasoners and rule engines) facilitates various applications on the Semantic Web. But, towards a unifying logic on top of ontologies and rules, as envisioned by [3], it makes sense to develop a novel algorithm specifically for the homogeneous integration of DL and general rules.

This paper extends a DL KB – consisting of a TBox $\mathcal{T}$ of subsumptions and an ABox $\mathcal{A}$ of assertions – with a PBox $\mathbb{P}$ of general rules, i.e., Datalog$^{\neg}$ rules permitting default negation for atoms in the body, in a homogeneous manner. Particularly, we show the following characteristics:

Sharing predicates. Rule predicates are exactly DL concepts and DL roles, taking advantage of the expressivity and reasoning power of both DL and rules.
Negative atoms. The default negation "not" is allowed to prefix atoms in the body, making non-monotonicity applicable. Note that the classical negation "$\neg$" is still preserved for DL's negative constructor.
Open Answer Set Semantics. Extended Herbrand structures are used for interpreting DL concepts and DL roles, while open answer sets hold for general rules, making a unique names assumption. Unnamed individuals, e.g. as introduced by DL existential restrictions, also occur in the open domain. To retain decidability, a well-known weak safeness condition [22] is employed, grounding variables in the rule head with named individuals.
Tableau-based algorithms. Decision procedures for the knowledge base (KB) satisfiability problem and the query entailment problem are designed on completion graphs, getting rules incorporated into classical DL tableaux algorithms (which originally work on completion forests or trees).

The remainder of this paper starts with preliminaries for integrating DL and general rules in our homogeneous language $\mathcal{ALC}^u_\mathbb{P}$. The syntax and semantics are defined in Section 3. Section 4 elaborates on algorithms, giving decision procedures for the KB satisfiability problem and the query entailment problem. Finally, Section 5 is our conclusion. Because of paper space limitations, detailed proofs are available in an Online Appendix.[1]

2   Preliminaries

Description Logic, as discussed in this paper, is a fragment of classical first-order logic (FOL). Therefore, the semantics for DL is based on first-order interpretations, of which the domain is arbitrary. However, a fixed domain, viz. the Herbrand universe, in which rule variables are instantiated, is the key to the semantics of logic programming (LP). When combining DL and rules, we first of all should figure out the domain in common. A good candidate is the so-called *open domain*, i.e., an arbitrary non-empty countable superset of the Herbrand universe, as proposed for open answer set programming to solve the lack of modularity in closed world answer set programming [12].

Moreover, in the context of LP, rule variables are ultimately substituted by constants, receiving a grounded version of rules. Within a combined signature of DL and rules [5], constants are referred to as *named individuals*, which are asserted explicitly into the corresponding KB, and the Herbrand universe exactly consists of those constants. Nevertheless, DL existential restrictions would introduce *unnamed individuals*, and unnamed individuals also act as constants but unfortunately are beyond the Herbrand universe. Again, the open domain appears to be the right place for capturing unnamed individuals. Referring to [6], if there are no unnamed individuals in the domain, we say the *parameter names assumption (PNA)* applies. Not surprisingly, we prefer not to adopt PNA.

Open answer set semantics adheres to a *unique names assumption (UNA)*, which is not the case for DL. However, if desired, the UNA can be made explicit in DL by adding an assertion $a \neq b$ for each pair of differently named individuals to the KB. In this respect, we also adopt UNA. Since, the combination of PNA and UNA is called the *standard names assumption (SNA)*, our proposal is under UNA but neither PNA nor SNA, while $\mathcal{DL} + log$ [22] etc. adopted SNA.

Next, we should point out the (un)decidability issue. Actually, a decade ago, the undecidability of an unrestricted combination of DL and rules was proved with CARIN [16]. For reobtaining decidability, safeness conditions were proposed, e.g., rule-safeness in [16], DL-safeness in [19] and weak safeness in [22], each of which ensures a certain separation between DL and rule predicates. Differing from those predicate-separated systems, this paper is based on rule predicates shared with DL concepts and DL roles. Thus, we merely require the most general Datalog safeness in the *syntax*, while we adopt a *semantic* weak safeness condition that relies on grounding variables in the rule head with named individuals to avoid undecidability.

---

[1] http://www.is.pku.edu.cn/~mayyam/proof.pdf

On the other hand, DL is a family with many layers [2][13]. Bottom up, $\mathcal{ALC}$ is a basic and simple language, permitting concept descriptions via $C_1 \sqcap C_2, C_1 \sqcup C_2, \neg C, \forall R.C$, and $\exists R.C$, where C, C_1, C_2 are concepts and R is a role. Augmented by transitive roles, $\mathcal{ALC}$ becomes $\mathcal{ALC}_{\mathcal{R}^+}$, denoted by $\mathcal{S}$ in the following. $\mathcal{SI}$ is an extension to $\mathcal{S}$ with inverse roles, followed by $\mathcal{SHI}$ with role hierarchies. It is called $\mathcal{SHIF}$ if extending by functional restrictions, $\mathcal{SHIN}$ if by cardinality restrictions, and $\mathcal{SHIQ}$ if by qualified number restrictions. Support for datatype predicates (e.g., string, integer) brings up the concrete domain of $\mathbf{D}$, and using nominals $\mathcal{O}$ helps construct concepts with singleton sets. With the expected pervasive use of OWL, $\mathcal{SHIF}(\mathbf{D})$ and $\mathcal{SHOIN}(\mathbf{D})$ are paid much attention: OWL Lite is a syntax variant of one, and OWL DL, of the other.

As the DL foundation, $\mathcal{ALC}$ is regarded as the right level for our homogeneous DL-rule integration, observing that the expressivity of extending $\mathcal{ALC}$ with Datalog rules covers that of $\mathcal{SHI}$, i.e., $\mathcal{ALC}_{\mathcal{R}^+}\mathcal{HI}$, except for the semantic weak safeness condition for rules. Specifically, the role hierarchy $\mathcal{H}$ of $R_1 \sqsubseteq R_2$ is captured by $R_2(x, y) \leftarrow R_1(x, y)$, and inverse roles $\mathcal{I}$ and transitive roles $\mathcal{R}^+$ are characterized, respectively, by $\text{Inv}(R)(y, x) \leftarrow R(x, y)$ and $S(x, z) \leftarrow S(x, y), S(y, z)$, where $R_1, R_2, R, \text{Inv}(R)$ and S are roles, in addition to $\text{Trans}(S)$ being $\mathbf{true}$.

At this point, we are ready for a proposal of $\mathcal{ALC}_{\mathbb{P}}^u$, where the superscript "u" denotes the adoption of UNA, and the subscript "$\mathbb{P}$" means a program of *general* (*normal* [17]) rules. Even if the "$\mathbf{not}$" operator of general rules in $\mathbb{P}$ is removed from $\mathcal{ALC}_{\mathbb{P}}^u$, our proposal develops $\mathcal{SHI}$ into a language with "more Datalog and less DL". The "more Datalog" characteristic is evident, since 'end-user' rules are integrated right into the foundation of the DL machinery. The "less DL" characteristic results from the '$\mathcal{SHI}$-desugaring' rules, translating the role hierarchy $\mathcal{H}$, inverse roles $\mathcal{I}$, and transitive roles $\mathcal{R}^+$, but because of their semantic weak safeness condition not providing full support for $\mathcal{SHI}$ on top of $\mathcal{ALC}$.

This finally brings us to the design of algorithms. DL tableaux algorithms yield completion trees (resp. forests) for checking DL concept satisfiability [13] (resp. ABox consistency [14]). Those completion trees or forests are finite, and represent a set of possibly infinite models. For getting general rules incorporated homogeneously into this setting, we will use a parameter l and develop l-completion graphs. Thus, our algorithm is still tableau-based, and we conclude that: (1) An $\mathcal{ALC}_{\mathbb{P}}^u$ KB $\mathcal{K}$ is satisfiable iff the algorithm yields a complete and clash-free $l_{\mathcal{K}}$-completion graph; and (2) a query Q is entailed by an $\mathcal{ALC}_{\mathbb{P}}^u$ KB $\mathcal{K}$ iff Q is mappable to all complete and clash-free $l_{\mathcal{K},Q}$-completion graphs that the algorithm yields. More technical details are discussed below.

3   The $\mathcal{ALC}_{\mathbb{P}}^u$ Language

Syntactically, $\mathcal{ALC}_{\mathbb{P}}^u$, built on $\mathcal{ALC}$-concepts and $\mathcal{ALC}$-roles, has three parts: a TBox $\mathcal{T}$ of subsumptions, an ABox $\mathcal{A}$ of assertions, and additionally, a PBox $\mathbb{P}$ of general rules. Semantically, open answer sets are associated with extended Herbrand structures, treating weak safeness as a semantic condition for rules.

3.1 Syntax

Let $\mathbf{I}$ be a finite set of named individuals, and $\mathcal{V} = \{x, y, z, x_1, \cdots\}$ a countable set of variables. A (Datalog) term is a named individual or a variable.

Let N_C be a set of concept names and N_R a set of role names. The set $\mathbf{R}$ of $\mathcal{ALC}$-roles is N_R. The set $\mathbf{C}$ of $\mathcal{ALC}$-concepts is the smallest set such that (1) The top concept $\top$ and the bottom concept $\bot$ are $\mathcal{ALC}$-concepts; (2) Every concept name in N_C is an $\mathcal{ALC}$-concept; (3) If C, C_1, C_2 are $\mathcal{ALC}$-concepts and R is an $\mathcal{ALC}$-role, then $\neg C, C_1 \sqcap C_2, C_1 \sqcup C_2, \exists R.C, \forall R.C$ are also $\mathcal{ALC}$-concepts.

A concept is said to be in *negation normal form* (NNF) if negation occurs only in front of concept names. By pushing negations inwards using a combination of DeMorgan's laws, any concept can be translated to NNF in linear time, and we will assume that all concepts are in NNF in this paper. Given a concept C, $\mathrm{clos}(C)$ is the smallest set that contains C and is closed under subconcepts and negation (in NNF). For a set of concepts M, $\mathrm{clos}(M) = \bigcup_{C \in M} \mathrm{clos}(C)$. The size of $\mathrm{clos}(C)$ is linear in the length of C, and the size of $\mathrm{clos}(M)$ is polynomial in the size of M.

Definition 1. *An $\mathcal{ALC}_\mathbb{P}^u$ KB has the form $\mathcal{K} = (\mathcal{T}, \mathcal{A}, \mathbb{P})$, where*
TBox $\mathcal{T}$: Subsumptions are $C_1 \sqsubseteq C_2$ with $C_1, C_2 \in \mathbf{C}$
ABox $\mathcal{A}$: Assertions are $C(a)$ or $R(a, b)$ with $C \in \mathbf{C}$, $R \in \mathbf{R}$, and $a, b \in \mathbf{I}$
PBox $\mathbb{P}$: Rules are $r : p(\boldsymbol{u}) \leftarrow q_1(\boldsymbol{v_1}), \cdots, q_m(\boldsymbol{v_m}), \mathrm{not}\, q_{m+1}(\boldsymbol{v_{m+1}}), \cdots \mathrm{not}\, q_n(\boldsymbol{v_n})$
with $p, q_i \in \mathbf{C} \cup \mathbf{R}$, and $\boldsymbol{u}, \boldsymbol{v_i}$ are vectors of terms in $\mathbf{I} \cup \mathcal{V}$, for each $1 \leqslant i \leqslant m \leqslant n$
(each vector has length 1 or 2 since concepts from $\mathbf{C}$ become unary predicates and roles from $\mathbf{R}$ become binary predicates)

We remark that weak safeness [22] for general rules originally assumes a lexical separation of DL and rule predicates, while $\mathcal{ALC}_\mathbb{P}^u$ permits rule predicates shared with DL concepts and DL roles. Later, we will show how weak safeness is moved into the semantics. Syntactically, rule variables in the PBox $\mathbb{P}$ are merely required to satisfy the most general Datalog safeness condition. That is, every variable in a rule r must appear among at least one of the $\boldsymbol{v_1}, \cdots, \boldsymbol{v_m}$.

3.2 Semantics

Referring to [6], we introduce first-order and (extended) Herbrand structures.

Given a function-free first-order language $\mathcal{L}$, an $\mathcal{L}$-structure is a pair $\mathcal{I} = \langle U, I \rangle$, where the universe $U = (\mathcal{D}, \sigma)$ consists of a non-empty domain $\mathcal{D}$ and a function $\sigma : \mathbf{I} \cup \mathcal{D}' \to \mathcal{D}$ which assigns a domain value to each individual, and $\sigma(d) = d$ for all $d \in \mathcal{D}'$, given $\mathbf{I} \cap \mathcal{D}' = \emptyset$. Elements of $\mathcal{D}'$ are called *unnamed* individuals. We remark that the corresponding definitions in [6] are less clear, where $\sigma : \mathbf{I} \cup \mathcal{D} \to \mathcal{D}$ and any $d \in \mathcal{D}$ is defined as an *unnamed* individual if there is no $i \in \mathbf{I}$ such that $\sigma(i) = d$.

Using σ, we formalize UNA, PNA, and SNA as follows: in case σ is injective, the UNA applies; in case $\mathcal{D}'$ is empty, the PNA applies; the SNA is exactly the combination of UNA and PNA.

We call I an $\mathcal{L}$-interpretation over $\mathcal{D}$, which assigns a relation $p^I \subseteq \mathcal{D}^n$ to each n-ary predicate symbol p (here $n \geq 1$). Being a fragment of function-free first-order logic, DL can also rely on structures for interpreting concepts (here $n = 1$) and roles (here $n = 2$).

Answer set semantics is usually defined in terms of a *Herbrand structure* that has a fixed universe, namely *Herbrand universe* $H = (\mathbf{I}, id)$, where $id : \mathbf{I} \to \mathbf{I}$ is the identity function. Obviously, by $\mathbf{I}$ and id, the SNA applies here.

Relaxing the PNA, open answer set semantics considers an *extended Herbrand structure* based on an *extended Herbrand universe* $eH = (\mathcal{D}, id)$, where $id : \mathbf{I} \cup \mathcal{D}' \to \mathcal{D}$ is still an identity function and $id(d) = d$ for all $d \in \mathbf{I} \cup \mathcal{D}'$, given $\mathbf{I} \cap \mathcal{D}' = \emptyset$. Thus, by id, the UNA applies, but unnamed individuals reside in $\mathcal{D}'$.

Definition 2. *An extended Herbrand structure* $\mathcal{I} = \langle (\mathcal{D}, id), I \rangle$ *is defined for a set of named individuals* $\mathbf{I}$, *a set of concepts* $\mathbf{C}$ *and a set of roles* $\mathbf{R}$, *where*

$id : \mathbf{I} \cup \mathcal{D}' \to \mathcal{D}$ *and* $id(d) = d$ *for all* $d \in \mathbf{I} \cup \mathcal{D}'$, *given* $\mathbf{I} \cap \mathcal{D}' = \emptyset$

$I : \mathbf{C} \to 2^{\mathcal{D}}$ *for concepts and* $I : \mathbf{R} \to 2^{\mathcal{D} \times \mathcal{D}}$ *for roles*

such that for concepts $C, C_1, C_2 \in \mathbf{C}$ *and roles* $R \in \mathbf{R}$, *the following are satisfied:*

$\top^I = \mathcal{D}$ $\bot^I = \emptyset$ $(\neg C)^I = \mathcal{D} \backslash C^I$ $(C_1 \sqcap C_2)^I = C_1^I \cap C_2^I$ $(C_1 \sqcup C_2)^I = C_1^I \cup C_2^I$

$(\exists R.C)^I = \{e_1 \in \mathcal{D} | \exists e_2.(e_1, e_2) \in R^I \text{ and } e_2 \in C^I\}$

$(\forall R.C)^I = \{e_1 \in \mathcal{D} | \forall e_2.(e_1, e_2) \in R^I \text{ implies } e_2 \in C^I\}$

An associated valuation v_I *of an interpretation* I *over* $\mathcal{D}$ *is a mapping s.t.*

$v_I(C(d)) = true$, *if* $d \in C^I$, *where* $C \in \mathbf{C}$ *and* $d \in \mathcal{D}$

$v_I(R(d_1, d_2)) = true$, *if* $(d_1, d_2) \in R^I$, *where* $R \in \mathbf{R}$ *and* $d_1, d_2 \in \mathcal{D}$

An extended Herbrand structure $\mathcal{I}$ satisfies a TBox $\mathcal{T}$ if, $C_1^I \subseteq C_2^I$ for all $C_1 \sqsubseteq C_2$ in $\mathcal{T}$, where $C_1, C_2 \in \mathbf{C}$. Such a structure $\mathcal{I}$ is called a model of $\mathcal{T}$, written as $\mathcal{I} \models \mathcal{T}$. An extended Herbrand structure $\mathcal{I}$ satisfies an ABox $\mathcal{A}$ if, $id(a) = a \in C^I$ and $(id(a_1), id(a_2)) = (a_1, a_2) \in R^I$ for all $C(a)$ and $R(a_1, a_2)$ in $\mathcal{A}$, where $C \in \mathbf{C}$, $R \in \mathbf{R}$ and $a, a_1, a_2 \in \mathbf{I}$. Such a structure $\mathcal{I}$ is called a model of $\mathcal{A}$, written as $\mathcal{I} \models \mathcal{A}$.

To define a model of a PBox $\mathbb{P}$, we start by grounding $\mathbb{P}$. The grounding $\mathbb{P}_g$ of $\mathbb{P}$ w.r.t. an extended Herbrand universe $eH = (\mathcal{D}, id)$ is the set of all rules obtained as follows. For every rule r in $\mathbb{P}$,

(1) keep each named individual $a \in \mathbf{I}$ appearing in r unchanged as $id(a) = a \in \mathcal{D}$,
(2) replace each variable $v \in \mathcal{V}$ appearing in r with a certain $d \in \mathcal{D}$,
(3) replace each variable $v \in \mathcal{V}$ appearing in the head of r with a certain $d \in \mathbf{I}$.

In order to guarantee decidability, the semantic condition of (3) is proposed. While $\mathcal{DL} + log$ [22] has defined such a (syntactical) weak safeness condition for hybrid rules, we rephrase it semantically for homogeneous rules here. That is, only named individuals are legal for grounding the head of rules, so unnamed individuals cannot be propagated by rules.

Below, given an extended Herbrand structure $\mathcal{I} = \langle (\mathcal{D}, id), I \rangle$, we will first consider the grounded PBox $\mathbb{P}_g$ of rules without **not**, i.e., $m = n$ for all rules r in $\mathbb{P}_g$. Put differently, $\mathbb{P}_g$ corresponds to the positive (function-free Horn) case of traditional logic programming. The *extended Herbrand model* of $\mathbb{P}_g$ is a set S such that, for any rule $r : p(\boldsymbol{u}) \leftarrow q_1(\boldsymbol{v_1}), \cdots, q_m(\boldsymbol{v_m})$ in $\mathbb{P}_g$, if $q_i(\boldsymbol{v_i}) \in S$ for all $1 \leqslant i \leqslant m$, then $p(\boldsymbol{u}) \in S$. By $\lambda(\mathbb{P}_g)$, we denote the least extended Herbrand model of $\mathbb{P}_g$ in which none of the rules contains **not**.

Next, suppose $\mathbb{P}_g$ is a grounded PBox of general rules and S a set. Similarly as in the Gelfond-Lifschitz transformation [10], we denote with $\Gamma(\mathbb{P}_g, S)$ the set of rules obtained from $\mathbb{P}_g$ by deleting

1. each rule $r \in \mathbb{P}_g$ that has a "not $q(v)$" in the rule body with $q(v) \in S$;
2. all "not $q(v)$" occurrences in the bodies of the remaining rules.

Clearly, $\Gamma(\mathbb{P}_g, S)$ does not contain "not" any more, and its extended Herbrand model is already defined above. If the least extended Herbrand model of $\Gamma(\mathbb{P}_g, S)$ coincides with S, then we say that S is an *open answer set* of $\mathbb{P}_g$. In other words, open answer sets of $\mathbb{P}_g$ are characterized by the equation $S = \lambda(\Gamma(\mathbb{P}_g, S))$.

An extended Herbrand structure $\mathcal{I}$ satisfies a PBox $\mathbb{P}$ if the set $S = \{C(d)|$ $v_I(C(d)) = true\} \cup \{R(d_1, d_2)|v_I(R(d_1, d_2)) = true\}$ is an open answer set of $\mathbb{P}_g$. Such a structure $\mathcal{I}$ is called a model of $\mathbb{P}$, written as $\mathcal{I} \models \mathbb{P}$.

An extended Herbrand structure $\mathcal{I}$ satisfies an $\mathcal{ALC}_{\mathbb{P}}^u$ KB $\mathcal{K} = (\mathcal{T}, \mathcal{A}, \mathbb{P})$ if $\mathcal{I}$ is a model of $\mathcal{T}, \mathcal{A}$ and $\mathbb{P}$. Such a structure $\mathcal{I}$ is called a model of $\mathcal{K}$, written as $\mathcal{I} \models \mathcal{K}$. A KB $\mathcal{K}$ is *satisfiable* if there is a model of $\mathcal{K}$. Two KBs $\mathcal{K}_1$ and $\mathcal{K}_2$ are *equivalent* if the models of $\mathcal{K}_1$ are also the models of $\mathcal{K}_2$, and vice versa.

3.3   An Example

We demonstrate an example in Table 1, about the policy of "one family, one child" for the current generation in China.

Disjunction is exemplified by (1), a cyclic TBox by (2) and existential restriction by (3), all of which state the properties of a person. Among persons, the current generation is described in (4) having OnlyChild as descendants.

Recursive rules are used for the "descend" relationship by (5) and (6), of which (5) is the base and (6) is the propagation. Rule (7) describes a symmetric relationship of "hasSpouse". Rules (8) and (9) reflect the disjunction of male and female, according to (1), while role subsumptions of having parents are shown in (10). Excluding unmarried parents, we suppose, in (11), someone having a child has a spouse. As for (12) and (13), the OnlyChild has no sibling, while someone whose parents both have no siblings has no cousin.

Default negation appears in (14) and (15), also DL existential restriction participates in the rule head. The current generation, in general, has siblings (resp. cousins), but not in the case when there is an explicit statement of having no sibling (resp. having no cousin).

Classical negation, serving for DL negative concepts, appears in the head of rules (16), (17) and (18). It seems redundant to state both (18) and (13), whose heads are complements of each other. We remark that "hasSibling", in the rule body of (18), is possibly derived from (14), while (13) helps to override the default in (14). However, (14) merely concerns the current generation, and (13) is for all.

In (19), classical negation gets along with default negation, stating that OnlyChild generally has another OnlyChild as his/her spouse.

So far, we conclude definitely that [1]: descendants of the current generation are those without any sibling, as derived from (4)(12). By default, we conclude that [2]: (14)(16) and (15)(17) respectively state the current generation has

Table 1. An example of an $\mathcal{ALC}_{\mathbb{P}}^u$ KB

(1) Person $\sqsubseteq$ Male $\sqcup$ Female	Person is male or female.
(2) $\sqsubseteq$ $\forall$ hasChild.Person	Any child of a person is a person.
(3) $\sqsubseteq$ $\exists$ hasFather.Male $\sqcap\exists$ hasMother.Female	Any person has a father and a mother.
(4) CCG $\sqsubseteq$ Person $\sqcap\forall$ descend.OnlyChild	CCG: The current generation.
(5) descend(x,y) $\leftarrow$ hasChild(x,y).	The relationship of descend is the
(6) descend(x,z) $\leftarrow$ descend(x,y), hasChild(y,z).	transitive closure of having children.
(7) hasSpouse(x,y) $\leftarrow$ hasSpouse(y,x).	Having spouse is symmetric.
(8) hasFather(x,y) $\leftarrow$ hasChild(y,x), Male(y).	A male having a child is the father.
(9) hasMother(x,y) $\leftarrow$ hasChild(y,x), Female(y).	A female having a child is the mother.
(10) hasFather $\sqsubseteq$ hasParent hasMother $\sqsubseteq$ hasParent	Parents consist of father and mother.
(11) $\exists$ hasChild.Person $\sqsubseteq$ $\exists$ hasSpouse.Person	One having a child has a spouse.
(12) NoSibling(x) $\leftarrow$ OnlyChild(x).	One in OnlyChild belongs to NoSibling.
(13) NoCousin(x) $\leftarrow$ hasFather(x,y), NoSibling(y).	One whose father and mother are both
$\quad$ hasMother(x,z), NoSibling(z).	in NoSibling belongs to NoCousin.
(14) $\exists$ hasSibling.Person(x) $\leftarrow$ CCG(x),	One CCG not being known as NoSibling
$\quad$ **not** NoSibling(x).	has some sibling.
(15) $\exists$ hasCousin.Person(x) $\leftarrow$ CCG(x),	One CCG not being known as NoCousin
$\quad$ **not** NoCousin(x).	has some cousin.
(16) $\neg$ NoSibling(x) $\leftarrow$ hasSibling(x,y).	One with sibling is outside of NoSibling.
(17) $\neg$ NoCousin(x) $\leftarrow$ hasCousin(x,y).	One with cousin is outside of NoCousin.
(18) $\neg$ NoCousin(x) $\leftarrow$ hasParent(x,y), hasSibling(y,z).	One special is outside of NoCousin.
(19) OnlyChild(y) $\leftarrow$ hasSpouse(x,y), OnlyChild(x),	The OnlyChild generally has
$\quad$ **not** $\neg$ NoSibling(y).	another OnlyChild as his/her spouse.

Therefore	

[1] CCG $\sqsubseteq$ $\forall$descend.NoSibling	
[2] CCG $\sqsubseteq$ $\neg$NoSibling $\sqcap\neg$NoCousin $\sqcap\forall$hasChild.$\forall$descend.NoCousin	

[3]		
	Antecedent(*)	CCG(a). CCG(b). OnlyChild(a). $\forall$hasParent.OnlyChild(b).
	Consequence(*)	NoSibling(a). $\neg$NoCousin(a). NoCousin(b). $\neg$NoSibling(b).
	Suppose	AmusingFamily $\leftarrow$ amusedBy(x,y).
		amusedBy(x_2,y_2) $\leftarrow$ hasSpouse(x_1,y_1), NoSibling(x_1), NoCousin(y_1),
		hasCousin(x_1,x_2), hasSibling(y_1,y_2), **not** amusedBy(y_2,x_2).
	Conclude	AmusingFamily when Antecedent(*) holds in addition to hasSpouse(a,b).

siblings and cousins, while (13) implies that children of the current generation will have descendants without any cousin. For [3], when the antecedent (*) arises, we have one person a and the other person b as the current generation. Being OnlyChild, a has no sibling – an exception to (14). An exception to (15) is b, whose parents are both OnlyChild, and b has no cousin.

Suppose an amusing family, in which one is amused by the other. For a couple, one has a cousin but no sibling, and the other has a sibling but no cousin. As to such a case, the cousin is amused by the sibling, or in the converse direction. Given the antecedent (*) plus hasSpouse(a,b), an amusing family does exist.

4   Algorithms

In the following, if not stated otherwise, for an $\mathcal{ALC}_{\mathbb{P}}^u$ KB $\mathcal{K} = (\mathcal{T},\mathcal{A},\mathbb{P})$, we denote that: (1) Σ_C is the closure of concepts occurring in $\mathcal{T}$, $\mathcal{A}$ and $\mathbb{P}$; (2) Σ_R

is the set of roles occurring in $\mathcal{T}$, $\mathcal{A}$ and $\mathbb{P}$; (3) Σ_I is the set of named individuals occurring in $\mathcal{A}$ and $\mathbb{P}$.

The algorithm first rewrites TBox subsumptions with rules, and $\mathcal{K} = (\mathcal{T}, \mathcal{A}, \mathbb{P})$ becomes $\mathcal{K}' = (\emptyset, \mathcal{A}, \mathbb{P}^\mathcal{T})$, followed by $\mathcal{K}'' = (\emptyset, \mathcal{A}, \mathbb{P}^{\mathcal{T},E})$ to compute extensions of complex $\mathcal{ALC}$-concepts. Upon that, we will establish completion graphs, towards the decision procedure for the KB satisfiability problem and the query entailment problem, respectively.

4.1 Preprocessing

Given an $\mathcal{ALC}_\mathbb{P}^u$ KB $\mathcal{K} = (\mathcal{T}, \mathcal{A}, \mathbb{P})$, concept subsumptions in the TBox $\mathcal{T}$ are rewritten such that $\mathbb{P}^\mathcal{T} = \mathbb{P} \cup \{C_2(x) \leftarrow C_1(x) | C_1 \sqsubseteq C_2 \in \mathcal{T}\}$, and the KB is updated to $\mathcal{K}' = (\emptyset, \mathcal{A}, \mathbb{P}^\mathcal{T})$.

Next, the computation, along with reasoning, is used to evaluate extensions of complex $\mathcal{ALC}$-concepts, and now the KB becomes $\mathcal{K}'' = (\emptyset, \mathcal{A}, \mathbb{P}^{\mathcal{T},E})$. Starting from $\mathbb{P}^\mathcal{T}$, we obtain $\mathbb{P}^{\mathcal{T},E}$ by appending rules for each computable $\mathcal{ALC}$-concept in Σ_C, that is $C_1 \sqcap C_2, C_1 \sqcup C_2$ and $\exists R.C$. We observe that classical negation appears in $\neg C$ and $\forall R.C$, where $\forall R.C$ concerns a case for the negation of R. Incomplete information possibly leads to neither positive nor negative atoms, which motivates us to introduce *universal* concepts of $C \sqcup \neg C$ and $\forall R.C \sqcup \exists R.\neg C$ for $\neg C$ and $\forall R.C$, respectively. So that, individuals in the top concept $\top$ are assigned into those universal concepts.

$$C_1 \sqcap C_2(x) \leftarrow C_1(x), C_2(x). \qquad C_1 \sqcup C_2(x) \leftarrow C_1(x). \qquad C_1 \sqcup C_2(x) \leftarrow C_2(x).$$
$$\exists R.C(x) \leftarrow R(x,y), C(y). \quad C \sqcup \neg C(x) \leftarrow \top(x). \quad \forall R.C \sqcup \exists R.\neg C(x) \leftarrow \top(x).$$

Above, computation rules are specified for every concept $\neg C, C_1 \sqcap C_2, C_1 \sqcup C_2, \exists R.C$ and $\forall R.C$ appearing in Σ_C. Since these 'system-level' rules are designed for DL concepts, named individuals and facts need not to stay here. We also realize that, in a similar but more elaborate manner, [12] simulates DLs via open answer set programming. Interestingly, support for DL reasoning totally replies on running simulation rules in [12], while we would develop DL tableaux-based algorithms getting the above computation rules involved.

In the Online Appendix[1], it shows that: The $\mathcal{ALC}_\mathbb{P}^u$ KB $\mathcal{K} = (\mathcal{T}, \mathcal{A}, \mathbb{P})$ and its updated version $\mathcal{K}' = (\emptyset, \mathcal{A}, \mathbb{P}^\mathcal{T})$ as well as $\mathcal{K}'' = (\emptyset, \mathcal{A}, \mathbb{P}^{\mathcal{T},E})$ are equivalent.

4.2 Completion Graphs

Observing that role assertions are possibly refreshed by rules when such a role occurs in the rule head, completion graphs instead of completion forests [14] or completion trees [13] are studied in this paper.

A *completion graph* is a (directed) graph G where each node u is labeled with a set $\mathcal{L}(u) \subseteq \Sigma_C$ and each edge $\langle u, v \rangle$ is labeled with a set $\mathcal{L}(\langle u, v \rangle) \subseteq \Sigma_R$. If there is an edge $\langle u, v \rangle$ in G, then we say that v is the successor of u and u is the predecessor of v. The transitive closure of predecessor (resp. successor) is called ancestor (resp. descendant). For a node u, $\mathcal{L}(u)$ is said to contain a *clash* if, for some concept C, $\{C, \neg C\} \subseteq \mathcal{L}(u)$.

Initially, we construct a graph $G_\mathcal{A}$ for an ABox $\mathcal{A}$ as follows.

- A node u_a is created, for each named individual $a \in \Sigma_I$.
- An edge $\langle u_a, u_b \rangle$ is created, if $R(a, b) \in \mathcal{A}$ for some role $R \in \Sigma_R$ and $a, b \in \Sigma_I$.
- The labels of these nodes and edges are initialized by
$\mathcal{L}(u_a) = \{C | C(a) \in \mathcal{A}\}$ and $\mathcal{L}(\langle u_a, u_b \rangle) = \{R | R(a, b) \in \mathcal{A}\}$.

Running CompGraph($G_\mathcal{A}$), the algorithm proceeds.

Procedure CompGraph
Input: A graph G_{in}
Output: A set of graphs G_{out}
begin $G_{out} := \emptyset$

      for each g in ExpGraph(G_{in}) **do**
          for each g' in SmsGraph(g) **do**
             if g' is *complete* **then** $G_{out} := G_{out} \cup \{g'\}$
                        else $G_{out} := G_{out} \cup$ CompGraph(g')
      return G_{out}
end

Expansion principles in Table 2 are ready for the procedure of ExpGraph. The application of ⊔-principle is non-deterministic, branching graphs. The ∃-principle is a generating principle since, possibly, fresh new nodes are inserted into the graph. Besides, we call nodes having been located in $G_\mathcal{A}$ as a-nodes, each of which represents a named individual, and b-nodes for the others, each of which represents a unnamed individual (e.g., being introduced by the ∃-principle).

Referring to definitions of n-tree equivalence, n-witness and n-blocking in [16][20], as restated below, we present l-blocking for the ∃-principle in Table 2. The parameter of l will take the value of $l_\mathcal{K}$ for the KB satisfiability problem and of $l_{\mathcal{K},Q}$ for the query entailment problem, given that

$l_\mathcal{K}$: The maximal of l_r for all r in $\mathbb{P}^{\mathcal{T},E}$ where l_r is the number of variables in r
l_Q: The length of a query Q and Section 4.4 presents more details
$l_{\mathcal{K},Q}$: The maximal of $l_\mathcal{K}$ and l_Q

Definition 3. *The n-tree of a node u is the tree that includes the node u and its descendants, whose distance from u is at most n successor edges. We denote the set of nodes in the n-tree of u by $V_n(u)$.*

Table 2. Expansion Principles for ExpGraph

⊓:	if $C_1 \sqcap C_2 \in \mathcal{L}(u)$ and $\{C_1, C_2\} \nsubseteq \mathcal{L}(u)$
	then $\mathcal{L}(u) := \mathcal{L}(u) \cup \{C_1, C_2\}$
⊔:	if $C_1 \sqcup C_2 \in \mathcal{L}(u)$ and $\{C_1, C_2\} \cap \mathcal{L}(u) = \emptyset$
	then $\mathcal{L}(u) := \mathcal{L}(u) \cup \{C_1\}$ or $\mathcal{L}(u) := \mathcal{L}(u) \cup \{C_2\}$
∀:	if $\forall R.C \in \mathcal{L}(u)$ and $R \in \mathcal{L}(\langle u, v \rangle)$ but $C \notin \mathcal{L}(v)$
	then $\mathcal{L}(v) := \mathcal{L}(v) \cup \{C\}$
∃:	if $\exists R.C \in \mathcal{L}(u)$ where u is an a-node or a b-node not being l-blocked,
	there does not exist any node v such that $R \in \mathcal{L}(\langle u, v \rangle)$ and $C \in \mathcal{L}(v)$
	then create a b-node v with $\mathcal{L}(v) := \{C\}$ and an edge $\langle u, v \rangle$ with $\mathcal{L}(\langle u, v \rangle) := \{R\}$

Two nodes u, v in a graph G are said to be n-tree equivalent if there is an isomorphism $\psi : V_n(v) \rightarrow V_n(u)$ s.t. (1) $\psi(v) = u$; (2) $\mathcal{L}(s) = \mathcal{L}(\psi(s))$, for every $s \in V_n(v)$; (3) $\mathcal{L}(\langle s, t \rangle) = \mathcal{L}(\langle \psi(s), \psi(t) \rangle)$, for every $s, t \in V_n(v)$.

A node u is an n-witness of a node v in a graph G if (1) u is an ancestor of v, (2) u is n-tree equivalent to v, and (3) v is not in the n-tree of u.

A node w is n-blocked in a graph G if (1) one of its ancestors is n-blocked, or (2) w is in an n-tree of which root has an n-witness. Suppose u be an n-witness of v and $\psi : V_n(v) \rightarrow V_n(u)$ the isomorphism. For any node w in the n-tree of v, w is n-blocked by $\psi(w)$.

A completion graph G is called *complete* when for some node u in G, $\mathcal{L}(u)$ contains a clash, or when none of the expansion principles is applicable. The output of ExpGraph consists of complete completion graphs, each of which again becomes the input of SmsGraph. Intuitively, the procedure of ExpGraph serves for DL constructors, while the procedure of SmsGraph for general rules.

With an input graph g to SmsGraph, a "bottom" set B_g and a "top" set T_g are built. The former collects those labels in g such that $B_g = \{C(u)|C \in \mathcal{L}(u)\} \cup \{R(u,v)|R \in \mathcal{L}(\langle u,v \rangle)\}$, and the latter concerns all possible constituents s.t. $T_g = \{C(u)|C \in \Sigma_C$ and u appears in $g\} \cup \{R(u,v)|R \in \Sigma_R$ and u, v appear in $g\}$. By the Gelfond-Lifschitz transformation [10], we denote a *stable set* S_g s.t.

1. $B_g \subseteq S_g \subseteq T_g$;
2. For a rule $r : p(\boldsymbol{u}) \leftarrow q_1(\boldsymbol{v}_1), \cdots, q_m(\boldsymbol{v}_m), \text{not } q_{m+1}(\boldsymbol{v}_{m+1}), \cdots \text{not } q_n(\boldsymbol{v}_n)$ satisfying all $q_j(\sigma(\boldsymbol{v}_j)) \notin S_g$ and $m + 1 \leqslant j \leqslant n$, in $\mathbb{P}^{T,E}$, where σ is a term assignment w.r.t. g and r, if $q_i(\sigma(\boldsymbol{v}_i)) \in S_g$ for each $1 \leqslant i \leqslant m$ then $p(\sigma(\boldsymbol{u})) \in S_g$.

A *term assignment* σ w.r.t. g and r is a mapping which assigns

(1) a node in g to every variable in r,
(2) an a-node u_a in g to every named individual a in r,
(3) an a-node in g to every variable appearing in the head of r.

Naturally, the assignment of (3) concerns the *semantic* weak safeness.

After receiving all stable sets, we "repay" the input graph g with an output set of graphs, SmsGraph(g), each of which is constructed by a stable set S_g s.t.

– Nodes are created the same as g;
– An edge $\langle u, v \rangle$ is created, if $R(u, v) \in S_g$ for some R;
– Labels are $\mathcal{L}(u) = \{C|C(u) \in S_g\}$ and $\mathcal{L}(\langle u, v \rangle) = \{R|R(u, v) \in S_g\}$.

Since, the completion graph g' in SmsGraph(g) updates g (e.g., having new edges or more labels of nodes and edges), those expansion principles in Table 2 are possibly again applicable to g'. When g' happens not to being complete, a call to CompGraph(g') is stacked. If completion graphs, obtained from procedures of both ExpGraph and SmsGraph, are totally complete, the algorithm terminates. We remark l-blocking, which occurs in the $\exists$-principle at Table 2, is crucial to termination, and the following two subsections will elaborate on the parameter l: one takes $l_{\mathcal{K}}$ for the KB satisfiability problem, and the other is $l_{\mathcal{K},Q}$ for the query entailment problem.

4.3   The KB Satisfiability Problem

The above algorithm that yields $l_\mathcal{K}$-completion graphs is shown up as a decision procedure for the satisfiability problem w.r.t. an $\mathcal{ALC}_\mathbb{P}^u$ KB $\mathcal{K} = (\mathcal{T}, \mathcal{A}, \mathbb{P})$.

Recalling that weak safeness plays a role in our algorithm, the Online Appendix[1] declares the termination: For an $\mathcal{ALC}_\mathbb{P}^u$ KB $\mathcal{K}$, the algorithm terminates.

As to the soundness, which states that if the algorithm yields a complete and clash-free $l_\mathcal{K}$-completion graph then $\mathcal{K}$ is satisfiable, we need to introduce canonical structures for completion graphs (cf. [16] and [20]).

Definition 4. *Suppose G be an $l_\mathcal{K}$-completion graph generated by the algorithm for $\mathcal{K}$. A canonical structure $\mathcal{I}_G = \langle (\mathcal{D}_G, id), I_G \rangle$ for G is defined such that*
1. $\mathcal{D}_G := \{u \mid u \text{ is a node in } G\}$
2. *For each named individual $a \in \Sigma_I$, $id(a) \in \mathcal{D}_G$ corresponds to its a-node u_a*
3. *For each concept $C \in \Sigma_C$, $C^{I_G} := \{u \mid C \in \mathcal{L}(u)\}$*
4. *For each role $R \in \Sigma_R$, $(u, v) \in R^{I_G}$ if and only if (1) $R \in \mathcal{L}(\langle u, v \rangle)$; or (2) $R \in \mathcal{L}(\langle \psi(u), v \rangle)$ where u is $l_\mathcal{K}$-blocked, t is the root of the $l_\mathcal{K}$-tree to which u belongs, s is the witness of t, $\psi : V_{l_\mathcal{K}}(t) \to V_{l_\mathcal{K}}(s)$ is an isomorphism between the $l_\mathcal{K}$-trees rooted with t and s.*

Note that, for an $l_\mathcal{K}$-blocked node u, *explicit* edges, e.g., $\langle u, v \rangle$, are not available, but *implicit* edges, e.g., $\langle \psi(u), v \rangle$, rather contribute to interpreting roles.

Specifically, if the algorithm yields a complete and clash-free $l_\mathcal{K}$-completion graph G for an $\mathcal{ALC}_\mathbb{P}^u$ KB $\mathcal{K}$, a canonical structure $\mathcal{I}_G = \langle (\mathcal{D}_G, id), I_G \rangle$ for G is proved (in the Online Appendix[1]) as the model of $\mathcal{K}$, so that $\mathcal{K}$ is satisfiable.

Next is the completeness, which states that if $\mathcal{K}$ is satisfiable, then the algorithm yields a complete and clash-free $l_\mathcal{K}$-completion graph.

Since, $\mathcal{K}$ is satisfiable, by definitions, there is an extended Herbrand structure $\mathcal{I} = \langle (\mathcal{D}, id), I \rangle$ satisfying the ABox $\mathcal{A}$, the TBox $\mathcal{T}$ and the PBox $\mathbb{P}$. Referring to [14], we use $\mathcal{I}$ to trigger the application of the expansion principles such that they yield a complete and clash-free $l_\mathcal{K}$-completion graph. To this propose, a function π is defined, mapping nodes in a graph G to the domain $\mathcal{D}$, as follows.

(1) For a named individual a, $\pi(u_a) := a$ where u_a is the corresponding a-node.
(2) If $\pi(u) = s$ is already defined, and a successor v of u was generated for $\exists R.C \in \mathcal{L}(u)$, then $\pi(v) := t$ for some $t \in \mathcal{D}$ with $t \in C^I$ and $(s, t) \in R^I$.

For all nodes u, v in a completion graph G, we claim a condition that
$$\mathcal{L}(u) \subseteq \{C \mid \pi(u) \in C^I\} \text{ and } \mathcal{L}(\langle u, v \rangle) \subseteq \{R \mid (\pi(u), \pi(v)) \in R^I\}. \tag{*}$$
As shown in the Online Appendix[1], the algorithm ends up with certain complete $l_\mathcal{K}$-completion graph, denoted by $G_\mathcal{I}$, satisfying the condition (*). Because $\mathcal{I} = \langle (\mathcal{D}, id), I \rangle$ is a model of $\mathcal{K}$, we have $C^I \cap (\neg C)^I = \emptyset$ for any concept $C \in \Sigma_C$, which implies $G_\mathcal{I}$ is clash-free. Otherwise, there exists a clash such that $\{D, \neg D\} \subseteq \mathcal{L}(u) \subseteq \{C \mid \pi(u) \in C^I\}$ in $G_\mathcal{I}$, for some concept D and some node u, making $\pi(u) \in D^I \cap (\neg D)^I$ conflict with the model $\mathcal{I}$. Summing up, $G_\mathcal{I}$ is the complete and clash-free $l_\mathcal{K}$-completion graph that the algorithm yields.

Theorem 1. *The algorithm is a decision procedure for the satisfiability of an $\mathcal{ALC}_\mathbb{P}^u$ KB $\mathcal{K} = (\mathcal{T}, \mathcal{A}, \mathbb{P})$, and decides the KB satisfiability problem in 3ExpTime w.r.t. the size of $\mathcal{K}$.*

4.4   The Query Entailment Problem

Before we address this problem, queries are formalized.

Definition 5. *A conjunctive query (CQ) q over an $\mathcal{ALC}_{\mathbb{P}}^u$ KB $\mathcal{K}$ is of the form being $\{p_1(\boldsymbol{w_1}), \cdots, p_n(\boldsymbol{w_n})\}$, where p_i is either a DL concept or a DL role, and $\boldsymbol{w_i}$ is a (unary, binary) vector of terms, for each $1 \leqslant i \leqslant n$. By l_q, we denote the length of a CQ $q = \{p_1(\boldsymbol{w_1}), \cdots, p_n(\boldsymbol{w_n})\}$, and $l_q = n$.*

A union of conjunctive queries (UCQ) q' over an $\mathcal{ALC}_{\mathbb{P}}^u$ KB $\mathcal{K}$ is of the form being $q_1 \vee \cdots \vee q_m$, where q_j is a CQ for each $1 \leqslant j \leqslant m$. By $l_{q'}$, we denote the length of an UCQ $q' = q_1 \vee \cdots \vee q_m$, and $l_{q'} = \max\{l_{q_j} | 1 \leqslant j \leqslant m\}$.

For simplification, Q is said to be a *query*, whether Q is a CQ or an UCQ. Queries are interpreted in a standard way. Given a query Q and an extended Herbrand structure $\mathcal{I} = \langle (\mathcal{D}, id), I \rangle$, the *variable substitution* w.r.t. Q and $\mathcal{I}$ is $\theta = \{x_1/t_1, \cdots, x_n/t_n\}$, which substitutes each variable $x_i \in \mathcal{V}$ appearing in Q with a (un)named individual $t_i \in \mathcal{D}$ and $1 \leqslant i \leqslant n$. We use the LP notation $\alpha\theta$ to apply θ to variables in an atom α. As for a CQ q, a structure $\mathcal{I}$ is a model of q, denoted by $\mathcal{I} \models q$, if there is a variable substitution θ w.r.t. q and $\mathcal{I}$ such that $\mathcal{I} \models p_i(\boldsymbol{w_i})\theta$ for each $p_i(\boldsymbol{w_i})$ in q, where $1 \leqslant i \leqslant n$. For an UCQ q', $\mathcal{I}$ is a model of q', denoted by $\mathcal{I} \models q'$, if $\mathcal{I} \models q_j$ for some q_j in q', where $1 \leqslant j \leqslant m$.

Given an $\mathcal{ALC}_{\mathbb{P}}^u$ KB $\mathcal{K}$ and a query Q, we say $\mathcal{K}$ *entails* Q, denoted by $\mathcal{K} \models Q$, if $\mathcal{I} \models Q$ for each model $\mathcal{I}$ of $\mathcal{K}$. The *query entailment* problem is to decide whether $\mathcal{K} \models Q$. We assume $\mathcal{K}$ being satisfiable, in this context; otherwise, everything can be entailed from a contradictory KB.

Now, for an $\mathcal{ALC}_{\mathbb{P}}^u$ KB $\mathcal{K} = (\mathcal{T}, \mathcal{A}, \mathbb{P})$ and a query Q, we redefine that: (1) Σ_C is the closure of concepts occurring in $\mathcal{T}, \mathcal{A}, \mathbb{P}$ and Q; (2) Σ_R is the set of roles occurring in $\mathcal{T}, \mathcal{A}, \mathbb{P}$ and Q; (3) Σ_I is the set of named individual occurring in $\mathcal{A}, \mathbb{P}$ and Q. The parameter $l_{\mathcal{K},Q}$ is the maximal of $l_\mathcal{K}$ and l_Q, and the previous algorithm, as described in Section 4.2, will yield $l_{\mathcal{K},Q}$-completion graphs.

Next, referring to [20], we establish mappings from the query to those obtained $l_{\mathcal{K},Q}$-completion graphs. For a CQ $q : \{p_1(\boldsymbol{w_1}), \cdots, p_n(\boldsymbol{w_n})\}$ and a graph G, a mapping δ maps named individuals and variables in q to nodes in G, s.t.
1. For each named individual $a \in \Sigma_I$ in q, $\delta(a) = u_a$ is the corresponding a-node;
2. For each $C(t)$ and $R(t_1, t_2)$ in q where t, t_1, t_2 are named individuals or variables, $C \in \mathcal{L}(\delta(t))$ and $R \in \mathcal{L}(\langle \delta(t_1), \delta(t_2) \rangle)$.

A CQ q is mappable to a graph G, denoted by $q \hookrightarrow G$, if there exists such a mapping δ. An UCQ $q' : q_1 \vee \cdots \vee q_m$ is mappable to a graph G, denoted by $q' \hookrightarrow G$, if $q_j \hookrightarrow G$ for some q_j in q' where $1 \leqslant j \leqslant m$.

Thus, the algorithm returns "Q is entailed by $\mathcal{K}$", denoted as $\mathcal{K} \vdash Q$, if for all complete and clash-free $l_{\mathcal{K},Q}$-completion graphs G that the algorithm yields, $Q \hookrightarrow G$ holds, otherwise the algorithm returns "Q is not entailed by $\mathcal{K}$".

We direct readers to the Online Appendix[1] for details on termination, soundness, completeness, and complexity etc. Below is the resulting theorem.

Theorem 2. *The updated algorithm is a decision procedure for the entailment of an $\mathcal{ALC}_{\mathbb{P}}^u$ KB $\mathcal{K}$ to a query Q, and decides the query entailment problem in 3ExpTime w.r.t. the size of $\mathcal{K}$.*

5   Conclusion

This paper presents an $\mathcal{ALC}_{\mathbb{P}}^{u}$ KB, consisting of a TBox of subsumptions and an ABox of assertions, augmented by a PBox of general rules sharing predicates with the DL concepts and roles. For its open answer set semantics, extended Herbrand structures are used to interpret DL concepts and roles, while open answer sets hold for general rules. To retain decidability, a well-known weak safeness [22] condition is employed. We extend DL tableaux-based algorithms to $\mathcal{ALC}_{\mathbb{P}}^{u}$ decision procedures for the KB satisfiability and query entailment problems.

By way of comparison, CARIN [16] builds completion trees, which are used to evaluate hybrid rules externally, so that the information flow is uni-directional, i.e., from DL to rules but not vice versa. Our $\mathcal{ALC}_{\mathbb{P}}^{u}$ constructs completion graphs shared homogeneously between the DL and rule components, which makes bi-directional information flow a characteristic of $\mathcal{ALC}_{\mathbb{P}}^{u}$.

Although existing DL reasoners and rule engines facilitate other related work (e.g., [8][18][22]), we believe that novel algorithms, specified for a homogeneous integration of DL and general rules, enable the newly envisioned unifying logic on top of ontologies and rules in the Semantic Web. The unary/binary $\mathcal{ALC}_{\mathbb{P}}^{u}$ logic could be extended for n-ary relations, which may be realized by decomposition into binary ones; this might also benefit from $\mathcal{DLR}$'s [4] extension of binary DL roles to n-ary DL relations; we currently explore which n-ary approach works best with our (extended) $\mathcal{ALC}_{\mathbb{P}}^{u}$ algorithms. On top of n-ary relations, further rule layers, such as undecidable (function-full) Horn rules, could be built. On the other hand, extensions of $\mathcal{ALC}_{\mathbb{P}}^{u}$ towards higher OWL layers, e.g., $\mathcal{SHIF}(\mathbf{D})$ and $\mathcal{SHOIN}(\mathbf{D})$, deserve more investigation w.r.t. corresponding DL tableaux-based algorithms that integrate general rules.

References

1. Antoniou, G., Damasio, C.V., Grosof, B., Horrocks, I., Kifer, M., Maluszynski, J., Patel-Schneider, P.F.: Combining Rules and Ontologies - A survey. Deliverables I3-D3, REWERSE, http://rewerse.net/deliverables/m12/i3-d3.pdf (March 2005)
2. Baader, F., Calvanese, D., McGuinness, D., Nardi, D., Patel-Schneider, P.: The Description Logic Handbook: Theory, Implementation and Applications. Cambridge University Press, Cambridge (2003)
3. Berners-Lee, T.: AAAI-06 Invited Talk: Artificial Intelligence and the Semantic Web. http://www.w3.org/2006/Talks/0718-aaai-tbl/Overview.html
4. Calvanese, D., De Giacomo, G., Lenzerini, M.: Conjunctive Query Containment in Description Logics with n-ary Relations. In: Proceedings of International Workshop on Description Logics, vol. 410 of URA-CNRS (1997)
5. de Bruijn, J., Eiter, T., Polleres, A., Tompits, H.: On Representational Issues About Combinations of Classical Theories with Nonmonotonic Rules. In: Lang, J., Lin, F., Wang, J. (eds.) KSEM 2006. LNCS (LNAI), vol. 4092, pp. 1–22. Springer, Heidelberg (2006)
6. de Bruijn, J., Pearce, D., Polleres, A., Valverde, A.: A Logic for Hybrid Rules. In: Proceedings of RuleML 2006 Workshop: Ontology and Rule Integration (November 2006)

7. Donini, F.M., Lenzerini, M., Nardi, D., Schaerf, A.: AL-log: Integrating Datalog and Description Logics. Journal of Intelligent Information Systems (JIIS) 10(3), 227–252 (1998)
8. Eiter, T., Ianni, G., Schindlauer, R., Tompits, H.: Effective Integration of Declarative Rules with External Evaluations for Semantic-Web Reasoning. In: Sure, Y., Domingue, J. (eds.) ESWC 2006. LNCS, vol. 4011, pp. 273–287. Springer, Heidelberg (2006)
9. Eiter, T., Lukasiewicz, T., Schindlauer, R., Tompits, H.: Combining Answer Set Programming with Description Logics for the Semantic Web. In: Proceedings of the 9th KR, pp. 141–151. AAAI Press, Stanford (2004)
10. Gelfond, M., Lifschitz, V.: The Stable Model Semantics for Logic Programming. In: Proceedings of the 5th International Conference and Symposium on Logic Programming (ICLP/SLP), pp. 1070–1080. MIT Press, Cambridge (1988)
11. Grosof, B.N., Horrocks, I., Volz, R., Decker, S.: Description Logic Programs: Combining Logic Programs with Description Logic. In: Proceedings of the 12th International World Wide Web Conference, pp. 48–57. ACM Press, New York (2003)
12. Heymans, S.: Decidable Open Answer Set Programming. Phd thesis, Theoretical Computer Science Lab (TINF), Vrije Universiteit Brussel (February 2006)
13. Horrocks, I., Sattler, U., Tobies, S.: A Description Logic with Transitive and Converse Roles, Role Hierarchies and Qualifying Number Restrictions. LTCS-Report 99–08, RWTH Aachen, Germany (1999)
14. Horrocks, I., Sattler, U., Tobies, S.: Reasoning with Individuals for the Description Logic SHIQ. In: McAllester, D. (ed.) Automated Deduction - CADE-17. LNCS, vol. 1831, pp. 482–496. Springer, Heidelberg (2000)
15. Hustadt, U., Motik, B., Sattler, U.: Reducing SHIQ-Description Logic to Disjunctive Datalog Programs. In: Proceedings of the 9th KR, pp. 152–162. AAAI Press, Stanford (2004)
16. Levy, A.Y., Rousset, M.-C.: Combining Horn Rules and Description Logics in CARIN. Artifician Intelligence 104(1-2), 165–209 (1998)
17. Lloyd, J.W.: Foundations of Logic Programming (second, extended edition). Springer, Heidelberg (1987)
18. Motik, B., Horrocks, I., Rosati, R., Sattler, U.: Can OWL and Logic Programming Live Together Happily Ever After? In: Cruz, I., Decker, S., Allemang, D., Preist, C., Schwabe, D., Mika, P., Uschold, M., Aroyo, L. (eds.) ISWC 2006. LNCS, vol. 4273, pp. 501–514. Springer, Heidelberg (2006)
19. Motik, B., Sattler, U., Studer, R.: Query Answering for OWL-DL with rules. Journal of Web. Semantics 3(1), 41–60 (2005)
20. Ortiz, M., Calvanese, D., Eiter, T.: Data complexity of Answering Unions of Conjunctive Queries in shiq. Technical report, Faculty of Computer Science, Free University of Bozen-Bolzano (2006)
21. Rosati, R.: On the Decidability and Complexity of Integrating Ontologies and Rules. Journal of Web Semantics 3(1), 61–73 (2005)
22. Rosati, R.: DL+log: Tight Integration of Description Logics and Disjunctive Datalog. In: Proceedings of the 10th KR, pp. 68–78. AAAI Press, Stanford (2006)
23. W3C. OWL: Web Ontology Language Semantics and Abstract Syntax. http://www.w3.org/TR/owl-absyn/
24. W3C. Rule Interchange Format Working Group. http://www.w3.org/2005/rules/
25. W3C. SWRL: A Semantic Web Rule Language Combining OWL and RuleML. http://www.w3.org/Submission/SWRL/

Evaluating Formalisms for Modular Ontologies in Distributed Information Systems

Yimin Wang[1], Jie Bao[2], Peter Haase[1], and Guilin Qi[1]

[1] Institute AIFB, University of Karlsruhe (TH), Karlsruhe, Germany
{ywa,pha,gqi}@aifb.uni-karlsruhe.de
[2] Artificial Intelligence Research Laboratory, Department of Computer Science
Iowa State University, Ames, IA 50011-1040, USA
baojie@cs.iastate.edu

Abstract. Modern semantic technology is one of the necessary supports for the infrastructure of next generation information systems. In particular, large international organizations, which usually have branches around the globe, need to manage web-based, complex, dynamically changing and geographically distributed information. Formalisms for modular ontologies offer the necessary mechanism that is needed to handle ontology-based distributed information systems in the aforementioned scenario. In this paper, we investigate state-of-the-art technologies in the area of modular ontologies and corresponding logical formalisms. We compare different formalisms for modular ontologies in their ability to support networked, dynamic and distributed ontologies, as well as the reasoning capability over these ontologies. The comparison results show the strength and limitation of existing formalisms against the needs of modular ontologies in the given setting, and possible future extensions to overcome those limitations.

Keywords: Distributed information systems, modular ontologies, semantic technology, requirements.

1 Introduction

Managing large-scale information systems in a distributed way is usually a challenging task in which each system may pertain only a subset of the information in question and the dynamically-changing information in local systems is difficult to detect or to control. A typical application scenario is that large international organizations, which may have branches around the globe and maintain multiple, distributed, large information systems for each of their branch. With the popularity of semantic technologies deployed in information system engineering, knowledge, often being represented as ontologies, is typically maintained by local branches of the organization in a collaborative way. While those ontologies are usually focused on the local information of particular local branches and are physically distributed around the world, they are also very likely to be linked together to offer the necessary global usage of information.

As a motivating example, we consider one of the case studies of the NeOn project[1] [8] – a fishery case study in the Food and Agriculture Organization (FAO) of the United

---

[1] http://www.neon-project.org

M. Marchiori, J.Z. Pan, and C. de Sainte Marie (Eds.): RR 2007, LNCS 4524, pp. 178–193, 2007.

Nations (UN). This case study aims to improve the interoperability of FAO information systems in the fishery domain, integrating and using *networked ontologies* [14], by creating and maintaining distributed ontologies (and ontology mappings) in the fishery domain. In particular, FAO has large sets of fishery ontology data with the following features and requirements:

1. *Networking.* The ontology data sets in FAO are intensively interconnected by different subjects, languages, countries and other geopolitical aspects in a secure networked environment with clear boundary for information hiding and encapsulation.
2. *Dynamics.* In FAO, the ontologies are large, interconnected and changing over time. Therefore, an approach that can handle ontology data in a dynamic way with change monitoring and propagation is required.
3. *Distribution.* Because FAO has many branches around the world, the ontologies in FAO are distributed rather than centralized, which arises challenges in loose coupling and autonomous management.
4. *Reasoning.* FAO ontologies, which usually consist of both terminologies and assertional data in FAO fishery case studyies, need reasoning support with high efficiency and good scalability.

We argue that such a scenario is common to typical large-scale distributed information systems that are deployed using semantic applications, especially for knowledge management in big international organizations. Hence, there have been considerable recent efforts to provide solutions for such a scenario. For example, the recent W3C recommendation, OWL Web Ontology Language [23] can represent and connect ontologies on the Web in a machine readable format, which is one of the central concerns of the Semantic Web [5,30]. Borgida and colleagues proposes Distributed Description Logics (DDL) to correspond the federated information sources [6] and a DDL implementation DRAGO [28]. However, these current technologies often have difficulties in handling ontological data against the requirements mentioned above:

1. Traditional ontology formalisms, e.g. Frame System or Description Logics, are designed for centralized ontologies rather than decentralized ones. Furthermore, most ontology management systems do not support processing large instance data represented in the form of ontologies in the decentralized scenario.
2. In a scenario with interconnected ontology modules, ideally, when one ontology module is updated, the depending ontology modules should be updated as well to reflect the changes. However, few current technologies can support such dynamic automatic updating.
3. What is still missing is a *principled* approach to support distributed ontologies, where the individual ontology modules are physically distributed, loosely coupled and autonomously managed.
4. Some reasoners are able to support either local TBox reasoning (e.g. FaCT++ [35]) or distributed TBox reasoning (e.g. DRAGO [28] and Pellet [31]), while others are good at ABox reasoning (e.g. KAON2 [24]). However, handling both TBox and ABox in a distributed, efficient and scalable way for modular ontologies is a challenging task for reasoners.

To manage information generated and maintained in such distributed settings, we need knowledge representation formalisms and tools to meet the following challenge:

How to properly manage multiple networked, distributed, dynamic ontologies and provide corresponding reasoning support? In this paper, we investigate approaches to represent and exploit such networked ontologies, considering the recent advances in formalisms for modular ontologies and distributed reasoning techniques.

In the following sections, we firstly introduce some preliminaries of description logics and modular ontologies in Section 2. We analyze requirements of networked ontologies and comparison criteria for different formalisms on their language functionality and expressivity in Section 3. We compare several formalisms for the need of networked ontologies in the light of the given set of requirements in Section 4 and identify some critical unsolved problems in modeling and reasoning with networked ontologies and discuss possible solutions to those problems Section 6. We summarize the paper and outline future work in Section 7.

2 Preliminaries

Formalisms of modular ontologies studied in this paper mainly aim to handle subsets of OWL-DL with Description Logics (DLs) as the underlying logical formalism. Therefore, we first introduce basic preliminaries of DLs to allow a better understanding of the formalisms introduced in Section 4. Furthermore, we also briefly introduce modular ontologies and their roles in the distributed information systems.

2.1 Description Logics

Syntax. Given $\mathcal{R}$ as a finite set of transitive and inclusion axioms with normal role names N_R, a $\mathcal{SHIQ}$-role is either some $R \in N_R$ or an *inverse role* R^- for $R \in N_R$. $\mathsf{Trans}(R)$ and $R \sqsubseteq S$ represent the transitive and inclusion axioms, respectively, where R and S are roles. A simple role is a $\mathcal{SHIQ}$-role that neither its sub-roles nor itself is transitive. Let N_C be a set of *concept names*, the set of $\mathcal{SHIQ}$-concepts is the minimal set such that every concept $C \in N_C$ is a $\mathcal{SHIQ}$-concept and for C and D are $\mathcal{SHIQ}$-concepts, R is a role, S a simple role and n a positive integer, then $(\neg C)$, $(C \sqcap D)$, $(C \sqcup D)$, $(\exists R.C)$, $(\forall R.C)$, $(\leqslant nSC)$ and $(\geqslant nSC)$ are also $\mathcal{SHIQ}$-concepts.

Therefore we have a knowledge base $\mathcal{KB}$ that is a triple $(\mathcal{R}, \mathcal{T}, \mathcal{A})$ where $\mathcal{R}$ is the RBox, TBox $\mathcal{T}$ is a finite set of axioms representing the concept inclusions with the

Table 1. Semantics of $\mathcal{SHIQ} - \mathcal{KB}$

Interpretation of Concepts
$(\neg C)^{\mathcal{I}} = \Delta^{\mathcal{I}} \backslash C^{\mathcal{I}}, (C \sqcap D)^{\mathcal{I}} = C^{\mathcal{I}} \cap D^{\mathcal{I}}, (C \sqcup D)^{\mathcal{I}} = C^{\mathcal{I}} \cup D^{\mathcal{I}}$
$(\exists R.C)^{\mathcal{I}} = \{x \in \Delta^{\mathcal{I}} \mid R^{\mathcal{I}}(x, C) \neq \emptyset\}, (\forall R.C)^{\mathcal{I}} = \{x \in \Delta^{\mathcal{I}} \mid R^{\mathcal{I}}(x, \neg C) = \emptyset\}$
$(\leqslant nS.C)^{\mathcal{I}} = \{x \in \Delta^{\mathcal{I}} \mid \mathbf{N} R^{\mathcal{I}}(x, C) \leqslant n\}, (\geqslant nS.C)^{\mathcal{I}} = \{x \in \Delta^{\mathcal{I}} \mid \mathbf{N} R^{\mathcal{I}}(x, C) \geqslant n\}$
Interpretation of Axioms
$(C \sqsubseteq D)^{\mathcal{I}} : C^{\mathcal{I}} \subseteq D^{\mathcal{I}}, (R \sqsubseteq S)^{\mathcal{I}} : R^{\mathcal{I}} \subseteq S^{\mathcal{I}}$
$(\mathsf{Trans}(R))^{\mathcal{I}} : \{\forall x, y, z \in \Delta^{\mathcal{I}} \mid R^{\mathcal{I}}(x, y) \cap R^{\mathcal{I}}(y, z) \rightarrow R^{\mathcal{I}}(x, z)\}$
$\mathbf{N} R$ is the number restriction of a set R and $R^{\mathcal{I}}(x, C)$ is defined as:
$\{y \mid \langle x, y \rangle \in R^{\mathcal{I}} \text{ and } y \in C^{\mathcal{I}}\}.$

form $C \sqsubseteq D$, ABox $\mathcal{A}$ is a finite set of axioms with the form $C(x)$, $R(x,y)$, and $x = y$ (or $x \neq y$) that consists (un)equality-relations.

Semantics. The semantics of $\mathcal{KB}$ is given by the interpretation $\mathcal{I} = (\Delta^{\mathcal{I}}, \cdot^{\mathcal{I}'})$ that consists of a non-empty set $\Delta^{\mathcal{I}}$ (the domain of $\mathcal{I}$) and the function $\cdot^{\mathcal{I}'}$ in the Table 1 [17]. The satisfiability checking of $\mathcal{KB}$ in expressive DLs is performed by reducing the subsumption, and the reasoning over TBox and role hierarchy can be reduced to reasoning over only role hierarchy [16]. The interpretation $\mathcal{I}$ is the model of $\mathcal{R}$ and $\mathcal{T}$ if for each $R \sqsubseteq S \in \mathcal{R}$, $R^{\mathcal{I}} \subseteq S^{\mathcal{I}}$ and for each $C \sqsubseteq D \in \mathcal{T}$, $C^{\mathcal{I}} \subseteq D^{\mathcal{I}}$.

2.2 Modular Ontologies

Syntax. A modular ontology usually contains a set of component theories (modules) from same or different languages, and a set of semantic connections between those component. Formally, an abstract modular ontology $\Sigma = \langle \{L_i\}, \{M_{ij}\}_{i \neq j} \rangle$ contains a set of modules L_i, each is a TBox of a subset of $\mathcal{SHIQ}$, and a set of semantic connections M_{ij} between L_i and L_j for some $i \neq j$.

Two broad types of modular ontology languages have been studied [3]. The linking or mapping approach requires signatures of modules to be disjoint, i.e. $\mathsf{Sig}(L_i) \cap \mathsf{Sig}(L_j) = \emptyset$, for $i \neq j$; M_{ij} serves as the *mapping* between L_i and L_j. On the other hand, the importing approach allows modules to share terms. Formally, for a module L_i, a subset of its symbols $\mathsf{Loc}(L_i) \subseteq \mathsf{Sig}(L_i)$ is called L_i's *local signature*; the set of terms in $\mathsf{Ext}(L_i) = \mathsf{Sig}(L_i) \backslash \mathsf{Loc}(L_i)$ is called L_i's *external signature*; a term $t \in \mathsf{Loc}(L_i) \cap \mathsf{Ext}(L_j)$ ($i \neq j$) is said an imported term of j. Hence, semantic connection M_{ij} in the importing approach only allows name reuse in the form of $L_i \xrightarrow{t} L_j$.

Semantics. An interpretation $\mathcal{I} = \langle \{\mathcal{I}_i\}, \{r_{ij}\}_{i \neq j} \rangle$ of abstract modular ontology $\Sigma = \langle \{L_i\}, \{M_{ij}\}_{i \neq j} \rangle$, where $\mathcal{I}_i = \langle \Delta^{\mathcal{I}_i}, (.)^{\mathcal{I}_i} \rangle$ is the *local interpretation* of module L_i; *domain relation* $r_{ij} \subseteq \Delta^{\mathcal{I}_i} \times \Delta^{\mathcal{I}_j}$ is the interpretation for the semantic connection from L_i to L_j. It should be noted that two domains $\Delta^{\mathcal{I}_i}$ and $\Delta^{\mathcal{I}_j}$ are *not necessarily* the same or are disjoint. A domain relation r_{ij} represents the capability of the module j to map the objects of $\Delta^{\mathcal{I}_i}$ into $\Delta^{\mathcal{I}_j}$. Some formalisms may allow multiple domain relations under names $\{R_1, ...R_m\}$ such that $r_{ij} = \bigcup_n r_{ij}^{R_n}$.

Different modular ontology languages provide different solutions to model component theories and semantic connections between them. In section 4, we will further introduce several representative families of modular ontologies.

3 Criteria for Evaluation

In this section, we discuss two categories of criteria for evaluating modular ontology formalisms: functionality criteria is driven by the requirements of applications of large-scale distributed information system, while the expressivity criteria is driven by the requirements on language modelling ability.

3.1 Functionality

We measure language functionalities supported by different formalisms in four dimensions as we introduced in Section 1.

Networking

- *Encapsulation.* In the networked ontology setting, each ontology module may represent knowledge in a subset of the domain in question. Those modules are usually autonomously created and maintained, while they may also be inter-connected to form a larger knowledge base. In other words, such ontology modules can *encapsulate* knowledge sub-domains, where the local domain is a subset of the global domain. Syntactically, instead of having a single logic theory L, we may have a set of local theories $\{L_i\}$ such that axioms will have clearly defined provenance from one of the local theory.
- *Reusability (Inheritance).* Ontologies are very likely to be reused. Thus, formalisms for modular ontologies should also support managing different modules and identifying module dependencies. Formally, if module L_1 reuses L_2 and if a subsumption $C \sqsubseteq D$ is entailed by L_2, such that for every model $\mathcal{I}_2$ of L_2, $C^{\mathcal{I}_2} \subseteq D^{\mathcal{I}_2}$, then we will have for every model $\mathcal{I}_1$ of L_1, $C^{\mathcal{I}_1} \subseteq D^{\mathcal{I}_1}$.

  In particular, ontology modules should be also transitively reusable, that is, if a module X uses module Y, and module Y uses module Z, then apparently, module X should use module Z.
- *Authorization.* Many applications call for controllable access of knowledge due to copyright, privacy or safety concerns. Formalisms for modular ontologies may also support authorization features to ensure authorized creation and usage of ontology modules. For example, to enable multi-user access to ontologies, the language supported by the formalism may secure the session by explicitly defined rights for accessing or editing of each module. Formally, for certain agent, an ontology module L_i with authorization may be divided into a hidden part L_i^H and visible part L_i^V, such that there is a reasoner for L_i such that if axiom $\alpha \in L_i^H$, then no any combination of L_i^V and previous answers from the same reasoner will entail α.

Dynamics

- *Networked Ontology Dynamics.* The dynamic role of networked ontologies reflects the importance of monitoring and propagating ontology changes and updating. Such a requirement is closely related to ontology evolution, while it is more focused on the identification and updating of module changes rather than managing ontology versions. Assume concept C is in ontology module L_1 and concept D is in module L_2, then we have can axioms to represent that C corresponds to D by certain intermodule correspondences. The dynamics of network ontology requires the changes on C to C' should be detectable by L_2 in order to preserve the global $(L_1 \sqcup L_2)$ consistency or satisfiability by changing D change to D' if necessary [32].

Distribution

- *Loose Coupling.* Modules in a modular ontology may only be loosely coupled, such that interconnections between different modules are well controlled, conflicts can be easily detected and eliminated, and communication cost in the reasoning process is minimized. On the other hand, two modules are not necessarily fully disjoint from each other. Syntactically, it can be measured by the *"connectedness"* notion [25], such that the size of axioms in mappings $\{M_{ij}\}$ or in component logics $\{L_i\}$ that contains terms from different components are minimized.
- *Self-Containment.* On the other hand, ontology modules may also be semantically loosely coupled such that a module could be self-contained in the sense that reasoning tasks may be locally preformed using only local knowledge when there is no required access for knowledge in other modules. It may be measured by the supporting to the "conservative extension"[22,11] property of ontology module, such that for any module L_i and L_j, for a query α in the language of L_i, $L_i \cup L_j \vDash \alpha$ iff $L_i \vDash \alpha$, i.e. the combination of logic modules will not change the internal knowledge structure of any module.

Reasoning

- *Complexity and Scalability.* Processing modular ontologies is typically more challenging than reasoning with a single ontology. Thus, a desirable formalism for modular ontologies should provide reasoning procedures that are efficient and scalable to large terminologies and instance sets. For example, the formalism should be able to scale when processing large number of modular ontology that are distributed.
- *Reasoning Support for Terminological and Assertional Knowledge.* A desirable feature for a modular ontology formalism is to supports both T-Box reasoning and ABox querying. Support for modular ABoxes is particularly important since our motivation applications involve knowledge that is represented in large and distributed instance sets.

3.2   Expressivity

Expressivity criteria of modular ontology formalisms include the following:

- *Module Correspondence.* As we mentioned in the functionality criteria, different modules may be partially coupled in their languages or interpretations. For example, an ontology module about academic department may borrow (inherit) some knowledge from another university ontology, which may be stated as:

$$\textsf{DepartmentModule } isInheritedFrom \textsf{ UniversityModule}$$

- *Concept Subsumption.* Having subsumption relations between concepts in different modules is one of the most needed features in modular ontologies. For example, MasterStudent in a university ontology module may be a subclass of Student in the people ontology module.
- *Concept Interconnection.* A concept in a module may be connected to concepts in foreign modules by roles. For example, PhDStudent in the university module may be related to the City concept from a geographic ontology module by *lives* role connection.

- *Role Subsumption.* It is used to allow the subsumption relationship between the local and the foreign role.
- *Role Transitivity.* A foreign transitive role may be used in a module, e.g., the module A reuses the property biggerThan which is defined in the module B.
- *Role Inversion.* It is required to specify inverse relations between local and foreign roles.
- *Individual Correspondence.* It is required to specify that some individuals in one module are related to individuals in other modules.

Given the above set of criteria on language functionality and expressivity, we will analyze candidate formalisms with details in the next section. Apparently, not all applications need all of the criteria above, which are mainly driven by the FAO fishery case study setting, nevertheless we still argue that this setting can be generalized and applied to many real world distributed information systems.

4   Candidates of Formalisms for Modular Ontologies

4.1   Modularization with OWL Import

The OWL ontology language provides limited support for modularizing ontologies: an ontology document – identified via its ontology URI – can be imported by another document using the *owl:imports* statement. The semantics of this import statement is that all definitions of the imported ontology (module) are logical part of the importing ontology (module) as if they were defined in the importing ontology directly. Thus, they are forced to share a classical DL semantics, i.e., a global model semantics. It should be noted that such an importing is directed: only the importing ontology is affected by the import statement; it is also transitive: if ontology A imports ontology B, and ontology B imports ontology C, then ontology A also imports ontology C. Cyclic imports are also allowed (e.g. A *owl:imports* B, B *owl:imports* A).

Terms of the importing and imported ontology module can be related to each other using legal primitives available in OWL. Typically these relation definitions are part of the importing ontology module. The *owl:imports* functionality provides no partial importing of modules, thus it is up to the user to decide the proper level of granularity of ontology modules.

4.2   Distributed Description Logics

Distributed Description Logics (DDL) [6] adopt a linking mechanism. In DDL, the *distributed knowledge base (D-KB)*, $\mathfrak{D} = \langle \{L_i\}_{i \in I}, \mathfrak{B} \rangle$ consists a set of local knowledge bases $\{L_i\}_{i \in j}$ and bridge rules $\mathfrak{B} = \{\mathfrak{B}_{ij}\}_{\{i \neq j\} \in I}$ that represent the correspondences between them. The semantic linkings between modules L_i and L_j are represented by cross-module *Bridge Rules* "INTO" and "ONTO" axioms in one of the following forms:

- INTO: $i : C \xrightarrow{\sqsubseteq} j : D$, with semantics: $r_{ij}(C^{\mathcal{I}_i}) \subseteq D^{\mathcal{I}_j}$
- ONTO: $i : C \xrightarrow{\sqsupseteq} j : D$, with semantics: $r_{ij}(C^{\mathcal{I}_i}) \supseteq D^{\mathcal{I}_j}$

where $\mathcal{I}_i$ and $\mathcal{I}_j$ are local interpretations of L_i and L_j, respectively, C, D are concepts, r_{ij} (called *domain relation*) is a relation that represents an interpretation of B_{ij}.

DDL bridge rules between concepts covers one of the most important scenarios in modular ontologies. They are intended to simulate concept inclusion with a special type of roles. However, a bridge rule cannot be read as concept subsumption, such as $i : A \sqsubseteq j : B$. Instead, it must be read as a classic DL axiom in the following way [6]:

- $i : A \xrightarrow{\sqsubseteq} j : B \Rightarrow (i : A) \sqsubseteq \forall R_{ij}.(j : B)$
- $i : A \xrightarrow{\sqsupseteq} j : B \Rightarrow (j : B) \sqsubseteq \exists R_{ij}^-.(i : A)$

where R_{ij} is a new role representing correspondences B_{ij} between L_i and L_j.

Such relations have semantic differences with respect to concept inclusion (interpreted in classic DLs as subset relations between concept interpretations, e.g. $A^{\mathcal{I}_i} \sqsubseteq B^{\mathcal{I}_j}$) in several ways. For example, empty domain relation r_{ij} is allowed in the original DDL proposal [6], while GCIs between satisfiable concepts enforce restrictions on non-empty interpretations. Arbitrary domain relations may not preserve concept unsatisfiability among different modules which may result in some reasoning difficulties [3]. Furthermore, while subset relations (between concept interpretations) is transitive, DDL domain relations are not transitive, therefore bridge rules cannot be *transitively reused* by multiple modules. Those problems are recently recognized in several papers [2,3,34,27] and it is proposed that arbitrary domain relations should be avoided. For example, domain relations should be one-to-one [27,3] and non-empty [34].

The requirements of practical applications raised in the previous section are not fully satisfied by the expressivity of DDL. For example, inter-module role correspondences, which are important to present relations between concepts in different modules, are not supported in DDL: assume an concept PhDStudent is included in one ontology module and another concept Thesis is include in another ontology module, we cannot define PhDStudent $\sqsubseteq \exists$writes.Thesis in DDL, where writes is a *inter-module* role.

4.3 Integrity and Change of Modular Terminologies in DDL

Influenced by DDL semantics, Stuckenschmidt and Klein [32] adopt a view-based information integration approach to express relationships between ontology modules. In particular, in this approach ontology modules are connected by correspondences between conjunctive queries. This way of connecting modules provides a tradeoff between the simplicity of one-to-one mappings between concept names and the unrestricted use of logical languages to connect different modules.

Stuckenschmidt and Klein [32] defines an ontology module – abstracted from a particular ontology language – as a triple $M = (\mathcal{C}, \mathcal{R}, \mathcal{O})$, where $\mathcal{C}$ is a set of concept definitions, $\mathcal{R}$ is a set of relation definitions and $\mathcal{O}$ is a set of object definitions. A conjunctive query Q over an ontology module $M = (\mathcal{C}, \mathcal{R}, \mathcal{O})$ is defined as an expression of the form $q_1 \wedge ... \wedge q_m$, where q_i is a query term of the form $C(x)$, $R(x, y)$ or $x = y$, C and R are concept and role names, respectively, and x and y are either variable or object names.

In a modular terminology it is possible to use conjunctive queries to define concepts in one module in terms of a query over another module. For this purpose, the set of concept definitions $\mathcal{C}$ is divided into two disjoint sets of internally and externally defined concepts $\mathcal{C}_I$ and $\mathcal{C}_E$, respectively, with $\mathcal{C} = \mathcal{C}_I \cup \mathcal{C}_E, \mathcal{C}_I \cap \mathcal{C}_E = \emptyset$. An *internal concept* definition is specified using regular description logics based concept expressions with the form of $C \sqsubseteq D$ or $C \equiv D$, where C and D are atomic and complex concepts, respectively. An *external concept* definition is an axiom of the form $C \equiv M : Q$, where M is a module and Q is a conjunctive query over M. It is assumed that such queries can be later reduced to complex concept descriptions using the query-rollup techniques from [19] in order to be able to rely on standard reasoning techniques. A modular ontology is then simply defined as a set of modules that are connected by external concept definitions. The semantics of these modules is defined using the notion of a distributed interpretation introduced in Section 4.2.

Although the definition of a module, in its abstract form shown above, may allow arbitrary concept, relation and object definitions, only concept definitions is studied in [32]. This is due to the focus of the approach to improve terminological reasoning with modular ontologies by pre-compiling implied subsumption relations. In that sense it can be seen as a restricted form of DDLs that enables improved efficiency for special TBox reasoning tasks.

4.4 $\mathcal{E}$-Connection

While DDL allows only one type of domain relations, the $\mathcal{E}$-connection approach allows multiple "connections" between two modules, such as liveIn and bornIn between 2 : Fishkind and 1 : Region, where "2" and "1" stand for different modules, respectively. $\mathcal{E}$-connections between DLs [20,13] divide roles into disjoint sets of *local roles* (connecting concepts in one module) and *links* (connecting inter-module concepts). Formally, given ontology modules $\{L_i\}$, a (one-way binary) link $E \in \mathcal{E}_{ij}$, where $\mathcal{E}_{ij}(i \neq j)$ is the set of all links from the module i to the module j, can be used to construct a concept in module i, with the syntax and semantics specified as follows:

- $\exists E.(j : C) : \{x \in \Delta_i | \exists y \in \Delta_j, (x, y) \in E^\mathcal{I}, y \in C^\mathcal{I}\}$
- $\forall E.(j : C) : \{x \in \Delta_i | \forall y \in \Delta_j, (x, y) \in E^\mathcal{I} \to y \in C^\mathcal{I}\}\}$
- $\leq nE.(j : C) : \{x \in \Delta_i | \mathbf{N}(\{y \in \Delta_j | (x, y) \in E^\mathcal{I}, y \in C^\mathcal{I}\}) \leq n\}$
- $\geq nE.(j : C) : \{x \in \Delta_i | \mathbf{N}(\{y \in \Delta_j | (x, y) \in E^\mathcal{I}, y \in C^\mathcal{I}\}) \geq n\}$

where C is a concept in L_j, with interpretation $C^\mathcal{I} = C^{\mathcal{I}_j}$; $E^\mathcal{I} \subseteq \Delta^{\mathcal{I}_i} \times \Delta^{\mathcal{I}_j}$ is the interpretation of a $\mathcal{E}$-connection E; and $\mathbf{N}$ is the cardinality of set; $\mathcal{I} = \langle \{\mathcal{I}_i\}, \{E^\mathcal{I}\}_{E \in \mathcal{E}_{ij}} \rangle$ is an interpretation of the $\mathcal{E}$-connected ontology, $\mathcal{I}_i$ is the local interpretation of L_i.

Existing $\mathcal{E}$-connection proposals [20,13] has required both local languages and local domains of ontology modules to be disjoint, which lead to several difficulties:

- The requirement for terminology disjointness and local domain disjointness in $\mathcal{E}$-connections enforce strong restrictions in some applications. For example, $\mathcal{E}$-connections is not able to refine role definitions in an existing module with a new module, e.g. i : hatchedIn is less general than j : bornIn, where j : bornIn is a role in an existing module and i : hatchedIn is a new role extended from j : bornIn.
- To enforce local domain disjointness, a concept cannot be declared as subclass of another concept in a foreign module thereby ruling out the possibility of asserting

inter-module subsumption and the general support for transitive usability; a property cannot be declared as sub-relation of a foreign property; neither foreign classes nor foreign properties can be instantiated; cross-module concept conjunction or disjunction are also illegal.

- $\mathcal{E}$-connected ontologies have difficulties to be used with OWL importing mechanism, since importing may actually "decouple" the combination and result in inconsistency [10].
- $\mathcal{E}$-connected ontologies do not allow a same term be used as both a link name and a local role name, nor role inclusions between links and roles, while such features are widely required in practice [10]. The"punning" approach [10], where a same name can have different interpretations, is rather as a syntactical sugar than a semantic solution to such problems.

4.5   Package-Based Description Logics

Package-based Description Logics (P-DL) [4], uses importing relations to connect local modules. In contrast to OWL, which forces the model of an imported ontology to be completely embedded in a global model, the P-DL importing relation is *partial* in that only commonly shared terms are interpreted in the overlapping part of local models. The semantics of P-DL is given as the follows: the *image domain relation* between local interpretations $\mathcal{I}_i$ and $\mathcal{I}_j$ (of package P_i and P_j) is $r_{ij} \subseteq \Delta^{\mathcal{I}_i} \times \Delta^{\mathcal{I}_j}$. P-DL domain relation is:

- one-to-one: for any $x \in \Delta_i$, there is at most one $y \in \Delta_j$, such that $(x, y) \in r_{ij}$, and vice versa.
- compositionally consistent: $r_{ij} = r_{ik} \circ r_{jk}$, where $\circ$ denotes function composition. In other words, domain relations in P-DL is transitive.

P-DL provide contextualized semantics such that different packages have contextualized top concepts $\top_i$ (for all i) instead of a universal top $\top$; for any concept C, $r_{ij}(C^{\mathcal{I}_i}) = C^{\mathcal{I}_j}$. Hence, axiom in a P-DL package P_i will only be interpreted in its domain $\Delta^{\mathcal{I}_i}$, and may be influence only the overlapped domain $r_{ij}(\Delta^{\mathcal{I}_i}) \cap \Delta^{\mathcal{I}_j}$ of another package. Therefore, knowledge in P-DL can be reused as well as keeping its contextuality.

P-DL also supports selective knowledge sharing by associating ontology terms and axioms with "scope limitation modifiers (SLM)". A SLM controls the visibility of the corresponding term or axiom to entities on the web, in particular, to other packages. The scope limitation modifier of a term or an axiom t_K in package K is a boolean function $f(p, t_K)$, where p is a URI of an entity, the entity identified by p can access t_K iff $f(p, t_K) - true$. For example, some representative SLMs can be defined as follows:

- $\forall p, public(p, t) := true$, means t is accessible everywhere.
- $\forall p, private(p, t) := (t \in p)$, means t is visible only to its home package.

P-DL semantics ensure that distributed reasoning with a modular ontology will yield the same conclusion as that obtained by a classical reasoning process applied to an integration of the respective ontology modules [3]. Reported result in [1] only supports reasoning in P-DL as extensions of $\mathcal{ALC}$ TBox. Reasoning algorithms for more expressive P-DL TBox and ABox reasoning still need to be investigated.

5 Evaluation

In this section, we first evaluate existing modular ontology formalisms, then we explain the results based on the evaluation criteria given in Section 3.

Table 2 evaluates different formalisms against the functionality requirements, and Table 3 compares the expressivity of the these formalisms. In this section, the integrity and change aspects related to modular ontologies investigated in [32] will be denoted as "DDL-IC", since it follows the semantics of DDL.

- *Encapsulation.* According to our criteria, All formalisms listed above support knowledge encapsulation at different level. OWL- DL provides a basic *owl:import* primitive to import foreign ontologies without formal encapsulated modules, hence OWL-DL partially supports this functionality; DDL, DDL-IC, $\mathcal{E}$-connection and P-DL allow a large knowledge base to be represented by a set of ontology modules each capturing a subset of the domain of interest, thus provide the support for knowledge encapsulation.
- *Reusability.* OWL-DL ontologies has only limited reusability, because it is difficult for users to partially reuse ontologies designed by others. DDL, DDL-IC and P-DL establish good reusability via well-defined encapsulation and their semantics also satisfy with our criteria. The reusability of $\mathcal{E}$-connection is marked with a "*" symbol because the experiment in [26] shows for some knowledge bases, $\mathcal{E}$-connection is not able to generate reusable ontology modules. The lack of support for inter-module concept inclusion presents restriction in reusing $\mathcal{E}$-Connection modules. By combining the scope limitation and importing mechanism provided by P-DL, ontology modules may be reused through selected "interface" which is similar to that of code reusing in software engineering (the "+" symbol in the Table 2 means this additional feature).
- *Authorization.* Bao et.al. [4] show that it is possible to integrate authorization information with modular ontologies to guarantee the secure access, editing and reasoning with ontology modules. To the best of our knowledge, there is no other reported formalisms support this functionality with semantics described in the criteria.

Table 2. Comparison on language functionality. "T" means this formalism supports terminological (TBox) reasoning and "A" stands for the assertional (ABox) reasoning support. We refer the reader to the corresponding analysis for explanations of the "+" and "*" symbols.

	OWL-DL	DDL	DDL-IC	P-DL	$\mathcal{E}$-Connection
Encapsulation	Partial	Yes	Yes	Yes	Yes
Reusability	Fair	Good	Good	Good$^+$	Good*
Authorization	No	No	No	Partial	No
Ontology Dynamics	Yes	No	Yes	Unclear	Unclear
Loose Coupling	No	Yes	Yes	Yes	Yes
Self-Containment	Partial	Yes	Yes	Partial	Yes
Scalability	Low	Fair	Fair	Fair	Low
Reasoning Support	T and A	T and Partial A	T	T	T

- *Ontology Dynamics*. There have been rich study with respect to the dynamics of OWL-DL [15], and DDL- IC developed a mechanism to monitor the changes of modular ontologies [32], but it is not clear that other formalisms support this functionality.
- *Loose Coupling*. It is supported at different levels by different formalisms except for OWL-DL. Stuckenschmidt and colleagues explicitly argued its importance and deployment in DDL-IC [32].
- *Self-containment*. Due to the lack of localized semantics, OWL-DL does not fully support knowledge self-containment. In particular, reasoning in an OWL ontology requires the integration of all directly or indirectly imported ontologies of the given ontology. DDL-IC [32] introduces the self-containment functionality based on traditional DDL, while $\mathcal{E}$-connections requires strict separation of knowledge terminologies of ontology modules as well as their local interpretation domains [10]. P-DL can maintain the autonomy of individual modules; however, since P-DL adopts a partial semantic importing approach, reasoning in a P-DL ontology may also depend on its imported ontologies. According to our arguments in Section 3, DDL, DDL-IC and $\mathcal{E}$-Connection provide full support to this functionality by preserving the local knowledge structure while combining with other foreign modules.
- *Scalability*. The worst time complexity of the four formalisms studied in this paper are all exponential [18,1,10,28] for standard reasoning tasks, thereby we mainly discuss the scalability of these formalisms in the distributed environment. DDL, DDL-IC and P-DL support reasoning in a distributed setting in which ontology modules can be kept strictly separate, thus the integration of component ontology modules is avoided to obtain higher scalability in handling large ontologies. On the other hand, the current reasoning strategy for $\mathcal{E}$-connection, which is implemented in the reasoner Pellet [31], adopts the "coloring" but not physical separation of tableaux of ontology modules, hence requires implicit ontology integration to a single location, which may deteriorate its scalability.
- *Reasoning Support*. Reasoning support for OWL-DL has been successfully implemented in several highly optimized reasoners, such as FaCT++[35], Pellet[31] and KAON2; in particular KAON2 is optimized for reasoning with large ABoxes. DDL recently supported large ABox reasoning in a limited form [29]. Other formalisms have reported the support for TBoxes [12] only.

In the following, we explain the expressivity comparison of the formalisms:

- DDL-IC and P-DL define modules that may be related to other modules before the integration, while other languages do not define correspondences between modules.
- All formalisms but DDL support concept interconnections across modules. OWL-DL allows arbitrarily complex relations between concepts in different ontologies (i.e. semantic connections have the same expressivity as that of the local ontology language in each module). On the other hand, other formalism restrict the expressivity of concept connections to obtain both localized semantics and decidability. DDL, DDL-IC support concept subsumptions. $\mathcal{E}$- connection does not allow cross-module subsumption relationships, but allows two concepts being connected by

Table 3. Comparison of expressivity

	OWL-DL	DDL	DDL-IC	P-DL	$\mathcal{E}$-Connection
Module Correspondence.	No	No	Partial	Partial	No
Concept Subsumption.	Yes	Yes	Yes	Yes	No
Concept Interconnection.	Yes	Yes	Yes	Yes	Yes
Role Subsumption.	Yes	Yes	Yes	No	No
Role Transitivity.	Yes	No	Yes	No	Partial
Role Inversion.	Yes	No	Yes	No	No
Individual Correspondence.	Yes	Yes	Yes	No	No

links. P-DL supports both inter-module concept subsumptions and inter-module concept connections by roles.

- Role subsumption is provided by DDL [9], DDL-IC and OWL-DL. $\mathcal{E}$-connection does not allow a same name being shared by links and roles, and it does not allow role inclusions between modules. Role transitivity and inversion are not supported by DDL, DDL-IC. Reported P-DL formalism [2] does not allow role name importing hence does not support inter-module role subsumption, inversion and the reuse of transitive roles.
- The predicate *owl:sameIndividualAs* in OWL-DL supports simple individual correspondence by predicate . Among other formalisms, only DDL has investigated individual correspondence between ontology modules [29]. $\mathcal{E}$-connections does not allow cross- module individual correspondence since local domains of ontology modules are strictly disjoint. Such a feature is also missing in reported P-DL formalism (which only allows concept importing among ontology modules). DDL-IC allows a view with no variable being defined, which may be used to establish individual correspondence between ontology modules.

6   Discussion

The survey in the previous sections shows that existing formalisms may provide solutions with strength and weakness on different aspects to meet the requirement from our motivated applications, i.e. the FAO fishery case study in NeOn project.

First of all, a commonly accepted definition of "What is a good ontology module?" is still missing. It has been argued that different application scenarios may require different set of modularity requirements [21]. Secondly, an efficient and scalable reasoning approach for large ABox data is currently not well provided by existing formalisms. Thirdly, most of the existing approaches can not support trust and authorization requirements. Finally, managing the dynamics of ontologies is only supported by the approach proposed by Stuckenschmidt and colleagues [33], which is still missing in other modular ontology formalisms.

Existing formalisms are also limited in expressivity. Most formalisms provide means to deal with concepts in terminology knowledge. However, mechanisms to handling other ontological entities, such as roles and individuals correspondences, is not supported by $\mathcal{E}$-connection or P-DL in their current forms. On the other hand, interconnections and relationships between modules, which is needed by many applications using modular ontologies, is currently not well-defined and lacks implementations.

Existing formalisms require further extensions, such as conservative extension [7], in order to be served as successful formalisms for modular ontologies as discussed in Section 3. Practical reasoning support for expressive formalisms for modular ontologies are also to be investigated.

7 Conclusions and Future Work

In this paper, we studied different formalisms for modular ontologies against the requirements within the context where deploys modern semantic technologies as a novel approach for large-scale distributed information system engineering. We presented a set of formal criteria based on the requirements of a typical networked ontology applications. We then compared several formalisms for modular ontologies against these requirements.

The comparison result suggests that no existing approach can satisfactorily meet all the requirements of our networked ontology applications. Several possible extension of existing formalisms were identified and discussed.

Work in progress includes the development of a networked ontology based formalism that meets the requirements raised in the Section 3, and the efficient and scalable reasoning support for such a formalism that is able to handle both large distributed ontology terminologies and instance data sets that are contained in the large-scale distributed information systems.

Acknowledgments

Research reported in this paper is partially support by the EU in the IST project NeOn (EU IST-2006-027595, http://www.neon-project.org/). We appreciate the fruitful discussion and comments from our colleagues.

References

1. Bao, J., Caragea, D., Honavar, V.: A distributed tableau algorithm for package-based description logics. In: The 2nd International Workshop On Context Representation And Reasoning (CRR 2006), co-located with ECAI 2006 (2006)
2. Bao, J., Caragea, D., Honavar, V.: Modular ontologies - a formal investigation of semantics and expressivity. In: Mizoguchi, R., Shi, Z., Giunchiglia, F. (eds.) ASWC 2006. LNCS, vol. 4185, pp. 616–631. Springer, Heidelberg (2006)
3. Bao, J., Caragea, D., Honavar, V.: On the semantics of linking and importing in modular ontologies. In: Cruz, I., Decker, S., Allemang, D., Preist, C., Schwabe, D., Mika, P., Uschold, M., Aroyo, L. (eds.) ISWC 2006. LNCS, vol. 4273, pp. 72–86. Springer, Heidelberg (2006)
4. Bao, J., Caragea, D., Honavar, V.: Towards collaborative environments for ontology construction and sharing. In: International Symposium on Collaborative Technologies and Systems (CTS 2006), pp. 99–108. IEEE Press, Orlando (2006)
5. Berners-Lee, T., Hendler, J., Lassila, O.: The semantic web. Scientific American 284, 34–43 (2001)

6. Borgida, A., Serafini, L.: Distributed description logics: Directed domain correspondences in federated information sources. In: OTM Federated Conference CoopIS/DOA/ODBASE. pp. 36–53 (2002)

7. Cuenca Grau, B., Kazakov, Y., Horrocks, I., Sattler, U.: A logical framework for modular integration of ontologies. In: Proc. of the 20th Int. Joint Conf. on Artificial Intelligence (IJCAI 2007) (2007)

8. Dzbor, M., Motta, E., Studer, R., Sure, Y., Haase, P., Gmez-Prez, A., Benjamins, R., Waterfeld, W.: Neon - lifecycle support for networked ontologies. In: Proceedings of 2nd European Workshop on the Integration of Knowledge, Semantic and Digital Media Technologies (EWIMT-2005), pp. 451–452 London, UK, IEE (2005)

9. Ghidini, C., Serafini, L.: Mapping properties of heterogeneous ontologies. In: 1st International Workshop on Modular Ontologies (WoMo 2006), co-located with ISWC (2006)

10. Grau, B.C.: Combination and Integration of Ontologies on the Semantic Web. PhD thesis, Dpto. de Informatica, Universitat de Valencia, Spain (2005)

11. Grau, B.C., Horrocks, I., Kazakov, Y., Sattler, U.: A logical framework for modular integration of ontologies. In: Proceedings of IJCAI'07 (2007)

12. Grau, B.C., Parsia, B., Sirin, E.: Tableau algorithms for e-connections of description logics. Technical report, University of Maryland Institute for Advanced Computer Studies (UMIACS), TR 2004-72 (2004)

13. Grau, B.C., Parsia, B., Sirin, E.: Working with multiple ontologies on the semantic web. In: International Semantic Web Conference. pp. 620–634 (2004)

14. Haase, P., Rudolph, S., Wang, Y., Brockmans, S., Palma, R., Euzenat, J., d'Aquin, M.: D1.1.1 networked ontology model. NeOn Deliverable 1.1.1, Universität Karlsruhe, UPM, INRIA-ALPES, Open University (2007)

15. Haase, P., Sure, Y.: State-of-the-art on ontology evolution. Technical report, SEKT informal deliverable 3.1.1.b, Institute AIFB, University of Karlsruhe (2004)

16. Horrocks, I., Patel-Schneider, P.F.: Optimizing description logic subsumption. Journal of Logic and Computation 9, 267–293 (1999)

17. Horrocks, I., Patel-Schneider, P.F., van Harmelen, F.: From SHIQ and RDF to OWL: The making of a web ontology language. J. of Web. Semantics 1, 7–26 (2003)

18. Horrocks, I., Sattler, U.: A Tableaux Decision Procedure for SHOIQ. In: Proceedings of the 19th International Joint Conference on Artificial Intelligence - IJCAI'05. pp. 448–453 (2005)

19. Horrocks, I., Tessaris, S.: A conjunctive query language for description logic aboxes. In: Proceedings of the Seventeenth National Conference on Artificial Intelligence and Twelfth Conference on Innovative Applications of Artificial Intelligence, pp. 399–404, AAAI Press / The MIT Press (2000)

20. Kutz, O., Lutz, C., Wolter, F., Zakharyaschev, M.: E-connections of description logics. In: Description Logics Workshop, CEUR-WS, Vol 81 (2003)

21. Loebe, F.: Requirements for logical modules. In: 1st International Workshop on Modular Ontologies (WoMo 2006), co-located with ISWC (2006)

22. Lutz, C., Walther, D., Wolter, F.: Conservative extensions in expressive description logics. In: Proceedings of the Twentieth International Joint Conference on Artificial Intelligence IJCAI-07, AAAI Press, Stanford (2007)

23. McGuinness, D.L., van Harmelen, F.: OWL Web Ontology Language Overview. Technical report, World Wide Web Consortium (W3C) (2003) Internet: http://www.w3.org/TR/owl-features/

24. Motik, B., Sattler, U.: A comparison of reasoning techniques for querying large description logic aboxes. In: Hermann, M., Voronkov, A. (eds.) LPAR 2006. LNCS (LNAI), vol. 4246, Springer, Heidelberg (2006)

25. Schlicht, A., Stuckenschmidt, H.: Towards structural criteria for ontology modularizationc. In: 1st International Workshop on Modular Ontologies (WoMo 2006), co-located with ISWC (2006)
26. Seidenberg, J., Rector, A.: Web ontology segmentation: Analysis, classification and use. In: Proceedings of the World Wide Web Conference (WWW), Edinburgh (2006)
27. Serafini, L., Stuckenschmidt, H., Wache, H.: A formal investigation of mapping languages for terminological knowledge. In: Proceedings of the 19th International Joint Conference on Artificial Intelligence - IJCAI'05, Edinburgh, UK (2005)
28. Serafini, L., Tamilin, A.: Drago: Distributed reasoning architecture for the semantic web. In: Gómez-Pérez, A., Euzenat, J. (eds.) ESWC 2005. LNCS, vol. 3532, pp. 361–376. Springer, Heidelberg (2005)
29. Serafini, L., Tamilin, A.: Instance retrieval over a set of heterogeneous ontologies. In: the 2nd International Workshop On Context Representation And Reasoning (CRR 2006), co-located with ECAI 2006 (2006)
30. Shadbolt, N., Berners-Lee, T., Hall, W.: The semantic web revisited. IEEE Intelligent Systems 21, 96–101 (2006)
31. Sirin, E., Parsia, B.: Pellet: An OWL DL Reasoner. In: Description Logics Workshop (2004)
32. Stuckenschmidt, H., Klein, M.C.A.: Integrity and change in modular ontologies. In: Proceedings of the 18th International Joint Conference on Artificial Intelligence - IJCAI'03. pp.900–908 (2003)
33. Stuckenschmidt, H., Klein, M.C.A.: Structure-based partitioning of large concept hierarchies. In: International Semantic Web Conference. pp.289–303 (2004)
34. Stuckenschmidt, H., Serafini, L., Wache, H.: Reasoning about ontology mappings. Technical report, Department for Mathematics and Computer Science, University of Mannheim; TR-2005-011 (2005)
35. Tsarkov, D., Horrocks, I.: Efficient reasoning with range and domain constraints. In: Description Logics. FaCT++ (2004)

Consistent Query Answering over Description Logic Ontologies

Domenico Lembo and Marco Ruzzi

Dipartimento di Informatica e Sistemistica,
Università di Roma "La Sapienza",
Via Salaria 113, 00198 Roma, Italy
{lembo,ruzzi}@dis.uniroma1.it

Abstract. Description Logics (DLs) have been widely used in the last years as formal language for specifying ontologies over the web. Due to the dynamic nature of this setting, it may frequently happen that data retrieved from the web contradict the intensional knowledge provided by the ontology through which they are collected, which therefore may result inconsistent. In this paper, we analyze the problem of consistent query answering over DL ontologies, i.e., the problem of providing meaningful answers to queries posed over inconsistent ontologies. We provide inconsistency tolerant semantics for DLs, and study the computational complexity of consistent query answering over ontologies specified in *DL-Lite*, a family of DLs specifically tailored to deal with large amounts of data. We show that the above problem is coNP-complete w.r.t. data complexity, i.e., the complexity measured w.r.t. the size of the data only. Towards identification of tractable cases of consistent query answering over *DL-Lite* ontologies, we then study the problem of consistent instance checking, i.e., the instance checking problem considered under our inconsistency-tolerant semantics. We provide an algorithm for it which runs in time polynomial in the size of the data, thus showing that the problem is in PTIME w.r.t. data complexity.

1   Introduction

In several Information and Communication Technology areas, ranging from the Semantic Web (SW) [23], to Enterprise Application Integration, or Data Integration [26], ontologies are nowadays considered as the ideal formal tool to provide a shared conceptualization of a particular domain of interest. Description Logics (DLs) [5] are logics that represent the domain in terms of *concepts* (sets of objects) and *roles* (binary relations between concepts), and that allow for the definition of knowledge bases (KBs) composed by a terminological component (*TBox*), specifying the intensional knowledge, and an assertional component (*ABox*), specifying the extensional knowledge. DLs have been widely used in the last years as formal language for specifying ontologies over the web, for their ability of combining modelling power and decidability of reasoning [24]. Recently, besides expressive DLs, which suffer from inherently worst-case exponential time behavior of reasoning [8], also DLs that allow for tractable reasoning have been proposed for ontology modelling [4,11]. The study on tractable DLs is motivated by the need of managing large amounts of data (e.g., from thousands to

M. Marchiori, J.Z. Pan, and C. de Sainte Marie (Eds.): RR 2007, LNCS 4524, pp. 194–208, 2007.

millions of instances) under the control of ontology-based systems, like data repositories over the web, in which data constitute the instances of the concepts in the ontology. Furthermore, in the SW community, a growing interest is being recently devoted to data integration [30], which in the SW context mainly means accessing, collecting, and exchanging data distributed over the web through the use of ontologies.

Due to the dynamic nature of the setting described above, it may frequently happen that data contradict the intensional knowledge provided by the ontology through which they are accessed, especially in those cases in which the ontology provides a conceptual view of a number of autonomous information sources, heterogeneous and widely distributed. In the above situation, ontologies may result inconsistent, and reasoning over them, according to classical first-order semantics of DL ontologies, may become meaningless, since whatever conclusion may be derived from an inconsistent theory. Then, besides handling inconsistency at the terminological/schema level, which has been a subject recently investigated for ontology-based applications [28,25,22], the need arises in this context to deal with inconsistency at the instance/data level. In the present paper we study this problem.

The approach commonly adopted to solve data inconsistency is through data cleaning [9]. This approach is procedural, and is based on domain-specific transformation mechanisms applied to the data. One of its problems is incomplete information on how certain conflicts should be resolved. This typically happens in systems which are not tailored for business logic support at the enterprise level, like systems for information integration on-demand over the web. In the last years, an alternative declarative approach has been investigated in the area of consistent query answering [3,17,7,10,20]. Such an approach relies on the notion of *repair* for a database instance that may violate integrity constraints specified over its schema. Roughly speaking, a repair is a new database instance which satisfies the constraints in the schema and minimally differs from the original one. In general multiple repairs are possible. Then, consistent query answering amounts to compute those answers to a user query that are in the evaluation of the query over each repair. It is well-known [10,15,21] that consistent query answering of conjunctive queries expressed over database schemas with (even simple forms of) integrity constraints is a coNP-complete problem in data complexity, i.e., the complexity measured only with respect to the size of the database instance [32]. Motivated by the high computational complexity of the problem, some works have recently faced the problem under the perspective of identifying tractable cases, by limiting both the form of integrity constraints allowed on the database schema, and the language used for specifying the queries [20,21,16].

In this paper, we study consistent query answering over DL ontologies. In particular, we provide a new semantic characterization for DLs, based on the notion of repair. We focus on a family of DLs called *DL-Lite* [11,12], which is specifically tailored to deal with large amounts of data. While the expressive power of the DLs in the *DL-Lite* family is carefully controlled to maintain low the complexity of reasoning, such DLs are expressive enough to capture the main notions of both ontologies, and conceptual modelling formalisms used in databases and software engineering (i.e., ER and UML class diagrams). We consider two DLs of the *DL-Lite* family, called *DL-Lite$_{\mathcal{F}}$* and *DL-Lite$_{\mathcal{R}}$*, which have as distinguish features the ability of specifying functionalities on roles, and subsumption between roles, respectively. We study consistent query answering for the class of union of conjunctive queries (UCQs), which is the most expressive class of queries for which decidability of query answering has been proved in DLs [14,27]. Notably, standard query answering of UCQs over *DL-Lite$_\mathcal{F}$* or *DL-Lite$_\mathcal{R}$*, can be solved by means of evaluation of suitable first-order logic queries over the underlying *DL-Lite* ABox considered as a flat relational database [11,12]. This allows for using well established Relational Data Base Management System (RDBMS) technology for reasoning over queries in such DLs. We point out that these DLs are maximal DLs that admit such a property, in the sense that we lose it as soon as we consider a DL that allows for constructs provided by both *DL-Lite$_\mathcal{F}$* and *DL-Lite$_\mathcal{R}$*. Notice also that *DL-Lite$_\mathcal{F}$* is a strict subset of OWL Lite[1], a DL version of the W3C OWL Web Ontology Language, whereas *DL-Lite$_\mathcal{R}$* can be seen as an extension of (the DL-like part of) the ontology language RDFS[2].

The contributions of the present paper can then be summarized as follows.

– We provide an inconsistency-tolerant semantics for DLs, which relies on the notion of repair of a DL ontology, and allows for meaningful reasoning in the presence of inconsistency;
– We study computational complexity of consistent query answering for conjunctive queries expressed over *DL-Lite$_\mathcal{R}$* and *DL-Lite$_\mathcal{F}$* ontologies, and show that such a problem is coNP-complete w.r.t. data complexity, for both such DLs;
– Towards identification of tractable cases of consistent query answering for *DL-Lite*, we study consistent instance checking over *DL-Lite$_\mathcal{R}$* and *DL-Lite$_\mathcal{F}$* ontologies, i.e., the instance checking problem under our inconsistency-tolerant semantics. Such a problem consists in establishing whether a knowledge base entails the fact that a certain constant (or pair of constants) is an instance of a concept (resp. of a role), according to our repair semantics. We provide a polynomial time algorithm for consistent instance checking for both *DL-Lite$_\mathcal{R}$* and *DL-Lite$_\mathcal{F}$*, then showing that such a problem is in PTIME w.r.t. data complexity, in both cases.

The rest of the paper is organized as follows. In Section 2 we describe the DLs *DL-Lite$_\mathcal{R}$* and *DL-Lite$_\mathcal{F}$*. In Section 3 we propose our repair semantics and define the consistent query answering and consistent instance checking problems. In Section 4 and in Section 5 we study computational complexity of consistent query answering and consistent instance checking over *DL-Lite$_\mathcal{F}$* and *DL-Lite$_\mathcal{R}$*, respectively. Finally, in Section 6 we discuss some related work and in Section 7, we conclude the paper.

2   The Description Logics *DL-Lite$_\mathcal{F}$* and *DL-Lite$_\mathcal{R}$*

In this section we present the syntax and the semantics of both *DL-Lite$_\mathcal{F}$* and *DL-Lite$_\mathcal{R}$*, the two DLs of to the *DL-Lite* family [11,12] that we mainly focus on in this paper.

At the core of both such DLs we have concepts and roles constructed according to the following syntax

$$B \longrightarrow A \mid \exists R \qquad R \longrightarrow P \mid P^- \qquad C \longrightarrow B \mid \neg B \qquad E \longrightarrow R \mid \neg R$$

---

[1] http://www.w3.org/TR/owl-features
[2] http://www.w3.org/RDF/

where A denotes an atomic concept, P an atomic role, and P^- the inverse of the atomic role P. B denotes a *basic concept*, i.e., a concept that can be either an atomic concept or a concept of the form $\exists R$, and R denotes a *basic role*, i.e., a role that is either an atomic role or the inverse of an atomic role. Sometimes we write R^- with the intended meaning that $R^- = P^-$ if $R = P$, and $R^- = P$, if $R = P^-$. Finally, C denotes a *(general) concept*, which can be a basic concept or its negation, whereas E denotes a *(general) role*, which can be a basic role or its negation. Sometimes we write $\neg C$ (resp., $\neg E$) with the intended meaning that $\neg C = \neg B$ if $C = B$ (resp., $\neg E = \neg R$ if $E = R$), and $\neg C = B$, if $C = \neg B$ (resp., $\neg E = R$, if $E = \neg R$).

Let B_1 and B_2 be basic concepts, and let R_1 and R_2 be basic roles, we call *positive inclusions (PIs)* assertions of the form $B_1 \sqsubseteq B_2$, and of the form $R_1 \sqsubseteq R_2$, whereas we call *negative inclusions (NIs)* assertions of the form $B_1 \sqsubseteq \neg B_2$ and $R_1 \sqsubseteq \neg R_2$.

A DL *knowledge base* (KB) $\mathcal{K}$ is a pair $\langle \mathcal{T}, \mathcal{A} \rangle$ which represents the domain of interest in terms of two parts, a *TBox* $\mathcal{T}$, specifying the intensional knowledge, and an *ABox* $\mathcal{A}$, specifying extensional knowledge. *DL-Lite$_\mathcal{F}$* and *DL-Lite$_\mathcal{R}$* differ from one another for the form of the TBoxes that they allow, whereas they admit the same form of ABoxes. In particular a *DL-Lite$_\mathcal{F}$* TBox is formed by: (i) a finite set of *concept inclusion assertions*, i.e., expressions of the form $B \sqsubseteq C$, meaning that all instances of the basic concept B are also instances of the generic concept C, and (ii) a finite set of *functionality assertions* on roles or on their inverses of the form (funct P) or (funct P^-), respectively, meaning that a relation P (resp. P^-) is functional. A *DL-Lite$_\mathcal{R}$* TBox is formed by: (i) concept inclusion assertions of the form $B \sqsubseteq C$ (as for *DL-Lite$_\mathcal{F}$*) and (ii) *role inclusion assertions* of the form $R \sqsubseteq E$ meaning that all instances of the basic role R are also instances of the general role E. *DL-Lite$_\mathcal{R}$* and *DL-Lite$_\mathcal{F}$* ABoxes are formed by a finite set of membership assertions on atomic concepts and atomic roles, of the form $A(a)$ and $P(a, b)$, stating respectively that the object denoted by the constant a is an instance of the atomic concept A and that the pair of objects denoted by the pair of constants (a, b) is an instance of the role P.

Before proceeding, we point out that *DL-Lite$_\mathcal{F}$* coincides with the DL presented in [11], in that paper simply called *DL-Lite*. In fact, other DLs with the same computational behavior of the DL presented in [11], but allowing for the use of different constructs, have been successively defined [12,13]. Thus, the term *DL-Lite* actually refers now to an entire family of DLs, which contains both *DL-Lite$_\mathcal{F}$* and *DL-Lite$_\mathcal{R}$*. In the following, for simplicity, we sometimes use the term *DL-Lite* to refer to either *DL-Lite$_\mathcal{F}$* or *DL-Lite$_\mathcal{R}$*.

The semantics of a DL is given in terms of interpretations, where an *interpretation* $\mathcal{I} = (\Delta^\mathcal{I}, \cdot^\mathcal{I})$ consists of a non-empty interpretation domain $\Delta^\mathcal{I}$ and an *interpretation function* $\cdot^\mathcal{I}$ that assigns to each concept C a subset $C^\mathcal{I}$ of $\Delta^\mathcal{I}$, and to each role R a binary relation $R^\mathcal{I}$ over $\Delta^\mathcal{I}$. In particular we have:

$$A^\mathcal{I} \subseteq \Delta^\mathcal{I} \qquad\qquad (\exists R)^\mathcal{I} = \{o \mid \exists o'. (o, o') \in R^\mathcal{I}\}$$
$$P^\mathcal{I} \subseteq \Delta^\mathcal{I} \times \Delta^\mathcal{I} \qquad\qquad (\neg B)^\mathcal{I} = \Delta^\mathcal{I} \setminus B^\mathcal{I}$$
$$(P^-)^\mathcal{I} = \{(o_2, o_1) \mid (o_1, o_2) \in P^\mathcal{I}\} \qquad (\neg R)^\mathcal{I} = \Delta^\mathcal{I} \times \Delta^\mathcal{I} \setminus R^\mathcal{I}$$

Furthermore, an interpretation $\mathcal{I}$ is a model of a concept inclusion assertion $B \sqsubseteq C$, if $B^\mathcal{I} \subseteq C^\mathcal{I}$, $\mathcal{I}$ is a model of a role inclusion assertion $R \sqsubseteq E$ if $R^\mathcal{I} \subseteq E^\mathcal{I}$, and is $\mathcal{I}$ is a model of an assertion (funct P) if $(o, o_1) \in P^\mathcal{I}$ and $(o, o_2) \in P^\mathcal{I}$ implies $o_1 = o_2$.

Analogously for (funct P^-). To specify the semantics of membership assertions, we extend the interpretation function to constants, by assigning to each constant a a *distinct* object $a^{\mathcal{I}} \in \Delta^{\mathcal{I}}$. Note that this implies that we enforce the *unique name assumption* on constants [5]. An interpretation $\mathcal{I}$ is a model of a membership assertion $A(a)$, (resp., $P(a, b)$) if $a^{\mathcal{I}} \in A^{\mathcal{I}}$ (resp., $(a^{\mathcal{I}}, b^{\mathcal{I}}) \in P^{\mathcal{I}}$).

Given an (inclusion, functionality, or membership) assertion α, and an interpretation $\mathcal{I}$, we denote by $\mathcal{I} \models \alpha$ the fact that $\mathcal{I}$ is a model of α, and also say that α is satisfied by $\mathcal{I}$. Given a (finite) set of assertions κ, we denote by $\mathcal{I} \models \kappa$ the fact that $\mathcal{I}$ is a model of every assertion in κ. A *model of a DL-Lite KB* $\mathcal{K} = \langle \mathcal{T}, \mathcal{A} \rangle$ is an interpretation $\mathcal{I}$ such that $\mathcal{I} \models \mathcal{T}$ and $\mathcal{I} \models \mathcal{A}$. With a little abuse of notation, we also write $\mathcal{I} \models \mathcal{K}$. A KB is *satisfiable* if it has at least one model, otherwise it is *unsatisfiable*.

Example 1. Consider the atomic concepts *Cat*, *Dog*, *Pet* and *Person* and the roles *hasOwner* and *feeds*. The following TBox $\mathcal{T}$ is an example of *DL-Lite$_{\mathcal{F}}$* TBox:

$$Dog \sqsubseteq Pet \qquad\qquad \exists hasOwner^- \sqsubseteq Person$$
$$Cat \sqsubseteq Pet \qquad\qquad Cat \sqsubseteq \neg Dog$$
$$Pet \sqsubseteq \exists hasOwner \qquad\quad (\text{funct} \quad hasOwner).$$

From the TBox above, we can obtain a *DL-Lite$_{\mathcal{R}}$* TBox by removing the functionality assertion (funct *hasOwner*) and adding the role inclusion assertion

$$hasOwner \sqsubseteq feeds^-.$$

In both TBoxes we say that cats and dogs are pets, every pet has an owner, a cat is not a dog and the owner of an animal is a person. Moreover in the *DL-Lite$_{\mathcal{F}}$* TBox we can say that a pet cannot have more then one owner, whereas in the *DL-Lite$_{\mathcal{R}}$* TBox we can say that an owner must feed her/his pet. Finally, we show a simple *DL-Lite* ABox $\mathcal{A}$:

$$Person(\text{John}), \quad Dog(\text{Bruto}), \quad hasOwner(\text{Tom, Leonard}). \qquad \blacksquare$$

A *union of conjunctive queries (UCQ)* q over a *DL-Lite* KB $\mathcal{K}$ is an expression of the form

$$q(\boldsymbol{x}) \leftarrow \bigvee_{i=1,\ldots,n} \exists \boldsymbol{y_i}.conj_i(\boldsymbol{x}, \boldsymbol{y_i}), \qquad\qquad (1)$$

where each $conj_i(\boldsymbol{x}, \boldsymbol{y_i})$ is a conjunction of atoms and equalities, with free variables $\boldsymbol{x}$ and $\boldsymbol{y_i}$. Variables in $\boldsymbol{x}$ are called *distinguished*, and the size of $\boldsymbol{x}$ is called the *arity* of q. The right-hand side of the Formula (1) is called the *body* of q. Atoms in each $conj_i$ are of the form $A(z)$ or $P(z_1, z_2)$, where A and P are respectively an atomic concept and an atomic role of $\mathcal{K}$, and z, z_1, z_2 are either constants in $\mathcal{K}$ or variables. A *Boolean* UCQ is a query with arity 0, written simply as a sentence of the form $\bigvee_{i=1,\ldots,n} \exists \boldsymbol{y_i}.conj_i(\boldsymbol{y_i})$. A UCQ with a single conjunction of atoms, i.e., with $n = 1$ in the Formula (1), is called *conjunctive query (CQ)*.

Let q be a Boolean UCQ over a *DL-Lite* KB $\mathcal{K}$. We say that q is *entailed* by $\mathcal{K}$, and write $\mathcal{K} \models q$, if, for every model $\mathcal{M}$ of $\mathcal{K}$, $\mathcal{M} \models q$, where $\models$ is the standard evaluation of first-order sentences in an interpretation. The *instance checking problem* corresponds to entailment of a Boolean ground CQ consisting of a single atom, i.e., a membership assertion of the form $A(a)$ or $P(a, b)^3$. Let q be a non-Boolean UCQ of arity n over $\mathcal{K}$, and let t be an n-tuple of constants. We say that t is a *certain answer* to q in $\mathcal{K}$ if $\mathcal{K} \models q(t)$, where $q(t)$ is the sentence obtained form the body of q by replacing its distinguished variables by constants in t. We denote by $Ans(q, \mathcal{K})$ the set of certain answers to q in $\mathcal{K}$.

Example 2. Let us consider the DL KB $\mathcal{K} = \langle \mathcal{T}, \mathcal{A} \rangle$, where the TBox $\mathcal{T}$ and the ABox $\mathcal{A}$ are as defined in Example 1, and the CQ $q(x) \leftarrow Person(x)$, posed over $\mathcal{K}$. It is easy to see that $Ans(q, \mathcal{K}) = \{\text{John}, \text{Leonard}\}$, where the certain answer John can be directly derived from the membership assertions of $\mathcal{A}$, whereas the certain answer Leonard is implied by the inclusion assertion $\exists hasOwner^- \sqsubseteq Person$ and by the role membership assertion $hasOwner(\text{Tom}, \text{Leonard})$. ∎

3 Inconsistency-Tolerant Semantics

Let us now consider the case in which a DL knowledge base $\mathcal{K}$ is unsatisfiable, i.e., $\mathcal{K}$ does not have any model. As already said in the introduction, reasoning over such a $\mathcal{K}$ is meaningless, since whatever consequence can be deduced from $\mathcal{K}$. In this section, we provide a new semantics for DL knowledge bases that is inconsistency-tolerant, i.e., it allows for "meaningful" reasoning over KBs that are unsatisfiable according to the classical first-order based semantics, as that considered in Section 2 for *DL-Lite*. In particular, our semantics is tolerant to the inconsistency that arises in a DL knowledge base $\mathcal{K} = \langle \mathcal{T}, \mathcal{A} \rangle$ in which a satisfiable TBox $\mathcal{T}$ may be contradicted by the extensional assertions in the ABox $\mathcal{A}$, thus resulting in possibly unsatisfiable KBs. This situation frequently happens in those systems that provide access to data (possibly integrated from autonomous sources) through DL ontologies, as in Semantic Web applications.

Formally, let $\mathcal{I}$ be an interpretation and let $\mathcal{A}$ be an ABox. We denote by $Sat(\mathcal{I}, \mathcal{A})$ the set of membership assertions from $\mathcal{A}$ that are satisfied in $\mathcal{I}$, i.e., $Sat(\mathcal{I}, \mathcal{A}) = \{\alpha \mid \alpha \in \mathcal{A} \text{ and } \mathcal{I} \models \alpha\}$.

Definition 1. *Let $\mathcal{K} = \langle \mathcal{T}, \mathcal{A} \rangle$ be a DL KB and let $\mathcal{I}$ be an interpretation. We say that $\mathcal{I}$ is a* repair *of $\mathcal{K}$ if:*

1. *$\mathcal{I}$ is a model for $\mathcal{T}$;*
2. *there exists no interpretation $\mathcal{I}'$ such that $\mathcal{I}'$ is a model for $\mathcal{T}$ and $Sat(\mathcal{I}', \mathcal{A}) \supset Sat(\mathcal{I}, \mathcal{A})$.*

In the following, we denote by $Rep(\mathcal{K})$ the set of repairs of $\mathcal{K}$. It is easy to see that when a KB $\mathcal{K}$ is satisfiable, repairs of $\mathcal{K}$ coincide with models of $\mathcal{K}$. Also, when the TBox of $\mathcal{K}$ is satisfiable, $\mathcal{K}$ has always at least one repair.

Following the lines of research in *consistent query answering* [3,17,7,10,20], in our semantics, intensional knowledge specified by the TBox of a knowledge base is considered stronger than data, i.e., the extensional knowledge provided by the ABox. Indeed,

---

[3] Obviously, we can also have consistent instance checking of an assertion of the form $P^-(a, b)$, by considering the assertion $P(b, a)$.

a repair $\mathcal{R}$ of a knowledge base $\mathcal{K} = \langle T, \mathcal{A} \rangle$ is an interpretation that needs to satisfy T and that at the same time satisfies a maximal set $\mathcal{A}_m$ of the membership assertions in $\mathcal{A}$, i.e., $\mathcal{R}$ is a model of the knowledge base $\langle T, \mathcal{A}_m \rangle$.

The notions of entailment of a Boolean query, instance checking and answers to a query in a DL knowledge base under the repair semantics given in this section are analogous to the corresponding ones given in Section 2. More precisely, we say that a Boolean UCQ q is *consistently entailed* by a DL knowledge base $\mathcal{K}$, and write $\mathcal{K} \models_{cons}$ q if, for every $\mathcal{R} \in Rep(\mathcal{K})$, $\mathcal{R} \models q$. Then, given a non-Boolean UCQ q of arity n over $\mathcal{K}$, we say that an n-tuple t of constants is a *consistent answer* to q in $\mathcal{K}$ if $\mathcal{K} \models_{cons} q(t)$. We denote by $ConsAns(q, \mathcal{K})$ the set of consistent answers to q in $\mathcal{K}$. Furthermore, the *consistent instance checking* problem corresponds to consistent entailment of a Boolean ground CQ consisting of a single atom.

We finally notice that, when a DL knowledge base $\mathcal{K} = \langle T, \mathcal{A} \rangle$ is a *DL-Lite* KB, $\mathcal{K}$ may result unsatisfiable only if the ABox $\mathcal{A}$ contradicts the intensional knowledge of the TBox T. Indeed, it is possible to show that a *DL-Lite* TBox admits always at least one model. As a consequence, we have that our inconsistency-tolerant semantics ensures that every *DL-Lite* KB has always at least one repair.

Example 3. Let us consider again the *DL-Lite$_F$* TBox T described in Example 1 and the following ABox $\mathcal{A}'$:

$$Person(\text{John}), \quad hasOwner(\text{Tom, John}), \quad hasOwner(\text{Tom, Leonard}).$$

It is easy to see that the knowledge base $\mathcal{K}' = \langle T, \mathcal{A}' \rangle$ is unsatisfiable, since the functionality assertion on $hasOwner$ is contradicted by the two role membership assertions of $\mathcal{A}'$. Then, each repair $\mathcal{I}$ of $\mathcal{K}'$ is such that $\mathcal{I} \models T$, and either $Sat(\mathcal{I}, \mathcal{A}') = \{hasOwner(\text{Tom, John})\}$, or $Sat(\mathcal{I}, \mathcal{A}') = \{hasOwner(\text{Tom, Leonard})\}$. Let us now consider the Boolean conjunctive query $q' = \exists y.hasOwner(\text{Tom}, y)$ over $\mathcal{K}'$, asking whether Tom is owned by someone. It is easy to see that q is consistently entailed by $\mathcal{K}'$. However, for the query $q'' = \{ x \mid hasOwner(\text{Tom}, x) \}$, we have that $ConsAns(q'', \mathcal{K}') = \emptyset$. In other words, we cannot establish who is the owner of Tom, but we can state that Tom has an owner. ∎

4 Consistent Query Answering

In this section we consider the problem of consistent query answering for conjunctive queries over both *DL-Lite$_F$* and *DL-Lite$_R$* KBs. In particular, we study the computational complexity of the problem, and show that for both such DLs it is coNP-hard w.r.t. data complexity, i.e., the complexity measured w.r.t. the size of the ABox only. Let us now first analyze *DL-Lite$_F$* KBs.

Theorem 1. *Let $\mathcal{K}$ be a DL-Lite$_F$ KB, q a conjunctive query of arity n over $\mathcal{K}$, and t an n-tuple of constants. Then, the problem of establishing whether $t \in ConsAns(q, \mathcal{K})$ is coNP-complete with respect to data complexity.*

Proof (sketch). We prove coNP-hardness by a reduction from the 3-COLORABILITY problem to the complement of our problem. Given a graph $G = (V, E)$, where V is the set of vertices of G, and E is the set of edges of G, we define a $DL\text{-}Lite_{\mathcal{F}}$ KB $\mathcal{K} = \langle \mathcal{T}, \mathcal{A} \rangle$, with basic roles $color$ and $edge$, as follows:

$$\mathcal{T} = \{(\text{funct } color)\}$$
$$\mathcal{A} = \{edge(v_1, v_2) \mid (v_1, v_2) \in E\} \cup \{color(v, R), color(v, G), color(v, B) \mid v \in V\}$$

Then, we consider the following Boolean conjunctive query q over $\mathcal{K}$:

$$\exists x, y, z.\, edge(x, y) \wedge color(x, z) \wedge color(y, z).$$

Since computing the consistent answers to the Boolean query q means establishing whether $\mathcal{K} \models_{cons} q$, we can prove our claim by showing that $\mathcal{K} \not\models_{cons} q$ iff G is 3-colorable.

Membership in coNP follows from an analogous result given in [21] for consistent query answering of conjunctive queries over relational databases with exclusion and key dependencies. Indeed, consistent answers in our setting can be computed by means of the algorithm of [21], which is based on an encoding of the problem in Datalog enriched with unstratified negation. Since, however, only relations with at most one key dependency are considered in [21], to be applied to the present setting, the algorithm has to be generalized to deal with the presence of both (funct P) and (funct P^-), for an atomic role P (this can be easily done by adding a proper rule to the encoding). ∎

We now consider $DL\text{-}Lite_{\mathcal{F}}$ KBs, and obtain the same complexity result, as stated by the theorem below.

Theorem 2. *Let $\mathcal{K}$ be a $DL\text{-}Lite_{\mathcal{R}}$ KB, q a conjunctive query of arity n over $\mathcal{K}$, and t an n-tuple of constants. Then, the problem of establishing whether $t \in ConsAns(q, \mathcal{K})$ is coNP-complete with respect to data complexity.*

Proof (sketch). The proof of coNP-hardness is as for Theorem 1. The only difference is in the form of the KB, which is in this case a $DL\text{-}Lite_{\mathcal{R}}$ KB $\mathcal{K} = \langle \mathcal{T}, \mathcal{A} \rangle$, with basic roles $color_r$, $color_g$, $color_b$, $color$ and $edge$, and TBox and ABox as follows:

$$\mathcal{T} = \{color_r \sqsubseteq color,\ color_g \sqsubseteq color,\ color_b \sqsubseteq color, \} \cup$$
$$\{\exists color_r \sqsubseteq \neg\exists color_g,\ \exists color_r \sqsubseteq \neg\exists color_b,\ \exists color_g \sqsubseteq \neg\exists color_b\}$$
$$\mathcal{A} = \{edge(v_1, v_2) \mid (v_1, v_2) \in E\} \cup$$
$$\{color_r(v, R), color_g(v, G), color_b(v, B) \mid v \in V\}$$

Membership in coNP follows again from the results of [21]. ∎

The above results tell us that consistent query answering over $DL\text{-}Lite$ KBs is in general intractable w.r.t. data complexity, differently from the problem of (standard) query answering over $DL\text{-}Lite$ KBs, i.e., the problem of computing certain answers to queries under the standard semantics given in Section 2, as shown in [11,12]. Notice that tractability of query answering (and of classical DL reasoning services) is a crucial property for DLs of the $DL\text{-}Lite$ family, since they are particularly suited for dealing with big amounts of data. Therefore, the problem arises of identifying interesting cases in which consistent query answering is tractable. As we will show in the next section, consistent instance checking is in fact tractable over both $DL\text{-}Lite_{\mathcal{F}}$ and $DL\text{-}Lite_{\mathcal{R}}$ KBs.

5 Consistent Instance Checking

In this section we study consistent instance checking over *DL-Lite* KBs, and show that, differently from consistent query answering, such a problem is in PTIME w.r.t. data complexity. For ease of exposition, and due to space limits, we show here only the case in which the KB is specified in *DL-Lite$_{\mathcal{F}}$*. However, the technical treatment below can be easily adapted to deal with *DL-Lite$_{\mathcal{R}}$* KBs, and therefore our results are valid also for KBs of this kind.

Let us first consider only KBs without positive inclusions (PIs), i.e., inclusions of the form $B_1 \sqsubseteq B_2$, where B_1 and B_2 are basic concepts. KBs without PIs are called *DL-Lite$_{\mathcal{F}}^-$* KBs, and as TBox assertions contain only functionality and negative inclusion (NIs) assertions, i.e., inclusions of the form $B_1 \sqsubseteq \neg B_2$.

Given a *DL-Lite$_{\mathcal{F}}^-$* knowledge base $\mathcal{K}$, we consider the problem of consistent entailment of a Boolean union of atoms q over $\mathcal{K}$, i.e., a Boolean UCQ $\bigvee_{i=1,\dots,n} \exists y_i.conj_i$ (y_i) such that, for each $i \in \{1, \dots, n\}$, $conj_i(y_i)$ consists of only a single atom. We are interested in studying this problem, since, as we will show in the following, solving it will allow us to easily solve consistent instance checking over *DL-Lite$_{\mathcal{F}}$* KBs. We start by introducing some preliminary notions.

Given a *DL-Lite$_{\mathcal{F}}^-$* KB $\mathcal{K} = \langle \mathcal{T}, \mathcal{A} \rangle$, a membership assertion α is called *inconsistent in $\mathcal{K}$* if there exist no repair R of $\mathcal{K}$ such that $R \models \alpha$. Otherwise α is called *consistent in $\mathcal{K}$*. Notice that consistent membership assertions may violate intensional assertions of the TBox only together with other membership assertions, whereas an inconsistent membership assertion contradicts alone the TBox. Then, it is easy to see that membership assertions in $\mathcal{A}$ that are inconsistent in $\mathcal{K}$ cannot contribute to the consistent entailment problem mentioned above.

In order to get rid of inconsistent membership assertions, we define the algorithm DeleteInconsistentFacts($\mathcal{K}$), which takes as input a *DL-Lite$_{\mathcal{F}}^-$* KB $\mathcal{K} = \langle \mathcal{T}, \mathcal{A} \rangle$ and returns a *DL-Lite$_{\mathcal{F}}^-$* KB $\mathcal{K}' = \langle \mathcal{T}, \mathcal{A}' \rangle$ where $\mathcal{A}'$ is obtained from $\mathcal{A}$ by deleting all membership assertions that are inconsistent in $\mathcal{K}$, i.e., the algorithm discards each membership assertion α such that the KB $\langle \mathcal{T}, \{\alpha\} \rangle$ is unsatisfiable. Intuitively, a membership assertion of the form $A(a)$ (resp. $P(a,b)$) is not satisfied by any repair, if there is an assertion on the TBox which implies that the concept A (resp. the role P) has to be interpreted by the empty set in any interpretation. More precisely, DeleteInconsistentFacts($\mathcal{K}$) computes the ABox $\mathcal{A}'$ by deleting assertions from $\mathcal{A}$ as follows:

- delete each assertion $A(a)$ such that the NI $A \sqsubseteq \neg A$ belongs to $\mathcal{T}$;
- delete each assertion $R(a,b)$ such that either the NI $\exists R \sqsubseteq \neg \exists R$ or the NI $\exists R^- \sqsubseteq \neg \exists R^-$ belongs to $\mathcal{T}$;
- delete each assertion $R(a,a)$ such that the NI $\exists R \sqsubseteq \neg \exists R^-$ or the NI $\exists R^- \sqsubseteq \neg \exists R$ belongs to $\mathcal{T}$.

It is easy to see that DeleteInconsistentFacts($\mathcal{K}$) deletes only assertions that are inconsistent in $\mathcal{K}$, and that every assertion that is not deleted by DeleteInconsistentFacts ($\mathcal{K}$) is satisfied by at leat one repair of $\mathcal{K}$ (i.e., every assertion in $\mathcal{A}'$ is consistent in $\mathcal{K}$). Furthermore, we easily have that $Rep(\mathcal{K}) = Rep(\mathcal{K}')$.

The following definition provides the important notion of $\mathcal{K}$-opponent to a membership assertion.

Definition 2. *Let* $\mathcal{K} = \langle \mathcal{T}, \mathcal{A} \rangle$ *be a DL-Lite$_{\mathcal{F}}^-$ KB, and let* α *be a membership assertion in* $\mathcal{A}$ *consistent in* $\mathcal{K}$. *Then, a membership assertion* β *is a* $\mathcal{K}$-opponent *to* α *if* $\beta \in \mathcal{A}$ *and the KB* $\langle \mathcal{T}, \{\alpha, \beta\} \rangle$ *is unsatisfiable.*

Intuitively, a $\mathcal{K}$-opponent to a membership assertion α is a membership assertion which together with α contradicts a functionality assertion or a negative inclusion assertion in the TBox $\mathcal{T}$.

Finally, we introduce the notion of an image of a query. Let $q = \bigvee_{i=1,\ldots,n} \exists \boldsymbol{y_i}.conj_i$ $(\boldsymbol{y_i})$ be a Boolean union of atoms. Then a membership assertion γ is an *image of* q if there is an $i \in \{1, \ldots, n\}$ such that there exists a substitution σ from the variables in $conj_i(\boldsymbol{y_i})$ to constants in γ such that $\sigma(conj_i(\boldsymbol{y_i})) = \gamma$. Roughly speaking, an image of q is a membership assertion γ such that q is entailed by the knowledge base constituted only by the assertion γ. Given a *DL-Lite* ABox $\mathcal{A}$ and a Boolean union of atoms q, *IMAGES*$(q, \mathcal{A})$, denotes the set of *images of* q *in* $\mathcal{A}$.

With this notion in place we can rephrase the problem of consistent entailment of a Boolean union of atoms q, and say that q is consistently entailed by a *DL-Lite$_{\mathcal{F}}^-$* KB $\mathcal{K} = \langle \mathcal{T}, \mathcal{A} \rangle$ if for each $\mathcal{R} \in Rep(\mathcal{K})$ there exists $\gamma \in$ *IMAGES*$(q, \mathcal{A})$ such that $\mathcal{R} \models \gamma$. Obviously, since an image is a membership assertion, it can be either consistent or inconsistent in $\mathcal{K}$. If it is consistent in $\mathcal{K}$, it may have opponents according to Defintion 2.

Example 4. Consider the KB $\mathcal{K} = \langle \mathcal{T}, \mathcal{A}' \rangle$ of Example 3, and the query $q' = \exists y.hasOwner(\mathsf{Tom}, y)$. It is easy to see that $hasOwner(\mathsf{Tom}, \mathsf{John})$ is a consistent image of q in $\mathcal{A}$, and that $hasOwner(\mathsf{Tom}, \mathsf{Leonard})$ is a $\mathcal{K}$-opponent to $hasOwner$ $(\mathsf{Tom}, \mathsf{John})$. Notice also that in this particular example also $hasOwner(\mathsf{Tom}, \mathsf{Leonard})$ is a consistent image of q in $\mathcal{A}$, and obviously $hasOwner(\mathsf{Tom}, \mathsf{John})$ is a $\mathcal{K}$-opponent to $hasOwner(\mathsf{Tom}, \mathsf{Leonard})$. ∎

In Figure 1, we provide an algorithm, called ConsAnswer, which takes as input a *DL-Lite$_{\mathcal{F}}^-$* KB $\mathcal{K}$ and a Boolean union of atoms q and verifies whether q is consistently entailed by $\mathcal{K}$.

Intuitively, after using the algorithm DeleteInconsistentFacts to drop all membership assertions of $\mathcal{A}$ that do not belong to any repair of $\mathcal{K}$, the algorithm ConsAnswer verifies whether there exists an image γ such that either (a) γ has no $\mathcal{K}$-opponents or (b) every $\mathcal{K}$-opponent β to γ is such that β has at least one $\mathcal{K}$-opponent β' which is not $\mathcal{K}$-opponent to γ and is in turn $\mathcal{K}$-opponent to a different image γ'. If the condition (a) succeeds, then the query q is consistently entailed by $\mathcal{K}$ since every repair of $\mathcal{K}$ satisfies the same image of q in $\mathcal{A}$. As for condition (b), it ensures that if a repair $\mathcal{R}$ does not satisfy the image γ, since it satisfies the opponent β of γ, $\mathcal{R}$ satisfies another image γ', whose satisfaction is guaranteed by the fact that $\mathcal{R}$ does not satisfy β'.

The following theorem states soundness and completeness of the algorithm ConsAnswer.

Theorem 3. *Let* $\mathcal{K}$ *be a DL-Lite$_{\mathcal{F}}^-$ KB and let* q *be a Boolean union of atoms. Then,* $\mathcal{K} \models_{cons} q$ *iff* ConsAnswer$(\mathcal{K}, q)$ *returns true.*

Algorithm ConsAnswer($\mathcal{K}, q$)
Input: $DL\text{-}Lite_{\mathcal{F}}^{-}$ KB $\mathcal{K} = (\mathcal{T}, \mathcal{A})$, Boolean union of atoms q
Output: *true* if $\mathcal{K} \models_{cons} q$, *false* otherwise
begin
   $\mathcal{K} :=$ DeleteInconsistentFacts($\mathcal{K}$);
   for each $\gamma \in IMAGES(q, \mathcal{A})$ **do**
     if
       for each $\mathcal{K}$-opponent β to γ
       there exists $\mathcal{K}$-opponent β' to β **such that**
         β' is not a $\mathcal{K}$-opponent to γ
       and there exists $\gamma' \in IMAGES(q, \mathcal{A})$ **such that**
         β' is a $\mathcal{K}$-opponent to γ'
       then return *true*;
     return *false*;
end

Fig. 1. The Algorithm ConsAnswer

Let us now turn our attention to the problem of consistent instance checking over $DL\text{-}Lite_{\mathcal{F}}$ KBs. We now show that it is possible to exploit the algorithm ConsAnswer to solve such a problem. The basic idea is to separate reasoning on PIs from reasoning on NIs and functionalities. Whereas for the latter form of reasoning we will make use of the algorithm ConsAnswer presented above, for the former we resort to the results of [11]. These results show that in the presence of satisfiable $DL\text{-}Lite_{\mathcal{F}}$ KBs, i.e., KBs in which the ABox does not contradict intensional knowledge of the TBox, (standard) query answering of a UCQ q can be solved by first processing PIs through a rewriting technique, which produces a new UCQ q_r, called perfect rewriting of q, and by then evaluating q_r over the ABox seen as a flat relational database.

To verify KB satisfiability, the use of the following construction is needed (cf. [11]).

Definition 3. *Let $\mathcal{T}$ be a $DL\text{-}Lite_{\mathcal{F}}$ TBox. We call* NI-closure *of $\mathcal{T}$, denoted by $cln(\mathcal{T})$, the TBox defined inductively as follows:*

1. *all negative inclusion assertions in $\mathcal{T}$ are in $cln(\mathcal{T})$;*
2. *all functionality assertions in $\mathcal{T}$ are in $cln(\mathcal{T})$;*
3. *if $B_1 \sqsubseteq B_2$ is in $\mathcal{T}$ and $B_2 \sqsubseteq \neg B_3$ or $B_3 \sqsubseteq \neg B_2$ is in $cln(\mathcal{T})$, then $B_1 \sqsubseteq \neg B_3$ is in $cln(\mathcal{T})$;*
4. *if one of the assertions $\exists P \sqsubseteq \neg \exists P$, or $\exists P^- \sqsubseteq \neg \exists P^-$ is in $cln(\mathcal{T})$, then both such assertions are in $cln(\mathcal{T})$.*

In other words, $cln(\mathcal{T})$ is a special TBox that does not contain PIs and is obtained by closing the NIs in $\mathcal{T}$ with respect to the PIs in $\mathcal{T}$ (notice, however, that not all NIs logically implied by $\mathcal{T}$ are inserted in $cln(\mathcal{T})$, but only those that are needed for our aims). The TBox $cln(\mathcal{T})$ results particularly useful for testing KB satisfiability, since it is possible to show that a $DL\text{-}Lite_{\mathcal{F}}$ KB $\mathcal{K} = \langle \mathcal{T}, \mathcal{A} \rangle$ is satisfiable if and only if the KB $\langle cln(\mathcal{T}), \mathcal{A} \rangle$ is satisfiable. Furthermore, satisfiability of $\langle cln(\mathcal{T}), \mathcal{A} \rangle$ can be carried out by simply issuing suitable first-order queries over the ABox $\mathcal{A}$.

In order to compute the perfect reformulation of a conjunctive query q, in [11] an algorithm is defined, called PerfectRef, which takes as input a UCQ q and a $DL\text{-}Lite_{\mathcal{F}}$ TBox $\mathcal{T}$. Roughly speaking, in PerfectRef, PIs in $\mathcal{T}$ are used as rewriting rules, iteratively applied from right to left to atoms occurring in the query, thus allowing for compiling away in the rewriting the intensional knowledge of $\mathcal{T}$ that is relevant for answering q. We do not give here the exact definition of the algorithm PerfectRef, and refer the reader to [11] for further details.

We now extend the results in [11] by considering generic $DL\text{-}Lite_{\mathcal{F}}$ KBs (either satisfiable or unsatisfiable), and provide the following theorem which shows that consistent query answering for UCQs over $DL\text{-}Lite_{\mathcal{F}}$ KBs can be reduced to consistent query answering of UCQs over $DL\text{-}Lite_{\mathcal{F}}^-$ KBs.

Theorem 4. *Let $\mathcal{T}$ be a $DL\text{-}Lite_{\mathcal{F}}$ TBox, q a UCQ over $\mathcal{T}$, and let q_r be the UCQ returned by* PerfectRef$(q, \mathcal{T})$. *Then, for each $DL\text{-}Lite_{\mathcal{F}}$ ABox $\mathcal{A}$, we have that* $ConsAns(q, \langle \mathcal{T}, \mathcal{A} \rangle) = ConsAns(q_r, \langle cln(\mathcal{T}), \mathcal{A} \rangle)$.

With the above result in place, we can now turn back to the problem of consistent instance checking over $DL\text{-}Lite_{\mathcal{F}}$ KBs. Figure 2 shows an algorithm, called ConsEntails, that takes as input a $DL\text{-}Lite_{\mathcal{F}}$ KB $\mathcal{K}$ and a membership assertion α and verifies whether α is consistently entailed by $\mathcal{K}$. Notice that the algorithm first computes the perfect reformulation q_r of the Boolean conjunctive ground query α, and then makes use of the algorithm ConsAnswer with the $DL\text{-}Lite_{\mathcal{F}}^-$ KB $\langle cln(\mathcal{T}), \mathcal{A} \rangle$ and the query q_r as input. Such an usage of ConsAnswer is possible since it can be shown that PerfectRef$(\alpha, \mathcal{T})$ returns always a Boolean union of atoms, whatever $DL\text{-}Lite_{\mathcal{F}}$ membership assertion α and TBox are taken as input.

Algorithm ConsEntails$(\mathcal{K}, \alpha)$
Input: $DL\text{-}Lite_{\mathcal{F}}$ KB $\mathcal{K} = \langle \mathcal{T}, \mathcal{A} \rangle$, membership assertion α
Output: *true* if $\mathcal{K} \models_{cons} \alpha$, *false* otherwise
begin
    $q_r := $ PerfectRef$(\alpha, \mathcal{T})$;
    return ConsAnswer$(\langle cln(\mathcal{T}), \mathcal{A} \rangle, q_r)$;
end

Fig. 2. The Algorithm ConsEntails

The following theorem states soundness and completeness of the algorithm ConsEntails.

Theorem 5. *Let $\mathcal{K}$ be a $DL\text{-}Lite_{\mathcal{F}}$ KB and let α be a membership assertion. Then, $\mathcal{K} \models_{cons} \alpha$ iff* ConsEntails$(\mathcal{K}, \alpha)$ *returns true.*

We finally exploit the algorithm ConsEntails to analyze the computational complexity of the consistent instance checking problem.

Theorem 6. *Let $\mathcal{K}$ be a $DL\text{-}Lite_{\mathcal{F}}$ KB and let α be a membership assertion. The problem of establishing whether $\mathcal{K} \models_{cons} \alpha$ is in* PTIME *with respect to data complexity.*

Proof (sketch). The proof is a consequence of Theorem 5 and of the fact that the algorithm $\mathsf{ConsAnswer}((\mathcal{T}, \mathcal{A}), q)$ runs in time polynomial with respect to the size of the ABox $\mathcal{A}$. Indeed, if n is the number of assertions in $\mathcal{A}$, then: (i) $\mathsf{DeleteInconsistentFacts}$ $(\mathcal{K})$ can be computed in time linear in n; (ii) for every atomic query q, the size of *IMAGES* $(q, \mathcal{A})$ is at most n, and for every membership assertion α, the number of $\mathcal{K}$-opponents to α is also at most n. Consequently, the algorithm has a cost of $O(n^4)$.   ∎

As said at the beginning of this section, we can also give the analogous of the theorem above for *DL-Lite$_\mathcal{R}$* KBs.

Theorem 7. *Let $\mathcal{K}$ be a DL-Lite$_\mathcal{R}$ KB and let α be a membership assertion. The problem of establishing whether $\mathcal{K} \models_{cons} \alpha$ is in* PTIME *with respect to data complexity.*

6   Related Work

Consistent query answering over ontologies can be seen as a particular problem of *belief revision* [2], the area of Artificial Intelligence that studies the problem of integrating new information with previous knowledge. However, from a computational perspective, results from belief revision concern a setting in which knowledge is specified in terms of propositional formulae of classical logic [18,19]. Therefore, no specific results are given for the particular kind of belief revision that we have considered in this paper.

Dealing with inconsistency in ontologies has also received recently a growing attention in the SW community. Many works in this field focus on the issue of locating inconsistencies in ontologies. In [28], a set of techniques for debugging OWL ontologies is given, which allows for detecting unsatisfiable concepts and inconsistent ontologies. In [29], diagnosing the causes of inconsistencies is investigated. In [6], a visual tool for consistency checking is described. In [1], consistency of a *DL-Lite* KB is checked through evaluation of first-order queries over the KB ABox. However, all these works provide no support (or limited) to inconsistency management. Furthermore, with the exception of [1], they are mainly focused on inconsistencies at the terminological level.

Other works are specifically tailored to handling inconsistent ontologies. In [31], integrity preserving in modular ontologies is investigated. In [25], a framework for reasoning with inconsistent ontologies is presented. The framework is based on the notion of selection function, which allows for choosing some consistent sub-theory from an inconsistent ontology. Standard reasoning is then applied to the selected sub-theory. An instantiation of the framework, based on a syntactic relevance-based selection function is also shortly described. In [22], a more extended framework that generalizes four approaches to inconsistency handling is presented. In particular, consistency ontology evolution, repairing inconsistency, reasoning with inconsistent ontologies, and ontology versioning are considered. Both the last mentioned papers are mainly definitional, and provide basic notions and abstract properties and algorithms. Furthermore, such papers pursue a syntactic-based approach, which seems more suitable for dealing with inconsistency at the terminological level, rather than at the instance level, as done in the present paper. Nonetheless, our work can be seen as a special case of the task of reasoning with inconsistent ontologies described in [22], where our notion of $\models_{cons}$ is adopted for non-standard entailment.

The relationship between the present work and the literature on consistent query answering [3,17,7,10,20] has been briefly discussed in the previous sections. We further point out that neither of the papers from this area considers the same combination of integrity constraints (in the present setting given in terms of TBox assertions) and reasoning services studied in the present paper.

7   Conclusions

The present paper can be extended in several directions. We are currently working on a completely intensional technique for consistent instance checking, with the aim of reducing this problem to query evaluation over a database instance representing the KB ABox. Such a technique would allow us to maintain reasoning at the intensional level, as can be already done for standard query answering over *DL-Lite* KBs. We are also working in the direction of identifying other tractable cases of consistent query answering over *DL-Lite* KBs. In this respect, we point out that results of the present paper immediately imply that consistent query answering of Boolean ground union of conjunctive queries is tractable. The same analysis is being carried out over other DLs that allow for tractable reasoning [4]. Finally, we are also studying the problem of consistent query answering over more expressive DLs.

Acknowledgments. This research has been partially supported by FET project TONES (Thinking ONtologiES), funded by the EU under contract number FP6-7603, by project HYPER, funded by IBM through a Shared University Research (SUR) Award grant, and by MIUR FIRB 2005 project "Tecnologie Orientate alla Conoscenza per Aggregazioni di Imprese in Internet" (TOCAI.IT). We finally thank Riccardo Rosati for fruitful discussions on the matter of the present paper, and his helpful comments.

References

1. Acciarri, A., Calvanese, D., De Giacomo, G., Lembo, D., Lenzerini, M., Palmieri, M., Rosati, R.: QuOnto: Querying ontologies. In: Proc. of AAAI 2005, pp. 1670–1671 (2005)
2. Alchourrón, C.E., Gärdenfors, P., Makinson, D.: On the logic of theory change: Partial meet contraction and revision functions. J. of Symbolic Logic 50, 510–530 (1985)
3. Arenas, M., Bertossi, L.E., Chomicki, J.: Consistent query answers in inconsistent databases. In: Proc. of PODS'99, pp. 68–79 (1999)
4. Baader, F., Brandt, S., Lutz, C.: Pushing the EL envelope. In: Proc. of IJCAI 2005, pp. 364–369 (2005)
5. Baader, F., Calvanese, D., McGuinness, D., Nardi, D., Patel-Schneider, P.F. (eds.): The Description Logic Handbook: Theory, Implementation and Applications. Cambridge University Press, New York (2003)
6. Baclawski, K., Kokar, M.M., Waldinger, R., Kogut, P.A.: Consistency checking of semantic web ontologies. In: Horrocks, I., Hendler, J. (eds.) ISWC 2002. LNCS, vol. 2342, Springer, Heidelberg (2002)
7. Bertossi, L.E., Hunter, A., Schaub, T. (eds.): Inconsistency Tolerance. LNCS, vol. 3300. Springer, Heidelberg (2005)
8. Borgida, A., Brachman, R.J.: Conceptual modeling with description logics. In: Baader, et al. [5] ch. 10, pp. 349–372
9. Bouzeghoub, M., Lenzerini, M.: Introduction to the special issue on data extraction, cleaning, and reconciliation. Information Systems 26(8), 535–536 (2001)

10. Cal ì, A., Lembo, D., Rosati, R.: On the decidability and complexity of query answering over inconsistent and incomplete databases. In: Proc. of PODS 2003, pp. 260–271 (2003)
11. Calvanese, D., De Giacomo, G., Lembo, D., Lenzerini, M., Rosati, R.: DL-Lite: Tractable description logics for ontologies. In: Proc. of AAAI 2005, pp. 602–607 (2005)
12. Calvanese, D., De Giacomo, G., Lembo, D., Lenzerini, M., Rosati, R.: Data complexity of query answering in description logics. In: Proc. of KR 2006, pp. 260–270 (2006)
13. Calvanese, D., De Giacomo, G., Lembo, D., Lenzerini, M., Rosati, R.: Tractable reasoning and efficient query answering in description logics: The DL-Lite family, 2007. (To Appear)
14. Calvanese, D., De Giacomo, G., Lenzerini, M.: Answering queries using views over description logics knowledge bases. In: Proc. of AAAI 2000, pp. 386–391 (2000)
15. Chomicki, J., Marcinkowski, J.: On the computational complexity of minimal-change integrity maintenance in relational databases. In: Bertossi, L., Hunter, A., Schaub, T. (eds.) Inconsistency Tolerance. LNCS, vol. 3300, pp. 119–150. Springer, Heidelberg (2005)
16. Chomicki, J., Marcinkowski, J., Staworko, S.: Computing consistent query answers using conflict hypergraphs. In: Proc. of CIKM 2004, pp. 417–426 (2004)
17. Eiter, T., Fink, M., Greco, G., Lembo, D.: Efficient evaluation of logic programs for querying data integration systems. In: Palamidessi, C. (ed.) ICLP 2003. LNCS, vol. 2916, pp. 163–177. Springer, Heidelberg (2003)
18. Eiter, T., Gottlob, G.: On the complexity of propositional knowledge base revision, updates and counterfactuals. Artificial Intelligence 57, 227–270 (1992)
19. Eiter, T., Gottlob, G.: The complexity of nested counterfactuals and iterated knowledge base revisions. J. of Computer and System Sciences 53(3), 497–512 (1996)
20. Fuxman, A., Miller, R.J.: First-order query rewriting for inconsistent databases. In: Eiter, T., Libkin, L. (eds.) ICDT 2005. LNCS, vol. 3363, pp. 337–351. Springer, Heidelberg (2004)
21. Grieco, L., Lembo, D., Ruzzi, M., Rosati, R.: Consistent query answering under key and exclusion dependencies: Algorithms and experiments. In: Proc. of CIKM 2005, pp. 792–799 (2005)
22. Haasa, P., van Harmelen, F., Huang, Z., Stuckenschmidt, H., Sure, Y.: A framework for handling inconsistency in changing ontologies. In: Gil, Y., Motta, E., Benjamins, V.R., Musen, M.A. (eds.) ISWC 2005. LNCS, vol. 3729, Springer, Heidelberg (2005)
23. Heflin, J., Hendler, J.: A portrait of the Semantic Web in action. IEEE Intelligent Systems 16(2), 54–59 (2001)
24. Horrocks, I., Patel-Schneider, P.F., van Harmelen, F.: From SHIQ and RDF to OWL: The making of a web ontology language. J. of Web. Semantics 1(1), 7–26 (2003)
25. Huang, Z., van Harmelen, F., ten Teije, A.: Reasoning with inconsistent ontologies. In: Proc. of IJCAI 2003 (2003)
26. Lenzerini, M.: Data integration: A theoretical perspective. In: Proc. of PODS 2002, pp. 233–246 (2002)
27. Ortiz, M.M., Calvanese, D., Eiter, T.: Data complexity of answering unions of conjunctive queries in SHIQ. In: Proc. of DL 2006. CEUR Electronic Workshop Proceedings (2006)
28. Parsia, B., Sirin, E., Kalyanpur, A.: Debugging OWL ontologies. In: Proc. of the 14th Int. World Wide Web Conf. (WWW 2005) (2005)
29. Schlobach, S., Cornet, R.: Non-standard reasoning services for the debugging of descritpion logic terminologies. In: Proc. of IJCAI 2003, pp. 355–360 (2003)
30. Shadbolt, N., Hall, W., Berners-Lee, T.: The semantic web revisited. IEEE Intelligent Systems 21(3), 96–101 (2006)
31. Stuckenschmidt, H., Klein, M.: Integrity and change in modular ontologies. In: Proc. of IJCAI 2003, pp. 900–908 (2003)
32. Vardi, M.Y.: The complexity of relational query languages. In: Proc. of STOC'82, pp. 137–146 (1982)

A Context-Based Architecture for RDF Knowledge Bases: Approach, Implementation and Preliminary Results*

Heiko Stoermer[1], Paolo Bouquet[1], Ignazio Palmisano[2], and Domenico Redavid[3]

[1] University of Trento,
Dept. of Information and Communication Tech.,
Trento, Italy
{stoermer, bouquet}@dit.unitn.it
[2] Liverpool University
Computer Science Department
Liverpool, UK
ignazio@csc.liv.ac.uk
[3] Università degli Studi di Bari
Dipartimento di Informatica
Bari, Italy
redavid@di.uniba.it

Abstract. In this paper we present a context-based architecture and implementation for supporting the construction and management of contextualized RDF knowledge bases. The goal of this work is to take explicitly into account any possible contextual dependency of a collection of RDF models, without losing sight of performance and scalability issues. We are illustrating motivations, as well as theoretical background, implementation details and test-results of our latest works.

1 Introduction

It is a well-known fact from past work on knowledge representation (see e.g. [11,8,6,1]) that any formalization of knowledge is somehow context dependent. In general, this means that the truth of a statement in a theory typically depends on a collection of assumptions which qualify its interpretation and its holding (or not holding). As the Semantic Web includes an attempt of making domain and top-level knowledge available to web based applications, the need for managing context-dependence is becoming more and more crucial, as it is proved by a few seminal papers on context and Semantic Web (see e.g. [2,7]).

Based on this foundational and theoretical works, this paper aims at contributing a first implementation of a context-based RDF management system

---

* This research was partially funded by the European Commission under the 6th Framework Programme IST Integrated Project VIKEF - Virtual Information and Knowledge Environment Framework (Contract no. 507173, Priority 2.3.1.7 Semantic-based Knowledge Systems; more information at http://www.vikef.net).

M. Marchiori, J.Z. Pan, and C. de Sainte Marie (Eds.): RR 2007, LNCS 4524, pp. 209–218, 2007.

built on top of *RDFCore* [5]. As discussed in other papers, the underlying intuitions of this work are the following: on the one hand, context can be used as a way for restricting the scope of statements to the circumstances with respect to which they are made; on the other hand, appropriate rules – which formalize compatibility relations (CRs) across context-dependent collections of RDF statements – can be used to specify the semantic relations which hold between different contexts, and therefore how statements from different contexts can be used to answer queries across a contextualized RDF knowledge base. Concretely, an RDF context is implemented as a named RDF graph (namely as a graph which can be addressed as a whole through a single URI), and compatibility relations are RDF statements which express relations between context URIs.

The contribution of this paper is to present one possible realization of a contextualized RDF knowledge base for the Semantic Web, and to illustrate our progress based on the RDF knowledge base management system (KBMS). We have conducted a more extensive experiment to investigate performance aspects of *RDFCore* and our extensions.

The paper is organized as follows: In Section 2 we present intuitive and technical motivations for our approach, as well as some related work. Section 3 describes our general proposal, whereas Section 4 contains a technical description of the steps taken to realize our ideas. In Section 5 we present our experimentation results, and we wrap up with a conclusion and a short mention of planned further works in Section 6.

2   Motivation and Related Work

One of the very appealing ideas of using ontologies in the Semantic Web is that – with a shared ontology – two RDF Aboxes provided by different applications can simply be merged, collapsed on identical URIs, and thus provide a new, bigger KB for answering a query.

However, simple cases can be constructed that unveil problems with this view, both on the practical and on the logical level. Take the example depicted in Fig. 1: imagine we have a TBox T with relations that have cardinality constraints (e.g. that a country can have at most one prime minister), and two ABoxes A and A' with assertions compliant to this TBox (e.g. that Berlusconi is the Italian prime minister and that Prodi is the Italian prime minister, respectively). The two ABoxes, when taken in isolation, are consistent with the cardinality constraint; however, when merged, they may produce a situation which is formally inconsistent, though intuitively it may be the case that the two statements implicitly refer to different points in time (e.g. 2005 and 2006 respectively).

Based on the literature on context in knowledge representation (see, for example, the classical papers cited in the introduction), we propose to address this general problem by binding consistent sets of assertions to the circumstances

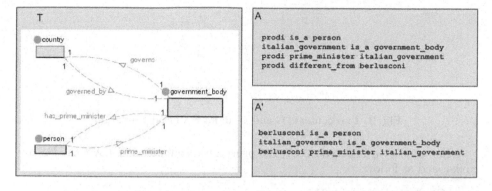

Fig. 1. Example formalization that produces an inconsistency when merged

they were made under, i.e. to limit their scope to a context, as we will describe in Section 3.

As discussed in [7,3,4], this contextualization can serve as a basis for a number of KR modelling aspects, such as temporal evolution, trust, beliefs and provenance. The contributions of our approach compared to the proposals made in [7,4,10,9] as well as compared to named graph implementations in current RDF triple stores are that (i) we do not propose or require an extension of the current RDF standard and (ii) we aim at providing support for managing cross-contextual inference via compatibility relations (CRs). These relations between contexts may have procedural semantics[1] and thus enable us to make explicit in which way the assertions in the related contexts are supposed to be combined for query answering, to provide for flexible and powerful contextual reasoning as envisioned in the mentioned bibliography.

3   An Exemplary Compatibility Relation

The EXTENDS relation we have chosen to illustrate is meant to describe a situation where we know that two contexts describe the same object, but assume that one context contains more information about it than the other.

Take the example of two Information Extraction processes P and P' that are run on the same document, at different points in time. Assume P' is a more advanced process and is able to extract more information from the document. We propose to model this as two contexts C (created by P) and C' (created by P') with a relation $EXTENDS$ that explicates that C' is an extension to C (a necessary condition for this relation is that both contexts describe the same object). Intuitively we want to keep the information derived from different sources separate and with explicit metadata, but have the possibility to combine the resulting information where necessary.

---

[1] And can therefore not be formalized in an OWL ontology.

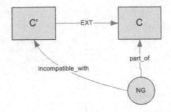

Fig. 2. Two contexts C and C' in an EXTENDS relation

When a query q is posed on C', the procedural semantics of $EXTENDS$ are envisioned as follows:

```
if q has results in C'
    then return result set
else
    propagate query to the union of C' and C.
```

One issue that becomes obvious immediately is the case where the union of C' and C produces an inconsistent ABox which makes query answering impossible. This can result from cardinality constraints in the TBox (see the Berlusconi-Prodi example in Sect. 2), or subsumption issues (an individual o is said to be instance of different classes). Our basic solution approach is to extract a minimal subgraph containing the statement(s) that caused the inconsistency into a named graph NG, as illustrated in Fig. 2. The result is that the query can be processed on the conflict-free part of the union of C' and C.

The case becomes of course slightly more complex when we take into account more than two contexts. We envision the $EXTENDS$ relation to be transitive. This can result in a reasoning chain i) when establishing the relation, as conflicts have to be detected and re-modelled and ii) when querying the contexts, as the necessary contexts and relevant subgraphs have to be traversed. This chain however is non-cyclic, as the relation is directional. Section 4 describes our first implementation of this relation.

We have chosen to attack and illustrate this specific relation due to its relative complexity. However, we are convinced that our basic approach as described in [13] is fairly general and can be used to implement relations of different kinds. In the course of the project we envision relations that make explicit temporal evolution, trust and a number of domain specific aspects.

4   Realization

4.1   The Compatibility Relations Ontology (CRO)

The CRO contains the definition of the main concepts used to describe the KB structure in terms of contexts; it contains the definition of Context and the definition of Graph, where both concepts represent entities that are named graphs; a Context has the (informal) property of representing something that has a meaning as a whole, e.g. the set of statements extracted from a specific

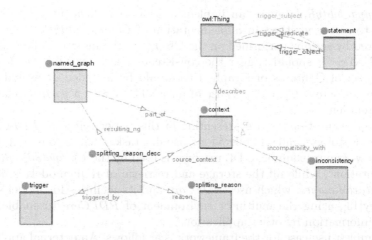

Fig. 3. Domain-range view of the CR Ontology

document, at a specific time, with a specific algorithm, while a Graph is a set
of statements that is included in one or more Contexts or other Graphs, but
has no specific meaning alone (e.g. the set of statements in a Context that cause
inconsistencies with another Context). A domain-range view of the CRO is given
in Fig. 3.

Moreover, the CRO contains the definition of the SplittingReason class, which
represents the reason that led to the isolation of a part of a Context and the storage of that fragment as a Graph; a SplittingReason instance includes references
to the Context from where the statements that are being split belonged, the
Graph that will hold these statements, the reason for which this split has been
done, e.g. because the statements create inconsistencies w.r.t. another context
(which is also linked to the reason), and the reification of the statements in the
CRO that triggered the split, if any. An example of SplittingReason generation
is illustrated in detail in Sect. 4.3.

The CRO also acts as a registry for *CompatibilityRelation* implementations,
since each declaration of a *CompatibilityRelation* amounts to the declaration of
a property in this ontology; an AnnotationProperty for this property, called *im-
plementation_uri*, gives the java class name of the corresponding implementation;
this is used to retrieve the set of *CompatibilityRelation* that *RDFContextManager*
will use when managing the CRO and the knowledge base.

4.2   RDFContextManager

The component we developed to manage contexts is called *RDFContextManager*; its architecture bases on the work we presented in [12]. *RDFContextManager* provides methods to i) manage the contents of the Compatibility Relation
Ontology (CRO) as described in 4.1, ii) add, remove or update Contexts and
Graphs in the underlying persistence layer and iii) obtain Views over a Context,
respecting all the relation chains involved.

A *CompatibilityRelation* is an implementation of a Java interface exposing methods to assess whether an implementation of *CompatibilityRelation* should be triggered by actions performed on the CRO (e.g. the insertion of a statement C_1 EXTENDS C_2 should trigger the consistency check over $C_1 \sqcup C_2$), and to provide a set of Contexts or Graphs that would be included or excluded in a View over a Context C_1, e.g. because of an EXTENDS or a *part_of* relation or chain of relations.

The implementation we are presenting in this paper relies on *RDFCore* for RDF models storage, and on Pellet[2] for reasoning tasks such as consistency check over a View. In our example, a DL reasoner is used by the *CompatibilityRelation* implementation[3], while all the storage and retrieval of RDF models is done on *RDFContextManager*, which uses *RDFCore* and its facilities for model storage and query[13], using the multiuser environment of *RDFCore* to enable use of Context information by other applications.

The simplest use case for the framework is as follows. An external application adds one or more different Contexts in *RDFContextManager*, assigning them URIs or letting *RDFContextManager* choose one. The external application asserts some relations between the contexts or specific to a context; the relations between the contexts are expressed through properties defined in the CRO, and are effected through the RDFContextManager API. *RDFContextManager* receives these new assertions, and triggers all the CR implementations available into first verifying if any of the new assertions is relevant (i.e. the asserted relation corresponds to the URI the implementation is attached to) and then checking whether the new relation is likely to cause reorganization of the knowledge base; if this is the case, corrective actions are undertaken. Finally, the external application makes a query over the CRO to find out all the contexts that satisfy some conditions (e.g. all the contexts which have been created in a specific date), and then asks to perform a query over the set of statements resulting from the union of the contexts; this involves creation of a View for each context that is selected by the query.

4.3   Implementation of EXTENDS

The algorithms involved in the EXTENDS relation are as follows:

Two contexts C_1 and C_2 are inserted in *RDFContextManager*, and C_1 is asserted to extend C_2 w.r.t a specific subject S_1 with the following statements in the CRO:

$$< C_1 \; EXTENDS \; C_2 >, \; < C_1 \; rdf : about \; S_1 >, \; < C_2 \; rdf : about \; S_1 >$$

The implementation of *EXTENDS* will be triggered to check for consistency and the necessity of knowledge base reorganization. If any inconsistency is detected, *EXTENDS* tries to isolate the responsible statements, selects those

---

[2] www.mindswap.org/2003/pellet/
[3] Note that different implementations could need – and are allowed to have – different reasoning settings, e.g. only RDFS or OWL Lite inference rather than OWL DL inference.

that appear in C_2 and removes them from C_2; the statements are then stored as a Named Graph G_1. The split is tracked by creating a SplittingReason object, connected to C_2, which is the *source*, and G_1, which is the *result*; it is also connected to a reason, which in this case is instance of the *Inconsistency* class, and in turn to C_1 which is related as *incompatible* w.r.t G_1. The statements added to the CRO are reified and attached to the SplittingReason as *triggers*, in order for the split to be traceable, and finally a *part_of* relation is asserted between C_2 and G_1. Since the *EXTENDS* relation is defined transitive, in case C_2 is already connected through a *EXTENDS* relation to other contexts, then the check is performed not against C_2 alone but over the resulting View; the generated splits in the KB can then be distributed along the *EXTENDS* chain, which is one of the scalability issues we analyze in Sect. 5.

When a View over C_1 is requested, all the CR implementations are requested to provide a set of Contexts or Graphs that *must not* appear in the final view (EXCLUDE set), i.e. are requested to forbid to follow some paths in the CRO assertions; this is because, when multiple CR are present, some of them may forbid the presence of a result that others would allow to appear in the results; simply removing all the forbidden results after all the paths are followed is not correct nor efficient, since this would require complex pruning strategies. After the EXCLUDE set has been computed, all the CR implementations are required to provide the set of Contexts or Graphs that should appear in the resulting View (INCLUDE set), and they will prune their visiting graph as soon as a forbidden result is reached. The final View is then computed as the INCLUDE set plus the resources connected through *part_of* to these elements (not including those in the EXCLUDE set). The View can now be viewed as a single model, or the set of URIs for the contexts and graphs can be used as dataset for the FROM part of a SPARQL query to be issued to *RDFCore*, which in turn uses ARQ[4] as SPARQL engine to interpret and answer it.

5   Results

In this section we presents the empirical evaluation we have conducted so far. In order to check the system for scalability, we needed to design a big knowledge base with non trivial contents, and at the same time divided in smaller chunks without changing the semantics of the content. This, however, seems a very difficult task, and so far we have not found real world ontologies that satisfy these requirements, so we used a homemade tool to generate individuals for a generic ontology; repeating the process many times gave us two well sized knowledge bases.

Using the SOFSEM ontology,[5] an ontology to describe the SOFSEM conference, we generated two knowledge bases, one composed of 30 models containing about 70000 statements each (for a total of more than 2 millions triples), and the other containing 900 models of about 2000 triples each (1.8 millions triples);

---

[4] http://jena.sourceforge.net
[5] http://nb.vse.cz/~svabo/oaei2006/data/Conference.owl

Table 1. Results for 70000 triples models

Model number	Consistency check (ms)	Model number	Consistency check (ms)
0 - 1	63476	10 - 11	60091
2 - 3	49529	12 - 13	62621
4 - 5	54184	14 - 15	59216
6 - 7	58410	16 - 17	58142
8 - 9	62342	18 - 19	62041

Table 2. Results for small sized models and long chains

Model number	View (ms)	Consistency check (ms)	Model number	View (ms)	Consistency check (ms)	Model number	View (ms)	Consistency check (ms)
0	91	2043	9	156	5913	18	208	9986
1	176	2542	10	152	6076	19	214	10950
2	111	2956	11	175	6497	20	218	10699
3	122	3185	12	166	7101	21	232	11434
4	153	3634	13	175	7383	22	267	11696
5	114	3894	14	186	8046	23	242	12064
6	132	4328	15	195	8421	24	244	12706
7	134	4907	16	208	8862	25	249	13095
8	149	5057	17	220	9486	26	276	13476

on the first one, we tried to chain the models with *EXTENDS* relations involving two models at a time, while in the second one we chained tirthy models at a time, obtaining many chains, and then joined the chains. The results are presented in Table 1, where the results for the first experiment are presented, in Table 2 for the second experiment. The second experiment is also depicted in Fig. 4.

As is evident from Fig. 4, the time elapsed to create a view over the graphs is almost constant, even if the number of relations to navigate increases, while the time elapsed to check the consistency of the models grows proportionally to their size. It is important to note that the consistency check runs only when new relations are enterend in the CRO; the most frequent operation, then, will

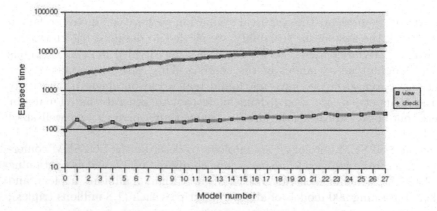

Fig. 4. Results trend for small sized models

be the request to create a View starting from some specified models, and the experimental evaluation shows that this operation is usually performed in less than half a second on the test machine (a laptop with 512 MB of RAM, which is not an adequate server setup). The time required to complete the consistency check and automatic splitting on models of greater size is around one minute, which is acceptable from our point of view if we consider that this operation has to be done only once, and occasionally as new relations are added.

The most relevant point, here, is that requesting a View operation will return a set of graph identifiers that can be used as dataset for a SPARQL query, ensuring that the model resulting from the union of the queried data is consistent, without having to check at the time of querying; this also means that the memory requirements (at query time) of the framework only depend on the number of relations between Contexts and Graphs, and not on the size of the contained data, or on their complexity. The memory needed by the SPARQL engine to run the query itself, instead, depends heavily on the specific query; still no complete evaluation of the behavior of the system w.r.t. the possible kind of queries has been performed.

6   Conclusion and Further Works

Basing on the opinion that contexts in Semantic Web KR are a way to tackle some of the current limitations of the languages available and provide for better scalability in some cases, we have presented a theoretical approach and an implementation of Contextual Reasoning in a Semantic Web KB and the associated testing results. We have not only implemented a context mechanism into our KBMS to be able to use a context as a first-class object in assertions, but also illustrated a way to provide for context relations with procedural semantics which – in our opinion – is required for a complete context functionality.

Our next steps will be directed towards the formal definition and implementation of more compatibility relations. Some of them will be as required by the VIKEF project, but we are also interested in exploring more general and domain independent relations between contexts and their properties.

On the implementational side, these planned steps will be accompanied by the development of a more standardized test set and a set of exemplary queries that specifically display and make use of contexts, to assess the practicability, performance and scalability of our implementations.

References

1. Benerecetti, M., Bouquet, P., Ghidini, C.: Contextual Reasoning Distilled. Journal of Theoretical and Experimental Artificial Intelligence 12(3), 279–305 (2000)
2. Bouquet, P., Giunchiglia, F., van Harmelen, F., Serafini, L., Stuckenschmidt, H.: Contextualizing ontologies. Journal of Web Semantics, vol. 1(4) (2005)

3. Bouquet, P., Serafini, L., Stoermer, H.: Introducing Context into RDF Knowledge Bases. In: Proceedings of SWAP 2005, the 2nd Italian Semantic Web Workshop, Trento, Italy, December 14-16, 2005. CEUR Workshop Proceedings, ISSN 1613-0073, online http://ceur-ws.org/Vol-166/70.pdf (December 2005)
4. Carroll, J., Bizer, C., Hayes, P., Stickler, P.: Named Graphs, Provenance and Trust. In: Proceedings of the Fourteenth International World Wide Web Conference (WWW2005), Chiba, Japan, vol.14, pp. 613–622 (May 2005)
5. Esposito, F., Iannone, L., Palmisano, I., Semeraro, G.: RDF Core: a Component for Effective Management of RDF Models. In: Cruz, I. F., Kashyap, V., Decker, S., Eckstein, R. (eds.), Proceedings of SWDB'03, The first International Workshop on Semantic Web and Databases, Co-located with VLDB 2003, Humboldt-Universität, Berlin, Germany, (September 7-8, 2003)
6. Ghidini, C., Giunchiglia, F.: Local Models Semantics, or Contextual Reasoning = Locality + Compatibility. Artificial Intelligence 127(2), 221–259 (2001)
7. Guha, R.V., McCool, R., Fikes, R.: Contexts for the semantic web. In: McIlraith, S.A., Plexousakis, D., van Harmelen, F. (eds.) ISWC 2004. LNCS, vol. 3298, pp. 32–46. Springer, Heidelberg (2004)
8. Guha, R.V.: Contexts: a Formalization and some Applications. Technical Report ACT-CYC-423-91, MCC, Austin, Texas (1991)
9. Klyne, G.: Contexts for RDF Information Modelling. Content Technologies Ltd, http://www.ninebynine.org/RDFNotes/RDFContexts.html (October 2000)
10. Klyne, G.: Circumstance, provenance and partial knowledge - Limiting the scope of RDF assertions, http://www.ninebynine.org/RDFNotes/UsingContextsWithRDF.html (2002)
11. McCarthy, J.: Notes on Formalizing Context. In: Proc. of the 13th International Joint Conference on Artificial Intelligence, pp. 555–560, Chambery, France (1993)
12. Stoermer, H., Palmisano, I., Redavid, D., Iannone, L., Bouquet, P., Semeraro, G.: Contextualization of a RDF Knowledge Base in the VIKEF Project. In: Sugimoto, S., Hunter, J., Rauber, A., Morishima, A. (eds.) ICADL 2006. LNCS, vol. 4312, pp. 101–110. Springer, Heidelberg (2006)
13. Stoermer, H., Palmisano, I., Redavid, D., Iannone, L., Bouquet, P., Semeraro, G.: RDF and Contexts: Use of SPARQL and Named Graphs to Achieve Contextualization. In: Proceedings of the First Jena User's Conference, Bristol, UK http://jena.hpl.hp.com/juc2006/proceedings/palmisano/paper.pdf (April 2006)

Towards a Hybrid System Using an Ontology Enriched by Rules for the Semantic Annotation of Brain MRI Images

Ammar Mechouche[1,2], Christine Golbreich[3], and Bernard Gibaud[1,2]

[1] INSERM, U746, Campus de Villejean, F-35043 Rennes, France,
[2] INRIA, VisAGeS, Univ. Rennes I, CNRS, UMR 6074, F-35042 Rennes, France
{Ammar.Mechouche,Bernard.Gibaud}@irisa.fr
[3] University of Versailles Saint-Quentin, 55 avenue de Paris - 78035 Versailles, France
Christine.Golbreich@uvsq.fr

Abstract. This paper describes an hybrid method combining symbolic and numerical techniques for annotating brain Magnetic Resonance images. Existing automatic labelling methods are mostly statistical in nature and do not work very well in certain situations such as the presence of lesions. The goal is to assist them by a knowledge-based method. The system uses statistical method for generating a sufficient set of initial facts for fruitful reasoning. Then, the reasoning is supported by an OWL DL ontology enriched by SWRL rules. The experiments described were achieved using the KAON2 reasoner for inferring the annotations.

1 Introduction

Identifying anatomical structures in brain Magnetic Resonance Images (MRI) is an important aspect of the preparation of a surgical intervention in neurosurgery, especially when the lesion is located in the cerebral cortex. A precise labelling of cortical structures (gyri, sulci) surrounding the lesion is particularly necessary to determine an optimal surgical strategy. Existing automatic approaches for annotating brain images are often statistical, e.g., based on Statistical Probability Anatomy Maps (SPAMs) [1]. A SPAM is a 3D probabilistic map associated to a particular anatomical structure. The value at each voxel position represents the probability of belonging to this structure at that location. The statistical data used in our system were derived from a database of 305 normal subjects, after re-alignment of MRI data into a common reference system (called stereotaxic space). SPAMs-like methods have an important drawback. They are not robust against deformations and shifts caused by a lesion in the brain. A symbolic method, using a priori knowledge about topological relations between the cerebral structures may be an alterative or a complement to compensate it, since in contrast topological relations are preserved. This paper describes a new hybrid method for annotating brain images where SPAMs are used to get a sufficient set of initial facts for reasoning. Reasoning is supported by an OWL[1] ontology

---

[1] http://www.w3.org/TR/owl-features/

M. Marchiori, J.Z. Pan, and C. de Sainte Marie (Eds.): RR 2007, LNCS 4524, pp. 219–228, 2007.

about the brain cortex anatomical structures and Horn rules capturing the topological dependencies between the brain structures. OWL offers several benefits. The labels get a clear and well-defined semantics. The brain ontology becomes interoperable. OWL provides useful services for its design and maintainance. Using Web standard languages makes the ontology and rules sharable on the Web. Thus, they can be used to annotate images distributed in multiple sources.

2   Method

The method consists of two main steps. The first step is the segmentation of the brain and the extraction of the sulci tracks from an MRI exam. The second step, is the annotation of a region of interest (ROI) selected from the sulci graph. This paper mainly focuses on the second step.

Reasoning is performed from an ontology of the brain structures enriched by rules representing their topological dependencies, and initial facts provided by numerical and statistical tools (SPAMs). The complete process of the application is: (1) acquiring the patient MRI ; (2) brain segmentation; (3) extraction of the external tracks of the sulci; (4) selection by the user of a region of interest and extraction of the corresponding subgraph of sulcus segments delimiting surfaces corresponding to the parts of gyrus (called patches) present in the region; (5) initialization of the ABox $\mathcal{A}$. The above numerical and statistical treatments lead to the initial facts, OWL individuals and role values representing their topological relations, as explained thereafter; (6) reasoning based on the brain ontology $\mathcal{O}$, the rule base $\mathcal{R}$, and the ABox $\mathcal{A}$ (with some user interaction), (7) Finally, the inferred labels of the structures are involved in the ROI.

2.1   Populating the Abox

First, the numerical tools extract the sulci of a ROI and delimit the surfaces limited by the sulci (patches). They also provide the topological relations and the orientations between the different patches and sulcus segments.

The yellow segments figure 1 (left) show the sulci of the ROI. The patches (e.g.; $P7$, $P8$, $P9$ etc.) are delimited by the sulci (e.g.; 178, 124 etc.) (right). The facts extracted by the numerical tools from this graph are represented in OWL DL (figure 2 left). For example $P9$ is an individual of the class Patch while 178 is a SulcusSegment. The property $isMAEBoundedBy$ has a value (individual of the class AttributedEntity) expressing that $P9$ is bounded by the segment 178 with a posterior orientation, and other segments 423, 424 etc.

These facts are then completed by data computed from the SPAMs. A SPAM is a 3D image file associated to a particular anatomical structure, for instance, a particular gyrus. The information at each point of this 3D image $pt(x, y, z)$ represents an estimate of the probability to belong to this particular structure. Each segment s_i of the ROI is a set of points. We first transform the points coordinates into coordinates of the reference space, i.e. the stereotaxic space. Then we calculate the probability p_{ij} of the segment s_i to belong to a SPAM sp_j by calculating the average of the probabilities of all its (transformed) points. For

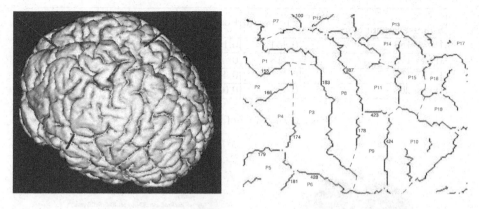

Fig. 1. Extraction of the ROI graph

```
<Patch rdf:ID="p9">
    ...
    <isMAEBoundedBy>

        <AttributedEntity rdf:ID="AttEntity1">
            <entity>
                <SulcusSegment rdf:ID="178"/>
            </entity>
            <orientation>
                <Posterior rdf:ID="posteriorTo"/>
            </orientation>
            <MAEBounds rdf:resource="#p9"/>
        </AttributedEntity>
    </isMAEBoundedBy>
    ...
</Patch>
```

```
<owl:Class redf:ID="Orientation">
    <rdfs:subClassOf>
        <owl:Class rdf:ID="Posterior"/>
    </rdfs:subClassOf>
</owl:Class>


<owl:ObjectProperty rdf:ID="isMAEBoundedBy">
    <inverseOf>
        <owl:objectProperty rdf:about="#MAEBounds">
    </inverseOf>
</owl:ObjectProperty>
```

Fig. 2. Facts in the ABox (left), OWL class and ObjectProperty (right)

each segment we store the two highest probabilities that have been computed (figure 3). These values computed from the SPAMs, and the abstractions rules presented below enable to automatically acquire the initial facts of the Abox $\mathcal{A}$.

Computing the boundaries and separations. Some heuristics have been defined to determine whether a sulcus 'bounds' a SPAM or 'separates' two SPAMs: if the two highest probabilities are small, over a given threshold MIN, then the segment is asserted to separate or to bound the corresponding SPAMs, else if they are very big, over a given threshold MAX, then the segment is asserted to be inside the corresponding SPAM. The thresholds MIN and MAX are defined empirically. More precisely, the rules that abstract the topological relations regarding the boundaries and separations are:

- if($p_{i1} \in [MIN, MAX]$ and $p_{i2} \in [MIN, MAX]$) then s_i separates sp_1 and sp_2. Indeed it means that s_i is located between sp_1 and sp_2 that is s_i separates them, e.g.; S_1 figure 4).
- $if(p_{i1} \in [MIN, MAX]$ and $p_{i2} < MIN)$ then s_i bounds sp_1, indeed low values mean that s_i is located at the extremity of the SPAM thus it is a boundary (e.g.; S_3 figure 4)

SulcusSegment \ Gyrus	Precentral	Postcentral	Angular	SupTemporal	...
ID = 183	0.384	0.186	0	0	.
ID = 178	0.218	0	0	0	.
ID = 155	0	0.477	0.105	0	.
ID = 298	0	0.038	0	0.076	.

Fig. 3. Example of probabilities

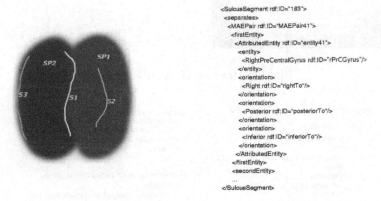

Fig. 4. Computing facts about separation and boundary from SPAMS

- $if(p_{i1} > MAX$ and $p_{i2} < MIN)$ then s_i isInside an instance sp_1, indeed these values indicate that s_i is within the SPAM (e.g.; S_2 figure 4)

Computing the orientations. Each entity has three orientations: (Right or Left), (Posterior or Anterior) and (Superior or Inferior). To determine the orientations of the segments w.r.t SPAMs, for example that a segment s_i bounds a SPAM sp_j with an anterior orientation, we compare the coordinates (x, y, z) of the centre of the segment, transformed into the reference space, to the coordinates (x', y', z') of the SPAM centre.

The heuristic rules below abstract the orientations:

- if $x > x'$ then s_i isRightTo sp_j else s_i isLeftTo sp_j
- if $y > y'$ then s_i isAnteriorTo sp_j else s_i isPosteriorTo sp_j
- if $z > z'$ then s_i isSuperiorTo sp_j else s_i isInferiorTo sp_j

Since such rules could not be used by KAON2, they were applied using a $C++$ procedural program. The resulting role values, e.g.; separates(s_0, ($prcgr$, $anteriorTo$, $rightTo$, $superiorTo$), ($pcgr$, $posteriorTo$, $leftTo$, $inferiorTo$)) are represented in OWL (figure 4).

2.2   Brain Ontology and Rules

The knowledge base consists of the brain ontology enriched with rules [6]. For the moment, the ontology about the sulci and gyri is represented in OWL DL,

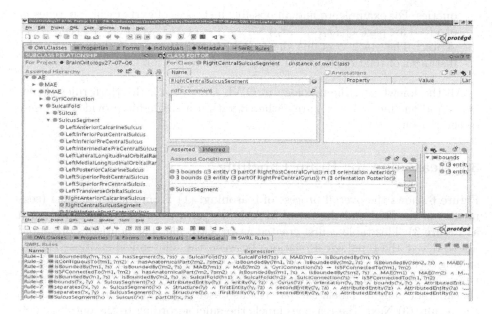

Fig. 5. Brain ontology and rules edited with Protégé

the rules in SWRL. They have been edited using Protégé OWL and the SWRL plugin[2] (figure 5). During the construction of the ontology we have been assisted by a neurosurgeon, and used the Ono Atlas [5] and other sources.[3]

- **Tbox:**The *Tbox* provides the logical definitions of concepts (classes), roles (properties) and the asserted axioms. For example, the necessary and sufficient condition to be a segment of the right central sulcus is[4]: $RightCentral-$ $SulcusSegment \equiv ((\exists MAEBounds (\exists entity (\exists partOf RightPost$ $CentralGyrus)) \sqcap (\exists orientation Anterior))) \sqcap ((\exists MAEBounds$ $(\exists entity (\exists partOf RightPreCentralGyrus)) \sqcap \exists orientation Poste-$ $rior))))$ (figure 5). This OWL definition expresses that a segment of central sulcus is bounded by a part of postcentral gyrus with an orientation which is an instance of Anterior, and is bounded by a part of precentral gyrus with an orientation which is an instance of Posterior.

- **Rule-box:** The *Rule-box* contains all the rules extending the ontology, for example the rule bellow expresses that a boundary is propagated from parts to whole: $isMAEBoundedBy(?x, ?y) \land hasSegment(?z, ?y) \land SulcalFold(?z) \land$ $SulcalFold(?y) \land MAE(?x) \rightarrow isMAEBoundedBy(?x, ?z)$. (figure 5) If a material anatomical entity x is bounded by a sulcal fold y, and y is a segment of z, then x is bounded by z. Such rules are needed to infer the missing knowledge of the classes definitions for instance retrieval. Rules are also useful to express

---

[2] http://protege.stanford.edu/

[3] http://www.med.univ-rennes1.fr/~dameron/thesis/dameronThesis.pdf

[4] This is not the exact definition but a simplification for the example.

queries. For example, to find all possible instances of gyri of which patches p_i of a ROI are part: $Q(?x_i, ..., ?x_n) \leftarrow \wedge_{i=1 \ to \ n}(AE(?x_i)) \wedge partOf(p_i, ?x_i)$.

– **Abox:** The *Abox* contains the individuals (instances of classes) and the instances of relations between them as defined section 2.1.

All the knowledge, the ontology in OWL DL (Tbox), the Horn rules (Rulebox), and the facts (Abox), are gathered within a single file provided as input to the reasoner.

3 Reasoning for Brain Labelling

Figure 6 shows the overall process of reasoning: (1) From the list of sulci (segments) of the ROI and the list of SPAMs we get a table of probabilities (such as Figure 3). This table is first created as an XML file. The heuristics presented above derive the topological relations between the anatomical entities. The resulting facts are stored in an OWL file. This file is merged with the ontology, the rules, and the other facts coming from the numerical tools. (2) From this file, the inference engine labels the patches as described below. The user validates the result. (3) Next, the reasoner labels the sulci according to the ontology definitions enriched by rules. The user validates this step, and finally the labelled image is obtained. The reasoning is performed as follows :

Labelling the patches. The patches are first labelled using the rules below. The main used is a rule ($\mathcal{R}_\mathcal{M}$) that makes a matching between the facts extracted from the images by the numerical tools and the facts computed about their boundaries and orientations w.r.t the SPAMs:

MAEBounds(?x, ?y) ∧ SulcusSegment(?x) ∧ AttributedEntity(?y) ∧ entity(?y, ?z) ∧ Gyrus(?z) ∧ orientation(?y, ?b) ∧ MAEBounds(?x, ?c) ∧ AttributedEntity(?c) ∧ entity(?c, ?d) ∧ Patch(?d) ∧ orientation(?c, ?b') ∧ Orientation(?b) ∧ Orientation(?b') ∧ sameAs(?b, ?b') → partOf(?d, ?z)

This rule expresses that if it is known from the extracted facts that a segment x bounds a given patch d with a given orientation b and it comes out from the computed orientation that x bounds a SPAM z with the same orientation, then

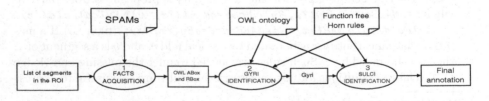

Fig. 6. Labelling process

this patch belongs to the gyrus corresponding to that SPAM. The probability associated to it is the probability p_i calculated as explained section 2.1.

As there is a possible incertitude in the computed orientations mainly due to the approximations caused by the SPAMs, it may occur that a segment bounds two SPAMs with the same orientation, hence a patch d is inferred to belong to several gyri z_i with probabilities p_i. To decide to which gyrus d finally belongs, we calculate $\sum(p_i)$ for each gyrus and keep the gyrus with the highest result. The second rule $(\mathcal{R}_\mathcal{S})$ below infers boundaries from a separation: if a given sulcus separates two gyri then it bounds each of them. This rule is used to infer boundaries from the known separations, information which is needed to fire the first rule above.

$separates(?x, ?y) \land SulcusSegment(?x) \land MAEPair(?y) \land firstEntity(?y, ?z) \land secondEntity(?y, ?a) \land AttributedEntity(?z) \land AttributedEntity(?a) \rightarrow MAEBounds(?x, ?z)$

Labelling the sulci. After the patches, the sulci are next labelled thanks to the ontology definitions and the rules. If a given segment s_i satisfies a definition of a given sulcus su_j in the ontology, i.e. if it meets the necessary and sufficient condition of su_j, then s_i is classified as an instance of su_j.

Simplified example.

– Let be a segment s_0 and two patches p_1, p_2 of the ROI.
– the facts provided by the numerical tools include the individuals p_1 and p_2 and the relation separates$(s_0, (p_1, anteriorTo, rightTo, superiorTo), (p_2, posteriorTo, leftTo, inferiorTo))$ where $anteriorTo, rightTo, superiorTo, posteriorTo, leftTo,$ and $inferiorTo$ are respective individuals of the classes Anterior, Right, Superior, Posterior, Left, and Inferior.
– the facts computed from the SPAMs include the relation separates$(s_0, (prcgr, anteriorTo, rightTo, superiorTo), (pcgr, posteriorTo, leftTo, inferiorTo))$ where prcgr: RightPreCentralGyrus and pcgr: RightPostCentralGyrus.

The labels of the patches are obtained by answering the query $Q(?x_i, ..., ?x_n) \leftarrow \wedge_{i=1 \; to \; n}(AE(?x_i)) \land \text{partOf}(p_i, ?x_i)$. Applying the rule $\mathcal{R}_\mathcal{S}$, facts about boundaries are derived from the initial facts about separations, then as the body of the matching rule $\mathcal{R}_\mathcal{M}$ can be satisfied by bindings its variable to known individuals, the reasoner infers: $partOf(p_1, prcgr)$ and $partOf(p_2, pcgr)$. Next, at a second step, the labels of the segments are obtained from the class definitions in the ontology. As s_0 satisfies the N&S condition of RightCentralSulcusSegment, the reasoner infers that s_0 is an instance of the RightCentralSulcusSegment.

4   Results and Discussion

This section presents some results obtained for real data with the method presented above. The experiments are achieved with the reasoner KAON2[5], which

---

[5] http://kaon2.semanticweb.org/

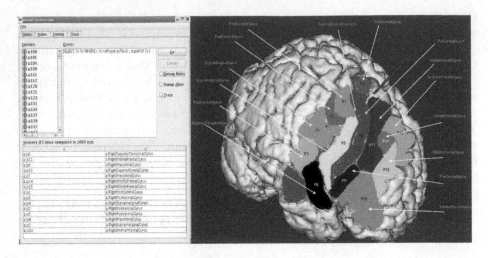

Fig. 7. Results obtained with KAON2

accepts ontologies extended with rules [2]. The region of interest is the automatically extracted region displayed figure 1. We used 45 SPAMs corresponding to the most important gyri of the brain. The MIN value approximated from the computations is 0.05 and the MAX value 0.75.

Labels of patches. The $SPARQL$ query[6] $SELECT$?x ?y WHERE ?x rdf:type a:Patch ; a:partOf ?y asks for each patch all entities it is part of. The answers of KAON2 to that query provide the labels of the patches, for example patch $P6$ is a part of the right superior temporal gyrus (figure 7).

Labels of sulcus segments. The query $SELECT$?x WHERE ?x rdf:type a:RightCentralSulcusSegment asks for the right central sulcus segments. KAON2 returns the segment 183 (figure 7), which is the single segment of the right central sulcus for this ROI.

The labels inferred by the system are exhibited in figure 7. Most of the labels are the same, except for $P3$ for which the label inferred by the system is wrong. For example the patch $P8$ is inferred to be a part of the right precentral gyrus, $P1$ is inferred to be a part of the right postcentral gyrus, and the segment 183 is inferred to be an instance of the right central sulcus segment, which is correct since it separates parts of the right precentral gyrus from parts of the right postcentral gyrus. This is an ongoing work. It will be interesting in the future to assess how this percentage is affected by various aspects of the ontology and rules, and the respective effect of the SPAMs and of the reasoning on the results. The proposed method was adapted to comply with some language and tools limitations, in particular with the version of the KAON2 reasoner available online and the Protégé SWRL editor, for example:

---

[6] The query language of KAON2.

- For the moment the ontology was simplified using OWL DL instead of OWL1.1[7]. We used existential restriction instead of qualified cardinality restrictions (QCR). But, it should be noted that the real Tbox requires both QCR, disjunctions, inverse. For example, the ontology should express that each right PostCentralGyrus is bounded exactly by one right CentralSulcus. Besides, the rules cannot be expressed as role inclusion axioms (cf. rule ($\mathcal{R_M}$) or the rules of the online Annex at http://www.med.univ-rennes1.fr/~cgolb/Brain/annexes.pdf). Thus the required knowledge is not expressible in the $\mathcal{EL}^{++}$ or in OWL1.1.
- we defined subclasses of Orientation, e.g.; Posterior, Anterior etc. with individual e.g., posteriorTo and used existential restrictions instead of enumeration or hasValue restrictions, because KAON2 does not support nominals.
- KAON2 reasoner is based on the DL-safe rules assumption [2]. Although the rules used for our system are not DL-safe, KAON2 provides the expected answers for the reported experiments. Indeed, in these cases the rules were fired, because given the initial facts asserted, their body was satisfied by bindings their variables to known individuals. However, this approach is not always relevant and situations may occur where solutions are missed because of the existential construct. For example, a patch is defined with an existential in the equivalent class expression (rhs). Hence, it may happen in some cases that a rule expressing the propagation of a property from parts to whole cannot be fired, because an instance of Patch is defined without being connected to a known instance of gyrus by the relation partOf [3]. KAON2 does not draw all the consequences according to the first order semantics of SWRL, but only consequences under the "the DL-safe semantics".
- all n-ary relations were transformed into binary relations, using reification for example we defined an artificial class AttributedEntity for it. The ontology was edited using Protégé rules editor which allows to edit only SWRL rules and does not support ordinary predicates that are not DL predicates. KAON2 extends the standard SWRL syntax and offers a swrl:PredicateAtom that allows ordinary predicates, but according to the authors their SWRL extensions were still experimental at the time of these experiments. It would be preferred to have a language extension and tools allowing n-ary relations. N-ary relations is a general needs for example also encountered with the Foundational Model of Anatomy ontology which exhibits more than 30 attributed relationships and where more than 2300 nested classes were generated for their values [4].
- The heuristic rules section 2.1 were implemented in $C + +$. A declarative approach was not possible with KAON2 since at the moment it does not handle OWL DL datatypes or OWL1.1 user-defined datatypes and restrictions involving datatype predicates.

5   Conclusion

This paper reports the current stage of development of an hybrid system combining numerical and symbolic techniques for brain MRI images description, and its present limitations. The method is based on an OWL DL ontology extended with rules, and facts coming from numerical tools and SPAMs. Future work will investigate how to overcome some of the work-arounds employed to circumvent the limitations encountered with the representation and tools used. At the moment the method was only tested over a limited set of brain images that did not exhibit a lesion. The experiments will be extended to more cases and to brain images exhibiting a lesion in order to assess its robustness.Automatizing the annotation of the semantic content of digital images presents promising perspectives for new applications such as retrieval of similar cases for decision support, or statistical medical studies in large populations.

Acknowledgement. We are grateful to Louis Collins of the Montreal Neurological Institute for the SPAMs database and to the Regional Council of Brittany for its support.

References

1. Collins, D.L., Zijdenbos, A.P., Baaré, W.F.C., Evans, A.C.: Improved cortical structure segmentation. In: Kuba, A., Sámal, M., Todd-Pokropek, A. (eds.) IPMI 1999. LNCS, vol. 1613, pp. 210–223. Springer, Heidelberg (1999)
2. Motik, B., Sattler, U., Studer, R.: Query answering for OWL DL with rules. In: McIlraith, S.A., Plexousakis, D., van Harmelen, F. (eds.) ISWC 2004. LNCS, vol. 3298, Springer, Heidelberg (2004) aUGll_TSNR0J:scholar.google.com/
3. Golbreich, C.: Web rules for Health Care and Life Sciences: use cases and requirements. In: RoW Workshop at WWW (2006)
4. Golbreich, C., Zhang, S., Bodenreider, O.: The Foundational Model of Anatomy in OWL: Experience and Perspectives. Journal of Web Semantics,vol. (4)3 http://www.idealibrary.com (2006)
5. Ono, M., Kubik, S., Abernathey, C.: Atlas of the Cerebral Sulci. Thieme Medical Publishers (1990)
6. Golbreich, C., Bierlaire, O., Dameron, O., Gibaud, B.: Use Case: Ontology with Rules for identifying brain anatomical structures, In: W3C Workshop on Rule Languages for Interoperability, Washington, D.C., USA (2005)
7. Patel-Schneider, P., Horrocks, I.: OWL 1.1 Web Ontology Language overview. W3C Member Submission. Available at http://www.w3.org/Submission/owl11-overview/. (December 19, 2006)

A Framework for Ontology Based Rule Acquisition from Web Documents

Sangun Park[1], Juyoung Kang[2], and Wooju Kim[3]

[1] Division of Business Administration, Kyonggi University
San 94-6 Yiui-Dong, Paldal-Gu, Suwon 442-760, South Korea
supark@kgu.ac.kr
[2] Department of E-Business, School of Business, Ajou University
San 5 Wonchun-dong, Suwon, Korea
jykang@ajou.ac.kr
[3] Department of Information and Industrial Engineering, Yonsei University
134 Shin-Chon Dong, Seoul 120-749, Korea
wkim@yonsei.ac.kr

Abstract. Rule based systems and agents are important applications of the Semantic Web constructs such as RDF, OWL, and SWRL. While there are plenty of utilities that support ontology generation and utilization, rule acquisition is still a bottleneck as an obstacle to wide propagation of rule based systems. To automatically acquire rules from unstructured texts, we develop a rule acquisition framework that uses a rule ontology. The ontology can be acquired from the rule base of a similar site, and then is used for rule acquisition in the other sites of the same domain. The procedure of ontology-based rule acquisition consists of rule component identification and rule composition. The former uses stemming and semantic similarity to extract variables and values from the Web page and the latter uses the best-first search method in composing the variables and values into rules.

1 Introduction

Semantic Web research has developed many meta-languages that can express the characteristics of information on the Web pages in a machine understandable form. Typical languages include RDF(S) [3, 11], OWL [17], and SWRL [7]. The descriptive ontology is extended to various types of logic [16], and reasoning tools are developed such as Jena [14], F-OWL [19], KAON [18], and OntoBroker [6]. These tools enable the Semantic Web to be widely used by software agents and rule based systems. However, rule extraction from Web pages that consists of unstructured texts and tables is a challenging issue in the same way that knowledge acquisition has been the bottleneck of the knowledge based system. Many researchers attempted to extract object type ontology from Web documents [1, 5]. But extracting rules from unstructured natural language texts is more complicated than ontology acquisition [9].

One of major applications that require rule acquisition is a comparison shopping portal. Comparison of various attributes of products in addition to price is currently required while general comparison shopping malls compare only price. However, the comparison of other factors usually requires more complicated reasoning process

M. Marchiori, J.Z. Pan, and C. de Sainte Marie (Eds.): RR 2007, LNCS 4524, pp. 229–238, 2007.

rather than simple calculation. For example, calculation of shipping costs depends on different free shipping rules and various delivery options of each mall. Rule based reasoning is essential to provide a service that supports the enhanced comparison.

Fig. 1 shows the framework of a comparison shopping portal based on a rule based reasoning system [9]. The portal builds a rule base with acquired rules about delivery options, shipping rules, and return policies from multiple shopping malls. Through a rule based reasoning system, the portal can provide an enhanced comparison service to customers. In this case, we should repeatedly acquire similar rules on shipping rates and return policies from multiple malls. The rules of the same domain are similar to each other in their shapes and contents.

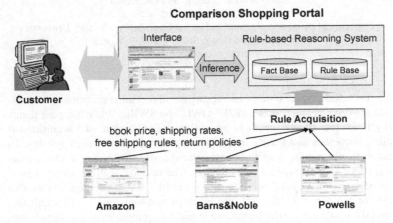

Fig. 1. Framework of Comparison Shopping Portal Based on Rule-Based System

Fig. 2 shows an example of rule acquisition from a sample Web page of BarnesAndNoble.com (in short BN) in the left part to a rule of our format in the right part. It is easy to notice that variables and values of the rule came from the words of the Web page.

Fig. 2. An Example of Rule Acquisition

The basic idea of our approach comes from the fact that we repeatedly acquire similar rules from multiple sites. In that case, we can easily acquire rules from a site by referencing previously acquired rules from the previous site. For example, if we have rules about return policies acquired from Amazon.com, we can use those rules in BN to detect similar rules. We designed and used a compact ontology generalized from the rules because the size of rules is getting bigger and it is difficult to refer the rules. The main objective of our research is to propose a rule acquisition procedure that automates repeated rule acquisition from similar sites by using the rule ontology.

There are three assumptions in our approach. The first one is that similar sites should exist in the target domain to utilize acquired ontology. Our approach works well in the domain where rules are repeatedly acquired from multiple sites which have similar rules. There are several domains which are desirable for our approach such as terms of agreement in various shopping malls, insurance rates and policies in insurance companies, and loan policies in banks. The second assumption is that the Web page should include practical and executable rules. The last assumption is that target application requires rule based reasoning.

2   Overview of Ontology Based Rule Acquisition

This section describes the idea of rule acquisition using the rule ontology. Rule acquisition consists of rule component identification and rule composition from the acquired rule components. We briefly describe the main idea of each step in Section 2.1 and 2.2. Also, we describe brief design of our proposed rule ontology in Section 2.3.

2.1   Rule Component Identification Using Ontology

How can we use the rule ontology in identification of rule components such as variables and values? Let us assume that we acquired rules from Aamzon.com as shown in Fig. 3. In that case, we can possibly generalize those rules into an ontology and use it in rule acquisition from a Web page of BN as shown in Fig. 3. We use a frame expression to represent the ontology because it is simple and easy to understand, and moreover it can be automatically transformed to other ontology representations such as RDF and OWL. From the ontology in Fig. 3, we can easily recognize that *refund* and *days of the shipment* in Fig. 2 are variables and *books*, *CDs*, and *VHS tapes* are values. This example is very simple, but the ontology can provide more information. For example, it can help to detect omitted components from the Web pages. We can perceive that *item* is omitted in the Web page of Fig. 3 because *books*, *CDs*, and *VHS tapes* are values of *item* in the ontology of Fig. 3. Also, it is possible to assign variables to corresponding values because every value has its matching variable in the ontology.

One of issues in rule component identification is the synonym issue. Even though the shape and content of rules are similar, different sites usually use different terms on the same meaning. They use synonyms in most cases, but they frequently use semantically similar terms in different rule structures. For example, Amazon is using the concept *region* for shipping destinations, but Powells is using each *country* in every shipping rate rules. *Country* is not the synonym of *region*, but semantically similar to *region*. Therefore, we use semantic similarity measure [4] in addition to synonyms when we identify variables and values to increase recall rate. We developed our own

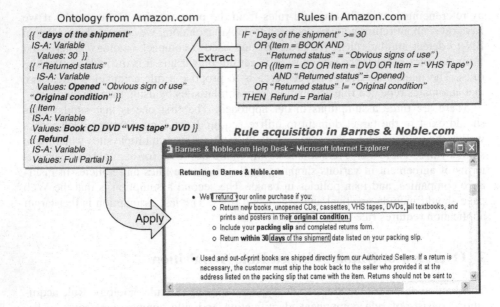

Fig. 3. An Example of Ontology and Rule Component Identification

semantic similarity measure [4] while there are several measures such as Resnik [15] and Lin [10].

2.2   Composing Rules from Variables Through the Best-First Search

The basic idea of rule composition is using patterns of rules in similar systems. We can extract an ontology by generalizing rules of another system. In that case, several rules can be generalized into one rule of the ontology. For example, 102 rules in the rule base of Amazon.com were generalized into 21 rules of the rule ontology in our experiment. Fig. 4 shows an example of a rule in the ontology. If we find a similar pattern of this rule from the identified variables in text, we can compose them into a rule by using the best-first search [13]. For example, if there are *item, refund*, and *days of the shipment* variables in the Web page, we can compose *Return Policy Rule* from those variables with the rule ontology in Fig. 4. The best-first search algorithm assigns variable instances one after another to a rule of the ontology by making a search tree.

> *{{ "Refund Policy Rule"*
>   *IS-A: Rule*
>   *IF: "days of the shipment" Item "Returned status"*
>   *THEN: Refund }}*

Fig. 4. An Example of Rule Ontology

There are several issues on composing rules through the best-first search as follows:

2.2.1 Complexity of Rule Composition

There can be many combinations for the cases of assigning variables to rule candidates that are extracted from the ontology. Therefore we need to reduce the complexity of choosing the next variable instance to assign. We imported the concept, *variable ordering* in the Constrained Heuristic Search [2]. One popular variable ordering heuristic is to choose the variable with the fewest number of remaining possible values [2]. We decided to adopt the same heuristic in our approach. When we assign variable instances to each rule, we start from a variable which has the smallest number of matching instances because it can reduce the number of options in the beginning. We call this heuristic variable ordering. In addition to setting the variable order in each rule, we should decide the order of candidate rules. We start from a rule which has the smallest number of combinations for assigning variable instances to the rule. We call this procedure rule ordering.

2.2.2 Evaluation Function of the Best-First Search

We need an appropriate method for the evaluation function of the best-first search. How can we evaluate the degree of suitability of a variable instance to a rule? We make an evaluation function under the assumption that variables comprising a rule are located in the neighborhood in text. Therefore, if a variable instance is closer to the already chosen instances for a rule than the other set of instances, we assign the instance to the rule. This geographic assumption plays a very important role in our approach.

2.3 Design of Rule Ontology

The ontology that is used in our approach is named *OntoRule*. OntoRule is domain specific knowledge that provides information about rule components and structures. While the ontology for rule component identification consists of variables, values and the relationship between them, the ontology for rule composition requires generalized rule structures as shown in Fig. 4. It includes variables for the *IF* part and *THEN* part of each rule. That is, *IF* and *THEN* slots of *Rule* class represents relationships between rules and variables. We excluded connectives like *AND* and *OR* from OntoRule because it is hard to represent the complex nested structure of connectives in simple frame representation, and there is no effect of generalization if we represent all connectives in the ontology.

In another viewpoint, it is possible to directly use rules of the previous system instead of the proposed ontology. But, it requires a large space and additional processes to utilize information on rules, while OntoRule is a generalized compact set of information for rule acquisition. That is the reason we use OntoRule instead of the rules themselves.

3 Ontology Based Rule Acquisition Procedure

In this section, we propose a procedure which automatically acquires rules by using OntoRule, and besides, we describe a brief summary of detailed rule component identification procedure in Section 3.2 and rule composition procedure in Section 3.3.

3.1 Overall Rule Acquisition Procedure

Fig. 5 shows the overall rule acquisition process. In step 1, the rule ontology is generated from a rule base which is acquired in another site. In step 2, the knowledge engineer selects Web pages for rule acquisition. In step 3, the tool named *RuleMiner* automatically identifies variables and values from the Web page using OntoRule and creates the first rule draft. In step 4, *RuleMiner* automatically generates rules with *IF* and *THEN* statements by composing the identified variables and values. A graph search method with the property of A* algorithm [13] is developed for this purpose. However, the generated rules may be incomplete. Therefore, the knowledge engineer needs to refine the second rule draft to make it complete in step 5.

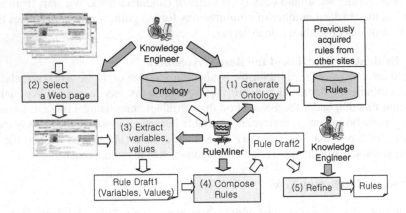

Fig. 5. Overall Rule Acquisition Process Using Ontology

3.2 Rule Component Identification Procedure

The goal of rule component identification is to elicit variables and values by comparing parsed words of the given text with the variables and values of the given rule ontology. For the first step, we expanded the rule ontology by adding synonyms of each term by using WordNet [12] as shown in Fig. 6 that describes the step 3 of Fig. 5 in detail. To implement the procedure, we transformed the frame-based ontology into OWL and parsed it through Jena API. After that, we applied the stemming algorithm [8] to the expanded ontology to normalize the terms in step 2. Also we parsed and stemmed the Web page for rule acquisition in step 3. In the comparison between the terms of the ontology and the terms of the Web page, we used semantic matching instead of simple string comparison as discussed in Section 2.1.

To find the semantic similarity between two terms, we used the hyponym structure of WordNet. The distance between two terms in the hyponym hierarchy is the main factor of our semantic similarity. We do not include the details of the algorithm [4] not to lose our focus.

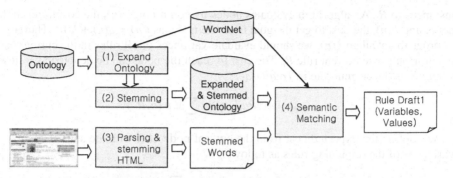

Fig. 6. Extracting Variables and Values by Using Ontology

3.3 Rule Composition Through the Best-First Search

This section describes the best-first search algorithm that composes rules from ex-tracted rule components by using the rule ontology. The input of the best-first search (BFS) algorithm is a set of identified variable instances, $VI=\{VI_1, VI_2, ..., VI_i, ..., VI_n\}$ in the given Web page. The output is a set of rule instances, $RI=\{ RI_1, RI_2, ..., RI_p, ..., RI_q\}$, where RI_p is a set of assigned variable instances to the rule. The ontology that is used in rule composition is made up of rule candidates from OntoRule, $RC=\{R_1, R_2, ..., R_j, ...,R_l\}$, where a rule candidate, R_j is $\{V_{j1}, V_{j2}, ..., V_{jk}, ..., V_{jm}\}$.

3.3.1 Rule Ordering and Variable Ordering

Before rule ordering, we need to extract rule candidates from OntoRule. If variables in R_j exist in VI, R_j is extracted for rule candidates. The first step of rule ordering is to calculate the number of possible combinations of variable instance assignments for each R_j with the following formula:

$$NC(R_j)= \prod_{k=1,Count(V_{jk})\neq0}^{m} Count(V_{jk})$$

The last step of rule ordering is to sort rules of RC with increasing order of $NC()$. Once the rule order is determined in rule ordering, the next step is making the order of variables within each rule. We use the same heuristic by choosing the variable with the smallest number of instances. After that, we sort variables within each rule with increasing order of $Count()$. By integrating $RuleOrder$ and $VariableOrder$, we can generate $TotalOrder(RC)$. $TotalOrder(RC)$ is a sorted list of rules that are sorted vari-able lists. BFS proceeds in the order of variables in $TotalOrder(RC)$.

3.3.2 Evaluation of Composed Rules

As discussed in Section 2.2, the suitability of a variable instance for a rule can be measured based on the distance between the variable instance and the already assigned instances. This distance can be calculated with the variance of positions of variable instances.

A low variance means that the instances gather around one place in the text. There-fore, the evaluation function of a current variable instance n for R_j is denoted as $Var(n, R_j)$, the variance of the set containing the instance n and already assigned instances to R_j. A* algorithm evaluates nodes by combining $g(n)$, the cost to reach the node, and $h(n)$, the cost to get the goal from the node, as $f(n) = g(n) + h(n)$. Therefore, in order to calculate $g(n)$, we should evaluate variances of all rules in the current path in addition to the current rule R_j. The cost to reach the node can be denoted as follows where R_r is the current rule in *TotalOrder*:

$$g(n) = Var(Path(n)) = \sum_{j=1}^{r} Var(n, R_j)$$

We define the expected cost from the current node $h(n)$ with the sum of minimum variances of the remaining rules as follows:

$$h(n) = ExpectedVar(PathToGoal(n)) = \sum_{j=r+1}^{l} MinVar(Comb(n, R_j))$$

Comb(n, R_j) means possible combinations for the rule R_j that locates behind the current instance n in *TotalOrder*, and *MinVar* means a minimum variance of them. Because $h(n)$ is always smaller than $h^*(n)$ that is the true cost, the evaluation function $f(n)$ satisfies A* algorithm.

3.3.3 The Best-First Search Algorithm for Rule Composition
Once the search order and evaluation function are determined, the best-first search algorithm is simple. In the first step, the algorithm extracts variable instances that match the first variable of *TotalOrder*(RC) and put them into OPEN. In the second step, it chooses the most suitable variable instance for the current variable of the candidate rule from OPEN with the evaluation function $f(n)$ and assigns it to the current candidate rule. After that, we generate the next variable instances with *TotalOrder*(RC), put them into OPEN, and go back to the second step. If *TotalOrder*(RC) is empty, the algorithm stops with the assigned variable instances to each candidate rule.

3.3.4 Assigning *IF* and *THEN*
This step is very simple. If an identified variable belongs to an *IF* part of the selected rule, we assign *IF* to the variable. We cannot assign *IF* or *THEN* to variables and values which are not in the selected rule of ontology.

4   Experiment Using Ontology in Rule Identification

This section shows the performance of our approach proposed in Section 3 by measuring the effect of automatic rule acquisition using OntoRule. In order to start the experiment, we first constructed the ontology from Amazon.com. We applied this ontology on acquiring rules from two online bookstores, BarnesAndNoble.com (in short BN) and Powells.com.

We use two performance measures to evaluate the performance of our approach. The first performance measure is precision, which is calculated by dividing the number of correct recommendations through ontology by the number of displayed recommendations through ontology. The second performance measure is recall, which is obtained by dividing the number of correct recommendations through ontology by the total number of true terms that should be identified.

Table 1. Experiment Results of Rule Acquisition

	Variable		Value	
	Precision	Recall	Precision	Recall
BN	70.88%	83.33%	88.55%	76.76%
Powells	84.78%	81.25%	99.65%	99.11%
Total	72.96%	82.96%	97.45%	94.16%

We obtained satisfactory performance of using ontology in rule component identification as shown in Table 1. Precision and recall of values in Powells are very high at 99.65% and 99.11% because Powells uses large tables for shipping rates which are well structured and easy to match with the ontology.

One major limitation of the evaluation is that there are only two sites in our experiment. The objective in this experiment is not to empirically verify the validity of our approach, but to show an example where our approach works. Therefore, an extended experiment with enough Web sites is surely required to verify and generalize our approach, so we are planning to do it. Another major limitation is that the above results came from just one domain of the comparison shopping portal for online bookstores. We should extend our approach to various domains.

5 Conclusions

To reduce the knowledge engineer's manual work in rule acquisition, we proposed a rule acquisition procedure using an ontology, named *OntoRule*, that includes information about the rule components and its structures. The procedure consists of rule component identification step and rule composition step. We used stemming and semantic similarity in the former and developed a Graph Search method with the property of A* Algorithm in the latter. Also, we demonstrate the possibility of our ontology-based rule acquisition approach with an experiment. We expect that the results show the potential of this approach even though the experiment is very limited in the domain and the number of sites.

There are several challenging research issues in order to meet the ultimate goal of our research. First, we need to test with many sites to understand the possibility of automatic rule acquisition. Second, we need to extend our research into various domains because the performance may depend upon the nature of Web pages in each domain. We expect that insurance rates and policies of insurance companies, and loan policies of banks would be good examples of such domain.

References

1. Alani, H., Kim, S., Millard, D.E., Weal, M.J., Hall, W., Lewis, P.H., Shadbolt, N.R.: Automatic Ontology-Based Knowledge Extraction from Web Documents. IEEE Intelligent Systems 18(1), 14–21 (2003)
2. Beck, J.C., Fox, M.: A Generic Framework for Constraint Directed Search and Scheduling. AI Magazine 19(4), 101–130 (1998)

3. Brickley, D., Guha, R.V.: RDF Vocabulary Description Language 1.0: RDF Schema. W3C Recommendation, <http://www.w3c.org/TR/rdf-schema/> (2004)
4. Chae, S.: Ontology-Based Intelligent Rule Component Extraction. Master Thesis, Yonsei University (2006)
5. Crow, L., Shadbolt, N.: Extracting Focused Knowledge from the Semantic Web. International Journal of Human-Computer Studies 54, 155–184 (2001)
6. Decker, S., Erdmann, M., Fensel, D., Studer, R.: Ontobroker: Ontology based Access to Distributed and Semi-Structured Information. In: Meersman, R. et al. (ed.) Database Semantics, Semantic Issues in Multimedia Systems, Kluwer Academic Publisher, Boston (1999)
7. Horrocks, I., Patel-Schneider, P.F., Boley, H., Tabet, S., Grosof, B., Dean, M.: SWRL: A Semantic Web Rule Language Combining OWL and RuleML, W3C Member Submission, <http://www.w3.org/Submission/2004/SUBM-SWRL-20040521/> (2004)
8. Jones, K.S., Willet, P., (eds.): Readings in Information Retrieval. Morgan Kaufmann Publishers, San Francisco (1997)
9. Kang, J., Lee, J.K.: Rule Identification from Web Pages by the XRML Approach. Decision Support Systems 41(1), 205–227 (2005)
10. Lin, D.: An information-theoretic definition of similarity. In: 15th International Conference on Machine Learning, pp. 296-304 (1998)
11. Manola, F., Miller, E.: Resource Description Framework (RDF) Primer. W3C Recommendation, <http://www.w3.org/TR/REC-rdf-syntax/> (2004)
12. Miller, G.A.: WordNet a Lexical Database for English. Communications of the ACM 38(11), 39–41 (1995)
13. Pearl, J.: Heuristics: Intelligent Search Strategies for Computer Problem Solving. Addison-Wesley, London (1984)
14. Reynolds, D.: Jena 2 Inference Support.<http://jena.sourceforge.net/inference> (2005)
15. Resnik, P.: Using information content to evaluate semantic similarity in a taxonomy. In: 14th International Joint Conference on Artificial Intelligence, pp. 448-453 (1995)
16. RuleML: The Rule Markup Initiative. <http://www.dfki.uni-kl.de/ruleml/> (2003)
17. Smith, M.K., Welty, C., McGuinness, D.: OWL Web Ontology Language Guide. W3C Recommendation, <http://www.w3c.org/TR/owl-guide/> (2004)
18. Volz, R., Oberle, D., Staab, S., Motik, B.: KAON SERVER - A Semantic Web Management System. In: Volz, R., Oberle, D., Staab, S., Motik, B. (eds.) Alternate Track Proceedings of the Twelfth International World Wide Web Conference, WWW2003, Budapest, Hungary, ACM Press, New York (2003)
19. Zou, Y., Finin, T., Chen, H.: F-OWL: an Inference Engine for Semantic Web. In: Hinchey, M.G., Rash, J.L., Truszkowski, W.F., Rouff, C.A. (eds.) FAABS 2004. LNCS (LNAI), vol. 3228, pp. 16–18. Springer, Heidelberg (2004)

A Fast Algebraic Web Verification Service*

M. Alpuente[1], D. Ballis[2], M. Falaschi[3], P. Ojeda[1], and D. Romero[1]

[1] DSIC, Universidad Politécnica de Valencia
Camino de Vera s/n, Apdo. 22012, 46071 Valencia, Spain
{alpuente, pojeda, dromero}@dsic.upv.es
[2] Dip. Matematica e Informatica
Via delle Scienze 206, 33100 Udine, Italy
demis@dimi.uniud.it
[3] Dip. di Scienze Matematiche e Informatiche
Pian dei Mantellini 44, 53100 Siena, Italy
moreno.falaschi@unisi.it

Abstract. In this paper, we present the rewriting-based, Web verification service WebVerdi-M, which is able to recognize forbidden/incorrect patterns and incomplete/missing Web pages. WebVerdi-M relies on a powerful Web verification engine that is written in Maude, which automatically derives the error symptoms. Thanks to the AC pattern matching supported by Maude and its metalevel facilities, WebVerdi-M enjoys much better performance and usability than a previous implementation of the verification framework. By using the XML Benchmarking tool xmlgen, we develop some scalable experiments which demonstrate the usefulness of our approach.

1 Introduction

The automated management of data-intensive Web sites is an area to which rule-based technology has a significant potential to contribute. It is widely accepted today that declarative representations are the best way to specify the structural aspects of Web sites as well as many forms of Web-site content. As an additional advantage, rule-based languages such as Maude [8] offer an extremely powerful, rewriting-based "reasoning engine" where the system transitions are represented/derived by rewrite rules indicating how a configuration is *transformed* into another.

In previous work [2,4], we proposed a rewriting-based approach to Web-site verification and repair. In a nutshell, our methodology w.r.t. a given formal specification is applied to discover two classes of important, semantic flaws in Web sites. The first class consists of correctness errors (forbidden information that occurs in the Web site), while the second class consist of completeness errors (missing and/or incomplete Web pages). This is done by means of a

---

* This work has been partially supported by the EU (FEDER) and Spanish MEC TIN-2004-7943-C04-02 project, the Generalitat Valenciana under grant GV06/285, and Integrated Action Hispano-Alemana HA2006-0007. Daniel Romero is also supported by ALFA grant LERNet AML/19.0902/97/0666/II-0472-FA.

M. Marchiori, J.Z. Pan, and C. de Sainte Marie (Eds.): RR 2007, LNCS 4524, pp. 239–248, 2007.
© Springer-Verlag Berlin Heidelberg 2007

novel rewriting-based technique, called *partial rewriting*, in which the traditional pattern matching mechanism is replaced by a suitable technique based on the *homeomorphic embedding* relation for recognizing patterns inside semistructured documents. The new prototype WebVerdi-M relies on a strictly more powerful Web verification engine written in Maude [8] which automatically derives the error symptoms of a given Web site. Thanks to the AC pattern matching supported by Maude and its metalevel features, we have significantly improved both the performance and the usability of the original system. By using SOAP messages and other Web-related standards, a Java Web client that interacts with Web verification service has been made publicly available within the implementation.

Although there have been other recent efforts to apply formal techniques to Web site management [10,12,14,18], only few works addressed the semantic verification of Web sites before. The key idea behind WebVerdi-M is that rule-based techniques can support in a natural way not only intuitive, high level Web site specification, but also efficient Web site verification techniques.

VeriWeb [18] explores interactive, dynamic Web sites using a special browser that systematically explores all paths up to a specified depth. The user first specifies some properties by means of *SmartProfiles*, and then the verifier traverses the considered Web site to report the errors as sequences of Web operations that lead to a page which violates a property. Navigation errors and page errors can be signaled, but tests are performed only at the http-level. In [14], a declarative verification algorithm is developed which checks a particular class of integrity constraints concerning the Web site's structure, but not the contents of a given instance of the site. In [10], a methodology to verify some semantic constraints concerning the Web site contents is proposed, which consists of using inference rules and axioms of natural semantics. The framework XLINKIT [12,19] allows one to check the consistency of distributed, heterogeneous documents as well as to fix the (possibly) inconsistent information. The specification language is a restricted form of first order logic combined with Xpath expressions [23] where no functions are allowed.

The paper is organized as follows. Section 2 presents some preliminaries, and in Section 3 we briefly recall the rewriting-based, Web-site verification technique of [2]. In Section 4, we discuss the efficient implementation in Maude (by means of AC pattern matching) of one of the key ingredients of our verification engine: the *homeomorphic embedding* relation, which we use to recognize patterns within semi-structured documents. Section 5 briefly describes the service-oriented architecture of our verification prototype WebVerdi-M. Finally, Section 6, we present an experimental evaluation of the system on a set of benchmarks which shows impressive performance (e.g. less than a second for evaluating a tree of some 30,000 nodes). An extended version of this work can be found in [3].

2   Preliminaries

By $\mathcal{V}$ we denote a countably infinite set of variables and Σ denotes a set of *function symbols* (also called *operators*), or *signature*. We consider varyadic signatures as in [9] (i.e., signatures in which symbols do not have a fixed arity).

$\tau(\Sigma, \mathcal{V})$ and $\tau(\Sigma)$ denote the *non-ground term algebra* and the *term algebra* built on $\Sigma \cup \mathcal{V}$ and Σ, respectively. Terms are viewed as labelled trees in the usual way. Given a term t, we say that t is *ground*, if no variable occurs in t. A *substitution* $\sigma \equiv \{X_1/t_1, X_2/t_2, \dots\}$ is a mapping from the set of variables $\mathcal{V}$ into the set of terms $\tau(\Sigma, \mathcal{V})$ satisfying the following conditions: (*i*) $X_i \neq X_j$, whenever $i \neq j$, (*ii*) $X_i\sigma = t_i$, $i = 1,..n$, and (*iii*) $X\sigma = X$, for all $X \in \mathcal{V} \setminus \{X_1, \dots, X_n\}$. An *instance* of a term t is defined as $t\sigma$, where σ is a substitution. By $Var(s)$ we denote the set of variables occurring in the syntactic object s. Syntactic equality between objects is represented by $\equiv$.

3   Rule-Based Web Site Verification

In this section, we briefly recall the formal verification methodology proposed in [2], which allows us to detect forbidden/erroneous information as well as missing information in a Web site. This methodology is able to recognize and exactly locate the source of a possible discrepancy between the Web site and the properties required in the Web specification. An efficient and elegant implementation in Maude of such a methodology is described in Section 4.

We assume a Web page to be a well-formed *XML document* [22], since there are plenty of programs and online services that are able to validate XML syntax and perform link checking (e.g. [24],[21]). Moreover, as XML documents are provided with a tree-like structure, we can straightforwardly model them as ground Herbrand terms of a given term algebra.

The Web specification language. A Web specification is a triple (I_N, I_M, R), where I_N and I_M are a finite set of correctness and completeness rules, and the set R contains the definition of some auxiliary functions.

The set I_N describes constraints for detecting erroneous Web pages (*correctNess rules*). A correctness rule has the following syntax: $l \rightharpoonup error \mid C$ where l is a term, *error* is a reserved constant, and C is a (possibly empty) finite sequence (wich could contains membership tests of the form $X \in rexp$ w.r.t. a given regular language $rexp$;[1] and/or equations/inequalities over terms). When C is empty, we simply write $l \rightharpoonup error$. Informally, the meaning of a correctness rule is the following: whenever (i) a "piece" of a given Web page can be "recognized" to be an instance $l\sigma$ of l, and (ii) the corresponding instantiated condition $C\sigma$ holds, then Web page p is marked as an incorrect page.

The third set of rules I_M specifes some properties for discovering incomplete/missing Web pages (*coMpleteness rules*). A completeness rule is defined as $l \rightharpoonup r \langle q \rangle$ where l and r are terms and $q \in \{E, A\}$. Completeness rules of a Web specification formalize the requirement that some information must be included in all or some pages of the Web site. We use attributes $\langle A \rangle$ and $\langle E \rangle$ to distinguish "universal" from "existential" rules, as explained below. Right-hand sides r of completeness rules can contain functions, which are defined in R. In addiction,

---

[1] Regular languages are represented by means of the usual Unix-like regular expression syntax.

some symbols in the right-hand sides of the rules may be marked by means of the symbol ♯. Marking information of a given rule r is used to select the subset of the Web site in order to check the condition formalized by r. Intuitively, the interpretation of a universal rule (respectively, an existential rule) w.r.t. a Web site W is as follows: if (an instance of) l is "recognized" in W, (an instance of) the irreducible form of r must also be "recognized" in *all* (respectively, *some*) of the Web pages that embed (an instance of) the marked structure of r.

Web Verification Methodology. Diagnoses are carried out by running Web specifications on Web sites. The operational mechanism is based on a novel, flexible matching technique [2] that is able to "recognize" the partial structure of a term (Web template) within another and select it by computing *homeomorphic embeddings* (cf. [16]) of Web templates within Web pages.

Homeomorphic embedding relations allow us to verify whether a template is somehow "enclosed" within another one. Our embedding relation $\trianglelefteq$ closely resembles the notion of *simulation* (for the formal definition, see [2]), which has been widely used in a number of works about querying, transformation, and verification of semistructured data (cf. [6,1,15,5]). Let us illustrate the embedding relation $\trianglelefteq$ by means of a rather intuitive example.

Example 1. Consider the following Web templates (called s_1 and s_2, respectively): $hpage(surname(Y), status(prof), name(X), teaching)$ and
$hpage(\ name(mario), surname(rossi), status(prof), teaching(course(logic1),$
$\qquad course(logic2)), hobbies(hobby(reading), hobby(gardening)))$
Note that $s_1 \trianglelefteq s_2$, since the structure of s_1 can be recognized inside the structure of s_2, while $s_2 \ntrianglelefteq s_1$.

It is important to have an efficient implementation of *homeomorphic embedding* because it is used repeatedly during the verification process as described in the following.

First, by using the homeomorphic embedding relation $\trianglelefteq$, we check whether the left-hand side l of some Web specification rule is embedded into a given page p of the considered Web site. When the embedding test $l \trianglelefteq p$ succeeds, by extending the proof, we construct the biggest substitution[2] σ for the variables in $Var(l)$, such that $l\sigma \trianglelefteq p$. Then, depending on the nature of the Web specification rule (correction or completeness rule), it is as follows:

(Correction rule) evaluating the condition of the rule (instantiated by σ); a correctness error is signalled in the case when the error condition is fulfilled.

(Completeness rule) by a new homeomorphic embedding test, checking whether the right-hand side of the rule (instantiated by σ) is recognized in some page of the considered Web site. Otherwise, a completeness error is signalled. Moreover, from the incompleteness symptom computed so far, a fixpoint computation is started in order to discover further missing information, which may involve the execution of other completeness rules.

---

[2] The substitution σ is easily obtained by composing the bindings X/t, which can be recursively gathered during the *homeomorphic embedding* test $X \trianglelefteq t$, for $X \in l$ and $t \in p$.

4   Verifying Web Sites Using Maude

Maude is a high-performance reflective language supporting both equational and rewriting logic programming, which is particularly suitable for developing domain-specific applications [20,11]. In addiction, the Maude language is not only intended for system prototyping, but it has to be considered as a real programming language with competitive performance. In the rest of the section, we recall some of the most important features of the Maude language which we have conveniently exploited for the optimized implementation of our Web site verification engine.

Equational attributes. Let us describe how we model (part of) the internal representation of XML documents in our system. The chosen representation slightly modifies the data structure provided by the Haskell HXML Library [13] by adding commutativity to the standard XML tree-like data representation. In other words, in our setting, the order of the children of a tree node is not relevant: e.g., $f(a, b)$ is "equivalent" to $f(b, a)$.

```
fmod TREE-XML is
sort XMLNode .
op RTNode : -> XMLNode .                    -- Root (doc) information item
op ELNode _ _ : String AttList -> XMLNode . -- Element information item
op TXNode _ : String -> XMLNode .           -- Text information item
--- ... definitions of the other XMLNode types omitted ...
sorts XMLTreeList XMLTreeSeq XMLTree .
op Tree (_) _ : XMLNode XMLTreeList - > XMLTree .
subsort XMLTree < XMLTreeSeq .
op _,_ : XMLTreeSeq XMLTreeSeq -> XMLTreeSeq    [comm assoc id:null] .
op null : -> XMLTreeSeq .
op [_] : XMLTreeSeq -> XMLTreeList .
op [] : -> XMLTreeList .
endfm
```

In the previous module, the XMLTreeSeq constructor `_,_` is given the equational attributes `comm assoc id:null`, which allow us to get rid of parentheses and disregard the ordering among XML nodes within the list. The significance of this optimization will be clear when we consider rewriting XML trees with AC pattern matching.

AC pattern matching. The evaluation mechanism of Maude is based on rewriting modulo an equational theory E (i.e. a set of equational axioms), which is accomplished by performing *pattern matching modulo* the equational theory E. More precisely, given an equational theory E, a term t and a term u, we say that t *matches* u *modulo* E (or that t E-*matches* u) if there is a substitution σ such that $\sigma(t) =_E u$, that is, $\sigma(t)$ and u are equal modulo the equational theory E. When E contains axioms for associativity and commutativity of operators, we talk about *AC pattern matching*. AC pattern matching is a powerful matching mechanism, which we employ to inspect and extract the partial structure of a term. That is, we use it directly to implement the notion of homeomorphic embedding of Section 3.

Metaprogramming. Maude is based on rewriting logic [17], which is reflective in a precise mathematical way. In other words, there is a finitely presented rewrite theory $\mathcal{U}$ that is universal in the sense that we can represent in $\mathcal{U}$ (as a data) any finitely presented rewrite theory $\mathcal{R}$ (including $\mathcal{U}$ itself), and then mimick in $\mathcal{U}$ the behavior of $\mathcal{R}$. We have used the metaprogramming capabilities of Maude to implement the semantics of correctness as well as completeness rules (e.g. implementing the homeomorphic embedding algorithm, evaluating conditions of conditional rules, etc.). Namely, during the partial rewriting process, functional modules are dynamically created and run by using the meta-reduction facilities of the language.

Now we are ready to explain how we implemented the homeomorphic embedding relation of Section 3, by exploiting the aforementioned Maude high-level features.

Homeomorphic embedding implementation. Let us consider two XML document templates l and p. The critical point of our methodology is to (i) discover whether $l \trianglelefteq p$ (i.e. l is embedded into p); (ii) find the substitution σ such that $l\sigma$ is the instance of l recognized inside p, whenever $l \trianglelefteq p$.

Given l and p, our proposed solution can be summarized as follows. By using Maude metalevel feactures, we first dynamically build a module M that contains a single rule of the form

$$\text{eq } 1 = \text{sub}("X_1"/X_1), \ldots, \text{sub}("X_n"/X_n), \qquad X_i \in \text{Var}(1), i = 1, \ldots n,$$

where **sub** is an associative operator used to record the substitution σ that we want to compute. Next, we try to reduce the XML template p by using such a rule. Since l and p are internally represented by means of the binary constructor $\_,\_$ that is given the equational attributes **comm assoc id:null** (see Section 4), the execution of module M on p essentially boils down to computing an AC-matcher between l and p. Moreover, since AC pattern matching directly implements the homeomorphic embedding relation. The execution of M corresponds to finding all the homeomorphic embeddings of l into p (recall that the set of AC matchers of two compatible terms is not generally a singleton). Additionally, as a side effect of the execution of M, we obtain the computed substitution σ for free as the sequence of bindings for the variables X_i, $i = 1, \ldots, n$ which occur in the instantiated rhs

$$\text{sub}("X_1"/X_1)\sigma, \ldots, \text{sub}("X_n"/X_n)\sigma, \qquad X_i \in \text{Var}(1), i = 1, \ldots n,$$

of the dynamic rule after the partial rewriting step.

Example 2. Consider again the XML document templates s_1 and s_2 of Example 1. We build the dynamic module M containing the rule

$$\text{eq } \text{hpage}(\text{surname}(Y), \text{status}(\text{prof}), \text{name}(X), \text{teaching}) = \text{sub}("Y"/Y), \text{sub}("X"/X) .$$

Since $s_1 \trianglelefteq s_2$, there exists an AC-match between s_1 and s_2 and, hence, the result of executing M against the (ground) XML document template s_2 is the computed substitution: $\text{sub}("Y"/\text{rossi}), \text{sub}("X"/\text{mario})$.

5 Prototype Implementation

The verification methodology presented so far has been implemented in the prototype WebVerdi-M (Web Verification and Rewriting for Debugging Internet sites with Maude). In developing and deploying the system, we fixed the following requirements: 1) define a system architecture as simple as possible, 2) make the Web verification service available to every Internet requestor, and 3) hide the technical details from the user. In order to fulfill the above requirements, we developed the Web verification system WebVerdi-M as a Web service.

5.1 WebVerdi-M Architecture

WebVerdi-M is a service-oriented architecture that allows one to access the core verification engine Verdi-M as a reusable entity. WebVerdi-M can be divided into two layers: *front-end* and *back-end*. The *back-end* layer provides web services to support the *front-end* layer. This architecture allow clients on the network to invoke the Web service functionality through the available interfaces.

Figure 1 illustrates the overall architecture of the system. For the reader interested in more detail, the types of messages and the specific message exchange patterns that are involved in interacting with WebVerdi-M can be found in [3].

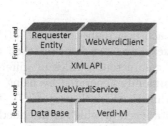

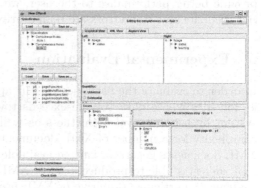

Fig. 1. Components of WebVerdi-M   **Fig. 2.** WebVerdiClient Snapshot

WebVerdiService. Our web service exports six operations that are network-accessible through standardized XML messaging. The Web service acts as a single access point to the core engine Verdi-M. Following the standards, the architecture is also platform and language independent so as to be accessible via scripting environment as well as via client applications across multiple platforms.

XML API. In order for successful communications to occur, both the WebVerdiService and WebVerdiClient (or any user) must agree to a common format for the messages being delivered so that they can be properly interpreted at each end. The WebVerdiService Web service is developed by defining an API that encompasses the executable library of the core engine. This is achieved by making use of Oracle JDeveloper, including the generation of WSDL for making the API available. The OC4J Server (the web server integrated in Oracle JDeveloper) handles all procedures common to Web service development. Synthesized error symptoms are also encoded as XML documents in order to be transferred from the WebVerdiService Web service to client applications as an XML response by means of the SOAP protocol.

Verdi-M. Verdi-M is the most important part of the tool. Here is where the verification methodology is implemented. This component is implemented in Maude language and is independent of the other system components.

WebVerdiClient. WebVerdiClient is a Web client that interacts with the Web service to use the capabilities of Verdi-M. Our main goal was to provide an *intuitive* and *friendly* interface for the user. WebVerdiClient is provided with a versatile, new graphical interface that offers three complementary views for both the specification rules and the pages of the considered Web site: the first one is based on the typical idea of accessing contents by using folders trees; the second one is based on XML, and the third one is based on term algebra syntax. A snapshot of WebVerdiClient is shown in Figure 2.

DB. The WebVerdiService Web service needs to transmit abundant XML data over the Web to and from client applications. In order to avoid overhead and to provide better performance to the user, we use a local *MySql* data base where the Web site and Web errors are temporarily stored at the server side.

6   Experimental Evaluation

In order to evaluate the usefulness of our approach in a realistic scenario (that is, for sites whose data volume exceeds toy sizes), we have benchmarked our system by using several correctness as well as completeness rules of different complexity for a number of XML documents randomly generated by using the XML documents generator xmlgen available within the XMark project [7]. The tool xmlgen is able to produce a set of XML data, each of which is intended to challenge a particular primitive of XML processors or storage engines by using different scale factors.

Table 1 shows some of the results we obtained for the simulation of three different Web specifications $WS1$, $WS2$ and $WS3$ in five different, randomly generated XML documents. Specifically, we tuned the generator for scaling factors from 0.01 to 0.1 to match an XML document whose size ranges from 1Mb –corresponding to an XML tree of about 31000 nodes– to 10Mb –corresponding to an XML tree of about 302000 nodes. An exhaustive evaluation, including comparison with related systems, can be found in

http://www.dsic.upv.es/users/elp/webverdi-m/.

Both Web specifications $WS1$ and $WS2$ aim at checking the verification power of our tool regarding data correctness, and thus include only correctness rules. The specification rules of $WS2$ contain more complex and more demanding constraints than the ones fomalized in $WS1$, with involved error patterns to match, and conditional rules with a number of membership tests and functions evaluation. The Web specification $WS3$ aims at checking the completeness of the randomly generated XML documents. In this case, some critical completeness rules have been formalized which recognize a significant amount of missing information.

Table 1. Verdi-M Benchmarks

Size	Nodes	Scale factor	Time		
			$WS1$	$WS2$	$WS3$
1 Mb	30,985	0.01	0.930 s	0.969 s	165.578 s
3 Mb	90,528	0.03	2.604 s	2.842 s	1768.747 s
5 Mb	150,528	0.05	5.975 s	5.949 s	4712.157 s
8 Mb	241,824	0.08	8.608 s	9.422 s	12503.454 s
10 Mb	301,656	0.10	12.458 s	12.642 s	21208.494 s

The results shown in Table 1 were obtained on a personal computer equipped with 1Gb of RAM memory, 40Gb hard disk and a Pentium Centrino CPU clocked at 1.75 GHz running Ubuntu Linux 5.10.

Let us briefly comment our results. Regarding the verification of correctness, the implementation is extremely time efficient, with elapsed times scaling lineary. Table 1 shows that the execution times are small even for very large documents (e.g. running the correctness rules of Web specification $WS1$ over a 10Mb XML document with 302000 nodes takes less than 13 seconds). Concerning the completeness verification, the fixpoint computation which is involved in the evaluation of the completeness rules typically burdens the expected performance (see [2]), and we are currently able to process efficiently XML documents whose size is not bigger than 1Mb (running the completeness rules of Web specification $WS3$ over a 1Mb XML document with 31000 nodes takes less than 3 minutes).

Finally, we want to point out that the current Maude implementation of the verification system supersedes and greatly improves our preliminary system, called GVerdi[2,4], that was only able to manage correctness for small XML repositories (of about 1Mb) within a reasonable time. We are currently working on further improving the performance of our system.

References

1. Abiteboul, S., Buneman, P., Suciu, D.: Data on the Web. From Relations to Semistructured Data and XML. Morgan Kaufmann (2000)
2. Alpuente, M., Ballis, D., Falaschi, M.: Automated Verification of Web Sites Using Partial Rewriting. Software Tools for Technology Transfer 8, 565–585 (2006)
3. Alpuente, M., Ballis, D., Falaschi, M., Ojeda, P., Romero, D.: The Web Verification Service WebVerdi-M. Technical Report DSIC-II/08/07, DSIC-UPV (2007)
4. Ballis, D., García, J.: A Rule-based System for Web Site Verification. In: ENTCS, Proc. of 1st Int'l Workshop on Automated Specification and Verification of Web Sites (WWV'05). vol. 157(2), Elsevier, North-Holland (2005)

5. Bertino, E., Mesiti, M., Guerrin, G.: A Matching Algorithm for Measuring the Structural Similarity between an XML Document and a DTD and its Applications. Information Systems 29(1), 23–46 (2004)
6. Bry, F., Schaffert, S.: Towards a Declarative Query and Transformation Language for XML and Semistructured Data: Simulation Unification. In: Stuckey, P.J. (ed.) ICLP 2002. LNCS, vol. 2401, Springer, Heidelberg (2002)
7. Centrum voor Wiskunde en Informatica. XMark – an XML Benchmark Project. Available at: http://monetdb.cwi.nl/xml/ (2001)
8. Clavel, M., Durán, F., Eker, S., Lincoln, P., Martí-Oliet, N., Meseguer, J., Talcott, C.: The maude 2.0 system. In: Nieuwenhuis, R. (ed.) RTA 2003. LNCS, vol. 2706, pp. 76–87. Springer, Heidelberg (2003)
9. Dershowitz, N., Plaisted, D.: Rewriting. Handbook of Automated Reasoning 1, 535–610 (2001)
10. Despeyroux, T., Trousse, B.: Semantic Verification of Web Sites Using Natural Semantics. In: Proc. of 6th Conference on Content-Based Multimedia Information Access (RIAO'00) (2000)
11. Eker, S., Meseguer, J., Sridharanarayanan, A.: The Maude LTL model checker and its implementation. In: Ball, T., Rajamani, S.K. (eds.) Model Checking Software. LNCS, vol. 2648, pp. 230–234. Springer, Heidelberg (2003)
12. Ellmer, E., Emmerich, W., Finkelstein, A., Nentwich, C.: Flexible Consistency Checking. ACM Transaction on Software Engineering 12(1), 28–63 (2003)
13. English, J.: The HXML Haskell Library. Available at: http://www.flightlab.com/~joe/hxml/ (2002)
14. Fernandez, M., Florescu, D., Levy, A., Suciu, D.: Verifying Integrity Constraints on Web Sites. In: Proc. of Sixteenth International Joint Conference on Artificial Intelligence (IJCAI'99). vol.2, pp. 614–619. Morgan Kaufmann, Washington (1999)
15. Fernandez, M.F., Suciu, D.: Optimizing Regular Path Expressions Using Graph Schemas. In: Proc. of Int'l Conf on Data Engineering (ICDE'98), pp. 14–23 (1998)
16. Leuschel, M.: Homeomorphic Embedding for Online Termination of Symbolic Methods. In: The Essence of Computation. LNCS, vol. 2566, pp. 379–403. Springer, Heidelberg (2002)
17. Martí-Oliet, N., Meseguer, J.: Rewriting Logic: Roadmap and Bibliography. Theoretical Computer Science 285(2), 121–154 (2002)
18. Michael, B., Juliana, F., Patrice, G.: Veriweb: automatically testing dynamic web sites. In: ENTCS. Proc. of 11th Int'l WWW Conference, Elsevier, North-Holland (2002)
19. Nentwich, C., Emmerich, W., Finkelstein, A.: Consistency Management with Repair Actions. In: Proc. of the 25th International Conference on Software Engineering (ICSE'03), IEEE Computer Society Press, Washington (2003)
20. Meseguer, J., Escobar, S., Meadows, C.: A Rewriting-Based Inference System for the NRL Protocol Analyzer and its Meta-Logical Properties. Theoretical Computer Science 367(1-2), 162–202 (2006)
21. Typke und Wicke GbR. Validate/Check XML. Available at: http://www.xmlvalidation.com/
22. World Wide Web Consortium (W3C). Extensible Markup Language (XML) 1.0, second edition. Available at: http://www.w3.org (1999).
23. World Wide Web Consortium (W3C). XML Path Language (XPath). Available at:http://www.w3.org (1999)
24. World Wide Web Consortium (W3C). Markup Validation Service. Available at: http://validator.w3.org/ (2005)

Proof Explanation in the DR-DEVICE System

Nick Bassiliades[1], Grigoris Antoniou[2], and Guido Governatori[3]

[1] Aristotle University of Thessaloniki, Greece
nbassili@csd.auth.gr
[2] FORTH-ICS, Greece and University of Crete, Greece
antoniou@ics.forth.gr
[3] University of Queensland, Australia
guido@itee.uq.edu.au

Abstract. Trust is a vital feature for the Semantic Web: If users (humans and agents) are to use and integrate system answers, they must trust them. Thus, systems should be able to explain their actions, sources, and beliefs, and this issue is the topic of the proof layer in the design of the Semantic Web. This paper presents the design of a system for proof explanation on the Semantic Web, based on defeasible reasoning. The basis of this work is the DR-DEVICE system that is extended to handle proofs. A critical aspect is the representation of proofs in an XML language, which is achieved by a RuleML language extension.

1 Introduction

The development of the Semantic Web proceeds in steps, each step building a layer on top of another. At present, the highest layer that has reached sufficient maturity is the ontology layer in the form of the description logic-based language OWL [8]. The next step in the development of the Semantic Web will be the logic and proof layers. The implementation of these two layers will allow the user to state any logical principles, and permit the computer to infer new knowledge by applying these principles on the existing data. Rule systems appear to lie in the mainstream of such activities.

Many recent studies have focused on the integration of rules and ontologies, and various solutions have been proposed. The Description Logic Programs is the approach followed in [13]; DLPs derive from the intersection of Description Logics and Horn Logic, and enable reasoning with available efficient LP inferencing algorithms over large-scale DL ontologies. We also distinguish the approaches presented in [16] and [20], which study the integration of Description Logics and Datalog rules. Two representative examples of rule languages for the Semantic Web are TRIPLE [22] and SWRL [14]. They both provide a model for rules on the Semantic Web. TRIPLE is based on F-Logic and provides support for RDFS and a subset of OWL Lite, while SWRL extends OWL DL with Horn-style rules.

Different, but equally interesting research efforts, deal with the standardization of rules for the Semantic Web. Works in this direction include (a) the RuleML Markup Initiative [9], whose ultimate goal is to develop a canonical Web language for rules using XML markup, formal semantics, and efficient implementations; and (b) the research conducted by the Rule Interchange Format (RIF) Working Group, which was recently launched by W3C.

M. Marchiori, J.Z. Pan, and C. de Sainte Marie (Eds.): RR 2007, LNCS 4524, pp. 249–258, 2007.

Apart from classical rules that lead to monotonic logical systems, recently researchers started to study systems capable of handling conflicts among rules and reasoning with partial information. Recently developed nonmonotonic rule systems for the Semantic Web include DR-Prolog [1], SweetJess [12], dlvhex [10] and DR-DEVICE [5], a defeasible reasoning system for the Semantic Web, implemented in CLIPS, which integrates well with RuleML and RDF.

The upper levels of the Semantic Web have not been researched enough and contain critical issues, like accessibility, trust and credibility. The next step in the architecture of the Semantic Web is the proof layer and little has been written and done for this layer. The main difference between a query posed to a traditional database system and a semantic web system is that the answer in the first case is returned from a given collection of data, while for the semantic web system the answer is the result of a reasoning process. While in some cases the answer speaks for itself, in other cases the user will not be confident in the answer unless he/she can trust the reasons why the answer has been produced. In addition it is envisioned that the semantic web is a distributed system with disparate sources of information. Thus a semantic web answering system, to gain the trust of a user must be able, if required, to provide an explanation or justification for an answer. Since the answer is the result of a reasoning process, the justification can be given as a derivation of the conclusion with the sources of information for the various steps.

In this work we describe the design of an extension of the nonmonotonic rules system DR-DEVICE, to extract and present explanations of answers. This work can be viewed as a contribution to the realization of a proof layer for a nonmonotonic rule language on the semantic web.

2   Defeasible Logics

The root of defeasible logics lies on research in knowledge representation, and in particular on inheritance networks. Defeasible logics can be seen as inheritance networks expressed in a logical rules language. In fact, they are the first nonmonotonic reasoning approach designed from its beginning to be implementable.

Being nonmonotonic, defeasible logics deal with potential conflicts (inconsistencies) among knowledge items. Thus they contain classical negation, contrary to usual logic programming systems. They can also deal with negation as failure (NAF), the other type of negation typical of nonmonotonic logic programming systems; in fact, [24] argues that the Semantic Web requires both types of negation. In defeasible logics, often it is assumed that NAF is not included in the object language. However, as [3] argues, it can be easily simulated when necessary. Thus, we may use NAF in the object language and transform the original knowledge to logical rules without NAF exhibiting the same behavior.

Conflicts among rules are indicated by a conflict between their conclusions. These conflicts are of local nature. The simpler case is that one conclusion is the negation of the other. The more complex case arises when the conclusions have been declared to be mutually exclusive, a very useful representation feature in practical applications.

Defeasible logics are skeptical in the sense that conflicting rules do not fire. Thus consistency of drawn conclusions is preserved.

Priorities on rules may be used to resolve some conflicts among rules. Priority information is often found in practice, and constitutes another representational feature of defeasible logics.

The logics take a pragmatic view and have low computational complexity. This is, among others, achieved through the absence of disjunction and the local nature of priorities: only priorities between conflicting rules are used, as opposed to systems of formal argumentation where often more complex kinds of priorities (e.g. comparing the strength of reasoning chains) are incorporated.

Generally speaking, defeasible logics are closely related to Courteous Logic Programs [11], as discussed in, e.g., [5].

The Language

A *defeasible theory D* is a couple $(R,>)$ where R a finite set of rules, and $>$ a superiority relation on R. Rules containing free variables are interpreted as the set of their variable-free instances.

There are three kinds of rules: *Strict rules* are denoted by $A \rightarrow p$, and are interpreted in the classical sense: whenever the premises are indisputable then so is the conclusion. An example of a strict rule is "Professors are faculty members". Written formally: `professor(X) → faculty(X)`. Inference from strict rules only is called *definite inference*. Strict rules are intended to define relationships that are definitional in nature, for example ontological knowledge.

Defeasible rules are denoted by $A \Rightarrow p$, and can be defeated by contrary evidence. An example of such a rule is `faculty(X) ⇒ tenured(X)` which reads as follows: "Professors are typically tenured".

Defeaters are denoted as $A \sim> p$ and are used only to prevent some conclusions, not to actively support conclusions. An example of such a defeater is `assistant-Prof(X) ~> ¬tenured(X)` which reads as follows: "Assistant professors may be not tenured".

A *superiority relation* on R is an acyclic relation $>$ on R (that is, the transitive closure of $>$ is irreflexive). When $r_1 > r_2$, then r_1 is called *superior* to r_2, and r_2 *inferior* to r_1. This expresses that r_1 may override r_2. For example, given the defeasible rules

```
r:  professor(X) =>  tenured(X)
r': visiting(X)  => ¬tenured(X)
```

which contradict one another, no conclusive decision can be made about whether a visiting professor is tenured. But if we introduce a superiority relation $>$ with r' $>$ r, then we can indeed conclude that a visiting professor is not tenured.

The system works roughly in the following way. to prove a conclusion A defeasibly, there must be a firing rule with A as its head (that is, all literals in the rule body have already been proved); in addition, we must rebut all attacking rules with head the (strong) negation of A. For each such attacking rule we must establish either (a) that this rule cannot fire because we have already established that one of the literals in its body cannot be proved defeasibly (finite failure), or (b) that there is a firing rule with head A superior to the attacking rule.

A formal definition of the proof theory is found in [3]. A model theoretic semantics is found in [17].

3   System Functionality

In this section we mainly concentrate on the functionality of the proof explanations facility of the DR-DEVICE system (Fig. 1). More details on the architecture and the implementation of the system can be found in [5].

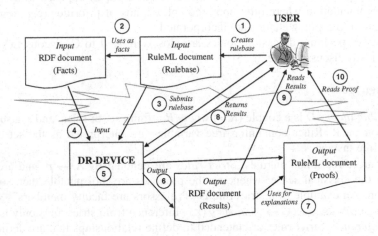

Fig. 1. Functionality of the DR-DEVICE system

The DR-DEVICE system accepts as input a defeasibe logic rulebase (step 4) in a RuleML-like syntax [9]. The rulebase has been created by a user (step 1) and its address is submitted to the DR-DEVICE system (step 3) through the stand-alone user interface of the system [6], or through a web-based interface hat we are currently developing. The rulebase contains only rules; the facts for the rule program are (input) RDF documents, whose addresses are declared in the rulebase header (step 2). The rule conclusions are materialized inside DR-DEVICE as objects (step 5) and when the inference procedure terminates, the instances of designated derived classes are exported as an RDF document (step 6). The RDF document includes:

- The RDF Schema definitions for the exported derived classes.
- Those instances of the exported derived classes, which have been proven, either positively or negatively, either defeasibly or definitely.

Furthermore, the system exports the grounds for all derived objects in a separate RuleML document (steps 6, 7). To this end we have extended RuleML with an XML schema for proofs of both classically (definitely) derived objects and defeasibly derived objects, which is discussed in the next section. DR-DEVICE returns to the user (step 8) the address of the RDF document with the results and the address of the RuleML document with the proof traces. Finally, the user can access the results (step 9) and the proofs (step 10) through a web browser or through a specialized software that can customize the visualization. Notice, that DR-DEVICE can also provide explanations about non-proved objects.

4 Proof Schema

The XML Schema for proof traces[1] explaining DR-DEVICE's results is an extension of the RuleML's 0.91 schema[2]. Actually, the rule language of DR-DEVICE is also an extension of RuleML. Extensions (for the rule language) deal with two aspects of DR-DEVICE, namely defeasible logic and its CLIPS implementation. Defeasible logic extensions include rule types, superiority relation among rules and conflicting literals, while CLIPS-related extensions deal with constraints on predicate arguments and functions. More details about the rule language can be found in [5].

The top-level element of the proof schema is the optional Grounds element, which is a top-level element of a RuleML document, although it should actually be an alternative to an Assert element. The latter could not be achieved using the redefinition mechanism of XML Schema, since element extensions deal only with sequences and not choices. Grounds consist of multiple proved or even not proved rule conclusions. Proofs can be either definite, i.e. using classical strict rules, or defeasible, which can use all three rule types of defeasible logic.

Definitely proved literals consist of the literal itself and the definite proof tree. The literal can be a positive atom or its negation, or even a reference to an RDF resource. Notice that DR-DEVICE uses RDF resources as facts and its conclusions are also materialized as RDF resources. A literal is definitely proved if there is a strict clause, either a strict rule or a fact, whose body literals are also definitely proven. Rules can either be in-lined in the proof tree or an external reference can exist to rules in another RuleML document. Similarly, the proofs for body literals can either be encapsulated in the proof tree of the rule head or can be referenced from another place of the proof document.

On the other hand, defeasible proofs are more complicated since they require either a defeasible or a strict rule (collectively called supportive rules), whose body literals are defeasibly proven. Notice that a definite proof subsumes a defeasible proof, that is why the Definite_Proof element is an alternative to the Defeasible_Proof element. Furthermore, the defeasibe conclusion must not be strongly attacked, i.e. the negation of the conclusion must not be definitely proved. Finally, the rules that defeasibly attack the current one must all be blocked, so the defeasible conclusion of this rules prevails.

A rule can be blocked in three ways. A defeasible rule (or a defeater) is blocked either when its body literals are not defeasibly proven or when it is attacked by another superior defeasible rule, whose body literals are defeasibly proven. A strict rule is blocked if its body literals are not definitely proven. Finally, inferior defeasible rules are considered as blocked.

Not proved conclusions follow a similar structure, i.e. the supportive rule that could not prove something must be included along with the reason why this happened. In the case of a defeasible non-proof, reasons include either the non-proof of some of the body literals or a definitely proved negated literal or an undefeated defeasible attacker. A defeasible attacker can be a defeasible rule or a defeater, whose body

---

[1] http://lpis.csd.auth.gr/systems/dr-device/dr-device-0.91.xsd
[2] http://www.ruleml.org/0.91/xsd/nafnegdatalog.xsd

literals are proven and whose possible attackers have been blocked. Notice that in order for a conclusion to not be defeasibly provable it must also be not definitely provable. The latter is similar to the blocked strict rule case above.

5 Proof Example

In this section we include a full example of the functionality of DR-DEVICE concerning both the inferencing and proof provision procedures. Assume that the user wants to submit the following rulebase (shown in simple logical notation) and wants to find out why the conclusion rich(antonis) is defeasibly derived.

```
wins_lotto(antonis)                owns(antonis)
r₁: wins_lotto(X) ⇒ rich(X)    r₂: paid_well(X) ⇒ rich(X)
r₃: owns(X) ⇒ ¬rich(X)           r₁ > r₃
r₄: gamble(X) ⇒ ¬rich(X)
```

The rulebase is submitted to DR-DEVICE as a RuleML document (Fig. 2). Notice that facts are not directly included in the RuleML document but in a separate input RDF document (Fig. 3), as indicated by the rdf_input attribute of the top-level RuleML element in Fig. 2. The rdf_export_classes attribute indicates which are the exported conclusions, the rdf_export attribute designates the output RDF document (Fig. 4) and the proof attribute designates the output RuleML document (Fig. 5) that contains the proofs for the exported conclusions.

DR-DEVICE atoms follow an object-oriented structure; the operator is a class name and the arguments are named slots. The DR-DEVICE system employs an object-oriented RDF data model ([5], [7]), where properties as normal encapsulated attributes of resource objects. The operator of an atom corresponds to the type of an RDF resource, the oid element to the URI of the resource and the slot arguments to the resource's properties.

The exported results in Fig. 4 contain the materialization of the derived object as an RDF resource, which also contains some system-defined properties, such as truthStatus that indicates if the conclusion was definitely or defeasibly proven, and proof that references the proof ID of the corresponding proof tree in the output proof document (Fig. 5). The latter indicates that the corresponding RDF resource was defeasibly proved using defeasible rule r₁, whose body literal was also defeasibly proved via a definitive proof due to the existence of a fact (RDF resource of the input RDF document). Furthermore, the negated conclusion was not definitely proven, because there are no appropriate strict rules, which is indicated by the fact that the not_strongly_attacked element is empty. Finally, defeasible rules r₃ and r₄ which attack r₁ are both blocked; r₃ is blocked because it is attacked by the superior rule r₁ and r₄ is blocked because its body literal cannot be proved.

```
<RuleML rdf_import="http://.../ex1.rdf" rdf_export_classes="rich"
        rdf_export="export-ex1.rdf" proof="http://.../proof-ex1.ruleml"
        xsi:schemaLocation="http://www.ruleml.org/0.91/xsd
                            http://.../dr-device/dr-device-0.91.xsd">
  <Assert>
    <Implies ruletype="defeasiblerule">
      <oid><Ind uri="&ex_rb;r1">r1</Ind></oid>
      <head>  <Atom>  <op><Rel>rich</Rel></op>
                      <slot><Ind>person</Ind> <Var>x</Var></slot> </Atom> </head>
      <body>  <Atom>  <op><Rel uri="ex:person"/></op>
                  <slot><Ind>ex:name</Ind><Var>x</Var></slot>
                  <slot>  <Ind>ex:wins_lotto</Ind>
                          <Data xsi:type="xs:string">true</Data>  </slot> </Atom> </body>
      <superior>  <Ind uri="&ex_rb;r3"/>  </superior>
    </Implies>
...
    <Implies ruletype="defeasiblerule">
      <oid><Ind uri="&ex_rb;r3">r3</Ind></oid>
      <head>  <Neg> <Atom>  <op><Rel>rich</Rel></op>
                      <slot><Ind>person</Ind><Var>x</Var></slot>  </Atom> </Neg>  </head>
      <body>  <Atom>  <op><Rel uri="ex:person"/></op>
                  <slot><Ind>ex:name</Ind><Var>x</Var></slot>
                  <slot>  <Ind>ex:owns</Ind>
                          <Data xsi:type="xs:string">true</Data>  </slot> </Atom> </body>
    </Implies>
...
  </Assert>
</RuleML>
```

Fig. 2. Rulebase example parts

```
<rdf:RDF ... >
    <ex:person    rdf:ID="Inst_6"
        ex:name="antonis"        ex:owns="false"
        ex:paid_well="true"      ex:wins_lotto="true"/>
</rdf:RDF>
```

Fig. 3. Input RDF document example

```
<rdf:RDF  xmlns:defeasible="http://.../defeasible.rdfs#"
          xmlns:dr-device="http://.../export-ex1.rdf#" ... >
...
  <dr-device:rich rdf:about="http://.../export-ex1.rdf#rich1">
    <dr-device:person>antonis</dr-device:person>
    <defeasible:truthStatus>defeasibly-proven</defeasible:truthStatus>
    <defeasible:proof
        rdf:datatype="&xsd;anyURI">'http://.../proof-ex1.ruleml#proof1'</defeasible:proof>
  </dr-device:rich>
</rdf:RDF>
```

Fig. 4. Output RDF document example.

6 Related Work

Besides teaching logic [4], not much work has been centered around explanation in reasoning systems so far. Rule-based expert systems have been very successful in applications of AI, and from the beginning, their designers and users have noted the need for explanations in their recommendations. In expert systems like [21] and Explainable Expert System [23], a simple trace of the program execution rule firing appears to provide a sufficient basis on which to build an explanation facility and they generate explanations in a language understandable to its users.

```
<RuleML rdf_import="http://.../ex1.rdf"          rdf_export="http://.../export-ex1.rdf"
        rulebase="http://.../dr-device/proof/ex/ex1.ruleml"
        xsi:schemaLocation="http://www.ruleml.org/0.91/xsd http://.../dr-device-0.91.xsd">
  <Grounds>
    <Proved>
      <Defeasibly_Proved> <oid><Ind uri="&pr_ex;proof1">proof1</Ind></oid>
        <Literal> <RDF_resource uri="http://.../export-ex1.rdf#rich1"/>
        <Defeasible_Proof>
          <supportive_rule> <rule_ref rule="&ex_rb;r1"/> </supportive_rule>
          <defeasible_body_grounds>
            <Defeasibly_Proved>
              <Literal> <Atom>  <op><Rel uri="ex:person"/></op>
                          <slot>  <Ind>ex:name</Ind>
                                  <Data xsi:type="xs:string">Antonis</Data></slot>
                          <slot>  <Ind>ex:wins_lotto</Ind>
                                  <Data xsi:type="xs:string">true</Data>  </slot> </Atom>
              </Literal>
              <Definite_Proof>
                <strict_clause>
                  <Fact>  <RDF_resource uri="http://...ex1.rdf#Inst_6"/>  </Fact>
                </strict_clause>
              </Definite_Proof>
            </Defeasibly_Proved>
          </defeasible_body_grounds>
          <not_strongly_attacked/>
          <defeasible_attackers_blocked>
            <Blocked>
              <Blocked_Defeasible_rule>
                <rule_ref rule="&ex_rb;r3"/>
                <Attacked_by_Superior>  <rule_ref rule="&ex_rb;r1"/>
                </Attacked_by_Superior> </Blocked_Defeasible_rule>  </Blocked>
            <Blocked>
              <Blocked_Defeasible_rule>
                <rule_ref rule="&ex_rb;r4"/>
                <not_defeasible_body_grounds>
                  <Not_Defeasibly_Proved>
                    <Literal> <Atom>  <op><Rel uri="ex:person"/></op>
                                <slot>  <Ind>ex:name</Ind>
                                        <Data xsi:type="xs:string">Antonis</Data></slot>
                                <slot>  <Ind>ex:gambles</Ind>
                                        <Data xsi:type="xs:string">true</Data>  </slot>
                    </Atom>    </Literal>
                    <Not_Defeasible_Proof/>
                    <Not_Definite_Proof/>
  ...
</RuleML>
```

Fig. 5. Proof example

Work has also been done in explaining the reasoning in description logics [18]. This research presents a logical infrastructure for separating pieces of logical proofs and automatically generating follow-up queries based on the logical format.

The most prominent work on proofs in the Semantic Web context is *Inference Web* [19]. The Inference Web (IW) is a Semantic Web based knowledge provenance infrastructure that supports interoperable explanations of sources, assumptions, learned information, and answers as an enabler for trust. It supports provenance, by providing proof metadata about sources, and explanation, by providing manipulation trace information. It also supports trust, by rating the sources about their trustworthiness.

IW simply requires inference rule registration and PML format. It does not limit itself to only extracting deductive engines. It provides a proof theoretic foundation on which to build and present its explanations, but any question answering system may be registered in the Inference Web and thus explained. So, in order to use the Inference Web infrastructure, a question answering system must register in the IWBase its inference engine along with its supported inference rules, using the PML specification format. The IW supports proof generation service that facilitates the creation of PML proofs by inference engines.

Closest to this paper is the work [2] that also focuses on explanation extraction and presentation for defeasible reasoning on the semantic web, but relies on an XSB-based reasoning engine and is embedded in a multi-agent environment, while it provides few details regarding the extensions of RuleML.

7 Conclusion and Future Work

This work presented a new system that aims to increase the trust of the users for Semantic Web applications. The system automatically generates an explanation for every answer to user's queries, in a formal and useful representation. It can be used by individual users who want to get a more detailed explanation from a reasoning system in the Semantic Web, in a more human readable way. Also, an explanation could be fed into a proof checker to verify the validity of a conclusion; this is important in a multi-agent setting. Our reasoning system is based on defeasible logic (a non-monotonic rule system) and we used the related reasoning engine DR-DEVICE. One contribution of our work is a RuleML extension for a formal representation of an explanation using defeasible logic.

In future work, we intend to improve the explanation facility to make it more intuitive and human-friendly, to suit users unfamiliar with logic. This effort includes proof visualization and visual rule execution tracing through integrating the work described in this paper with a tool for rule visualization [15] we have developed. Also, integration with the Inference Web infrastructure will be explored. Finally, we will investigate the use of the system in semantic web applications in which explanation and trust are essential elements.

Acknowledgments

This work was partially supported by the REWERSE Network of Excellence, and a GSRT Greek-Australian Project "Defeasible Reasoning for Semantic Web e-Commerce Applications".

References

[1] Antoniou, G., Bikakis, A.: DR-Prolog: A System for Defeasible Reasoning with Rules and Ontologies on the Semantic Web. IEEE Tran on Knowledge and Data Engineering 19(2), 233–245 (2007)

[2] Antoniou, G., et al.: Proof Explanation for the Semantic Web Using Defeasible Logic.(submitted)

[3] Antoniou, G., Billington, D., Governatori, G., Maher, M.J.: Representation results for defeasible logic. ACM Trans. on Computational Logic 2(2), 255–287 (2001)

[4] Barwise, J., Etchemendy, J.: The Language of First-Order Logic. Center for the study of Language and Information (1993)

[5] Bassiliades, N., Antoniou, G., Vlahavas, I.: A Defeasible Logic Reasoner for the Semantic Web. Int. Journal on Semantic Web and Information Systems 2(1), 1–41 (2006)

[6] Bassiliades, N., Kontopoulos, E., Antoniou, G.: A Visual Environment for Developing Defeasible Rule Bases for the Semantic Web. In: Adi, A., Stoutenburg, S., Tabet, S. (eds.) RuleML 2005. LNCS, vol. 3791, pp. 172–186. Springer, Heidelberg (2005)

[7] Bassiliades, N., Vlahavas, I.: R-DEVICE: An Object-Oriented Knowledge Base System for RDF Metadata. Int. Journal on Semantic Web and Information Systems 2(2), 24–90 (2006)

[8] Bechhofer, S., van Harmelen, F., Hendler, J., Horrocks, I., McGuinness, D.L., Patel-Schneider, P.F., Stein, L.A.: OWL web ontology language reference, W3C Recommendation www.w3.org/TR/owl-ref/ (February 10 2004)

[9] Boley, H., Tabet, S.: The Rule Markup Initiative, www.ruleml.org

[10] Eiter, T., Ianni, G., Schindlauer, R., Tompits, H.: dlvhex: A System for Integrating Multiple Semantics in an Answer-Set Programming Framework. In: Proc. WLP2006 , pp. 206-210 (2006)

[11] Grosof, B.N.: Prioritized conflict handing for logic programs. In: Proc. of the 1997 Int. Symposium on Logic Programming, pp. 197-211 (1997)

[12] Grosof, B.N., Gandhe, M.D., Finin, T.W.: SweetJess: Translating DAMLRuleML to JESS. In: Proc. RuleML (2002)

[13] Grosof, B.N., Horrocks, I., Volz, R., Decker, S.: Description Logic Programs: Combining Logic Programs with Description Logic. In: In: Proc. 12th Intl. Conf. on the World Wide Web (WWW-2003), pp. 48–57. ACM Press, New York (2003)

[14] Horrocks, I., Patel-Schneider, P.F., Bechhofer, S., Tsarkov, D.: OWL Rules: A Proposal and Prototype Implementation. Journal of Web Semantics 3(1), 23–40 (2005)

[15] Kontopoulos, E., Bassiliades, N., Antoniou, G.: Visualizing Defeasible Logic Rules for the Semantic Web. In: Mizoguchi, R., Shi, Z., Giunchiglia, F. (eds.) ASWC 2006. LNCS, vol. 4185, pp. 278–292. Springer, Heidelberg (2006)

[16] Levy, A., Rousset, M.-C.: Combining Horn rules and description logics in CARIN. Artificial Intelligence 104(1-2), 165–209 (1998)

[17] Maher, M.J.: A Model-Theoretic Semantics for Defeasible Logic. In: Proc. Workshop on Paraconsistent Computational Logic, pp. 67-80 (2002)

[18] McGuinness, D.L., Borgida, A.: Explaining Subsumption in Description Logics. In: Proc. IJCAI , pp. 816-821 (1995)

[19] McGuinness, D.L., da Silva, P.: Explaining answers from the Semantic Web: the Inference Web approach. Journal of Web Semantics 1(4), 397–413 (2004)

[20] Rosati, R.: On the decidability and complexity of integrating ontologies and rules. Journal of Web Semantics 3(1), 41–60 (2005)

[21] Shortliffe, E.: Computer-based medical consultations: MYCIN. Elsevier, North-Holland (1976)

[22] Sintek, M., Decker, S.: TRIPLE - A Query, Inference, and Transformation Language for the Semantic Web. In: Proc. Int. Semantic Web Conference, pp. 364-378 (2002)

[23] Swartout, W., Paris, C., Moore, J.: Explanations in Knowledge Systems: Design for Explainable Expert Systems. IEEE Expert 6(3), 58–64 (1991)

[24] Wagner, G.: Web Rules Need Two Kinds of Negation. In: Bry, F., Henze, N., Małuszyński, J. (eds.) PPSWR 2003. LNCS, vol. 2901, pp. 33–50. Springer, Heidelberg (2003)

Rule-Based Active Domain Brokering for the Semantic Web

Erik Behrends, Oliver Fritzen, Tobias Knabke, Wolfgang May,
and Franz Schenk

Institut für Informatik, Universität Göttingen
{behrends,fritzen,knabke,may,schenk}@informatik.uni-goettingen.de

Abstract. We investigate the use of domain ontologies that also include actions and events of that domain. Such ontologies do not only cover the static aspects of an ontology, but also activities and behavior in the given domain. We analyze what information has to be contained in such an ontology and show that large parts of the behavior can be expressed preferably by rules. We show how the tasks can be integrated and handled by a service infrastructure in the Semantic Web.

1 Introduction

For a powerful Semantic Web, a *domain ontology* should provide a comprehensive computer-processable characterization of an application domain. When considering the Semantic Web not only as a set of passive data sources (as by e.g. the OWL language design that provides powerful modeling concepts for expressing *static* issues of ontologies), but as a *living organism* of autonomous nodes, ontologies also have to supply notions of behavior. In this paper, we investigate ontologies for *active* nodes in the Semantic Web. For that we define first an abstract ontology of active concepts which is based on the concepts of *events* and *actions*. By having a set of agreed events and actions in an ontology, both local and global behavior in the Semantic Web can be expressed and implemented in a modular and declarative way by *Event-Condition-Action (ECA) Rules*.

MARS (Modular Active Rules for the Semantic Web) is a proposal for a framework for modular specification of active rules in the Semantic Web. From that point of view, it deals with languages and services for processing ECA rules and their components. For this paper, we take languages and services for running ECA rules (ECA-ML and an ECA engine [BFMS06b]), composite event descriptions and algorithmic event detection, as well as process specifications and execution [BFMS06a] as given.

The paper is structured as follows: In the next section, we describe how ontologies are extended with events and actions. In Section 3, we show how the subontology of events and actions in a domain can be described by different types of rules. The remaining sections describe how an active Semantic Web is realized upon such ontologies: Section 4 presents an architecture for individual

M. Marchiori, J.Z. Pan, and C. de Sainte Marie (Eds.): RR 2007, LNCS 4524, pp. 259–268, 2007.

domain nodes that support actions and events, and Section 5 describes the Domain Brokers that organize the communication between nodes contributing to a domain. Section 6 concludes the paper.

2 Domain Ontologies Including Dynamic Aspects

A *complete* ontology of an application domain requires to describe not only the static part, but also the dynamic part, including actions and events. Figure 1 depicts the structure of an ontology and the interferences between its components. Static concepts can be partitioned into classes, relationships and individuals. Actions influence classes, relationships, and individuals, and raise events.

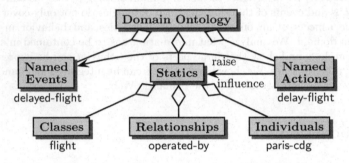

Fig. 1. Structure and Interference in Ontologies

An ontology relates the notions of a domain, as provided by the RDFS and OWL vocabularies. When including events and actions, further constraints, derivations and *interferences* can be described that –if rich enough– can even serve for reasoning and verification of workflows: describe actions in terms of agents, preconditions, and effects/postconditions; describe events, i.e., correlating actions and the resulting events; specify composite events and composite actions (processes); and in the end, business rules themselves can also be seen as parts of the ontology of an application.

2.1 Actions

The notion of actions is already established in modeling formalisms (e.g., UML). For describing atomic actions in an ontology, the main aspects are what classes the arguments belong to, the preconditions when an action is applicable, and the state that is guaranteed to hold afterwards. For composite actions, their definition in terms of reduction rules to processes over simpler actions has to be given, e.g., "implement a money transfer of amount x from A to B by a debit of x at A, and a deposit of x at B". This can e.g. be done by using CCS [Mil83, BFMS06a].

2.2   Events

Application Domain Events. Domain events are the basic events in a particular application domain. They are used by high-level rules, e.g., *business rules*. Such events must be described by the ontology of an application.

Events vs. Actions. In contrast to simple RDF or XML data-level events, on the application-level there is an important difference between *actions* and *events*: an event is a visible, possibly indirect or derived, consequence of an action. For instance, the action is to "book person P on flight LH123 on 17.2.2007" which results in the internal action "book person P for seat 42C of flight LH123 on 17.2.2007" and the events "a person has been booked for a seat behind the kitchen", "flight LH123 on 17.2.2007 is fully booked", "all flights from X to Y on 17.2.2007 are fully booked" (*) , or "person P has now more than 10.000 bonus miles". Note that there may be several rules for the same derived event; e.g., (*) can also be raised by canceling flight AF678 on the same day. All these events can be used for formulating (business) rules.

Use and Communication of Events. In contrast to the static information that is evaluated by *queries*, events are not queried, but are subject to *event detection*. This means, that a node that wants to "use" an event has to become aware of it. For that, events are *emitted* by the nodes and they are objects in the Semantic Web that are communicated between nodes (e.g. as XML fragments).

Derived and Composite Events. Derived events can be defined in terms of a temporal condition on (one or more) subevents and optionally a test of a condition: The event "flight LH123 on 17.2.2007 is fully booked" is actually raised by a single final booking event and a query against the current bookings. In contrast, the event "flight LH456 is first delayed, and later canceled" is a composite event defined as a sequence of subevents. Composite events are subject of heterogeneity since there are multiple formalisms for describing them. In most cases, *event algebras*, e.g., SNOOP [CKAK94] are used. Derived events are defined by *derivation rules* that can be expressed as ECA rules where the event component describes the triggering (atomic or composite) event, the condition part contains the query, and the action consists of raising/signaling the derived event; this will be discussed in Section 3.

Localization of Events. While basic application-level events are associated with a certain node, derived events can either involve subevents and queries at a single node, or they can happen "Web-wide", i.e., involve knowledge from several nodes: the event "flight LH123 on 17.2.2007 is fully booked" is only concerned with local knowledge of the according airline node. In contrast, the event that *all* flights between two places on a given day are fully booked can only be derived "Web-wide" – doing this will be one of the tasks of the domain broker.

3   Defining and Relating Events and Actions of an Ontology in Terms of Rules

In the MARS approach, the behavior of domains is specified and implemented by several types of rules on different abstraction levels (cf. Figure 2). Rules that axiomatize the *ontology*, i.e., mandatory relationships between actions, objects, and events that are inherent to the domain must be validated against the ontology. Additionally, there are rules that specify a given *application* on this domain.

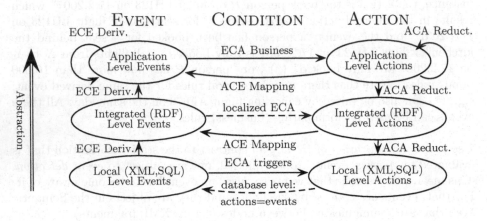

Fig. 2. Types of Rules

3.1   ECA Rules

From the external user's point of view, *ECA-Business Rules* specify the actual behavior and run application services: "when something happens and some conditions are satisfied, something has to be done". Here, events and actions refer to a very high and abstract level of the ontology. Internally, ECA rules are also used for implementing mechanisms e.g. for integrity maintenance.

3.2   ECE Event Derivation Rules: Providing High-Level Events

For implementing high-level rules, high-level events need to be *derived* according to their definition in the ontology. This is done by *ECE (event-condition-event)* rules where the "action" actually consists of deriving/raising an event.

ECE rules can be horizontal, i.e., the event is derived from another high-level event under certain conditions, e.g., *"when a booking for a flight is done, and this is the last seat, then the plane is completely booked"*.

In upward vertical ECE rules, an abstract event is derived from a less abstract one. This case covers both the derivation of global events from local ones, and the derivation of events from changes in the underlying database, e.g., *"when the arrival time in a database of a flight of today is changed (database-level update), signal 'delay of a flight'"*.

While ECA rules are *active* rules, the *logical* semantics of ECE rules corresponds to the *bottom-up* semantics of derivation rules: Given the body, "derive" the head event. *Event derivation rules* "fire" only once when an event is detected and another event is raised.

3.3   ACA/ACE Rules: Talking About High-Level Actions

High-level actions like "book a travel by plane from Hanover to Lisbon" are *reduced* by rules that provide an *implementation* (by searching for (indirect) connections). Such reduction *ACA (action-condition-action)* rules correspond to SQL's INSTEAD-triggers. Considering Transaction Logic Programming [BK93]), they are also closely related to the *top-down* semantics of derivation rules: To obtain the head, realize the body. Some of these rules are inherent to the ontology of the underlying domain, others specify only the behavior of a given application (including e.g. local policies that are not inherent to the domain).

Event Derivation instead of Detection. Since high-level events can also be seen as consequences of high-level actions, it is also reasonable to raise them when a certain action is executed. In most cases, this amounts to a simple mapping from high-level actions to high-level events: the action "cancel-flight($flight)" directly raises the event "cancelled-flight($flight)" at the same node (and is internally executed by inserting a fact into a database by a downward ACA rule).

ACA and ACE on higher level are located in the Domain Brioker, whereas ACA rules that provide the actual implementation of atomic actions are located in the individual domain nodes.

3.4   Low-Level Rules

The base is provided by update actions on the database level (to which all abstract actions must eventually be reduced in order to actually change the state of any node) and low-level ECA rules, e.g., database triggers. Here, neither the event nor the action is part of the application ontology, but both exist and are related only due to the physical implementation of the application.

3.5   Responsibility for Rule Processing

As depicted in Fig. 2, the actual processing of the rules takes place on different levels: only local rules can be processed in the individual domain nodes, this includes low-level ECE and ACA rules. For higher-level rules, e.g., ECE that define global events, or ACA that distribute actions, the *Domain Brokers* are responsible. Such rules belong to the globally agreed ontology of the domain. Additionally, the domain brokers have to know the individual domain application nodes (via registration or search), and have to be aware of events. They also serve as "primary" contact to users and higher-level services (such as the general, application-independent ECA engines) for queries and execution of actions in a domain.

4   Domain Application Nodes

Domain application nodes are the "leaves" of the Semantic Web architecture. They represent services in the application domain, e.g., airlines or train companies. As such, they usually have some kind of database or knowledge base. According to their task as services, they are able to execute actions of that domain (e.g., booking a flight). Extending known Web Service functionality, domain nodes also *emit* events as defined by the domain ontology (e.g. that a flight is *now* fully booked).

The Jena [Jen] Framework provides an API for dealing with RDF and OWL data. In our implementation, the node core consists of a Jena instance that uses an external database (e.g. PostgreSQL) for storing base data, and the DL reasoner Pellet. The handling of ontology-level behavior and mapping it to the RDF model level is located in a wrapper as shown in Fig. 3.

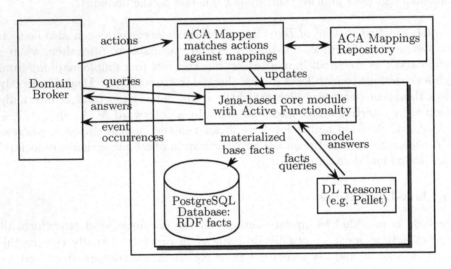

Fig. 3. Architecture of the Domain Node

Functionality of the Node Core. An RDF/OWL domain node with local active behavior has been implemented and is described in [MSvL06]: Queries over concepts and properties are directly stated in SPARQL against the RDF/OWL core. The basic functionality has been extended with a simple update language for RDF data and with support for RDF-level database triggers reacting upon *database update actions*. With this, local ECA rules *inside* the database (that are also required to support actual updates, e.g., when deleting an instance $p(x, y)$ of a property that is symmetric and stored as $p(y, x)$) as well as ECE rules raising simple events can be implemented. In the MARS Framework, atomic events are communicated in a straightforward XML format to the domain brokers, e.g.,

```
<travel:delayed-flight flight="iata://flights/LH123" time="30 min" /> .
```

Functionality of the Node Wrapper. Execution of Actions. Ontology-level actions are communicated to the domain nodes according to an agreed downward communication format, consisting of the action as an XML fragment, and optionally tuples of variable bindings (cf. [MAA05]), e.g.,

```
<travel:schedule-flight flight="iata://flights/LH123"
  captain="travel://.../airlines/lufthansa/people/jameskirk" >
  <travel:cabincrew name="..." />
  <travel:cabincrew name="..." />
</travel:schedule-flight>
```

The ACA reduction rules implement the actions similar to INSTEAD-triggers that update the local database. The local implementation of the mapping from actions (that are atomic from the ontology level) onto actual database update statements for a given XML input can be seen as a transformation that generates a sequence of database updates:

```
## sample rule using XQuery-style
IMPLEMENT <schedule-flight/> BY
let $flight := /schedule-flight/@flight
let $captain := /schedule-flight/@captain
return concat(
  "INSERT ($flight has-captain $captain);",
  for $name in /schedule-flight/cabincrew/@name
  let $cabincrew := local:make-person-uri($name)
  return "INSERT ($flight has-cabincrew $cabincrew);")
```

Note that the implementation of an action must match the specification of the action in terms of preconditions and postconditions, if such a specification is given in the ontology. Such specifications that can then also serve for reasoning about workflows are future work. A domain node for a certain domain ontology is set up by instantiating the generic architecture with a set of ACA mappings.

5 Domain Brokering

The MARS domain broker architecture has been implemented in [Kna05]. Brokering –often also known as (query) mediation– is a well-known issue in distributed environments. In addition to query brokering, domain brokers also have to collect events coming from domain nodes and to forward them to event consumers such as ECA engines and composite event detection services. Additionally, actions requested by ECA engines are forwarded to domain nodes to be executed.

5.1 Query Brokering

Domain brokers are responsible as mediators for answering queries by querying domain nodes and integrating the answers. For that, domain brokers know the respective ontology that consists of OWL statements and derivation rules (here, current developments like SWRL [SWRL] or DL+log [Ros05] can be used). To get the MARS infrastructure running, a simple approach is followed first (query evaluation is not in the focus of the MARS framework – it will be ready to adapt any distributed query answering algorithm): Given a query, all static notions (concepts and properties) that are relevant for answering the query are identified. For this, declarations like owl:inverseOf and owl:equivalentProperty must be considered. Moreover, if the ontology contains rules (or OWL class definitions and axioms) of the form *head ← body*, and the notion in the head is asked, notions occurring in the bodies have to be answered. Each of the notions is forwarded to the relevant domain nodes. The domain broker collects the answers (as RDF triples) and uses them for answering the original query.

5.2 Event Brokering

Event Brokering functionality provides the mediation between event providers (i.e., domain nodes) and event consumers. We give only an abstract sketch of the event handling, see [AAB+06, Chapter A.4.2] for details: The event component of an ECA (or ECE) rule is a specification of a (possibly composite) event pattern using an event algebra (which can be seen as a certain ontology for composite events) over *atomic event specifications (AESs)*, which are simple queries or patterns of event instances, binding (free) variables, e.g.,

<travel:delayed-flight flight="{$FlightNo}" time="{$Time}" /> .

Given a composite event specification, the *composite event detection service (CED)* registers each contained AES at an *Atomic Event Matcher (AEM)* for the respective (matching) formalism. The AEM then registers at the *Domain Brokers* for the relevant *event types* (e.g., travel:delayed-flight). From then on, the domain broker will forward every element of that type to the AEM. Note that when using more sophisticated ontologies and RDF/OWL-based AES formalisms, event classes and subclasses can be defined and OWL reasoning about events has to be applied.

Derived events are explicitly raised by ECE rules encoded as ECA rules that can be registered at any ECA engine to enable the detection of the derived event:

```
<eca:Rule>
  <!-- eca:Event and eca:Query: body of the ECE rule definition -->
  <eca:Action>
    <eca:raise-event> <!-- head of the ECE rule --> </eca:raise-event>
  </eca:Action>
</eca:Rule>
```

5.3 Action Brokering

Clients request actions either at certain domain nodes, or at the domain broker. The broker then forwards the (sub)tasks to all relevant domain nodes.

Example 1. Consider the case that the domain node representing *Frankfurt Airport* decides to delay a given flight by one hour due to bad weather conditions, e.g., by a rule

```
<eca:Rule xmlns:travel="http://www.semwebtech.org/domains/2006/travel" >
  <eca:Event>bad snow conditions detected </eca:Event>
  <eca:Query>all $flights departing in the next hour </eca:Query>
  <eca:Action>
    <travel:delay-flight flight="{$flight}" delay="1h" reason="snow" />
  </eca:Action>
</eca:Rule>
```

The action instances (submitted e.g. as XML or RDF/XML)

```
<travel:delay-flight flight="LH123" delay="1h" reason="snow" />
<travel:delay-flight flight="AF789" delay="1h" reason="snow" />
```

are sent to a domain broker for the travel domain. The broker then checks which nodes are potentially concerned by that action.

Mapping of the Action by the Domain Nodes. The domain ontology contains an ACA rule that specifies how the action is mapped to RDF-level updates, e.g.

```
## sample rule in the local RDF and RDF updates style
IMPLEMENT { a travel:delay-flight;
       travel:flight $Flight; travel:delay $Time; travel:reason $Reason }
BY   ASSERT (make-uri($Flight) travel:is-delayed $Time)
     ANNOTATE WITH (travel:reason $Reason)
```

5.4   Handling of Composite Actions by ACA Rules

As discussed above, ACA rules are a suitable paradigm for expressing actions on a higher abstraction level by defining them as composite actions. The structure and the information flow through the components (in MARS done by variable bindings [MAA05]) of ACA rules is closely related to ECA rules – both use an "ON ... DO": "*on invocation of an action do ...*" and "*on occurrence of an event do ...*". The specification of the invoking action (an atomic action given by some action name with parameters) uses the same AES/AEM mechanisms as for atomic event specification. Thus, the available ECA engine architecture can be used. When a domain broker is initialized with an ontology, it registers all ACA rules of the ontology at an ECA engine. It registers the atomic action specification (analogous to AES) at an AEM. The AEM registers at one or more domain brokers (for *domain:action-name*), and the domain brokers submit these actions like events to the AEM. Thus, only the domain broker must be aware if a registration by the AEM is concerned with an event or an action (this information is contained in the ontology).

6 Conclusion

We have described the domain brokering level for the MARS (Modular Active Rules for the Semantic Web) Framework. By being completely rule-based, it extends and uses the infrastructure that has been defined and implemented for processing ECA rules.

Related Work. There is a lot of related work on query brokering and mediators in the data integration and peer data management areas, but we are not aware of approaches for event brokering and action brokering in the above style.

Acknowledgements. This research has been funded by the European Commission within the 6th Framework Programme project REWERSE, no. 506779.

References

[AAB⁺06] Alferes, J.J., Amador, R., Behrends, E., Eckert, M., Fritzen, O., May, W., Pătrânjan, P.L., Schenk, F.: A First Prototype on Evolution and Behavior at the XML Level. Deliverable I5-D5, REWERSE EU FP6 NoE, 2006. Available at http://www.rewerse.net

[BFMS06a] Behrends, E., Fritzen, O., May, W., Schenk, F.: Combining ECA Rules with Process Algebras for the Semantic Web. In: RuleML, IEEE Press, New York (2006)

[BFMS06b] Behrends, E., Fritzen, O., May, W., Schubert, D.: An ECA Engine for Deploying Heterogeneous Component Languages in the Semantic Web. In: Grust, T., Höpfner, H., Illarramendi, A., Jablonski, S., Mesiti, M., Müller, S., Patranjan, P.-L., Sattler, K.-U., Spiliopoulou, M., Wijsen, J. (eds.) EDBT 2006. LNCS, vol. 4254, pp. 887–898. Springer, Heidelberg (2006)

[BK93] Bonner, A.J., Kifer, M.: Transaction Logic Programming. ICLP (1993)

[CKAK94] Chakravarthy, S., Krishnaprasad, V., Anwar, E., Kim, S.-K.: Composite events for active databases: Semantics, contexts and detection. VLDB (1994)

[Jen] Jena: A Java Framework for Semantic Web Applications. http://jena.sourceforge.net

[Kna05] Knabke, T.: Development of a domain broker. Master's Thesis, Univ. Göttingen (2006)

[MAA05] May, W., Alferes, J.J., Amador, R.: Active Rules in the Semantic Web: Dealing with Language Heterogeneity. In: Adi, A., Stoutenburg, S., Tabet, S. (eds.) RuleML 2005. LNCS, vol. 3791, Springer, Heidelberg (2005)

[MSvL06] May, W., Schenk, F., von Lienen, E.: Extending an OWL Web Node with Reactive Behavior. In: Alferes, J.J., Bailey, J., May, W., Schwertel, U. (eds.) PPSWR 2006. LNCS, vol. 4187, Springer, Heidelberg (2006)

[Mil83] Milner, R.: Calculi for synchrony and asynchrony. Theoretical Computer Science, pp. 267–310 (1983)

[Ros05] Rosati, R.: On the decidability and complexity of integrating ontologies and rules. Journal of Web. Semantics 3(1), 61–73 (2005)

[SWRL] Horrocks, I., Patel-Schneider, P., Boley, H., Tabet, S., Grosof, B., Dean, M.: SWRL: A Semantic Web Rule Language Combining OWL and RuleML, http://www.w3.org/Submission/SWRL/ (2004)

Decidability Under the Well-Founded Semantics*

Natalia Cherchago[1], Pascal Hitzler[2], and Steffen Hölldobler[3]

[1] Department of Computer Science, Technische Universität Dresden, Germany
[2] Institute AIFB, Universität Karlsruhe, Germany
[3] International Center for Computational Logic, Technische Universität Dresden, Germany

Abstract. The well-founded semantics (WFS) for logic programs is one of the few major paradigms for closed-world reasoning. With the advent of the Semantic Web, it is being used as part of rule systems for ontology reasoning, and also investigated as to its usefulness as a semantics for hybrid systems featuring combined open- and closed-world reasoning. Even in its most basic form, however, the WFS is undecidable. In fact, it is not even semi-decidable, which means that it is a theoretical impossibility that sound and complete reasoners for the WFS exist.

Surprisingly, however, this matter has received next to no attention in research, although it has already been shown in 1995 by John Schlipf [1]. In this paper, we present several conditions under which query-answering under the well-founded semantics is decidable or semi-decidable. To the best of our knowledge, these are the very first results on such conditions.

1 Introduction

Logic programming under the well-founded semantics (WFS) [2] is one of the most prominent paradigms for knowledge representation and reasoning. It has recently found applications in the area of Semantic Web reasoning, in particular in the form of the logic programming variant of F-Logic [3], on which systems like FLORA-2, Florid, and the commercial ontobroker are based. As such, it complements standardized ontology languages such as the description logics and open-world based Web Ontology Language OWL[1], in that it provides a rule-based modeling paradigm under a non-monotonic closed-world semantics.

However, while decidability of the language was a major design criterion for OWL, logic programming under the WFS is undecidable — indeed, it is not even semi-decidable in the presence of function symbols [1], which is a rather unpleasant fact because this means that sound and complete implementations of the semantics are not possible in principle. Hence, existing systems like XSB

---

* This work is partially supported by the German Federal Ministry of Education and Research (BMBF) under the SmartWeb project (grant 01 IMD01 B), by the Deutsche Forschungsgemeinschaft (DFG) under the ReaSem project and by the EU in the IST project NeOn (IST-2006-027595), http://www.neon-project.org/
[1] http://www.w3.org/2004/OWL/

M. Marchiori, J.Z. Pan, and C. de Sainte Marie (Eds.): RR 2007, LNCS 4524, pp. 269–278, 2007.
© Springer-Verlag Berlin Heidelberg 2007

Prolog [4] only realize a decidable or semi-decidable fragment of the WFS. Surprisingly, however, there exists hardly any literature[2] describing such decidable or semi-decidable fragments, or literature describing in detail the fragment(s) of the WFS actually realized in implementations in terms which are not procedural.

The issue of (semi-)decidable fragments of not semi-decidable non-monotonic reasoning paradigms indeed has been neglected to a considerable extent, which is a severe theoretical obstacle in trying to realize expressive practical approaches. The only work we know which addresses this is due to Bonnatti [5] concerning Answer Set Programming, which is not readily adaptable to our setting.

In this paper, we study conditions under which query-answering is decidable or semi-decidable under the well-founded semantics. We obtain such conditions by combining the notion of *relevance* of semantics [6] with a new characterization of the well-founded semantics by means of stratification with level-mappings [7].

The paper is organized as follows. Section 2 introduces key notions and terminology. In Section 3 we combine *relevance* [6] and *stratification* [7] to define a new meta-level property of *stratified relevance*. In Section 4 we present two classes of programs with semi-decidable query evaluation and provide examples. The classes of *programs finitely recursive on lower levels* and of *programs of finite level* are completely new. We prove semi-decidability results in Section 5. In Section 6 we discuss related literature and conclude.

2   Preliminaries

In this section we introduce our notation and basic definitions. We assume the reader to be familiar with the classical theory of logic programming. *Literals* are atoms or negated atoms. We denote atoms by A, B, C or D and literals by L; all symbols may be indexed. A (*normal*) *logic program* is a finite set of (normal) rules of the form $A \leftarrow B_1, ..., B_l, \neg C_1, ..., \neg C_m$. As usual, by *head* and *body* of such a rule we mean A and $B_1, ..., B_l, \neg C_1, ..., \neg C_m$ respectively. A rule with empty body is called a *fact*. A *query* or *goal* is an expression of the from $\leftarrow B_1, ..., B_l, \neg C_1, ..., \neg C_m$.

We will assign a *Herbrand universe* U_P and a *Herbrand base* B_P to a program P as usual while assuming that the underlying first-order language consists of exactly the constants, function symbols and predicate symbols occurring in P. The ground instantiation $ground(P)$ of P consists of all ground instances (w.r.t. the Herbrand base B_P) of all rules in P. For a consistent $I \subseteq B_P \cup \neg B_P$, we say that A is *true in I* if $A \in I$, we say that A is *false in I* if $\neg A \in I$, otherwise we say that A *is undefined in I*. A *(partial) Herbrand interpretation* I for P is a consistent subset of $B_P \cup \neg B_P$. (Partial) Herbrand interpretations are ordered by set-inclusion; this is usually called the *knowledge ordering* on Herbrand interpretations.

Let P be a program. $A > B$ iff there is a rule in $ground(P)$ with head A and B occurring in its body. The *dependency graph* $\mathcal{G}_P$ is a directed graph whose

---

[2] In fact, we found none such literature at all, despite a considerable effort invested into searching for it. Nevertheless, some other results carry over from other semantics.

vertices are the atoms from $ground(P)$ and there is an *edge* from A to B iff $A > B$. We say that A *depends on* B, in symbols $A \rhd B$ iff there is a path from A to B in $\mathcal{G}_P$.

By a *semantics* we mean a mapping $\mathcal{S}$ from the class of all programs into the power set of the set of all partial Herbrand models. $\mathcal{S}$ assigns to every program P a set of partial Herbrand models of P.

Given a normal program P and a partial interpretation I, we say that $\mathcal{A} \subseteq B_P$ is an *unfounded set of P w.r.t. I*, if for every $A \in \mathcal{A}$ and every $A \leftarrow \mathcal{B} \in ground(P)$ one of the following conditions holds: (i) either at least one body literal $L \in \mathcal{B}$ is false in I, or (ii) at least one positive body literal $B \in \mathcal{B}$ is contained in $\mathcal{A}$. Under the greatest unfounded set of P w.r.t. I we understand the union of all unfounded sets of P w.r.t. I.

Given a program P, $T_P(I)$ is the set of all $A \in B_P$ such that there is a clause $A \leftarrow \mathcal{B}$ in $ground(P)$ such that $\mathcal{B}$ is true in I. Let $U_P(I)$ is the greatest unfounded set of P w.r.t. I. The operator $W_P(I)$ is defined by $W_P(I) := T_P(I) \cup \neg U_P(I)$. This operator is due to van Gelder et al. [2]. The least fixed point of $W_P(I)$ is called the *well-founded model of P*, determining its *well-founded semantics*.

The property of *relevance* states intuitively that a goal G can be answered w.r.t. P using only those atoms occurring in $ground(P)$ on which the atoms occurring in G depend.

Definition 1. *(Relevant Universe and Subprogram [5]) Let P be a program and G a ground goal. The* relevant universe for P and G *is*

$$U_{rel}(P, G) = \{B \mid \text{there occurs and atom } A \text{ in } G \text{ such that } A \rhd B\}.$$

The relevant subprogram of P for G *is*

$$P_G = \{R \mid R \in ground(P) \text{ and } head(R) \in U_{rel}(P, G)\}.$$

Definition 2. *(Relevance [6]) Relevance states that for all ground literals L we have $\mathcal{S}(P)(L) = \mathcal{S}(P_L)(L)$, where P_L is a relevant subprogram of P w.r.t. L (and L is understood as a query in the formation of P_L).*

Relevance states that for all normal logic programs P and all ground atoms A, P entails A under semantics $\mathcal{S}$ iff $P_{\leftarrow A}$ entails A under $\mathcal{S}$. One should observe that the relevant subprogram P_G w.r.t. a ground goal G contains all rules that could ever contribute to the derivation of G or to its non-derivability.

Technically, our approach rests on a new characterization of the well-founded semantics by means of level-mappings, which is due to [7]. Level-mapping characterizations expose the dependency structures between literals underlying a given semantics. The relevance of level-mapping characterizations for decidability analysis is obvious, but we employ them in this paper for the first time.

For an interpretation I and a program P, an *I-partial level mapping for P* is a partial mapping $l : B_P \to \alpha$ with domain $dom(l) = \{A \mid A \in I \text{ or } \neg A \in I\}$, where α is some (countable) ordinal. A *total level mapping* is a total mapping $l : B_P \to \alpha$ for some (countable) ordinal α. We extend every level mapping to literals by setting $l(\neg A) = l(A)$ for all $A \in dom(l)$.

Definition 3. *(WF-properties [7]) Let P be a normal logic program, I a model for P, and l an I-partial level mapping for P. P satisfies WF with respect to I and l if each $A \in \mathrm{dom}(l)$ satisfies one of the following conditions.*

(WFi) $A \in I$ *and there is a clause $A \leftarrow L_1, .., L_n$ in $\mathrm{ground}(P)$ such that $L_i \in I$ and $l(A) > l(L_i)$ for all i.*
(WFii) $\neg A \in I$ *and for each clause $A \leftarrow A_1, .., A_n, \neg B_1, .., \neg B_m$ in $\mathrm{ground}(P)$ (at least) one of the following conditions holds:*
   (WFiia) *There exists i with $\neg A_i \in I$ and $l(A) \geq l(A_i)$.*
   (WFiib) *There exists j with $B_j \in I$ and $l(A) > l(B_j)$.*

If $A \in \mathrm{dom}(l)$ satisfies (WFi), then we say that A satisfies (WFi) with respect to I and l, and similarly if $A \in \mathrm{dom}(l)$ satisfies (WFii).

Theorem 1. *([7]) Let P be a normal logic program with well-founded model M_P. Then, in the knowledge ordering, M_P is the greatest model amongst all models I for which there exists an I-partial level mapping l for P such that P satisfies (WF) with respect to I and l.*

In the following, we shall often refer to the property of the well-founded semantics stated in Theorem 1 as the property of *stratification*. By slight abuse of language, we call such a level mapping as in Theorem 1 a *level mapping characterization* of P (or of the well-founded semantics of P).

3   Stratified Relevance

Given any semantics $\mathcal{S}$, it is reasonable to expect that the truth value of a ground goal G only depends on the relevant subprogram P_G for G with respect to P. As we have seen in Section 2, this idea was formalized by Dix [6] in the property of *relevance*. We can prove an even stronger property with the help of level mappings and Theorem 1 from ([7]).

Suppose P has a well-founded model M_P. Define an M_P-partial level mapping l_P as follows: $l_P(A) = \alpha$, where α is the least ordinal such that A is not undefined in $W_P \uparrow (\alpha + 1)$. Let $l^{-1}(\alpha) = \Lambda_\alpha \subseteq M_P$ be a set of ground literals of level α, $W_P \uparrow (\alpha + 1) \backslash W_P \uparrow (\alpha) = \Lambda_\alpha$. In the following and when it is clear from the context, we call a set of literals of some level simply a *level*.

If we evaluate a ground goal of the form $\leftarrow A$, we start from some set Λ_α such that $A \in \Lambda_\alpha$. According to the WF-properties that a model M_P enjoys by Theorem 1, every evaluation step either "goes down" to the previous level, or "stays" at the same level. Therefore we define a new relevant universe $U_{rel}^*(P, G)$ and, likewise, the relevant subprogram P_G^*, in such a way that the levels are limited to those ones which are less than or equal to the level of atoms occurring in a ground goal G w.r.t the level mapping l_P.

Definition 4. *(Stratified Relevant Universe) Let P be a logic program and G a ground goal. The* stratified relevant universe *for P and G is $U_{rel}^*(P, G) =$*

$$\{B \mid there\ occurs\ an\ atom\ A\ in\ G\ such\ that\ A \triangleright B\ and\ l_P(A) \geq l_P(B)\}.$$

To define stratified relevant subprogram, we need the following definition:

Definition 5. *Let P be a logic program and G be a ground goal. P'_G is the set of all rules $R\sigma$ such that there exists a rule R in P and a substitution σ meeting the following conditions:*

- *The head of $R\sigma$ is in $U^*_{rel}(P, G)$.*
- *At least one atom occurring in the body of $R\sigma$ is contained in $U^*_{rel}(P, G)$.*
- *Let $A_1, \ldots, A_n$ be all atoms occurring in R, such that $A_i\sigma \in U^*_{rel}(P, F)$ for all $1 \le i \le n$. Then the following must hold:*
  - *σ is a most general unifier for the unification problem $\{A_i = A_i\sigma \mid i = 1, \ldots, n\}$.*
  - *There does not exist an atom B occurring in R, which is distinct from all A_i $(i = 1, \ldots, n)$ such that there is a substitution ϑ with $B\sigma\vartheta \in U^*_{rel}(P, G)$.*

Definition 6. *(Stratified Relevant Subprogram) Let P be a program and G a ground goal. The stratified relevant subprogram for P and G w.r.t. an I-partial level mapping l_P, denoted by P^*_G, is the set of all rules R' defined as follows: For any rule R in P'_G, let R' be the rule which is obtained by removing all non-ground literals from R. Note that by definition the head and at least one of the body literals of R' are never removed.*

The underlying intuition is that we use rules from $ground(P)$ where the head and all body atoms are contained in $U^*_{rel}(P, G)$, as they are those which contribute to the well-founded semantics in the sense of condition (WFi) in Definition 3. In order to accommodate condition (WFii) from Definition 3 it suffices if one *witness of unusability*[3] remains in the body or the rule, which is the rationale behind the remaining definition of stratified relevant subprogram.

Definition 7. *(Stratified Relevance) Stratified Relevance states that for all ground queries F and all normal logic programs G we find that P entails G under semantics S iff P^*_G entails G under S.*

Proposition 1. *The well-founded semantics satisfies Stratified Relevance.*

Proof. (Proof Sketch) Given a normal program P and its well-founded model M, we have that by Theorem 1, there exists an M-partial level mapping l for P such that P satisfies (WF) with respect to M and l. Let this level mapping be l_P as defined above. The proof follows by induction on the evaluation of L under the well-founded semantics. We have to consider two cases: $L = A$ is a positive literal and $L = \neg A$ is a negative literal. Let $A \in dom(l_P)$, suppose $l_P(A) = \alpha$ and let $M(L) = M^*(L)(induction\ hypothesis)$.

Case i. $A \in M$. By (WFi) we have that there is at least one rule $R = A \leftarrow L_1, .., L_n$ in $ground(P)$ such that $L_i \in M$ and $l_P(A) \ge l_P(L_i)$ for all i. We have that $A \in T_P(W_P \uparrow \alpha)$ and all $L_i \in body(R)$ are true in $W_P \uparrow \alpha$. We see that A refers to all these literals or, in other words, $A > L_i, i = 1, .., n$.

---

[3] These are literals satisfying one of the unfoundedness conditions [2].

Induction step: prove that $L_i \in M^*$ for all i. By definition of $P^*_{\leftarrow L}$, $R \in P^*_{\leftarrow L}$ and by induction hypothesis we have that $A \in M^*$. By definition of W_P and by relevance, from $R \in P^*_{\leftarrow L}$ and $A \in M^*$, it follows that $L_i \in M^*$ for all i.

Case ii is similar to **Case i**.   □

The proposition shows that $P^*_{\leftarrow L}$ by its definition contains all the necessary information for L's derivation or non-derivability.

The next proposition concerns computability of the stratified relevant subprogram and is also crucial for our decidability results.

Proposition 2. *Let P be a program with a level mapping characterization l and let G be a goal such that $U^*_{rel}(P,G)$ is finite. Then P^*_G is finite and computable in finite time.*

Proof. P consists of finitely many rules, so it suffices to show the proposition for a program consisting of a single rule R. Let n be the number of body literals occurring in R, and let A be the head of R. A finite computation of P^*_G is possible by means of the following algorithm:

1. For all selections of m atoms $A_1, \ldots, A_m$ occurring in the body of P, where $1 < m \leq n$, do the following.
   (a) For all selections of $m+1$ elements $B, B_1, \ldots, B_m$ from $U^*_{rel}(P,G)$ do the following
      i. If the unification problem $\{A = B\} \cup \{A_i = B_i \mid i = 1, \ldots, m\}$ is solvable with most general unifier σ, then do the following.
         A. If $m = n$ then add $R\sigma$ to P'.
         B. If $m < n$ then for all selections of a body literal C from R which is distinct from $A_1, \ldots, A_m$ and for all selections of an element D from $U^*_{rel}(P,G)$, check whether there is a substitution ϑ such that $C\sigma\theta = D$. If such a ϑ does *not* exist, then add $r\sigma$ to P'.
2. For every rule R in P', add to P^*_G the rule R' obtained from R by removing all non-ground literals.

It is straightforward to check that all selections made in the algorithm are selections from finite sets. Furthermore, the computation of the most general unifiers is terminating by well-known algorithms. So the algorithm terminates after finite time. The reader will also have no difficulties verifying that the program resulting from the algorithm is indeed the desired stratified relevant subprogram.   □

4   Program Classes with Semi-decidable Query Evaluation

4.1   Programs Finitely Recursive on Lower Levels

In this subsection we define a class of normal logic programs whose consequences under the well-founded semantics are semi-decidable, even though they admit function symbols (and, hence, infinite domains) and recursion. The idea is to restrict recursion to prevent infinite sequences of recursive calls without repeats.

This follows the ideas presented in [5] by Bonatti, where a class of *finitary programs* under the stable model semantics was defined. The intuition behind it is the following: a literal is brought into the well-founded model M in two ways: either by T_P or U_P. But in both cases there must exist a dependency between the consequence atom and the precedence atoms in the dependency graph. With the help of *stratified relevance* from Section 3 we can define the relevant subprogram in such a way that it contains only rules with literals of the same or lower level than that of query atoms.

The following definition captures the desired restriction on recursion.

Definition 8. *(Programs Finitely Recursive On Lower Levels)* A program P is finitely recursive on lower levels w.r.t a ground query G iff there exists a level mapping characterization l of the well-founded model of P such that each ground atom A depends on finitely many ground atoms of level less then or equal to the level of G. In other words, the cardinality of the set $\{B \mid A \triangleright B$ and $l(B) \le l(G)\}$ is finite for all A.

Now, given a program which is finitely recursive on lower levels, we can prove finiteness of the stratified relevant universe and subprogram.

Proposition 3. *Given a program P, a (partial) interpretation I and an I-partial level mapping l_P. The following condition holds: if P is finitely recursive on lower levels, then for all ground queries G, $U^*_{rel}(P, G)$ and P^*_G are finite.*

Example 1. (Programs Finitely Recursive On Lower Levels)
$$P : \{p(f(X)) \leftarrow p(X), q(X),$$
$$q(a) \leftarrow s(f(X)), r(X),$$
$$r(a) \leftarrow r(a).\} \qquad G :\leftarrow p(f(a)).$$
Both $U_{rel}(P, G)$ and P_G are infinite for this program. It happens because of the second rule: $q(a)$ depends on an infinite sequence of atoms of the form $s(f^m(X)), m > 0$ and $r(f^n(X)), n \ge 0$. However, given a level mapping characterization l_P(as defined above), we have $l_P(p(f(a))) = 3$ and $l_P(r(a)) = 1$, and at the same time $\{s(f^m(a)), r(f^n(a)) | m > 1, n > 0\} \not\subseteq dom(l)$. It leaves all the rules $q(a) \leftarrow s(f^m(a)), r(f^n(a))$ with $m > 1, n > 0$ out of our P^*_G:
$$P'_G : \{p(f(a)) \leftarrow p(X), q(a), \qquad P^*_G : \{p(f(a)) \leftarrow q(a),$$
$$q(a) \leftarrow s(f(X)), r(a), \qquad q(a) \leftarrow r(a),$$
$$r(a) \leftarrow r(a)\} \qquad\qquad r(a) \leftarrow r(a)\}$$

4.2   Programs of Finite Level

In this subsection we define another class of programs with semi-decidable query evaluation: programs of finite level. The property of *stratified relevance* is also central for their definition, but instead of limiting certain dependency paths to be finite, we now require finiteness of every level in the level mapping characterization of the well-founded model. Indeed, if we drop the "finite recursiveness" condition, we have to use other means that would guarantee semi-decidability.

To provide "safe" query evaluation, we have to take care of two aspects. First, when we "stay" within the same level, then a dependency path which we might take must be finite. Second, there is only a finite number of levels to look at. The first condition given above can be solved by introducing a class of programs with finite levels, the second by restricting the level of query atoms.

Definition 9. *(Programs of Finite Level)* A logic program P is called of finite level *if there exists a level mapping characterization of the well-founded model of P with a level mapping l such that $l^{-1}(\alpha)$ is finite for all ordinals α.*

In other words, in programs of finite level, the number of atoms of level α, denoted as Λ_α, is finite for all α.

Definition 10. *(ω-Restricted Query or Goal)* A query or goal G is ω-restricted *(w.r.t. some I-partial level mapping l) iff all its atoms are of level less than ω.*

Suppose P is a program and G a ground ω-restricted query. Due to the stratification of the well-founded semantics, we can use the stratified relevant universe, viz. the relevant universe restricted to the levels less than or equal to those of query atoms.

Proposition 4. *Given a program P, a (partial) interpretation I and an I-partial level mapping l_P. If P is a program of finite level and G an ω-restricted ground query, then $U^*_{rel}(P, G)$ and P^*_G are finite.*

Example 2. (Programs Of Finite Level)
$$P : \{p(a),$$
$$p(f(X)) \leftarrow p(X),$$
$$q(a) \leftarrow \neg p(X),$$
$$q(f(X)) \leftarrow q(X),$$
$$r(a) \leftarrow \neg p(a), q(X).\} \quad G :\leftarrow r(a).$$
An example level mapping characterization of the well-founded model of P is given by l_P (as defined in Section 3):

l_P	l_P^{-1}
$\vdots$	$\vdots$
n	$p(f^{n-1}(a)), \neg q(f^{n-2}(a))$
$\vdots$	$\vdots$
2	$p(f(a)), \neg r(a), \neg q(a)$
1	$p(a)$
0	$\emptyset$

The level mapping l_P for this program has finite levels, even though its dependency graph contains infinite dependency chains of atoms with predicates q and p. We see that it leaves us with a finite stratified relevant subprogram, P^*_G:
$$U^*_{rel}(P, G) : \{r(a), p(a), q(a), p(f(a))\}$$
$$P^*_G : \quad \{p(a); p(f(a)) \leftarrow p(a); q(a) \leftarrow \neg p(a);$$
$$q(a) \leftarrow \neg p(f(a)); r(a) \leftarrow \neg p(a), q(a)\}$$

5 Decidability Results

Due to finiteness of $U^*_{rel}(P,G)$ and P^*_G shown for both classes of programs in Propositions 3 and 4, we prove that query evaluation for programs is decidable.

Theorem 2. *Given a program P and a level mapping characterization l_P of the well-founded model of P, the following conditions hold:*

i *if P is finitely recursive on lower levels, then for all ground queries G, the truth value of G under the well-founded model of P is decidable.*

ii *if P is a program of finite level and G a ground ω-restricted query, then the truth value of G under the well-founded model of P is decidable.*

It follows immediately that existentially quantified goals are semi-decidable. The existential closure of G is denoted by $\exists G$.

Corollary 1. *Given a program P and a level mapping characterization l_P of the well-founded model of P, the following conditions hold:*

i *if P is finitely recursive on lower levels, then for all ground queries of the form $\exists G$, the truth value of $\exists G$ under the well-founded model of P is semi-decidable.*

ii *if P is of finite level, then for all ω-restricted queries $\exists G$, the truth value of $\exists G$ under the well-founded model of P is semi-decidable.*

6 Related Work and Conclusions

The work on programs finitely recursive on lower levels and of finite level was inspired by the paper of Bonatti [5] on finitary programs. Work in a similar direction comprises papers on acyclic programs [8], acceptable programs [9], Φ-accessible programs [10,11], and (locally) stratified programs [12,13]. This work concerns Prolog or semantics other than the well-founded semantics. Nevertheless, some results carry over directly to the well-founded semantics by means of well-known relationships between different semantics.

Methods for top-down computation of queries under the WFS are presented in [14,4], lacking, however, a satisfactory non-procedural characterization of the fragment of the well-founded semantics which is being computed.

We presented (semi-)decidable fragments of the well-founded semantics. The corresponding program classes constitute expressive fragments of logic programming under the well-founded semantics. Our results show how queries can be answered by using only a strict subprogram of the ground instantiation of the program, that is, the (stratified) relevant subprogram.

While our results are–to the best of our knowledge–the very first ones which address decidability under the well-founded semantics, we also notice a major drawback of the initial results presented in this paper: Decidability under the described fragments rests on the knowledge of a suitable level mapping characterization, the computation of which is in general itself undecidable. However, our results simplify the matter considerably, as programmers usually keep track of the syntactic and semantic dependencies between literals occurring in their programs, which essentially boils down to keeping track of a suitable level mapping. We therefore believe that this restriction of our results–albeit not entirely satisfactory from a theoretical perspective–is much less severe in practice. This issue, however, will need to be investigated in future work.

References

1. Schlipf, J.S.: The expressive powers of the logic programming semantics. In: Selected papers of the 9th annual ACM SIGACT-SIGMOD-SIGART symposium on Principles of database systems, Orlando, FL, USA, pp. 64–86. Academic Press, Inc. London (1995)
2. van Gelder, A., Ross, K.A., Schlipf, J.S.: The well-founded semantics for general logic programs. Journal of the ACM 38(3), 620–650 (1991)
3. Kifer, M., Lausen, G., Wu, J.: Logical Foundations of Object-Oriented and Frame-Based Languages. Journal of the ACM 42, 741–843 (1995)
4. Rao, P., Sagonas, K., Swift, T., Warren, D., Freire, J.: XSB: A System for Effciently Computing WFS. In: Logic Programming and Non-monotonic Reasoning, pp. 431–441 (1997)
5. Bonatti, P.A.: Reasoning with infinite stable models. Artificial Intelligence 156(1), 75–111 (2004)
6. Dix, J.: A classification theory of semantics of normal logic programs: II. Weak Properties. Fundamenta Informaticae 22(3), 257–288 (1995)
7. Hitzler, P., Wendt, M.: A uniform approach to logic programming semantics. Theory and Practice of Logic Programming 5(1–2), 123–159 (2005)
8. Apt, K.R., Bezem, M.: Acyclic programs. New Generation Computing 9(3-4), 335–365 (1991)
9. Apt, K., Pedreschi, D.: Reasoning about termination of pure prolog programs. Information and Computation 106, 109–157 (1993)
10. Hitzler, P., Seda, A.K.: Generalized Metrics and Uniquely Determined Logic Programs. Theoretical Computer Science 305(1–3), 187–219 (2003)
11. Hitzler, P., Seda, A.K.: Characterizations of classes of programs by three-valued operators. In: Gelfond, M., Leone, N., Pfeifer, G. (eds.) LPNMR 1999. LNCS (LNAI), vol. 1730, pp. 357–371. Springer, Heidelberg (1999)
12. Apt, K.R., Blair, H.A., Walker, A.: Towards a theory of declarative knowledge. In: Minker, J. (ed.) Foundations of Deductive Databases and Logic Programming, pp. 89–148. Morgan Kaufmann, Los Altos (1988)
13. Przymusinski, T.: On the declarative semantics of deductive databases and logic programs. In: Minker, J. (ed.) Foundations of Deductive Databases and Logic Programming, pp. 193–216. Morgan Kaufmann, Los Altos (1988)
14. Chen, W., Swift, T., Warren, D.: Efficient Top-Down Computation of Queries under the Well-Founded Semantics. Journal of Logic Programming 24(3), 161–199 (1995)

A Rule-Based Approach for Reasoning About Collaboration Between Smart Web Services

Marco Alberti[1], Federico Chesani[2], Marco Gavanelli[1], Evelina Lamma[1],
Paola Mello[2], Marco Montali[2], and Paolo Torroni[2]

[1] Dipartimento di Ingegneria – Università di Ferrara – Italy
{marco.gavanelli,marco.alberti,lme}@unife.it
[2] DEIS – Università di Bologna – Italy
{fchesani,pmello,mmontali,ptorroni}@deis.unibo.it

Abstract. We present a vision of smart, goal-oriented web services that reason about other services' policies and evaluate the possibility of future interactions. We assume web services whose behavioural interface is specified in terms of reactive rules. Such rules can be made public, in order for other web services to answer the following question: "is it possible to inter-operate with a given web service and achieve a given goal?". In this article we focus on the underlying reasoning process, and we propose a declarative and operational abductive logic programming-based framework, called WAV^e. We show how this framework can be used for a-priori verification of web services interaction.

1 Introduction

Service Oriented Computing (SOC) is rapidly emerging as a new programming paradigm, propelled by the wide availability of network infrastructures, such as the Internet. Web service-based technologies are an implementation of SOC, aimed at overcoming the intrinsic difficulties of integrating different platforms, operating systems, languages, etc., into new applications. It is in the spirit of SOC to take off-the-shelf solutions, like web services, and compose them into new applications. Service composition is very attractive for its support to rapid prototyping and possibility to create complex applications from simple elements.

If we adopt the SOC paradigm, how to exploit the potential of a growing base of web services, in order to decide which service could be used for inter-operating, becomes a strategic issue. A partial answer is given by service discovery through yellow pages or other registries. This solves part of the problem: as through discovery we only know that there are some potentially useful services, but understanding whether interacting with them will be profitable or detrimental is far from being a trivial question. In this article we consider web serivces that need to understand, pairwise, and based on a run-time exchange of policies, if they can inter-operate or not. We present a vision of smart, goal-oriented web services that reason about other services' specifications, with the aim to separate out those that can lead to a fruitful interaction. We assume that each web service publishes, alongside with its WSDL, its *behavioural interface specification*.

M. Marchiori, J.Z. Pan, and C. de Sainte Marie (Eds.): RR 2007, LNCS 4524, pp. 279–288, 2007.

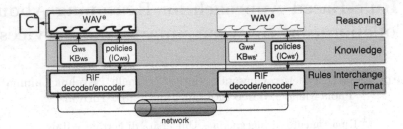

Fig. 1. The architecture of WAV^e

By reasoning on the information available about other web services' behavioural interface, each web service can verify which goals can be reached by interacting.

To achieve our vision, we propose a proof theoretic approach, based on computational logic – in fact, on abductive logic programming. We formalise service policies in a declarative language which is a modification of the $\mathcal{S}$CIFF language [7]. Policies are defined with *integrity constraints* ($\mathcal{IC}$s): a sort of reactive rules used to generate and reason about expectations on possible evolutions of a given interaction. We believe that, as advocated by Alferes et al. [9], an approach based on logic programming allows us to express knowledge in form of rules and to make inference with them. As claimed in [11], a rule-based approach to reactivity on the Web provides several benefits over conventional approaches. Rules are easy to understand for humans, and requirements often already come in the form of rules; they are well-suited for processing and analyzing by machines, and can be managed in a centralized knowledge base or distributed over the Web.

Based on $\mathcal{S}$CIFF, we propose a new declarative semantics and a proof-procedure that combines forward, reactive reasoning with backward, goal-oriented reasoning. The new framework, called WAV^e (Web-service Abductive Verification), features a language for logically defining the behavioural interface of web services (suitably encoded in RuleML), primitives for acquiring rules from the web and reasoning about them, and goal-directed discovery of web services with whom interaction could be successful.

2   The WAV^e Framework

Fig. 1 depicts our general reference architecture. The layered design of a web service has WAV^e at the top of the stack, performing reasoning based on its own knowledge and on the specifications of other web services. Web services exchange their specifications/policies encoded in a Rule Interchange Format (RIF).

In WAV^e, the observable behaviour of web services is represented by *events*:
$$Event ::= \mathbf{H}(Sender, Receiver, Message, Time).$$
Since we focus on (explicit) interaction between web services, events represent exchanged messages. Events are hypothesised, when reasoning about the capabilities of a given service. Each web service tries to foresee the future course of events that will happen, assuming that its own policies, encoded in the published

specifications, will be respected by the other peers. Expected events are atoms that represent a message that the web service ws is expecting will be exchanged:

$$Expectation ::= \mathbf{E}_{ws}(Sender, Receiver, Message, Time).$$

The subscript indicates the web service holding the expectation. If a corresponding event ($\mathbf{H}$) indeed happens, the expectation is *fulfilled*, otherwise it is *violated*.

Web service specifications in WAV^e are relations among happened and expected events, expressed by an Abductive Logic Program (ALP). In general, an ALP [15] is a triplet $\langle P, Ab, IC \rangle$, where P is a logic program, Ab is a set of predicates named *abducibles*, and IC is a set of integrity constraints. Intuitively, P contains definitions of predicates, Ab represents unknown predicates (not defined in P), and IC constrains the way elements of Ab are hypothesised, or "abduced". Reasoning in ALP is usually goal-directed: given a goal $\mathcal{G}$, the aim is to find a set of hypotheses $\Delta \subseteq Ab$ such that $P \cup \Delta \models \mathcal{G}$ and $P \cup \Delta \models IC$.

Definition 1 (Behavioural Interface Specification). *Given a web service ws, its behavioural interface specification $\mathcal{P}_{ws}$ is the ALP $\langle \mathcal{KB}_{ws}, \mathcal{E}_{ws}, \mathcal{IC}_{ws} \rangle$, where $\mathcal{KB}_{ws}$ is ws's Knowledge Base, $\mathcal{E}_{ws}$ is ws's set of abducible predicates, and $\mathcal{IC}_{ws}$ is ws's set of Integrity Constraints.*

$\mathcal{E}_{ws}$ includes predicates not defined in $\mathcal{KB}_{ws}$, as well as expectations.

$\mathcal{KB}_{ws}$ is a set of clauses which declaratively specifies pieces of knowledge of the web service. In WAV^e, clauses can contain abducible literals (with signature in $\mathcal{E}_{ws}$), as well as constraints à la Constraint Logic Programming (CLP) [13].

$$
\begin{aligned}
IC &::= Body \rightarrow Head \\
Body &::= (Event|Expectation)[\wedge(Event|Expectation|Atom|Constr)]^* \\
Head &::= Disjunct\ [\ \vee Disjunct\ ]^*\ |\ false \\
Disjunct &::= (Expectation\ |\ Constr)[\ \wedge (Expectation\ |\ Constr\ |\ Atom)]^*
\end{aligned}
\tag{1}
$$

Integrity Constraints ($\mathcal{IC}s$) are forward rules, that can involve the various types of literals in our language, namely expectations, happened events, literals of predicates defined in the $\mathcal{KB}$, other abducible predicates, and CLP constraints. The syntax of $\mathcal{IC}_{ws}$ (Eq. 1) is a modification of the integrity constraints in the $\mathcal{SCIFF}$ language [7]. In particular, in WAV^e each expectation is labelled with the name of the web service that is expecting the event. Happened events ($\mathbf{H}$) are always acquired from the external in $\mathcal{SCIFF}$, while in WAV^e they are abducible during reasoning phase. Intuitively, the operational behaviour of $\mathcal{IC}s$ is similar to forward rules: whenever the body is true, the head should also be proven true.

3   Modeling in WAV^e

Let us consider the following running example, showing how the involved services are modeled in WAV^e. *Evelyn* is a customer who wants to obtain an electronic book by tomorrow, encrypted with algorithm *best*; she can pay cash or by credit card (cc), and knows two shops potentially able to satisfy her requirements.

The first shop accepts payments only with credit card and supports the encryption of goods. In our syntax, we can express that if a request arrives, then the shop will plan to reply asking for a payment, and expect the customer to pay for the good. Thus, the *eShop1* raises an expectation about its own behaviour (I should ask for money), and one about the behaviour of the peer (you should pay)[1]:

$$\mathbf{H}(X, eShop1, request(Item, enc(Alg)), T_s)$$
$$\rightarrow \mathbf{E}_{eShop1}(eShop1, X, ask(pay(Item, cc)), T_a) \qquad \text{(eShop1.1)}$$
$$\wedge \mathbf{E}_{eShop1}(X, eShop1, pay(Item, cc), T_{cc}).$$

If the shop received the money at least 48 hours earlier, it will deliver the item:

$$\mathbf{H}(X, eShop1, request(Item, enc(Alg)), T_s)$$
$$\wedge \mathbf{H}(X, eShop1, pay(Item, How), T_p) \qquad \text{(eShop1.2)}$$
$$\rightarrow \mathbf{E}_{eShop1}(eShop1, X, deliver(Item, enc(Alg)), T_s), T_p + 48 < T_s$$

eShop2 accepts payments either by cash or credit card:

$$\mathbf{H}(X, eShop2, request(Item, enc(Alg)), T_s)$$
$$\rightarrow \mathbf{E}_{eShop2}(X, eShop2, pay(Item, How), T_p), How::[cc, cash] \qquad \text{(eShop2.1)}$$
$$\wedge \mathbf{E}_{eShop2}(X, eShop2, pay(Item, How), T_{cc}).$$

Furthermore, it delivers goods in encrypted form only if the client has paid with credit card:

$$\mathbf{H}(X, eShop2, pay(Item, cash), T_p)$$
$$\rightarrow \mathbf{E}_{eShop2}(eShop2, X, deliver(Item, enc(none)), T_s) \qquad \text{(eShop2.2)}$$

$$\mathbf{H}(X, eShop2, pay(Item, cc), T_p)$$
$$\rightarrow \mathbf{E}_{eShop2}(eShop2, X, deliver(Item, enc(best)), T_s) \qquad \text{(eShop2.3)}$$

In this simple example, *Evelyn* knows the two shops and their URL. In a real world situation, the addresses could be collected from a yellow-pages service, or by advertisements broadcasted by the shops or sent directly to *Evelyn*. The known services, togheter with their corresponding URL, can be recorded in *Evelyn*'s $\mathcal{KB}$ by using a list of facts of the type $known\_service(Service, URL)$ (e.g. $known\_service(eShop1, "http://www.eShop1.com")$).

Evelyn's goal is to find a web service that provides her the book within 24 hours

$$\mathcal{G}_{evelyn} = \mathbf{E}_{evelyn}(S, evelyn, deliver(book, enc(best)), T), T \leq 24. \qquad \text{(Goal)}$$

Evelyn's $\mathcal{IC}$s say that upon request of payment, she will perform the payment, either by credit card or by cash:

$$\mathbf{H}(X, evelyn, ask(pay(Item, How)), T_p)$$
$$\rightarrow \mathbf{E}_{evelyn}(evelyn, X, pay(Item, How), T_p), How::[cc, cash] \qquad \text{(evelyn1)}$$

---

[1] The symbol "::" represents a domain constraint.

Moreover, *Evelyn* has a plan about how she could get an item; if she wants an item to be delivered her, she should *request* someone to deliver it:

$$\mathbf{E}_{evelyn}(S, evelyn, deliver(Item, enc(How)), T_d)$$
$$\rightarrow \mathbf{E}_{evelyn}(evelyn, S, request(Item, enc(How)), T_r), T_r < T_d, \qquad \text{(evelyn2)}$$
$$find\_conformant(S).$$

Predicate $find\_conformant$ is also defined in *Evelyn*'s $\mathcal{KB}$:

$$find\_conformant(Service) \leftarrow known\_service(Service, URL),$$
$$download(URL, ICS), impose\_ics(ICS).$$

Primitive *download* retrieves information from the web (and can be implemented, e.g., with the PiLLoW library [12]). In our framework, web services expose their behavioural interface on the web, so in this case *Evelyn* downloads the $\mathcal{IC}$s of the peer she wants to interact with. Finally, *impose_ics* is a meta-predicate that adds a set of implications to the current set of $\mathcal{IC}$s, and is used by *Evelyn* to put its own policies togheter with those of the other peer.

4   Declarative and Operational Semantics

We assume that all web services have their own behavioural interface specified in the language of $\mathcal{IC}$s. This behavioural interface could be thought of as an extension of WSDL, that can be used by other web services to reason about the specifications, or to check if inter-operability is possible.

The web service initiating the interaction has a goal $\mathcal{G}$, which is a given state of affairs. Typical goals are to access resources, retrieve information, or obtain services from another web service. $\mathcal{G}$ can be any conjunction of expectations, CLP constraints, and any other literals, in the syntax of $\mathcal{IC}_{ws}$ *Disjuncts* (Eq. 1).

A web service ws reasons about the possibility to achieve a goal $\mathcal{G}$ by interacting with a peer ws' using $\mathcal{KB}_{ws}$, $\mathcal{IC}_{ws}$, $\mathcal{G}$, and the information obtained about ws''s policies, $\mathcal{IC}_{ws'}$ (Fig. 1). The idea is to obtain, through abductive reasoning, a possible course of events that together with $\mathcal{KB}_{ws}$ entails $\mathcal{IC}_{ws} \cup \mathcal{IC}_{ws'}$ and $\mathcal{G}$.

Definition 2 (Possible interaction about $\mathcal{G}$). *A possible interaction about a goal $\mathcal{G}$ between two web services ws and ws' is an $\mathcal{A}$-minimal [6] set $\mathbf{HAP} \cup \mathbf{EXP} \cup \Delta A$ such that Eq. 2, 3 and 4 hold:*

$$\mathcal{KB}_{ws} \cup \mathbf{HAP} \cup \mathbf{EXP} \cup \Delta A \models \mathcal{G} \qquad (2)$$
$$\mathcal{KB}_{ws} \cup \mathbf{HAP} \cup \mathbf{EXP} \cup \Delta A \models \mathcal{IC}_{ws} \cup \mathcal{IC}_{ws'} \qquad (3)$$
$$\mathcal{KB}_{ws} \cup \mathbf{HAP} \cup \mathbf{EXP} \cup \Delta A \models \mathbf{E}_X(X, Receiver, Action, Time) \rightarrow \qquad (4)$$
$$\mathbf{H}(X, Receiver, Action, Time).$$

where $\mathbf{HAP}$ is a conjunction of $\mathbf{H}$ atoms, $\mathbf{EXP}$ a conjunction of $\mathbf{E}$ atoms, and ΔA a conjunction of abducible atoms.

We ground the notion of entailment on a model theoretic semantics defined for Abductive Disjunctive Logic Programs [6], a slight modification of the semantics presented in [17]. Rule 4 means that we assume all the web services will behave rationally, i.e., they will perform all actions that fulfil their own expectations.

Note that currently in our framework web services do not expose their knowledge base, but only the integrity constraints. However, in general integrity constraints can involve predicates defined in the $\mathcal{KB}$. In this case, the web service ws that reasons upon the specifications of ws' will make hypotheses on the possible truth value of the predicates defined in the (unknown) $\mathcal{KB}_{ws'}$; such hypotheses are abduced and recorded in the set ΔA. [2]

Among all possible interactions about $\mathcal{G}$, some of them are fruitful, and some are not. An interaction only based on expectations which are not matched by corresponding events is not fruitful: for example, the goal of ws might not have a corresponding event, thus $\mathcal{G}$ is not actually reached, but only *expected*. Or, one of the web services could be waiting for a message from the other fellow, which will never arrive, thus undermining the inter-operability.

We select, among the possible interactions, those whose history satisfies all the expectations of both the web services. After the abductive phase, we have a verification phase in which there are no abducibles, and in which the previously abduced predicates **H** and **E** are now considered as defined by atoms in **HAP** and **EXP**, and they have to match. If there is a possible interaction satisfying all expectations, then ws has found a sequence of actions that obtains the goal.

Definition 3 (Possible interaction achieving $\mathcal{G}$). *Given two web services, ws and ws', and a goal $\mathcal{G}$, a possible interaction achieving $\mathcal{G}$ is a possible interaction about $\mathcal{G}$ satisfying (for all $X \in \{ws, ws'\}$)*

$$\mathbf{HAP} \cup \mathbf{EXP} \models \mathbf{E}_X(S, R, Action, T) \leftrightarrow \mathbf{H}(S, R, Action, T) \tag{5}$$

Intuitively, the "$\rightarrow$" implication in Eq. 5 avoids situations in which a web service waits for an event that the peer will never produce. The "$\leftarrow$" implication avoids that one web service sends unexpected messages, which in the best case may not be understood (and in the worst cases may lead to faulty behaviour).

4.1   Operational Semantics

The operational semantics is a modification of the $\mathcal{S}$CIFF proof-procedure [7]. $\mathcal{S}$CIFF was initially developed to specify and verify agent interaction protocols in open environments. It processes events drawing from **HAP** and abduces expectations, checking that all of them are fulfilled by a happened event.

WAV^e extends $\mathcal{S}$CIFF and abduces **H** events as well as expectations. The events history is not taken as input, but all possible interactions are hypothesised. Moreover, in WAV^e events not matched by an expectation (acceaptble in an open scenario) cannot be part of a *possible interaction achieving* the goal. For this reason, in WAV^e a new transition labels each **H** events with an *expected* flag as soon as a matching expectation is abduced. At the end of the derivation,

---

[2] Possibly, the result of the abductive phase can be sent to the peer ws', that can accept or refuse such a proposal. In other words, a contracting phase could be initiated.

unflagged **H** will cause failure. Also, in WAV^e new $\mathcal{IC}s$ can be dinamically added. A transition accounts for this need: if the selected literal is $impose\_ics(X)$ it adds the set X to the $\mathcal{IC}s$.

Finally, note that soundness and completeness results, proven for the $\mathcal{S}$CIFF proof-procedure under reasonable assumptions, also hold for WAV^e. In particular, adding dynamically new $\mathcal{IC}s$ can be performed in $\mathcal{S}$CIFF, because the success nodes do not change if $\mathcal{IC}s$ are dynamically added with respect to the case in which they are stated from the beginning of the derivation. [3]

5   Verification

WAV^e supports different types of verification, using the same description of web services in terms of $\mathcal{IC}s$. For space reasons, we will consider only the a-priori verification, in which web services check whether there exists a possible interaction for obtaining the desired goal. After finding the possible interactions achieving its goal, the service can submit them to the other party, to establish an agreement, which could be considered as a contract, where the allowed interactions are (implicitly) listed. At this step both web services know which are the approved communications, so if they stick to what has been agreed the interaction should be successful. However, at execution time violations could always happen: on-the-fly verification aims at finding such possible violations. We have addressed this issue in [5], where the same web service specification is used to verify if the interacting parties actually behave in a conformant manner.

5.1   A-Priori Verification

Starting from her goal (Eq. Goal), *Evelyn* abduces that she wants the electronic *book* delivered to her within one day (24 hours):

$$\mathbf{E}_{evelyn}(S, evelyn, deliver(book, enc(best)), T), T \leq 24. \tag{6}$$

This expectation triggers the Rule evelyn2, and another expectation is abduced. By *rationality* (Eq. 4), such expectation becomes a happened event

$$\mathbf{H}(evelyn, S, request(book, enc(best)), T_r), T_r < 24. \tag{7}$$

Now, *Evelyn* invokes $find\_conformant$, that will choose one of the shops, download its interface, and test if it is conformant. Let us suppose to start with *eShop*1: rule eShop1.1 will trigger, as its antecedent is true because of event (7).

*eShop*1 is thus supposed to generate two expectations: it will ask *Evelyn* to pay by *cc*, and will expect *Evelyn* to do it. Again, by rationality, the expectation

---

[3] One way to see this property is using a lemma of the soundness theorem [7]. To prove that an $\mathcal{IC}$ can be added dynamically, it is enough to insert in the body a fictitious event and add such event dynamically. Propagation of this $\mathcal{IC}$ is thus delayed until such event occurs. The effect is the same as adding the $\mathcal{IC}$ dynamically.

of *eShop*1 about its own behaviour becomes a happened event, and *Evelyn* will react to it by performing the payment:

$$\mathbf{H}(eShop1, evelyn, ask(pay(book, cc)), T_a) \wedge How :: [cc, cash]$$
$$\mathbf{H}(evelyn, eShop1, pay(book, cc), T_p).$$

*eShop*1 can now trigger its Rule eShop1.2, generating an expectation about its own behaviour, that will be translated by *rationality* into the event:

$$\mathbf{H}(eShop1, evelyn, deliver(book, enc(best)), T_s) \wedge T_p + 48 < T_s.$$

Now the proof-procedure tries to match such event with *Evelyn*'s expectation (6). The propagation of CLP constraints infers $T_p < -24$, reminding *Evelyn* that she should have made her request one day earlier. The proof-procedure signals a deadline violation: there is no way to obtain the book on time from *eShop*1.

Evelyn can now download the behavioural interface of *eShop*2. Since the behaviour of *eShop*2 depends on the chosen payment method, we have two possible interactions. In the first one she pays by cash, obtaining the following history:

$$\mathbf{H}(evelyn, eShop2, request(book, enc(best)), T_r), T_r < 24$$
$$\mathbf{H}(eShop2, evelyn, ask(pay(book, cash)), T_a)$$
$$\mathbf{H}(evelyn, eShop2, pay(book, cash), T_p)$$
$$\mathbf{H}(eShop2, evelyn, deliver(book, enc(none)), T_s).$$

This time there are no missed deadlines, but the book is sent unencrypted: *Evelyn*'s expectation (6) is not matched by any event. Luckily, *Evelyn* has another branch to explore, i.e. the one in which she actually pays by *cc*. In this case, *eShop*2 will use the *best* algorithm (rule eShop2.3): the generated history satisfies all expectations of both peers, thus *eShop*2 is considered conformant.

6   Rule Mark-Up

In WAV^e, the $\mathcal{IC}$s can be exchanged between web services, as well as advertised together with their WSDL. As the exchanged information is made of rules, the natural choice for the web-friendly interchange format is RuleML [3].

WAV^e embeds two types of rules: $\mathcal{IC}$s and clauses. $\mathcal{IC}$s are forward rules, used to react to events and generate new expectations. Clauses are backward rules, used to plan, reason upon events and perform proactive reasoning. RuleML 0.9 contains a *direction* attribute to represent both kinds of rules. Being based on abduction, WAV^e can deal both with negation as failure and negation by default, that have an appropriate tagging in RuleML. In this work, we only used standard RuleML syntax; in future work we might be interested in distinguishing between defined and abducible predicates, or between expectations and events.

WAV^e was implemented in SICStus Prolog, which contains an implementation of PiLLoW [12], making it easy to access information on the web, and an XML parser, useful to easily implement a bidirectional RuleML parser.

7   Discussion and Related Work

WAV^e is a framework for defining declaratively the behavioural interface of web services, and for testing the possibility of fruitful interaction between them. It uses and extends a technology initially developed for online compliance verification of agent interaction to protocols [7]. The extension of $\mathcal{S}$CIFF to the context of web services, centering around the concept of policies seems very promising.

In a companion paper [6] we propose the use of $\mathcal{S}$CIFF in the context of discovery engines. We present a fundamentally different architecture, in which a third party (i.e. a discovery engine) reasons on behalf of the requesting web service. Specifically, we focus on the "contracting" stage of service discovery, in which, following ontological matchmaking, the third party needs to understand if there exists a concrete interaction between the "requestor" and a "provider" web service that achieves a given requestor's objective. D ifferently from what we show here, such interaction is not defined based on a "total expectation" concept (see Section 4, Eq. 5), but it may include "unexpected" events, which leads to a different semantics. This is due to the different architecture, in which the third party has to reason under the assumption of incomplete knowledge – thus even sequences of events that are not totally expected by the third party may lead to achieving the requestor's objective. We are working on the combination of the two proposed approaches into a unified architecture.

The idea of policies for web services and policy-based reasoning is also adopted by many other authors, among which Finin et al. [14], and Bradshaw et al. [18]. The first has an emphasis on representation of actions, the latter on the deontic semantic aspects of web service interaction. Previous work on $\mathcal{S}$CIFF addressed the links between deontic operators and expectation-based reasoning [8].

The outcome of the WAV^e reasoning process could be intended as a sort of "contract agreement", provided that each peer is tightly bounded to the policies it has previously published. The dynamic agreement on contracts (e-contracting) is addressed in [10], where Situated Courteous Logic is adopted for reasoning about rules that define business provisions policies.

In this work we mainly focus on the reasoning process upon the policies of both the peers, without considering ontologies. Many other approaches focus on the latter issue (as for example OWL-S [2]), hence our proposal could be seen as a complementary functionality. In [1] it is proposed a language for semantic web service specification (using logic), and a notion of *mediator* is introduced to overcome differences between ontologies. In [16], the authors present a framework for automated web service discovery that uses the Web Service Modeling Ontology (WSMO) as the conceptual model, and distinguishes between a discovery phase and a contracting phase. Both the approaches perform hypothetical reasoning; however, in [16,1], only the client's goal is considered, while in WAV^e also behavioural interfaces are taken into account. Therefore, our framework can be exploited to verify interoperability between behavioural interfaces [4].

Acknowledgements. This work has been partially supported by the MIUR PRIN 2005 projects *Specification and verification of agent interaction proto-*

cols and *Vincoli e preferenze come formalismo unificante per l'analisi di sistemi informatici e la soluzione di problemi reali*, and by the MIUR FIRB project *Tecnologie Orientate alla Conoscenza per Aggregazioni di Imprese in Internet.*

References

1. http://www.w3.org/Submission/SWSF-SWSL
2. OWL-S. http://www.daml.org/services/owl-s
3. Adi, A., Stoutenburg, S., Tabet, S. (eds.): RuleML 2005. LNCS, vol. 3791. Springer, Heidelberg (2005)
4. Alberti, M., Chesani, F., Gavanelli, M., Lamma, E., Mello, P., Montali, M.: An abductive framework for a-priori verification of web services. In: PPDP (2006)
5. Alberti, M., Chesani, F., Gavanelli, M., Lamma, E., Mello, P., Montali, M., Storari, S., Torroni, P.: In: Bravetti, M., Núñez, M., Zavattaro, G. (eds.) WS-FM 2006. LNCS, vol. 4184, Springer, Heidelberg (2006)
6. Alberti, M., Chesani, F., Gavanelli, M., Lamma, E., Mello, P., Montali, M., Torroni, P.: Contracting for dynamic location of web services: specification and reasoning with SCIFF. In: Franconi, E., Kifer, M., May, W. (eds.) ESWC. LNCS, Springer, Heidelberg (2007)
7. Alberti, M., Chesani, F., Gavanelli, M., Lamma, E., Mello, P., Torroni, P.: Verifiable agent interaction in abductive logic programming: the SCIFF framework. ACM Transactions on Computational Logics. Accepted for publication.
8. Alberti, M., Gavanelli, M., Lamma, E., Mello, P., Sartor, G., Torroni, P.: Mapping deontic operators to abductive expectations. Computational and Mathematical Organization Theory 12(2–3), 205–225 (2006)
9. Alferes, J., Damásio, C., Pereira, L.: Semantic web logic programming tools. In: Bry, F., Henze, N., Małuszyński, J. (eds.) PPSWR 2003. LNCS, vol. 2901, pp. 16–32. Springer, Heidelberg (2003)
10. Bhansali, S., Grosof, N.: Extending the sweetdeal approach for e-procurement using sweetrules and ruleml. In: Adi. et al. [3]
11. Bry, F., Eckert, M.: Twelve theses on reactive rules for the web. In: Proc. of the Workshop on Reactivity on the Web, Munich, Germany (March 2006)
12. Gras, D., Hermenegildo, M.: Distributed WWW programming using CiaoProlog and the PiLLoW library. TPLP 1(3), 251–282 (2001)
13. Jaffar, J., Maher, M.: Constraint logic programming: a survey. Journal of Logic Programming 19–20, 503–582 (1994)
14. Kagal, L., Finin, T.W., Joshi, A.: A policy based approach to security for the semantic web. In: Fensel, D., Sycara, K.P., Mylopoulos, J. (eds.) ISWC 2003. LNCS, vol. 2870, Springer, Heidelberg (2003)
15. Kakas, A.C., Kowalski, R.A., Toni, F.: Abductive Logic Programming. Journal of Logic and Computation 2(6), 719–770 (1993)
16. Kifer, M., Lara, R., Polleres, A., Zhao, C., Keller, U., Lausen, H., Fensel, D.: A logical framework for web service discovery. In: ISWC Worshop, Hiroshima (2004)
17. Sakama, C., Inoue, K.: Abductive logic programming and disjunctive logic programming: their relationship and transferability. Journal of Logic Programming 44(1-3), 75–100 (2000)
18. Uszok, A., Bradshaw, J., Jeffers, R., Tate, A., Dalton, J.: Applying KAoS services to ensure policy compliance for semantic web services workflow composition and enactment. In: McIlraith, S.A., Plexousakis, D., van Harmelen, F. (eds.) ISWC 2004. LNCS, vol. 3298, pp. 425–440. Springer, Heidelberg (2004)

Tightly Integrated Fuzzy Description Logic Programs Under the Answer Set Semantics for the Semantic Web

Thomas Lukasiewicz[1],* and Umberto Straccia[2]

[1] DIS, Università di Roma "La Sapienza", Via Salaria 113, I-00198 Rome, Italy
lukasiewicz@dis.uniroma1.it
[2] ISTI-CNR, Via G. Moruzzi 1, I-56124 Pisa, Italy
straccia@isti.cnr.it

Abstract. We present a novel approach to fuzzy dl-programs under the answer set semantics, which is a tight integration of fuzzy disjunctive programs under the answer set semantics with fuzzy description logics. From a different perspective, it is a generalization of tightly integrated disjunctive dl-programs by fuzzy vagueness in both the description logic and the logic program component. We show that the new formalism faithfully extends both fuzzy disjunctive programs and fuzzy description logics, and that under suitable assumptions, reasoning in the new formalism is decidable. Furthermore, we present a polynomial reduction of certain fuzzy dl-programs to tightly integrated disjunctive dl-programs. We also provide a special case of fuzzy dl-programs for which deciding consistency and query processing have both a polynomial data complexity.

1 Introduction

The *Semantic Web* [1,6] aims at an extension of the current World Wide Web by standards and technologies that help machines to understand the information on the Web so that they can support richer discovery, data integration, navigation, and automation of tasks. The main ideas behind it are to add a machine-readable meaning to Web pages, to use ontologies for a precise definition of shared terms in Web resources, to use KR technology for automated reasoning from Web resources, and to apply cooperative agent technology for processing the information of the Web.

The Semantic Web consists of several hierarchical layers, where the *Ontology layer*, in form of the *OWL Web Ontology Language* [29,11], is currently the highest layer of sufficient maturity. OWL consists of three increasingly expressive sublanguages, namely, *OWL Lite*, *OWL DL*, and *OWL Full*. OWL Lite and OWL DL are essentially very expressive description logics with an RDF syntax [11]. As shown in [9], ontology entailment in OWL Lite (resp., OWL DL) reduces to knowledge base (un)satisfiability in the description logic $\mathcal{SHIF}(\mathbf{D})$ (resp., $\mathcal{SHOIN}(\mathbf{D})$). As a next step in the development of the Semantic Web, one aims especially at sophisticated representation and reasoning capabilities for the *Rules*, *Logic*, and *Proof layers* of the Semantic Web.

---

* Alternate address: Institut für Informationssysteme, Technische Universität Wien, Favoritenstraße 9-11, A-1040 Vienna, Austria; e-mail: lukasiewicz@kr.tuwien.ac.at

M. Marchiori, J.Z. Pan, and C. de Sainte Marie (Eds.): RR 2007, LNCS 4524, pp. 289–298, 2007.
© Springer-Verlag Berlin Heidelberg 2007

In particular, there is a large body of work on integrating rules and ontologies, which is a key requirement of the layered architecture of the Semantic Web. Significant research efforts focus on hybrid integrations of rules and ontologies, called *description logic programs* (or *dl-programs*), which are of the form $KB = (L, P)$, where L is a description logic knowledge base and P is a finite set of rules involving either queries to L in a loose integration (see especially [4,5,3]) or concepts and roles from L as unary resp. binary predicates in a tight integration (see especially [21,22,16]).

Other works explore formalisms for *handling uncertainty and vagueness/imprecision* in the Semantic Web. In particular, formalisms for dealing with uncertainty and vagueness in ontologies have been applied in ontology mapping and information retrieval. Vagueness and imprecision also abound in multimedia information processing and retrieval. Moreover, handling vagueness is an important aspect of natural language interfaces to the Web. There are several recent extensions of description logics, ontology languages, and dl-programs for the Semantic Web by probabilistic uncertainty and by fuzzy vagueness. In particular, dl-programs under probabilistic uncertainty and under fuzzy vagueness have been proposed in [14,13] and [27,28,15], respectively.

In this paper, we continue this line of research. We present *tightly integrated fuzzy description logic programs* (or simply *fuzzy dl-programs*) *under the answer set semantics*, which are a tight integration of fuzzy disjunctive programs under the answer set semantics with fuzzy generalizations of $\mathcal{SHIF}(\mathbf{D})$ and $\mathcal{SHOIN}(\mathbf{D})$. Even though there has been previous work on fuzzy positive dl-programs [27,28] and on loosely integrated fuzzy normal dl-programs [15], to our knowledge, this is the first approach to tightly integrated fuzzy disjunctive dl-programs (with default negation in rule bodies). The main contributions of this paper can be summarized as follows:

- We present a novel approach to fuzzy dl-programs, which is a tight integration of fuzzy disjunctive programs under the answer set semantics with fuzzy description logics. It is a generalization of the tightly integrated disjunctive dl-programs in [16] by fuzzy vagueness in both the description logic and the logic program component.
- We show that the new fuzzy dl-programs have nice semantic features. In particular, all their answer sets are also minimal models, and the cautious answer set semantics faithfully extends both fuzzy disjunctive programs and fuzzy description logics. Furthermore, the new approach also does not need the unique name assumption.
- As an important property, in the large class of fuzzy dl-programs that are defined over a finite number of truth values, the problems of deciding consistency, cautious consequence, and brave consequence are all decidable.
- In the extended report [17], we also present a polynomial reduction for certain fuzzy dl-programs to the tightly integrated disjunctive dl-programs in [16]. Furthermore, we delineate a special case of fuzzy dl-programs where deciding consistency and query processing have both a polynomial data complexity.

The rest of this paper is organized as follows. Section 2 recalls combination strategies and fuzzy description logics. Section 3 introduces the syntax of fuzzy dl-programs and defines their answer set semantics. In Section 4, we analyze some semantic properties of fuzzy dl-programs under the answer set semantics. Section 5 summarizes our main results and gives an outlook on future research. Note that further results and technical details are given in the extended report [17].

Table 1. Combination strategies of various fuzzy logics

	Łukasiewicz Logic	Gödel Logic	Product Logic	Zadeh Logic
$a \otimes b$	$\max(a + b - 1, 0)$	$\min(a, b)$	$a \cdot b$	$\min(a, b)$
$a \oplus b$	$\min(a + b, 1)$	$\max(a, b)$	$a + b - a \cdot b$	$\max(a, b)$
$a \rhd b$	$\min(1 - a + b, 1)$	$\begin{cases} 1 & \text{if } a \leqslant b \\ b & \text{otherwise} \end{cases}$	$\min(1, b/a)$	$\max(1 - a, b)$
$\ominus a$	$1 - a$	$\begin{cases} 1 & \text{if } a = 0 \\ 0 & \text{otherwise} \end{cases}$	$\begin{cases} 1 & \text{if } a = 0 \\ 0 & \text{otherwise} \end{cases}$	$1 - a$

2 Preliminaries

In this section, we illustrate the notions of combination strategies and fuzzy description logics through some examples; more details are given in the extended report [17].

Combination Strategies. Rather than being restricted to an ordinary binary truth value among **false** and **true**, *vague propositions* may also have a truth value strictly between **false** and **true**. In the sequel, we use the unit interval $[0, 1]$ as the set of all possible truth values, where 0 and 1 represent the ordinary binary truth values **false** and **true**, respectively. For example, the vague proposition "John is a tall man" may be more or less true, and it is thus associated with a truth value in $[0, 1]$, depending on the body height of John.

In order to combine and modify the truth values in $[0, 1]$, we assume *combination strategies*, namely, *conjunction, disjunction, implication,* and *negation strategies*, denoted $\otimes, \oplus, \rhd$, and $\ominus$, respectively, which are functions $\otimes, \oplus, \rhd \colon [0, 1] \times [0, 1] \to [0, 1]$ and $\ominus \colon [0, 1] \to [0, 1]$ that generalize the ordinary Boolean operators $\wedge, \vee, \to$, and $\neg$, respectively, to the set of truth values $[0, 1]$. As usual, we assume that combination strategies have some natural algebraic properties [17]. Note that conjunction and disjunction strategies are also called *triangular norms* and *triangular co-norms* [8], respectively.

Example 2.1. The combination strategies of various fuzzy logics are shown in Table 1.

Fuzzy Description Logics. We now illustrate fuzzy $\mathcal{SHIF}(\mathbf{D})$ and fuzzy $\mathcal{SHOIN}(\mathbf{D})$ [25,26] (see also [23]) through an example. There also exists an implementation of fuzzy $\mathcal{SHIF}(\mathbf{D})$ (the *fuzzyDL* system; see http://gaia.isti.cnr.it/~straccia). Intuitively, description logics model a domain of interest in terms of concepts and roles, which represent classes of individuals and binary relations between classes of individuals, respectively. A description logic knowledge base encodes in particular subset relationships between classes of individuals, subset relationships between binary relations between classes, the membership of individuals to classes, and the membership of pairs of individuals to binary relations between classes. In fuzzy description logics, these relationships and memberships then have a degree of truth in $[0, 1]$.

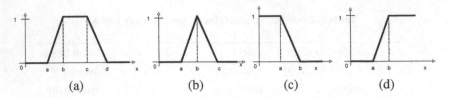

(a)   (b)   (c)   (d)

Fig. 1. (a) *Tra*-function, (b) *Tri*-function, (c) *L*-function, and (d) *R*-function

Example 2.2 (Shopping Agent). The following axioms are an excerpt of the description logic knowledge base L that conceptualizes a car selling web site:

$$Cars \sqcup Trucks \sqcup Vans \sqcup SUVs \sqsubseteq Vehicles\,; \tag{1}$$

$$PassengerCars \sqcup LuxuryCars \sqsubseteq Cars\,; \tag{2}$$

$$CompactCars \sqcup MidSizeCars \sqcup SportyCars \sqsubseteq PassengerCars\,; \tag{3}$$

$$Cars \sqsubseteq (\exists hasReview.Integer) \sqcap (\exists hasInvoice.Integer)$$
$$\sqcap (\exists hasResellValue.Integer) \sqcap (\exists hasMaxSpeed.Integer)$$
$$\sqcap (\exists hasHorsePower.Integer) \sqcap \dots\,; \tag{4}$$

$$MazdaMX5Miata: SportyCar \sqcap (\exists hasInvoice.18883)$$
$$\sqcap (\exists hasHorsePower.166) \sqcap \dots\,; \tag{5}$$

$$MitsubishiEclipseSpyder: SportyCar \sqcap (\exists hasInvoice.24029)$$
$$\sqcap (\exists hasHorsePower.162) \sqcap \dots. \tag{6}$$

Eqs. 1–3 describe the concept taxonomy of the site, while Eq. 4 describes the datatype attributes of the cars sold in the site. Eqs. 5–6 describe the properties of some sold cars.

We may then encode "costs at most about 22 000 €" and "has a power of around 150 HP" in a buyer's request through the following concepts C and D, respectively:

$$C = \exists hasInvoice.LeqAbout22000 \quad \text{and} \quad D = \exists hasHorsePower.Around150,$$

where $LeqAbout22000 = L(22000, 25000)$ and $Around150 = Tri(125, 150, 175)$ (see Fig. 1). The latter two equations define the fuzzy concepts of "at most about 22 000 €" and "around 150 HP". The former is modeled as a left shoulder function stating that if the prize is less than 22 000 €, then the degree of truth (degree of buyer's satisfaction) is 1, else the truth is linearly decreasing to 0 (reached at 25 000 €). In fact, we are modeling a case were the buyer would like to pay less than 22 000 €, though may still accept a higher price (up to 25 000 €) to a lesser degree. Similarly, the latter models the fuzzy concept "around 150 HP" as a triangular function with vertice in 150 HP.

The following fuzzy axioms are (tight) logical consequences of the above description logic knowledge base L (under the Zadeh semantics of the connectives):

$$C(MazdaMX5Miata) \geqslant 1.0\,; \quad C(MitsubishiEclipseSpyder) \geqslant 0.32\,;$$
$$D(MazdaMX5Miata) \geqslant 0.36\,; \quad D(MitsubishiEclipseSpyder) \geqslant 0.56\,.$$

3   Fuzzy Description Logic Programs

In this section, we present a tightly integrated approach to *fuzzy disjunctive description logic programs* (or simply *fuzzy dl-programs*) under the answer set semantics.

We extend the tightly integrated disjunctive description logic programs in [16], which have very nice features compared to other tightly integrated description logic programs; see [16] for more details and a comparison to related works in the literature. Observe that differently from [15] (in addition to being a tightly integrated approach to fuzzy dl-programs), the fuzzy dl-programs here are based on fuzzy description logics as in [26]. Furthermore, they additionally allow for disjunctions in rule heads. We first introduce the syntax of fuzzy dl-programs and then their answer set semantics.

The basic idea behind the tightly integrated approach in this section is as follows. Suppose that we have a fuzzy disjunctive program P. Under the answer set semantics, P is equivalent to its grounding $ground(P)$. Suppose now that some of the ground atoms in $ground(P)$ are additionally related to each other by a fuzzy description logic knowledge base L. That is, some of the ground atoms in $ground(P)$ actually represent concept and role memberships relative to L. Thus, when processing $ground(P)$, we also have to consider L. However, we only want to do it to the extent that we actually need it for processing $ground(P)$. Hence, when taking a fuzzy Herbrand interpretation $I \subseteq HB_\Phi$, we have to ensure that I represents a valid truth value assignment relative to L. In other words, the main idea behind the semantics is to interpret P relative to Herbrand interpretations that also satisfy L, while L is interpreted relative to general interpretations over a first-order domain. Thus, we modularly combine the standard semantics of fuzzy disjunctive programs and of fuzzy description logics as in [15], which allows for building on the standard techniques and the results of both areas. However, our new approach here allows for a much tighter integration of L and P.

Syntax. We assume a function-free first-order vocabulary Φ with nonempty finite sets of constant and predicate symbols. We use Φ_c to denote the set of all constant symbols in Φ. We also assume pairwise disjoint (nonempty) denumerable sets $\mathbf{A}$, $\mathbf{R}_A$, $\mathbf{R}_D$, $\mathbf{I}$, and $\mathbf{M}$ of *atomic concepts, abstract roles, datatype roles, individuals*, and *fuzzy modifiers*, respectively; see [17]. We assume that Φ_c is a subset of $\mathbf{I}$. This assumption guarantees that every ground atom constructed from atomic concepts, abstract roles, datatype roles, and constants in Φ_c can be interpreted in the description logic component. We do not assume any other restriction on the vocabularies, that is, Φ and $\mathbf{A}$ (resp., $\mathbf{R}_A \cup \mathbf{R}_D$) may have unary (resp., binary) predicate symbols in common.

Let $\mathcal{X}$ be a set of variables. A *term* is either a variable from $\mathcal{X}$ or a constant symbol from Φ. An *atom* is of the form $p(t_1, \ldots, t_n)$, where p is a predicate symbol of arity $n \geqslant 0$ from Φ, and $t_1, \ldots, t_n$ are terms. A *literal* l is an atom p or a default-negated atom $not\, p$. A *disjunctive fuzzy rule* (or simply *fuzzy rule*) r is of the form

$$a_1 \vee_{\oplus_1} \cdots \vee_{\oplus_{l-1}} a_l \leftarrow_{\otimes_0} b_1 \wedge_{\otimes_1} b_2 \wedge_{\otimes_2} \cdots \wedge_{\otimes_{k-1}} b_k \wedge_{\otimes_k}$$
$$not_{\ominus_{k+1}} b_{k+1} \wedge_{\otimes_{k+1}} \cdots \wedge_{\otimes_{m-1}} not_{\ominus_m} b_m \geqslant v, \tag{7}$$

where $l \geqslant 1$, $m \geqslant k \geqslant 0$, $a_1, \ldots, a_l, b_{k+1}, \ldots, b_m$ are atoms, $b_1, \ldots, b_k$ are either atoms or truth values from $[0,1]$, $\oplus_1, \ldots, \oplus_{l-1}$ are disjunction strategies, $\otimes_0, \ldots, \otimes_{m-1}$ are conjunction strategies, $\ominus_{k+1}, \ldots, \ominus_m$ are negation strategies, and $v \in [0,1]$. We refer to $a_1 \vee_{\oplus_1} \cdots \vee_{\oplus_{l-1}} a_l$ as the *head* of r, while the conjunction $b_1 \wedge_{\otimes_1} \ldots \wedge_{\otimes_{m-1}} not_{\ominus_m} b_m$ is the *body* of r. We define $H(r) = \{a_1, \ldots, a_l\}$ and $B(r) = B^+(r) \cup B^-(r)$, where $B^+(r) = \{b_1, \ldots, b_k\}$ and $B^-(r) = \{b_{k+1}, \ldots, b_m\}$. A *disjunctive fuzzy program* (or simply *fuzzy program* P is a finite set of fuzzy rules of the form (7). We say P is a *normal fuzzy program* iff $l = 1$ for all fuzzy rules (7) in P. We say P is a *positive fuzzy program* iff $l = 1$ and $m = k$ for all fuzzy rules (7) in P.

A *disjunctive fuzzy description logic program* (or simply *fuzzy dl-program*) $KB = (L, P)$ consists of a fuzzy description logic knowledge base L and a disjunctive fuzzy program P. It is called a *normal fuzzy dl-program* iff P is a normal fuzzy program. It is called a *positive fuzzy dl-program* iff P is a positive fuzzy program.

Example 3.1 (Shopping Agent cont'd). A fuzzy dl-program $KB = (L, P)$ is given by the fuzzy description logic knowledge base L in Example 2.2 and the set of fuzzy rules P, which contains only the following fuzzy rule (where $x \otimes y = \min(x, y)$):

$$query(x) \leftarrow_\otimes SportyCar(x) \wedge_\otimes hasInvoice(x, y_1) \wedge_\otimes hasHorsePower(x, y_2) \wedge_\otimes$$
$$LeqAbout22000(y_1) \wedge_\otimes Around150(y_2) \geqslant 1 .$$

Informally, the predicate $query$ collects all sports cars, and ranks them according to whether they cost at most around 22 000 € and have around 150 HP (such a car may be requested by a car buyer with economic needs). Another fuzzy rule is given as follows (where $\ominus x = 1 - x$ and $Around300 = Tri(250, 300, 350)$):

$$query'(x) \leftarrow_\otimes SportyCar(x) \wedge_\otimes hasInvoice(x, y_1) \wedge_\otimes hasMaxSpeed(x, y_2) \wedge_\otimes$$
$$not_\ominus LeqAbout22000(y_1) \wedge_\otimes Around300(y_2) \geqslant 1 .$$

Informally, this rule collects all sports cars, and ranks them according to whether they cost at least around 22 000 € and have a maximum speed of around 300 km/h (such a car may be requested by a car buyer with luxurious needs). Another fuzzy rule involving also a disjunction in its head is given as follows (where $x \oplus y = \max(x, y)$):

$$Small(x) \vee_\oplus Old(x) \leftarrow_\otimes Car(x) \wedge_\otimes hasInvoice(x, y) \wedge_\otimes not_\ominus GeqAbout15000(y) \geqslant 0.7 .$$

This rule says that a car costing at most around 15 000 € is either small or old. Observe here that *Small* and *Old* may be two concepts in the fuzzy description logic knowledge base L. That is, the tightly integrated approach to fuzzy dl-programs under the answer set semantics also allows for using the rules in P to express relationships between the concepts and roles in L. This is not possible in the loosely integrated approach to fuzzy dl-programs under the answer set semantics in [15], since the dl-queries of that framework can only occur in rule bodies, but not in rule heads.

Semantics. We now define the answer set semantics of fuzzy dl-programs via a generalization of the standard Gelfond-Lifschitz transformation [7].

In the sequel, let $KB = (L, P)$ be a fuzzy dl-program. A *ground instance* of a rule $r \in P$ is obtained from r by replacing every variable that occurs in r by a constant symbol from Φ_c. We denote by $ground(P)$ the set of all ground instances of rules in P. The *Herbrand base* relative to Φ, denoted HB_Φ, is the set of all ground atoms constructed with constant and predicate symbols from Φ. Observe that we define the Herbrand base relative to Φ and not relative to P. This allows for reasoning about ground atoms from the description logic component that do not necessarily occur in P. Observe, however, that the extension from P to Φ is only a notational simplification, since we can always make constant and predicate symbols from Φ occur in P by "dummy" rules such as *constant*(c) ← and $p(\mathbf{c}) \leftarrow p(\mathbf{c})$, respectively. We denote by DL_Φ the set of all ground atoms in HB_Φ that are constructed from atomic concepts in $\mathbf{A}$, abstract roles in $\mathbf{R}_A$, concrete roles in $\mathbf{R}_D$, and constant symbols in Φ_c.

We define Herbrand interpretations and the truth of fuzzy dl-programs in them as follows. An *interpretation* I is a mapping $I : HB_\Phi \rightarrow [0,1]$. We write $\mathbf{HB_\Phi}$ to denote the interpretation I such that $I(a) = 1$ for all $a \in HB_\Phi$. For interpretations I and J, we write $I \subseteq J$ iff $I(a) \leqslant J(a)$ for all $a \in HB_\Phi$, and we define the *intersection* of I and J, denoted $I \cap J$, by $(I \cap J)(a) = \min(I(a), J(a))$ for all $a \in HB_\Phi$. Observe that $I \subseteq \mathbf{HB_\Phi}$ for all interpretations I. We say that I is a *model* of a ground fuzzy rule r of the form (7), denoted $I \models r$, iff

$$I(a_1) \oplus_1 \cdots \oplus_l I(a_l) \geqslant I(b_1) \otimes_1 \cdots \otimes_{k-1} I(b_k) \otimes_k \\ \ominus_{k+1} I(b_{k+1}) \otimes_{k+1} \cdots \otimes_{m-1} \ominus_m I(b_m) \otimes_0 v. \tag{8}$$

Here, we implicitly assume that the disjunction strategies $\oplus_1, \ldots, \oplus_l$ and the conjunction strategies $\otimes_1, \ldots, \otimes_{m-1}, \otimes_0$ are evaluated from left to right. Notice also that the above definition implicitly assumes an implication strategy $\triangleright$ that is defined by $a \triangleright b = \sup\{c \in [0,1] \mid a \otimes_0 c \leqslant b\}$ for all $a, b \in [0,1]$ (and thus for $n, m \in [0,1]$ and $a = n$, it holds that $a \triangleright b \geqslant m$ iff $b \geqslant n \otimes_0 m$, if we assume that the conjunction strategy $\otimes_0$ is continuous). Observe that such a relationship between the implication strategy $\triangleright$ and the conjunction strategy $\otimes$ (including also the continuity of $\otimes$) holds in Łukasiewicz, Gödel, and Product Logic (see Table 1). We say that I is a *model* of a fuzzy program P, denoted $I \models P$, iff $I \models r$ for all $r \in ground(P)$. We say I is a *model* of a fuzzy description logic knowledge base L, denoted $I \models L$, iff $L \cup \{a = I(a) \mid a \in HB_\Phi\}$ is satisfiable. An interpretation $I \subseteq HB_\Phi$ is a *model* of a fuzzy dl-program $KB = (L, P)$, denoted $I \models KB$, iff $I \models L$ and $I \models P$. We say KB is *satisfiable* iff it has a model.

The *Gelfond-Lifschitz transform* of a fuzzy dl-program $KB = (L, P)$ relative to an interpretation $I \subseteq \mathbf{HB_\Phi}$, denoted KB^I, is defined as the fuzzy dl-program (L, P^I), where P^I is the set of all fuzzy rules obtained from $ground(P)$ by replacing all default-negated atoms $not_{\ominus_j} b_j$ by the truth value $\ominus_j I(b_j)$. We are now ready to define the answer set semantics of fuzzy dl-programs as follows.

Definition 3.1. Let $KB = (L, P)$ be a fuzzy dl-program. An interpretation $I \subseteq \mathbf{HB_\Phi}$ is an *answer set* of KB iff I is a minimal model of KB^I. We say that KB is *consistent* (resp., *inconsistent*) iff KB has an (resp., no) answer set.

We finally define the notions of *cautious* (resp., *brave*) *reasoning* from fuzzy dl-programs under the answer set semantics as follows.

Definition 3.2. Let $KB = (L, P)$ be a fuzzy dl-program. Let $a \in HB_\Phi$ and $n \in [0,1]$. Then, $a \geqslant n$ is a *cautious* (resp., *brave*) *consequence* of a fuzzy dl-program KB under the answer set semantics iff $I(a) \geqslant n$ for every (resp., some) answer set I of KB.

Example 3.2 (Shopping Agent cont'd). Consider again the fuzzy dl-program $KB = (L, P)$ of Example 3.1. The following holds for the answer set M of KB:

$$M(query(MazdaMX5Miata)) = 0.36; \qquad M(query(MitsubishiEclipseSpyder)) = 0.32.$$

4   Semantic Properties

In this section, we summarize some semantic properties (especially those relevant for the Semantic Web) of fuzzy dl-programs under the above answer set semantics.

Minimal Models. The following theorem shows that, like for ordinary disjunctive programs, every answer set of a fuzzy dl-program KB is also a minimal model of KB, and the answer sets of a positive fuzzy dl-program KB are the minimal models of KB.

Theorem 4.1. *Let $KB = (L, P)$ be a fuzzy dl-program. Then, (a) every answer set of KB is a minimal model of KB, and (b) if KB is positive, then the set of all answer sets of KB is given by the set of all minimal models of KB.*

Faithfulness. An important property of integrations of rules and ontologies is that they are a faithful [18,19] extension of both rules and ontologies.

The following theorem shows that the answer set semantics of fuzzy dl-programs faithfully extends its counterpart for fuzzy programs. That is, the answer set semantics of a fuzzy dl-program $KB = (L, P)$ with empty fuzzy description logic knowledge base L coincides with the answer set semantics of its fuzzy program P.

Theorem 4.2. *Let $KB = (L, P)$ be a fuzzy dl-program such that $L = \emptyset$. Then, the set of all answer sets of KB coincides with the set of all answer sets of the fuzzy program P.*

The next theorem shows that the answer set semantics of fuzzy dl-programs also faithfully extends the first-order semantics of fuzzy description logic knowledge bases. That is, for $a \in HB_\Phi$ and $n \in [0, 1]$, it holds that $a \geqslant n$ is true in all answer sets of a positive fuzzy dl-program $KB = (L, P)$ iff $a \geqslant n$ is true in all fuzzy first-order models of $L \cup ground(P)$. The theorem holds also when a is a ground formula constructed from HB_Φ using $\wedge$ and $\vee$, along with conjunction and disjunction strategies $\otimes$ resp. $\oplus$.

Theorem 4.3. *Let $KB = (L, P)$ be a positive fuzzy dl-program, and let $a \in HB_\Phi$ and $n \in [0, 1]$. Then, $a \geqslant n$ is true in all answer sets of KB iff $a \geqslant n$ is true in all fuzzy first-order models of $L \cup ground(P)$.*

As an immediate corollary, we obtain that $a \geqslant n$ is true in all answer sets of a fuzzy dl-program $KB = (L, \emptyset)$ iff $a \geqslant n$ is true in all fuzzy first-order models of L.

Corollary 4.1. *Let $KB = (L, P)$ be a fuzzy dl-program with $P = \emptyset$, and let $a \in HB_\Phi$ and $n \in [0, 1]$. Then, $a \geqslant n$ is true in all answer sets of KB iff $a \geqslant n$ is true in all fuzzy first-order models of L.*

Unique Name Assumption. Another aspect that may not be very desirable in the Semantic Web [10] is the *unique name assumption* (which says that any two distinct constant symbols in Φ_c represent two distinct domain objects). It turns out that we actually do not have to make this assumption, since the fuzzy description logic knowledge base of a fuzzy dl-program may very well contain or imply equalities between individuals.

This result is included in the following theorem, which shows an alternative characterization of the satisfaction of L in $I \subseteq HB_\Phi$: Rather than being enlarged by a set of axioms of exponential size, L is enlarged by a set of axioms of polynomial size. This characterization essentially shows that the satisfaction of L in I corresponds to checking that (i) I restricted to DL_Φ satisfies L, and (ii) I restricted to $HB_\Phi - DL_\Phi$ does not violate any equality axioms that follow from L. In the theorem, an equivalence relation $\sim$ on Φ_c is *admissible* with an interpretation $I \subseteq HB_\Phi$ iff $I(p(c_1, \ldots, c_n)) = I(p(c'_1, \ldots, c'_n))$ for all n-ary predicate symbols p, where $n > 0$, and constant symbols $c_1, \ldots, c_n, c'_1, \ldots, c'_n \in \Phi_c$ such that $c_i \sim c'_i$ for all $i \in \{1, \ldots, n\}$.

Theorem 4.4. *Let L be a fuzzy description logic knowledge base, and let $I \subseteq HB_\Phi$. Then, $L \cup \{a = I(a) \mid a \in HB_\Phi\}$ is satisfiable iff $L \cup \{a = I(a) \mid a \in DL_\Phi\} \cup \{c \neq c' \mid c \not\sim c'\}$ is satisfiable for some equivalence relation $\sim$ on Φ_c admissible with I.*

5   Summary and Outlook

We have presented an approach to tightly integrated fuzzy dl-programs under the answer set semantics, which generalizes the tightly integrated disjunctive dl-programs in [16] by fuzzy vagueness in both the description logic and the logic program component. We have shown that the new formalism faithfully extends both fuzzy disjunctive programs and fuzzy description logics, and that under suitable assumptions, reasoning in the new formalism is decidable. Furthermore, in [17], we have presented a polynomial reduction for certain fuzzy dl-programs to tightly integrated disjunctive dl-programs. Finally, in [17], we have also provided a special case of fuzzy dl-programs for which deciding consistency and query processing have both a polynomial data complexity.

An interesting topic for future research is to analyze the computational complexity of the main reasoning problems in fuzzy dl-programs, and to implement the approach. Another interesting issue is to extend fuzzy dl-programs by classical negation.

Acknowledgments. This work has been partially supported by a Heisenberg Professorship of the German Research Foundation (DFG). We thank the reviewers for their constructive comments, which helped to improve this work.

References

1. Berners-Lee, T.: Weaving the Web. Harper, San Francisco (1999)
2. Bobillo, F., Delgado, M., Gómez-Romero, J.: A crisp representation for fuzzy SHOIN with fuzzy nominals and general concept inclusions. In: Proc. URSW-2006 (2006)
3. Eiter, T., Iauui, G., Schindlauer, R., Tompits, H.: Effective integration of declarative rules with external evaluations for Semantic Web reasoning. In: Sure, Y., Domingue, J. (eds.) ESWC 2006. LNCS, vol. 4011, Springer, Heidelberg (2006)
4. Eiter, T., Lukasiewicz, T., Schindlauer, R., Tompits, H.: Combining answer set programming with description logics for the Semantic Web. In: Proc. KR-2004, pp. 141–151 (2004)
5. Eiter, T., Lukasiewicz, T., Schindlauer, R., Tompits, H.: Well-founded semantics for description logic programs in the Semantic Web. In: Proc. RuleML-2004, pp. 81–97 (2004)
6. Fensel, D., Wahlster, W., Lieberman, H., Hendler, J. (eds.): Spinning the Semantic Web: Bringing the World Wide Web to Its Full Potential. MIT Press, Cambridge (2002)

7. Gelfond, M., Lifschitz, V.: Classical negation in logic programs and disjunctive databases. New. Generation Comput 9(3/4), 365–386 (1991)
8. Hájek, P.: Metamathematics of Fuzzy Logic. Kluwer, Dordrecht (1998)
9. Horrocks, I., Patel-Schneider, P.F.: Reducing OWL entailment to description logic satisfiability. In: Fensel, D., Sycara, K.P., Mylopoulos, J. (eds.) ISWC 2003. LNCS, vol. 2870, pp. 17–29. Springer, Heidelberg (2003)
10. Horrocks, I., Patel-Schneider, P.F.: Position paper: A comparison of two modelling paradigms in the Semantic Web. In: Proc. WWW-2006, pp. 3–12 (2006)
11. Horrocks, I., Patel-Schneider, P.F., van Harmelen, F.: From SHIQ and RDF to OWL: The making of a web ontology language. J. Web. Sem. 1(1), 7–26 (2003)
12. Horrocks, I., Sattler, U., Tobies, S.: Practical reasoning for expressive description logics. In: Ganzinger, H., McAllester, D., Voronkov, A. (eds.) LPAR 1999. LNCS, vol. 1705, pp. 161–180. Springer, Heidelberg (1999)
13. Lukasiewicz, T.: Stratified probabilistic description logic programs. In: Proc. URSW-2005, pp. 87–97 (2005)
14. Lukasiewicz, T.: Probabilistic description logic programs. In: Proc. ECSQARU-2005, pp. 737–749, 2005. Extended version in Int. J. Approx. Reason. (in press) 2007
15. Lukasiewicz, T.: Fuzzy description logic programs under the answer set semantics for the Semantic Web. In: Proc. RuleML-2006, pp. 89–96 (2006)
16. Lukasiewicz, T.: A novel combination of answer set programming with description logics for the Semantic Web. In: Proc. ESWC-2007,To appear (2007)
17. Lukasiewicz, T., Straccia, U.: Tightly integrated fuzzy description logic programs under the answer set semantics for the Semantic Web. Report 1843-07-03, Institut für Informationssysteme, TU Wien (February 2007)
18. Motik, B., Horrocks, I., Rosati, R., Sattler, U.: Can OWL and logic programming live together happily ever after. In: Cruz, I., Decker, S., Allemang, D., Preist, C., Schwabe, D., Mika, P., Uschold, M., Aroyo, L. (eds.) ISWC 2006. LNCS, vol. 4273, pp. 501–514. Springer, Heidelberg (2006)
19. Motik, B., Rosati, R.: A faithful integration of description logics with logic programming. In: Proc. IJCAI-2007, pp. 477–482 (2007)
20. Poole, D.: The independent choice logic for modelling multiple agents under uncertainty. Artif.Intell. 94(1–2), 7–56 (1997)
21. Rosati, R.: On the decidability and complexity of integrating ontologies and rules. J. Web. Sem. 3(1), 61–73 (2005)
22. Rosati, R.: DL+log: Tight integration of description logics and disjunctive datalog. In: Proc. KR-2006, pp. 68–78 (2006)
23. Stoilos, G., Stamou, G., Tzouvaras, V., Pan, J., Horrocks, I.: Fuzzy OWL: Uncertainty and the Semantic Web. In: Proc. OWLED-2005 (2005)
24. Straccia, U.: Transforming fuzzy description logics into classical description logics. In: Proc. JELIA-2004, pp. 385–399 (2004)
25. Straccia, U.: Towards a fuzzy description logic for the Semantic Web (preliminary report). In: Gómez-Pérez, A., Euzenat, J. (eds.) ESWC 2005. LNCS, vol. 3532, pp. 167–181. Springer, Heidelberg (2005)
26. Straccia, U.: A fuzzy description logic for the Semantic Web. In: Sanchez, E. (ed.) Fuzzy Logic and the Semantic Web, Capturing Intelligence, pp. 73–90. Elsevier, Amsterdam (2006)
27. Straccia, U.: Uncertainty and description logic programs over lattices. In: E. Sanchez. (ed.) Fuzzy Logic and the Semantic Web, Capturing Intelligence, chapter 7, pp. 115–133 (2006)
28. Straccia, U.: Fuzzy description logic programs. In: Proc. IPMU-2006, pp. 1818–1825 (2006)
29. W3C. OWL web ontology language overview, W3C Recommendation. Available at www.w3.org/TR/2004/REC-owl-features-20040210 (February 10 (2004))

AceRules: Executing Rules in Controlled Natural Language

Tobias Kuhn

Department of Informatics, University of Zurich, Switzerland
tkuhn@ifi.uzh.ch
http://www.ifi.uzh.ch/cl/tkuhn

Abstract. Expressing rules in controlled natural language can bring us closer to the vision of the Semantic Web since rules can be written in the notation of the application domain and are understandable by anybody. AceRules is a prototype of a rule system with a multi-semantics architecture. It demonstrates the formal representation of rules using the controlled natural language ACE. We show that a rule language can be executable and easily understandable at the same time. AceRules is available via a web service and two web interfaces.

1 Introduction

The idea of the *Semantic Web* [4] is to transform and extend the current World Wide Web into a system that can also be understood by machines, at least to some degree. Ideally, the Semantic Web should become as pervasive as the traditional World Wide Web today. This means that a large part of the society should be able to participate and contribute, and thus we have to deal with the problem that most people feel uncomfortable with technical notations. Controlled natural languages seem to be a promising approach to overcome this problem by giving intuitive and natural representations for ontologies and rules. We present *AceRules* as a prototype of a front-end rule system to be used in the context of the Semantic Web or other environments.

The goal of AceRules is to show that controlled natural languages can be used to represent and execute formal rule systems. *Attempto Controlled English* (ACE) [9,8] is used as input and output language. ACE looks like English but avoids the ambiguities of natural language by restricting the syntax [15] and by defining a small set of interpretation rules [1]. The ACE parser[1] translates ACE texts automatically into *Discourse Representation Structures* (DRS) [7] which are a syntactical variant of first-order logic. Thus, every ACE text has a single and well-defined formal meaning. Among other features, ACE supports singular and plural noun phrases, active and passive voice, relative phrases, anaphoric references, existential and universal quantifiers, negation, and modality. ACE has successfully been used for different tasks, e.g. as a natural language OWL front-end [17] and as an ontology language for the biomedical domain [19].

---

[1] http://attempto.ifi.uzh.ch/ape

M. Marchiori, J.Z. Pan, and C. de Sainte Marie (Eds.): RR 2007, LNCS 4524, pp. 299–308, 2007.

In the following section, we will introduce the AceRules system and we will point out some of the problems involved (Sect. 2). Next, we will explain the interfaces available for AceRules (Sect. 3), and finally we will draw the conclusions (Sect. 4).

2   The AceRules System

AceRules is a multi-semantics rule system prototype using the controlled natural language ACE as input and output language. AceRules is designed for forward-chaining interpreters that calculate the complete answer set. The general approach of AceRules, however, could easily be adopted for backward-chaining interpreters. AceRules is publicly available as a web service and through two different web interfaces (see Sect. 3).

In order to clarify the functionality of AceRules, let us have a look at the following simple program. We use the term *program* for a set of rules and facts.

> If a customer has a card and does not have a code then CompanyX sends a letter
> to the customer.
> Every customer has a card.
> John is a customer.
> John does not have a code.

Submitting this program to AceRules, we get the answer shown below.[2] We use the term *answer* for the set of facts that can be derived from a program.

> John is a customer.
> CompanyX sends John a letter.
> John has a card.
> It is false that John has a code.

As we can see, the program and the answer are both in English. No other formal notations are needed for the user interaction. Even though inexperienced users might not be able to understand how the answer is inferred, they are certainly able to understand input and output and to verify that the output is some kind of conclusion of the input. This is the essential advantage of ACE over other formal knowledge representation languages.

Existing work to use natural language representations for rule systems is based on the idea of verbalizing rules that already exist in a formal representation [13,16,20]. In our approach, the controlled natural language is the *main* language that can be translated into a formal representation (parsing) and backwards (verbalizing). It is not necessary that the rules are first formalized in another language.

The rest of this section explains some of the important properties of AceRules, namely its multi-semantics architecture (Sect. 2.1), the representation of negation (Sect. 2.2), and the construction of valid programs (Sect. 2.3).

---

[2] The courteous interpreter is used here. See Sect. 2.1 for details.

2.1   Multi-semantics Architecture

AceRules is designed to support various semantics. The decision of which semantics to choose should depend on the application domain, the characteristics of the available information, and on the reasoning tasks to be performed. At the moment, AceRules incorporates three different semantics: courteous logic programs [12], stable models [10], and stable models with strong negation [11].

The original stable model semantics supports only negation as failure, but it has been extended to support also strong negation. Courteous logic programs are based on stable models with strong negation and support therefore both forms of negation. Section 2.2 will take a closer look at this issue.

None of the two forms of stable models guarantee a unique answer set. Thus, some programs can have more than one answer. In contrast, courteous logic programs generate always exactly one answer. In order to achieve this, priorities are introduced and the programs have to be acyclic.

On the basis of these properties, one should decide which semantics to choose. Since we do not want to restrict AceRules to a certain application or domain, we decided to make the semantics exchangeable.

The three semantics are implemented in AceRules as two interpreter modules. The first interpreter module handles courteous logic programs and is implemented natively.[3] For the stable model semantics with and without strong negation there is a second interpreter module that wraps the external tools *Smodels* [21] and *Lparse* [25].

There are various other semantics that could be supported, e.g. defeasible logic programs [22] or disjunctive stable models [23]. Only little integration effort would be necessary to incorporate these semantics into AceRules.

2.2   Two Kinds of Negation

In many applications, it is important to have two kinds of negation [27]. Strong negation (also called *classical negation* or *true negation*) indicates that something can be proven to be false. Negation as failure (also called *weak negation* or *default negation*), in contrast, states only that the truth of something cannot be proven.

However, there is no such general distinction in natural language. It depends on the context, what kind of negation is meant. This can be seen with the following two examples in natural English:

> If there is no train approaching then the school bus can cross the railway tracks.
> If there is no public transport connection to a customer then John takes the company car.

In the first example (which is taken from [11]), the negation corresponds to strong negation. The school bus is allowed to cross the railway tracks only if the available information (e.g. the sight of the bus driver) leads to the conclusion that

---

[3] The implementation of the courteous interpreter is based on [6].

no train is approaching. If there is no evidence whether a train is approaching or not (e.g. because of dense fog) then the bus driver is not allowed to cross the railway tracks.

The negation in the second sentence is most probably to be interpreted as negation as failure. If one cannot conclude that there is a public transport connection to the customer on the basis of the available information (e.g. public transport schedules) then John takes the company car, even if there is a special connection that is just not listed.

As long as only one kind of negation is available, there is no problem to express this in controlled natural language. As soon as two kinds of negation are supported, however, we need to distinguish them somehow. We found a clean and natural way to represent the two kinds of negation in ACE. Strong negation is represented with the common negation constructs of natural English:

- does not, is not (e.g. John is not a customer)
- no (e.g. no customer is a clerk)
- nothing, nobody (e.g. nobody knows John)
- it is false that (e.g. it is false that John waits)

To express negation as failure, we use the following constructs:

- does not provably, is not provably (e.g. a customer is not provably trustworthy)
- it is not provable that (e.g. it is not provable that John has a card)

This allows us to use both kinds of negation side by side in a natural looking way. The following example shows a rule using strong negation and negation as failure at the same time.

If a customer does not have a credit-card and is not provably a criminal then the customer gets a discount.

This representation is compact and we believe that it is well understandable. Even for persons that have never heard of strong negation and negation as failure, this rule *makes some sense*, even though they are probably not able to grasp all its semantic properties. Of course, if users want to create or modify rules containing negation then they have to learn first how the two kinds of negation have to be represented in ACE.

2.3 Intelligent Grouping

ACE is an expressive language, in fact more expressive than most rule languages. Thus, some sentences have to be rejected by AceRules because they cannot be mapped to an acceptable rule of the respective rule theory. However, in some situations the formal structure is not directly compliant with the rule theory, but can be translated in a meaningful way into a valid rule representation. This translation we call *intelligent grouping*.

To make this point clear, we present some simple examples using stable model semantics with strong negation. The described procedure can be used in the same way for the other semantics. Rules of the stable model semantics with strong negation have the form

$$L_0 \leftarrow L_1 \wedge \ldots \wedge L_m \wedge \sim L_{m+1} \wedge \ldots \wedge \sim L_n$$

with $0 \leq m \leq n$ and each L_i being a literal. A literal is an atomic proposition (A_i) or its strong negation $(\neg A_i)$. Negations are allowed to be applied only to atomic propositions or — in the case of negation as failure $(\sim)$ — to literals. Furthermore the heads of rules must contain nothing but a single literal. These restrictions we have to keep in mind when we translate an ACE text into a rule representation. As a first example, let us consider the following AceRules program:

> John owns a car.
> Bill does not own a car.
> If someone does not own a car then he/she owns a house.

The ACE parser transforms this text into its logical representation[4]

> $owns(john, X)$
> $car(X)$
> $\neg(owns(bill, Y) \wedge car(Y))$
> $\neg(owns(A, B) \wedge car(B)) \rightarrow (owns(A, C) \wedge house(C))$

which is not yet compliant with the rule theory. It contains complex terms inside of a negation and in the head of a rule. But considering the initial text, we would expect this example to be acceptable. In fact, it was just formalized in an inappropriate way. This is the point where the intelligent grouping is applied. If we aggregate some of the predicates then we end up with a simpler representation that has a correct rule structure:

> $owns\_car(john)$
> $\neg owns\_car(bill)$
> $\neg owns\_car(X) \rightarrow owns\_house(X)$

This transformation is based on a set of grouping patterns that are collected in a first step, and then these patterns are used to perform the actual grouping. For our example, the following two patterns have been used:

> $owns(X_1, I_1), car(I_1) \quad \Rightarrow owns\_car(X_1)$
> $owns(X_2, I_2), house(I_2) \Rightarrow owns\_house(X_2)$

In such patterns, there can be two kinds of placeholders: Each X_i stands for any variable or atom, and each I_i stands for a variable that does not occur outside of the group. This allows us to omit the variables I_i after the transformation. From a more intuitive point of view, we can say that the phrases "owns a car" and "owns

---

Throughout this article we will use a simplified form of the logical representation. For a more precise description, consult [7].

a house" are considered as atomic propositions. This means that the car and the house do not have an independent existence, and thus references to these objects are not allowed. If this restriction is violated then a consistent transformation into a valid rule structure is not possible. For example, the program

> Bill does not own a car.
> John owns a car X.
> Mary sees the car X.

that leads to the logical representation

$$\neg(owns(bill, A) \wedge car(A))$$
$$owns(john, B)$$
$$car(B)$$
$$sees(mary, B)$$

cannot be translated into a valid rule structure. An error message has to be raised in such cases informing the user that the program has an invalid structure. It has still to be evaluated how hard it is for normal users to follow this restriction and how often such situations actually occur. We are considering to develop authoring tools [3] that automatically enforce these restrictions.

Concerning the grouping step, one might think that the text was just translated into a too complex representation in the first place and that the parser should directly create a grouped representation. The following program shows that this is not the case:

> John owns a car.
> The car contains a suitcase.
> If someone X owns something that contains something Y then X owns Y.

It is transformed by the ACE parser into:

$$owns(john, H)$$
$$car(H)$$
$$contains(H, S)$$
$$suitcase(S)$$
$$owns(Z, X) \wedge contains(X, Y) \rightarrow owns(Z, Y)$$

In this case, we need the more fine-grained representation and no grouping has to be done since the program is already in a compliant form. This and the first example start both with the sentence "John owns a car", but in the end it has to be represented differently. Thus, the grouping is *intelligent* in the sense that it must consider the whole program to find out which predicates have to be grouped.

Another important property of the grouping step is that the transformation has to be reversible. Before verbalizing an answer set, we need to ungroup the predicates that were grouped before.

Altogether, the intelligent grouping gives us much flexibility. A sentence like "John owns a car" is treated as an atomic property of an object (John) or as a relation between two objects (John and a car), whichever makes sense in the respective context.

3   Interfaces

There are different existing interfaces that use controlled natural languages, e.g. query interfaces like *Querix* [18] or *LingoLogic* [26]. Other interfaces can also be used as editors like *ECOLE* [24], *GINO* [5], or *AceWiki*[5], but none of them concerns rule systems. There are applications like *NORMA* [14] which can verbalize formal rules, but no tool exists that uses a controlled natural language as a full-blown rule language.

AceRules comes with three interfaces. A webservice [2] facilitates the integration of the AceRules functionality into any other program. Furthermore, there are two web interfaces for human interaction. One is a technical interface[6] that is intended for advanced users that are interested in the technical background of the system. The main web interface[7] aims at end-users who are not familiar with formal notations. For the rest of this section, we will take a closer look at this main interface of which Fig. 1 shows a screenshot.

We claim that a Semantic Web interface for end-users (in the sense of an editor interface) should fulfill the following three properties which partly overlap.

1. Technical notations should be hidden. The users should not see any technical language (e.g. any XML-based language), but instead there should be a well-understandable and intuitive representation. Novice users should be able to understand the semantic representations after a very short learning phase.
2. The interface should guide the users during modification and creation of the formal representations. The users should not need to read any manuals or other documentation before they can start using the system, but they should be able to learn how to interact with the system while using it.
3. The users should be supported by a context-sensitive and comprehensive help feature. Especially in the case of errors, the users should be led immediately to a corresponding help article. These articles should be concise suggestions how to solve the problem.

Altogether, these three properties ensure that the Semantic Web interface has a shallow learning curve which we consider to be crucial for the success of the Semantic Web.

AceRules uses ACE as input and output language. No other notations are needed. Thus, AceRules fully satisfies the first condition. Furthermore, AceRules has a help feature which is shown in a browser-internal window. There is a help article for every error that can occur. If an error has occurred, then the user is directed to the respective article. Thus, AceRules fulfills the third condition as well.

AceRules gives also some help for the modification of existing programs and for the creation of new sentences. Nevertheless, we have to admit that it can only partially fulfill the second condition. For a real guidance of the user, a predictive

---

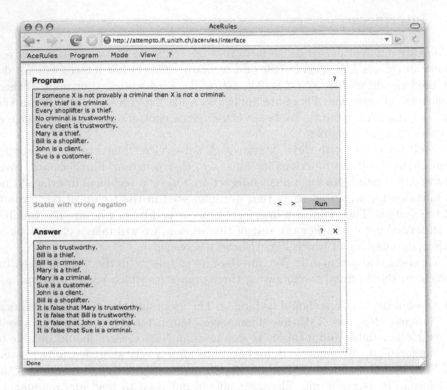

Fig. 1. The figure shows a screenshot of the AceRules web interface. The upper text box is the input component and contains the program to be executed. The result of the program is then displayed in the text box below.

authoring tool [3] would be needed, as provided by ECOLE and AceWiki. Such an authoring tool guides the user step by step through the creation of a sentence and makes it impossible to create syntactically incorrect representations.

4   Conclusions

We demonstrated that it is possible to use controlled natural languages for the formal representation of rule systems. Negation as failure and strong negation can be used side by side in a natural way. We introduced intelligent grouping as a method of transforming formal structures into valid rule representations. The AceRules web interface proves that a controlled natural language like ACE is well suited for the communication with the user and that no other formal language is needed.

AceRules is still a prototype and not yet ready for the use in real world applications. For example, the underlying theories do not support procedural attachments or arithmetics that would probably be needed in a real world environment. We believe that ACE and AceRules can be extended to support such constructs in a natural way. On the interface level, a predictive authoring tool would be very helpful. We referred to existing tools that demonstrate how this could be done.

Acknowledgement

This research has been funded by the European Commission and the Swiss State Secretariat for Education and Research within the 6th Framework Programme project REWERSE, and by the University of Zurich within the research grant program 2006 (Forschungskredit). I would like to thank Norbert E. Fuchs and Kaarel Kaljurand for their inputs.

References

1. ACE 5 Interpretation Rules. Attempto Documentation,
   `http://attempto.ifi.uzh.ch/site/docs/ace_interpretationrules.html`
   (December 13 2006)
2. AceRules Webservice. Attempto Documentation,
   `http://attempto.ifi.uzh.ch/site/docs/acerules_webservice.html` (March 15 2007)
3. Authoring Tools for ACE. Attempto Documentation,
   `http://attempto.ifi.uzh.ch/site/docs/authoring_tools.html` (March 23 2007)
4. Berners-Lee, T., Hendler, J., Lassila, O.: The semantic web. Scientific American (2001)
5. Bernstein, A., Kaufmann, E.: GINO - A Guided Input Natural Language Ontology Editor. In: Cruz, I., Decker, S., Allemang, D., Preist, C., Schwabe, D., Mika, P., Uschold, M., Aroyo, L. (eds.) ISWC 2006. LNCS, vol. 4273, pp. 144–157. Springer, Heidelberg (2006)
6. Dörflinger, M.: Interpreting Courteous Logic Programs, Diploma Thesis. Department of Informatics, University of Zurich (2005)
7. Fuchs, N.E., Hoefler, S., Kaljurand, K., Kuhn, T., Schneider, G., Schwertel, U.: Discourse Representation Structures for ACE 5, Technical Report ifi-2006.10. Department of Informatics, University of Zurich (2006)
8. Fuchs, N.E., Kaljurand, K., Schneider, G.: Attempto Controlled English Meets the Challenges of Knowledge Representation, Reasoning, Interoperability and User Interfaces. In: The 19th International FLAIRS Conference (FLAIRS'2006) (2006)
9. Fuchs, N.E., Schwertel, U., Schwitter, R.: Attempto Controlled English — Not Just Another Logic Specification Language. In: Flener, P. (ed.) LOPSTR 1998. LNCS, vol. 1559, Springer, Heidelberg (1999)
10. Gelfond, M., Lifschitz, V.: The stable model semantics for logic programming. In: Proceedings of the 5th International Conference on Logic Programming, pp. 1070–1080. MIT Press, Cambridge (1988)
11. Gelfond, M., Lifschitz, V.: Classical negation in logic programs and disjunctive databases. New Generation Computing 9, 365–385 (1990)
12. Grosof, B.N.: Courteous Logic Programs: Prioritized Conflict Handling For Rules. IBM Research Report RC 20836. Technical report, IBM T.J. Watson Research Center (1997)

13. Halpin, T.: Business Rule Verbalization. In: Doroshenko, A., Halpin, T., Liddle, S. W., Mayr, H.C. (eds.), In: Proceedings of Information Systems Technology and its Applications, 3rd International Conference ISTA 2004, Lecture Notes in Informatics (2004)

14. Halpin, T., Curland, M.: Automated Verbalization for ORM 2. In: Meersman, R., Tari, Z., Herrero, P. (eds.) On the Move to Meaningful Internet Systems 2006: OTM 2006 Workshops. LNCS, vol. 4278, pp. 1181–1190. Springer, Heidelberg (2006)

15. Hoefler, S.: The Syntax of Attempto Controlled English: An Abstract Grammar for ACE 4.0, Technical Report ifi-2004.03. Department of Informatics, University of Zurich (2004)

16. Jarrar, M., Keet, M., Dongilli, P.: Multilingual verbalization of ORM conceptual models and axiomatized ontologies. Technical report, Vrije Universiteit Brussel (2006)

17. Kaljurand, K., Fuchs, N.E.: Bidirectional mapping between OWL DL and Attempto Controlled English. In: Fourth Workshop on Principles and Practice of Semantic Web Reasoning, Budva, Montenegro (2006)

18. Kaufmann, E., Bernstein, A., Zumstein, R.: Querix: A Natural Language Interface to Query Ontologies Based on Clarification Dialogs. In: 5th International Semantic Web Conference (2006)

19. Kuhn, T., Royer, L., Fuchs, N.E., Schroeder, M.: Improving Text Mining with Controlled Natural Language: A Case Study for Protein Interactions. In: Leser, U., Naumann, F., Eckman, B. (eds.) DILS 2006. LNCS (LNBI), vol. 4075, Springer, Heidelberg (2006)

20. Lukichev, S., Wagner, G.: Verbalization of the REWERSE I1 Rule Markup Language, Deliverable I1-D6. Technical report, REWERSE (2006)

21. Niemelä, I., Simons, P.: Smodels — an implementation of the stable model and well-founded semantics for normal logic programs. In: Fuhrbach, U., Dix, J., Nerode, A. (eds.) LPNMR 1997. LNCS, vol. 1265, pp. 420–429. Springer, Heidelberg (1997)

22. Nute, D.: Defeasible Logic. In: Handbook of Logic in Artificial Intelligence and Logic Programming. Nonmonotonic Reasoning and Uncertain Reasoning, vol. 3, pp. 353–395. Oxford University Press, Oxford (1994)

23. Przymusinski, T.C.: Stable Semantics for Disjunctive Programs. New Generation Computing 9(3/4), 401–424 (1991)

24. Schwitter, R., Ljungberg, A., Hood, D.: ECOLE: A Look-ahead Editor for a Controlled Language. In: Proceedings of EAMT-CLAW03, Controlled Language Translation, Dublin City University, pp. 141–150 (2003)

25. Syrjänen, T.: Lparse 1.0 User's Manual (2000)

26. Thompson, C.W., Pazandak, P., Tennant, H.R.: Talk to Your Semantic Web. IEEE Internet Computing 9(6), 75–79 (2005)

27. Wagner, G.: Web Rules Need Two Kinds of Negation. In: Bry, F., Henze, N., Małuszyński, J. (eds.) PPSWR 2003. LNCS, vol. 2901, pp. 33–50. Springer, Heidelberg (2003)

Bridging Concrete and Abstract Syntax of Web Rule Languages

Milan Milanović[1], Dragan Gašević[2], Adrian Giurca[3],
Gerd Wagner[3], Sergey Lukichev[3], and Vladan Devedžić[1]

[1] FON-School of Business Administration, University of Belgrade, Serbia
milan@milanovic.org, devedzic@etf.bg.ac.yu
[2] School of Computing and Information Systems, Athabasca University, Canada
dgasevic@acm.org
[3] Institute of Informatics, Brandenburg Technical University at Cottbus, Germany
{Giurca, G.Wagner Lukichev}@tu-cottbus.de

Abstract. This paper proposes a solution for bridging abstract and concrete syntax of a Web rule language by using model transformations. Current specifications of Web rule languages such as Semantic Web Rule Language (SWRL) define its abstract syntax (e.g., EBNF notation) and concrete syntax (e.g., XML schema) separately. Although the recent research in the area of Model-Driven Engineering demonstrates that such a separation of two types of syntax is a good practice (due to the complexity of languages), one should also have tools that check validity of rules written in a concrete syntax with respect to the abstract syntax of the rule language. In this study, we use analyze the REWERSE I1 Rule Markup Language (R2ML) whose abstract syntax is defined by using metamodeling, while its textual concrete syntax is defined by using XML schema. We bridge this gap by a bi-directional transformation defined in a model transformation language (i.e., ATL).

1 Introduction

Using and sharing rules on the Web are some of the main challenges that the Web community tries to solve. The first important stream of research in this area is related to the Semantic Web technologies where researchers try to provide formally-defined rule languages (e.g., Semantic Web Rule Language, SWRL [7]) that are used for reasoning over Semantic Web ontologies. The main issue to be solved is the type (e.g., open of closed world) of reasoning that will be used, so that formal-semantics of such languages can be defined. However, as in constructing any other language, defining abstract syntax (independent of machine encoding) and concrete syntax (machine-dependent representation) is an unavoidable part of the language definition. An important characteristic of Semantic Web rule languages is that they are primarily not dealing with interchange of rules between various types of rules on the Web. This means that Semantic Web rule languages do not tend to compromise their reasoning characteristics for the broader syntactic expressivity. This is actually the main focus on the second stream of research on the Web that is chiefly articulated through the W3C effort called Rule Interchange Format (RIF) [6], while the most known effort in

M. Marchiori, J.Z. Pan, and C. de Sainte Marie (Eds.): RR 2007, LNCS 4524, pp. 309–318, 2007.

that area is the RuleML language [4]. The primary result expected from this research stream is to define an XML-based concrete syntax for sharing rules on the Web. Although the XML syntax for such a language is certainly the pragmatic expectation of the Web users, for a good definition of such a language is also important to have a well-designed abstract syntax.

In this paper, we try to address the problem of bridging the gap between an abstract and concrete syntax of a Web rule interchange language, i.e., the REWERSE I1 Rule Markup Language (R2ML) [18], one of the most-known RIF proposals. Since this language leverages the benefits of a new software engineering discipline Model-Driven Engineering (MDE) [3], the abstract syntax R2ML is defined by a metamodel. Furthermore, the R2ML XML schema, i.e., R2ML concrete syntax, has been developed for encoding rules by domain experts. However, there is no solution that enables transforming XML documents compliant to the R2ML XML documents into representation compliant to the R2ML metamodel (simply R2ML models). This gap between the R2ML metamodel and the R2ML XML schema causes the following problems:

1. Rules represented in the R2ML XML format cannot be stored in MOF-based model repositories, thus cannot be validated w.r.t. the R2ML metamodel.
2. The R2ML metamodel can not be instantiated based on rules encoded in the R2ML XML schema, and thus the R2ML metamodel can not be validated with real-world rules.

2 Model Driven Engineering

Model Driven Engineering is a new software engineering discipline in which the process heavily relies on the use of models [3]. A model defined is a set of statements about some system under study [16]. Models are usually specified by using modeling languages (e.g., UML), while modeling languages can be defined by metamodels. A metamodel is a model of a modeling language. That is, a metamodel makes statements about what can be expressed in the valid models of a certain modeling language [16]. The OMG's Model Driven Architecture (MDA) is one possible architecture for MDE [11]. One important characterestic of MDA is its organization. In fact, it consists of three layers, namely: M1 layer or model layer where models are defined by using modeling languages; M2 layer or metamodel layer where models of modeling languages (i.e. metamodels) are defined (e.g., UML) by using metamodel languages; and M3 layer or metametamodel layer where only one metamodeling language is defined (i.e. MOF) by itself [12].

The relations between different MDA layers can be considered as instance-of or conformant-to, which means that a model is an instance of a metamodel, and a metamodel is an instance of a metametamodel. The rationale for having only one language on the M3 layer is to have a unique grammar space for defining various modeling languages on the M2 layer. Thus, various modeling language can be processesed in the same way by using the same API. An example of such an API's are Java Metadata Interface (JMI)[1] that enables the implementation of a dynamic, platform-independent

---

[1] http://java.sun.com/products/jmi/

infrastructure to manage the creation, storage, access, discovery, and exchange of metadata. The most comprehensive implementation of JMI is NetBeans Metadata Repository (MDR).

Although MDE principles of defining modeling languages seems quite promising, the reality is that languages related can be defined and represented by using various technologies such as XML, databases, and MOF. In fact, the MDE theory introduces a concept of technical spaces, where a technical space is a working context with a set of associated concepts, body of knowledge, tools, required skills, and possibilities [9]. Although some technical spaces are difficult to define, they can be easily recognized (e.g. XML, MDA). In the case of the problem analyzed in this paper, we have to bridge between two technical spaces, since the R2ML metamodel and R2ML XML schema are defined in the MOF and XML technical spaces, respectively.

We should also mention the model transformations that represent the central operation for handling models in the MDA. Model transformations are the process of producing one model from another model of the same system [11]. In our research, we have decided to use ATLAS Transformation Language (ATL) [1] as the model transformations tool, which is based on OMG's QVT specification [13].

3 R2ML Metamodel and R2ML XML Schema

This section is devoted to the description of the R2ML language [15] [18] by explaining the R2ML abstract syntax and R2ML XML-based concrete syntax. Due to the size of the R2ML language, we only give an excerpt of the language related to integrity rules in this section. For the complete definition of the R2ML metamodel and R2ML XML schema, we advise readers to see [15].

3.1 The R2ML Abstract Syntax: R2ML Metamodel

The R2ML metamodel is defined by using the MOF metamodeling language. In Fig. 1, we give a UML class diagram depicting the MOF definition of integrity rules. An integrity rule, also known as (integrity) constraint, consists of a constraint assertion, which is a sentence (or formula without free variables) in a logical language such as first-order predicate logic. R2ML supports two kinds of integrity rules: the *alethic* and *deontic* ones. An alethic integrity rule can be expressed by a phrase, such as "*it is necessarilly the case that*" and a deontic one can be expressed by phrases, such as "*it is obligatory that*" or "*it should be the case that.*"

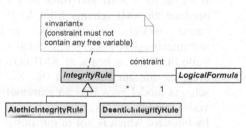

Fig. 1. The metamodel of integrity rules

Example 1 (Integrity rule). *If rental is not a one way rental then return branch of rental must be the same as pick-up branch of rental.*

R2ML defines the general concept of *LogicalFormula* (see Fig. 2) that can be Conjunction, Disjunction, NegationAsFailure, StrongNegation, and Implication. The concept of a *QuantifiedFormula* is essential for R2ML integrity rules, and it subsumes existentially quantified formulas and universally quantified formulas. Fig. 2 also contains elements such as *AtLeastQuantifiedFormula*, *AtMostQuantifiedFormula*, and *AtLeastAndAtMostQuantifiedFormula* that allow defining cardinality constrains in the R2ML rules.

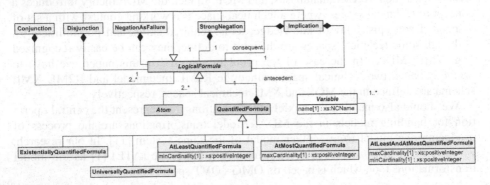

Fig. 2. The MOF model of LogicalFormula

3.2 R2ML XML Schema

The concrete syntax of the R2ML language is defined in a form of an XML schema. This XML schema is defined based on the R2ML MOF-based metamodel by using the following mapping rules presented in Table 1, while the full definition of the R2ML XML schema can be found [15]. In Fig. 3, we give the integrity rules defined in Example 1 in a form of an XML document compliant to the R2ML XML schema.

```
<r2ml:AlethicIntegrityRule r2ml:id="IR001">
  <r2ml:constraint>
    <r2ml:UniversallyQuantifiedFormula>
      <r2ml:ObjectVariable r2ml:name="r1" r2ml:classID="Rental"/>
      <r2ml:Implication>
        <r2ml:antecedent>
          <r2ml:NegationAsFailure>
            <r2ml:ObjectClassificationAtom r2ml:classID="OneWayRental">
              <r2ml:ObjectVariable r2ml:name="r1"/>
            </r2ml:ObjectClassificationAtom>
          </r2ml:NegationAsFailure>
        </r2ml:antecedent>
        <r2ml:consequent>
          <r2ml:EqualityAtom>
            <r2ml:ReferencePropertyFunctionTerm
              r2ml:referencePropertyID="returnBranch">
              <r2ml:contextArgument>
                <r2ml:ObjectVariable r2ml:name="r1"/>
              </r2ml:contextArgument>
            </r2ml:ReferencePropertyFunctionTerm>
            <r2ml:ReferencePropertyFunctionTerm
              r2ml:referencePropertyID="pickupBranch">
              <r2ml:contextArgument>
                <r2ml:ObjectVariable r2ml:name="r1"/>
              </r2ml:contextArgument>
            </r2ml:ReferencePropertyFunctionTerm>
          </r2ml:EqualityAtom>
        </r2ml:consequent>
      </r2ml:Implication>
    </r2ml:UniversallyQuantifiedFormula>
  </r2ml:constraint>
</r2ml:AlethicIntegrityRule>
```

Fig. 3. R2ML XML representation of the integrity rule from Example 1

One may raise a natural question: What do we need an XML schema for R2ML and the above design rules when there is XMI and rules how to produce an XMI schema from MOF-based models, metamodels, and metametamodels [14]. We decided to build this XML schema, as XMI is too complex for our needs and the XMI schema model goes into an extremely verbose XML syntax, hard to be used by humans, which is not in our design goals. However, the benefit of the use of XMI is that they can be processed by model repositories, thus we can test out the validity of XMI documents w.r.t. MOF-based metamodels.

4 Transformations Between the R2ML XML Schema and the R2ML Metamodel

In this section, we explain the transformation steps undertaken to transform R2ML XML documents into the models compliant to the R2ML metamodel. The R2ML concrete syntax is located in the XML technical space. However, the R2ML metamodel is defined by MOF, so the metamodel is located in the MOF technical space. To develop transformations between these two rule representations, we should put them into the same technical space. One alternative is to develop transformations in the XML technical space by using XSLT. This means that documents in the R2ML XML formant have to be transformed into the documents represented in the XMI format, compliant to the R2ML metamodel. However, the present practice has demonstrated that the use of XSLT as a solution is hard to maintain [8], since small modifications of the input and output XML formats can completely invalidate the XSLT transformation. This is especially amplified when transforming highly verbose XML formats such as XMI. On the other hand, we can perform this transformation in the MOF technical space by using model transformation languages such as ATL that are easier to maintain and have better tools for managing MOF-based models. We base our solution on the second alternative, i.e., in the MOF technical space by using ATL. The overall organization of the transformation process is shown in Fig. 4. It is obvious that transformation between the R2ML XML schema and the R2ML metamodel consists of two transformations, namely: 1. From the R2ML metamodel to the R2ML XML schema (i.e., from the XML technical space to the MOF technical space); and 2. From the R2ML XML schema to the R2ML metamodel.

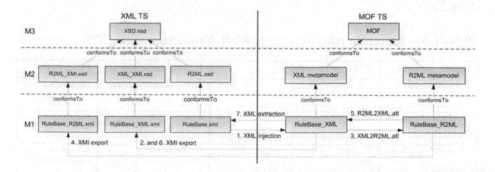

Fig. 4. The transformation scenario: R2ML XML into the R2ML metamodel and vice versa

4.1 Transforming the R2ML XML Schema into the R2ML Metamodel

The transformation process consists of two primary steps as follows.

Step 1. XML injection from the XML technical space to the MOF technical space. This means that we have to represent R2ML XML documents (RuleBase.xml from Fig. 4) into the form compliant to MOF. We use the XML injector that transforms R2ML XML documents (written w.r.t. the R2ML XML Schema, i.e., R2ML.xsd from Fig. 4) into the models conforming to the MOF-based XML metamodel (step 1 in Fig. 4). This has an extremely low cost, since the XML injector is distributed as a general-purpose tool together with ATL, which performs the XML injection automatically. An XML model (RuleBase_XML in Fig. 4), created by the XML injector, is located on the M1 layer of the MDA. This means that the XML injector instantiates the MOF-based XML metamodel (i.e., abstract syntax of XML). We can manipulate with these models like with any other type of MOF-based metamodels. Thus, such XML models can be represented in the XMI format (step 2 in Fig. 4). This XMI format can be regarded as an implicitly defined XML schema (XML_XMI.xsd) compliant to the XML metamodel.

Step 2. A transformation of XML models into R2ML models. We transform an XML model (RuleBase_XML) created in Step 1 into an R2ML model (RuleBase_R2ML) by using an ATL transformation named XML2R2ML.atl (step 3 in Fig. 4). The output R2ML model (RuleBase_R2ML) conforms to the R2ML metamodel. In the XML2R2ML.atl transformation, source elements from the XML metamodel are transformed into target elements of the R2ML metamodel. The XML2R2ML.atl transformation is done on the M1 level (i.e., the model level) of the MDA. This transformation uses the information about elements from the M2 (metamodel) level, i.e., metamodels defined on the M2 level (i.e., the XML and R2ML metamodels) in order to provide transformations of models on the level M1. It is important to point out that M1 models (both source and target ones) must be conformant to the M2 metamodels. This principle is well-know as metamodel-driven model transformations [2]. In Table 1, we give an excerpt of mappings between the R2ML XML Schema, XML metamodel, and R2ML metamodel. For XML Schema complex types, an instance of the XML metamodel element is created through the XML injection described in Step 1 above. Such an XML element is then transformed into an instance of the R2ML metamodel element by using the XML2R2ML.atl transformation (Step 2).

Table 1. An excerpt of mappings between the R2ML XML schema and the R2ML metamodel

R2ML schema	XML metamodel	R2ML metamodel	Description
IntegrityRule-Set	Element name = 'r2ml:IntegrityRuleSet'	IntegrityRuleSet	Captures a set of integrity rules.
AlethicInteg-rityRule	Element name = 'r2ml:AlethicIntegrityRule'	AlethicIntegri-tyRule	Represents an alethic integrity rule.
ObjectVariable	Element name = 'r2ml:ObjectVariable'	basCont-Voc.ObjectVariable	Represents an object variable.

Mappings between elements of the XML metamodel and elements of the R2ML metamodel are defined as a sequence of rules in the ATL language. These rules use additional helpers functions in defining mappings. Each rule in the ATL has one input element (i.e., an instance of a metaclass from a MOF-based metamodel) and one or more output elements. In fact, the ATL transformation takes an input XML model from a model repository and creates a new model compliant to the R2ML metamodel.

After applying the above ATL rules to the input XML models, R2ML models (RuleBase_R2ML) are stored in the model repository. Such R2ML models can be exported in the form of R2ML XMI documents (e.g., RuleBase_R2ML.xmi in Fig. 4).

4.2 Transforming the R2ML Metamodel into the R2ML XML Schema

Along with the transformation of the R2ML XML schema to the R2ML metamodel, we have also defined a transformation in the opposite direction, i.e., from the R2ML metamodel to the R2ML XML schema (R2ML2XML). This transformation process consists also of two primary steps as follows.

Step 1. The transformation of R2ML models to XML models. We transform an R2ML model (RuleBase_R2ML from Fig. 4) into an XML model (RuleBase_XML) by using an ATL transformation named R2ML2XML.atl (step 5 in Fig. 4). After applying this transformation to the input R2ML models, XML models (RuleBase_XML) are stored in the model repository (RuleBase_XML.xmi in Fig. 4). The output XML model conforms to XML metamodel. Mappings from Table 1 apply here with no changes. So, for the R2ML rules given the R2ML XMI format, we get an XML model which can be serialized back into the XML XMI format (step 6 in Fig. 4).

Step 2. The XML extraction from the MOF technical space to the XML technical space. In this step, we transforms XML model (RuleBase_XML in Fig. 4) which conforms to MOF-based XML metamodel and is generated in step 1 above, to RuleBase.xml document (Step 7 in Fig. 4). The XML extractor is a part of the ATL toolkit.

Creating a transformation from the R2ML metamodel to the R2ML XML schema (R2ML2XML), appeared to be easier to implement than the XML2R2ML transformation. For the R2ML2XML transformation, we needed only one helper for checking the negation of Atoms. All the ATL matched transformation rules are defined straightforward similar to the XML2R2ML transformation, except for unique elements (like *ObjectVariable*).

5 Experiences

The transformation is tested on a set of real world rules collected by the REWERSE Working Group I1 at the Brandenburg University of Technology at Cottbus. In this section, we report on some lessons we learned in developing and applying the transformation. These lessons also helped us to validate the R2ML MOF-based metamodel as well as to propose some changes of the R2ML metamodel.

Missing associations. Our goal was to transform rules from the R2ML XML format into the R2ML metamodel. This helped us identify some associations missing in the R2ML metamodel without which we could not represent all relations existing in the R2ML XML format. For example, the IntegrityRuleSet and DerivationRuleSet complex types are sequences of IntegrityRule and DerivationRule, respectively, in the R2ML XML schema. This implicated that in the R2ML metamodel we had to add an association between IntegrityRuleSet and IntegrityRule as well as another association between DerivationRuleSet and DerivationRule.

Abstract classes. Originally, some classes of the R2ML metamodel were defined as abstract classes (e.g., Disjunction, Conjunction, and Implication) [18]. When we attempted to transform rules form the R2ML XML format into the R2ML metamodel, we faced the problem that ATL engine refused executing the ATL transformation. The problem was that some classes should not actually be abstract, as the MDR model repository prevented their instantiation by strictly following the R2ML metamodel definition. This was an obvious indicator to change such classes not to be abstract.

Conflicting compositions. Since the meaning of MOF compositions is fully related to instances of classes connected by compositions, it is very hard to validate the use of compositions in MOF-based metamodels without instantiating metamodels. This means that for a class A that composes a class B, an instance of the class B can be only composed by one and only one instance of the class A. It is also correct to say that a class C also composes the class B. However, the same instance of the class B can not be composed by two other instances, regardless of the fact that one of them is a instance of the class A and another one of the class C. Since ATL uses the MDR as model repository, MDR does not allow us to execute ATL transformations that break the MOF semantics including the part related to compositions. This actually helped us identify some classes (e.g., *term* association from the ObjectClassificationAtom class to the ObjectTerm class, *objectArguments* association from the AssociationAtom class to the ObjectTerm class, etc.) in the R2ML metamodel breaking this rule. To overcome this problem, we have changed ("relaxed") the composition with a regular association relation. This makes sense, since a variable should be declared once, while all other elements should refer to that variable (not compose it).

Multiple inheritance conflict. During the implementation of the injection and transformation from the R2ML XML to the R2ML metamodel, we noticed the well-known "diamond" problem [17], i.e. a multiple inheritance conflict, in the object-oriented paradigm. Such a conflict arises when a class, say N, obtains the same attribute *attr* from two or more parent class; let us say classes A and B. These both parent classes A and B have the same parent class C from which both of them inherit the *attr*, thus there is a conflict to determine from which of them the attribute is inherited and how to access it at the class N. In the previous version of the R2ML metamodel, we defined three types of Variables: ObjectVariable, DataVariable and Variable which is parent from first two Variables. The problem occurred because ObjectVariable inherited ObjectTerm (which inherited Term), but it also inherited Variable, which also inherited Term, as shown in Fig. 5a. In this way, ObjectVariable inherited the class Term's attributes (i.e., *isMultivalued*) from two parents, namely, ObjectTerm and Variable. The same situation was with DataVariable and DataTerm. We solved this situation (Fig. 5b), as follows. First, we introduced the GenericTerm class which inherits the Term class, and the GenericVariable class which inherits GenericTerm. Next, we changed the Variable class, which is now an abstract class and it is a parent class for the GenericVariable and ObjectVariable classes. In this way, ObjectVariable only inherits Term's attributes from one parent only (ObjectTerm). Finally, we should note that we have a similar solution for DataVariable.

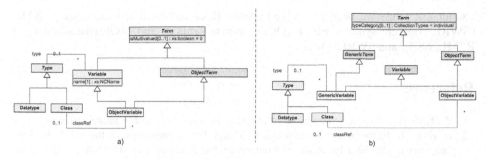

Fig. 5. The multiple inheritance conflict with (a) and its solution (b)

6 Conclusions

To the best of our knowledge, there is no solution to transforming rule languages based on model transformation languages. Most of previous solutions to transforming rule languages such as RuleML and SWRL are implemented by using XSLT or programming languages (Java) [5]. By the nature, our solution is the most similar to those based on the use of XSLT, as a general purpose transformation language for the XML technical space. Examples of transformations for the R2ML which are developed by using XSLT [15] such as translators from R2ML to F-Logic, between the F-Logic XML format and R2ML, from R2ML to Jess (rule engine), R2ML to RuleML, etc.

In this paper, we have demonstrated potentials of model transformations for transforming rule languages. First, the use of model transformation languages forces us to use valid source and target models. This means that the transformation can not be executed properly if either of rule models is not fully conformant to its metamodel. In our case, the source R2ML XML rules have to be conformant to the XML metamodel, while R2ML models have to be conformant to the R2ML metamodel. Second, every time we execute the model transformation, the elements of the target model are instantiated in the model repository. This means that the model transformation provided us with the mechanism for instantiation of the R2ML metamodel. This helped us detect some issues in the R2ML metamodel such as conflicting compositions and inappropriate abstract classes. Third, instances of rule metamodels are stored into MOF-based repositories. Since model repositories have generic tools for exporting/importing (meta)models in the XMI format, we employ them to export instances of the R2ML metamodel in the XMI format, and thus share R2ML models with other MOF-compliant applications. Finally, the use of ATL is more appropriate than XSLT when transforming rules between the XML and MOF technical spaces, since ATL supports advanced features for transforming languages based on metamodels.

In the future work, we will use real-world rules that we have transformed into the R2ML metamodel to evaluation transformations between the R2ML metamodel and other rule languages. Currently, we are implementing a bi-directional model transformation between the R2ML metamodel and the MOF-based OCL metamodel and between the R2ML metamodel and the SWRL language whose abstract syntax is defined by a metamodel. Of course, in this research we have to address even more challenges, since we need to bridge between three technical spaces, namely, XML (SWRL concrete syntax), EBNF (OCL concrete syntax), and MOF (metamodels of R2ML, OCL, and SWRL) [10].

References

1. ATLAS Transformation Language (ATL), http://www.sciences.univ-nantes.fr/lina/atl
2. Bézivin, J.: From Object Composition to Model Transformation with the MDA. In: Proceedings of the 39th International Conference and Exhibition on Technology of Object-Oriented Languages and Systems, Santa Barbara, USA, pp. 350–355 (2001)
3. Bézivin, J.: On the unification power of models. Software and System Modeling 4(2), 171–188 (2005)
4. Boley, H.: The Rule Markup Language: RDF-XML Data Model, XML Schema Hierarchy, and XSL Transformations. In: INAP 2001. LNCS (LNAI), vol. 2543, pp. 5–22. Springer, Heidelberg (2003)
5. Gandhe, M., Finin, T., Grosof, B.: SweetJess: Translating DamlRuleML to Jess. In: Proceedings of the International Workshop on Rule Markup Languages for Business Rules on the Semantic Web at 1st International Semantic Web Conference, the Sardinia, Italy (2002)
6. Ginsberg, A.: RIF Use Cases and Requirements, W3C Working Draft, http://www.w3.org/TR/rif-ucr (2006)
7. Horrocks I., Patel-Schneider, P. F., Boley, H., Tabet, S., Grosof, B., Dean, M.: SWRL: A Semantic Web Rule Language Combining OWL and RuleML, W3C Member Submission, http://www.w3.org/Submission/SWRL (2004)
8. Jovanović, J., Gašević, D.: XML/XSLT-Based Knowledge Sharing. Expert Systems with Applications 29(3), 535–553 (2005)
9. Kurtev, I., Bézivin, J., Aksit, M.: Technological Spaces: an Initial Appraisal, CoopIS, DOA'2002, Industrial track (2002)
10. Milanović, M., Gašević, D., Guirca, A., Wagner, G., Devedžić, V.: On Interchanging between OWL/SWRL and UML/OCL. In: Proceedings of 6th Workshop on OCL for (Meta-) Models in Multiple Application Domains (OCLApps) at the 9th ACM/IEEE International Conference on Model Driven Engineering Languages and Systems (MoDELS), Genoa, Italy, pp. 81–95 (2006)
11. Miller, J., Mukerji, J. (eds.): MDA Guide Version 1.0.1, OMG (2003)
12. Meta Object Facility (MOF) Core, v2.0, OMG Document formal/06-01-01, http://www.omg.org/cgi-bin/doc?formal/2006-01-01 (2005)
13. MOF QVT Final Adopted Specification, OMG document 05-11-01, (2005)
14. Meta Object Facility (MOF) 2.0 XMI Mapping Specification, v2.1, OMG Document formal/2005-09-01, http://www.omg.org/cgi-bin/doc?formal/2005-09-01 (2005)
15. The REWERSE I1 Rule Markup Language (R2ML), http://oxygen.informatik.tu-cottbus.de/rewerse-i1/?q=node/6 (2006)
16. Seidewitz, E.: What Models Mean, IEEE Software, pp. 26–32 (2003)
17. Simons, A.J.H.: The Theory of Classification, Part 17: Multiple Inheritance and the Resolution of Inheritance Conflicts. Journal of Object Technology 4(2), 15–26 (2005)
18. Wagner, G., Giurca, A., Lukichev, S., R2ML: A General Approach for Marking-up Rules", In Proceedings of Dagstuhl Seminar 05371. In Bry, F., Fages, F., Marchiori, M., Ohlbach, H. (Eds.) Principles and Practices of Semantic Web Reasoning, http://drops.dagstuhl.de/opus/volltexte/2006/479 (2005)

Completing Queries: Rewriting of Incomplete Web Queries Under Schema Constraints

Sacha Berger, François Bry, Tim Furche, and Andreas J. Häusler

Institute for Informatics, University of Munich,
Oettingenstraße 67, D-80538 München, Germany
http://www.pms.ifi.lmu.de/

Abstract. Web queries have been and will remain an essential tool for accessing, processing, and, ultimately, reasoning with data on the Web. With the vast data size on the Web and Semantic Web, reducing costs of data transfer and query evaluation for Web queries is crucial. To reduce costs, it is necessary to narrow the data candidates to query, simplify complex queries and reduce intermediate results.

This article describes a static approach to optimization of web queries. We introduce a set of rules which achieves the desired optimization by schema and type based query rewriting. The approach consists in using schema information for removing incompleteness (as expressed by 'descendant' constructs and disjunctions) from queries. The approach is presented on the query language Xcerpt, though applicable to other query languages like XQuery. The approach is an application of rules in many aspects—query rules are optimized using rewriting rules based on schema or type information specified in grammar rules.

1 Introduction

Web queries have been and, by all accounts, will remain an essential tool for accessing, processing, and, ultimately, reason with data on the Web. They are an essential component of many Web rule languages for expressing conditions on the information available on the Web. Web queries occur in so diverse rule languages as XSLT, CSS, Xcerpt, WebSQL, RVL, and dlvhex. The perceived strength and main contribution of Web queries and their underlying semi-structured data model is the ability to model data with little or no (a priori) information on the data's schema. In this spirit, all semi-structured query languages are distinguished from traditional relational query languages in providing core constructs for expressing *incomplete* queries, i.e., queries where only some of the sought-for data is specified but that are not affected by the presence of additional data. Examples of such constructs are regular path expressions in Lorel, the **descendant** and **following** closure axis in XPath and XQuery, descendant and adjacency selectors in CSS, or Xcerpt's **desc** and partial query patterns. Incompleteness constructs often, in particular if concerned with navigation in the graph, resemble to reachability or transitive closure constructs.

Incomplete query constructs have proved to be both essential tools for expressing Web queries and a great convenience for query authors able to focus better on the parts of the query he or she is most interested in. Though some evaluation approaches,

M. Marchiori, J.Z. Pan, and C. de Sainte Marie (Eds.): RR 2007, LNCS 4524, pp. 319–328, 2007.

e.g., [5] (usually limited to tree-shaped data) can handle certain incomplete queries (viz., those involving **descendant** or **following**) efficiently, most approaches suffer from lower performance for evaluating incomplete queries than for evaluating queries without incompleteness. The latter is particularly true for query processors with limited or no index support (a typical case in a Web context where query processors are often used in scenarios where data is transient rather than persistent).

In this paper, we propose a set of equivalences for removing (or introducing) queries with incomplete constructs. Our main contributions are as follows:

First, we discuss the types of incompleteness that occur in Web query languages and how they can be rewritten in Section 1.1. In this and the following parts, we have chosen our own query language Xcerpt for providing examples, mostly as it is able to express all forms of incompleteness that we consider in this article conveniently. We do not, however, rely on any specialized evaluation engine. The query rewriting equivalences are purely static and can be applied separately in a pre-processing step or during logical query optimization. It is worth noting that, where XQuery allows the distinction between complete and incomplete queries as in the case of the descendant axis, our equivalences can as well be used for rewriting XQuery expressions.

Second, in Section 2, we introduce the query language Xcerpt and its types, based on a graph schema language and a convenient automaton model for specifying and checking schema constraints on graph-shaped semi-structured data. The automaton model is exploited to be able to specify the equivalences introduced in the second part of the article concisely.

Third, we introduce a collection of equivalences for removing all forms of incompleteness discussed in the first part. These equivalences (Section 3) can actually be used in both directions, i.e., they could also be used to introduce incompleteness into a complete query. In contrast to previous work on minimization and containment under schema constraints, these equivalences operate on graph schemata and graph queries instead of tree schemata and queries.

Fourth, we discuss briefly how these equivalences can be exploited for query optimization (Section 4), both in a context where incompleteness is undesirable from the point of evaluation cost and in a context where at least certain incomplete queries can be evaluated as fast as equivalent complete queries, e.g., [5].

1.1 Three Forms of Incompleteness

In Web queries, incompleteness occurs in three forms: breadth, depth, and order. In this article, we focus mostly on breadth and depth though we briefly consider also order incompleteness.

1. Incompleteness in depth allows a query to express restrictions of the form "there is a path between the paper and the author" without specifying the path's exact shape. The most common construct for expressing depth incompleteness is XPath's **descendant** or Xcerpt's **desc**, an unqualified, arbitrary-length path between two nodes. Regular path expressions and Xcerpt's qualified **desc** allow more specific restrictions, e.g., "there is a path between paper and author and it contains no institutions".

2. Incompleteness in breadth allows a query to express restrictions on some children of a node without restricting others ("there is an author child of the paper but there may be other unspecified children"). Breadth incompleteness is an essential ability of all query languages. Indeed, in many languages breadth completeness is much harder to express than incompleteness. Nevertheless, breadth completeness allows e.g. indexed access to a node's children (often preferable to a "search-always" model).

3. Incompleteness in order allows a query to express that the children order of a node is irrelevant ("there is an author child of the paper and a title child of the same paper but don't care about their order").

In Section 3, we discuss how the first two forms of incompleteness can be rewritten and briefly mention how the last form could be treated as well.

2   Preliminaries–Brief Introduction to Xcerpt and R_2G_2 Types

The query and transformation language Xcerpt [15], is a declarative, logic based Web query language. Its salient features are **pattern based query** and **construction** of graph-shaped semi-structured data, possibly **incomplete query patterns** reflecting the *heterogeneity* and the *semi-structured* nature of Web data, **rules** relating query and construction, and **rule chaining** enabling simple inference and query modularization.

As we focus on query rewriting and optimization in this article, Xcerpt queries will be introduced, construct terms and rules are omitted. For more details about the Xcerpt query language refer, e.g., to [15].

An Xcerpt term (query- construct- or data term) represents a tree- or graph-like structure, it consists of a label and a sequence of child terms enclosed in braces or brackets. Square brackets (i.e., [ ]) denote *ordered term specification* (as in standard XML), curly braces (i.e., { }) denote *unordered term specification* (as is common in databases). Double braces (i.e., [[ ]] and {{ }}) are used to denote that a term's content is just partially specified—this concept only applies to query terms. This so called *incompleteness in breadth* denotes, that additional child terms may be interspersed in data matching this incomplete query term, among the ones specified in the query.

Graph structure can be expressed using a reference mechanism, but is not further introduced as not considered in the current rewriting rules.

Queries. are connections of zero or more query terms using the n-ary connectives *and* and *or*. A query is always (implicitly or explicitly) associated with a *resource*.

Query terms are similar to (possibly) *non-ground* functional programming expressions and logical atoms. Query terms are Xcerpt terms, Xcerpt terms prefixed by the **desc**-Keyword, query variables, or ★. A query term l[desc a[]] may match a data term with label l and child term a[] or with any child term that contains a[] at arbitrary depth as descendant or child term. A variable, e.g. var X, may match any term, multiple occurrences of the same variable have to match equivalent data terms. Variables can be restricted, e.g. var X ->q denotes, that the variable may only match with terms matching the query term q. The term ★ denotes the most general query matching any data term. It can also be seen as an anonymous variable. While not formally part of Xcerpt, it is under current investigation for further versions of Xcerpt and it is a short hand for a query term of constant length.

Query terms are *unified* with database or construct terms using a non-standard unification called *simulation unification*, which has been investigated in [7]. Simulation unification is based on *graph simulation* [1] which is similar to graph homomorphisms.

Typed Xcerpt. is the basis for (static and dynamic) type checking of Xcerpt and for the optimization presented in this article. In a (fully) typed Xcerpt program, every term t is annotated with a disjunction of types $\tau_1, \ldots, \tau_n$, denoted as $t : (\tau_1 | \ldots | \tau_n)$. Types are defined using a so called "regular rooted graph grammar", short R_2G_2. Internally, types are represented as automata, type automata are used for query rewriting. A type represents a set of data terms valid w.r.t. the given term. A well typed query w.r.t. a given type is a query that may match some data terms that are valid w.r.t. the given type.

R_2G_2 is a slight extension of regular tree grammars [6], the extensions cope with typed references (not introduced here) used to model graph shaped data and unordered child lists (neither introduced) as defined in Xcerpt.

While R_2G_2 grammars are convenient for the user, R_2G_2 is translated into an instance of a tree automaton model appropriate for processing. Tree automata for ranked trees are well established [10]. As Xcerpt and XML is based on an unranked tree model, a new automaton model specially tailored for unranked trees has been proposed [2]. A nondeterministic regular tree automaton M is a 5-tuple $(Q, \Delta, F, R, \Sigma)$ with label alphabet Σ, states Q, final states F where $F \subseteq Q$, transitions Δ where $\Delta \subseteq (Q \times \Sigma \times Q \times Q)$ and a set of root transitions R with $R \subseteq \Delta$. [1] The unorthodox about these automata are the edges—they are hyper edges of arity 3. An edge (s, l, c, e) represents a transition from state s to state e consuming (in the sense of automata acceptance) a data term with label l and a sequence of child terms accepted by a part of the automaton with start state c. Figure 1 shows an example automaton used through out the reminder of this article as example type.

In practice, various atomic data types like string, integer, and boolean also exist, but as they are arguably not relevant for structure based optimization they are omitted here.

In this article, in a typed term of the shape $t : \tau$ we will consider τ to correspond to an edge in the automaton. The example data term in the caption of figure 1 is hence type annotated under M as

```
z[ a[ c[]:(6,c,8,9),d[]:(9,d,10,11)]:(2,a,6,7)]:(1,z,2,3).
```

3   Rules for Completing Queries Under a Schema

The previous sections have established the formal aspects of the query and schema language employed and intuitively established the aim of rewriting incomplete queries under a given schema. The following section defines in a precise and formal manner a set of rules for this task.

Recall, that these are merely equivalence rules and not a full optimization algorithm. Note also, that for simplicity these rules apply only to non-recursive schemata (no recursion in either depth or breadth). However, this is only needed due to the naive application of the rules until no further expansion of rules is possible. This limitation is

---

[1] Usually we need just one root transition, but for technical reasons it is convenient to have a set of root transitions.

$M = (\ \{\ 1,\dots,20\},$
$\quad\ \{\ (1,z,2,3),$
$\qquad (2,y,4,5),$
$\qquad (2,a,6,7),$
$\qquad (6,c,8,9),$
$\qquad (9,d,10,11),$
$\qquad (6,b,12,13),$
$\qquad (13,d,14,15),$
$\qquad (6,b,16,17),$
$\qquad (17,c,18,19),$
$\qquad (19,d,20,21)\},$
$\quad\ \{\ 3,4,7,8,10,12,14,16,18,20\},$
$\quad\ (1,z,2,3),$
$\quad\ \{\ a,b,c,d,y,z\})$

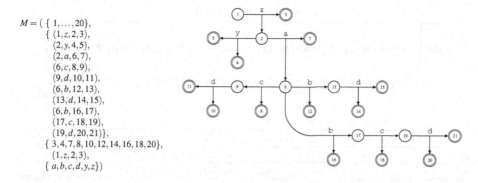

Fig. 1. This automaton represents the type used in the following rewriting rule example. An example data term valid w.r.t. this type is e.g. `z[ a[ d[],c[] ] ].`

not needed if these rules are part of an optimization algorithm that chooses when to further expand and when to stop (e.g., because the size increase offsets the gain from the reduction of incompleteness—cf. Section 5). Furthermore, no order of application for the rules is given—see also the outlook for a brief discussion on possible optimization strategies incorporating our rules. For the examples in this article, we have chosen to apply the rules in the most convenient way.

3.1 Prerequisites

There are a number of convenience functions that allow more concise rule definitions:

(1) HORIZONTALPATHSTOENDSTATES(s) (*hptes*): The *hptes* function takes as argument a state s and returns a set $\{\tau_1 = [t_{1_1},\dots,t_{1_{m_1}}],\dots,\tau_n = [t_{n_1},\dots,t_{n_{m_n}}]\}$ containing lists of paths τ_i from s to all end states reachable from s.

(2) HORIZONTALPATHSTOSTATES(s_1, s_2) (*hpts*): For a given state s_1 of an R_2G_2 graph, the *hpts* function returns a set of all paths τ_i through the graph which begin with s_1 and end with state s_2.

(3) MAP(T, E): Given an Xcerpt term t and a sequence of transitions (edges) $E = [e_1,\dots,e_n]$ in a given R_2G_2 graph, *map* returns the sequence $[t : e_1,\dots,t : e_n]$.

3.2 The Set of Rules

Now the rules for rewriting queries are defined. Afterwards, and before describing how the rules actually work, we give an example demonstrating the effects of rule application to an example query (Figure 3.2).

$$\frac{(\textbf{desc}\ t : \tau) : (s,1,c,e)}{1[[(\textbf{desc}\ t : \tau) : (s',1',c',e')]] : (s,1,c,e)}\ (\text{DESC1}) \qquad \frac{\textbf{var}\ X : \tau}{\textbf{var}\ X \to \bigstar : \tau}\ (\text{VAR})$$

$$\frac{(\textbf{desc}\ t : \tau) : (s,1,c,e)}{t : (s,1,c,e)}\ (\text{DESC2}) \qquad \frac{\bigstar : (s,1,c,e)}{1\ [[\ ]] : (s,1,c,e)}\ (\text{STAR})$$

$$1[[t_1, t_2, \ldots, t_q]] : (s, 1, c, e)$$

$$\text{or} \left[\begin{array}{c} \cdots \\ 1[map(\bigstar, z_1), t_1, map(\bigstar, z_2), t_2, \ldots, map(\bigstar, z_q), t_q, map(\bigstar, z_{q+1})] \\ \cdots \\ z_1, \ldots, z_{q+1} \in hpts(c, s_{t_1}) \times hpts(e_{t_1}, s_{t_2}) \times \ldots \times hpts(e_{t_{q-1}}, s_{t_q}) \times hptes(e_{t_q}) \end{array} \right]$$

(PARTIAL)

$$
\begin{array}{ll}
1: & \textbf{desc } (\texttt{a[[var X} \rightarrow \texttt{c]]} : (2, \texttt{a}, 6, 7)) : (1, \texttt{z}, 2, 3) \\
 & \rule{10cm}{0.4pt} \quad \text{DESC1} \\
2: & \texttt{z[[(\textbf{desc} (a[[var X} \rightarrow \texttt{c]]} : (2, \texttt{a}, 6, 7)) : (2, \texttt{a}, 6, 7))]] : (1, \texttt{z}, 2, 3) \\
 & \rule{10cm}{0.4pt} \quad \text{DESC2} \\
3: & \texttt{z[[(a[[var X} \rightarrow \texttt{c]]} : (2, \texttt{a}, 6, 7))]] : (1, \texttt{z}, 2, 3) \\
 & \rule{10cm}{0.4pt} \quad \text{PARTIAL} \\
4: & \texttt{z[(a[[var X} \rightarrow \texttt{c]]} : (2, \texttt{a}, 6, 7))] : (1, \texttt{z}, 2, 3) \\
 & \rule{10cm}{0.4pt} \quad \text{PARTIAL} \\
5: & \texttt{z[\textbf{or}[a[var X} \rightarrow \texttt{c, d], a[b, var X} \rightarrow \texttt{c, d]]} \\
\end{array}
$$

Fig. 2. Application of our rules to an example query. The applied rules are stated at each line to illustrate the way the query changed from line to line.

The example query **1** binds elements of type c occurring immediately beneath any a to the variable x. The cs may occur at any position within the list of a's children. Therefore, the query contains incompleteness in depth (the desc construct) and in breath (the double brackets).

The first step in our example applies the DESC1 rule (responsible for descendent expansion) in order to remove the depth incompleteness. This rule expands a desc t which is queried against a node with label 1 by replacing it with a partial subterm specification for the node with label 1. Please note that because of the subterm specification of the 1 labelled node being partial after applying this rule, the R_2G_2 graph node s' might be any of the states connected (horizontally) to c. Applying the rule results in an "inwards moved" desc, illustrated in line **2** of Figure 3.2.

Type checking now reveals that a second iteration of this rule is not necessary, because elements with label a are only allowed to occur immediately beneath z labelled nodes. This means that the desc in step **2** is not needed anymore and could be removed. This is achieved by applying rule DESC2 and results in query **3**.

Now the depth incompleteness has completely been removed, but the query still contains incompleteness in breath. In Xcerpt incompleteness in breath means partial subterm specification. Using the list of "subpaths" provided by the *hptes* function, a partial content model can be expanded to become total by the help of the most general node ★. (The ★s themselves can then in turn be specialized in a possible follow-up step.) However, in general the double brackets or braces may contain a list of the subterms the regarding node must possess, but do not preclude additional subterms in the data (as double brackets or braces indicate partial query terms). The PARTIAL rule ("partial specification expansion") covers this (using s_t as possible start states of the term t and e_t as its possible end states). Intuitively, it states that any partial query term t with sub-terms $t_1, \ldots, t_q$ and content model start state c can be complete to a disjunction of total query terms in the following way: for each path through the content model of t that touches also the given sub-terms $t_1, \ldots, t_q$ (in that order), we generate one disjunct where that path is explicitly unfolded. More precisely, the $z_1, \ldots, z_{q+1}$ represent one such path through the content model of t that touches, in order, each of the $t_1, \ldots, t_q$:

the path is partitioned at the $t_1, \ldots, t_q$ with z_1 being any possible path from the content model start state c to s_{t_1} (the start state of t_1), z_i for $1 < i <= q$ the path from the end state of t_{i-1} to the start state of t_i, and z_n the path from the end state of t_q to an end state of the schema automaton. Each of the z_is is a sequence of types representing its segment. For each combinations of z_i's a disjunct is generated where the actual z_i is unfolded into the missing siblings (using, as above, the ★ notation for elements restricted only by their type).

In the example query **3** this rule can be applied twice: once for the outermost partial term and once for the inner (with a label). The outermost can be simply dropped as there is just one possible path containing an a label in the $R_2 G_2$ graph of our schema *on the "child level" of* z (omitting the superfluous **or** which could be rewritten by general normalization rule, cf. Section 5). This results in step **4**, of which the inner partial term can be addressed. Here, however, we have a choice of several paths through the $R_2 G_2$ graph containing the required c labelled edge. The final result of the rule application to our example query is thus step **5**, which the expanded list of all a elements possible under the query's constraints.

The rules VAR and STAR are added merely for convenience in handling ★ in the rewriting process. They have been implicitly applied in steps **4** and **5** and will therefore not be illustrated with examples themselves. With VAR (variable specialization), a variable X of type τ (as might be used in a typed Xcerpt query) can be transformed to a variable binding, where X is bound to a (concrete) node ★ of type τ. Here one can also recognize the flexibility of ★: it can represent a node of any type and nevertheless be handled like any other concretely given node. With the rule of star specialization, STAR, we can transform the general ★ to an explicitly labelled term.

To conclude the discussion of the rewriting rules, please note that though we have given only rewriting rules concerning *ordered* subterm specifications, this is no limitation to the approach. On the level of the rewriting rules, the difference between ordered and unordered subterms is just notationally. In each of the above rules, the brackets may be replaced by braces. Therefore, the details of handling unordered subterm specifications are left out.

4 Related Work

Rewriting and minimization of queries is as central to Web queries as it has been to queries on relational databases. Often some form of normalization to rewrite undesirable language features into equivalent expressions is employed, e.g., the removal of reverse axis in XPath optimization [14].

On the remaining language, previous work has mostly concentrated on removing depth incompleteness (in form of regular path expressions (short RPEs) or XPath's descendant axis).

For Web queries using regular path expressions (short RPEs), [11] gives a practical algorithm for rewriting RPEs containing wild cards and a closure axis like XPath's **descendant**. They employ, as we do in this work, graph schemata and automata for processing such schemata. However, as the queries they consider are only regular path expressions, they can also use an automaton for (each of) the regular path expressions to be rewritten. Our approach is at the same time broader and more focused: Due to the limitation to RPEs they can only consider rewriting of depth incompleteness, whereas we consider also breadth (and briefly order) incompleteness. However, their approach can obtain rewritings in cases where our approach fails or produces undesirably large results.

On XPath containment and minimization, the essential results for our work are positive (polynomial time algorithms exist) if only tree pattern queries (understood as XPath queries with only child and descendant axis and no wild card labels) are considered, for details see [16].

Our approach differs from these works in rewriting not only vertical path expressions (involving only child and descendant) axis, but in considering also breadth (and briefly order) incompleteness. In this aspect, it is more closely related to approaches from area (3) such as [9], where a heuristic optimization technique for XQuery is proposed: Based on the PAT algebra, a number of normalizations, simplification, reordering, and access path equivalences are specified and a deterministic algorithm developed. Though the algorithm does not necessarily return an optimal query plan it is expected and experimentally verified to return a reasonably good one. Our approach could be employed in such a framework assuming a cost model where depth, breadth or order incompleteness is considered more expensive than complete, but under a given schema equivalent queries.

Whereas none of the above discussed approaches considers breadth and order incompleteness in the way we do in this work, some relation regarding such incompleteness to works on using schema information for pruning query processing against XML streams is noticeable. [17] proposes such a use of schema information.

Again, our proposed techniques for removing breadth incompleteness can be exploited in such a scenario. In case the schemata are rather regular, our techniques might even give rise to fixed memory constraints for the streamed processing, cf. [13]. However, the details of such an exploitation are still open.

5   Outlook and Conclusion

The previous section concludes the discussion of the equivalences for reducing or introducing (depending on the reading direction) incompleteness in Web queries. These equivalences, however, are only the first step to an automatic optimization of Web queries w.r.t. incompleteness. To be of practical use, they need to be integrated into an (necessarily heuristic, cf. Section 4) optimization algorithm such as [9].

It is worth noting, that elimination of any kind of incompleteness leads to no practically useful heuristic: Eliminating all breadth incompleteness, i.e., rewriting all partial subterm lists in total subterm lists. This is clearly infeasible, if types may occur in many different combinations as siblings of a node, as, e.g., in HTML where most element types may be combined with most other element types. In many cases it is even impossible, as repetition in breadth (i.e., any content model with kleene-stars involved) of a schema gives rise to infinite disjunctive query completions. A practical heuristic needs to implement some cut-off point where this expansion is no longer useful. Similar arguments apply for the elimination of all depth and order incompleteness. Infinite query completions arise with recursive schemata in depth, though completion of depth incompleteness is often more promising, as most practical Web documents and schemata have rather limited nesting depths. Despite these remarks, simple heuristics may be applicable if certain assumptions on the schemata are made such as upper limits on the number of possible parent and sibling types a given schema type may combine with.

The proposed equivalences are a small, though, in our opinion, important part of the optimization rules applicable for Web queries. Combination and integration with other forms of query optimization and rewriting for Web queries has not yet been considered.

If the proposed equivalences are to be employed in an XPath or XQuery context, the rewriting of reverse axes such as **ancestor**, cf. [14], in XPath is required as a precondition, since the discussed rules assume forward-only expressions (since these have mostly the same expressiveness as expressions allowing also reverse axes).

We have not yet integrated the discussed equivalences into an optimization algorithm, and thus experimental results on their practical use are still open.

Conclusion

In this paper, we present a novel look on incompleteness in Web queries expressed, e.g., in Xcerpt or XQuery. Incompleteness is one of the distinguishing features of Web query languages compared to languages such as SQL. However, incomplete queries are often considerably more expensive to evaluate than complete queries. Moreover, manually eliminating incompleteness robs Web query languages of one of the most used and most convenient features, the ability to specify data of interest without considering the context. Therefore, we propose to exploit schema information for *automatic* rewriting of Web queries containing incompleteness where applicable.

We propose a set of equivalences for rewriting graph-shaped Web queries on graph-shaped semi-structure data that allows the introduction or removal of all three forms of incompleteness (though order incompleteness is only briefly discussed). These equivalences form the foundation of a flexible treatment of incomplete Web queries beyond just the treatment of depth incompleteness as in previous work.

Ongoing work is on the development of an heuristic optimization algorithm that chooses when to apply these equivalences and to experimentally verify the practical improvement to query evaluation that can be obtained through these equivalences.

Acknowledgments. This research has been funded by the European Commission and by the Swiss Federal Office for Education and Science within the 6th Framework Programme project REWERSE number 506779 (cf. http://rewerse.net).

References

1. Abiteboul, S., Buneman, P., Suciu, D.: Data on the Web: From Relations to Semistructured Data and XML. Morgan Kaufmann Publishers Inc. San Francisco (2000)
2. Berger, S.: An Automaton Model for Xcerpt Type Checking and XML Schema Validation. REWERSE-TR-2007-01, Inst. for Computer Science, Univ. of Munich, Germany (2007)
3. Berger, S., Bry, F.: Towards Static Type Checking of Web Query Language. In: Proc. Workshop über Grundlagen von Datenbanken (GvD) (2005)

4. Berger, S., Coquery, E., Drabent, W., Wilk, A.: Descriptive Typing Rules for Xcerpt. In: PPSWR 2005. LNCS, vol. 3703, Springer, Heidelberg (2005)
5. Boncz, P., Grust, T., van Keulen, M., Manegold, S., Rittinger, J., Teubner, J.: MonetDB/X-Query: a fast XQuery Processor powered by a Relational Engine. In: SIGMOD (2006)
6. Brüggemann-Klein, A., Murata, M., Wood, D.: Regular tree and regular hedge languages over unranked alphabets. HKUST-TCSC-2001-0, Hongkong Univ. of Science and Tech. (2001)
7. Bry, F., Schaffert, S.: Towards a Declarative Query and Transformation Language for XML and Semistructured Data: Simulation Unification. In: Stuckey, P.J. (ed.) ICLP 2002. LNCS, vol. 2401, Springer, Heidelberg (2002)
8. Chamberlin, D., Frankhauser, P., Florescu, D., Marchiori, M., Robie, J.: XML Query Use Cases. Working draft, W3C (2005)
9. Che, D., Aberer, K., Özsu, T.: Query Optimization in XML Structured-document Databases. The VLDB Journal 15(3), 263–289 (2006)
10. Common, H., Dauchet, M., Gilleron, R., Lugiez, F.J.D., Tison, S., Tommasi, M.: Tree automata techniques and applications. http://www.grappa.univ-lille3.fr/tata (1999)
11. Fernandez, M.F., Suciu, D.: Optimizing Regular Path Expressions Using Graph Schemas. In: Proc. Int'l. Conf. on Data Engineering (ICDE) (1998)
12. Koch, C.: On the Complexity of Nonrecursive XQuery and Functional Query Languages on Complex Values. In: Proc. ACM Symp. on Principles of Database Sys. (PODS) (2005)
13. Olteanu, D.: SPEX: Streamed and Progressive Evaluation of XPath. IEEE Transactions on Knowledge and Data Engineering (2007)
14. Olteanu, D., Meuss, H., Furche, T., Bry, F.: XPath: Looking Forward. In: Chaudhri, A.B., Unland, R., Djeraba, C., Lindner, W. (eds.) EDBT 2002. LNCS, vol. 2490, Springer, Heidelberg (2002)
15. Schaffert, S., Bry, F.: Querying the Web Reconsidered: A Practical Introduction to Xcerpt. In: Proc. Extreme Markup Languages (2004)
16. Schwentick, T.: XPath Query Containment. SIGMOD Record 33(1), 101–109 (2004)
17. Su, H., Rundensteiner, E.A., Mani, M.: Semantic Query Optimization for XQuery over XML Streams. In: Proc. Int'l. Conf. on Very Large Data Bases (VLDB) (2005)

Attaining Higher Quality for Density Based Algorithms

Morteza Haghir Chehreghani[1], Hassan Abolhassani[1],
and Mostafa Haghir Chehreghani[2]

[1] Department of CE, Sharif University of Technology, Tehran, Iran
{haghir,abolhassani}@ce.sharif.edu
[2] Department of ECE, University of Tehran, Tehran, Iran
m.haghir@ece.ut.ac.ir

Abstract. So far several methods have been proposed for clustering the web. On the other hand, many algorithms have been developed for clustering the relational data, but their usage for the Web is to be investigated. One main category of such algorithms is density based methods providing high quality results. In this paper first, a new density based algorithm is introduced and then it is compared with other algorithms of this category. The proposed algorithm has some interesting properties and capabilities such as hierarchical clustering and sampling, making it suitable for clustering the web data.

1 Introduction

Clustering the data is an important task in data mining that can be done as a pre-processing phase. This task has a great significance on the web; because it can be used for improving the search engines and the web crawling operations. Up to now various methods have been introduced for clustering the web, more of which use techniques such as link analysis [6], [7], [10], content mining [11], [12], and combination of them [13], [17]. At first these methods were based on the text mining techniques. Then gradually link based algorithms such as hub and authority concepts [10], Graph and Spectral Clustering [18] and Page Rank [3] were developed. In continuation another category of algorithms have been developed that use combination of link and content.

For structured data various methods have been developed [8], [12], [15] with the density based algorithms as one important category among them. The main idea of these algorithms is that first a core point is found and then the associated neighborhood distance is investigated. Then according to various criteria, other neighborhoods are found and this process continues until creation of all of clusters [1], [5], [14].

One thing that until now does not have dealt with enough is the use of these algorithms for clustering the web data. We need to apply some improvements on existing algorithms to be consistent with new requirements of the web environment. Density based algorithms are mainly used for clustering the spatial data and since web documents have a large number of dimensions, it seems that using these algorithms in web will be difficult. As we will deal in this paper, we can reduce the number of dimensions by using techniques such as LSI and then prepare the web data for applying density based clustering.

M. Marchiori, J.Z. Pan, and C. de Sainte Marie (Eds.): RR 2007, LNCS 4524, pp. 329–338, 2007.

Density based algorithms try to find clusters according to the density of the points in different regions. Some examples of density based clustering methods are DBSCAN [5], GDBSCAN [14], Optics [1], and DBRS [16]. DBSCAN is the first density-based algorithm. In this algorithm for creation of a new cluster or extending an existing cluster, a neighborhood distance with radius *Eps* must contain at least a minimum number of points denoted by *MinPts*. This algorithm uses R*-tree [2] data structure to find the neighborhood distance of a point in *log n* time complexity.

DBSCAN first, selects a random point *q*. If its neighborhood is sparse then *q* is labeled as noise. Otherwise, a cluster is created and all points in *q*'s neighborhood are placed in this cluster. Then the neighborhood of each *q*'s neighbors is examined to see whether it can be added to the cluster. This process continues to extend an initial cluster as far as possible. Then another unlabelled point is selected and the process continues. If a dataset has clusters with widely varying densities, DBSCAN is not able to handle them efficiently. Since all neighbors are checked, much time may be spent in dense clusters for examining the neighborhoods of all points.

For overcoming this problem, Optics [1] after finding the neighborhood, orders its points. By finding new dense neighborhoods, the points of these regions are also sorted with previously ordered points and then for next expansion, one point with minimum distance within the set of ordered points is selected. If there is no point for expansion, a new un-clustered point is selected and the process continues. However, Optics doesn't solve the problem completely. In fact, there is no difference between regions with high and low densities from the point of view of this algorithm. DBSCAN is not suitable for finding approximate clusters in very large datasets. So, DBRS has been offered in [16]. DBRS iteratively picks an un-clustered point randomly and checks its neighborhood. If it was sparse, considers it as noise. Otherwise, if one or more points from the neighborhood belong(s) to a previously created cluster(s) all points of this neighborhood join to that cluster(s). Otherwise, a new cluster with these points is created. In this algorithm, the next point for expansion is selected from un-clustered points and so DBRS can find several clusters simultaneously.

The proposed algorithm in this paper is a density based algorithm that uses advantages of both Optics and DBRS. The algorithm has another advantage too: It can create hierarchical clusters making it useful for clustering the web data. The remaining of the paper is organized as follows: In section 2, the proposed algorithm is presented with time and memory analysis as well as other properties. Section 3 contains experimental results and finally conclusion and possible future improvements are given in sections 4 and 5.

2 Proposed Algorithm

In this section first we describe the algorithm and its time and memory complexity analysis. Then we explain the advantages of the algorithm.

2.1 Introducing the Algorithm

The informal description of the algorithm is as follows. At first, the algorithm for each point finds its neighborhood points. Then it checks whether this neighborhood satisfies dense condition or not. In the case that the neighborhood would not be dense, another point is selected by random and its neighborhood is found. But if it satisfies dense conditions, the points inside the neighborhood participate in the process of ordering. In this sorting process, all the points inside neighborhood distances of all potential cores are ordered incrementally based on their distance to the nearest associated core. To keep such ordering a MinHeap data structure is used. Every time a dense neighborhood distance is found, the points existing in this region are inserted into the MinHeap, which contains previous sorted points. Of course if a smaller distance for a point (border point) would be discovered, this point and its distance in the MinHeap are updated.

Algorithm: (Data , R , MinPts , MaxPts , IR , LNum)
//R: neighborhood radius
//MinPts: minimum required points for being a dense distance
//MaxPts: maximum points from a neighborhood that can be inserted in the heap
//IR: Internal Radius for decreasing the neighborhood distance in the dense regions
//LNum: Number of desired Levels
```
1     for each object in Data:
2        NList = FindNeighbors( object , R , MinPts );
3        if (NList.count > MaxPts):
4           NList = FindNeighbors( object , IR , MinPts );
5           SortByMinHeap(NList);   // while insertion, updates the previously inserted border
          points.
6        else:
7           SortByMinHeap(NList);  // while insertion, updates the previously inserted border points.
        // Inserts each point of seed in MinHeap in a form: (CoreID,BorderID,Distance)
8     Initialize e by R/LNum or other values that is dependent to application And MaxLevel by 1;
9     while (! EmptyMinHeap):
10       d=GetMin(MinHeap);
11       isFirst = true;
12       for each Cluster Cᵢ in ClusterList that Cᵢ.Active is true:
13          if ( hasIntersection ( d.Neighbors,Cᵢ ) ) :
14             if (isFirst == true):
15                isFirst = false;
16                if ( d.Distance –Cᵢ.Distance > e ):
17                   AddNewLevel(Cᵢ,d);
18                else:
19                   merge( Cᵢ,d.Neighbors );
20             else:
21                if ( d.Distance –Cᵢ.Distance > e ):
22                   AddNewLevel( Cᵢ,d );
23                else:
24                   merge( Cᵢ,d.Neighbors );
25                   deleteCluster( Cᵢ,ClusterList );
26       if (isFirst == true):
27          CreateNewCluster( null , d.Neighbors, d.Distance , MaxLevel )
Add NewLevel(&Cᵢ, &d):
28       Cᵢ.Active = false;
29       newCluster = CreateNewCluster( Cᵢ , d.Neighbors , d.Distance , Cᵢ.Level+1 );
30       if ( newCluster.Level > MaxLevel )
31          MaxLevel = newCluster.Level
```

Fig. 1. Representation of proposed algorithm

When all neighborhood regions are found and their corresponding points are inserted to the heap, this stage is finished.

Then in the second stage, the elements stored in MinHeap are retrieved one by one to construct the clusters. In every extraction, the extracted element (newly created cluster = neighborhood distance) is checked, if it has intersection with a previously constructed cluster, this neighborhood distance joins to it. This process is repeated for all previously constructed clusters. Therefore in joining process it is possible to join more than two clusters because the newly constructed one is filling the gap between some previously constructed ones. Also, in joining process it is possible that the composite cluster would be a more general cluster that should be located in a higher level. This happens when the extracted distance extends a cluster to a more general one or it fills the gap between the two or more clusters. For these situations a new cluster is created in a higher level that includes the new neighborhood distance and the specific (joined) cluster(s). This process enables the algorithm to create the clusters in a hierarchy manner.

Joining smaller clusters and creating larger ones is a property that algorithms such as DBSCAN and Optics which scan data points locally can not provide and hence they can not construct hierarchical clusters. Also it should be noted that DBRS operates randomly, while the proposed algorithm prioritize dense clusters (or dense parts of clusters) and so opposite of DBRS, provides the possibility of hierarchical clustering. The detail of the algorithm is presented in Fig. 1 in details.

When a neighborhood distance is very dense, a considerable number of points are associated to a core point. In such a case, if we operate naively, many points are inserted to the heap and hence the performance of the algorithm is highly degraded. To prevent this problem, condition *if (NList.count > MaxPts)* in line 3 of the algorithm handles it by considering a smaller neighborhood distance. Since this neighborhood is very dense, therefore other points (points that are reside inside the original neighborhood but outside the shorter neighborhood) will exist also in the neighborhood of some other core points which will be inserted into the heap later.

2.2 Time and Memory Complexity Analysis of the Algorithm

By examining the algorithm it is clear that lines 2 and 4 have the most complexity. Line 2 is related to the query *FindNeighbors(object , R , MinPts)* that can be done in $O(log\ n)$ by using the indexed data structures such as *R*-tree* [2] and *SR-tree*[9]. In the worst case the algorithm executes $O(n)$ query and therefore the time complexity for that part would be $O(n\ log\ n)$. The function *SortByMinHeap()* that inserts data into a MinHeap, performs an insertion in $O(log\ n)$ and therefore in average the time complexity for n data insertion would be $O(n\ log\ n)$. Hence the total complexity of the first section is not more than $O(n\ log\ n)$. In the second part of the algorithm, all elements of the heap are retrieved by using the function *GetMin()* which has $O(log\ n)$ complexity (with $O(1)$ the minimum element of heap is taken and the reconstruction cost of heap is $O(log\ n)$). Then next operations for finding the intersections will not have a significant complexity. Of course by using in place sorting methods for Heap Sort algorithm [4], there is no need for such additional memory.

2.3 The Advantages of the Algorithm Compared with Similar Algorithms

With respect to global sorting, the algorithm has several interesting properties:

1- By selecting a suitable radius we can create clusters in several levels. The combined cluster contains more general concepts, its intra cluster similarity is reduced, and the only parameters for controlling the number of levels of hierarchy are the neighborhood radius and the least needed points in the neighborhood distance.

2- As mentioned before, this algorithm contains the advantages of both Optics and DBRS algorithms. Even the algorithm can do better, because DBRS operates almost blindly whereas this algorithm follows a more awareness approach.

3- It is possible to do clustering with sampling by selecting some representative points from each cluster and then continue the process for determining the higher level clusters. In the implementation it is only needed to instead of finding the neighborhood distances for all points (in *for* loop, line 1 Fig. 1), continue while satisfying the condition. Then sorting process for the construction of higher level clusters continues. This scenario performs well in conditions like in Fig. 2. In the left part of the Fig. 2 there is a sample data set for clustering with densities relatively similar. For clustering, first the points of neighborhood regions are ordered. Then proportional with the kind of hierarchy and by applying a greater radius, a large neighborhood distance is found that joins clusters of previous stage.

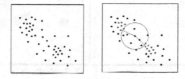

Fig. 2. Clustering with limited sampling

4- Another advantage of the algorithm is its incremental ability. It can construct the data structure for sorting in an off-line process. Later if new items are added, it only needs to add them to the stored data structure. This is not possible in Optics.

3 Experimental Results

3.1 Test 1

In first test we apply the algorithm on a data set; start from $MinPts-3$ and $R=2$ and then increase the values of each parameter. Results are shown in Fig. 3. Clusters created by our algorithm are larger than Optics. It is because of joining method in our algorithm. We assume that the goal is to reach clusters of parts f and g of Fig. 3. So our algorithm reaches faster (with smaller radius), which means it has faster convergence.

However, the most important result is the ability of clustering in several levels. In Fig. 3, three clusters exist that must be combined to construct a larger and more general cluster. Optics doesn't find all of three clusters at first. About Optics, only one cluster has related with two others and other clusters are disjointed with themselves. While our algorithm first creates three base clusters and then combines then in higher level.

3.2 Test 2

I this section, we study the behavior of the algorithm for sampling. So we stop the running after a limited time (about 700 extractions from Min Heap). These conditions happen whenever we are restricted by time or processing limitations which are

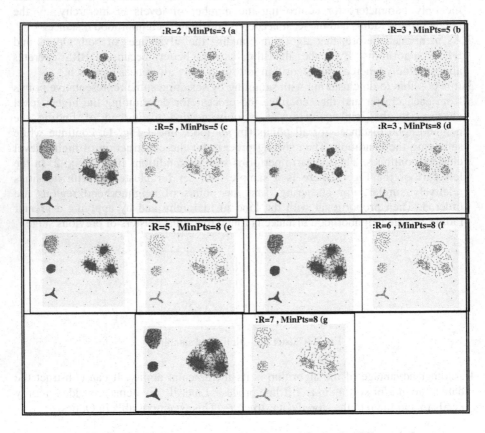

Fig. 3. Results of applying the algorithm and Optics for different values

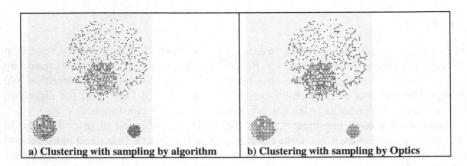

Fig. 4. The performance of sampling from clusters instead of clustering completely

common in clustering task. Results are presented in Fig. 4 part *a* for our algorithm and in part *b* for Optics. It is clear from results that the algorithm works much better than Optics and offers better representatives from clusters. This is because our algorithm performs a global ordering of the points while Optics works locally.

3.3 Test 3

In this test we apply the algorithm to the web data and evaluate the results. Also, since it may be seemed that the algorithm has several parameters which setting them is difficult, in following we argue about the setting of parameters. So, at first 424 web documents are selected in *Politics* domain and after creating frequency vectors, LSI (Latent Semantic Indexing) technique is applied on vectors to reduce the number of dimensions to 2 (this provides a good opportunity for applying spatial data mining algorithms). This is done using MATLAB (The Language of Technical Computing). LSI transforms the original document vectors to a lower dimensional space by analyzing the correlational structure of terms in that document collection such that similar documents that do not share the same terms are placed in the same category. In the next step, these vectors are given to the algorithm to create desired clusters. Since the value of different parameters can affect the quality of clustering, we perform the clustering with parameters *R=20*, *MinPts=7*, and *mutation=1.8* and evaluate the results. The result clusters are shown in Fig. 5 part (b). We number the clusters in a top-down and left to right BFS order.

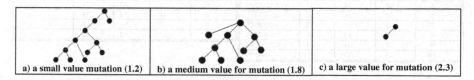

| a) a small value mutation (1.2) | b) a medium value for mutation (1.8) | c) a large value for mutation (2.3) |

Fig. 5. The effect of *mutation* on the hierarchy and on the number of levels

For evaluating the results, several methods have been presented that the most important methods are entropy-based methods and F-measure. F-measure combines two measures, *precision* and *recall*. This measure is defined by (1) and precision (*P*) and recall (*R*) are obtained by (2). In (2) n_j shows the size of cluster *j*, g_i shows the size of class *j* and $N(i,j)$ shows the number of pages of class *i* in cluster *j*.

F-measure (and entropy) only is developed for evaluation of flat clusters (or lowest level of hierarchical clusters). So we must adapt F-measure for evaluation of hierarchical clustering. We first apply F-measure on clusters without any child (lowest level) and then obtain the F-measure of higher clusters from their children. We define the *Precision* of a parent cluster from *Precision* of its children using (3).

$$F(i,j) = \frac{2(P(i,j)*R(i,j))}{(P(i,j)+R(i,j))}, \quad F = \sum_i \frac{g_i}{n} \max_j \{F(i,j)\} \tag{1}$$

$$P(i,j) = N(i,j)/n_j, \quad R(i,j) = N(i,j)/g_i \tag{2}$$

$$P_C = \sum_{\forall k \in C.children} \frac{n_k}{n} P_k + \frac{n - \sum_{\forall k \in C.children} n_k}{n} P_R \tag{3}$$

P_R shows the precision of cluster members that do not belong to sub-clusters. For *recall* we can calculate it from a similar method. But since for finding *recall* we must calculate the R_R by traversing all relevant web pages, so a more simple way can be done by calculating *Recall* straightly and without considering pre-calculated values for sub-clusters. Using this process the results are shown in Table 1. For more evaluation, we apply *K-Means* and compare the results. *K-Means* [19] selects *K* points as cluster centers and assigns each data point to the nearest center. The reassigning is kept until a convergence criterion is met. Since *K-Means* is sensitive to the value of *K* (number of clusters), it is executed with *K=8, 10, and 12,* and the best result is selected (Table 2, with *K=8*). Total F-measure for proposed algorithm is *0.710853* while for *K-Means* is *0.603258*. These values show the efficiency of the proposed algorithm.

Table 1. Results of applying algorithm on web data

CLUSTER ID	N	P	R	F
1	407	.67	.81	0.7333783
2	44	.79	.61	0.6884285
3	209	.68	.75	0.7132867
4	131	.53	.79	0.6343939
5	98	.74	.71	0.7246896
6	57	.56	.63	0.5929411
7	41	.62	.78	0.6908571
8	19	.84	.86	0.8498823
9	32	.81	.74	0.7734193
10	53	.77	.76	0.7649673

Table 2. Results of applying *K-Means* on web data

CLUSTER ID	N	P	R	F
1	17	.59	.41	0.4838
2	68	.52	.58	0.5483636
3	34	.68	.58	0.6260317
4	117	.47	.72	0.5687394
5	26	.63	.71	0.6676119
6	41	.52	.58	0.5483636
7	37	.61	.65	0.6293650
8	84	.62	.82	0.7061111

In following we pay attention to the effect of parameters on the efficiency of the algorithm. Our experiments show that the value of the *R* is not important and selecting an approximate value that can cover the ranges is enough. So we argue on the *mutation* and *MinPts* parameters. We first apply the algorithm with values *R=20*, *MinPts=7*, and *mutation=1.2, 1.8,* and *2.3.* The results are shown in Fig. 5.

As it is obvious from Fig. 5 part *b*, the value *mutation=1.8* constructs appropriate clusters. If we decrease *mutation* (Fig. 5 part *a* with *mutation = 1.2*), the number of clusters and levels will increase, that some clusters will be created by only some extension of a lower cluster. In contrast, by increasing *mutation* to 2.3 (Fig. 5 part *c*), the mutation from one level to higher one will not occur and the constructed clusters will be in one or some limited levels. In following we set *MinPts=5* and by changing the value of *mutation*, investigate the effect of this parameter on the results. The results are shown in Fig. 6 and Fig. 7. It is shown that both of the number of clusters and the number of levels have a reverse relation with *mutation*. Also it is clear that selecting rather near values, doesn't cause a deep change on the number of levels and clusters. So we can only have an estimation of *MinPts* and it is not necessary to determine its value precisely. We can find it by some experiments easily.

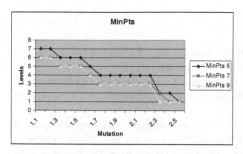

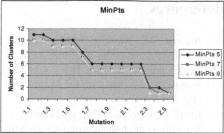

Fig. 6. Number of levels vs. *mutation*   **Fig. 7.** Number of clusters vs. *mutation*

4 Conclusion

In this paper we proposed a new density based algorithm and then explained its advantages compared to other clustering algorithms, i.e. DBSCAN, Optics, and DBRS. Main idea behind this algorithm is that by ordering data before starting clustering and by combining advantages of both Optics and DBRS algorithms, interesting capabilities such as hierarchical clustering and sampling and is provided.

While examining the algorithm and Optics, in addition to the capability of creating clusters in multi levels, faster convergence for clusters was observed. Also this algorithm provides a good way for limited clustering by sampling. Finally we performed some experiments on the web data and concluded that the effect of different parameters on the quality of clustering is very low in near ranges and so we can find parameters values easily by some simple experiments. Also we extended the F-measure for evaluating hierarchical clusters and by comparing the results with *K-Means;* the efficiency of the algorithm was concluded.

5 Future Works

The proposed algorithm has interesting properties, but also it needs some improvements, especially in setting suitable values for different parameters. It seems that we can improve the efficiency of the algorithm in two directions: finding the base dense units with a more flexible method that would be adaptive for different dense regions (associated with R and *MinPts*), and developing a method for doing hierarchy in a better and more precise manner (associated with *mutation*). It is expected that by applying this enhancements the efficiency of the algorithm will considerably improved.

Acknowledgement

This research is supported by Iran Telecommunication Research Center (ITRC).

References

1. Ankerst, M., Breunig, M.M., Kriegel, H.-P., Sander, J.: OPTICS: ordering points to identify the clustering structure. ACM SIGMOD'99, pp. 49–60 (1999)
2. Beckmann, N., Kriegel, H-P., Schneider, R., Seeger, B.: The R*-Tree: An Efficient and Robust Access Method for Points and Rectangles. ACM SIGMOD'90 19(2), 322–331 (1999)
3. Brin, S., Page, L.: The anatomy of a large scale hypertextual web search engine. In: Seventh international conference on World Wide Web 7, Australia, pp. 379–388 (1998)
4. Cormen, T.H., Leiserson, C.E., Rivest, R.L., Stein, C.: Introduction To Algorithms, 2nd edn. p. 136. McGraw-Hill, New York (2001)
5. Ester, M., Kriegel, H.-P., Sander, J., Xu, X.: A Density-Based Algorithm for Discovering Clusters in Large Spatial Databases with Noise. KDD'96, pp. 226–231 (1996)
6. Getoor, L.: Link Mining: A New Data Mining Challenge. ACM SIGKDD Explorations Newsletter 5(1), 84–89 (2003)
7. Henzinger, M.: Hyperlink analysis on the world wide web. Sixteenth ACM conference on Hypertext and hypermedia HYPERTEXT '05, Austria, pp. 1–3 (2005)
8. Jain, A.K., Murty, M.N., Flynn, P.J.: Data Clustering: A Review. ACM Computing Surveys (CSUR) 31(3), 264–323 (1999)
9. Katayama, N., Satoh, S.: The SR-tree: An Index Structure for High-Dimensional Nearest Neighbor Queries. ACM SIGMOD, USA 26(2), 369–380 (1997)
10. Kleinberg, M.: Authoritative sources in a hyperlinked environment. In: Ninth Annual ACM-SIAM Symposium on Discrete Algorithms, SODA (1998)
11. Liu, B., Chang, K.C.-C.: Editorial: Special Issue on Web Content Mining. ACM SIGKDD Explorations Newsletter 6(2), 1–4 (2004)
12. Mueller, C.: Data Clustering Overview. Oral Quals, http://www.osl.iu.edu/~chemuell/projects/presentations/data-clustering-overview.pdf (2004)
13. Nurminen, M., Honkaranta, A., Kärkkäinen, T.: ExtMiner: Combining Multiple Ranking and Clustering Algorithms for Structured Document Retrieval. In: Sixteenth Workshop on Database and Expert Systems Applications, pp. 1036-1040 (2005)
14. Sander, J., Ester, M., Kriegel, H.-P., Xiaowei, X.: Density-based clustering in spatial databases, the algorithm gdbscan and its applications. Data Mining and Knowledge Discovery(KDD) 2(2), 169–194 (1998)
15. Stein, B., Busch, M.: Density-based Cluster Algorithms in Low-dimensional and High-dimensional Applications. In: Second International Workshop on Text-Based Information Retrieval (TIR 05), Fachberichte Informatik, pp. 45–56 (2005)
16. Wang, X., Hamilton, H.J.: DBRS: A Density-Based Spatial Clustering Method with Random Sampling, PAKDD, Korea, pp. 563–575 (2003)
17. Weiss, R., Vélez, B., Sheldon, M.A.: HyPursuit: A Hierarchical Network Search Engine that Exploits Content-Link Hypertext Clustering. In: Proceedings of the seventh ACM conference on Hypertext, USA, pp. 180-193 (1996)
18. Hea, X., Zhaa, H., Ding, C.H.Q., Simon, H.D.: Web document clustering using hyperlink structures. Computational Statistics & Data Analysis 41(1), 19–45 (2002)
19. McQueen, J.: Some methods for classification and analysis of multivariate observations. Berkeley Symposium on Mathematical Statistics and Probability, pp. 281-297 (1967)

Correlation Rules and Ontologies Acquisition in Knowledge Extraction of Image

Hyung Moo Kim and Jae Soo Yoo

Chungbuk National University BK21, Chungbuk Information Technology Center,
Dept. of JeongboTongsin 48 Gaeshin-dong, Cheongju, Korea
kimhyungmoo@chonbuk.ac.kr
yjs@chungbuk.ac.kr

Abstract. After quantization and classification of the deviations between TM and ETM+ images based on approved thresholds, a correlation analysis method for the compared calibration is suggested in this paper. Four time points of raster data for 15 years of the highest group of land surface temperature and the lowest group of vegetation of the Kunsan city, are observed and analyzed their correlations for the change detection of urban land cover. This experiment detected strong and proportional correlation relationship between the highest group of land surface temperature and the lowest group of vegetation index which exceeded R=(+)0.9478, so the proposed correlation analysis model between land surface temperature and vegetation will be able to give proof an effective suitability to the land cover change detection and monitoring.

Keywords: LST, NDVI, Correlation Analysis, Landsat ETM+, Classification.

1 Introduction

This paper suggests a correlation analysis model between the NDVI(Normalized Difference Vegetation Index) lowest area and the highest land surface temperature area which uses Landsat-5 TM(thematic mapper) with Landsat-7 ETM+(enhanced thematic mapper plus) satellite image in order to extract change pattern for the change detection and the spatio-temporal change patterns of urban area surface temperature, suburban area land cover and vegetation. The experiment results of applying the proposed model into change detection in Chollapuk_do Kunsan city area shows that correlation analysis model between the NDVI lowest area and the highest land surface temperature area which uses Landsat-5 TM with Landsat-7 ETM+ satellite image was very efficient in land cover change detection.

Markham and Baker presented post-validation coefficient index value for the substitution of Planck's function at each sensor quality, which was needed to apply into the equation conversion between DN (Digital Number) and spectral radiation of black body when to calculate land surface temperature (LST) using Landsat MSS and Landsat TM[3]. Also, Chander and Markham proposed a new revision process and dynamic segment range of specific constant like gain or offset in each band of radiation correction which reflects the changes of Markham and Baker's equation relationship condition[1]. NASA suggested the approval dynamic scope of gain and offset in Landsat ETM+ which had not been proposed by Chander and Markham[5]. Melesse extracted land cover specific coefficient which was

M. Marchiori, J.Z. Pan, and C. de Sainte Marie (Eds.): RR 2007, LNCS 4524, pp. 339–347, 2007.

calculated and analyzed from NDVI (Normalized vegetation index) then, explained rainfall outflow which reflects the flow changes for 28 years due to the water which was melted at snowed mountains where land and the cities were located beneath[4]. This paper is based on NASA method [2] and applies Melesse model to Kunsan city area then extract a continuous distribution pattern between LST and NDVI using ERDAS IMAGINE 8.7.

2 Study Area and Data

Industrial jar is located in the west bound of the study area, Kunsan city, and the agricultural plain is located in the south bound. Saemangeum reclamation district of 401.00 km² is located between the south bound of Kunsan city and Yellow Sea. North and east bound of Kunsan is relatively forest area.

Fig. 1. Study area: Kunsan city Chollabuk_do, Korea

Table 1. Landsat 7 TM/ETM+ band specifications

Band / Feature / Name	Band1	Band2	Band3	Band4	Band5	Band 7	Band8	Band 6	
	TM/ETM+						ETM+	TM/ETM+	
	Visible			NIR	MIR	SIR	Pan-chromatic	TIR	
	B	G	R					TM	ETM+
Spectral Resolution(μm)	0.45-0.52	0.53-0.61	0.63-0.69	0.78-0.90	1.55-1.75	2.09-2.35	0.52-0.90	10.40-12.50	
Spatial Resolution (m*m)	30*30	30*30	30*30	30*30	30*30	30*30	15*15	120*120	60*60
Temporal Resolution (day)	16	16	16	16	16	16	16	16	

From band 1 to band 5 and band 7 have same sensor characteristics among Landsat TM and ETM+. Band 6 of ETM+ has two sub bands named low and high. Only ETM+ has panchromatic band 8.

Table 2. Landsat TM/ETM+ image pre-processing

No.	Year	Sensor	Pre-processing
1	1987.04.18	Landsat5TM	Geo-rectification
2	1995.10.17	Landsat5TM	Geo-rectification
3	1999.05.21	Landsat5TM	Geo-rectification
4	2002.02.14	Landsat7ETM+	Geo-rectification

The specification detail of 4 time points images are described at table 1. 4 images are selected for representing each 4 unique seasons spring, fall, summer and winter, respectively. Acquired time of each image is ten to twelve o'clock a.m.

3 Image Pre-processing

3.1 Land Cover Pre-processing

The satellite images used in this study, are distributed by ETRI and pre-processed by their image pre-processing component, then extracted the region of interest according to the 1:25,000 scale administrative boundary layer of National Geographic Intelligence Agency of Korea. After the geo-rectification, all images are classified by non-supervised ISODATA clustering algorithm which is built in the ERDAS IMAGINE 8.7.

3.2 NDVI Pre-processing

NDVI is the post-calibrated index of green intensity on the vegetation cover[6]. The principal of NDVI is that the reflexes rates are differ at the NIR and band 3, so these differences can produce an image which represents the conditions of green plant. This equation is denoted as following formula (1)[4].

$$NDVI = (NIR - Red) / (NIR + Red) \tag{1}$$

Following figure 2 shows the algorithm to get the land surface temperature, NDVI specific coefficient ε (land cover specific coefficient ε), then, analyze the correlation between LST (land surface temperature) and NDVI of continuously changing land cover.

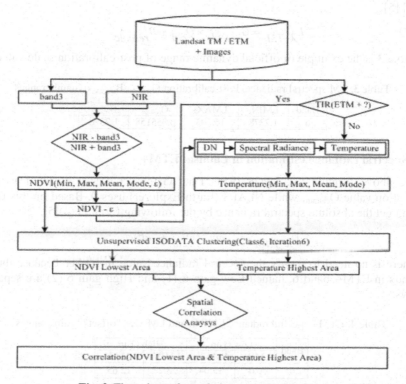

Fig. 2. Flow chart of correlation analysis algorithm

In the figure 2 when the NDVI of ETM+ images are greater than zero, we extract land cover specific coefficient ε, the substitute it as constant K_1 to get the LST, otherwise we get the LST directly from TM or ETM+ images. The rest of the proposed algorithm is correlation analysis between LST highest area and NDVI lowest area after ISODATA clustering.

3.3 LST Pre-processing

1) NASA equation between spectral radiance and temperature

Based on NASA model, this study calibrates surface temperature from the DN (Digital Number) which represents the absolute radiation of land cover. First of all, when each DN of TM and ETM+ images is given, we can subtract the spectral radiance L_λ ($L_{\lambda\text{-TM}}$, $L_{\lambda\text{-ETM+}}$) using the official NASA approval ranges $LMIN_\lambda$ and $LMAX_\lambda$ in following formula (2)[1] [4] [5].

$$L_\lambda = \frac{LMAX_\lambda - LMIN_\lambda}{(Q_{cal\,max} - Q_{cal\,min}) \times (Q_{cal} - Q_{cal\,min})} + LMIN_\lambda \qquad (2)$$

a. Spectral radiance estimation in Landsat TM

By the above formula (2). In case of the least post-calibration value Q_{calmin} (DN) is equal to zero, the $L_{\lambda\text{-TM}}$ is able to be calculated by following linear expression formula (3)[1] [5].

$$L_{\lambda-TM} = G_{rescale} \times Q_{cal} + B_{rescale} \qquad (3)$$

Table 3 is the example of official dynamic range of post-calibration scale values.

Table 3. TM spectral radiance, Post-calibration $G_{rescale}$, $B_{rescale}$ dynamic ranges

Band	$LMIN_\lambda$	$LMAX_\lambda$	$G_{rescale}$	$B_{rescale}$
6	1.2378	15.303	0.055158	1.2378

b. Spectral radiance estimation in Landsat ETM+

In the above formula (2), LPGS (ESO Data Gateway) uses 1 as the least post-calibration value Q_{calmin}, while NLAPS (Earth Explorer) uses 0. Based on this folicy, we can get the absolute spectral radiance by the following formula (4)[5].

$$L_{\lambda-ETM} = "gain" \times Q_{cal} + "offset" \qquad (4)$$

There is no need to rectify the spectral radiance value in ETM+ because the two subbands in ETM+ band 6, named Low gain 6 (1) and High gain 6 (2) are separated always.

Table 4. ETM+ spectral radiance $LMIN\lambda$ and $LMAX\lambda$ "offset" "gain" ranges

Band	Low Gain		High Gain	
	$LMIN_\lambda$	$LMAX_\lambda$	$LMIN_\lambda$	$LMAX_\lambda$
6	0.0	17.04	3.2	12.65

2) Landsat TM/ETM+ Temperature

a. NASA model to extract temperature from TM/ETM+ images

As discussed in the above formulas (1) to (4), there is the relationship between the spectral radiance value L_λ ($L_{\lambda\text{-TM}}$, $L_{\lambda\text{-ETM+}}$) and the absolute temperature $°K$(Kelvin). This can be denoted like following formula (5)[4] [5].

$$T(°K) = \frac{K_2}{ln((K_1/L_\lambda)+1)} \tag{5}$$

In the formula (5), DN means raster pixel value, L_λ ($L_{\lambda\text{-TM}}$, $L_{\lambda\text{-ETM+}}$) means the energy strength of solar light, and T means the absolute temperature of the land surface. K_1 is the post-calibration constant of spectral radiance, and k_2 is the post-calibration constant of absolute temperature.

Table 5. Landsat 5/7, TM/ETM+ thermal band calibration constants

constants \ sensors	K_1	K_2
Landsat-5 TM	607.76	1260.56
Landsat-7 ETM+	666.09	1282.71

b. Melesse model to extract temperature from NDVI coefficient

Melesse model uses NDVI coefficient, the extract temperature from the same Planck function presented at formula (6)[4].

$$T_{NDVI}(°K) = \frac{K_2}{ln((\varepsilon \times K_1/L_\lambda)+1)} \tag{6}$$

In the formula (6), T means absolute temperature of land surface, L_λ is calibrated by formula (2) with options like $Q_{calmin} = 1$, $Q_{calmax} = 255$, $L_{max} = 17.04$ [W/(m^{2}sr^1 μ m^1)], and $L_{min} = 0$ [W(m^{2}sr^1 μ m^1)]. ε means band specific coefficient and is came from NDVI which is calculated by formula (1).

In case of NDVI > 0, ε is 1.009 + 0.047 * (ln NDVI), otherwise ε takes constant 1. K_1 means spectral radiance post-calibration constant 666.09 (Landsat-7 ETM+), and K_2 means temperature post-calibration constant 1282.71K (Landsat-7 ETM+).

4 Experiment Result and Evaluation

Land cover specific coefficient εs that canbe substitute spectral radiance post-calibration constant K_1 of ETM+ images are presented at table 6. NDVI-means in the study area are in the range of positive until 1995, then are in the range of negative from 1999. In the year 2002, since the image is an ETM+ and the NDVI-mean indicates -0.014 and the NDVI-mode indicates -0.00044, NDVI- ε should be 1. However we separate 2002.02.14 as 2002.02.14-a and 2002.02.14-b.

Table 6. NDVI ranges and NDVI-εfor estimation of land surface temperature

NDVIs \ Year	NDVI-Min	Max	Mode	Mean	ε
1987.04.18	-0.5	0.543	-0.00095	0.0013	0.6966
1995.10.17	-0.705	0.688	-0.00024	0.0533	0.8712
1999.05.21	-0.571	0.591	-0.00146	-0.0003	1
2002.02.14-a	-0.508	0.496	-0.00044	-0.014	1
2002.02.14-b	0.113	0.113	0.113	0.113	0.9065

In case of 2002.02.14-b, land cover specific coefficient $\varepsilon^* K_1$ substitute K_1. As the result of this substitution, temperature increases from +6.55 to +11.817, and the deviation increases -1.452 to -6.717. These means that 2002.02.14-b method is worse than 2002.02.14-a.

Table 7. Observed temperature and estimated land surface temperature(unit: °C)

Temps \ Year	Observed	Landsat TM/ETM+ LST	Dev.
2002.02.14-a	5.1	6.552	-1.452
Avr.	17.3	16.45	0.85
2002.02.14-b	5.1	11.817	-6.717
Avr.	17.30	17.77	-0.47

This paper applied the method 2002.02.14-a to get the land surface temperature from satellite images and the method of 2002.02.14-b was not applied.

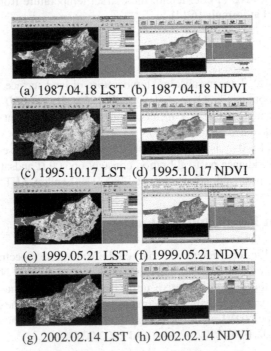

(a) 1987.04.18 LST (b) 1987.04.18 NDVI

(c) 1995.10.17 LST (d) 1995.10.17 NDVI

(e) 1999.05.21 LST (f) 1999.05.21 NDVI

(g) 2002.02.14 LST (h) 2002.02.14 NDVI

Fig. 3. Land cover clustering of LST and NDVI

Four time points of Kunsan city area images representing four unique seasons are selected and pre-processed, then classified by the non-supervised ISODATA clustering algorithm. (b), (d), (f) and (h) of figure 3 show that NDVI lowest areas are changing to the changes of compared LST.

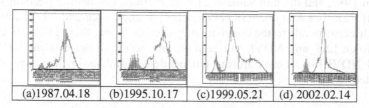

| (a)1987.04.18 | (b)1995.10.17 | (c)1999.05.21 | (d) 2002.02.14 |

Fig. 4. Kunsan city NDVI histogram

When it sees figure 4, the left half from NDVI zero is growing sharpen more as the time passing. The result of experiment that analyze the correlation between this NDVI lowest area and the LST highest area is presented at table 8.

Table 8. Correlation coefficient between the highest LST and the lowest NDVI

Variables Year	LST Highest (km²)	NDVI Lowest (km²)
LST Highest	1	
NDVI Lowest	R=(+)0.947822772	1

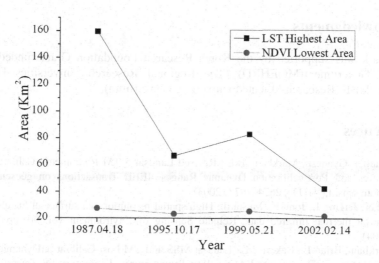

Fig. 5. Correlation scattergram between the highest LST and the lowest NDVI

In the Kunsan city area, LST highest area changes within the range of 42.40 km² - 159.51 km², the median is 75.02km², the standard error is 25.26km², and the SD is 50.53km².

Also, NDVI lowest area changes within the range of 21.60km² – 27.37 km², the median is 24.27km², the standard error is 1.25km², and the SD is 2.50km².

The result of experiment shows that the max value of LST highest area is 112.1 km² in 1997, the min value is 67.9 km² in 1995, the max value of NDVI lowest area is 27.3 km² in 1987, and the min value is 21.6 km² in 2002. The overall pearson's correlation coefficient is r = (+) 0.9478 between LST highest area and NDVI lowest area. The result corresponds to the conventional researches that there is negative correlation between LST and NDVI. Furthermore our result shows that the LST highest area and NDVI lowest area are the independent variables in the study of surface change detection.

5 Conclusion

In order to find out the efficient method to detect the changes of cities, this study observed land surface temperature of land cover and vegetation pattern after designing a correlation analysis between LST highest area and NDVI lowest area. This paper defined the process to convert the land surface temperature from satellite images, those are varying Landsat7 TM/ETM+ respectively. Especially, in case of ETM+ we adopted Mellesse's NDVI specific LST calculation coefficient then we applied them to Chollabuk_do Kunsan city land cover change detection. This experiment shows the result that there is the overall pearson's correlation coefficient is r = (+) 0.9478. With this result we suggest that the raster based LST highest area-NDVI lowest area model is very efficient in the field of land cover detection.

Acknowledgments

This work was supported by the Korea Research Foundation Grant funded by the Korean Government(MOEHRD) (The Regional Research Universities Program/ Chungbuk BIT Research-Oriented University Consortium).

References

[1] Chander, Gyanesh, Markham, B.L.: Revised Landsat-5 TM Radiometric Calibration Procedures and Post-calibration Dynamic Ranges. IEEE Transactions on geoscience and remote sensing 41(11), 2674–2677 (2003)
[2] Fisher, Jeremy I., John F., Mustard.: High spatial resolution sea surface climatology from Landsat thermal infrared data, Remote Sensing of Environment vol. 90, pp. 293–307 (2004)
[3] Markham, Brian L., Bakerl, J.L.: Landsat MSS and TM Post-CalibrationDynamic Ranges, Atmospheric Reflectance and At-Satellite Temperatures, Laboratory for Terrestrial Physics-NASA/Goddard Space Flight Center, Greenbelt, MD. 20771, pp.3-7 (1986)
[4] Melesse, Assefa, M.: Spatiotemporal dynamics of land surface parameters in the Red river of the north basin. Physics and Chemistry of the Earth 29, 795–810 (2004)

[5] NASA. Landsat Project Science Office. Landsat 7 Science Data Users Handbook. Chapt.11-Data Products, http://ltpwww.gsfc.nasa.gov/IAS/handbook/handbook_htmls/ chapter11/chapter11.html:11.1-11.4 (2004)

[6] Rouse, J. W., Haas, R. H., Schell, J. A.: Monitoring vegetation systems in the Great Plains with ERTS. In: Proc. Third Earth Resources Technology Satellite-1 Symposium, Greenbelt, NASA SP-351, pp.3010–3017 (1974)

[7] Suga, Y., Ohno, H., Ogawa, K., Ohno, K., Yamada.: Detection of surface temperature from Landsat-7/ETM+. Adv. Space Res. 32(11), 2235–2240 (2003)

Hybrid Reasoning with Rules and Constraints under Well-Founded Semantics

Włodzimierz Drabent[1,3], Jakob Henriksson[2], and Jan Małuszyński[3]

[1] Institute of Computer Science, Polish Academy of Sciences,
ul. Ordona 21, Pl – 01-237 Warszawa, Poland
drabent@ipipan.waw.pl
[2] Fakultät für Informatik, Technische Universität Dresden
jakob.henriksson@tu-dresden.de
[3] Department of Computer and Information Science,
Linköping University, S 581 83 Linköping, Sweden
janma@ida.liu.se

Abstract. The paper presents an architecture and implementation techniques for hybrid integration of normal clauses under well-founded semantics with ontologies specified in Description Logics. The described prototype uses XSB Prolog both for rule reasoning and for controlling communication with the ontology reasoner RacerPro. The query answering techniques for hybrid rules implemented in this prototype are sound wrt. the declarative semantics, extending the well-founded semantics of normal programs and are faithful wrt. FOL.

1 Introduction

The objective of this paper is to demonstrate a case of re-use of existing reasoners for a logically sound integration of rules supporting non-monotonic reasoning with ontologies formalized in Description Logic (DL).

The paper discusses implementation of a hybrid reasoner that combines XSB Prolog [8] with any DIG-compatible ontology reasoner. The objective is to extend normal logic programs under well-founded semantics by allowing ontological constraints in the body. We consider *hybrid programs*, each of which is a pair (T,P) where T is an ontology specified as a set of DL axioms, and P is a set of normal clauses extended with queries to T in the bodies. In this paper we consider hybrid programs extending Datalog, but the presented implementation techniques are applicable to the general case.

A declarative semantics of hybrid programs was defined in our previous work [2] and is briefly summarized in Section 2. The implementation is based on the operational semantics of [2] which answers queries by combining SLS-resolution with ontological reasoning. The operational semantics is sound wrt. the declarative one and complete for a restricted class of hybrid programs (see [2] for details). In the special case when the rules of P do not involve negation a hybrid program can be seen as a set of axioms in FOL. In that case the semantics of a hybrid program is a set of atomic logical consequences of the axioms, and is thus faithful to the semantics of FOL. A related work based on well-founded semantics does not have this property [4].

The presented prototype extends our previous work [1] where negation in the rules was not allowed.

M. Marchiori, J.Z. Pan, and C. de Sainte Marie (Eds.): RR 2007, LNCS 4524, pp. 348–357, 2007.

2   Hybrid Programs

In this section we first introduce the syntax of hybrid programs. We then briefly discuss the declarative semantics of hybrid programs and its operational semantics.

The Syntax. The syntax of hybrid programs is derived from the syntax of the component languages. The component languages considered here are Datalog with negation and some DL-based ontology language. We assume that the alphabets of predicate letters of Datalog and of the ontology language are disjoint, but both languages have common variables and constants. A standard Datalog syntax is extended by allowing ontological constraints to appear in the rule bodies. At the moment we only allow constraints of the form $C(x)$ or $\neg C(x)$ where C is a concept of the ontology and x is a variable or a constant. Conjunction of such constraints will be called a conjunctive constraint. By a disjunctive constraint we will mean a disjunction of conjunctive constraints. Thus, a hybrid rule looks as follows:

$$R_0 :- R_1, \ldots, R_k, \sim R_{k+1}, \ldots, \sim R_n, C_1, \ldots, C_m.$$

where $R_0, R_1, \ldots, R_n$ are rule literals and $C_1, \ldots, C_m$ are constraints. A hybrid program is a pair (T, P) where T is an ontology (a finite set of axioms of a DL) and P is a finite set of hybrid rules with constraints over the alphabet of T. In practice T will be provided by a declaration associating a short name (prefix) with the URI of the ontology. This is here done by using the syntax use '[ontology uri]' as '[prefix]'. Any symbol a that appears in the ontology is represented in the hybrid rules as prefix#a.

The example used throughout this paper consists of the hybrid program P shown in Listing 1.1. The program P references an ontology modelling a geographical domain shown in Listing 1.2.

Listing 1.1. An example hybrid program describing a two-person game

```
use 'http://dev.metajungle.info/owl/geography.owl' as 'g'.

win(X) :- move(X,Y), ~win(Y).

move(g#e,g#f) :- g#Europe(g#f).
move(g#c,g#f) :- g#ComplFinland(g#f).

move(g#b,g#a).  move(g#a,g#b).  move(g#a,g#c).  move(g#c,g#d).  move(g#d,g#e).
```

The hybrid program in Listing 1.1 describes a two-person game, where each of the players, in order, moves a token from a node of a directed graph, over an edge of the graph. The nodes correspond to geographical objects specified in an ontology (e.g. cities) and are represented by constants. Some axioms of the ontology are given in Listing 1.2. Some edges of a graph (represented in the example by the *move* facts) are labelled by constraints (added as constraints to the respective facts). The constraints refer to the ontology. A move from a position x to a position y is enabled if there is an edge from x to y and the constraint is satisfied. The predicate *win*/1 characterizes the winning positions of the game, as described below.

Listing 1.2. DL axioms of an ontology modelling a geographical domain

---
T–Box : *Finland* ⊑ *Europe* , *ComplFinland* ≡ ¬*Finland*
A–Box : *Finland*(*b*) , *Europe*(*c*) , *Europe*(*d*) , *Europe*(*e*) , *Top*(*f*) , *Top*(*a*) , *Top*(*b*)

A position is winning if a move is enabled to a position which is not winning (call it losing). Obviously a position where no moves are enabled is losing. Thus, position f is losing. The move from e to f is enabled only if f is in Europe. This cannot be concluded from the ontology. Consequently we cannot conclude that e is a winning position. Similarly, we cannot conclude that f is not in Finland which is required for the move from c to f. However, it follows from the ontology that if f is not in Europe it is also not in Finland. Hence one of the conditions holds for f. Consequently c is a winning position: if f is in Europe, e is winning, d is losing and c is winning. Otherwise f is not in Finland and c is winning.

The positions a and b cannot be classified as winning or losing, since from a one can always move to b where the only enabled move is back to a. The status of d and e is also not clear, but for different reasons discussed above. In some, but not all models of the ontology e is winning and d is losing and in the remaining ones the opposite holds.

The Declarative Semantics. In [2] we define a formal semantics of hybrid programs, extending the well-founded semantics of normal programs. Here we survey informally the main ideas. The well-founded semantics of normal programs is three-valued and gives a fixpoint formalization of the way of reasoning illustrated by the game example, when the constraints are neglected. It assigns to every element of the Herbrand base one of the logical values *true* (e.g. $win(c)$), *false* (e.g. $win(f)$) or *undefined* (e.g. $win(a)$).

The constraints added to the rule bodies refer to the ontology. As illustrated by the example, a ground instance of a constraint may have different truth values in different models of the ontology. Given a hybrid program (T, P) and a model M of T consider the set $ground(P)$ of all ground instances of the rules in P. Each of the ground constraints is either true or false in M. Denote by P/M the set obtained from $ground(P)$ by removing each rule including a constraint false in M and by removing all constraints (which are thus true) from the remaining rules. As P/M is a normal program it has a standard well-founded model. A ground literal p ($\sim p$) is said to follow from the program iff p is true (p is false) in the well-founded model of P/M for every M. The declarative semantics of P is defined as the set of all ground literals which follow from the program. Notice that there may be cases where neither p nor $\sim p$ follows from the program. This happens if there exist models M_1 and M_2 of T such that the logical values of p in the well-founded models of P/M_1 and P/M_2 are different, or if the logical value of p in the well-founded model of P/M is *undefined* for every model M of T.

The Operational Semantics. The implementation discussed below focuses on answering atomic queries and ground negated literal queries. We now informally sketch the principles of computing answers underlying our implementation. They are based on the operational semantics of hybrid programs presented in [2] by abstract notions of two kinds of derivation trees, called *t-tree* and *tu-tree* which are defined by a mutually recursive definition. These notions extend the well-known concept of SLD-trees to the case of hybrid programs, to handle negation and constraints. In the presentation below the term *derivation tree (d-tree)* is used whenever the statement applies to both kinds of trees.

The nodes of d-trees are labelled by goals, consisting of rule literals and constraints. The conjunction of all constraints of a node will be called *the constraint of the node*. The label of the root is called *the initial goal* of the tree. A leaf of a d-tree is called *successful* if it does not include rule literals and if its constraint is satisfiable. The other leaf nodes are called *failed* nodes. In every non-leaf node one of the rule-literals is distinguished. This literal is called a *selected literal* of the node. As usual, we assume existence of a selection function that determines the selected literals of the nodes.

For the sake of simplicity we restrict the presentation to the case of ground initial goals. For a formal general treatment the reader is referred to [2]. In the case when the initial goal g of a d-tree is ground the tree has the following property. Let $C_1, \ldots, C_k$ be the constraints of all successful leaves of a d-tree t. Then:

- If t is a t-tree then $(\exists (C_1 \vee \ldots \vee C_k)) \rightarrow g$. Thus g follows from the program if $\exists (C_1 \vee \ldots \vee C_k)$ is a logical consequence of the ontology.
- If t is a tu-tree then $(\neg \exists (C_1 \vee \ldots \vee C_k)) \rightarrow \neg g$. Thus the negation of g follows from the program if $\neg \exists (C_1 \vee \ldots \vee C_k)$ (or equivalently $\neg \exists C_1 \wedge \ldots \wedge \neg \exists C_k$) is a logical consequence of the ontology.

Thus to answer a ground query g our prototype constructs a t-tree with g as its initial goal and checks if the respective disjunctive constraint, existentially quantified, is a logical consequence of the ontology.

We now explain how d-trees are constructed for a given ground initial goal g. This is very similar to construction of an SLD-tree. Every step is an attempt to extend a tree which initially has only one node labelled by g. At every step one node n, not marked as failed, is considered. Let q be the goal of the node, let s be its selected literal and let C be the conjunction of its constraints. The following cases are considered separately:

1. *s is positive.* Let $h \text{ :- } B, Q$ be a (renamed) rule of the hybrid program, where B are rule literals and Q are constraints, such that:
   - it was not used yet for n,
   - a most general unifier θ of h and s exists,
   - the constraint $(C \wedge Q)\theta$ is satisfiable.
   Then a child is added to n with the label obtained from q by replacing s by $(B, Q)\theta$. If no child of n can be created n is marked as a failed node.
2. *s is negative, i.e. of the form* $\sim l$. Two subcases are:
   (a) If l is non-ground, or recursion through negation has been discovered (see below) then:
      - If the d-tree is a t-tree then the node n is marked as a failed node and won't be considered in the next steps of the derivation.
      - If the d-tree is a tu-tree then a child is added to n with the label obtained be removing s from q.
   (b) Otherwise l is ground; the step is completed after construction of a separate d-tree t for l. The kind of the separately constructed tree is different from the kind of the main tree, thus it is a tu-tree if the latter is a t-tree, and t-tree if the

latter is a tu-tree. Let $C_1, \ldots, C_k$ be the constraints of the successful leaves of t. If the constraint $C' = C \wedge \neg \exists C_1 \wedge \ldots \wedge \neg \exists C_k$ is satisfiable then a child is added to node n with the label obtained from q by removing s and replacing C by C'. Otherwise the node is marked as failed. In particular, if $k = 0$ (no successful leaf) C' is equivalent to C. On the other hand, if some $C_i (1 \le i \le k)$ is *true*, the constraint C' is equivalent to *false* and is not satisfiable.

In general the construction of a d-tree may not terminate for recursive rules. Recursion not involving negative literals may produce infinite branches of the constructed d-tree. Recursion through negation may require construction of infinite number of d-trees. In our implementation tabling is used and allows to cut the loops in the case when the same goal re-appears in the process.

3   Reasoner for Datalog with Ontological Constraints

In this section we describe a prototype reasoner for hybrid programs integrating Datalog with negation and ontological theories. The main objective is to show how existing rule reasoners and ontology reasoners are re-used for reasoning on hybrid programs. The prototype re-uses the Prolog engine XSB [8] and a DIG-compliant ontology reasoner (e.g. RacerPro [5]) for answering queries to hybrid programs.

In Section 3.1 we discuss a transformation technique for re-using an existing rule reasoner for handling hybrid programs without negation. In Section 3.2 we generalize this idea to programs with negation.

3.1   Reusing a Prolog Engine for Hybrid Rules

Since XSB cannot handle the ontological predicates in a hybrid program P, we transform P into a standard Prolog program $P' = t(P)$ via a transformation function t. The transformed program encapsulates the ontological predicates in Prolog lists. In this way the variables referred to by the ontology predicates will be processed by the engine during resolution, but the predicates themselves will never be selected by the engine's selection function. At a later stage, the semi-processed ontology predicates can properly be processed by an ontology reasoner. Thus, after applying the transformation t on a hybrid program P we can execute the transformed rules P' using an XSB engine.

An answer produced by XSB for a goal g provides a conjunction of constraints C, and a substitution θ for the variables of g. For a program P without negation, C implies $g\theta$ in the well-founded semantics of P. (This follows from the soundness of the operational semantics [2], as obtaining such an answer by XSB corresponds to constructing a branch of a t-tree for g.)

The original idea of this transformation technique was described in our previous work [1] and we refer the reader there for more details. Here we demonstrate the technique on an example. Consider the hybrid program S in Listing 1.3, referencing an ontology using the prefix o.

Listing 1.3. Hybrid program S

```
use 'http://owl.org/example.owl' as 'o'.

p(X,Y) :-
    q(X,Y), r(Y,X), o#C(X).
q(o#a,o#b).
r(o#b,o#a).
q(o#c,o#d).
r(o#d,o#c).
```

Listing 1.4. Prolog program $S' = t(S)$

```
p(X,Y,[o__C(X)|Var_0]) :-
    q(X,Y,Var_1), r(Y,X,Var_2),
    append(Var_1,Var_2,Var_0).

q(o__a,o__b,[]).
r(o__b,o__a,[]).
q(o__c,o__d,[]).
r(o__d,o__c,[]).
```

The hybrid program S in Listing 1.3 is transformed via t to the Prolog program S' shown in Listing 1.4. The program in Listing 1.4 may now be executed by a Prolog engine and its resulting constraints (collected as a Prolog list) can be verified at a later stage using an ontology reasoner. Notice the ontology declaration being dropped by the transformation. This information is however remembered by the controlling system executing the transformation. For practical reasons, in the transformed program, all ontology references are prefixed by the ontology declaration prefix (here o) followed by the characters __.

3.2 Implementing the Operational Semantics

The approach described in [1] and outlined above is applicable to programs without negation. Now we describe how to extend it to implement the operational semantics of hybrid programs with negation, described in Section 2. We have to construct d-trees (i.e. t- and tu-trees) for ground goals, and collect the constraints of their successful leaves. The top-level computation is a construction of a t-tree for a possibly non-ground goal. Top-level computations are similar to those described above, i.e., of a program without negation.

To separate constraints from rule literals we employ a program transformation which is an extension of the one described above. To construct a d-tree and collect its answers, we use a metainterpreter executing a transformed program.

A main technical problem is that a d-tree may be infinite, and that an infinite recursion through negation may lead to an attempt to construct an infinite set of d-trees. To cut infinite branches of a d-tree we apply the native tabulation of XSB Prolog. However, it turns out that the tabulation of XSB cannot be used to discover an infinite loop of the metainterpreter, related to an infinite set of d-trees (the details are explained later). Thus, tabulation for this purpose is implemented by the metainterpreter.

Each predicate of a transformed program has three additional arguments (in contrast to one extra argument in the case without negation outlined above). The first is a table for tabulating recursive calls of the metainterpreter, the second is the resulting conjunction of constraints and the third indicates whether the tree under construction is a t-tree or a tu-tree.

A query interface to the transformed program is shown in Listing 1.5. The predicate hgoal/2 executes a given goal G, with the additional arguments being an empty table, a variable to carry the resulting constraint, and a mark t indicating that a (branch of a) t-tree is to be built. As a result it provides an instance of G and the obtained constraint. This is a simple interface, producing the answers for G one by one. To obtain the disjunction of all the answers for a ground goal G, we have to augment it with additional

Listing 1.5. Query interface

```
hgoal(G,Const) :-
    % Append extra arguments. Start with an empty table and a t-tree.
    G =.. ListG, append(ListG, [[],Const,t], ListGoal), Goal =.. ListGoal,
    % Execute the goal with the transformed program.
    Goal.
```

arguments, as in Listing 1.5 and construct a t-tree, as described below. We do not here discuss how to obtain a disjunction of all the answers for a non-ground goal.

The program transformation is illustrated in Listing 1.6 by a Prolog program obtained from the example hybrid program of Listing 1.1. As long as negative literals are not involved, the transformation is similar to the one described previously; just two more arguments are added to each predicate. Negative rule literals are translated according to the semantics of Section 2, a tree is being built for the goal under negation. The kind of tree built is tu if the kind of the current tree is t, and vice versa. If the construction of the tree fails then the current computation fails if we are within a t-tree, and continues without changing the constraints if we are within a tu-tree[1]. If the tree is successfully constructed then a disjunction Const of constraints is obtained. The existential quantification of the disjunction is negated and the result is added to the accumulated constraints.

Listing 1.6. A transformed hybrid program

```
win(X,Tbl,Var_T0,Mode) :-
    move(X,Y,Tbl,Var_T1,Mode),
    swapmode(Mode,Mode1),                  % Change t into tu, and tu into t
    ( tree( win(Y,Tbl,_,Mode1), Const )    % Construct new derivation tree.
    ->     negateConstraintDisj( Const, ConstNeg ),
           append(Var_T1,ConstNeg,Var_T0)
    ;
      Mode = tu  ->  Var_T0 = Var_T1       % When the tree not constructed.
    ).

move(g__e,g__f,_,[g__Europe(g__f)],_).
move(g__c,g__f,_,[g__ComplFinland(g__f)],_).
move(g__b,g__a,_,[],_).
move(g__a,g__b,_,[],_).
move(g__a,g__c,_,[],_).
move(g__c,g__d,_,[],_).
move(g__d,g__e,_,[],_).
```

In order to perform different actions depending on success or failure of construction of a tree, the tree constructing predicate has to appear as the first argument of ->. Alternatively, some other programming construct eventually related to cut (!) has to be used. In all such cases XSB Prolog refuses to tabulate such predicates. This is why we have to take care about discovering attempts to construct an infinite set of trees.

The main predicate of the metainterpreter constructing t- and tu-trees for ground goals is tree/2 (Listing 1.7). It takes a ground atomic goal Goal and a variable to be unified with (disjunction of conjunctive) constraints resulting from the constructed tree for Goal wrt. the transformed program. The last argument of Goal tells which kind of

---

[1] This is case 2a of the operational semantics of Section 2.

tree is to be constructed. The tree is constructed and the constraints collected by the built-in predicate findall/3.

Listing 1.7. Metainterpreter, collecting the successful leaves of trees

```
tree ( Goal , Const )  :−
     groundGoal ( Goal ) ,                        % Check for no floundering
     getTable ( Goal , Table , GoalWithoutTable ) ,
     ( inTable ( GoalWithoutTable , Table )
     −> fail                                      % Recursion through negation
     ;
         addToTable ( Table , GoalWithoutTable , Table2 ) ,
         insertTable ( GoalWithoutTable , Table2 , Goal2 ) ,
         get_constraint_var ( Goal2 , CArg ) , % Argument for findall
         findall ( CArg , Goal2 , Const )      % Construct derivation tree
     ).
```

Additionally, tree/2 performs tabulation to discover whether the current invocation of tree/2 has occurred previously. The first of the extra arguments of the goal contains a table of all goals for which tree/2 has been invoked so far. If the current goal is found in the table it signifies infinite recursion of tree/2. In such a case the attempt to construct a tree should be abandoned. Otherwise, the goal has to be remembered and added to the table. The predicate getTable/3 extracts the table argument from a given goal. The predicate inTable/2 checks if a goal occurs in a table and addToTable/3 adds a goal to a table. The predicate insertTable/3 performs the reverse task to that of getTable/3, by adding a table argument to a goal lacking it.

The predicate groundGoal/1 checks whether or not the root of the tree to be constructed is ground. It checks groundness of the original arguments of the goal, i.e. not those added in the program transformation. Predicate get_constraint_var/2 gets the constraint argument of the goal (which is a variable when get_constraint_var/2 is used). Thus, findall/3 can collect the values of the constraint argument of the successes of the goal.

Our description above does not discuss when the constraints should be checked for satisfiability. This is a matter of implementation strategy. Our first choice is to check satisfiability of the obtained disjunction of the constraints from the leaves of a tree. In such a case, a satisfiability check is to be added at the end of the clause for tree/2 (Listing 1.7). (If predicate hgoal/2 is used at the top-level to produce answers one by one, then checking satisfiability of Const should be added at the end of the clause for hgoal/2, Listing 1.5.) During construction of a tree constraints are only collected. Unsatisfiability of the constraints collected so far would make it possible to prune the search space. However, checking this would require increased communication with the ontology reasoner.

The obtained constraints may be quite complicated, in particular they may contain quantifiers. Section 3.4 of [2] presents conditions under which the constraints are ground.

We are interested in the disjunction of the constraints of tree leaves. Thus, if some of these constraints, existentially quantified, is a logical consequence of the ontology then computing the remaining part of the tree is not necessary. Similarly, if the existential quantification of the disjunction of the constraints obtained up to now is a logical consequence of the ontology then construction of the tree may be abandoned.

3.3   Prototype Implementation

Our prototype implements a controlling system for coupling the involved reasoners to allow querying of hybrid programs. An overview of the architecture of the system is shown in Figure 1. The integrated reasoners are the XSB Prolog engine for handling the rule component and an ontology reasoner (e.g. RacerPro) for handling the ontological constraints in the hybrid program.

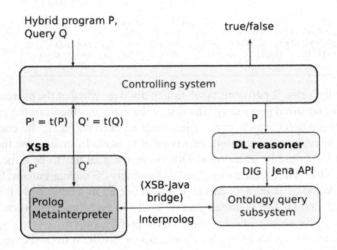

Fig. 1. Hybrid reasoning architecture overview

It is important to make the connection between the Prolog metainterpreter presented in Section 3.2 and the ontology query subsystem shown in Figure 1 for communicating with DL reasoners when verifying constraints. As discussed in Section 3.3, one can employ different computational strategies wrt. verifying constraints. Towards this goal one should augment the metainterpreter, in particular the predicates hgoal/2 and tree/2, with calls to the ontology query subsystem. Augmenting the prototype with such abilities is part of ongoing work.

We are currently working on finalizing the above presented implementation and releasing it as a usable, web-accessible, prototype.

4   Related Work and Conclusions

The paper presents an architecture and implementation techniques for a hybrid reasoning system for hybrid programs, integrating normal clauses and ontologies specified in Description Logics. The described prototype uses XSB Prolog both for rule reasoning and for controlling communication with RacerPro. The query answering techniques for hybrid rules implemented in this prototype are sound wrt. the declarative semantics, extending the well-founded semantics of normal programs, as discussed in a separate paper [2].

The problem of hybrid integration of rules and ontologies has recently been addressed by many authors (see e.g. [3,7,6,4] and references therein). None of them are based on well-founded semantics, save [4]. However, in the declarative semantics of [4] the *truth value* of a rule wrt. an interpretation depends on dl-queries in the rule being *logical consequences* of the respective ontologies. This makes the semantics incompatible with the standard semantics of the first order logic. For example consider two dl-queries Q_1, Q_2 such that in each model of the ontology at least one of them is true, but none of them is a logical consequence of the ontology. Add the rules $p \leftarrow Q_1$ and $p \leftarrow Q_2$, which can be seen as axioms in FOL. Then p is a logical consequence of the ontology and rules combined, but will not follow from the declarative semantics of [4]. In contrast, our approach is compatible with FOL. For achieving this our operational semantics requires collection of constraints which makes possible reasoning by cases.

In the continuation of the presented work we plan:

- to perform experimental evaluation of the prototype on examples referring to large ontologies.
- to experiment with alternative constraint solving strategies; in particular reasoning by cases necessary in our example may not be needed in some applications. In these cases there will be no need in construction and answering of disjunctive DL queries.
- to experiment with hybrid programs based on normal programs rather than on Datalog, using non-nullary term constructors for data structuring.

Acknowledgement

This research has been co-funded by the European Commission and by the Swiss Federal Office for Education and Science within the 6th Framework Programme project REWERSE number 506779 (cf. http://rewerse.net).

References

1. Aßmann, U., Henriksson, J., Maluszynski, J.: Combining safe rules and ontologies by interfacing of reasoners. In: Alferes, J.J., Bailey, J., May, W., Schwertel, U. (eds.) PPSWR 2006. LNCS, vol. 4187, pp. 33–47. Springer, Heidelberg (2006)
2. Drabent, W., Maluszynski, J.: Well-founded semantics for hybrid rules. In: Marchiori, M., Pan, J.Z., de Sainte Marie, C. (eds.) RR 2007. LNCS, vol. 4524, Springer, Heidelberg (To appear 2007)
3. Eiter, T., Ianni, G., Schindlauer, R., Tompits, H.: Effective integration of declarative rules with external evaluations for semantic-web reasoning. In: Proc. of European Semantic Web Conference, pp. 273–287 (2006)
4. Eiter, T., Lukasiewicz, T., Schindlauer, R., Tompits, H.: Well-founded semantics for description logic programs in the semantic web. In: RuleML, pp. 81–97 (2004)
5. Haarslev, V., et al.: RacerPro. WWW Page. http://www.racer-systems.com/products/racerpro/ Accessed (February 10 2007)
6. Motik, B., Sattler, U., Studer, R.: Query Answering for OWL-DL with Rules. J. of Web. Semantics 3, 41–60 (2005)
7. Rosati, R.: DL+log: Tight integration of description logics and disjunctive datalog. In: KR, pp. 68–78 (2006)
8. XSB. WWW Page. http://xsb.sourceforge.net/ Accessed (February 7 2007)

Extending SWRL to Enhance Mathematical Support

Alfonso Sánchez-Macián[1,*], Encarna Pastor[1], Jorge E. López de Vergara[2],
and David López[3]

[1] Dept. Ingeniería de Sistemas Telemáticos, Univ. Politécnica de Madrid
{aasmp, encarna}@dit.upm.es
[2] Dept. Ingeniería Informática, Univ. Autónoma de Madrid
jorge.lopez_vergara@uam.es
[3] Dept. Ingeniería Eléctrica y Electrónica, Univ. de León
david.lopez@unileon.es

Abstract. This paper presents an extension to the Semantic Web Rule
Language and a methodology to enable advanced mathematical support
in SWRL rules. This solution separates mathematical and problem semantics allowing the inclusion of integration, differentiation and other
operations not built-in to SWRL. Using this approach, it is possible to
create rules to cope with complex scenarios that include mathematical
relationships and formulas that exceed the SWRL capabilities.

1 Introduction

Current Semantic Web languages provide a way to represent knowledge formally
and exchange information. Some of these languages introduce Horn-like rules or
First-order-logic support, so they enable declarative programming. One example
is the Semantic Web Rule Language (SWRL) [2].

Developing complex systems will require the use of mathematical functions
that are not currently supported in the Semantic Web languages. An example can
be the implementation of real-time systems for emergency care units or vehicular
control. Semantic Web languages do not provide the tools to cope with these
scenarios. They usually include some mathematical built-ins to perform simple
operations such as addition or subtraction. However, they are not designed to
work with complex formulas.

This paper presents a methodology and a practical approach to add the required functionality to SWRL. The strategy is based on the separation between
mathematical and problem semantics.

2 SWRL and Mathematical Semantics in the Web

The OWL Web Ontology Language [4] provides the base for knowledge representation by means of the definition of classes, properties and individuals. SWRL

---

* Now at University of Southampton IT Innovation Centre, UK.

M. Marchiori, J.Z. Pan, and C. de Sainte Marie (Eds.): RR 2007, LNCS 4524, pp. 358–360, 2007.
© Springer-Verlag Berlin Heidelberg 2007

is based on OWL, adding high level abstract syntax to support Horn-like rules that can be used to deduce new facts in the knowledge-base. SWRL built-ins are used to perform specific mathematical computation (e.g. add, subtract, round, sin), comparisons (e.g. equal) and operations on different types of data value (e.g. strings).

Mathematical built-ins are useful, but the problem arises when the relationship to be presented implies unsupported operators (e.g summations). An example could be the calculation of a cumulative value of a Gaussian distribution as it requires the use of integration operators. There is also a problem of clarity due to mixing mathematical and problem semantics in the same rule. Furthermore, when the formula implies a high number of operations, the memory requirements for the reasoner increase as it has to store many temporary variables. The reason is that SWRL built-ins were designed as predicates. However, the capabilities of the existing reasoners allow us to use the built-ins as functions.

It becomes necessary to find a different way to represent mathematical formulas in SWRL. One of the main efforts to represent mathematical equations and formulas on the Web is OpenMath [1]. OpenMath is formed by a set of tags and content dictionaries. The tags allow the definition of primitive types, variables, symbols (e.g. π) and operators. Content dictionaries (CD) group mathematical symbols and define their semantics including arithmetic functions, transcendental functions, polynomials, differentiation and integration.

3   Working with SWRL and OpenMath

In order to overcome the issues pointed out in Section 2, we propose a combination of SWRL and OpenMath.

The solution uses SWRL to select the information to be included in the formulas and the formula itself. OpenMath is used to represent the formula and pass the information to a mathematical software tool. It is necessary to perform a binding between both languages in order to relate the information located by SWRL and the variables included in the OpenMath expression.

A new class is created called *Formula* with a datatype property (*hasOMExpression*) to hold the OpenMath expression in XML. Additionally, a new built-in (*mathext*) is defined in a new namespace (*swrlbext*). This built-in has a minimum of three arguments. The first one is the result of the formula. The second one is the OpenMath formula. The rest of the arguments are the values that correspond to the variables in the formula. The reason for having a Formula instance rather than just passing the OpenMath expression to mathext is to allow reuse of the formula.

The classes, rules and formulas are written using an OWL editor. The formula, written in OpenMath, is set as the value of the hasOMExpression property of an instance of the Formula class.

When the reasoner uses a rule (Figure 1), it selects the appropriate values, placing them as values of the variables used in the rule. When it finds a customized SWRL built-in, it calls a built-in handler function that delegates

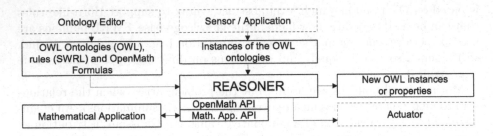

Fig. 1. SWRL-OpenMath Architecture

mathematical computation to programs specially prepared for it. It links to a mathematical application through existing tools (OpenMath and syntax translation APIs), gets the result and returns it to the reasoner. The reasoner resumes the rule execution and generates new statements depending on the values computed using the formula. The proposed architecture has been implemented using Bossam [3] and Mathematica[5].

4   Conclusions

This paper has identified the limitations of Semantic Web Languages to cope with complex scenarios that require the use of advanced mathematical expressions and conditions to deduce new facts. A new practical approach and architecture has been presented to add the required functionality to SWRL. The strategy is based on the separation between mathematical (OpenMath) and problem semantics (SWRL).

Acknowledgement. This work has been partially supported by the Spanish National Plan of Research, Development and Innovation (Ministry of Education and Science) under grants TIC2003-04406 and TSI2005-07306-C02-01.

References

1. Buswell, S., Caprotti, O., Carlisle, D.P., Dewar, M.C., Gaëtano, M., Kohlhase, M.: The OpenMath Standard version 2.0., Technical Report, The OpenMath Society, (June 2004) http://om-candidate.activemath.org/standard/om20-2004-06-30/
2. Horrocks, I., Patel-Schneider, P., Boley, H., Tabet, S., Grosof, B., Dean, M.: SWRL: A Semantic Web Rule Language Combining OWL and RuleML, W3C Member Submission, (May 2004) http://www.w3.org/Submission/SWRL
3. Jang, M., Sohn, J.: Bossam: an extended rule engine for the web. In: Antoniou, G., Boley, H. (eds.) RuleML 2004. LNCS, vol. 3323, pp. 128–138. Springer, Heidelberg (2004)
4. McGuinness, D.L., van Harmelen, F.: OWL Web Ontology Language Overview, W3C Recommendation, (February 2004) http://www.w3.org/TR/owl-features
5. Wolfram, S.: The Mathematica Book, 5th edn. Wolfram Media, Champaign, Illinois, US, (2003) http://documents.wolfram.com/mathematica

Efficiently Querying Relational Databases
Using OWL and SWRL

Martin O'Connor, Ravi Shankar, Samson Tu, Csongor Nyulas, Amar Das,
and Mark Musen

Stanford Medical Informatics, Stanford University School of Medicine,
Stanford, CA 94305
martin.oconnor@stanford.edu

Abstract. For the foreseeable future, most data will continue to be stored in
relational databases. To work with these data in ontology-based applications,
tools and techniques that bridge the two models are required. Mapping all
relational data to ontology instances is often not practical so dynamic data
access approaches are typically employed, though these approaches can still
suffer from scalability problems. The use of rules with these systems presents
an opportunity to employ optimization techniques that can significantly reduce
the amount of data transferred from databases. To illustrate this premise, we
have developed tools that allow direct access to relational data from OWL
applications. We express these data requirements by using extensions to OWL's
rule language SWRL. A variety of optimization techniques ensure that this
process is efficient and scales to large data sets.

1 Introduction

As ontology development tools have been increasingly used to address real-world
problems, scalability has become an important topic [4]. Initially, ontologies were
stored in flat files and fully loaded into application memory when in use. This
approach worked well for small ontologies, but it did not scale well. One of the first
approaches to this problem was to store ontology information directly in relational
databases. However, this approach generally used application-specific storage
formats, and ontologies stored this way could not be used easily by other tools. More
recent approaches have focused on triple stores [http://simile.mit.edu/reports/stores/],
which use native representation of RDF triples to store ontologies. Triple stores are
analogous to relational database management systems and provide efficient storage
and retrieval of ontology information. RDF query languages like RDQL
[http://www.w3.org/Submission/RDQL/] and SPARQL [http://www.w3.org/TR/rdf-
sparql-query/] can provide SQL-like query functionality on triple stores. OWL
ontologies can be stored in triple-store back ends without loss of semantics.

One approach to the problem would be to statically map a relational database to a
triple-store. This approach suffers from several shortcomings, however. First, there is an
issue of data duplication. Furthermore, there are questions about how frequently to

M. Marchiori, J.Z. Pan, and C. de Sainte Marie (Eds.): RR 2007, LNCS 4524, pp. 361–363, 2007.

update triple stores to reflect changes in associated relational database. Knowledge-driven applications requiring up-to-date information require frequent synchronization, which may be cumbersome and problematic. And, of course, supporting knowledge-driven updates, means that synchronization issues arise in the reverse direction.

Ideally, knowledge-driven data requests would retrieve data from live relational databases. This approach requires automatic or semi-automatic dynamic mapping between relational databases and triple-based formats. It also requires a software layer to rewrite knowledge-level queries into SQL-queries for retrieving required data from a database. Further reasoning with retrieved knowledge could be performed in memory. If updates were allowed, the reverse transformation would also be supported. Many recent systems have implemented this approach or variants of it [6,7].

2 Implementation

To support knowledge-driven querying of relational databases, we have developed tools to map data dynamically from relational databases to concepts described in an OWL ontology. Our tools make extensive use of OWL's rule language SWRL [2]. SWRL is used both to specify the OWL-to-relational mapping and to provide a knowledge-level query interface to the system.

This work extends ontology development technologies that we have been producing over the past decade. In particular, we have used Protégé-OWL [5], an open source framework that provides a suite of tools for constructing OWL ontologies and knowledge-based applications, and an associated development environment called SWRLTab for working with SWRL rules [1]. SWRLTab supports the editing and execution of SWRL rules. It also supports the incorporation of user-defined libraries of methods—called *built-ins*—that can be used in rules. Several standard libraries are provided, including implementations for the core SWRL built-ins defined by the SWRL submission [2], a temporal library that can be used to reason with temporal information in SWRL rules, and libraries that allow Abox and Tbox querying. A query library is also provided, and can be used to effectively turn SWRL into a query language.

We used the query extensions provided by SWRLTab to develop a set of tools that can be used to perform knowledge-level queries on data stored in a relational database. We have devised an array of optimization strategies to improve the performance of the underlying relational-to-ontology mapping process. Our primary goal is to offload as much work as possible to the underlying RDBMS by exploiting knowledge of SWRL rules as well as additional information provided by a rule base author. A secondary goal is to reduce the amount of data retrieved from databases during rule processing.

Our optimization strategies include: (1) adding annotations to built-ins to describe the nature of the operations they perform and then using them to rewrite the underlying data retrieval SQL queries to exclude unnecessary data; (2) annotating individual SWRL rules to describe their major 'axis of evaluation' and using these annotated rules to exclude as much unneeded data as possible; (3) using the same annotation technique at the rule base level to control overall relational data access during rule evaluation; (4) making rule engine optimizations by providing a late binding mechanism for mapped data so that information is retrieved only when needed; and finally, (5) using standard database optimization techniques, which are then enhanced by a knowledge-driven process to create database views based on the expected access pattern to data.

3 Conclusions

We have implemented an efficient dynamic OWL-to-relational mapping method and used SWRL to provide a high-level language that uses these mappings. An important benefit of our approach is that it allows knowledge-driven applications to work directly with relational data. We believe that SWRL provides a rich high-level language to specify the data requirements of these applications. In conjunction with relational-to-OWL mapping technology, it can also serve as an efficient means of dealing with legacy relational data.

Acknowledgements. This work was supported in part by the Centers for Disease Control and Prevention under grant number SPO-34603.

References

1. O'Connor M.J., Knublauch, H., Tu, S.W., Grossof, B., Dean, M., Grosso, W.E., Musen, M.A.: Supporting Rule System Interoperability on the Semantic Web with SWRL. In: Fourth International Semantic Web Conference Galway, Ireland (2005)
2. SWRL Submission: http://www.w3.org/Submission/SWRL
3. Crubezy, M., O'Connor, M.J., Buckeridge, D.L., Pincus, Z.S., Musen, M.A.: Ontology-Centered Syndromic Surveillance for Bioterrorism. IEEE Intelligent Systems 20(5), 26–35 (2005)
4. Lopez, V., Sabou, M., Motta, E.: PowerMap: Mapping the Real Semantic Web on the Fly. In: 5th International Semantic Web Conference, Athens, GA, USA (2006)
5. Knublauch, H., Fergerson, R.W., Noy, N.F., Musen, M.A.: The Protégé OWL Plugin: An Open Development Environment for Semantic Web applications. In: McIlraith, S.A., Plexousakis, D., van Harmelen, F. (eds.) ISWC 2004. LNCS, vol. 3298, pp. 229–243. Springer, Heidelberg (2004)
6. Bizer, C.: D2R MAP: A Database to RDF Mapping Language. WWW 2003, Budapest, Hungary (2003)
7. Chen, H., Wang, Y., Wang, H., Mao, Y., Tang, J., Zhou, C., Yin, A., Wu, Z.: Towards a Semantic Web of Relational Databases: a Practical Semantic Toolkit and an In-Use Case from Traditional Chinese Medicine. In: Fifth International Semantic Web Conference (2006)

Top-Down Computation of the Semantics of Weighted Fuzzy Logic Programs

Alexandros Chortaras*, Giorgos Stamou, and Andreas Stafylopatis

School of Electrical and Computer Engineering
National Technical University of Athens,
Zografou 157 80, Athens, Greece
{achort,gstam}@softlab.ntua.gr, andreas@cs.ntua.gr

Abstract. We describe a procedural, query answering-oriented semantics for weighted fuzzy logic programs. The computation of the semantics combines resolution with tabling methodologies and is done by constructing and evaluating an appropriate resolution graph.

1 Introduction

The handling of uncertainty is an important requirement for logic programming languages and has influenced the activities of W3C and RuleML (URW3 Incubator Group and Fuzzy RuleML Technical Group). Fuzzy logic is a way to provide logic programs with the ability to reason under uncertainty (e.g. [5,3]). Weighted fuzzy logic programs (wflps) [1] further extend fuzzy logic programs by introducing weights that allow each atom in a rule to have a different significance.

In this paper we describe a procedural semantics for wflps based on resolution and tabling [4]. A resolution-based query answering procedure for ground *implication based* programs is desribed in [3] and a tabling-based one for *residuated logic programs* in [2]. The latter is developed for programs that combine the several truth values inferred for the same atom using the max *s*-norm only. Wflps allow the use of any *s*-norm instead. We also do not require ground programs.

2 Weighted Fuzzy Logic Programs

A *weighted fuzzy logic program* $\mathcal{P}$ is a finite set of safe fuzzy rules of the form $w : B \leftarrow (w_1; A_1), \ldots, (w_n; A_n)$, where B and A_i are fuzzy atoms, the weight $w \in [0,1]$ is the rule confidence and the weight $w_i \in [0,1]$ the significance of A_i. The rule body is evaluated using a weighted conjunction operator (wco) $\widetilde{\wedge}_{[w_1,\ldots,w_n]}(a_1,\ldots,a_n)$ [1]. Since there is no negation, the semantics of $\mathcal{P}$ are defined similarly to logic programming. The *Herbrand base* $B_\mathcal{P}$ is as in logic programs and an *interpretation* I is a mapping $B_\mathcal{P} \to [0,1]$. We denote a ground

---

* A. Chortaras is on a scholarship from the Alexander S. Onassis Public Benefit Foundation. This work was partially funded by the X-Media project, sponsored by the European Comission under contract no. IST-FP6-26978.

M. Marchiori, J.Z. Pan, and C. de Sainte Marie (Eds.): RR 2007, LNCS 4524, pp. 364–366, 2007.

atom by $\underline{A}$ and by $\underline{A}^I$ its value in I. An atom A is *subsumed* by atom B $(A \sqsubseteq B)$ if there is a substitution θ such that $A = B\theta$. The *inference base* R_A of atom A is the set of all the rules whose head unifies with A by a mgu θ. The *ground inference base* $\underline{R}_{\underline{A}}$ of ground atom $\underline{A}$ consists of the ground instances of $R_{\underline{A}}$. Given a wco $\widetilde{\wedge}$, a t-norm T and an s-norm S, I is a *model* of $\mathcal{P}$ if for all $\underline{B} \in B_{\mathcal{P}}$

$$S\left(\left\{T(w, \widetilde{\wedge}_{[w_1,\ldots,w_n]}(\underline{A}_1^I, \ldots, \underline{A}_n^I))\right\}_{w:\underline{B}\leftarrow(w_1;\underline{A}_1),\ldots,(w_n;\underline{A}_n)\in R_{\underline{B}}}\right) \leq \underline{B}^I \quad (1)$$

If $V(\underline{B}^I)$ is the lhs of (1), the consequence operator $FT_{\mathcal{P}}$, defined by the equations $\underline{B}^{FT_{\mathcal{P}}(I)} = V(\underline{B}^I)$, has a least fixpoint $FT_{\mathcal{P}}^{\uparrow\omega}$ equal to the minimal model $FM_{\mathcal{P}}$ of $\mathcal{P}$, which, if $\widetilde{\wedge}, T, S$ are continuous, is obtained by a process of ω iterative applications of $FT_{\mathcal{P}}$ starting from the interpretation $I_{\perp}$ that maps all atoms to 0. If $FT_{\mathcal{P}}^{\uparrow\omega}$ is unreachable in less than ω steps, only an approximation of it is computable: given an interpretation distance metric, an approximation of $FM_{\mathcal{P}}$ by $FT_{\mathcal{P}}^{\uparrow k}$ at any accuracy level is computable in $k < \omega$ steps (cf. [5]).

3   Procedural Semantics

Given a wflp $\mathcal{P}$ and an atom A, the procedural semantics answer the query $?A$ by effectively computing all the ground atoms $\underline{A} \sqsubseteq A$ that have a non zero value in $FM_{\mathcal{P}}$. Given the preceding discussion, it may be possible to answer a query only approximatively: if $\underline{A} = A\theta$, we say that (θ, v) is an ϵ-*correct* answer to $?A$ for some $\epsilon > 0$ if $\underline{A}^{FM_{\mathcal{P}}} < v + \epsilon$ and a *correct* answer if $\underline{A}^{FM_{\mathcal{P}}} = v$.

In logic programming, query answering is performed by SLD-resolution, a process that tries to find a sequence of substitutions $\theta = \theta_1 \ldots \theta_k$ along a path of rules by which a ground atom $\underline{A} = A\theta$ subsumed by the query can be inferred. If such a sequence is found for $\underline{A}$, it is the correct answer for $\underline{A}$ and any alternative way to obtain θ along another path offers no additional information. This is not the case with wflps: according to (1) all the paths by which $\underline{A}$ may be inferred have to be taken into account. As a result, a resolution process for a fuzzy programming language has in general to consider all the alternative ways of inferencing the ground atoms subsumed by the query (cf. [3]).

For this reason, we propose a query answering algorithm for wflps that relies on the construction of a *resolution graph* G that models in a directed graph all the dependencies between the query and the program rules. The graph has a skeleton $G^{\sharp}$, which is a tree that encodes the non recursive dependencies. The skeleton is augmented into a cyclic graph if the program contains recursive rules. The skeleton is closely related with the *disjunctive derivation trees* of [3].

Given a wflp $\mathcal{P}$ and a query $?A$, G is constructed by creating the root of $G^{\sharp}$, which corresponds to the initial goal A, and then by adding step by step new edges and nodes by computing the inference base of each intermediate goal. The nodes are either *atom* or *rule* nodes. An atom node is labeled by an atom and a rule node by a rule of $\mathcal{P}$, possibly with some of its variables bound to constants. When an atom node α with label B is added to G, it constitutes a new goal, so it is given as children a new rule node ρ for each rule R in the inference base

R_B. If $R_B = \oslash$ then α is a leaf of $G^\sharp$. The connecting edges are marked by the confidence of R and the mgu θ for which the head of $R\theta$ equals $B\theta$. The label of ρ is $R\theta$. In its turn, a rule node ρ with label $w : B \leftarrow (w_1; A_1), \ldots, (w_n; A_n)$ is given n children atom nodes. The label of the i-th child is A_i. The edge connecting ρ with its i-th child is marked by the weight w_i. During the construction, if an atom node α is added in G whose label is subsumed through a substitution θ by the label of an already existing in G atom node α', α is connected with a *subsuming* edge, marked with θ, with α', and α is given no rule node children and becomes a leaf of $G^\sharp$. Each atom node with label B maintains also a set of ground substitution-value pairs (θ, v) which store the truth values v (if $v > 0$) that are computed during the evaluation of G for the ground atoms $B\theta$.

Given an initial interpretation I to initialize the leaves, the evaluation of G is performed bottom-up, moving from the leaves of $G^\sharp$ towards root$(G^\sharp)$. During this process, the substitution-value pairs of each atom node are computed by considering the already completed computations of its children. A rule node with n children, for each ground instance $R\theta$ of its label, computes a multiset with the values $\widetilde{\wedge}_{[w_1,\ldots,w_n]}(a_1, \ldots, a_n)$ where w_i is the weight of the i-th outcoming edge and a_i the value computed by the respective atom node child for a substitution compatible with θ. A non leaf atom node, for each ground instance $B\theta$ of its label, computes the pair $(\theta, S(\{T(w_i, a_i)\}_{i=1}^k))$ where w_i is an outcoming edge weight and a_i the value computed by the respective rule node child for a rule instance with head $B\theta$. A leaf atom with a subsuming outcoming edge obtains its substitution-value pairs directly from the linked atom node. If G is acyclic this process terminates once root$(G^\sharp)$ is reached. Otherwise, an iterative evaluation of G taking each time as initial interpretation the results of the previous evaluation of G may be necessary in order to exactly or approximately answer ?A. It can be shown that the process is sound and complete, so that for any substitution θ such that $\underline{A} = A\theta$ there is a resolution graph G and an iterative valuation of it starting from $I_\perp$, such that (θ, v) is a correct or an ϵ-correct answer for any $\epsilon > 0$ to ?A, where (θ, v) is the substitution-value pair held in root$(G^\sharp)$ for θ.

The above-described construction and evaluation process of G may be subject to optimizations that exploit the particular weight values and structure of $\mathcal{P}$.

References

1. Chortaras, A., Stamou, G., Stafylopatis, A.: Adaptation of weighted fuzzy programs. Lecture Notes in Computer Science, vol. 4132, pp. 45–54 (2006)
2. Damásio, C.V., Medina, J., Ojeda Aciego, M.: A tabulation proof procedure for first-order residuated logic programs: Soundness, completeness and optimizations. In: FUZZ'06: International Conference on Fuzzy Systems, pp. 9576–9583 (2006)
3. Lakshmanan, L.V.S., Shiri, N.: A parametric approach to deductive databases with uncertainty. IEEE Transactions on Knowledge and Data Engineering 13(4), 554–570 (2001)
4. Tamaki, H., Sato, T.: OLD resolution with tabulation. Lecture Notes in Computer Science, vol. 225, pp.84–98 (1986)
5. Vojtáš, P.: Fuzzy logic programming. Fuzzy Sets and Systems 124, 361–370 (2001)

A Visualization Algorithm for Defeasible Logic Rule Bases over RDF Data

Efstratios Kontopoulos[1], Nick Bassiliades[1], and Grigoris Antoniou[2]

[1] Department of Informatics
Aristotle University of Thessaloniki
GR-54124 Thessaloniki, Greece
{skontopo,nbassili}@csd.auth.gr
[2] Institute of Computer Science, FO.R.T.H.
P.O. Box 1385, GR-71110,
Heraklion, Greece
antoniou@ics.forth.gr

Abstract. This work presents a visualization algorithm for defeasible logic rule bases as well as a software tool that applies this algorithm, according to which, a directed graph is produced that represents the rule base. The graph features distinct node types for rules and atomic formulas and distinct connection types for the various rule types of defeasible logic.

1 Introduction

Logic and proofs posses a key role in the acceptance of the Semantic Web on behalf of the users. *Defeasible reasoning* [3] represents a rule-based approach to reasoning with incomplete, changing and conflicting information. Nevertheless, it is based on solid mathematical formulations and is, thus, not fully comprehensible by users, who often need graphical trace and explanation mechanisms for the derived conclusions.

This paper presents a visualization algorithm for defeasible logic rule bases and a software tool that applies this algorithm. For the representation of the rule base, *directed graphs* are applied that feature distinct node and connection types. The tool is called *dl-RuleViz* and is implemented as part of *VDR-DEVICE* [1], an environment for modeling and deploying defeasible logic rule bases on top of RDF ontologies.

2 Visualizing a Defeasible Logic Rule Base

The full theoretical approach, regarding the graphical representation of defeasible reasoning elements was discussed in a previous work of ours [2]. For every class in the rule base, a *class box* with the same name is constructed. Class boxes are containers, which are dynamically populated with one or more *class patterns*. Class patterns express conditions on *filtered subsets* of instances of the specific class and are populated with one or more *slot patterns*. Slot patterns represent conditions on slots (or class properties) and they consist of a slot name and, optionally, a variable and a list of value constraints. The variable is used for unifying the slot value, with the latter having to satisfy the list of constraints.

M. Marchiori, J.Z. Pan, and C. de Sainte Marie (Eds.): RR 2007, LNCS 4524, pp. 367–369, 2007.

For the placement of each element in the graph, an algorithm (Fig. 1) for the visualization of the defeasible logic rule base is proposed that takes advantage of common rule stratification techniques. Unlike the latter, however, that focus on computing the minimal model of a rule set, our algorithm aims at the optimal *visualization* outcome.

```
str:=1
foreach cb∈CBb do stratum(cb):=str
while |RS|≠0 do
    RuleTemp:=∅
    str:=str+1
    foreach R∈RS do
        if   ((∀p∈premises(R) → stratum(class(p))<str) ∧
             (∃p'∈premises(R) ∧ stratum(class(p'))=str-1))
        then stratum(R):=str, RS:=RS-{R}, RuleTemp:=RuleTemp∪{R}
    foreach R∈RuleTemp do
        foreach p∈premises(R) do
            if stratum(class(p))=str-1 then Type:=plain else Type:=expandable,
            in-arrow(R):=in-arrow(R)∪{<p,Type>},
            out-arrow(p):=out-arrow(p)∪{<R,Type>},
    str:=str+1
    CbTemp:=∅
    foreach R∈RuleTemp do
        if unknown(stratum(class(conclusion(R))))
        then stratum(class(conclusion(R))):=str, CbTemp:=CbTemp∪{class(conclusion(R))}
    foreach R∈RuleTemp do
        if type(R)=strictrule then Type:= strict
        else if type(R)=defeasible then Type:=defeasible
        else Type:=defeater,
        if class(conclusion(R))∈CbTemp then Orient:=plain else Orient:=dotted,
        out-arrow(R):=out-arrow(R)∪{<conclusion(R),Orient,Type>},
        in-arrow(class(conclusion(R))):=in-arrow(conclusion(R))∪{<R,Orient,Type>}
```

Fig. 1. The rule stratification algorithm

The algorithm gives a left-to-right orientation to the flow of information in the graph by "*stratifying*" the graph elements, i.e. by calculating the optimal stratum, where each graph element has to be placed. The following steps can be distinguished:

1. All base class boxes are placed in stratum #1.
2. The algorithm enters a loop, consecutively assigning strata to rule circles and derived class boxes, incrementing each time the stratum counter by 1.
   a. A rule circle is assigned to a stratum, if all its premises belong to previous strata, with at least one of them belonging to the immediately previous stratum.
   b. A class box is assigned to a stratum, if it contains the conclusions of rules in the immediately previous stratum.

When a conclusion of a rule serves as a premise for another rule in a previous stratum, the conclusion is not drawn again and the arrow connecting the rule with the conclusion is not drawn backwards. Instead, a "*dotted*" arrow is drawn, commencing from the rule circle and ending in three dots "...", to reduce complexity. By clicking on the arrow, a pop-up window shows the rule isolated in its completeness.

Only the arcs that connect two *consecutive* graph elements are drawn by default. When the stratum difference between a class pattern and a rule circle is greater than 1, the arrow that connects them is "*expandable*". To prevent graph cluttering, expandable arrows are drawn only at the user's request.

For example, suppose that we have the following rule base:

r_1: novel(X) → book(X)
r_2: book(X) ⇒ hardcover(X) r_3: novel(X) ⇒ ¬hardcover(X)

```
r₄: novel(X),collectible(X,"yes") ⇒ rare(X)
r₅: novel(X),author(X,"Asimov"),price(X,Y),Y>18 ⇒ hardcover(X)
```

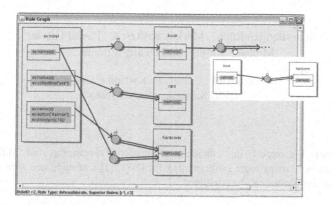

Fig. 2. Implementation of the visualization algorithm by dl-RuleViz

After applying the algorithm, it comes up that four strata (or columns) are needed to display all the graph elements. The resulting graph (Fig. 2), produced by dl-RuleViz, is compliant with the algorithm presented. The pop-up window displays the premises and conclusion of rule r_2.

3 Future Work

Potential improvements of dl-RuleViz and the visualization algorithm include enhancing the derived graph with negation-as-failure and variable unification, for simplifying the display of multiple unifiable class patterns. Expressive visualization of a defeasible logic rule base can then lead to proof explanations. By adding visual rule execution tracing, proof visualization and validation to the dl-RuleViz module, we can delve deeper into the Proof layer of the Semantic Web architecture, implementing facilities that would increase the trust of users towards the Semantic Web.

References

[1] Bassiliades, N., Kontopoulos, E., Antoniou, G.: A Visual Environment for Developing Defeasible Rule Bases for the Semantic Web. In: Adi, A., Stoutenburg, S., Tabet, S. (eds.) RuleML 2005. LNCS, vol. 3791, pp. 172–186. Springer, Heidelberg (2005)

[2] Kontopoulos, E., Bassiliades, N., Antoniou, G.: Visualizing Defeasible Logic Rules for the Semantic Web, 1st Asian Semantic Web Conference (ASWC'06). In: Mizoguchi, R., Shi, Z., Giunchiglia, F. (eds.) ASWC 2006. LNCS, vol. 4185, pp. 278–292. Springer, Heidelberg (2006)

[3] Nute, D.: Defeasible Reasoning. In: Proc. 20th Int. Conference on Systems Science, pp. 470–477. IEEE Press, New York (1987)

Efficient OWL Reasoning with Logic Programs – Evaluations*

Sebastian Rudolph[1], Markus Krötzsch[1], Pascal Hitzler[1],
Michael Sintek[2], and Denny Vrandecic[1]

[1] Institute AIFB, Universität Karlsruhe, Germany
[2] DFKI Kaiserslautern, Germany

Abstract. We report on efficiency evaluations concerning two different approaches to using logic programming for OWL [1] reasoning and show, how the two approaches can be combined.

Introduction

Scalability of reasoning remains one of the major obstacles in leveraging the full power of the Web Ontology Language OWL [1] for practical applications. Among the many possible approaches to address scalability, one of them concerns the use of logic programming for this purpose. It was recently shown that reasoning in Horn-$\mathcal{SHIQ}$ [2,3,4] can be realised by invoking Prolog systems on the output of the KAON2-transformations [5]. Still, performance experiments had not been reported yet.

An entirely different effort to leveraging logic programming for OWL reasoning rests on the idea of approximate reasoning, by allowing some incorrect inferences in order to speed up the reasoning. First experiments with an implementation – called Screech [6], have been encouraging.

In this paper, we report on evaluations concerning the feasibility of the two mentioned approaches. We performed corresponding experiments using the ontologies GALEN, DOLCE, WINE and SEMINTEC.

The KAON2-Transformation

Reasoning with KAON2 is based on special-purpose algorithms which have been designed for dealing with large ABoxes, detailed in [2]. The KAON2 approach transforms OWL DL ontologies to disjunctive datalog, and applies established algorithms for dealing with this formalism. The program returned by the transformation algorithm is in general not logically equivalent to the input TBox, but equisatisfiable, which is sufficient for most reasoning problems.

---

* This work is partially supported by the German Federal Ministry of Education and Research (BMBF) under the SmartWeb project (grant 01 IMD01), by the Deutsche Forschungsgemeinschaft (DFG) under the ReaSem project and by the EU in the IST project NeOn (IST-2006-027595), http://www.neon-project.org/.

M. Marchiori, J.Z. Pan, and C. de Sainte Marie (Eds.): RR 2007, LNCS 4524, pp. 370–373, 2007.

Convenient access to the KAON2 transformation algorithm is given by means of the KAON2 OWL Tool[1] dlpconvert,[2] which can also produce F-Logic serialisations which can be used with F-Logic engines like OntoBroker.

Approximate OWL-Reasoning with Screech

SCREECH uses a modified notion of *split program* [7] to deal with disjunctive datalog: for any rule $H_1 \vee \cdots \vee H_m \leftarrow A_1, \ldots, A_k$, from the output of the KAON2 transformation algorithm, the *derived split rules* are defined as: $H_1 \leftarrow A_1, \ldots, A_k \ \ldots \ H_m \leftarrow A_1, \ldots, A_k$. The *split program* P' of a given program P, obtained by splitting all its rules, is complete but may be unsound wrt. instance retrieval tasks. Note that the data complexity for this is polynomial since P' is (non-disjunctive) datalog. A prototype implementation of our approach is available as the SCREECH OWL approximate reasoner.[3]

Experiments and Evaluation

An approximate reasoning procedure needs to be evaluated on real data from practical applications. So we evaluated the following popular publicly available ontologies: the GALEN Upper Ontology,[4] DOLCE,[5] the WINE ontology,[6] and SEMINTEC.[7] For each of these ontologies, we measured the time and precision for retrieving the extensions of all named classes. The results of our evaluations are summarized in the table below, where also the fraction of disjunctive rules in the KAON2 output can be found for each ontology.

ontology	time saved	correct instances	correct class extensions	disjunctive rules
GALEN	38.0%	91.8%	138/175	54/1449
DOLCE	29.1%	62.1%	93/123	47/1797
WINE	34.5%	95.8%	131/140	26/559
SEMINTEC	67.3%	100%	59/59	0/221

The Data-Tractable OWL Fragment Horn-$\mathcal{SHIQ}$

Horn-$\mathcal{SHIQ}$ is defined as the fragment of OWL DL for which the disjunctive datalog program obtained from the KAON2 transformation is in fact non-disjunctive, i.e. Horn [2,3]. A direct definition using a grammar is due to [4]. Horn-$\mathcal{SHIQ}$'s data complexity is polynomial, qualifying it as a tractable description logic [8]. Its combined complexity is still exponential [4].

---

[1] http://owltools.ontoware.org/

[2] http://logic.aifb.uni-karlsruhe.de/wiki/Dlpconvert

[3] http://logic.aifb.uni-karlsruhe.de/screech

[4] http://www.cs.man.ac.uk/~rector/ontologies/simple-top-bio/

[5] http://www.loa-cnr.it/DOLCE.html

[6] http://www.schemaweb.info/schema/SchemaDetails.aspx?id=62

[7] http://www.cs.put.poznan.pl/alawrynowicz/semintec.htm

In [5] was shown that using off-the shelf Prolog implementations for reasoning with Horn-$\mathcal{SHIQ}$ after the KAON2-transformation is possible in principle by using Prolog with tabling, as implemented e.g. in the XSB system.

It turns out, however, that tabling is too expensive for our test ontologies. For none of our test ontologies, XSB with tabling was able to produce answers to the queries, which shows that it cannot be used naively on realistic data.

Using OntoBroker 5.0 build 690, the results were similar. OntoBroker could be used with our test ontologies only with bottom-up reasoning, which is the least efficient of the reasoning strategies. Consequently, performance was much worse if compared with SCREECH on the KAON2 datalog engine, with about factor 20 for SEMINTEC and factor 100 for WINE. For the GALEN ontology, however, OntoBroker performed drastically better than the KAON2 datalog engine: querying for the extensions of all classes, on average, OntoBroker performed better than the KAON2 datalog engine on the screeched version, by a factor of 3.9. In this experiment, the speedup by SCREECH compared to the unscreeched version on KAON2 was at a factor of 11.4. Overall, using a combination of SCREECH and OntoBroker we obtained a speedup of factor 44.7 compared to using KAON2 on the unscreeched version.

Discussion

The two approaches which we presented can be combined in a straightforward manner, namely by first screeching a given TBox and then performing the subsequent reasoning on a logic programming engine. The results presented for the GALEN ontology indicate that a significant speedup is possible, in this case by an overall factor of 44.7 (i.e. 97.8% time saved), while 91.8% of the retrieved instances are correct.

The SCREECH part of the performance improvement is stable over all tested ontologies. The gain varied between 29.1 and 67.3 %, the amount of correctly retrieved instances was above 91.8% for all but one of the ontologies. It is encouraging that the approach appears to be feasible even for the sophisticated WINE ontology.

Concerning the use of logic programming systems for improving Horn-$\mathcal{SHIQ}$ performance, the results were mostly discouraging, because a naive application of such systems was not possible. However, the drastic speed-up of factor 11.4 (i.e. 91.2% time saved) compared to SCREECH obtained with OntoBroker in bottom-up setting on the GALEN ontology indicates that a special-purpose logic programming system should frequently be able to outperform KAON2 on Horn-$\mathcal{SHIQ}$. But specialised implementations may be needed for this purpose as the off-the-shelf systems are currently not applicable in general.

References

1. McGuinness, D.L., van Harmelen, F.: OWL web ontology language overview (February 2004) http://www.w3.org/TR/owl-features/
2. Motik, B.: Reasoning in Description Logics using Resolution and Deductive Databases. PhD thesis, Universität Karlsruhe (2006)

3. Hustadt, U., Motik, B., Sattler, U.: Data Complexity of Reasoning in Very Expressive Description Logics. In: Kaelbling, L.P., Saffiotti, A. (eds.) Proceedings of the Nineteenth International Joint Conference on Artificial Intelligence, Edinburgh, Scotland, pp. 466–471(2005)
4. Krötzsch, M., Rudolph, S., Hitzler, P.: On the complexity of Horn description logics. In: Grau, B.C., Hitzler, P., Shankey, C., Wallace, E. (eds.) Proceedings of the 2nd Workshop on OWL: Experiences and Directions. CEUR Workshop Proceedings, vol. 216 (November 2006)
5. Krötzsch, M., Hitzler, P., Vrandecic, D., Sintek, M.: How to reason with OWL in a logic programming system. In: Eiter, T., Franconi, E., Hodgson, R., Stephens, S. (eds.) Proceedings of the Second International Conference on Rules and Rule Markup Languages for the Semantic Web, RuleML2006, Athens, Georgia, pp. 17–26. IEEE Computer Society Press, Los Alamitos (2006)
6. Hitzler, P., Vrandecic, D.: Resolution-Based Approximate Reasoning for OWL DL. In: Gil, Y. (ed.) ISWC 2005. LNCS, vol. 3729, pp. 383–397. Springer, Heidelberg (2005)
7. Sakama, C., Inoue, K.: An alternative approach to the semantics of disjunctive logic programs and deductive databases. Journal of Automated Reasoning 13, 145–172 (1994)
8. Grau, B.C.: OWL 1.1 web ontology language tractable fragments (2004)
   http://owl1-1.cs.manchester.ac.uk/tractable.html

Reasoning About XML Schema Mappings in the Presence of Key Constraints and Value Dependencies*

Tadeusz Pankowski[1,2], Jolanta Cybulka[1], and Adam Meissner[1]

[1] Institute of Control and Information Engineering,
Poznań University of Technology, Poland
[2] Faculty of Mathematics and Computer Science,
Adam Mickiewicz University, Poznań, Poland
`tadeusz.pankowski@put.poznan.pl`

1 Introduction

Schema mappings play a central role in both data integration and data exchange, and are understood as high-level specifications describing the relationships between data schemas. Based on these specifications, data structured under a source schema can be transformed into data structured under a target schema. During the transformation some structural constraints, both context-free (the structure) and contextual (e.g. keys and value dependencies) should be taken into account. In this work, we present a formalism for schema mapping specification taking into account key constraints and value dependencies. The formalism extends results from [1,2], and our previous work [3,4]. We illustrate the approach by an example.

2 XML Schema Mappings and Transformations

In data exchange settings, the following *second-order source-to-target dependencies* (SO STDs) are usually used to express schema mappings [1]:

$$\mathcal{M}_{S \to S'} := \exists \mathbf{f} \forall \mathbf{x}(\Phi(\mathbf{x}) \wedge \chi(\mathbf{x}, \mathbf{y}) \Rightarrow \Psi(\mathbf{x}, \mathbf{y})), \tag{1}$$

where: $\mathbf{f}$ is a vector of function symbols, $\mathbf{x}$, $\mathbf{y}$ are vectors of variables; Φ is a conjunction of atoms over the source schema S; $\chi(\mathbf{x}, \mathbf{y})$ is a conjunction of equalities of the form $t = t'$ where t and t' are terms over $\mathbf{f}$, $\mathbf{x}$ and $\mathbf{y}$; Ψ is a conjunction of atoms over the target schema S'; each variable is safe.

In relational data exchange [1], atoms in (1) are restricted to atomic relational formulas. In the case of XML, so called *tree-pattern formulas* can be used instead of atoms. In [2] tree-pattern formulas express mappings between XML schemas. However, these mappings are restricted only to the structure of the schemas and

* The work was supported in part by the Polish Ministry of Science and Higher Education under Grant N516 015 31/1553.

M. Marchiori, J.Z. Pan, and C. de Sainte Marie (Eds.): RR 2007, LNCS 4524, pp. 374–376, 2007.
© Springer-Verlag Berlin Heidelberg 2007

do not consider any contextual constraints, i.e. ignore the $\chi(\mathbf{x}, \mathbf{y})$ part of (1), thus they are restricted to DTD's only. In this paper we additionally consider such contextual constraints as *keys* and *key references*, which can be specified within XSD (XML Schema Definition) [5], as well as so-called *value dependencies* that can be easily incorporated into XSD by means of annotations. As we discussed in our previous works [3,4] such features are useful in data integration processes and should be taken into account for:

- a unique target instance satisfying all imposed constraints can be obtained, in [4] we proposed a suitable algorithm for that based on Skolem functions;
- some missing data may be inferred while merging data from different sources; a solution to this problem was discussed in [3].

Let L be a set of labels of a schema S. A *tree-pattern formula* (TPF) over L is an expression π conforming to the syntax ($l \in L$, *top* $\in L$ and *top* is the outermost label in the schema, x is a string-valued variable):
$$\pi ::= /top[E]; \qquad E ::= l = x \mid l[E] \mid E \wedge E.$$
A label l in TPF may be followed by a *key expression* $\{(P_1, ..., P_k)\}$ providing information about *key paths* which uniquely identify subtrees rooted in l in any instance of the schema S (possibly in a context determined by a *context path* P). This corresponds to the key for XML $(P, (l, (P_1, ..., P_k)))$, as proposed by Buneman *et al.* [6]. A TPF extended with key expressions will be referred to as a *key-pattern formula* (KPF). We distinguish among three kinds of schema mappings: *automappings*, *correspondences*, and *transformations*. As in (1), function symbols are quantified existentially, while variables universally.

An *automapping* describes how an instance of a schema S is transformed onto an equivalent instance of S satisfying all the key constraints defined in δ_S:
$$\mathcal{A}_S := \pi_S(\mathbf{x}) \wedge \psi_S(\mathbf{x}) \Rightarrow \delta_S(\mathbf{x}),$$
where: $\pi_S(\mathbf{x})$ is a TPF capturing the structure of the schema; $\psi_S(\mathbf{x})$ is a conjunction of atoms of the form $x = x'$ and $x = f(x_1, ..., x_n)$, where the former captures a key reference and the latter a value dependence; $\delta_S(\mathbf{x})$ is a KPF.

A *correspondence* states how patterns in the source schema tree S correspond to patterns in the target schema tree S':
$$\mathcal{M}_{S \to S'} := \pi_S(\mathbf{x}) \wedge \phi_{S,S'}(\mathbf{x}, \mathbf{y}) \Rightarrow \pi_{S'}(\mathbf{x}, \mathbf{y}),$$
$\pi_S(\mathbf{x})$ and $\pi_{S'}(\mathbf{x}, \mathbf{y})$ are TPFs over S and S', respectively; $\phi_{S,S'}(\mathbf{x}, \mathbf{y})$ is a conjunction of atoms of the form $x = x'$, $y = y'$ and $y = f(x_1, ..., x_n)$, i.e. restricts variable values and defines target variables as functions over source variables.

A *transformation* describes how data structured under the source schema is to be transformed into data structured under the target schema preserving keys in the target. The transformation can be derived automatically based on both the correspondence $\mathcal{M}_{S \to S'}$ from S to S' and the automapping $\mathcal{A}_{S'}$ over S':

$$\mathcal{M}_{S \to S'} := \pi_S(\mathbf{x_1}) \wedge \phi_{S,S'}(\mathbf{x_1}, \mathbf{y_1}) \Rightarrow \pi_{S'}(\mathbf{x_1}, \mathbf{y_1})$$
$$\mathcal{A}_{S'} := \pi_{S'}(\mathbf{x_2}) \wedge \psi_{S'}(\mathbf{x_2}) \Rightarrow \delta_{S'}(\mathbf{x_2})$$

$$\overline{\mathcal{T}_{S \to S'} := (\pi_S(\mathbf{x_1}) \wedge \phi_{S,S'}(\mathbf{x_1}, \mathbf{y_1}))[(\mathbf{x_1}, \mathbf{y_1}) \mapsto \mathbf{x_2}] \wedge \psi_{S'}(\mathbf{x_2}) \Rightarrow \delta_{S'}(\mathbf{x_2}),}$$

$(\pi_S(\mathbf{x_1}) \wedge \phi_{S,S'}(\mathbf{x_1}, \mathbf{y_1}))[(\mathbf{x_1}, \mathbf{y_1}) \mapsto \mathbf{x_2}]$ arises from $\pi_S(\mathbf{x_1}) \wedge \phi_{S,S'}(\mathbf{x_1}, \mathbf{y_1})$ by replacing variables in $(\mathbf{x_1}, \mathbf{y_1})$ with corresponding variables in $\mathbf{x_2}$. Replacement is made according to occurrences of variables within $\pi_{S'}(\mathbf{x_1}, \mathbf{y_1})$ and $\pi_{S'}(\mathbf{x_2})$.

Example 1. In Fig. 1, there are sample XML trees and XML schema trees representing bibliographical data. The node labels are as follows: paper (P) and title (T) of the paper; author (A), name (N) and university (U) of the author; year (Y) of publication the paper P. We can define the following mappings for these schemas:

$$\mathcal{A}_{S_2} := \pi_{S_2} \wedge \psi_{S_2} \Rightarrow \delta_{S_2}, \text{ or, alternatively, } \mathcal{A}'_{S_2} := \pi_{S_2} \wedge \psi_{S_2} \Rightarrow \delta'_{S_2}, \text{ where:}$$
$$\pi_{S_2}(x_1, x_2, x_3, x_4) := /S2[A[N = x_1 \wedge U = x_2 \wedge P[T = x_3 \wedge Y = x_4]]],$$
$$\psi_{S_2} := x_2 = f_U(x_1) \wedge x_4 = f_Y(x_3),$$
$$\delta_{S_2} := /S2[A\{N\}[N = x_1 \wedge U = x_2 \wedge P\{T\}[T = x_3 \wedge Y = x_4]]],$$
$$\delta'_{S_2} := /S2[A\{(N, P/T)\}[N = x_1 \wedge U = x_2 \wedge P\{T\}[T = x_3 \wedge Y = x_4]]],$$
$$\mathcal{M}_{S_1 \to S_2} := \pi_{S_1}(z_1, z_2, z_3) \wedge z_4 = f_Y(z_1) \Rightarrow \pi_{S_2}(z_1, z_2, z_3, z_4), \text{ where}$$
$$\pi_{S_1}(z_1, z_2, z_3) := /S1[P[T = z_1 \wedge A[N = z_2 \wedge U = z_3]]],$$
$$\mathcal{T}_{S_1 \to S_2} := \pi_{S_1}(x_3, x_1, x_2) \wedge x_4 = f_Y(x_1) \wedge x_2 = f_U(x_1) \Rightarrow \delta_{S_2}(x_1, x_2, x_3, x_4),$$
$$\mathcal{T}'_{S_1 \to S_2} := \pi_{S_1}(x_3, x_1, x_2) \wedge x_4 = f_Y(x_1) \wedge x_2 = f_U(x_1) \Rightarrow \delta'_{S_2}(x_1, x_2, x_3, x_4).$$

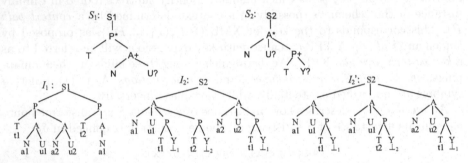

Fig. 1. XML schemas S_1, S_2, and their instances: I_1 of S_1, and I_2 and I'_2 of S_2; $I_2 = \mathcal{T}_{S_1 \to S_2}(I_1)$, $I'_2 = \mathcal{T}'_{S_1 \to S_2}(I_1)$

References

1. Fagin, R., Kolaitis, P.G., Popa, L.: Data exchange: getting to the core. ACM Trans. Database Syst. 30(1), 174–210 (2005)
2. Arenas, M., Libkin, L.: XML Data Exchange: Consistency and Query Answering. In: PODS Conference. pp. 13–24 (2005)
3. Pankowski, T.: Management of executable schema mappings for XML data exchange. In: Grust, T., Höpfner, H., Illarramendi, A., Jablonski, S., Mesiti, M., Müller, S., Patranjan, P.-L., Sattler, K.-U., Spiliopoulou, M., Wijsen, J. (eds.) EDBT 2006. LNCS, vol. 4254, pp. 264–277. Springer, Heidelberg (2006)
4. Pankowski, T., Cybulka, J., Meissner, A.: XML Schema Mappings in the Presence of Key Constraints and Value Dependencies. In: ICDT 2007 Workshop EROW'07, CEUR Workshop Proceedings CEUR-WS.org Vol. 229, pp. 1–15 (2007)
5. XML Schema Part 1: Structures. www.w3.org/TR/xmlschema-1 (2004)
6. Buneman, P., Davidson, S.B., Fan, W., Hara, C.S., Tan, W.C.: Reasoning about keys for XML. Information Systems 28(8), 1037–1063 (2003)

Context in Rules Used in P2P Semantic Data Integration System

Grażyna Brzykcy and Jerzy Bartoszek

Technical University of Poznań, Institute of Control and Information Engineering,
Pl. M. Skłodowskiej-Curie 5, 60-965 Poznań, Poland
{Grazyna.Brzykcy, Jerzy.Bartoszek}@put.poznan.pl

Abstract. We use situation theory to model context of agents' actions in heterogeneous P2P system of semantic data integration. This formal basis is also suitable to cope with information partiality, open-world and non-monotonic reasoning. Operational semantics of asking and answering queries by the agents is presented as a set of context-dependent rules. Situations are represented by facts and rules and Prolog-like reasoning mechanisms are used in the system. Specification of sample actions is presented.

Keywords: P2P system, situation theory, context-aware processes, Prolog-like computations, operational semantics.

1 Introduction

In this paper we consider systems consisted of agents (peers), which manage local data and can cooperate with other agents by asking them and answering queries. We assume that an agent performs actions with respect to all data and metadata it posses (its context or mental state [7]). To cope with data heterogeneity and semantic data processing in the system we choose situation theory [3, 4] and Prolog-like inference mechanisms. Precisely, (1) we adopt abstract situations as context of agents' actions, (2) we propose a set of rules, which describe evaluation of these actions with respect to explicitly shown context and (3) we outline a Prolog specification of some actions executed by agents in the semantic data integration system SIX-P2P [2].

The most elementary construct in the situation theory is infon – a discrete item of information. If R is an n-place relation and $a_1,...,a_n$ are objects appropriate for the respective argument places of R, then a tuple $<<R,r_1 \rightarrow a_1,...,r_n \rightarrow a_n,p>>$ with p=+ denotes the informational item that $a_1,...,a_n$ are standing in the relation R, and with p=– the informational item that $a_1,...,a_n$ are not standing in the relation R. To represent partial information one can omit some arguments of R. A real situation s (a limited structured part of the world individuated by a cognitive agent) is modeled by an abstract situation – the set $\{\sigma \mid s \models \sigma\}$ of infons, which are true in the situation s. Inferences in the situation theory are realized via constraints on situation types. With the infon $<<S1 \Rightarrow S2,+>>$, where $\Rightarrow$ is a relation written in infix style, an agent knows that if it is in mental state of type S1 than it is also in state of type S2. In general, any

M. Marchiori, J.Z. Pan, and C. de Sainte Marie (Eds.): RR 2007, LNCS 4524, pp. 377–380, 2007.

constraint may depend on a set B of background conditions ([S1 => S2] / B) and then allows to capture a phenomenon like non-monotonicity in commonsense reasoning.

Situations and constraints constitute a context in situation theory [1].

2 Reasoning with Rules over Abstract Situations

Agents (peers) have unique names. The mental state of the peer p is denoted by $\underline{p}$. Queries issued by a peer take a form of Prolog-like goals, e.g., the agent p executes q*G if it wants the agent q to evaluate the goal G. If the evaluation succeeds, then some substitution θ is returned to p (following [5] we denote it as $p/\underline{p} \vdash_\theta q*G$). The evaluation of goals can be described by the following rules, where conclusions hold when all premises hold.

$$\frac{}{p \: / \: \underline{p} \: \vdash_\epsilon \: true} \tag{1}$$

$$\frac{q \: / \: \underline{q} \: \vdash_\theta \: G}{p \: / \: \underline{p} \: \vdash_\theta \: q * G} \tag{2}$$

Any agent p with mental state $\underline{p}$ always can execute the empty goal denoted by *true*. The rule (2) shows what happens when the agent p sends the goal G to the agent q.

$$\frac{\underline{p} \: \vDash \: << R(t_1, \ldots, t_n)\theta, + >>}{p \: / \: \underline{p} \: \vdash_\theta \: R(t_1, \ldots, t_n)} \tag{3}$$

$$\frac{\underline{p} \: \vDash \: << R(t_1, \ldots, t_n)\theta, - >>}{p \: / \: \underline{p} \: \vdash_\theta \: \neg R(t_1, \ldots, t_n)} \tag{4}$$

If the agent p "knows" the fact $<<R(t_1,\ldots,t_n)\theta, \pm>>$, than it can execute, respectively, goal $R(t_1,\ldots,t_n)$ or $\neg R(t_1,\ldots,t_n)$. So, an agent can correctly act in the "open world".

$$\frac{\gamma = mgu(A, H) \wedge << H : -G, + >> \in \underline{p} \wedge p \: / \: \underline{p} \: \vdash_\delta \: G\gamma}{p \: / \: \underline{p} \: \vdash_{\gamma\delta} \: A} \tag{5}$$

The above rule shows how the agent p executes the goal A when it has the Prolog rule H:-G in his mental state. The assignment γ is the most general unifier of A and H. If the unifier does not exist, execution of A fails.

$$\frac{p/\underline{p} \vdash_\theta G_1 \wedge p/\underline{p} \vdash_\gamma G_2\theta}{p/\underline{p} \vdash_{\theta\gamma} G_1, G_2} \tag{6}$$

$$\frac{p/\underline{p} : Q \wedge \left[p/\underline{p} : Q \Rightarrow p/\underline{r} : R \right] \wedge p/\underline{p} \cup \underline{r} \vdash_\theta G}{p/\underline{p} \vdash_\theta G} \tag{7}$$

In the rule (6) a conjunctive query is described. The successful execution of G_1 with a new substitution θ appears. It is used then in the execution of the goal G_2. The rule (7) shows how the agent p ought to evaluate the goal G with respect to the constraint [Q =>R]. It executes this goal in the new mental state p$\cup$r.

3 Specification of Sample Actions

A query in SIX-P2P system may be propagated to partners of each peer inducing a cooperative evaluation of the query in the set of possible "knowledge sources".

There are two types of agents in the system: peers and brokers. Introduction of the Agent consists of registration, which is an action executed by the Broker, and results in replying a list of Agent's partners. The Agent stores the list as a part of its context.

```
introduce(Agent, Broker, Parts) :-
  Broker * register(Agent, Parts),   % registration is done by a broker
  assert(partners(Parts)).           % list of partners is stored
```

Note that metapredicate assert/1 is used to change the current context of the agent.

To gain information from any partner an agent has to prepare suitable mapping (create_map/2) between schemas.

```
create_map(Part, Mpa) :-
  schema(self, Scha),                % local schema
  Part * schema(self, Schp),         % partner's schema is taken
  map(Scha, Schp, Mpa),              % mapping is constructed
  assert(mapping(Part, Mpa)).        % mapping is stored
```

Querying and answering (ask/3) consists of local (query/2), and collective (ask_partners/2) query processing and merging of answers (merge/3).

```
ask(Agent, Query, Answer) :-
  query(Query, Ans1),                % local query is answered
  ask_partners(Query, Ansr),         % collective query is answered
  merge(Ans1, Ansr, Answer).         % answers are merged
```

To ask a partner an agent has to convert (q_reformulate/3) the original Query to the appropriate form Qp, directed to the partner P.

```
ask_qparts(_, [ ], _).                  % all partners are asked
ask_qparts(Query, [P|Ps], [A|As]) :- % partner P is asked
  mapping(P, Mpa),
  q_reformulate(Qp, Map, Qp1),          % query is converted
  P ^ ask(Qp1, A),                      % query is answered
  ask_qparts(Query, Ps, As).
```

References

1. Akman, V., Surav, M.: The Use of Situation Theory in Context Modeling. Computational Intelligence vol. 12 (4) (1996)
2. Brzykcy G., Bartoszek J., Pankowski T.: Semantic data integration in P2P environment using schema mappings and agent technology. In: Proceedings of AMSTA 2007, to appear (2007)

3. Barwise, J., Perry, J.: Situations and attitudes. MIT Press, Cambridge (1983)
4. Devlin, K.: Logic and information. Cambridge University Press, New York (1991)
5. Loke, S.W.: Declarative programming of integrated peer-to-peer and Web based systems: the case of Prolog. Journal of Systems and Software 79(4), 523–536 (2006)
6. Manzalini, A., Zambonelli, F.: Towards Autonomic and Situation-Aware Communication Services: the CASCADAS Vision. IEEE DIS Workshop, Prague (2006)
7. Zambonelli, F., Van Dyke Parunak, H.: Towards a Paradigm Change in Computer Science and Software Engineering: A Synthesis. The Knowledge Engineering Review (2004)

Author Index

Lecture Notes in Computer Science

For information about Vols. 1–4421

please contact your bookseller or Springer